Professional ASP.NET 2.0 XML

Professional ASP.NET 2.0 XML

Thiru Thangarathinam

Wiley Publishing, Inc.

Professional ASP.NET 2.0 XML

Published by
Wiley Publishing, Inc.
10475 Crosspoint Boulevard
Indianapolis, IN 46256
www.wiley.com

About the Author

Thiru Thangarathinam works for Intel Corporation in Phoenix, Arizona. He is an MCAD (Microsoft Certified Application Developer) and specializes in architecting and building Distributed N-Tier applications using ASP.NET, Visual C#.NET, VB.NET, ADO.NET, and SQL Server 2000. He has co-authored a number of books for Wrox Press in .NET technologies. Thiru is also a regular contributor to print and online magazines such as *Visual Studio Magazine,* Visual Studio .NET Professional, SQL Server Professional, DevX, ASPToday.com, 15seconds.com, and Developer.com. At Intel, he is part of the team that is focused on developing the Enterprise Architecture and Service Oriented Architectures for Intel. He can be reached at `thiru.thangarathinam@intel.com`.

Credits

Senior Acquisitions Editor
Jim Minatel

Development Editor
Ed Connor

Technical Editor
Kirk Evans

Production Editor
Pam Hanley

Copy Editor
Susan Hobbs

Editorial Manager
Mary Beth Wakefield

Production Manager
Tim Tate

Vice President and Executive Group Publisher
Richard Swadley

Vice President and Executive Publisher
Joseph B. Wikert

Project Coordinator
Ryan Steffen

Graphics and Production Specialists
Carrie A. Foster
Lauren Goddard
Denny Hager
Barbara Moore
Alicia B. South

Quality Control Technician
Brian H. Walls, Joe Niesen

Proofreading and Indexing
TECHBOOKS Production Services

Contents

Contents

Contents

Contents

Contents

Acknowledgments

I would like to acknowledge my wife Thamiya, my parents and my family for their constant support and encouragement throughout while I spent nights and weekends working on this book.

Introduction

This book will cover the intersection between two great technologies: ASP.NET and XML.

XML has been a hot topic for some time. The massive industry acceptance of this W3C Recommendation, which allows data communication and information storage in a platform independent manner, has been astounding. XML is seen and used everywhere—from the display of data on various browsers using the transformation language XSLT, to the transport of messages between Web services using SOAP.

.NET is Microsoft's evolutionary and much vaunted new vision. It allows programming of applications in a language independent manner, the sharing of code between languages, self-describing classes, and self-documenting program code to name but a few of its capabilities. .NET, in particular ASP.NET, has been specifically designed with Web services and ease of development in mind. With the release of .NET 2.0 Framework, .NET includes significant enhancements to all areas of ASP.NET. For Web page development, new XML data controls like XmlDataSource, and TreeView make it possible to display and edit data on an ASP.NET Web page without writing code reducing the required amount of code by as much as 70% in some cases. ADO.NET 2.0 includes many new features that allow you to leverage the new XML features introduced with SQL Server 2005 (the next major release of SQL Server).

To achieve this exciting new Web programming environment, Microsoft has made extensive use of XML. In fact, no other technology is so tightly bound with ASP.NET as XML. It is used as the universal data format for everything from configuration files to metadata, Web Services communication, and object serialization. All the XML capabilities in the System.Xml namespace were significantly enhanced for added performance and standards support. The new model for processing in-memory XML data, editable XPathNavigator, new XSLT processor, strong typed support for XmlReader, and XmlWriter classes, are some of the key XML related improvements. Connected to this is the new support for XML that ADO.NET 2.0 has. Because of the new ADO.NET 2.0 features, the programmer now has the ability to access and update data in both hierarchical XML and relational database form at the same time.

Who This Book Is For

This book is aimed at intermediate or experienced programmers who have started on their journey toward ASP.NET development and who are already familiar with XML. While I do introduce the reader to many new ASP.NET 2.0 concepts in Chapter 2, this book is not intended as a first port of call for the developer looking at ASP.NET, since there are already many books and articles covering this area. Instead, I cut straight to the heart of using XML within ASP.NET Web applications. To get the most out of the book, you will have some basic knowledge of C#. All the code examples will be explained in C#.

In a similar vein, there are many books and articles that cover the XML technologies that you will need to use this book. I assume a general knowledge of XML, namespaces, and XSLT, and a basic understanding of XML schemas.

What This Book Covers

This book explores the array of XML features and how they can be used in ASP.NET for developing Web applications. XML is everywhere in the .NET Framework, from serialization to Web services, and from data access to configuration. In the first part of this book, you'll find in-depth coverage of the key classes that implement XML in the .NET platform. Readers and writers, validation, schemas, and XML DOM are discussed with ASP.NET samples and reference information. Next the book moves on to XPath and XSL Transformations (XSLT), XML support in ADO.NET and the use of XML for data display.

The final part of this book focuses on SQL Server 2005 XML Features, XML Serialization, XML Web services, and touches on XML based configuration files and its XML extensions. You'll also find a couple of case studies on the use of XML related features of ASP.NET and Web services that provide you with a real life example on how to leverage these features.

How This Book Is Structured

The book consists of 15 chapters including two case studies. The book is structured to walk the reader through the process of XML development in ASP.NET 2.0. I take a focused approach, teaching readers only what they need at each stage without using an excessive level of ancillary detail, overly complex technical jargon, or unnecessary digressions into detailed discussion of specifications and standards. A brief explanation of each of the chapters is as follows:

An Introduction to XML

XML finds several applications in business and, increasingly, in everyday life. It provides a common data format for companies that want to exchange documents using Web services. This chapter is about XML as a language and its related technologies. The XML technologies that I will specifically introduce in this chapter are: XML document elements, namespaces, entities, DTD, XDR, XSD, XSD schema data types, XSLT, XML DOM, XPath, SAX, XLink, XPointer, and XQuery.

An Introduction to ASP.NET 2.0

In Chapter 2, I aim to give the reader an overview of the new features of ASP.NET 2.0. I will highlight the new ASP.NET page architecture, new data controls, and code sharing features. I ask, "What is master pages" and go on to talk about how master pages and themes aid in creating consistent Web sites. Later on, I look at security controls and Web parts framework and illustrate how ASP.NET 2.0 enables 70% code reduction. Finally, I will look at the new caching and administration and management functionalities of ASP.NET 2.0.

XML Classes in the .NET Framework

In Chapter 3, I take a brisk walk through all the new XML classes in the .NET Framework, which will be discussed in more detail throughout the rest of the book.

Microsoft has introduced several new applications of XML in .NET 2.0 and has also done some innovative work to improve the core XML API. I start with a discussion on the use of XML in configuration files, DOM, XSD schema validation, XSLT transformations, XML serialization, Web services, and XML support in ADO.NET and look at the namespaces and classes that are available for this purpose. I will also illustrate the new ASP.NET configuration enhancements and take a quick look at the configuration classes in .NET Framework 2.0.

Reading and Writing XML

Chapter 4 starts a section of chapters (4 through 6) that look at the functionality contained within the System.Xml in more detail.

In particular, here I look at the fast, forward-only read-only mechanisms provided by the .NET Framework for reading and writing XML documents, namely the XmlReader and XmlWriter classes. I explore the new XML reading and writing model and talk about the various ways using, which you can read and write XML data. I also go onto discuss node order, parsing attributes, customizing reader and writer settings, white spaces handling, and namespace handling, and other namespace support.

Validating XML

In Chapter 5, I take a look at different options for the XML validation grammars: DTDs, XDR schemas, and XSD schemas. I also go on to look at all the ways you can create an XSD schema in Visual Studio 2005: using the XML designer, from a DTD, using the XSD generator, from an XML document, from an XDR schema, or from an assembly. I also discuss the schema object and see how to link XML documents to DTDs, XDR schemas, and XSD schemas, and how to then perform validation using the XmlReaderSettings in conjunction with the XmlReader class. I also illustrate the use of the XmlSchemaSet class to keep a cache of schemas in memory, to optimize performance, and also deal with unqualified/namespace-qualified content in XML documents.

XML DOM Object Model

In Chapter 6, I look at the DOM functionality within the .NET Framework provided within the System.Xml namespace of classes. I look at programmatically creating XML documents, opening documents from URLs, or strings in memory, and searching and accessing the contents of these documents, before serializing them back out to XML strings. I also take a look at the differences between the XmlDocument object and the XmlReader and XmlWriter classes, and where using each is more appropriate. Finally, I demonstrate the XPath capabilities of the XmlDocument class and also highlight the new editing capabilities of the XPathNavigator class to modify an XML document in memory.

Transforming XML Data with XSLT

The .NET Framework provides robust support for XSLT and XPath processing and with .NET Framework 2.0, the XSL support has been completely redesigned and a new XSLT processor is introduced. In Chapter 7, I look at the technologies used for XSL transformations in the .NET Framework, namely the System.Xml.Xsl namespace, and System.Xml.XPath namespaces, as well as the newly introduced XslCompiledTransform class. The .NET Framework fully supports the XSLT and XPath specification as defined by the W3C, but also provides more helpful extensions to these specifications, which enhance the usability of style sheets within .NET applications. To this end, I look at using embedded script with <msxsl:script> for transforming XML documents and show how to extend style sheets with extension objects. Towards the end of the chapter, I discuss advanced XSLT operations such as how to pass a node set to a style sheet and how to resolve external style sheets using XmlResolver.

XML Support in ADO.NET

In Chapter 8, I start to move away from the realm of the System.Xml namespace of classes, to explore the broader picture of how XML is used in .NET specifically from ADO.NET, the data access technology of choice.

Chapter 8 looks at the role of XML in ADO.NET 2.0 and highlights the new XML related features of ADO.NET. I cover the capabilities of the DataSet and DataTable classes, including reading and writing XML, and programmatically accessing or changing its XML representation. I highlight how to synchronize DataSets with XmlDataDocuments and why you would do so. I also cover the creation of strongly typed DataSets and their advantages. Finally, I take a glimpse at how to access some of the new XML features available in SQL Server 2005 from ADO.NET.

XML Data Display

The XML support in ASP.NET provides excellent support for storing, retrieving and rendering XML. I start with looking at the new web.sitemap file that allows you to store the hierarchy of a Web site and leverage that to drive the navigation structure of a Web site. Then, I go on to discuss the features of new XML data controls such as XmlDataSource, TreeView, and GridView for consuming and displaying native XML directly in the browser. Finally, I also introduce the new ASP.NET 2.0 script callback feature for retrieving XML data directly from the browser without refreshing the page.

SQL Server 2005 XML Integration

With the release of SQL Server 2005, XML support just got better and SQL Server 2005 provides powerful XML query and data modification capabilities over XML data. To start with, I introduce the new XML features of SQL Server 2005 including the FOR XML clause enhancements, XQuery support, and the XML data type. Then I go on to discuss the execution of FOR XML queries from within ADO.NET both synchronously and asynchronously. I also discuss the steps involved in working with typed and untyped XML data type columns. Finally, I illustrate how to retrieve XSD schemas from a typed column using ADO.NET and also focus on MARS and OPENXML() functions.

Building an Airline Reservation System using ASP.NET 2.0 and SQL Server 2005

This case study ties together all the concepts including XML DOM, XML support in ADO.NET, XSLT features in .NET, XML data display, that have been covered so far in this book. The focus of this case study is on incorporating these XML features in a real world airline reservations Web site and showcasing the best practices of using these XML features. I also discuss the N-Tier design methodology and illustrate how to leverage that to create an extensible and flexible airline reservations system.

XML Serialization

In Chapter 12, I look at serializing XML documents as XML data using the XmlSerializer class from the System.Xml.Serialization namespace. More specifically, you create serializers, and then serialize and deserialize generic types, complex objects, properties, enumeration values, arrays and composite objects. I also look at serializing and deserializing with nested objects, followed by formatting XML documents, XML attributes, and text content. Towards the end of the chapter, I discuss the steps involved in improving the serialization performance by pregenerating assemblies using the new XML serializer generator tool.

XML Web Services

Web Services are objects and methods that can be invoked from any client over HTTP. Web Services are built on the Simple Object Access Protocol (SOAP). In this chapter, I provide a thorough understanding of XML Web Services by showing the creation of XML Web Services using .NET Framework 2.0 and Visual Studio 2005. After the initial discussion, I also go on to discuss advanced Web service concepts such as SOAP headers, SOAP extensions, XML serialization customization, schema importer extensions, asynchronous Web service methods, and asynchronous invocation of Web service methods.

ASP.NET 2.0 Configuration

In Chapter 14, I introduce the new configuration management API of ASP.NET 2.0 that enables users to programmatically build programs or scripts that create, read, and update settings in web.config and machine.config files. I also go on to discuss the new comprehensive admin tool that plugs into the existing IIS Administration MMC, enabling an administrator to graphically read or change any setting within our XML configuration files. Throughout this chapter, I focus on the new configuration management classes, properties, and methods of the configuration API and also provide examples on how to use them from your ASP.NET applications.

Building a ShoppingAssistant using XML Web Services

This chapter is based on a case study named ShoppingAssistant, which provides one stop shopping for consumers that want to find out information such as the products that are on sale, availability of products in different stores, comparison of the price of the product across different stores and so on. In this case study, I demonstrate how to leverage Web services in a real world Web application by using asynchronous Web service invocation capabilities in conjunction with other .NET features such as XML Serialization, FileSystemWatcher, and Timer component.

What You Need to Use This Book

All of the examples in this book are ASP.NET samples. The key requirements for running these applications are the .NET Framework 2.0 and Microsoft Visual Studio 2005. You also need to have SQL Server 2005 server along with the AdventureWorks sample database installed to make most of the samples work. A few examples make use of SQL Server 2005 Express database.

The SQL Server examples in this book utilize integrated security to connect to the SQL Server database, so remember to enable integrated authentication in your SQL Server. This will also require you to turn on integrated Windows authentication (as well as impersonation depending on your configuration) in ASP.NET Web sites.

Conventions

To help you get the most from the text and keep track of what's happening, I've used a number of conventions throughout the book.

> **Boxes like this one hold important, not-to-be forgotten information that is directly relevant to the surrounding text.**

Tips, hints, tricks, and asides to the current discussion are offset and placed in italics like this.

As for styles in the text:

- ❏ We *highlight* new terms and important words when we introduce them.
- ❏ We show keyboard strokes like this: Ctrl+A.
- ❏ We show file names, URLs, and code within the text like so: `persistence.properties`.

Source Code

As you work through the examples in this book, you may choose either to type in all the code manually or to use the source code files that accompany the book. All of the source code used in this book is available for download at `http://www.wrox.com`. Once at the site, simply locate the book's title (either by using the Search box or by using one of the title lists) and click the Download Code link on the book's detail page to obtain all the source code for the book.

Because many books have similar titles, you may find it easiest to search by ISBN; this book's ISBN is 0-7645-9677-2 (changing to 978-0-7645-9677-3 as the new industry-wide 13-digit ISBN numbering system is phased in by January 2007).

Once you download the code, just decompress it with your favorite compression tool. Alternately, you can go to the main Wrox code download page at `http://www.wrox.com/dynamic/books/download.aspx` to see the code available for this book and all other Wrox books.

Errata

We make every effort to ensure that there are no errors in the text or in the code. However, no one is perfect, and mistakes do occur. If you find an error in one of our books, like a spelling mistake or faulty piece of code, we would be very grateful for your feedback. By sending in errata you may save another reader hours of frustration and at the same time you will be helping us provide even higher quality information.

To find the errata page for this book, go to `http://www.wrox.com` and locate the title using the Search box or one of the title lists. Then, on the book details page, click the Book Errata link. On this page you can view all errata that has been submitted for this book and posted by Wrox editors. A complete book list including links to each book's errata is also available at `www.wrox.com/misc-pages/booklist.shtml`.

If you don't spot "your" error on the Book Errata page, go to www.wrox.com/contact/techsupport .shtml and complete the form there to send us the error you have found. We'll check the information and, if appropriate, post a message to the book's errata page and fix the problem in subsequent editions of the book.

p2p.wrox.com

For author and peer discussion, join the P2P forums at p2p.wrox.com. The forums are a Web-based system for you to post messages relating to Wrox books and related technologies and interact with other readers and technology users. The forums offer a subscription feature to e-mail you topics of interest of your choosing when new posts are made to the forums. Wrox authors, editors, other industry experts, and your fellow readers are present on these forums.

At http://p2p.wrox.com you will find a number of different forums that will help you not only as you read this book, but also as you develop your own applications. To join the forums, just follow these steps:

1. Go to p2p.wrox.com and click the Register link.

2. Read the terms of use and click Agree.

3. Complete the required information to join as well as any optional information you wish to provide and click Submit.

4. You will receive an e-mail with information describing how to verify your account and complete the joining process.

You can read messages in the forums without joining P2P but in order to post your own messages, you must join.

Once you join, you can post new messages and respond to messages other users post. You can read messages at any time on the Web. If you would like to have new messages from a particular forum e-mailed to you, click the Subscribe to this Forum icon by the forum name in the forum listing.

For more information about how to use the Wrox P2P, be sure to read the P2P FAQs for answers to questions about how the forum software works as well as many common questions specific to P2P and Wrox books. To read the FAQs, click the FAQ link on any P2P page.

Professional ASP.NET 2.0 XML

Introduction to XML

Extensible Markup Language (XML) is a language defined by the World Wide Web Consortium (W3C, `http://www.w3c.org`), the body that sets the standards for the Web. You can use XML to create your own elements, thus creating a customized markup language for your own use. In this way, XML supersedes other markup languages such as Hypertext Markup Language (HTML); in HTML, all the elements you use are predefined — and there are not enough of them. In fact, XML is a metamarkup language because it lets you create your own markup languages.

XML is the next logical step in developing the full potential of the Internet and the Web. Just as HTML, HyperText Transfer Protocol (HTTP), and Web browsers paved the way for exciting new methods of communications between networked computers and people, XML and its associated technologies open new avenues of electronic communications between people and machines. In the case of XML, however, the promise is for both human-machine and machine-machine communications, with XML as the "lowest-common-denominator" language that all other systems — proprietary or open — can use.

XML derives much of its strength in combination with the Web. The Web provides a collection of protocols for moving data; XML represents a way to define that data. The most immediate effect has been a new way to look at the enterprise. Instead of a tightly knit network of servers, the enterprise is now seen as encompassing not just our traditional networks but also the Web itself, with its global reach and scope. XML has become the unquestionable standard for generically marking data to be shared. As XML continues to grow in popularity, so too are the number of ways in which XML is being implemented. XML can be used for a variety of purposes, from obvious tasks such as marking up simple data files and storing temporary data to more complex tasks such as passing information from one program or process to another.

XML finds several applications in business and, increasingly, in everyday life. It provides a common data format for companies that want to exchange documents. It's used by Web services to encode messages and data in a platform-independent manner. It's even used to build Web sites, where it serves as a tool for cleanly separating content from appearance.

This chapter is about XML as a language and its related technologies. A comprehensive treatment of the subject could easily fill 300 pages or more, so this chapter attempts to strike a reasonable balance between detail and succinctness. In the pages that follow, you learn about the different XML-related technologies and their usage. But before that, take a brief look at XML itself.

A Primer on XML

XML is derived from the Standard Generalized Markup Language (SGML), a rich language used mostly for huge documentation projects. The designers of XML drew heavily from SGML and were guided by the lessons learned from HTML. They produced a specification that was only about 20 percent the size of the SGML specification, but nearly as powerful. Although SGML is typically used by those who need the power of an industrial-strength language, XML is intended for everyone.

One of the great strengths of XML is the extensibility it brings to the table. XML doesn't have any tags of its own and it doesn't constrain you like other markup languages. Instead, XML defines rules for developing semantic tags of your own. The tags you create form vocabularies that can be used to structure data into hierarchical trees of information. You can think of XML as a metamarkup language that enables developers, companies, and even industries to create their own, specific markup languages.

One of the most important concepts to grasp in XML is about content, not presentation. The tags you create focus on organizing your data rather than displaying it. XML isn't used, for example, to indicate a particular part of a document in a new paragraph or that another part should be bolded. XML is used to develop tags that indicate a particular piece of data is the author's first name, another piece is the book title, and a third piece is the published year of the book.

Self-Describing Data

As mentioned before, the most powerful feature of XML is that it doesn't define any tags. Creating your own tags is what makes XML extensible; however, defining meaningful tags is up to you. When creating tags, it isn't necessary to abbreviate or shorten your tag names. It doesn't make processing them any faster. but it can make your XML documents more confusing or easier to understand. Remember, developers are going to be writing code against your XML documents. On the one hand, you could certainly define tags like the following:

```
<H1>XSLT Programmers Reference
<p><b>Michael Kay</b></p>
</H1>
```

Using these HTML-based tags might make it easy to be displayed in a browser, but they don't add any information to the document. Remember, XML is focused on content, not presentation. Creating the following XML would be far more meaningful:

```
<books>
  <book>
    <title>XSLT Programmers Reference</title>
    <author>Michael Kay</author>
  </book>
</books>
```

The second example is far more readable in human terms, and it also provides more functionality and versatility to nonhumans. With this set of tags, applications can easily access the book's title or author name without splitting any strings or searching for spaces. And, for developers writing code, searching for the author name in an XML document becomes much more natural when the name of the element is title, for example, rather than H1.

Indenting the tags in the previous example was done purely for readability and certainly isn't necessary in your XML documents. You may find, however, when you create your own documents, indentation helps you to read them.

To process the previous XML data, no special editors are needed to create XML documents, although a number of them are available. And no breakthrough technology is involved. Much of the attention swirling around XML comes from its simplicity. Specifically, interest in XML has grown because of the way XML simplifies the tasks of the developers who employ it in their designs. Many of the tough tasks software developers have to do again and again over the years are now much easier to accomplish. XML also makes it easier for components to communicate with each other because it provides a standardized, structured language recognized by the most popular platforms today. In fact, in the .NET platform, Microsoft has demonstrated how important XML is by using it as the underpinning of the entire platform. As you see in later chapters, .NET relies heavily on XML and SOAP (Simple Object Access Protocol) in its framework and base services to make development easier and more efficient.

Basic Terminology

XML terminology is thrown around, sometimes recklessly, within the XML community. Understanding this terminology will help you understand conversations about XML a little more.

Well-Formed

A document is considered to be well-formed if it meets all the well-formedness constraints defined by XML specification. These constraints are as follows:

- ❏ The document contains one or more elements.
- ❏ The document consists of exactly one root element (also known as the document element).
- ❏ The name of an element's end tag matches the name defined in the start tag.
- ❏ No attribute may appear more than once within an element.
- ❏ Attribute values cannot contain a left-angle bracket (<).
- ❏ Elements delimited with start and end tags must nest properly within each other.

Validity

First and foremost, a valid XML document must be well-formed before it can even think about being a valid XML document. The well-formed requirement should be fairly straightforward, but the key that makes an XML document leap from well-formed to valid is slightly more difficult. To be valid, an XML document must be validated. A document can be validated through a Document Type Definition (DTD), or an XML Schema Definition (XSD). For the XML document to be valid, it must conform to the constraints expressed by the associated DTD or the XSD schema.

A valid document does not ensure semantic perfection. Although XML Schema defines stricter constraints on element and attribute content than XML DTDs do, it cannot catch all errors. For example, you might define a price datatype that requires two decimal places; however, you might enter 1600.00 when you meant to enter 16.00, and the schema document wouldn't catch the error.

When dealing with validity, you need to keep in mind that there are three ways an XML document can exist:

❏ As a free-form, well-formed XML document that does not have DTD or schema associated with it

❏ As a well-formed and valid XML document, adhering to a DTD or schema

❏ As a well-formed document that is not valid because it does not conform to the constraints defined by the associated DTD or schema

Now that you have a general understanding of the XML concepts, the next section examines the constituents of an XML document.

Components of an XML Document

As mentioned earlier in this chapter, XML is a language for describing data and the structure of data. XML data is contained in a document, which can be a file, a stream, or any other storage medium, real or virtual, that's capable of holding text. A proper XML document begins with the following XML declaration, which identifies the document as an XML document and specifies the version of XML that the document's contents conform to:

```
<?xml version="1.0"?>
```

The XML declaration can also include an encoding attribute that identifies the type of characters contained in the document. For example, the following declaration specifies that the document contains characters from the Latin-1 character set used by Windows 95, 98, and Windows Me:

```
<?xml version="1.0" encoding="ISO-8859-1"?>
```

The next example identifies the character set as UTF-16, which consists of 16-bit Unicode characters:

```
<?xml version="1.0" encoding="UTF-16"?>
```

The encoding attribute is optional if the document consists of UTF-8 or UTF-16 characters because an XML parser can infer the encoding from the document's first five characters: '<?xml'. Documents that use other encodings must identify the encodings that they use to ensure that an XML parser can read them. XML declarations are actually specialized forms of XML processing instructions that contain commands for XML processors. Processing instructions are always enclosed in <? and ?> symbols. Some browsers, such as Internet Explorer, interpret the following processing instruction to mean that the XML document should be formatted using a style sheet named Books.xsl before it's displayed:

```
<?xml-stylesheet type="text/xsl" href="Books.xsl"?>
```

The XML declaration is followed by the document's root element, which is usually referred to as the document element. In the following example, the document element is named books:

```
<?xml version="1.0"?>
<books>
   ...
</books>
```

The document element is not optional; every document must have one. The following XML is legal because book elements are nested within the document element books:

```
<?xml version="1.0"?>
<books>
   <book>
      ...
   </book>
   <book>
      ...
   </book>
</books>
```

The document in the next example, however, is not legal because it lacks a document element:

```
<?xml version="1.0"?>
<book>
   ...
</book>
<book>
   ...
</book>
```

If you run the previous XML through a parser, the XML will not load properly, complaining about the non-existence of the root element.

Elements

Element names conform to a set of rules prescribed in the XML specification that you can read at http://www.w3.org/TR/REC-xml. The specification essentially says that element names can consist of letters or underscores followed by letters, digits, periods, hyphens, and underscores. Spaces are not permitted in element names. Elements are the building blocks of XML documents and can contain data, other elements, or both, and are always delimited by start and end tags. XML has no predefined elements; you define elements as needed to adequately describe the data contained in an XML document. The following document describes a collection of books:

```
<?xml version="1.0"?>
<books>
   <book>
      <title>XSLT Programmers Reference</title>
      <author>Michael Kay</author>
      <year>2003</year>
   </book>
   <book>
```

```
        <title>ASP.NET 2.0 Beta Preview</title>
        <author>Bill Evjen</author>
        <year></year>
    </book>
</books>
```

In this example, `books` is the document element, book elements are children of books, and title, and author are children of book. The book elements contain no data (just other elements), but title, and author contain data. The following line in the second book element contains neither data nor other elements.

```
<year></year>
```

Empty elements are perfectly legal in XML. An empty year element can optionally be written this way for conciseness:

```
<year/>
```

Unlike HTML, XML requires that start tags be accompanied by end tags; therefore, the following XML is never legal:

```
<year>2003
```

Also unlike HTML, XML is case-sensitive. A `<year>` tag closed by a `</ Year>` tag is not legal because the cases of the `Y`s do not match.

Because XML permits elements to be nested within elements, the content of an XML document can be viewed as a tree. By visualizing the document structure in a tree, you can clearly understand the parent-child relationships among the document's elements.

Attributes

XML allows you to attach additional information to elements by including attributes in the elements' start tags. Attributes are name/value pairs. The following book element expresses year as an attribute rather than as a child element:

```
<book year="2003">
   <title>XSLT Programmers Reference</title>
   <author>Michael Kay</author>
</book>
```

Attribute values must be enclosed in single or double quotation marks and may include spaces and embedded quotation marks. (An attribute value delimited by single quotation marks can contain double quotation marks and vice versa.) Attribute names are subject to the same restrictions as element names and therefore can't include spaces. The number of attributes an element can be decorated with is not limited.

> **When defining a document's structure, it's sometimes unclear — especially to XML newcomers — whether a given item should be defined as an attribute or an element. In general, attributes should be used to define out-of-band data and elements to define data that is integral to the document. In the previous example, it probably makes sense to define year as an element rather than an attribute because year provides important information about the book in question.**

Now consider the following XML document:

```
<book image="xslt.gif">
  <title>XSLT Programmers Reference</title>
  <author>Michael Kay</author>
  <year>2003</year>
</book>
```

The image attribute contains additional information that an application might use to display the book information with a picture. Because no one other than the software processing this document is likely to care about the image, and because the image is an adjunct to (rather than a part of) the book's definition, image is properly cast as an attribute instead of an element.

CDATA, PCDATA, and Entity References

Textual data contained in an XML element can be expressed as Character Data (CDATA), Parsed Character Data (PCDATA), or a combination of the two. Data that appears between <![CDATA[and]]> tags is CDATA; any other data is PCDATA. The following element contains PCDATA:

```
<title>XSLT Programmers Reference</title>
```

The next element contains CDATA:

```
<author><![CDATA[Michael Kay]]></author>
```

And the following contains both:

```
<title>XSLT Programmers Reference <![CDATA[Author - Michael Kay]]></title>
```

As you can see, CDATA is useful when you want some parts of your XML document to be ignored by the parser and not processed at all. This means you can put anything between <![CDATA[and]]> tags and an XML parser won't care; however data not enclosed in <![CDATA[and]]> tags must conform to the rules of XML. Often, CDATA sections are used to enclose code for scripting languages like VBScript or JavaScript.

XML parsers ignore CDATA but parse PCDATA — that is, interpret it as markup language. You might wonder why an XML parser distinguishes between CDATA and PCDATA. Certain characters, notably <, >, and &, have special meaning in XML and must be enclosed in CDATA sections if they're to be used verbatim. For example, suppose you wanted to define an element named range whose value is '0 < counter < 1000'. Because < is a reserved character, you can't define the element this way:

```
<range>0 < counter < 1000</range>
```

You can, however, define it this way:

```
<range><[CDATA[0 < counter < 100]]></range>
```

As you can see, CDATA sections are useful for including mathematical equations, code listings, and even other XML documents in XML documents.

Another way to include <, >, and & characters in an XML document is to replace them with entity references. An entity reference is a string enclosed in & and ; symbols. XML predefines the following entities:

Symbol	Corresponding Entity
<	lt
>	gt
&	amp
'	apos
"	quot

Using the entity references, you can alternatively define a range element with the value '0 < counter < 1000':

```
<range>0 &lt; counter &lt; 100</range>
```

You can also represent characters in PCDATA with character references, which are nothing more than numeric character codes enclosed in &# and ; symbols, as in

```
<range>0 &#60; counter &#60; 100</range>
```

Character references are useful for representing characters that can't be typed from the keyboard. Entity references are useful for escaping the occasional special character, but for large amounts of text containing arbitrary content, CDATA sections are far more convenient.

Namespaces

A namespace groups elements together by partitioning elements and their attributes into logical areas and providing a way to identify the elements and attributes uniquely. Namespaces are also used to reference a particular DTD or XML Schema. Namespaces were defined after XML 1.0 was formally presented to the public. After the release of XML 1.0, the W3C set out to resolve a few problems, one of which is related to naming conflicts. To understand the significance of this problem, first think about the future of the Web.

Shortly after the W3C introduced XML 1.0, an entire family of languages such as Mathematical Markup Language (MathML), Synchronized Multimedia Integration Language (SMIL), Scalable Vector Graphics (SVG), XLink, XForms, and the Extensible Hypertext Markup Language (XHTML) started appearing. Instead of relying on one language to bear the burden of communicating on the Web, the idea was to present many languages that could work together. If functions were modularized, each language could do what it does best; however the problem arises when a developer needs to use multiple vocabularies within the same application. For example, one might need to use a combination of languages such as SVG, SMIL, XHTML, and XForms for an interactive Web site. When mixing vocabularies, you have to have a way to distinguish between element types. Take the following example:

```
<html>
  <head>
    <title>Book List</title>
  </head>
```

```
      <body>
        <books>
          <book>
            <title>XSLT Programmers Reference</title>
            <author>Michael Kay</author>
          </book>
        </books>
      </body>
    </html>
```

In this example, there's no way to distinguish between the two title elements even though they are semantically different. A namespace can solve this problem by providing a unique identifier for a collection of elements and/or attributes. This is accomplished by prefixing each member element and attribute with a name, uniquely identifying them as part of that namespace. Grouping elements into a namespace allows them to be referenced easily by many XML documents and allows one XML document to reference many namespaces. XML namespaces are a form of qualifying attribute and element names. This is done within XML documents by associating them with namespaces that are identified with Universal Resource Indicators (URIs).

> *A URI is a unique name recognized by the processing application that identifies a particular resource. URIs includes Uniform Resource Locators (URL) and Uniform Resource Numbers (URN).*

The following is an example of using a namespace declaration that associates the namespace `http://www.w3.org/1999/xhtml` with the HTML element.

```
<html xmlns ="http://www.w3.org /1999/xhtml">
```

The `xmlns` keyword is a special kind of attribute that indicates you are about to declare an XML namespace. The information between the quotes is the URI, pointing to the actual namespace — in this case, a schema. The URI is a formal way to differentiate between namespaces; it doesn't necessarily need to point to anything at all. The URI is used only to demarcate elements and attributes uniquely. The `xmlns` declaration is placed inside the element tag using the namespace.

> *Namespaces can confuse XML novices because the namespace names are URIs and therefore often mistaken for a Web address that points to some resource; however, XML namespace names are URLs that don't necessarily have to point to anything. For example, if you visit the XSLT namespace (http://www .w3.org/1999/XSL/Transform), you would find a single sentence: "This is an XML Namespace defined in the XSL Transformations (XSLT) Version 1.0 specification." The unique identifier is meant to be symbolic; therefore, there's no need for a document to be defined. URLs were selected for namespace names because they contain domain names that can work globally across the Internet and they are unique.*

The following code shows the use of namespaces to resolve the name conflict in the preceding example.

```
<html xmlns="http://www.w3.org/1999/xhtml">
  <head>
    <title>Book List</title>
  </head>
  <body>
    <books xmlns="http://www.wrox.com/books/xml">
      <book>
        <title>XSLT Programmers Reference</title>
        <author>Michael Kay</author>
      </book>
```

```
      </books>
    </body>
  </html>
```

The books element belongs to the namespace `http://www.wrox.com/books/xslt`, whereas all the XHTML elements belong to the XHTML namespace `http://www.w3.org/1999/xhtml`.

Declaring Namespaces

To declare a namespace, you need to be aware of the three possible parts of a namespace declaration:

❑   `xmlns` — Identifies the value as an XML namespace and is required to declare a namespace and can be attached to any XML element.

❑   `prefix` — Identifies a namespace prefix. It (including the colon) is only used if you're declaring a namespace prefix. If it's used, any element found in the document that uses the prefix (prefix:element) is then assumed to fall under the scope of the declared namespace.

❑   `namespaceURI` — It is the unique identifier. The value does not have to point to a Web resource; it's only a symbolic identifier. The value is required and must be defined within single or double quotation marks.

There are two different ways you can define a namespace:

❑   `Default namespace` — Defines a namespace using the xmlns attribute without a prefix, and all child elements are assumed to belong to the defined namespace. Default namespaces are simply a tool to make XML documents more readable and easier to write. If you have one namespace that will be predominant throughout your document, it's easier to eliminate prefixing each of the elements with that namespace's prefix.

❑   `Prefixed namespace` — Defines a namespace using the xmlns attribute with a prefix. When the prefix is attached to an element, it's assumed to belong to that namespace.

> **Default namespaces save time when creating large documents with a particular namespace; however, they don't eliminate the need to use prefixes for attributes.**

The following example demonstrates the use of default namespaces and prefixed namespaces.

```
<html xmlns="http://www.w3.org/1999/xhtml">
<head>
<title>Book List</title>
</head>
<body>
  <blist:books
    xmlns:blist="http://www.wrox.com/books/xml">
    <blist:book>
      <blist:title>XSLT Programmers Reference</blist:title>
      <blist:author>Michael Kay</blist:author>
    </blist:book>
  </blist:books>
</body>
</html>
```

The `xmlns` defined at the root HTML element is the default namespace applied for all the elements that don't have an explicit namespace defined; however the books element defines an explicit namespace using the prefix `blist`. Because that prefix is used while declaring the books elements, all of the elements under books are considered to be using the prefixed namespace.

Role of Namespaces

A namespace is a set of XML elements and their constituent attributes. As you dive deep into XML, such as creating interactive XML Web pages for the Web and establishing guidelines for transporting data and so on, you will find that XML namespaces are incredibly important. Here are some of the uses of namespaces.

Reuse

Namespaces can allow any number of XML documents to reference them. This allows namespaces to be reused as needed, rather than forcing developers to reinvent them for each document they create. For instance, consider the common business scenario wherein you have two applications that exchange a common XML format: the server that generates the XML, relying on a particular namespace, and the client that consumes this XML, which also must rely on the same namespace. Rather than generating two namespaces (one for each application), a single namespace can be referenced by both applications in the XML they generate. This enables namespaces to be reused, which is an important feature. Not only can namespaces be reused by different parts of one application, they can be reused by different parts of any number of applications. Therefore, investing in developing a well thought out namespace can pay dividends for some time.

Multiple Namespaces

Just as multiple XML documents can reference the same namespace, one document can reference more than one namespace. This is a natural by-product of dividing elements into logical, ordered groups. Just as software development often breaks large processes into smaller procedures, namespaces are usually chunked into smaller, more logical groupings. Creating one large namespace with every element you think you might need doesn't make sense. This would be confusing to develop and it certainly would be confusing to anyone who had to use such an XML element structure. Rather, granular, more natural namespaces should be developed to contain elements that belong together.

For instance, you can create the namespaces as building blocks, assembled together to form the vocabularies required by a large program. For example, an application might perform services that help users to buy products from an e-commerce Web site. This application would require elements that define product categories, products, buyers, and so on. Namespaces make it possible to include these vocabularies inside one XML document, pulling from each namespace as needed.

Ambiguity

Namespaces can sometimes overlap and contain identical elements. This can cause problems when an XML document relies on the namespaces in question. An example of such a collision might be a namespace containing elements for book orders and another with elements for book inventories. Both might use elements that refer to a book's title or an author's name. When one document attempts to reference elements from both namespaces, this creates ambiguity for the XML parser. You can resolve this problem by wrapping the elements of book orders and book inventories in separate namespaces. Because elements and attributes that belong to a particular namespace are identified as such, they don't conflict with other elements and attributes sharing the same name. This solves the previously mentioned ambiguity. By prefacing a particular element or attribute name with the namespace prefix, a parser can correctly reconcile any potential name collisions. The process of using a namespace prefix creates qualified names for each of the elements and attributes used within a document.

XML Technologies

As the popularity of XML grows, new technologies that complement XML's capabilities also continue to grow. The following section takes a quick tour of the important XML technologies that are essential to the understanding and development of XML-based ASP.NET Web applications.

DTD

One of the greatest strengths of XML is that it allows you to create your own tag names. But for any given application, it is probably not meaningful for any kind of tags to occur in a completely arbitrary order. If the XML document is to have meaning, and certainly if you're writing a style sheet or application to process it, there must be some constraint on the sequence and nesting of tags. DTDs are one way using which constraints can be expressed.

DTDs, often referred to as doctypes, consist of a series of declarations for elements and associated attributes that may appear in the documents they validate. If this target document contains other elements or attributes, or uses included elements and attributes in the wrong way, validation will fail. In effect, the DTD defines a grammar for the documents it validates.

The following shows an example of what a DTD looks like:

```
<?xml version="1.0" ?>
<!-- DTD is not parsed as XML, but read by parser for validation -->
<!DOCTYPE book [
<!ELEMENT book (title, chapter+)>
<!ATTLIST book author CDATA #REQUIRED>
<!ELEMENT title (#PCDATA)>
<!ELEMENT chapter (#PCDATA)>
<!ATTLIST chapter id #REQUIRED>
]>
```

From the preceding DTD, you can already recognize enough vocabulary to understand this DTD as a definition of a book document that has elements book, title, and chapter and attributes author and id. A DTD can exist inline (inside the XML document), or it can be externally referenced using a URL.

A DTD also includes information about data types, whether values are required, default values, number of allowed occurrences, and nearly every other structural aspect you could imagine. At this stage, just be aware that your XML-based applications may require an interface with these types of information if your partners have translated documents from SGML to XML or are leveraging part of their SGML infrastructure.

As mentioned before, DTDs may either be stored internally as part of the XML document or externally in a separate file, accessible via a URL. A DTD is associated with an XML document by means of a `<!DOCTYPE>` declaration within the document. This declaration specifies a name for the doctype (which should be the same as the name of the root element in the XML document) along with either a URL reference to a remote DTD file, or the DTD itself.

It is possible to reference both external and internal DTDs, in which case the internal DTD is processed first, and duplicate definitions in the external file may cause errors. To specify an external DTD, use either the SYSTEM or PUBLIC keyword as follows:

```
<!DOCTYPE docTypeName SYSTEM "http://www.wrox.com/Books.dtd">
```

Using SYSTEM as shown allows the parser to load the DTD from the specified location. If you use PUBLIC, the named DTD should be one that is familiar to the parser being used, which may have a store of commonly used DTDs. In most cases, you will want to use your own DTD and use SYSTEM. This method enables the parsing application to make its own decisions as to what DTD to use, which may result in a performance increase; however, specific implementation of this is down to individual parsers, which might limit the usefulness of this technique.

> **As useful as DTDs are, they also have their shortcomings. The major concern most developers have with DTDs is the lack of strong type-checking. Also, DTDs are created using a strange and seemingly archaic syntax. They have only a limited capability in describing the document structure in terms of how many elements can nest within other elements.**

Because of the inherent disadvantages of DTDs, XML Schemas are the commonly used mechanism to validate XML documents. XML schemas are discussed in detail in a later section of this chapter.

XDR

XML Data Reduced (XDR) schema is Microsoft's own version of the W3C's early 1999 work-in-progress version of XSD. This schema is based on the W3C Recommendation of the XML-Data Note (http://www.w3.org/TR/1998/NOTE-XML-data), which defines the XML Data Reduced schema.

The following document contains the same information that you could find in a DTD. The main difference is that it has the structure of a well-formed XML document. This example shows the same constraints as the DTD example, but in an XML schema format:

```xml
<?xml version="1.0" ? >
<!-- XML-Data is a standalone valid document-->
<Schema xmlns="urn:schemas-microsoft-com:xml-data">
  <AttributeType name="author" required="yes"/>
  <AttributeType name="id" required="yes"/>
  <ElementType name="title" content="textOnly"/>
  <ElementType name="chapter" content="textOnly"/>
  <ElementType name="book" content="eltOnly">
    <attribute type="author" />
    <element type="title" />
    <element type="chapter" />
  </ElementType>
</Schema>
```

There are a few things that an XDR schema can do that a DTD cannot. You can directly add data types, range checking, and external references called namespaces.

XSD

The term *schema* is commonly used in the database community and refers to the organization or structure for a database. When this term is used in the XML community, it refers to the structure (or model) of a class of documents. This model describes the hierarchy of elements and allowable content in a valid XML document. In other words, the schema defines constraints for an XML vocabulary.

New standards for defining XML documents have become desirable because of the limitations imposed by DTDs. XML Schema Definition (XSD) schema, sometimes referred to as an XML schema, is a formal definition for defining a schema for a class of XML documents. The sheer volume of text involved in defining the XML schema language can be overwhelming to an XML novice, or even to someone making the move from DTDs to XML schema. As previously stated before our detour into namespaces, XML schemas have evolved as a response to problems with the W3C's first attempt at data validation, DTDs. DTDs are a legacy inherited from SGML to provide content validation and, although DTDs do a good job of validating XML, certainly room does exist for improvement. Some of the more important concerns expressed about DTDs are the following:

- ❑ DTD uses Extended Backus Naur Form syntax, which is dissimilar to XML.
- ❑ DTDs aren't intuitive, and they can be difficult to interpret from a human-readable point of view.
- ❑ The metadata of DTDs is programmatically difficult to consume.
- ❑ No support exists for data types.
- ❑ DTDs cannot be inherited.

To address these concerns, the W3C developed a new validating mechanism to replace DTDs called XML schemas. Schemas provide the same features DTDs provide, but they were designed with the previous issues in mind and thus are more powerful and flexible. The design principles outlined by the XML Schema Requirements document are fairly straightforward. XML schema documents should be created so they are as follows:

- ❑ More expressive than XML DTDs
- ❑ Expressed in XML
- ❑ Self-describing
- ❑ Usable in a wide variety of applications that employ XML
- ❑ Straightforwardly usable on the Internet
- ❑ Optimized for interoperability
- ❑ Simple enough to implement with modest design and runtime resources
- ❑ Coordinated with relevant W3C specs, such as XML Information Set, XML Linking Language (XLink), Namespaces in XML, Document Object Model (DOM), HTML, and the Resource Description Framework (RDF) schema

As mentioned earlier in this chapter, an XML schema is a method used to describe XML attributes and elements. This method for describing the XML file is actually written using XML, which provides many benefits over other validation techniques, such as DTD. These benefits include the following:

❑ Because the schema is written in XML, you don't have to know an archaic language to describe your document. Because you already know XML, using XSD schema is fairly easy and straightforward.

❑ The same engines to parse XML documents can also be used to parse schemas.

❑ Just as you can parse schemas in the same fashion as XML, you can also add nodes, attributes, and elements to schemas in the same manner.

❑ Schemas are widely accepted by most major parsing engines.

❑ Schemas allow you to data type with many different types. DTD only allows type content to be a string.

Now that you have had a brief look at the XSD schemas, the next section provides an in-depth look at schemas.

In-Depth Look at Schemas

One of the best ways to understand the XML schema language is to take a look at it; therefore, this section provides you with a brief example of a simple XML schema document followed by the XML document instance that conforms to the schema.

```
<?xml version="1.0" encoding="utf-8"?>
<xsd:schema
  xmlns:xsd="http://www.w3.org/2001/XMLSchema"
  elementFormDefault="qualified"
  targetNamespace="http://www.wrox.com/books/xml"
  xmlns="http://www.wrox.com/books/xml">
<xsd:element name="books">
  <xsd:complexType>
    <xsd:sequence>
      <xsd:element name="book" maxOccurs="unbounded">
        <xsd:complexType>
          <xsd:sequence>
            <xsd:element name="title" type="xsd:string"/>
            <xsd:element name="author" type="xsd:string"/>
          </xsd:sequence>
        </xsd:complexType>
      </xsd:element>
    </xsd:sequence>
  </xsd:complexType>
</xsd:element>
</xsd:schema>
```

Notice that schemas look similar to XML, and are usually longer than a DTD; typically, schemas are longer because they contain more information. Here is the XML document instance that conforms to the schema declaration.

```
<?xml version="1.0"?>
<books>
  <book>
    <title>XSLT Programmers Reference</title>
    <author>Michael Kay</author>
  </book>
</books>
```

Starting at the top with the preamble, the schema can be dissected as follows. A schema preamble is found within the element, schema. All XML schemas begin with the document element, schema. The first `xmlns` attribute is used to reference the namespace for the XML schema specification; it defines all the elements used to write a schema. The second `xmlns` attribute declares the namespace for the schema you are creating. Three letters is usually good for a namespace, but it can be longer. XML schemas can independently require elements and attributes to be qualified. The `elementFormDefault` attribute specifies whether or not elements need to be qualified with a namespace prefix. The default value is "unqualified." This schema, like most schemas, assigns the value of "qualified," which means that all locally declared elements must be qualified. This attribute also allows schemas to be used as the default schema for an XML document without having to qualify its elements. The `targetNamespace` attribute indicates the namespace and URI of the schema being defined.

> *The attribute targetNamespace is important because it's used to indicate this schema belongs to the same vocabulary as other schemas that reference the same namespace. This is how large vocabularies can be built, stringing them together with the schema keyword include.*

Now that you have a general understanding of the xsd:schema element, consider the following two constructs:

```
<xsd:element name="books">
<xsd:sequence>
```

The `xsd:element` uses the name attribute to define an element name (books); then, the sequence element is a compositor that tells the processor that the child elements nested with the sequence element must occur in that order when used as a part of an XML document instance.

XML Schema Datatypes

Datatypes provides document authors with a robust, extensible datatype system for XML. This datatype system is built on the idea of derivation. Beginning with one basic datatype, others are derived. In total, the datatypes specification defines 44 built-in datatypes (datatypes that are built into the specification) that you can use. In addition to these built-in datatypes, you can derive your own datatypes using techniques such as restricting the datatype, extending the datatype, adding datatypes, or allowing a datatype to consist of a list of datatypes.

XML Schema Usage Scenarios

There are many reasons document authors are turning to XML schema as their modeling language of choice. If you have a schema model, you can ensure that a document author follows it. This is important if you're defining an e-commerce application and you need to make sure that you receive exactly what you expect — nothing more and nothing less — when exchanging data. The schema model also ensures that data types are followed, such as rounding all prices to the second decimal place, for example. Another common usage for XML schema is to ensure that your XML data follows the document model before the data is sent to a transformation tool. For example, you may need to exchange data with your parent company, and because your parent company uses a legacy document model, your company uses different labeling (`bookPrice` versus `price`). In this case, you would need to transform your data so it conforms to the parent company's document model; however, before sending your XML data to be transformed, you want to be sure that it's valid because one error could throw off the transformation process. Another possible scenario is that you're asked to maintain a large collection of XML documents and then apply a style sheet to them to define the overall presentation (for example, for a CD-ROM or Web site). In this case, you need to make sure that each document follows the same document model. If one document uses a para instead of a p element (the latter of which the style sheet expects), the desired style may not be applied. These are only a few scenarios that require the use of XML schema (or a schema alternative).

There are countless other scenarios that would warrant their use. The XML Schema Working Group carefully outlined several usage scenarios that it wanted to account for while designing XML schema. They are as follows:

- ❏ Publishing and syndication
- ❏ E-commerce transaction processing
- ❏ Supervisory control and data acquisition
- ❏ Traditional document authoring/editing governed by schema constraints
- ❏ Using schema to help query formulation and optimization
- ❏ Open and uniform transfer of data between applications, including databases
- ❏ Metadata interchange

As defined by the XML Schema Requirements Document, the previous usage scenarios were used to help shape and develop XML schema.

XSLT

Extensible Stylesheet Language Transformations (XSLT) is a language used for converting XML documents from one format to another. Although it can be applied in a variety of ways, XSLT enjoys two primary uses:

- ❏ Converting XML documents into HTML documents
- ❏ Converting XML documents into other XML documents

The first application — turning XML into HTML — is useful for building Web pages and other browser-based documents in XML. XML defines the content and structure of data, but it doesn't define the data's appearance. Using XSLT to generate HTML from XML is a fine way to separate content from appearance and to build generic documents that can be displayed however you want them displayed. You can also use Cascading Style Sheets (CSS) to layer appearance over XML content, but XSLT is more versatile than CSS and provides substantially more control over the output.

Here is how the transformation works: You feed a source XML document and an XSL style sheet that describes how the document is to be transformed to an XSLT processor. The XSLT processor, in turn, generates the output document using the rules in the style sheet. You see an in-depth discussion on XSLT and its usage in .NET in Chapter 7.

As mentioned earlier in this chapter, XSLT can also be used to convert XML document formats. Suppose company A expects XML invoices submitted by company B to conform to a particular format (that is, fit a particular schema), but company B already has an XML invoice format and doesn't want to change it to satisfy the whims of company A. Rather than lose company B's business, company A can use XSLT to convert invoices submitted by company B to company A's format. That way, both companies are happy, and neither has to go to extraordinary lengths to work with the other. XML-to-XML XSLT conversions are the cornerstone of middleware applications such as Microsoft BizTalk Server that automate business processes by orchestrating the flow of information.

XML DOM

The W3C has standardized an API for accessing XML documents known as XML DOM. The DOM API represents an XML document as a tree of nodes. Because an XML document is hierarchical in structure, you can build a tree of nodes and subnodes to represent an entire XML document. You can get to any arbitrary node by starting at the root node and traversing the child nodes of the root node. If you don't find the node you are looking for, you can traverse the grandchild nodes of the root node. You can continue this process until you find the node you are looking for.

The DOM API provides other services in additional to document traversal. You can find the full W3C XML DOM specification at http://www.w3.org/DOM. The following list shows some of the capabilities provided by the DOM API:

- ❏ Find the root node in an XML document.
- ❏ Find a list of elements with a given tag name.
- ❏ Get a list of children of a given node.
- ❏ Get the parent of a given node.
- ❏ Get the tag name of an element.
- ❏ Get the data associated with an element.
- ❏ Get a list of attributes of an element.
- ❏ Get the tag name of an attribute.
- ❏ Get the value of an attribute.
- ❏ Add, modify, or delete an element in the document.
- ❏ Add, modify, or delete an attribute in the document.
- ❏ Copy a node in a document (including subnodes).

The DOM API provides a rich set of functionality to programmers as is shown in the previous list. The .NET Framework provides excellent support for the XML DOM API through the classes contained in the namespace System.Xml, which you will see later in this book. The DOM API is well suited for traversing and modifying an XML document, but, it provides little support for finding an arbitrary element or attribute in a document. Fortunately another XML technology is available to provide this support: XML Path Language (XPath).

XPath

XML is technically limited in that it is impossible to query or navigate through an XML document using XML alone. XPath language overcomes this limitation. XPath is a navigational query language specified by the W3C for locating data within an XML document. You can use XPath to query an XML document much as you use SQL to query a database. An XPath query expression can select on document parts, or types, such as the document's elements, attributes, and text. It was created for use with XSLT and XPointer, as well as other components of XML such as the upcoming XQuery specification. All of these technologies require some mechanism that enables querying and navigation within the structure of an XML document.

The word *path* refers to XPath's use of a location path to locate the desired parts of an XML document. This concept is similar to the path used to locate a file in the directories of a file system, or the path specified in a URL in a Web browser to locate a specific page in a complex Web site. One of the most important uses of XPath is in conjunction with XSLT. For example, you can utilize XPath to query XML documents and then leverage XSLT to transform the resulting XML into an HTML document (for display in any format desired) or any other form of XML (for import into another program that may use a different set of XML tags). XPath is very powerful in that you can not only use it to query an XML document for a list of nodes matching a given criteria, but also apply Boolean operators, string functions, and arithmetic operators to XPath expressions to build extremely complex queries against an XML document. XPath also provides functions to do numeric evaluations, such as summations and rounding. You can find the full W3C XPath specification at `http://www.w3.org/TR/xpath`. The following list shows some of the capabilities of the XPath language:

❑   Find all children of the current node.

❑   Find all ancestor elements of the current context node with a specific tag.

❑   Find the last child element of the current node with a specific tag.

❑   Find the nth child element of the current context node with a given attribute.

❑   Find the first child element with a tag of `<tag1>` or `<tag2>`.

❑   Get all child nodes that do not have an element with a given attribute.

❑   Get the sum of all child nodes with a numeric element.

❑   Get the count of all child nodes.

The preceding list just scratches the surface of the capabilities available using XPath. Once again, the .NET Framework provides excellent built-in support for XPath queries against XML DOM documents and read-only XPath documents. You will see examples of this in later chapters.

SAX

In sharp contrast to XML DOM, the Simple API for XML (SAX) approaches its manipulation of a document as a stream of data parts instead of their aggregation. SAX requires the programmer to decide what nodes the application will recognize to trigger an event. DOM uses a parallel approach to the document, meaning it can access several different level nodes with one method. SAX navigates an XML document in serial, starting at the beginning and responding to its contents once for each node and in the order they appear in the document.

Because it has a considerably smaller memory footprint, SAX can make managing large documents (usually one measured in megabytes) and retrieving small amounts from them much easier and quicker. Because a SAX application approaches a document in search of nested messages for which it generates responses, aborting a load under SAX is easier than doing so under DOM. The speed by which you can find a certain type of node data in a large document is also improved.

XLink and XPointer

It's hard to imagine the World Wide Web without hyperlinks, and, of course, HTML documents excel at letting you link from one to another. How about XML? In XML, it turns out, you use XLinks and XPointers.

XLinks enables any element to become a link, not just a single element as with the HTML <A> element. That's a good thing because XML doesn't have a built-in <A> element. In XML, you define your own elements, and it only makes sense that you can define which of those represent links to other documents. In fact, XLinks are more powerful than simple hyperlinks. XLinks can be bidirectional, allowing the user to return after following a link. They can even be multidirectional — in fact, they can be sophisticated enough to point to the nearest mirror site from which a resource can be fetched.

XPointers, on the other hand, point not to a whole document, but to a part of a document. In fact, XPointers are smart enough to point to a specific element in a document, or the second instance of such an element, or any instance. They can even point to the first child element of another element, and so on. The idea is that XPointers are powerful enough to locate specific parts of another document without forcing you to add more markup to the target document.

On the other hand, the whole idea of XLinks and XPointers is relatively new and not fully implemented in any browser. Here are some XLink and XPointer references online that will provide you more information on these topics.

❏　`http://www.w3.org/TR/xlink/` — The W3C XLink page

❏　`http://www.w3.org/TR/xptr` — The W3C XPointer page

XQuery

XQuery (XML Query) is a language for finding and extracting (querying) data from XML documents. XQuery is a query language specification under development by the W3C that's designed to query collections of XML data — not just XML files, but anything that can appear as XML, including relational databases. Using XQuery, you can easily and efficiently extract information from native XML databases and relational databases. XQuery uses the structure of XML intelligently to express queries across all these kinds of data, whether physically stored in XML or viewed as XML via middleware.

XQuery makes heavy use of XPath. In fact, XQuery 1.0 and XPath 2.0 are under development by the same W3C working group, and their specifications are intertwined. XQuery 1.0 and XPath 2.0 share the same data model, the same functions, and the same syntax. Because the XQuery 1.0 specification is still in draft status, .NET Framework 2.0 does not provide support for XQuery 1.0 specification.

The XML Advantage

XML has had an impact across a broad range of areas. The following is a list of some of the factors that have influenced XML's adoption by a variety of organizations and individuals.

❑ XML files are human-readable. XML was designed as text so that, in the worst case, someone can always read it to figure out the content. Such is not the case with binary data formats.

❑ Widespread industry support exists for XML. Numerous tools and utilities are being provided with Web browsers, databases, and operating systems, making it easier and less expensive for small and medium-sized organizations to import and export data in XML format. For example, the .NET Framework has XML support available everywhere in the framework enabling the developers to easily and effectively utilize the power of the XML.

❑ Major relational databases such as SQL Server 20005 have the native capability to store, read and generate XML data.

❑ A large family of XML support technologies is available for the interpretation and transformation of XML data for Web page display and report generation.

Summary

Much more can certainly be written about XML and a number of books have done just that. This chapter just scratched the surface of XML by providing an overview of XML, highlighting important features related to XML. This chapter also discussed the related XML technologies used later in this book. To summarize this chapter:

❑ XML is extensible. It provides a specification for creating your own tags. XML is a metamarkup language.

❑ To be well formed, XML must essentially conform syntactically to the W3C specification, and all elements within the document must be children of one and only one document element.

❑ You have the ability to create your own tags, so make them meaningful. Because XML doesn't define any tags, creating tags that make sense to other developers is crucial.

❑ Namespaces provide a way to group elements and attributes into one vocabulary using a unique name. Using the xmlns attribute, a namespace prefix is bound to a unique namespace name.

❑ XML schemas offer developers a rich language to describe and define the structure, cardinality, datatypes, and overall content of their XML documents.

❑ Two object models exist for processing the content in any XML document: the DOM and SAX. The DOM allows random access and the capability to modify, delete, and replace nodes in the XML hierarchy. SAX provides a simple, efficient way to process large XML documents.

❑ XSLT provides a way to transform an XML document to another format such as HTML or another type of XML.

❑ XPath is a language that permits you to address the parts of an XML document.

2

Introduction to ASP.NET 2.0

With the release of ASP.NET 1.0, Microsoft revolutionized Web application development by providing a rich set of features aimed at increasing developer productivity. Now with ASP.NET 2.0, Microsoft increased the bar to a much higher level by providing excellent features out-of-the-box that are not only geared towards increasing the productivity of the developers but also simplifying the administration and management of ASP.NET 2.0 applications. These new features combined with the increased speed and performance of ASP.NET 2.0, arm the developers with a powerful platform that can make a significant impact in the way Web applications are developed, deployed, and maintained.

This chapter takes a quick tour of the new ASP.NET 2.0 features. Specifically, this chapter discusses the features of this new improved platform that will help you in designing, developing, and deploying enterprise class Web applications.

ASP.NET 2.0 Features

When Microsoft started designing the feature-set of ASP.NET 2.0, they had the following three core themes in mind:

- ❑ Developer Productivity
- ❑ Administration and Management
- ❑ Speed and Performance

The next few sections examine the features of ASP.NET 2.0 based on these categories.

Developer Productivity

One of the goals of ASP.NET 2.0 is to enable developers to easily and quickly build feature-rich Web applications. To accomplish this, Microsoft has looked at the existing ASP.NET 1.x applications to identify the common features, patterns, and code that developers build over and over today. After they have identified those features, they have componentized those features and included them as built-in functionality of ASP.NET. With ASP.NET 2.0, the ASP.NET team has a goal of reducing the number of lines of code required for an application by a whopping 70 percent. To this end, Microsoft has introduced a collective arsenal of new features that are now available to developers in ASP.NET 2.0.

Using these features, you can spend your time building richer, more fully featured applications by leveraging the new controls and infrastructure services built into the core platform as opposed to writing a lot of infrastructure code as is the case with ASP.NET 1.x. For example, ASP.NET 2.0 now includes built-in support for membership (user name/password credential storage) and role management services out of the box. The new personalization service provides for quick storage/retrieval of user settings and preferences, enabling rich customization with minimal code. With ASP.NET 2.0, Microsoft has introduced a new concept known as Master Pages that now enable flexible page UI inheritance across sites. The new site navigation system enables developers to quickly build link structures consistently across a site. Site counters enable rich logging and instrumentation of client browser access patterns. Themes enable flexible UI skinning of controls and pages. And the new ASP.NET Web Part framework enables rich portal-style layout and end user customization features that would require tens of thousands of lines of code to write today. Along with all these features, ASP.NET 2.0 also brings with it 45 new server controls that enable powerful declarative support for data access, login security, wizard navigation, image generation, menus, treeviews, portals, and more. The next few sections provide you with a glimpse of these features.

Master Pages

ASP.NET 2.0 introduces a new concept known as Master Pages, in which a common base master file contains the common look and feel and standard behavior for all the pages in your application. After the common content is available in the Master Page, the content pages (child pages) can inherit content from the Master Pages apart from adding their content to the final output. To allow the content page to add its own content, you add placeholders (known as ContentPlaceHolder control) in the Master Page that will be utilized by the content pages (or child pages) to add their custom content. When users request the content pages, the output of the content pages are merged with the output of the Master Page, resulting in an output that combines the layout of the Master Page with the output of the content page.

> In ASP.NET 1.x, you could achieve similar effects by creating user controls that abstract the common look and behavior of all the pages in the application and then declaring user control in each and every page. Even though this approach was useful, it required a lot of cut and paste of code across all the pages in a Web application. Master Pages take this approach of reusable user controls to the next level by providing a much cleaner approach to reusing common look and feel across all the pages.

Master Pages are saved with the file extension .master. Apart from containing all the contents that are required for defining the standard look and feel of the application, the master pages also contain all the top-level HTML elements for a page, such as <html>, <head>, and <form>. As mentioned earlier in this chapter, the Master Pages also contain one or more content placeholders that are used to define regions that will be rendered through the content pages. Now that you have had a general understanding of Master Pages, let us look at an example. First, create a Master Page named BasePage.master and add the code shown in Listing 2-1.

Listing 2-1: A Master Page Example

```
<%@ master language="C#" %>
<html xmlns="http://www.w3.org/1999/xhtml">
<head runat="server">
  <title>Master Page</title>
</head>
<body>
  <form runat="server">
    Master Page Content
    <br/>
    <b>
      <asp:ContentPlaceHolder id="MiddleContent" runat="server">
      </asp:ContentPlaceHolder>
    </b>
  </form>
</body>
</html>
```

Apart from looking at the file extension, you can also identify a master file by looking at the new page directive named master at the top of the page. This declarative is used to identify that the current page is a Master Page and prevents the users from requesting the page from a browser. Inside the code, the code contains an element named `asp:ContentPlaceHolder` that will be used by all the content pages to render appropriate content that is specific to their pages. That's all there is to creating the Master Page. To create a content page, add a new ASP.NET page named `ContentPage.aspx` and modify the code to look like the following:

```
<%@ page language="c#" MasterPageFile="~/BasePage.master" %>
<asp:Content id="Content1" ContentPlaceHolderID="MiddleContent"
  runat="server">
  Child Page Content
</asp:Content>
```

The code required for the content page is very simple and straightforward. As part of the Page directive, specify a new attribute named `MasterPageFile` that is used to identify the name of Master Page you want to utilize. This example uses the Master Page created in the previous example. Next you have a new element named `asp:Content` that is used to associate the `asp:ContentPlaceHolder` element in the Master Page with the content page. This is done through the use of the ContentPlaceHolderID attribute. That's all there is to creating a Master Page and using the Master Page from a content page.

Creating and Sharing Reusable Components in ASP.NET 2.0

Prior to ASP.NET 2.0, if you were to reference a reusable class from your ASP.NET application, you had to compile the assembly and place it in the bin folder (or place it in the GAC) of the Web application. But now with ASP.NET 2.0, creating a reusable class is very simple and straightforward. All you need to do is to create the class in a pre-defined subdirectory called App_Code. Any class placed in this directory will be automatically compiled at runtime into a single assembly. This assembly is automatically referenced and will be available to all the pages in the site. Note that you should only put classes in the App_Code subdirectory.

New ASP.NET 2.0 Controls

ASP .NET 2.0 introduces several new controls that help create data-driven Web applications. These controls perform actions, such as connecting to a database, executing commands against the database, and so on without you even having to write a single line of code. To start with, the next section explores the new data source controls supplied with ASP.NET 2.0.

Data Controls

One of the important goals of ASP.NET 2.0 is 70 percent code reduction. The data controls supplied with ASP.NET 2.0 play an important role in making this ambitious goal a reality. Data source controls provide a consistent and extensible method for declaratively accessing data from Web pages. Data source controls supplied with ASP.NET 2.0 are as follows:

❑   `<asp:SqlDataSource>` — This data source control is designed to work with SQL Server, OLE DB, ODBC, and Oracle databases. Using this control, you can also enable select, update, delete, and insert data using SQL commands.

❑   `<asp:ObjectDataSource>` — N-Tier methodology allows you to create Web applications that are not only scalable and but also easier to maintain. N-Tier principle also enables clean separation thereby allowing you to easily add new functionalities. In an N-Tier application, the middle tier objects may return complex objects that you have to process in your ASP.NET presentation layer. Keeping this requirement in mind, Microsoft has created this new control that allows you to seamlessly integrate the data returned from the middle layer objects with the ASP.NET presentation layer.

❑   `<asp:AccessDataSource>` — This is similar to the `SqlDataSource` control, except that it is designed to work with Access databases.

❑   `<asp:XmlDataSource>` — The `XmlDataSource` control allows you to bind to XML data, which can come from a variety of sources such as an external XML file, a DataSet object and so on. After the XML data is bound to the `XmlDataSource` control, this control can then act as a source of data for data-bound controls such as `TreeView` and Menu.

❑   `<asp:SiteMapDataSource>` — The `SiteMapDataSource` control provides a site navigation framework that makes the creation of a site navigation system a breezy experience. Accomplishing this requires the use of a new XML file named web.sitemap that lays out the pages of the site in a hierarchical XML structure. After you have the site hierarchy in the web.sitemap file, you can then data-bind the `SiteMapDataSource` control with the web.sitemap file. The contents of the `SiteMapDataSource` control can then be bound to data-aware controls such as `TreeView`, Menu control, and so on.

Now that you have had a look at the data source controls supplied with ASP.NET 2.0, this section examines the data-bound controls that you will normally use to display data contained in the data source controls. These data-bound controls bind data automatically.

One of the nice things about data-bound control is that the development environment automatically guides developers through the process of binding a data control to a data source. Developers are prompted to select the particular data source to use for selecting, inserting, updating, and deleting data. The feature that walks the developers through this process is called Smart Tasks. This is explained in detail in the Visual Studio Improvements section in the later part of this chapter.

Some data-bound controls introduced in ASP .NET 2.0 are:

❑ `<asp:GridView>` — This control is successor to the `DataGrid` control that was part of ASP.NET 1.0, and is used to display multiple records in a Web page; however the `GridView` also enables you to add, update, and delete a record in a database without writing a single line of code. As similar to the `DataGrid` control, in a `GridView` control each column represents a field, while each row represents a record. As you would expect, you can bind a `GridView` control to a `SqlDataSource` control, as well as to any data source control as long as that control implements the `System.Collections.IEnumerable` interface.

❑ `<asp:DetailsView>` — The `DetailsView` control can be used in conjunction with the `GridView` control to display a specific record in the data source.

❑ `<asp:FormView>` — Provides a user interface to display and modify the data stored in a database. The `FormView` control provides different templates, such as `ItemTemplate` and `EditItemTemplate` that you can use to view and modify the database records.

❑ `<asp:TreeView>` — The `TreeView` control provides a seamless way to consume information from hierarchical data sources such as an XML file and then display that information. You can use the `TreeView` control to display information from a wide variety of data sources such as an XML file, site-map file, string, or from a database.

❑ `<asp:Menu>` — The Menu control, similar to the `TreeView` control, can be used to display hierarchical data. You can use the Menu control to display static data, site map data, and database data. The main difference between the two controls is their appearance.

Listing 2-2 demonstrates how to use the combination of `SqlDataSource` and `GridView` controls to retrieve and display data from the Categories table in the Northwind database without even having a single line of code.

Listing 2-2: Using SqlDataSource Control to Retrieve Categories Information

```
<%@ page language="C#" %>
<html xmlns="http://www.w3.org/1999/xhtml">
<head id="Head1" runat="server">
  <title>Data Binding using SqlDataSource control</title>
</head>
<body>
  <form id="Form1" runat="server">
    <asp:SqlDataSource id="categoriesSource" runat="server"
      ConnectionString="server=localhost;database=AdventureWorks;
      uid=user1;pwd=password1
      SelectCommand="SELECT * From Production.ProductCategory">
    </asp:SqlDataSource>
    <asp:GridView DataSourceID="categoriesSource" runat="server"
      id="gridCategories">
    </asp:GridView>
  </form>
</body>
</html>
```

The code declares a `SqlDataSource` control and a `GridView` control. The `SqlDataSource` control declaration also specifies the connection string and the `Sql` statement to be executed as attributes. The `DataSourceID` attribute in the `GridView` is the one that links the `SqlDataSource` control to the

`GridView` control. That's all there is to retrieving the data from the database and displaying it in a Web page. Figure 2-1 shows the output produced by the page when requested from the browser.

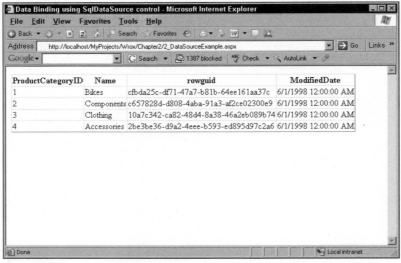

Figure 2-1

Security Controls

With the large amount of business being done on the Web, security is vitally important for protecting not only confidential information such as credit card numbers but also users' personal details and preferences. Thus most of the Web applications require the capability to authenticate users on their Web sites. Although this was easy to do it in ASP.NET 1.x, you still had to write code. With ASP.NET 2.0, things have changed for the better. For security related functionalities, ASP.NET 2.0 introduces a wide range of new controls:

- ❑ `<asp:Login>` — Provides a standard login capability that allows the users to enter their credentials
- ❑ `<asp:LoginName>` — Allows you to display the name of the logged-in user
- ❑ `<asp:LoginStatus>` — Displays whether the user is authenticated or not
- ❑ `<asp:LoginView>` — Provides various login views depending on the selected template
- ❑ `<asp:PasswordRecovery>` — Provides the Web site administrators with the capability of emailing the users their lost password

These login controls abstract most of the common tasks performed by developers when writing code for a secured Web site. Although this could be achieved in ASP.NET 1.x, you still had to add controls manually and write code. Apart from providing the user interface, ASP.NET 2.0 also provides the ability to retrieve and validate user information using Membership functionality. To this end, ASP.NET ships with a new Membership API, whose aim is to abstract the required membership functionality from the storage of the member information.

Validation Groups

In ASP.NET 1.x, you assign validation controls to input controls such as text boxes, password fields, radio buttons, and check boxes and the validation controls will automatically validate the data entered by an end user to input controls. With ASP.NET 2.0, Microsoft introduces a new feature, known as Validation Groups, which enables you to create different groups of validation controls and assign them to input controls, such as text boxes. You can assign a Validation Group to a collection of input controls if you want to validate the collection of input controls on the same criteria. For example, you can assign the button control to a group of input controls and validate the data entered to each group of input controls on a criterion. This feature is handy when you have multiple forms on a single Web page. For example, you can create a Web page that contains login and password text boxes for registered end users, and another set of controls for new end users to register with the Web site. In this case, you can use the `ValidationGroup` property to perform different actions, such as logging on to the Web site and registering an end user.

Themes

One of the neat features of ASP.NET 2.0 is Themes, which enables you to define the appearance of a set of controls once and apply the appearance to your entire Web application. For example, you can utilize themes to define a common appearance for all of the `CheckBox` controls in your application, such as the background and foreground color, in one central location. By leveraging themes, you can easily create and maintain a consistent look throughout your Web site. Themes are extremely flexible in that they can be applied to an entire Web application, to a page, or to an individual control. Theme files are stored with extension `.skin` and all the themes for a Web application are stored in the special folder named `App_Themes`.

> As you read this, you might be wondering if themes are another variation of Cascading Style Sheets. Themes are not the same thing as Cascading Style Sheets. Using Cascading Style Sheets, you can control the appearance of HTML tags on the browser; themes are applied on the server and they apply to the properties of ASP.NET controls. Another difference is that themes can also include external files such as images and so on.

The implementation of themes in ASP.NET 2.0 is built around two areas: skins and themes. A skin is a set of properties and templates that can be applied to controls. A theme is a set of skins and any other associated files (such as images or style sheets). Skins are control specific, so for a given theme there could be a separate skin for each control within that theme. Any controls without a skin inherit the default look. There are two types of themes.

- ❑ Customization-themes — These types of themes are applied after the properties of the control are applied meaning that the properties of the themes override the properties of the control itself.

- ❑ Style sheet-themes — You can apply this type of theme to a page in exactly the same manner as a customization-theme; however, style sheet themes don't override control properties, thus allowing the control to use the theme properties or override them.

Characteristics of ASP.NET 2.0 Themes

Some of the important characteristics of ASP.NET 2.0 themes are as follows:

❑ Themes make it simple to customize the appearance of a site or page, using the same design tools and methods used when developing the page itself thus obviating the need to learn any special tools or techniques to add and apply themes to a site.

❑ You can apply themes to controls, pages, and even entire sites. You can leverage this feature to customize parts of a Web site while retaining the identity of the other parts of the site.

❑ Themes allow all visual properties to be customized, thus ensuring that when themed, pages and controls can achieve a consistent style.

❑ Customization themes override control definitions, thus changing the look and feel of controls. Customization themes are applied with the Theme attribute on the Page directive.

❑ Style sheet themes don't override control definitions, thus allowing the control to use the theme properties or override them. Style sheet themes are applied with the StylesheetTheme attribute on the Page directive.

Now that you have an understanding of the concepts behind themes, the next section provides you with a quick example of creating a theme and utilizing it from an ASP.NET page.

Creating a Simple Theme

To create a theme and apply it to a specific page, go through the following steps.

❑ Create a folder called ControlThemes under the App_Themes folder.

❑ Create a file with the extension .skin and add all the controls (that you want to use in a page) and their style properties. Or you can also create individual skin files for each and every control. When you are defining skin files, remember to remove the ID attribute from all of the controls declaration. For example, you can use the following code to define the theme for a button control.

```
<asp:Button runat="server" BackColor="Black" ForeColor="White"
    Font-Name="Arial" Font-Size="10px" />
```

❑ Name the skin file as Button.skin and place it under the ControlThemes folder. After you have created the .skin file, you can then apply that theme to all the pages in your application by using appropriate settings in the web.config file. To apply the theme to a specific page, all you need to do is to add the Theme attribute to the Page directive as shown here.

```
<%@Page Theme="ControlThemes" %>
```

That's all there is to creating a theme and utilizing it in an ASP.NET page. It is also possible for you to programmatically access the theme associated with a specific page using the Page.Theme property. Similarly, you can also set the SkinID property of any of the control's to specify the skin. If the theme does not contain a SkinID value for the control type, no error is thrown and the control simply defaults to its own properties. For dynamic controls, it is possible to set the SkinID property after they are created.

Web Parts Framework

There are many times where you would want to allow the users of your Web site to be able to customize the content by selecting, removing, and rearranging the contents in the Web page. Traditionally implementing this capability required a lot of custom code or you had to depend on third-party products to accomplish this. To address this shortcoming, ASP.NET 2.0 ships with a Web Parts Framework that provides the infrastructure and the building blocks required for creating modular Web pages that can be easily customized by the users. You can use Web Parts to create portal pages that aggregate different types of content such as static text, links, and content that can change at runtime. It is also possible for the users to change the layout of the Web Parts by dragging and dropping from one place to another, providing a rich user experience.

> **Web Parts are reusable pieces of code that allows you to logically group related functionality together into one unit. After the Web Parts are added to an ASP.NET page, they can then be shown, hidden, moved around, and redesigned all by the user.**

By taking advantage of Web Parts, you as a developer can empower your users with the ability to perform the following operations.

- ❑ Personalize page content
- ❑ Personalize the page layout by allowing the users to drag Web parts from one zone to another zone, or change its appearance, look, and feel and so on
- ❑ Users can also export and import Web Part controls so that the Web parts can be effectively shared among other sites
- ❑ Users can create connections between two Web Parts by establishing communication between Web Part controls

As a developer, you will typically work with Web Parts in one of the three ways: creating pages that use Web Parts controls, creating individual Web Parts controls, or creating complete personalizable Web portals. There are two kinds of Web Parts that you can create in ASP.NET 2.0:

- ❑ Custom Web Part — Custom Web Parts are those Web Part controls that derive from the `System.Web.UI.WebParts.WebPart` class.
- ❑ Generic Web Part — A custom control that does not inherit from the WebPart class and still used as a Web Part is called `GenericWebPart`. For example, if you place a textbox control inside a `WebPartZone` (`WebPartZone` is a zone on the page that hosts the Web parts control) control, the textbox control will be wrapped to a `GenericWebPart` class.

Creating a Simple Web Part

This section provides you with a simple generic Web Part creation example followed by the code examination. Listing 2-3 shows the code required to implement the Web Part.

Listing 2-3: Creating a Simple Generic Web Part

```
<%@ Page Language="C#" %>
<html xmlns="http://www.w3.org/1999/xhtml" >
<head runat="server">
  <title>Example of a Generic Web Part</title>
</head>
<body>
<form id="form1" runat="server">
```

```
<asp:WebPartManager id="WebPartManager1" runat="Server">
</asp:WebPartManager>
<table cellspacing="0" cellpadding="0" border="0">
  <tr>
    <td valign="top">
      <asp:WebPartZone id="MainZone" runat="server"
        headertext="Main">
        <ZoneTemplate>
          <asp:Label id="contentPart" runat="server"
            title="Generic Web Part">
            <h4>Generic Web part that uses a label control
              to generate the contents of the Web part
            </h4>
          </asp:Label>
        </ZoneTemplate>
      </asp:WebPartZone>
    </td>
  </tr>
</table>
</form>
</body>
</html>
```

To start with, you declare a `WebPartManager` control. The `WebPartManager` control is a must for any ASP.NET page that utilizes Web Parts. This control must be the first element in an ASP.NET Web form, above all other Web Parts, zones, or any other custom or specialized Web Part controls. The `WebPartManager` has no visual element associated with it; however it is very crucial because of the required plumbing it provides for managing the interactions between Web Parts. The code then declares a `WebPartZone` control, which in turn includes a label control that consists of all the HTML elements that make up the display of the Web Part. `WebPartZone` control is the one that provides overall layout for the Web Part controls that compose the main UI of a page. Before navigating to the page using the browser, enable Windows Authentication for the Web site through IIS Manager. Now run the page and you will see the following output shown in Figure 2-2.

Figure 2-2

In Figure 2-2, you can choose to minimize or close the Web part by clicking on the appropriate links.

Personalization Framework

There are times when you want to store and present information that is unique to a specific user. For instance, when a user visits your site, you can collect information from the user about his preference such as color scheme, styles, and so on. After you have that information, you can use it to present the user with a personalized version of your Web application. To implement this with ASP.NET 1.x, you had to go through the following steps.

❑ Store the information about the user using a unique user identifier. This information is used to uniquely identify the user when the user visits again.

❑ Fetch the user information as needed.

❑ Present the user with the personalized content.

Now with the introduction of ASP.NET 2.0 personalization, all of these complexities are handled by the personalization framework itself. In ASP.NET personalization, information about a specific user is stored in a persistent format. Also ASP.NET personalization allows you to easily manage user information without requiring you to create and maintain your own database. In addition, the personalization system makes the user information available using a consistent, easy-to-use, strongly typed API that you can access from anywhere in your application. You can also store objects of any type in the personalization system, including user information, user preferences, or business information. The personalization system uses a generic storage system for storing the data and makes that data available to the users in a type-safe manner. By default, ASP.NET 2.0 uses SQL Server as the storage mechanism.

Visual Studio 2005 Improvements

Visual Studio 2005 is the best development tool for building data driven Web applications. As part of the Visual Studio 2005 suite of tools, Microsoft is introducing a new tool called Visual Web Developer that is designed to work with the current and next generation of ASP.NET. Visual Web Developer provides powerful new features for the Web developer. Visual Web Developer is also tuned to the specific needs of the Web developer through a new Web profile that exposes a menu and window layout optimized for Web development. The environment includes a best-of-breed HTML source editor, an improved visual page designer, better Intellisense support, a new project system, better support for working with data, and full XHTML standards support. Collectively, these features enable you to develop data-driven Web applications faster than ever before. The next few sections explore some of the important Web development improvements coming with Visual Web Developer.

> Intellisense is the pop-up code hints that automatically appear when you type in the development environment.

Better Source Code Editing

Visual Web Developer provides an improved HTML source editor which enables you to write and modify your pages faster. The source editor provides full Intellisense throughout your files and has new features for navigating and validating your markup.

Although Visual Studio.NET provides excellent Intellisense support, it gets even better with Visual Studio 2005. In Visual Studio 2005, Intellisense pops up everywhere. For example, you can take full advantage of Intellisense within the script blocks, page directives, inline CSS style attributes, Web.config configuration file, as well as in any generic XML file that contains a DTD or XML schema reference.

HTML Source Preservation

Visual Studio 2005 preserves the formatting of your HTML markup, including all white space, casing, indention, carriage returns, and word wrapping. The formatting is preserved exactly even when switching back and forth between the Design view and Source view of the page. This is one of the important features that developers have been clamoring for in the previous versions of Visual Studio.

Tag Navigator

Visual Studio 2005 comes with a new Tag Navigator feature that enables developers to easily track their location in an HTML document, thereby providing excellent navigation support. The Tag Navigator displays the current path within the source of an HTML page by displaying a list of all the HTML tags that contain the tag where your cursor is currently located. Clicking on any of the nodes enables developers to optionally change the source level selection, and quickly move up and down a deep HTML hierarchy. This feature can be very handy, especially when you are editing multiple nested HTML elements. For example, when you are editing multiple nested HTML tables, it is very easy to get lost, and you can leverage Tag Navigator to easily identify the current path within the hierarchy of table elements.

Targeting Specific Browsers and HTML Validation

Using Visual Studio 2005, you can easily target a specific HTML standard or browser when writing your HTML pages. For example, you can target your HTML pages to work with a particular browser such as Internet Explorer 5.0 or Netscape Navigator 4.0. Alternatively, you can target a particular HTML standard such as XHTML 1.0 Strict or XHTML 1.0 Transitional. As you type your HTML in the source editor, it is automatically validated in real time. Invalid HTML is automatically underlined with a red squiggly and all the validation errors are also summarized in real time within the Task List window.

Code Refactoring

Code Refactoring allows you to change the code structure without changing or affecting what the code itself actually does. For example, changing a variable name or packaging a few lines of code into a method are part of Code Refactoring. The main difference between Code Refactoring and a mere edit or find-and-replace is that you can harness the intelligence of the compiler to distinguish between code and comments, and so on. Code Refactoring is supported everywhere that you can write code, including both code-behind and single-file ASP.NET pages.

Smart Tasks

Smart Task is a new feature that displays a popup list of common tasks that you can perform on an ASP.NET control. For example, when you add a `GridView` control to a page, a common task list appears, which enables you to quickly enable sorting, paging, or editing for the `GridView`. Visual Studio 2005 enables you to perform many of the most common programming tasks directly from the designer surface. When you drag new controls onto the designer surface, a popup list of common tasks automatically appears. You can use the common tasks list to quickly configure a control's properties, as well as walk through common operations you might perform with it. Smart Tasks can go a long way in increasing the productivity of the developers, allowing developers to create feature-rich, database-driven Web application without writing a single line of code.

Creating Web Projects

With Visual Studio 2005, you have more flexibility and features for managing the files in your Web projects. When you bring up the New Web Site dialog box and click on the Browse button, you see the dialog box shown in Figure 2-3.

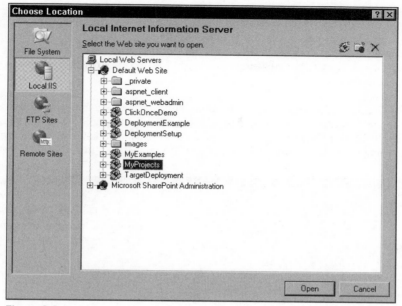

Figure 2-3

As you can see from Figure 2-3, you have the following options when creating Web projects.

❏ File System Support — With Visual Studio 2005, you now have the option of creating a new Web application within any folder on your computer. Note that neither IIS nor Front Page Server Extensions are required to be installed on your computer. You can simply point the Web application to a specific folder and start building Web pages. This is made possible through the new built-in ASP.NET enabled Web server that ships with Visual Studio 2005. Using this new Web server, you can develop and debug Web applications without requiring Administrator access. Note that the built-in Web server cannot be accessed remotely and it automatically shuts down when you close the Visual Studio 2005 development environment.

❏ Local IIS Support — In addition to file system projects, Visual Studio 2005 enables you to more easily manage projects that are hosted in an IIS Web server. When you create a new IIS project, you can now view all of the Web sites and applications configured on your machine. You can even create new IIS Web applications or virtual directories directly from the New Web Site dialog box. Figure 2-3 shows an example of this in action. FrontPage Server Extensions (FPSE) is no longer required for locally developed IIS Web applications.

❏ FTP Support — Visual Studio 2005 now has out of the box support for editing and updating remote Web projects using the standard File Transfer Protocol (FTP). The New Web Site and Open Web Site dialog boxes allow you to quickly connect to a remote Web site using FTP.

Administration and Management

One of the key goals of ASP.NET 2.0 is to ease the effort required to deploy, manage, and operate ASP.NET Web sites. To this end, ASP.NET 2.0 features a new Configuration Management API that enables users to programmatically build programs or scripts that create, read, and update configuration files such as `web.config` and `machine.config`. In addition, there is a new comprehensive admin tool that plugs into the existing IIS Administration MMC, enabling an administrator to graphically read or change any setting within the configuration files. ASP.NET 2.0 also provides new health-monitoring support to enable administrators to be automatically notified when an application on a server starts to experience problems. New tracing features enable administrators to capture runtime and request data from a production server to better diagnose issues.

Visual Studio 2005 also ships with a new Web-based tool that provides an easy way to administer an ASP.NET Web site. You can access this by selecting ASP.NET Configuration from the Web site menu in Visual Studio 2005. This Web-based tool wraps much of the Management API, thereby providing an easy and effective way to remotely administer a site. Figure 2-4 shows the ASP.NET Configuration tool in action.

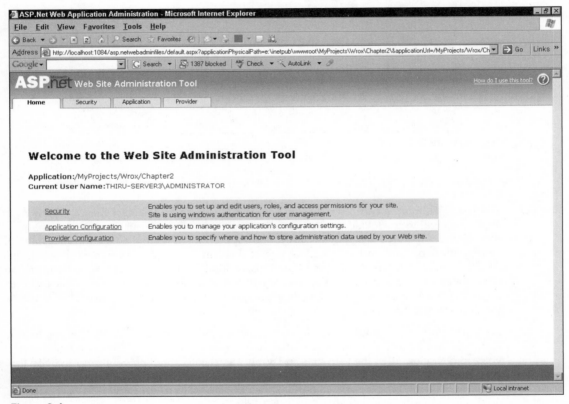

Figure 2-4

As you can see from Figure 2-4, it provides a simple Web interface that allows configuration of all aspects of a site. The interface is designed to be customized, so corporations and hosts can give it a company look.

Precompilation

One of the significant improvements in ASP.NET 2.0 is the capability to request a Web form (`.aspx` file) from a browser without having to compile the code even once. When the page is first requested, ASP.NET compiles the page on the fly, dynamically generating the assembly. This makes it possible for you to resort to the "Just Hit Save" programming model (as similar to ASP) wherein you just develop the page and test the page without having to compile it. After the initial compilation, the compiled page is cached, which is used to satisfy the subsequent requests for the same page. Although this approach is flexible, it does result in a performance hit, especially when the page is requested for the first time because ASP.NET requires a bit of extra time to compile the code. You can avoid this overhead by leveraging a new feature known as Precompilation, which you can use to compile an ASP.NET Web site before making the Web site available to the users. Precompilation also allows you to catch all the compilation errors before deploying the application onto the production servers. ASP.NET 2.0 provides the following two options for precompiling a site.

❑   In-Place Precompilation — When you perform in-place precompilation, all ASP.NET files are compiled and stored in a special folder. The precompilation process follows the same logic that ASP.NET uses for dynamic compilation, also taking into consideration the dependencies between files. During precompilation, the compiler creates assemblies for all executable output and places them in a special folder. After the compiled output is created, ASP.NET fulfills requests for pages using the assemblies contained in this folder. One of the important advantages of precompilation is the ability to check the Web site for compilation errors. For example, to precompile a Web application named Chapter2, enter the following command in the .NET Framework 2.0 SDK command prompt.

```
aspnet_compiler -v /myprojects/wrox/chapter2
```

This command precompiles the Web site and displays the compilation errors in the command prompt, if there are any.

❑   Precompiling a site for deployment — Using this option, you can create a special deployable output of your Web application that can be deployed to production servers. After the output is created, you can deploy the output using various mechanisms such as XCOPY, or FTP, or Windows installers onto the production servers. To precompile a Web site for deployment, use the same aspnet_compiler utility and specify the target path as well. This type of precompilation enables applications to be deployed without any source being stored on the server (even the content of .aspx files is removed as part of the precompilation), further protecting your intellectual property.

```
aspnet_compiler -v /myprojects/wrox/chapter2 C:\Chapter2\Output
```

Speed and Performance

Although ASP.NET 1.x is one of the World's fastest Web application servers, Microsoft aims to make it even faster by bundling the performance improvements in ASP.NET 2.0. ASP.NET 2.0 is now 64-bit enabled, meaning it can take advantage of the full memory address space of new 64-bit processors and servers. Developers can simply copy existing 32-bit ASP.NET applications onto a 64-bit ASP.NET 2.0 server and the Web application is automatically JIT compiled and executed as native 64-bit applications. As part of the performance improvements, ASP.NET 2.0 also enhances the caching feature set by providing new functionalities. The next section provides you with a quick overview of the caching improvements in ASP.NET 2.0.

Caching Feature

Caching is defined as temporary storage of data for faster retrieval on subsequent requests. In ASP.NET 2.0, the caching support is integrated with the DataSource controls to cache data in a Web page. ASP.NET 2.0 also now includes automatic database server cache invalidation. This powerful and easy-to-use feature allows developers to aggressively output cache database-driven page and partial page content within a site and have ASP.NET automatically invalidate these cache entries and refresh the content whenever the back-end database changes. ASP .NET 2.0 also introduces a new control, called Substitution control, which allows you to link dynamic and cached content in a Web page.

Caching with the DataSource Controls

The `DataSource` controls enable you to cache database data while connecting a .NET application to a database. The `DataSource` control provides various properties, such as `EnableCaching`, which you can use to automatically cache the data represented by a `DataSource` control. The syntax to cache a database table in a memory for 120 seconds is:

```
<asp:SqlDataSource ID="SqlDataSource1" EnableCaching="True" CacheDuration="120"
ConnectionString="Server=localhost;database=AdventureWorks;
uiduser1;pwd=password1" SelectCommand="SELECT * FROM Production.ProductCategory"
Runat="server"/>
```

This syntax caches a database table, `Production.ProductCategory` by setting the `EnableCaching` property of the `DataSource` control to `True`. The `CacheDuration` property of the `DataSource` control specifies the time, in seconds, for caching the data before it is updated in a database containing the `Production.ProductCategory` table. The value of the Time parameter is set to 120 to cache data for two minutes.

Using SQL Cache Invalidation

The Cache API introduced with ASP.NET 1.x was a powerful feature that can be immensely useful in increasing the performance of a Web application. The Cache API also allows you to invalidate items in the cache based on some pre-defined conditions such as change in an XML file, change in another cache item, and so on. Using this feature, you can remove or invalidate an item from the cache when the data or another cached item changes; however, the Cache API in ASP.NET 1.x versions did not provide a mechanism to invalidate an item in the cache when data in a SQL Server database changes. This is a common capability that many Web applications require. Now with ASP.NET 2.0, Microsoft has introduced a new cache invalidation mechanism that works with SQL Server as well. Using this new capability, you can invalidate an item in the Cache object whenever the data in a SQL Server database changes. This built-in cache invalidation mechanism works with SQL Server 7.0 and above; however, with SQL Server 7.0 and 2000, only Table level cache invalidation mechanism is supported. The next release of SQL Server (named SQL Server 2005) will also feature row-level cache invalidation mechanism providing a finer level of accuracy over the cached data. To enable SQL Server based cache invalidation mechanism, you need to do the following.

❑ Add `<caching>` element to the `web.config` file and specify the polling time and the connection string information.

❑ Enable SQL cache invalidation at the database and table levels by using either the `aspnet_regsql` utility or the `SqlCacheDependencyAdmin` class. This is not required if you are using SQL Server 2005 as your database.

❑ Specify the `SqlCacheDependency` attribute in the `SqlDataSource` control.

That's all you need to do to leverage SQL Server cache invalidation from your ASP.NET pages.

Using Substitution Control

ASP .NET 2.0 provides a new control, called the Substitution control, which enables you to insert dynamic content into a cached Web page. For example, you can display the name of an end user, which is dynamically generated in a cached Web page containing some text or images. The Substitution control provides a property called `MethodName` that represents the method called to return the dynamic content. Listing 2-4 shows an example of Substitution control in action.

Listing 2-4: Partial Page Caching Using Substitution Control

```
<%@ Page Language="C#" %>
<%@ OutputCache Duration="6000" VaryByParam="none" %>
<script runat="server">
  static string GetRandomNumber(HttpContext context)
  {
    int randomNumber;
    randomNumber = new System.Random().Next(1, 10000);
    return randomNumber.ToString();
  }
</script>
<html xmlns="http://www.w3.org/1999/xhtml">
<head>
  <title>Use of Substitution control to implement Partial Caching</title>
</head>
<body>
  <form id="form1" runat="server">
    The random number generated is:
    <asp:Substitution ID="Substitution1" MethodName="GetRandomNumber"
    Runat="Server" />
    <p>
      The current time is <%= DateTime.Now.ToString("t") %>.
      It never changes since the page is cached.
    </p>
  </form>
</body>
</html>
```

At the top of the page, the `OutputCache` directive is used to cache the contents of the page in memory. The duration attribute of the `OutputCache` directive is set to 6000 seconds. The `VaryByParam` attribute indicates whether or not ASP.NET should consider the parameters passed to the page when caching. When `VaryByParam` is set to none, no parameters will be considered; all users receive the same page no matter what additional parameters are supplied. The `MethodName` attribute of the Substitution control is set to a method named `GetRandomNumber`, which simply returns a random number between 1 and 10000. Note that the return value of `GetRandomNumber` method is string because the `HttpResponseSubstitutionCallback` delegate always requires a return type of string. When you make a request for the page through the browser, you will find that the displayed current time always remains the same whereas the portion of the page that is generated by the substitution control keeps changing every time. In this case, it displays a random number between 1 and 10000 every time someone requests the page.

Summary

This chapter provided you with a quick tour of the features of ASP.NET 2.0. Specifically, this chapter discussed the number of new productivity enhancements of ASP.NET 2.0 that are exciting for the developers. In addition, this chapter also discussed the configuration and management of ASP.NET Web applications as well as the performance improvement features. Apart from the features discussed so far, ASP.NET 2.0 provides the following features.

❑ ASP.NET 2.0 is 64-bit enabled.

❑ ASP.NET 2.0 will be almost completely backward compatible with ASP.NET 1.0 and ASP.NET 1.1.

❑ You can also define a single class in multiple files and at runtime will be compiled together to create a single assembly.

❑ With ASP.NET 2.0, you can perform postback across pages, meaning that you can postback to another page from one page. To perform cross-postback when the user clicks a button, set the `PostTargetUrl` property on the button control to the URL of the new page. From within the new page, you can reference the original page using the `PreviousPage` property.

❑ In the health monitoring space, it provides support for automated notification when exceptions occur in the Web site. For example, ASP.NET can automatically send an email to the admin when an exception occurs in the Web site.

XML Classes in the .NET Framework

The first two chapters provided you with an introduction to XML and ASP.NET 2.0, respectively. In this chapter, you get an understanding of the XML support in the .NET Framework. The initial release of .NET Framework provided excellent support for working with XML in .NET applications. The .NET Framework 2.0 builds on the foundation of .NET 1.x by providing new classes and features such as better standards support, increased performance improvements, and so on. In addition, XML core classes are tightly integrated with key areas of the .NET Framework, including data access, serialization, and applications configuration.

This chapter discusses the overall support for XML in the .NET Framework. Specifically, this chapter focuses on the XML classes in the .NET Framework that provide support for standards such as XML 1.0, XML namespaces, Document Object Model (DOM) Level 2 Core, XML Schema Definition (XSD) Language, Extensible Stylesheet Language Transformations (XSLT), and XPath expressions.

XML Support in the .NET Framework 2.0

Microsoft is serious about .NET's commitment to XML. This is made obvious by the extent to which XML is used in the .NET architecture and supported through several feature-rich namespaces. In this chapter, you are introduced to the XML API in the .NET Framework. Before looking at the XML support in the .NET Framework, it is important to examine the design goals of .NET Framework 2.0.

Design Goals for XML Support in .NET Framework 2.0

Through the XML namespaces and classes present in the .NET Framework 2.0 base class library, you can easily build XML support into your applications. These classes enable you to read, write, manipulate, and transform XML. Because XML manipulation is inevitable in application development, it is recommended that all developers have an understanding of these core XML classes. When the XML team in Microsoft started designing the XML feature set for the .NET Framework 2.0, they had the following design goals in mind:

❑ Better Standards compliance — Support for the major W3C XML standards that provide cross-platform interoperability, such as XML 1.0, XML Namespaces 1.0, XSLT 1.0, XPath 1.0, and W3C XML schema 1.0.

❑ Usability — XML API should be not only easy-to-use but also intuitive.

❑ Seamless Integration with ADO.NET — The classes in the XML API can really be considered part of ADO.NET as an XML data access API. The combination of `System.Data.DataSet` and the `System.Xml.XmlDataDocument` classes provide a seamless experience when moving between XML and relational data.

❑ Significant Performance Improvements — This was the number one requirement for the .NET Framework 2.0 release. The new XSLT processor through the introduction of the new `System.Xml.Xsl.XslCompiledTransform` class is one of the many performance improvements with XML API in .NET Framework 2.0.

❑ Developer Productivity enhancements — These enhancements are geared towards increasing the productivity of the developers by allowing them to perform common tasks even easier to do in less lines of code.

❑ Support for Strong Types and XML schema — In the .NET Framework 1.x, almost all of the XML API were untyped in that the data was both stored and retrieved as string types. This is enhanced in .NET Framework 2.0 by integrating schema information deeply across the XML namespaces. This provides for more efficient storage, improved performance, and better integration with the .NET programming languages.

XML Namespaces

XML API in .NET Framework 2.0 is mainly encapsulated in five namespaces. These namespaces house all of the XML functionality within the .NET Framework class library. Table 3-1 describes these namespaces at a high level.

Table 3-1. XML Namespaces in .NET Framework 2.0

Namespace	Description
System.Xml	Contains the classes that provide the core of all XML functionality
System.Xml.Schema	Provides support for XML Schema Definition Language (XSD) schemas
System.Xml.Serialization	Provides classes that allow you to serialize and deserialize objects into XML formatted documents
System.Xml.XPath	Provides support for the XPath parser and evaluation functionality
System.Xml.Xsl	Provides support for XSLT transformations

The next few sections provide an overview of the classes and functionalities contained in these namespaces.

The System.Xml Namespace

The classes in the `System.Xml` namespace are designed to fully support your XML needs. Your needs may range from reading and writing XML to storing XML. In fact, your application's needs may even extend to querying XML or transforming XML. There are many feature-rich classes available in this namespace that provide reading, writing, and manipulating XML documents.

The System.Xml.Schema Namespace

This namespace offers classes, delegates, and enumerations used to support your XSD language needs. It strongly supports the W3C Recommendations for XML schemas for structures and XML schemas for data types. The classes in this namespace service the Schema Object Model (SOM).

The System.Xml.XPath Namespace

This namespace offers support for the XPath parser (query support) via several classes, interfaces, and enumerations. Two commonly used classes from this namespace are `XPathDocument` (fast, read-only cache, optimized for XSLT) and `XPathNavigator` (editable, random access, cursor model). Note that the `XPathNavigator` class can now be used to edit XML data in addition to providing a cursor model for navigating XML data.

The System.Xml.Xsl Namespace

This namespace provides full support for the Extensible Stylesheet Transformation (XSLT) technology. Although several classes and interfaces are offered in this namespace, you will likely use the `XslCompiledTransform` class and `XsltArgumentList` classes most often.

The System.Xml.Serialization Namespace

This namespace offers classes and delegates to assist with object serialization. Among the many managed classes offered, you will use the `XmlSerializer` class the most. Using the `XmlSerializer` class, you can serialize and deserialize instantiated objects to and from XML documents or streams. Object serialization is a useful technique for persisting (or saving) the state of an object so that you can later re-create an exact copy of the object. Object serialization is also useful when you want to pass the object (marshal by value) during .NET Remoting scenarios.

The preceding list of namespaces is provided to give you a more complete picture of the XML support available through the .NET Framework and platform. Combining this information with that of the classes in the `System.Xml` namespace, you are certainly off to an informed start. Now that you have understood the different XML namespaces, you are ready to examine the different XML-related capabilities such as XML Parsing, XML Validation, `XPath`, XML Serialization, XML Web Services, and so on, and how they are supported in .NET Framework 2.0. The next section examines how XML is enabled in .NET Framework.

XML Parsing

Parsing is not always as simple as just reading through an XML document and verifying it for ASCII text. The structure and rules of your governing DTD, or XSD schemas can be verified when processing these instance documents if you utilize a validating parser. You need this parsing application to evaluate the instance document and determine if it's valid and then make it available for secondary applications to utilize the data contained therein.

Parsing is an essential task for any application that uses language-based data or code as input. XML processors, which rely heavily on parsers, provide a standard mechanism for navigating and manipulating XML documents. If you have an XML document and need to get data out of it, change the data, or modify the XML document structure, you don't need to write code to load the XML file, validate it for specific characters and elements, and process this information accordingly. You can use an XML parser instead, which will load the document and give you access to its contents in the form of objects.

Validating and Non-Validating Parsers

A validating parser can use a DTD or schema to verify that a document is properly constructed according to the rules for the XML application, and it is supposed to complain loudly if the rules aren't followed. A DTD or XML schema can also specify default values for the attributes of various elements, and a validating parser can fill them in when it encounters elements with no attributes listed. This capability can be important when you are processing XML documents that you have received from the outside world. For example, if vendors send XML-marked invoices to your company, you'll want to ensure that they contain the right elements in the right order.

A non-validating parser only requires that the document be well-formed. Because of the design of XML, it's possible to parse well-formed documents without referring to a DTD or XSD schema. Non-validating parsers are simpler, and many of the free parsers available over the Web are non-validating. They are usually sufficient for processing XML documents generated within the same organization or documents whose validity constraints are so complex that they can't be expressed by a DTD and need to be verified by application logic instead.

XML Parsing Support in .NET Framework

Implementing XML with the .NET Framework class library requires referencing the `System.Xml.dll` assembly. The .NET Framework class library provides two ways of parsing XML data:

- ❑ Fast, non-cached, forward-only access
- ❑ Random access via an in-memory DOM tree

Both methods of processing XML data are equally valid; however, each has a definite time when it is better suited. At other times, both work equally well, and the decision of which to use is up to the developer's taste. The next sections explore both of these methods in detail.

Forward-Only Access

Forward-only access to XML is amazingly fast. If you can live with the restriction that you can process the XML data only in a forward-only method, this is the way to go. The core class for implementing this method of read-only, forward-only access is named `System.Xml.XmlReader`. The `XmlReader` class allows you to access XML data from a stream or XML document. The `XmlReader` class conforms to the W3C XML 1.0 and the Namespaces in XML recommendations.

> **In .NET 1.x, the `XmlReader` class is an abstract class and provides methods that are implemented by the derived classes to provide access to the elements and attributes of XML data. With .NET Framework 2.0, however, the `Create()` method of the `XmlReader` class returns an instance of the `XmlReader` object that you can directly use to read an XML document.**

You can also use `XmlReader` classes to determine various factors such as the depth of a node in an XML document, whether the node has attributes, the number of attributes in a node, and the value of an attribute. To perform validation while reading the XML data using the `XmlReader` class, use the new `System.Xml.XmlReaderSettings` class that exposes properties which can be set to appropriate values to validate XML data using DTD and XSD schemas. The `XmlReaderSettings` class is described in detail in Chapter 5.

> *Although the .NET Framework includes concrete implementations of the* `XmlReader` *class, such as the* `XmlTextReader, XmlNodeReader,` *and the* `XmlValidatingReader` *classes, the recommended practice in .NET Framework 2.0 is to create* `XmlReader` *instances using the* `Create()` *method. The* `XmlReader` *object returned by the Create method has better conformance checking and compliance to the XML 1.0 recommendation.*

SAX Vs XmlReader

When you first look at it, the .NET Framework class library's implementation of forward-only access seems very similar to the Simple API for XML (SAX), but actually they are fundamentally different. Where SAX uses a more complex push model, the class library uses a simple pull model. This means that a developer requests or pulls data one record at a time instead of having to capture the data using event handlers. Coding using the .NET Framework class library's implementation of forward-only access is more intuitive because you can handle the processing of an XML document as you would a simple file, using a good old-fashioned while loop. There is no need to learn about event handlers or SAX's complex state machine.

Random Access via DOM

The XML DOM class, `System.Xml.XmlDocument`, is a representation of the XML document in memory. The .NET Framework DOM implementation provides classes that enable you to navigate through an XML document and obtain relevant information. Every XML document consists of parent and child nodes. The `XmlDocument` class has the capability to read in XML files, streams, or `XmlReader` objects. Among the many public methods of the `XmlDocument` class, you will want to start with the `Load()` method. Using this method, you can easily load XML data into an `XmlDocument` object.

Choosing the Right XML Reader

Basically, you could take an either/or approach when you choose your XML class for reading. For example, either you choose the `XmlReader` class for fast, forward-only, read-only, non-cached type reading. Or you can choose the DOM class `XmlDocument` for full-featured XML document reading and manipulation. The major deciding factors for choosing one method over the other are whether all data needs to be in memory at one time (large files take up large amounts of memory, which in many cases isn't a good thing) and whether random access to the data is needed. When either of these factors is a requirement, the DOM tree should probably be used because the process of repeatedly reading forward sequentially through a document to find the right place in the stream of XML to read, update, or write random data is time consuming.

Is XML API in .NET a Replacement for MSXML 6.0?

Microsoft's XML parser, MSXML 6.0 (now known as Microsoft XML Core Services), has historically provided much of the XML DOM support described in this section. The .NET XML managed objects largely overlap the functionality exposed in the COM-based MSXML 6.0 library. Generally, you want to use the managed objects offered in the various .NET XML namespaces. There are occasions, however, when you should use the MSXML 6.0 implementation when you need backward compatibility with legacy applications. For example, if you want backward compatibility with legacy applications, you could utilize the .NET COM Interop feature and reference the MSXML 6.0 library and take advantage of its features.

> *Possibly the most frequently asked question regarding XML support in the .NET Framework is if there is support for the SAX. SAX is an API that provides access to XML documents like XML DOM. The advantage of SAX API over XML DOM is that XML DOM parsers typically read the whole XML tree into memory. This can be very slow and can impact the performance when dealing with extremely large XML files. SAX provides a streaming forward-only event-based push mode, in which you register a series of callbacks that are called by the parser when events occur, such as the beginning of an element, the end of an element, and so on. Although SAX itself is not supported in the .NET Framework, you can utilize the* XmlReader *class to write applications that use a streaming model like SAX.*

Writing XML

Your choice for writing is much simpler, and you want to explore the methods of the System.Xml .XmlWriter for your XML output needs. The XmlWriter class is the core class that enables you to create XML streams and write data to well-formed XML documents. XmlWriter is used to perform tasks such as writing multiple documents into one output stream, writing valid names and tokens into the stream, encoding binary data and writing text output, managing output, and flushing and closing the output stream.

XPath Support

The XPath is used in an XML document to access a node or a set of nodes. After you create an XML document, you might need to access a value from a certain node, and you can accomplish this using XPath. In addition, XPath enables you to create expressions that can manipulate strings, numbers, and Boolean values. XPath treats an XML document as a tree containing different types of nodes, which include elements, attributes, and text. You can create XPath expressions that identify these nodes in an XML document based on their type, name, and value. In addition, an XPath expression can identify the relationship between the nodes in a document. The XPath implementation recognizes several node types in an XML document, such as Root, Element, Attribute, Namespace, Text, ProcessingInstruction, Comment, SignificantWhitespace, Whitespace, and All. The XPath functionality in the .NET Framework is encapsulated in the System.Xml.XPath namespace. Table 3-2 describes the classes and interfaces of the System.Xml.XPath namespace that not only enable you to perform an XPath query on an XML document, but also update the XML document.

Table 3-2. Classes and Interfaces of the System.Xml.XPath Namespace

Classes and Interfaces	Description
XPathDocument	This class provides a read-only cache for a fast and highly optimized processing of XML documents using XSLT.
XPathException	This class represents the exception that is thrown when an error occurs during the processing of an XPath expression.
XPathExpression	This class encapsulates a compiled XPath expression. An XPathExpression object is returned when you call the Compile method. The Select, Evaluate, and Matches methods use this class.

Classes and Interfaces	Description
XPathItem	Represents an item in the XQuery 1.0 and XPath 2.0 data model.
XPathNavigator	This class provides a cursor model for navigating and editing XML data.
XPathNodeIterator	This class enables you to iterate a set of nodes that you select by calling the XPath methods such as Select, SelectDescendants, and so on.
IXPathNavigable	This interface contains a method that provides an accessor to the XPathNavigator class.

In the list of classes in Table 3-2, the XPathNavigator class is the core of the XPath implementation that contains the methods that you use to perform XPath queries on an XML document. In addition, the XPathNavigator also allows you to edit XML information. The .NET Framework 1.x version of the XPathNavigator class was based on the XPath 1.0 Data Model and the .NET Framework 2.0 version of the XPathNavigator class is based on the XQuery 1.0 and XPath 2.0 Data Model.

You can create an XPathNavigator object for an XML document using the CreateNavigator() methods of the XPathDocument, and XmlDocument classes, which implement the IXPathNavigable interface. An XPathNavigator object created from an XPathDocument object is read-only; the XPathNavigator object created from an XmlDocument object can be edited.

> One of the new XML features in .NET Framework 2.0 is the ability to use the XPathNavigator **object to edit XML documents. You can determine the read-only or edit status of an** XPathNavigator **object by examining the** CanEdit **property of the** XPathNavigator **class.**

The CreateNavigator() method returns an XPathNavigator object. You can then use the XPathNavigator object to perform XPath queries or edit XML data. The XPathNavigator object reads data from an XML document by using a cursor that enables forward and backward navigation within the nodes. In addition, XPathNavigator provides random access to nodes. You can use XPathNavigator to select a set of nodes from any data store as long as that data source implements the IXPathNavigable interface. A data store is the source of data, which may be a file, a database, an XmlDocument object, or a DataSet object. You can also create your own implementation of the XPathNavigator class that can query over other data stores.

XML Schema Object Model (SOM)

The structure of XML documents is based on rules that are also known as grammar. These rules are specified in an XSD file, which is also known as an XML schema. An XSD file contains the definitions of elements, attributes, and data types. The schema is an XML file and has an .xsd file name extension. The XSD file uses valid XML objects to describe the contents of a target XML document. These XML objects include elements and attributes, which are declared in the XSD file using element and attribute elements. The structure of the XML document is created using simpleType and complexType elements.

A `simpleType` element is defined using the built-in data types or existing simple types and cannot contain elements or attributes. A `complexType` definition can consist of elements and attributes.

You use XML schema to create and validate the structure of XML documents. XML schema provides a way to define the structure of XML documents. To specify the structure of an XML document, you specify the following:

❑ Names of elements that you can use in documents

❑ The structure and types of elements to be valid for that specific schema

The SOM consists of a set of classes that enable you to read the schema definition from a file. In addition, you can use the classes in the SOM to create the schema definition files programmatically. These SOM classes are part of the `System.Xml.Schema` namespace. When you create a schema using the classes in the `System.Xml.Schema` namespace, the schema resides in memory. You need to validate and compile the schema before writing it to a file. The Schema object model implementation in the .NET Framework 2.0 supports the following standards.

❑ XML Schemas for Structures - `http://www.w3.org/TR/xmlschema-1/`

❑ XML Schemas for Data Types - `http://www.w3.org/TR/xmlschema-2/`

Features of the SOM can be summarized as follows:

❑ You can load valid XSD schemas from files, and also save valid XSD schemas to files.

❑ You can create in-memory schemas using strongly typed classes.

❑ You can cache and retrieve schemas by using the `XmlSchemaSet` class.

❑ You can validate XML instance documents against the schemas by using the `XmlReader` class in conjunction with `XmlReaderSettings` class.

❑ You can build editors to create and maintain schemas.

❑ You can use the `XmlSchema` class to build a schema programmatically. After you create a schema definition file, you can use the SOM to edit these files. The way in which you edit schema definition files using the SOM is similar to the way in which you edit XML documents using the DOM.

> In `System.Xml` **version 1.0, you loaded XML schemas into an** `XmlSchemaCollection` **class and referenced them as a library of schemas. In** `System.Xml` **version 2.0, the** `XmlValidatingReader` **and the** `XmlSchemaCollection` **classes are replaced by the** `Create()` **method of the** `XmlReader` **class and the** `XmlSchemaSet` **class, respectively. The new** `XmlSchemaSet` **class provides better standards compatibility and improved performance.**

In .NET 1.x version, to validate the XSD file you created using the `XmlSchema`, you used the `Compile()` method of the `XmlSchema` class. The `Compile()` method verifies that the schema is semantically correct and also ensures that the types are derived correctly. In addition, it also ensures that the constraints are correctly applied. In .NET 2.0, however, the `Compile()` method of the `XmlSchema` class is made obsolete by the Compile() method of the `XmlSchemaSet` class. This `Compile()` method is called automatically when validation is needed and the `XmlSchemaSet` has not been previously compiled. If the `XmlSchemaSet` is already in the compiled state, this method will not recompile the schemas. Also successful execution of this method results in the `IsCompiled` property being set to true.

Understanding XML Validation

Validation is the process of enforcing rules on the XML content either via a DTD, a XSD schema or a XDR schema. An XML file is generally validated for its conformance to a particular schema or a DTD. For example, if you specify the age of an employee to be an integer data type in the schema of your XML document, the actual data in your XML document must conform to the data type or it will be considered invalid. The XML schema file usually is an XML-Data Reduced (XDR) or XML Schema Definition language (XSD) file. XSD schema-based validation is the industry accepted standard and will be the primary means of validating XML data in most of the newly developed .NET applications.

You can perform the validation of XML documents by using the validation settings supplied with the `System.Xml.XmlReaderSettings` class. The `XmlReaderSettings` class provides the DTD and XSD schema validation services that allow you to validate an XML document or a fragment of an XML document. The Create method of the `XmlReader` class takes an `XmlReaderSettings` object as one of the inputs and applies the properties that you specify in the `XmlReaderSettings` class while reading the XML document.

The following code shows how to use the `XmlReaderSettings` class to add validation support to the `XmlReader` class.

```
XmlReaderSettings settings = new XmlReaderSettings();
settings.ValidationEventHandler += new
  ValidationEventHandler(this.ValidationEventHandler);
settings.ValidationType = ValidationType.Schema;
settings.Schemas.Add(null, XmlReader.Create("Employees.xsd"));
reader = XmlReader.Create("Employees.xml", settings);
while(reader.Read()){}
```

To validate an XML document, you first create an instance of the `XmlReaderSettings` class and assign an event handler for the `ValidationEventHandler` event. You then set the `ValidationType` enumeration to `ValidationType.Schema` to indicate that you are validating the XML data against the XSD schema. Next, load the XSD schema object utilizing the `Add()` method of the `XmlSchemaSet` class and then supply the `XmlReaderSettings` object to the `Create()` method of the `XmlReader` class. For in-depth information on XML Data validation, please refer to Chapter 5.

Transforming XML Data using XSLT

XSLT is the transformation component of the XSL specification by W3C (www.w3.org/Style/XSL). It is essentially a template-based declarative language that can be used to transform an XML document to another XML document or to documents of other types (such as HTML and Text). You can develop and apply various XSLT templates to select, filter, and process various parts of an XML document. Figure 3-1 demonstrates the XSL transformation process.

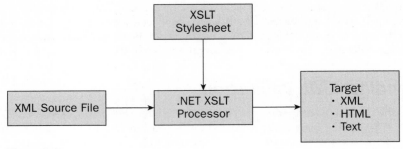

Figure 3-1

Figure 3-1 shows the use of the XSLT processor in transforming an input XML document into another format.

XSLT in .NET Framework 2.0

.NET Framework 2.0 augments the XSLT support provided by the .NET Framework 1.x by providing a very rich and powerful set of XML classes that allow the developers to easily tap into XML and XSLT in their applications. Although .NET 1.x provided built-in support for transforming XML documents using XSLT, .NET 2.0 provides huge performance gains by introducing new classes to the base class library.

XSLT uses the XPath language to perform queries on an XML document to select a particular part of the document. You can also use XSLT to transform the existing XML structure into one that can be easily processed. To accomplish this, you use an XSLT processor and an XSLT style sheet (XSLT file) that defines how to carry out the transformation. The classes in the System.Xml.Xsl namespace that are mainly utilized for transforming XML data using an XSLT style sheet are as follows:

❏   XslCompiledTransform — This class is the new .NET XSLT processor and provides the core services for transforming XML data using XSLT style sheet. Its implementation is based on the XML query architecture and this class provides significant performance gains when compared to the obsolete XslTransform class. This class supports the XSLT 1.0 syntax.

❏   XsltArgumentList — As the name suggests, this class is used to supply values of runtime parameters to the XSLT query processor. Runtime parameters are very useful in scenarios wherein you want to utilize the same compiled query multiple times with different parameters. You can also use this class to add a new extension object to the list and associate it with the given namespace.

❏   XsltException — This class encapsulates the exception that is thrown when an error occurs while processing an XSLT transform.

> *The XslTransform class used with .NET 1.x is now obsolete in .NET Framework 2.0. The new XslCompiledTransform class is the .NET XSLT processor and provides the implementation of the XSLT engine. In addition to the performance improvements, this new class also brings with it a host of new security features.*

Chapter 7 provides an in-depth discussion on transforming XML data using XSLT with .NET classes.

XML Serialization

Often, you'll need to convert an object from the internal format used in an application to a format suitable for persistence or transportation. The process of converting an object into such a form is called serialization. The reverse process is called deserialization. Serialization is an important part of any distributed system. For example, in the Microsoft .NET Framework, serialization is an important technology that is employed when you use the .NET Remoting architecture or access Web services. The .NET Framework offers two types of serialization technologies that can you can use from any of the languages that execute in the common language runtime. These are as follows:

❑ Binary Serialization — A compact format that's useful for sharing data between managed applications.

❑ XML Serialization — A more open but less dense format that is typically used when you build Web services.

The next section provides you with an overview of the .NET support for XML Serialization.

.NET Support for XML Serialization

The .NET Framework Class Library has built-in support for converting objects to and from an XML format through the `XmlSerializer` class of the `System.Xml.Serialization` namespace. The `XmlSerializer` class allows you to serialize and deserialize objects into XML documents while providing you with a fine degree of control over the shape of the output. When you use the XmlSerializer object to serialize an object, the object's public properties and public fields are converted into XML elements and/or attributes.

To serialize an object, instantiate an `XmlSerializer` object, specifying the type of the object to serialize; then instantiate a stream/writer object to write the file to a stream/document. The final step is to call the `Serialize()` method on the `XmlSerializer`, passing it the stream/writer object, and the object to serialize. Data that can be serialized are primitive types, fields, arrays, and embedded XML in the form of `XmlElement` and `XmlAttribute` objects.

To deserialize an object from an XML document, you go through the reverse process of the above. You create a stream/reader and an `XmlSerializer` object and then pass the stream/reader to the `Deserialize()` method. This method returns the deserialized object, although it needs to be cast to the correct type.

> The `XmlSerializer` **cannot convert private data and also it cannot serialize object graphs; however, these should not be serious limitations; by carefully designing your classes, you can easily overcome them. If you do need to be able to serialize public and private data as well as an object graph containing many nested objects, you will want to use the** `BinaryFormatter` **class in the** `System.Runtime.Serialization.Formatters.Binary` **namespace or take control of the XML serialization of your types using the** `IXmlSerializable` **interface.**

Some of the other things that you can do with `System.Xml.Serialization` classes are:

❑ Determine if the data should be an attribute or element

❑ Specify the namespace

❑ Change the attribute or element name

The links between your object and the XML document are the custom C# attributes that annotate your classes. These attributes are what are used to inform the serializer how to write out the data. Included with the .NET Framework is the tool called xsd.exe that can help create these attributes for you. Using `xsd.exe`, you can do the following:

❑ Generate an XML schema from an XDR schema file

❑ Generate an XML schema from an XML file

❑ Generate `DataSet` class from an XSD schema file

❑ Generate run-time classes that have the custom attributes for `XmlSerialization`

❑ Generate an XSD file from classes that you have already developed

❑ Limit which elements are created in code

❑ Determine which programming language the generated code should be in (C#, VB.NET, or JScript.NET)

❑ Create schemas from types in compiled assemblies

The .NET Framework 2.0 introduces a new tool called XML Serializer Generator (Sgen.exe) that can create an XML serialization assembly for types in a specified assembly. The pre-generated assemblies can help improve the performance of an `XmlSerializer` *object when it serializes or deserializes objects of the specific types contained in the assembly.*

An in-depth discussion of XML serialization is provided in Chapter 12.

XML Web Services

XML Web services are programmable components that allow you to build scalable, loosely coupled, platform-independent applications. XML Web services enable disparate applications to exchange messages using Internet standard protocols such as HTTP, XML, XSD, SOAP, and Web Services Description Language (WSDL). In this section, you learn about the Web services programming model and the support .NET provides for developing Web services.

An Overview of XML Web Services

An XML Web service is a component that implements program logic and provides functionality for disparate applications. These applications use standard protocols, such as HTTP, XML, and SOAP, to access the functionality. XML Web services use XML-based messaging to send and receive data, which enables heterogeneous applications to interoperate with each other. You can use XML Web services to integrate applications that are written in different programming languages and deployed on different platforms. In addition, you can deploy XML Web services within an intranet as well as on the Internet.

From the highest level, one can simply define an XML Web service as a unit of code that can be invoked via HTTP requests. Unlike a traditional Web application however, XML Web services are not (necessarily) used to emit HTML back to a browser for display purposes. Rather, an XML Web service exposes the same sort of functionality found in a standard .NET code library, in that it defines computational objects that execute a unit of work for the consumer (such as crunch some numbers, read information from a data source, etc.), return a result (if necessary), and wait for the next request.

XML Web services provide a way for unrelated platforms, operating systems, and programming languages to exchange information in harmony. One important feature of the XML Web services-based computing model is that a client need not know the language in which XML Web services are implemented. The client just needs to know the location of an XML Web service and the methods that the client can call on the service. The only requirement on the client side is that the client should be able to parse a well-formed XML document and then map the underlying XML elements into platform and/or language specific types. In a nutshell, XML Web services offer a way to let the Web provide information that can be pieced together to build a platform and language-agnostic distributed system.

XML Web Services Infrastructure

One of the important features of the XML Web services-based computing model is that both clients and XML Web services are unaware of the implementation details of each other. The XML Web services infrastructure provides several components that enable client applications to locate and consume XML Web services. These components include the following.

XML Web Services Directories

These directories provide a central place to store published information about XML Web services. These directories might also be XML Web services that allow you to search for information about other XML Web services programmatically. The Universal Description, Discovery, and Integration (UDDI) specifications define the guidelines for publishing information about XML Web services. The XML schemas associated with UDDI define four types of information that you must publish to make your XML Web service accessible. This information includes business information, service information, binding information, and service specifications. Microsoft provides its own implementation of UDDI specification, which is located at `http://uddi.microsoft.com`.

XML Web Services Discovery

Using this process, clients locate the documents that describe an XML Web service using WSDL. The discovery process enables clients to know about the presence of an XML Web service and about the location of a particular XML Web service.

XML Web Services Description

This component provides information that enables you to know which operations to perform on an XML Web service. The XML Web service description is an XML document that specifies the format of messages that an XML Web service can understand. For example, the description document specifies the SOAP message schemas that you use when invoking methods on an XML Web service.

XML Web Service Wire Formats

To enable communication between disparate systems, XML Web services use open wire formats. Open wire formats are the protocols that can be understood by any system that is capable of supporting common Web standards, such as HTTP and SOAP. The HTTP-GET and HTTP-POST protocols are the standard Web protocols that allow you to send parameters as name-value pairs. The HTTP-GET protocol allows you to send URL-encoded parameters as name-value pairs to an XML Web service. The HTTP-GET protocol requires you to append the parameter name-value pairs to the URL of the XML Web service. You can also use the HTTP-POST protocol to URL-encode and pass parameters to the XML Web service as name-value pairs; however, the parameters are passed inside the actual request message and not appended to the URL of the XML Web service.

The SOAP protocol allows you to exchange structured and typed information between the applications on the Internet. The SOAP protocol consists of four parts. The first part is mandatory and defines the envelope that contains the message. The SOAP envelope is the basic unit of exchange between the processors of SOAP messages. The second part defines the optional data encoding rules that you use to encode application-specific data types. The third part defines the request/response pattern of message exchanges between XML Web services. The fourth part, which is optional, defines the bindings between the SOAP and HTTP protocols.

Communication between the Client and the XML Web Service

The process of communication between a client and an XML Web service is similar to a remote procedure call (RPC) invocation. The client uses a proxy object of the XML Web service on the local computer to call methods on the XML Web service. Figure 3-2 shows the process of communication between a client and an XML Web service.

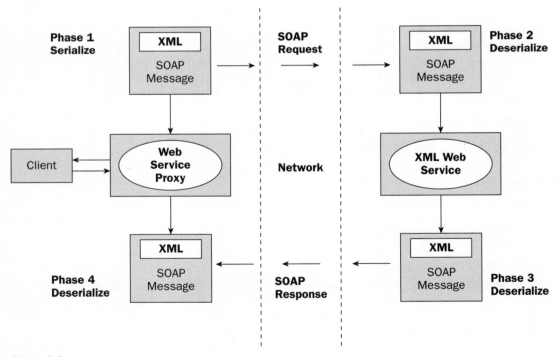

Figure 3-2

As shown in Figure 3-2, the interaction between a client and an XML Web service consists of several phases. Tasks performed during those phases are as follows:

1. The client creates an instance of the XML Web service proxy class on the same computer on which the client resides.

2. The client calls a method on the proxy object.

3. The XML Web services infrastructure on the client system serializes the method call and the arguments to the method into a SOAP request message and sends it to the XML Web service over the network.

4. The infrastructure on the server on which the XML Web service resides deserializes the SOAP message and creates an instance of the XML Web service. The infrastructure then calls the actual web service method passing in the arguments on the XML Web service.

5. The XML Web service executes the method and returns the value with any output parameters to the infrastructure.

6. The infrastructure serializes the return value and the output parameters into a SOAP response message and sends them back to the client over the network.

7. The infrastructure on the client computer deserializes the SOAP response containing the return value and the output parameters and sends them to the proxy object.

The proxy object sends the return value and the output parameters to the client.

As you can see from the preceding steps, the XML Web Services infrastructure provided by the .NET Framework plays an important role in building, deploying, and consuming Web services. In addition, Visual Studio 2005 provides tools that allow you to easily and effectively build, deploy, and publish your XML Web services using ASP.NET.

The .NET XML Web Service Namespaces

XML Web Service capabilities are primarily provided by the five namespaces shown in Table 3-3.

Table 3-3. XML Web Service Namespaces

Namespace	Description
System.Web.Services	Contains the minimal and complete set of classes needed to build a Web service, such as the WebMethodAttribute, WebService, and WebServiceAttribute
System.Web.Services.Configuration	Provides classes that allow you to configure the runtime behavior of an ASP.NET XML Web service
System.Web.Services.Description	Contains classes that allow you to programmatically interact with the WSDL document that is used to describe a Web service
System.Web.Services.Discovery	Consists of classes that allow you to programmatically discover the Web services available on a given Web server
System.Web.Services.Protocols	Provides classes that define the protocols such as HTTP GET, HTTP POST, and SOAP that are used to transmit data between an XML Web service and its consumer

More information on these namespaces and Web services will be provided in detail in Chapter 13.

XML and ADO.NET

Databases are used to store and manage organization's data; however, it is not a simple task to transfer data from the database to a remote client or to a business partner, especially when you do not clearly know how the client will use the sent data. Well, you may send the required data using XML documents. That way, the data container is independent of the client's platform. The databases and other related data stores are here to stay and XML will not replace these data stores. XML will undoubtedly provide a common medium for exchanging data among sources and destinations. It will also allow various applications to exchange data among themselves. In this context, the XML forms a bridge between ADO.NET and other applications. Because XML is integrated in the .NET Framework, the data transfer using XML is much easier than it is in other software development environments. Data can be exchanged from one source to another via XML. The ADO.NET Framework is essentially based on DataSets, which, in turn, relies heavily on XML architecture.

Role of XML Schemas in Typed DataSets

A `System.Data.DataSet` can either be typed or untyped. A typed `DataSet` is a class that is derived from a `DataSet` class and has an associated XML schema. On the other hand, an untyped `DataSet` does not have an XML schema associated with it. In a typed `DataSet`, you can make changes to the XSD file, which are reflected in the underlying `DataSet`. XML schema is similar to the typed `DataSet` representation because both are available as XSD files in the XML designer in Visual Studio; however, a typed `DataSet` has an associated class file and a predefined root node.

When you load an XML document into a `DataSet`, XML schema validates the data that is fetched from the XML document. The XML schema contains all the information about the relational structure, such as tables, constraints, and relations that is necessary to validate an XML document. This information is stored in the XSD file. The .NET Framework uses the XSD files to generate the object representation of the `DataSet` object.

The `DataSet` class has a rich collection of methods that are related to processing XML. Some of the widely used ones are `ReadXml`, `WriteXml`, `GetXml`, `GetXmlSchema`, `InferXmlSchema`, `ReadXmlSchema`, and `WriteXmlSchema`.

To use ADO.NET and XML together, you need to create a DataSet and create a `System.Xml.XmlDataDocument` object with it. Then you can manipulate the database data just as you did with `XmlDocument`. The `XmlDataDocument` class extends the `XmlDocument` class and enables you to load either relational data or XML data and manipulate that data using the W3C DOM. Because the `XmlDataDocument` implements the `IXPathNavigable` interface, it can also be used as the source document for the `XslCompiledTransform` class.

> `XmlDataDocument` **has a close affiliation with the DataSet class that provides a relational view of the loaded XML data. The** `DataSet` **and** `XmlDataDocument` **objects provide a synchronized view of the same data using a relational and hierarchical model, respectively. Any changes made to the** `XmlDataDocument` **are reflected in the DataSet and vice versa. The** `XmlDataDocument` **class adds properties and members to streamline some activities and to make them more like "relational database." A detailed discussion of XML support in ADO.NET is provided in Chapter 8.**

ASP.NET Configuration

Configuration information for an ASP.NET Web application is stored in a file named `Web.config`. The configuration file contains a nested hierarchy of XML tags and subtags with attributes that specify the configuration settings. This configuration file is deployed when the ASP.NET application is deployed on a Web server. Configuring a Web site requires configuration of settings according to the server's capabilities and requirements. Configuring a Web site might also require developers to write code. At a later stage, the site administrator might need to change the settings of the site or the server on which the site has been deployed so as to enhance the performance of the site. If the change in settings involves embedding values into code, however, it becomes very complicated and difficult for both the developer and the administrator to reconfigure the application.

As you can see, the application deployment process requires a rich and flexible configuration system. The configuration system should enable developers to easily associate settings with an installable application without having to embed values into code. The system should also enable administrators to easily adjust or customize these values after the deployment of the application on the application Web server. The ASP.NET configuration system based on `Web.config` file fulfills both these requirements. To accomplish this, ASP.NET provides a rich set of configuration settings that you can specify in the `Web.config` file.

ASP.NET Configuration Architecture

ASP.NET uses a hierarchical configuration architecture that uses an XML format. In the hierarchical configuration architecture, whenever a client makes a request for an ASP.NET application or a specific ASP.NET resource, ASP.NET checks the settings for the URL requested by the client in a hierarchical fashion. The check is carried out using the configuration files located in the path for the requested URL. These settings are then logged or cached by the application Web server to speed up any future requests for ASP.NET resources.

All configuration information resides between the `<configuration>` and `</configuration>` root XML tags. Configuration information between the tags is grouped into two main areas: the configuration section handler declaration area and the configuration section settings area.

Web.config versus Machine.config

Consider a scenario wherein the Web site has only one `Web.config` file in the root directory. Although the Web site has only one `Web.config` file in the directory structure, the Web site actually uses two configuration files because a file named `machine.config` exists in the `%windir%\Microsoft .NET\Framework\v2.0.<buildnumber>\CONFIG` directory. In this path, `<buildnumber>` represents the build number of the Microsoft .NET Framework. In future releases, this build number will change, and therefore the actual name of the folder might also change. This `machine.config` file is at the highest level and is called the machine-level configuration file. This machine-level configuration file comes with the .NET Framework and contains the default settings for all the applications built using .NET Framework.

> *All ASP.NET directories and subdirectories inherit settings from this machine-level configuration file; however, a* `Web.config` *file can also be located at the Web site level, and if it is not overridden at a lower level, it will apply to all ASP.NET resources on the Web site.*

ASP.NET 2.0 Support for Accessing Configuration Settings

ASP.NET 2.0 provides enhanced support for accessing configuration settings from a configuration file through the new class called `System.Web.Configuration.WebConfigurationManager`, which provides seamless access to configuration files and configuration sections. This new class renders obsolete the ASP.NET 1.x class `ConfigurationSettings` that was utilized to access configuration settings from a configuration file. The functionality provided by the methods of this class fall into any of the following three categories.

❑ Easy and quick access to the configuration sections such as `appSettings` and `connectionStrings` sections through the use of properties such as `AppSettings` and `ConnectionStrings`

❑ Quick access to specific configuration sections of the configuration files through methods such as `GetSection()`, and `GetWebApplicationSection()`

❑ Ability to open the specified configuration files using methods such as `OpenMappedWebConfiguration()`, `OpenWebConfiguration()` and so on

More information on how to utilize this new class is provided in Chapter 14.

Benefits of ASP.NET Configuration System

The XML based ASP.NET configuration system features an extensible infrastructure that not only enables you to define configuration settings at the time of deploying your ASP.NET applications but also allows you to add or revise configuration settings at any time with minimal impact to the operational Web application. The ASP.NET configuration system provides the following benefits:

❑ The hierarchical configuration architecture provides a flexible and rich configuration system that enables extensible configuration settings to be defined and used throughout the ASP.NET applications.

❑ The configuration information for the ASP.NET applications is stored in plain XML-based configuration files, which makes it easy to read and write. Administrators and developers can use a standard text editor such as Notepad for updating of the configuration settings of the application.

❑ Because the configuration files are stored in the same directory tree as the rest of the application files, the configuration files can be easily deployed along with the rest of ASP.NET application.

❑ The configuration system is highly flexible and allows developers to create new configuration sections, and store customized configuration criteria and settings in the configuration system. This extensibility feature can then be used at runtime to affect the processing of the HTTP requests.

❑ The configuration system allows the automation of any configuration updates made to the ASP.NET configuration files meaning that whenever changes are made to a configuration file, the application can pick up the new changes instantaneously without requiring user intervention.

❑ The configuration information contained in the XML file is applied hierarchically with regard to the virtual directory structure, which is provided at the time of Web site creation. Subdirectories under the virtual directory inherit or override the configuration settings from their parent directories. This allows different settings for different applications or for different parts of a single application.

❑ Now with the introduction of the new `WebConfigurationManager` class, you can programmatically interact with the different sections in the configuration files such as `Web.config`, `machine.config` with minimal effort.

Summary

This chapter introduced the basic concepts of XML in .NET Framework, and provided a concise overview of the .NET classes available to read, store, and manipulate XML documents. The System.Xml namespaces contain probably the richest collection of XML-related classes available thus far in any other software development platform. The XML support in .NET Framework 2.0 has been further enriched by the recent addition of XslCompiledTransform class that provides improved functionality and performance enhancements. To summarize this chapter:

❑ The System.Xml namespace provides the XmlReader and XmlWriter classes that enable you to parse and write XML data from streams or XML documents.

❑ The XmlReader class enables you to access XML data from a stream or XML document. This class provides fast, non-cacheable, read-only, and forward-only access to XML data.

❑ The XmlWriter class is the core class that enables you to create XML streams and write data in well-formed XML documents. You use XmlWriter to perform tasks such as writing multiple documents into one output stream, writing valid names and tokens into the stream, encoding binary data and writing text output, managing output, and flushing and closing the output stream.

❑ The XmlDocument class is a representation of the XML document in memory. The XmlDocument class allows you to read, write, and manipulate an XML document. The DOM includes a set of libraries that contain classes, which enable you to navigate through an XML document and obtain relevant information. Every XML document consists of parent and child nodes.

❑ In an XML document, you use XPath to access a node or a set of nodes. The XPathNavigator class of the .NET Framework contains the methods that you use to perform XPath queries on an XML document. XPath support in .NET Framework 2.0 is enhanced by the editing support added to the XPathNavigator.

❑ The structure of valid XML documents is specified by XSD files. You can ensure the validation of XML documents by using the XmlReaderSettings class. The XmlReaderSettings class in conjunction with the XmlSchemaSet class provides the DTD, and XSD schema validation services that enable you to validate an XML document or a fragment of an XML document.

❑ The SOM consists of a set of classes that enable you to read the schema definition from a file. In addition, you can use the classes in the SOM to create the schema definition files programmatically. These SOM classes are part of the System.Xml.Schema namespace.

❑ When you load an XML document into a DataSet, XML schema validates the data that is fetched from the XML document. The XML schema contains all the information about the relational structure, such as tables, constraints, and relations that are necessary to validate an XML document.

4

Reading and Writing XML Data Using XmlReader and XmlWriter

One of the major features of the .NET Framework is that it enables you to easily produce distributed applications that are language-independent, and that are platform-independent when .NET is ported to other platforms. XML plays a major part in this plan by acting as a simple, portable glue layer that is used to pass data around in distributed applications. Microsoft has XML-enabled many parts of the .NET Framework and it is crucial for the developers to get an understanding of how to work with XML data using the .NET Framework classes. This chapter discusses the different ways of reading and writing XML data utilizing the `System.Xml` classes. Specifically, this chapter covers:

❑ XML reading and writing support provided by the .NET Framework 2.0

❑ How to parse an XML file using the `XmlReader` class

❑ How to parse the attributes and data contained in the XML file

❑ How to customize the settings of the `XmlReader` object through the use of the reusable `XmlReaderSettings` class

❑ How to write to an XML file using the `XmlWriter` class

❑ How to customize the output produced by the `XmlWriter` object using the `XmlWriterSettings` class

❑ How to write namespaces using the `XmlWriter` class

❑ How to embed images in an XML document using the `XmlWriter` class

The following section starts by discussing the different XML reader and writer classes in the .NET Framework 2.0.

XML Readers and Writers

.NET Framework provides two important core classes named XmlReader and XmlWriter classes for reading and writing XML data. These classes will feel familiar to anyone who has ever used SAX. XmlReader class provides a very fast, forward-only, read-only cursor that streams the XML data for processing. Because it is a streaming model, the memory requirements are not very demanding; however, you don't have the navigation flexibility and the read/write capabilities that would be available from a DOM-based model. The DOM-based model implemented through the XmlDocument class is discussed in Chapter 6 of this book. The hierarchy of XmlReader and XmlWriter classes and their derived classes are shown in Figure 4-1.

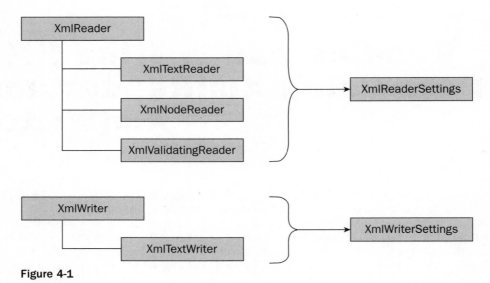

Figure 4-1

In Figure 4-1, the XmlReaderSettings and XmlWriterSettings classes allow you to configure the set of features available through the reader and writer, respectively. As you can see from Figure 4-1, the .NET framework provides the following four built-in reader classes for reading XML data.

❏ XmlReader — The XmlReader class behaves as a "forward-only, non-cached reader" that not only provides an efficient way to read XML data, but also much more standards compliant than any other readers.

❏ XmlTextReader — The plain-vanilla XmlTextReader class behaves as a "forward-only, non-cached reader" to read XML data. It is versatile enough to allow you to access XML from different input sources, including flat files, data streams, or URLs.

❏ XmlValidatingReader — The XmlReader has one little drawback – it doesn't allow you to validate the data present in the XML source. If you are looking for a foolproof way to maintain the sanctity of your data, you are better off using the XmlValidatingReader class. This class comes with built-in features to validate your XML data against external DTDs, XDR, or XSD schemas. With the release of .NET Framework 2.0, however, this class is made obsolete and replaced by the new XmlReaderSettings class that provides all the validation services except for the DTD based validation. So the only situation where you would use XmlValidatingReader class is when you want to perform DTD based validation with your XML data. Chapter 5, "XML Validation Data," provides more information on this.

❑ XmlNodeReader — In case you are looking to implement the pull model on a DOM tree that's already present in memory, you can consider using the XmlNodeReader class. Best-suited only for the very specialized application previously mentioned, this class allows you to read the data from specific nodes of the tree and enjoy a double benefit — the speed associated with the XmlReader class and the ease of use of the DOM. You see usage of this class in Chapter 6.

Typically, you would create objects of these classes and use their methods and properties. If warranted, you may also extend these classes to provide further specific functionalities. The XmlWriter class has only one derived class: XmlTextWriter. The XmlWriter can be used to write XML document on a forward-only basis. The classes utilized for writing XML data are as follows:

❑ XmlWriter — Is an abstract class that provides a "forward-only, read-only, non-cached" way of generating XML streams. By creating the XmlWriter object using the static Create() method, you can take advantage of the new features of XmlWriter object in .NET Framework 2.0.

❑ XmlTextWriter — Provides a writer that provides a "forward-only, read-only, non-cached" way of generating XML streams. Note that this class is obsolete in .NET Framework 2.0 and should only be used in situations where you require backward compatibility with an application created using .NET 1.x versions.

Now that you have an overview of the different classes available for reading and writing, the following section focuses on reading XML data with the XmlReader class.

Reading XML with XmlReader

XmlReader provides you with a way to parse XML data that minimizes resource usage by reading forward through the document, recognizing elements as it reads. This approach results in very little data being cached in memory, but the forward-only style has two main consequences. The first is that it isn't possible to go back to an earlier point in the file without starting to read from the top again. The second consequence is slightly more subtle: elements are read and presented to you one by one, with no context. If you need to keep track of where an element occurs within the document structure, you'll need to do it yourself. If either of these shortcomings sounds like limitations to you, you might need to use the DOM style XmlDocument class, which is discussed later in Chapter 6 of this book.

Overview of XmlReader

The XmlReader class allows you to access XML data from a stream or XML document. This class provides fast, non-cacheable, read-only, and forward-only access to XML data. In .NET Framework 1.x, the XmlReader is an abstract class that provides methods that are implemented by the derived classes to provide access to the elements and attributes of XML data. With the release of .NET Framework 2.0, however, the XmlReader class is a full-featured class similar to the XmlTextReader class and provides standards-based support to read XML data. You use XmlReader classes to determine various factors such as the depth of a node in an XML document, whether the node has attributes, the number of attributes in a node, and the value of an attribute.

Although you can use the XmlTextReader class to read XML data, the preferred approach to reading XML data is to use the XmlReader object that is created through the static Create() method of the XmlReader object. This is because of the fact that the XmlReader object obtained through the Create() method is much more standards compliant than the XmlTextReader implementation. For example, the XmlTextReader class does not expand entities by default and does not add default attributes.

The XmlTextReader class is one of the derived classes of the XmlReader class and implements the methods defined by the XmlReader class. The XmlValidatingReader is another class in .NET Framework 1.x that is derived from the XmlReader class, allowing you to not only read XML data but also support DTD and schema validation. Note that in .NET Framework 2.0, both XmlTextReader and XmlValidatingReader classes are obsolete, whose functionalities are now provided by the XmlReader and XmlReaderSettings class, respectively.

Steps Involved in Using XmlReader to Read XML Data

The XmlReader class is designed for fast, forward-only access to the contents of an XML file, and is not suited for making modifications to the file's contents or structure (for that you will use the XmlDocument class). The XmlReader class works by starting at the beginning of the file and reading one node at a time. As each node is read, you can either ignore the node or access the node information as dictated by the needs of the application.

The steps for using the XmlReader class are as follows:

1. Create an instance of the class using the Create() method of the XmlReader class, passing to the method the name of the XML file to be read.

2. Set up a loop that calls the Read() method repeatedly. This method starts with the first node in the file and then reads all remaining nodes, one at a time, as it is called. It returns true if there is a node to read, false when the end of the file has been reached.

3. In the loop, examine the properties and methods of the XmlReader object to obtain information about the current node (its type, name, data, and so on). Loop back until Read() returns False.

The XmlReader class has a large number of properties and methods. The ones that you will need most often are explained in Table 4-1 and Table 4-2.

Table 4-1. Important Properties of the XmlReader Class

Property	Description
AttributeCount	Returns the number of attributes in the current node
Depth	Returns the depth of the current node; used to determine if a specific node has child nodes
EOF	Indicates if the reader is positioned at the end of the stream
HasAttributes	Returns a boolean value indicating if the current node has attributes
HasValue	Returns a boolean value indicating if the current node can have a value
IsEmptyElement	Indicates if the current node is an empty element
LocalName	Returns the local name of the current node
Name	Returns the qualified name of the current node

Property	Description
NamespaceURI	Returns the namespace URI of the current node
NodeType	Returns the type of the current node in the form of an XmlNodeType enumeration
Prefix	Returns the namespace prefix associated with the current node
ReadState	Returns the current state of the reader in the form of ReadState enumeration
Settings	Returns the XmlReaderSettings object used to create the XmlReader instance
Value	Gets the value of the current node
ValueType	Gets the CLR type of the current node

Now that you have an understanding of the important properties of the XmlReader class, Table 4-2 outlines the important methods of the XmlReader class.

Table 4-2. Important Methods of the XmlReader **Class**

Method	Description
Close	Closes the XmlReader object by setting the ReadState enumeration to Closed
Create	Factory method that creates an instance of the XmlReader object and returns it to the caller; the preferred mechanism for obtaining XmlReader instances
GetAttribute	Gets the value of an attribute
IsStartElement	Indicates if the current node is a start tag
MoveToAttribute	Moves the reader to the specified attribute
MoveToContent	Moves the reader to the next content node if the current node is not a content node
MoveToElement	Moves the reader to the element that contains the current attribute; used when you are enumerating through the attributes and you want to switch back to the element that contains all these attributes
MoveToFirstAttribute	Moves the reader to the first attribute of the current node
MoveToNextAttribute	Moves the reader to the next attribute; used especially when you are enumerating through the attributes in a node
Read	Reads the next node from the stream
ReadContentAs	Reads the content as an object of the supplied type

Method	Description
ReadElementContentAs	Reads the current element and returns it contents as an object of the type specified
ReadEndElement	Moves the reader past the current end tag and moves onto the next node
ReadInnerXml	Reads all of the node's content including the markup as a string
ReadOuterXml	Reads the node's content including the current node markup and all its children
ReadToDescendant	Moves the reader to the next matching descendant element
ReadToFollowing	Reads until the named element is found
ReadToNextSibling	Advances the reader to the next matching sibling element
ReadValueChunk	Allows you to read large streams of text embedded in an XML document

In addition to the methods described in Table 4-2, XmlReader also exposes a variety of ReadContentAsXXX() methods such as:

❑   ReadContentAsBase64()

❑   ReadContentAsBinHex()

❑   ReadContentAsBoolean()

❑   ReadContentAsDateTime()

❑   ReadContentAsDouble()

❑   ReadContentAsInt()

❑   ReadContentAsLong()

❑   ReadContentAsObject()

❑   ReadContentAsString()

As the name suggests, these methods return the node value as an object of the type specified in the method name. For instance, the ReadContentAsString() method returns the node value as an object of type string. Similar to the ReadContentAsXXX() methods, there are also a number of variations of the ReadElementContentAsXXX() method. These methods are:

❑   ReadElementContentAsBase64()

❑   ReadElementContentAsBinHex()

❑   ReadElementContentAsBoolean()

❑   ReadElementContentAsDateTime()

❑   ReadElementContentAsDouble()

❑   `ReadElementContentAsInt()`

❑   `ReadElementContentAsLong()`

❑   `ReadElementContentAsObject()`

❑   `ReadElementContentAsString()`

The most important function in all of these functions is `Read()`, which tells the `XmlReader` to fetch the next node from the document. After you've got the node, you can use the `NodeType` property to find out what you have. The `NodeType` property returns one of the members of the `XmlNodeType` enumeration, whose members are listed in the Table 4-3.

Table 4-3. Members of the `XmlNodeType` Enumeration

Member	Description
Attribute	An attribute, for example id=1
CDATA	A CDATA section, for example `<![CDATA[Some text]]>`
Comment	An XML comment, for example `<!-- Some comment -->`
Document	The document object, representing the root of the XML tree
DocumentFragment	A fragment of XML that isn't a document in itself
DocumentType	A document type declaration
Element, EndElement	The start and end of an element
Entity, EndEntity	The start and end of an entity declaration
EntityReference	An entity reference (for example, <)
None	Used if the node type is queried when no node has been read
Notation	A notation entry in a DTD
ProcessingInstruction	An XML processing instruction
SignificantWhitespace	White space in a mixed content model document, or when `xml:space=preserve` has been set
Text	The text content of an element
Whitespace	White space between markup
XmlDeclaration	The XML declaration at the top of a document

Now that you have understood the important properties and methods, take a look at the different ways of creating documents, elements, attributes, and other data in the next few sections.

Chapter 4

Start Reading a Document

To begin reading an XML document, you can call any of the Read() methods to extract data from the document. For example, this code snippet uses the ReadStartElement() to move to the first element in the document:

```
XmlReader reader = XmlReader.Create("Employees.xml");
//Skip the XML declaration and go to the first element
reader.ReadStartElement();
```

Alternatively, you can just jump straight to the document content by calling MoveToContent(), which skips to the next content node if the current node is not a content node. (Content nodes are the CDATA, Element, Entity, and EntityReference nodes.) If positioned on an attribute, the reader will move back to the element that contains the attribute.

```
XmlReader reader = XmlReader.Create("Employees.xml");
reader.MoveToContent();
```

In the examples shown, if Employees.xml looks as follows

```
<?xml version="1.0"?>
<!--Employee Details -->
<firstName>
  Nancy
</firstName>
```

the previous code would advance to the <firstName> element and skip everything before it in the prolog.

Reading Elements

The Read(), ReadString(), ReadStartElement(), and ReadEndElement() methods can all be used to read Element nodes from the XML source. After reading the element, each method advances to the next node in the document. In comparison, the MoveToElement() method moves to the next Element, but does not read it.

The Read() method is the simplest: It reads the next node in the source whether or not it is an Element node. When using this method, you should check the node's name and type to make sure you are processing an appropriate node. For example, the following code uses the Read() method and the NodeType property of the XmlReader to read only Comment nodes:

```
XmlReader reader = XmlReader.Create("Employees.xml");
//Read the nodes in a loop
while (reader.Read())
{
    if (reader.NodeType == XmlNodeType.Comment)
    {
      //Code to process Comments
    }
}
```

As you read through the XML document using the XmlReader object, if you examine the ReadState property of the XmlReader object, you will find that it provides different values depending on the state of the XmlReader. Table 4-4 summarizes the states of the XmlReader as it reads through the various portions of an XML document.

Table 4-4. Members of the ReadState Enumeration

State	Description
Closed	The reader enters this state when the Close method is called
EndOfFile	Signals the end of the XML document
Error	Specifies that an error has occurred and the error prevents the reader from continuing the read operation
Initial	The reader is in this state before the invocation of the Read method
Interactive	The reader is in this state after the Read method has been called and can respond to the additional methods

Reading Attributes

Before you attempt to read attributes in an element node, you should first use the `HasAttributes` property to make sure that the element node contains attributes. Attributes in an element node can be accessed directly by their name or index. They can also be accessed by the `MoveToAttribute()`, `MoveToFirstAttribute()`, and `MoveToNextAttribute()` methods.

For example, to process an attribute by name, you can call `MoveToAttribute()` with the name of the attribute.

```
XmlReader reader = XmlReader.Create("Employees.xml");
//Move to the first element
reader.MoveToElement();
if (reader.HasAttributes)
{
  reader.MoveToAttribute("id")
  //Code to do something with the attribute value stored in id attribute
}
```

You see a complete example on the use of attributes in a later section of this chapter.

Reading Content and Other Data

Your application can use the `ReadString()` method to read the content of the current node as a string. You can also read the content of the element using the various forms of the `ReadElementContentAsXXX` methods. In addition to those methods, you also have the `ReadContentAsXXX` methods that allow you to read the text content at the current position. For example, using the `ReadContentAsDouble()` method, you can read the text content at the current position as a Double value. The `ReadString()` method behaves differently depending on the element the reader is currently positioned in.

❑   If the current node is an Element node, `ReadString()` concatenates all text, significant white space, white space, and CDATA section node types within the Element node and returns the concatenated data as the Element node's content.

❑   If the current node is a Text node, `ReadString()` performs the same concatenation on the Text node's end tag as it did on the Element node.

❑   If the current node is an Attribute node, `ReadString()` behaves as though the reader were currently positioned on the starting tag of the Element node and returns data as described for Element nodes.

❑   For all other node types, `ReadString()` returns an empty string.

> Microsoft has greatly enhanced XML support in the .NET Framework 2.0 by adding strong type support to all the XML processing classes. An example of this is the introduction of methods like `ReadElementContentAsInt()` to the `XmlReader` class that allow you to read the contents of an XML node in a strongly typed manner. Accomplishing this in .NET 1.x would mean that you read the XML node as a string and then convert that to appropriate data type using a helper class such as `XmlConvert`. This is no longer required in .NET Framework 2.0 because of the native support that is available for almost all of the XML processing classes. In addition to the strongly typed support, Microsoft also has greatly enhanced the performance of the `XmlReader` and `XmlWriter` classes.

Now that you have a complete understanding of the various methods and properties of the `XmlReader` class, it is time to look at examples that exercise all of these concepts.

Reading an XML File Using XmlReader

Now that you know the theory, this section begins with an example to demonstrate how to read an XML document using an `XmlReader` object. This simple example leverages the functionalities of the `XmlReader` class to parse a static XML file named `Employees.xml`. Here's the XML file, a list of employees in an organization, shown in Listing 4-1.

Listing 4-1: Employees.xml File

```xml
<?xml version='1.0'?>
<employees>
  <employee id="1">
    <name>
      <firstName>Nancy</firstName>
      <lastName>Davolio</lastName>
    </name>
    <city>Seattle</city>
    <state>WA</state>
    <zipCode>98122</zipCode>
  </employee>
  <employee id="2">
    <name>
      <firstName>Andrew</firstName>
      <lastName>Fuller</lastName>
    </name>
    <city>Tacoma</city>
    <state>WA</state>
    <zipCode>98401</zipCode>
  </employee>
</employees>
```

Now that you have seen the contents of the `Employees.xml` file, Listing 4-2 shows the ASP.NET code that allows you to parse the `Employees.xml` file.

Listing 4-2: Processing the Elements of the Employees XML File Using `XmlReader` **Class**

```csharp
<%@ Page Language="C#" %>
<%@ Import Namespace="System.Xml" %>
<script runat="server">
  void Page_Load(object sender, EventArgs e)
  {
    //Location of XML file
    string xmlFilePath = @"C:\Data\Employees.xml";
    try
    {
      //Get reference to the XmlReader object
      using (XmlReader reader = XmlReader.Create(xmlFilePath))
      {
        string result;
        while (reader.Read())
        {
          //Process only the elements
          if (reader.NodeType == XmlNodeType.Element)
          {
            //Reset the variable for a new element
            result = "";
            for (int count = 1;count <= reader.Depth; count++)
            {
              result += "===";
            }
            result += "=> " + reader.Name + "<br/>";
            lblResult.Text += result;
          }
        }
      }
    }
    catch(Exception ex)
    {
      lblResult.Text = "An Exception occurred: " + ex.Message;
    }
  }
</script>

<html xmlns="http://www.w3.org/1999/xhtml" >
<head runat="server">
    <title>Reading an XML File using XmlReader</title>
</head>
<body>
    <form id="form1" runat="server">
    <div>
        <asp:label id="lblResult" runat="server" />
    </div>
    </form>
</body>
</html>
```

Before examining the code, here is the output produced by Listing 4-2.

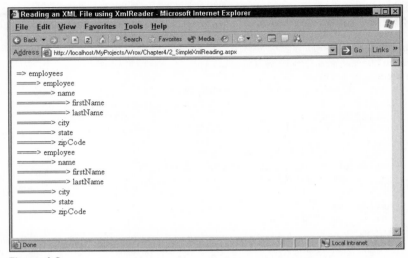

Figure 4-2

The first step is to import all the namespaces required to execute the page — the .NET libraries for the XML parser, most of which are primarily contained in the `System.Xml` namespace.

```
<%@ Import Namespace="System.Xml" %>
```

Next, within the `Page_Load` function, a variable containing the location of the XML file is defined. The code then declares an `XmlReader` object within the scope of a using block by invoking the Create method of the `XmlReader` object.

```
using (XmlReader reader = XmlReader.Create(xmlFilePath))
```

> **Among the many enhancements made to the** `XmlReader` **class in .NET Framework 2.0, an important feature is the ability to dispose of the resources used by the** `XmlReader` **by invoking the Dispose method. This is made possible by the fact that the** `XmlReader` **class now implements the IDisposable interface. Because of this, you can now enclose the creation of the** `XmlReader` **object within the scope of a using block and the resources utilized by the** `XmlReader` **will be automatically released at the end of the using block.**

Note that `XmlReader` object isn't limited to reading from files. Various overloads of the `Create()` method enable you to take XML input from URLs, streams, strings, and other Reader objects. The next step is to read the XML file — a simple matter because the `XmlReader` object provides a `Read()` method for just this purpose. This method returns true if it encounters a node in the XML file. After it is finished with the file, it returns false. This makes it easy to process an entire file simply by wrapping the method call in a "while" loop. Inside the while loop, there is code to process element nodes and format them for display.

The `NodeType` property of the current node can be used to filter out the elements for further processing.

```
if (reader.NodeType == XmlNodeType.Element)
```

The rest of the code in the "while" loop ensures that the output is formatted properly for display in the browser. Pay special attention to the use of the Depth property, which holds an integer value specifying the depth of the current node in the tree hierarchy. Simply put, the element `<employees>` is at depth 0; the element `<employee>` is at depth 1, and so on.

It is important to realize that a node read by the Read method does not correspond to an entire XML element. For example, look at this XML element:

```
<city>Seattle</city>
```

From the perspective of the `XmlReader`, the three nodes will be read in the following order:

1. A node corresponding to the opening tag. This node has type `Element` and local name 'city'.

2. A node corresponding to the data. This node has type `Text` and value 'Seattle'.

3. A node corresponding to the closing tag. This node has type `EndElement` and local name 'city'.

That takes care of handling elements. But what about the attributes contained within each element? In a later section, you see the steps involved in processing attributes using the `XmlReader` class.

Dealing with Exceptions

When the `XmlReader` class processes an XML file, it checks the XML file for well-formedness and also resolves external references (if any). Problems can crop up in many places, aside from the obvious one where the specified file is not found or cannot be opened. Any XML syntax error will raise an exception of type `System.Xml.XmlException`. The Message property of this class returns a descriptive message about the error (as is the case with all Exception classes). This message also includes the line number and position where the error was found. The `XmlException` class has two additional properties — `LineNumber` and `LinePosition` — that return the line number and character position of the error, respectively. You can use this information as needed. For example, your program could open and display the offending XML file with a pointer indicating where the error occurred.

Exception handling in programs that use the `XmlReader` class (and other XML-related classes) follows this general scheme:

1. Catch exceptions of type XmlException to deal with XML parsing errors.
2. Catch other exceptions to deal with other types of errors.

For reasons of brevity, the previous example shown in Listing 4-2 handled all the exceptions including the `XmlException` in a single catch block as opposed to creating two catch blocks.

Handling Attributes in an XML File

XML elements can include attributes, which consist of name/value pairs and are always string data. In the sample XML file, the employee element has an id attribute. As you play with the sample code in Listing 4-2, you may notice that when the nodes are read in, you don't see any attributes. This is because attributes are not considered part of a document's structure. When you are on an element node, you can check for the existence of attributes, and optionally retrieve the attribute values. For example, the `HasAttributes` property returns `true` if there are any attributes; otherwise, `false` is returned. The `AttributeCount` property tells you how many attributes there are, and the `GetAttribute()` method gets an attribute by name or by index. If you want to iterate through the attributes one at a time, there are also `MoveToFirstAttribute()` and `MoveToNextAttribute()` methods.

This section builds on the previous example by adding the capability to process attributes in the XML file. Listing 4-3 discusses the code required to add attributes processing to the previous example.

Listing 4-3: Processing Attributes in an XML File

```
<%@ Page Language="C#" %>
<%@ Import Namespace="System.Xml" %>
<script runat="server">
  void Page_Load(object sender, EventArgs e)
  {
    //Location of XML file
    string xmlFilePath = @"C:\Data\Employees.xml";
    try
    {
      //Get reference to the XmlReader object
      using (XmlReader reader = XmlReader.Create(xmlFilePath))
      {
        string result;
        while (reader.Read())
        {
          //Process only the elements
          if (reader.NodeType == XmlNodeType.Element)
          {
            //Reset the variable for a new element
            result = "";
            for (int count = 1; count <= reader.Depth; count++)
            {
              result += "===";
            }
            result += "=> " + reader.Name;
            lblResult.Text += result;
            //Check if the element has any attributes
            if (reader.HasAttributes)
            {
              lblResult.Text += " (";
              for (int count = 0; count < reader.AttributeCount; count++)
              {
                //Read the current attribute
                reader.MoveToAttribute(count);
                lblResult.Text += reader.Name;
              }
              lblResult.Text += ")";
              //Instruct the parser to go back the element
```

```
            reader.MoveToElement();
        }
        lblResult.Text += "<br/>";
    }
  }
}
}
catch(Exception ex)
{
    lblResult.Text = "An Exception occurred: " + ex.Message;
}
}
</script>
<html xmlns="http://www.w3.org/1999/xhtml" >
<head runat="server">
  <title>Reading an XML File and attributes using XmlReader</title>
</head>
<body>
  <form id="form1" runat="server">
    <div>
      <asp:label id="lblResult" runat="server" />
    </div>
  </form>
</body>
</html>
```

As you can see, Listing 4-3 contains only one major change to the original code Listing 4-2 — handling attributes for each element that the reader encounters in the XML file.

Listing 4-3 begins with a check for attributes in the current node using the `HasAttributes` property. Note that this property is set to true if the current node has at least one attribute.

```
if (reader.HasAttributes)
```

The `XmlReader`'s `AttributeCount` property stores the total number of attributes and is useful for looping through the collection of attributes. The `MoveToAttribute()` method positions the reader at the next attribute in the collection, and the Name property is then used to get the name of the attribute.

```
for (int count = 0; count < reader.AttributeCount; count++)
{
  //Read the current attribute
  reader.MoveToAttribute(count);
  lblResult.Text += reader.Name;
}
```

After iteration through the attributes of the current node is complete, the `MoveToElement()` method resets the position of the reader, and it then proceeds to the next node, if one exists. Figure 4-3 shows the output of code Listing 4-3.

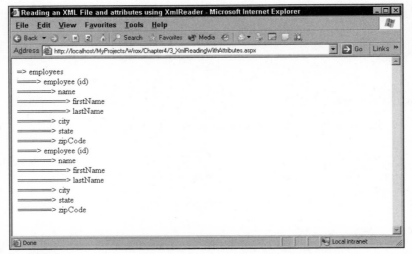

Figure 4-3

The last two examples have shown you how to study the information structures in the XML file, but completely ignore the data contained within each attribute and element. In the real world, you're usually as concerned about the data within each element as about the element and attribute names. The next section explores this aspect and shows you how to read the data contained in those elements and attributes.

Processing the Data in an XML File Using XmlReader

This section completes the circle by showing you how to process the data stored within each element and attribute of an XML file. Listing 4-4 shows the required implementation.

Listing 4-4: Processing Data in an XML File Using XmlReader

```
<%@ Page Language="C#" %>
<%@ Import Namespace="System.Xml" %>
<script runat="server">
  void Page_Load(object sender, EventArgs e)
  {
    //Location of XML file
    string xmlFilePath = @"C:\Data\Employees.xml";
    string employeeID = "";
    try
    {
      //Get reference to the XmlReader object
      using (XmlReader reader = XmlReader.Create(xmlFilePath))
      {
        lblResult.Text = "<b>Employees</b>";
        lblResult.Text += "<ul/>";
        string result;
        while(reader.Read())
        {
          if(reader.NodeType == XmlNodeType.Element)
```

```
        {
            if(reader.Name == "employee")
            {
                employeeID = reader.GetAttribute("id");
            }
            if(reader.Name=="name")
            {
                lblResult.Text += "<li>" + "Employee - " + employeeID;
                lblResult.Text += "<ul>";
                lblResult.Text += "<li>ID - " + employeeID + "</li>";
            }
            if (reader.Name == "firstName")
            {
                lblResult.Text += "<li>First Name - " + reader.ReadString()
                    + "</li>";
            }
            if (reader.Name == "lastName")
            {
                lblResult.Text += "<li>Last Name - " + reader.ReadString()
                    + "</li>";
            }
            if(reader.Name=="city")
            {
                lblResult.Text += "<li>City - " + reader.ReadString() + "</li>";
            }
            if(reader.Name=="state")
            {
                lblResult.Text += "<li>State - " + reader.ReadString() + "</li>";
            }
            if(reader.Name=="zipCode")
            {
                lblResult.Text += "<li>Zipcode - " +
                    reader.ReadElementContentAsInt().ToString() + "</li>";
            }
        }
        else if(reader.NodeType == XmlNodeType.EndElement)
        {
            if(reader.Name == "employee" )
            {
                //Close the open tags
                lblResult.Text += "</ul>";
                lblResult.Text += "</li>";
            }
        }
    }
    lblResult.Text += "</ul>";
}
catch(Exception ex)
{
    lblResult.Text = "An Exception occurred: " + ex.Message;
}
}
</script>
<html xmlns="http://www.w3.org/1999/xhtml" >
<head runat="server">
```

```
      <title>Processing the Data in an XML File</title>
  </head>
  <body>
    <form id="form1" runat="server">
      <div>
        <asp:label id="lblResult" runat="server" />
      </div>
    </form>
  </body>
</html>
```

Before examining the code, take a look at the output produced by Listing 4-4 in Figure 4-4.

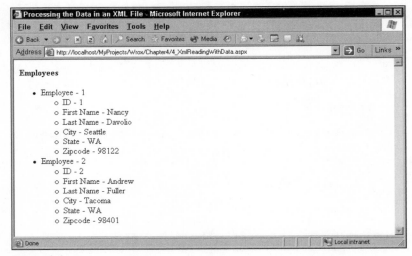

Figure 4-4

The `Page_Load()` function in Listing 4-4 begins by declaring two variables—one for storing the location of the XML file and the other one for storing the employee id. The `employeeID` variable will be used further down in the script to store the ID of the employee.

Now, the process of reading the XML file starts with the `Read()` method of the `XmlReader` object. The code inside the while loop does the dirty work of processing the data that is read by the object.

```
while(reader.Read())
{
  if(reader.NodeType == XmlNodeType.Element)
```

It all starts with a check to see if the current node is an element. This test returns true when the reader encounters the starting tag of an element in the XML file. After this is confirmed, the script checks the name of each element so that it can be processed appropriately. Element processing starts with the `<employee>` element. Because the `<employee>` contains the `employeeID`, the `GetAttribute()` method of the `XmlReader` object is used to fetch the value stored in the id attribute. If you know which attribute you want, this is a convenient way to avoid having to unnecessarily iterate through the collection of attributes, as demonstrated earlier. The ID retrieved is stored in the "`employeeID`" variable created earlier.

```
if(reader.Name == "employee")
{
   employeeID = reader.GetAttribute("id");
}
```

During the next pass, the script encounters the other parameters associated with a particular employee such as `firstName`, `lastName`, `city`, `state`, and `zipCode`. For each of these elements except for the `zipCode` element, the `ReadString()` method can be used to retrieve the text stored in the corresponding element.

```
if(reader.Name=="zipCode")
{
   lblResult.Text += "<li>Zipcode - " +
   reader.ReadElementContentAsInt().ToString() + "</li>";
}
```

Although you can use the `ReadString()` method to retrieve the value contained in the `zipCode` element, the preceding code takes advantage of the type safe `ReadElementContentAsInt()` method so that the value contained in the `zipCode` can be read in a type-safe manner.

> Type safe methods such as `ReadElementContentAsInt()` are specifically designed for reading typed element content into a .NET CLR typed variable. Use of these methods will result in error-free code as you read through the different elements in an XML document using the `XmlReader` object.

After a particular employee has been dealt with, the tags used to format the output of the XML file must be reset for the next employee element in the XML file. A good place to do this is when the reader encounters the closing `</employee>` element. How do you know when this happens? It's simple—just check if a particular node is a closing element with the `EndElement` property and if its name is employee.

```
if(reader.Name == "employee" )
{
   //Close the open formatting tags
   lblResult.Text += "</ul>";
   lblResult.Text += "</li>";
}
```

In Listing 4-4, note that you can also use the `IsStartElement()` method of the `XmlReader` object to check whether an element is indeed the opening element.

Configuring the `XmlReader` Object to Support Specific Features

`XmlReaderSettings` class is an important class used for validating the XML data. Chapter 5 shows you how to use the `XmlReaderSettings` class to validate an XML file. This chapter demonstrates the use of the `XmlReaderSettings` object to configure the output of the `XmlReader`. Important properties of the `XmlReaderSettings` object are shown in Table 4-5.

Table 4-5. Important Properties of the XmlReaderSettings **Class**

Property	Description
CheckCharacters	Allows you to get or set a value indicating whether character checking is carried out
ConformanceLevel	Gets or sets the conformance requirements for the XmlReader object
IgnoreComments	Allows you to get or set a value that indicates whether to ignore comments
IgnoreProcessingInstructions	Specifies whether to ignore processing instructions
IgnoreWhitespace	Specifies whether to ignore insignificant white space
ProhibitDtd	Specifies if DTD processing are allowed
Schemas	Specifies the XmlSchemaSet to use when performing XSD validation; more on this is covered in Chapter 5
ValidationFlags	Gets or sets a value that specifies the schema validation settings
ValidationType	Gets or sets a value that specifies the type of validation to perform
XmlResolver	Sets the XmlResolver that is used to access external documents

Through the XmlReaderSettings class, you can specify a set of features that will be supported on the XmlReader object. You can accomplish this by passing in the XmlReaderSettings object as an argument to the Create() method of the XmlReader object. Listing 4-5 shows an example of how to use the XmlReaderSettings object in conjunction with the XmlReader object to customize the reader settings.

Listing 4-5: Using the XmlReaderSettings **Object to Customize the Output of the** XmlReader **Object**

```
<%@ Page Language="C#" %>
<%@ Import Namespace="System.Xml" %>
<script runat="server">
  void Page_Load(object sender, EventArgs e)
  {
    //Location of XML file
    string xmlFilePath = @"C:\Data\Employees.xml";
    //Create the XmlReaderSettings object and set appropriate properties
    XmlReaderSettings settings = new XmlReaderSettings();
    settings.IgnoreComments = true;
    settings.IgnoreWhitespace = true;
    try
    {
      //Get reference to the XmlReader object
      using (XmlReader reader = XmlReader.Create(xmlFilePath,settings))
      {
```

```
        string result;
        while (reader.Read())
        {
          //Process only the elements
          if (reader.NodeType == XmlNodeType.Element)
          {
            //Reset the variable for a new element
            result = "";
            for (int count = 1;count <= reader.Depth; count++)
            {
              result += "===";
            }
            result += "=> " + reader.Name + "<br/>";
            lblResult.Text += result;
          }
        }
      }
    }
    catch(Exception ex)
    {
      lblResult.Text = "An Exception occurred: " + ex.Message;
    }
  }
</script>
<html xmlns="http://www.w3.org/1999/xhtml" >
<head runat="server">
  <title>Reading an XML File using XmlReader with XmlReaderSettings</title>
</head>
<body>
  <form id="form1" runat="server">
    <div>
      <asp:label id="lblResult" runat="server" />
    </div>
  </form>
</body>
</html>
```

An important thing to note in Listing 4-5 is the creation of the XmlReaderSettings object.

```
XmlReaderSettings settings = new XmlReaderSettings();
```

After an instance of the XmlReaderSettings object is created, you can then set its various properties.

```
settings.IgnoreComments = true;
settings.IgnoreWhitespace = true;
```

After that, you need to supply the XmlReaderSettings object to the Create() method of the XmlReader object.

```
using (XmlReader reader = XmlReader.Create(xmlFilePath,settings))
```

That's all you need to do to be able to utilize the XmlReaderSettings object.

SAX XML Reader versus .NET XmlReader

If you are at all familiar with XML programming, you will be aware that there are two basic approaches to parsing an XML document. The SAX is one; it parses an XML document in a sequential manner, generating and throwing events for the application layer to process as it encounters different XML elements. This sequential approach enables rapid parsing of XML data, especially in the case of long or complex XML documents; the downside is that a SAX parser cannot be used to access XML document nodes in a random or non-sequential manner. Also keep in mind that the .NET Framework does not provide native SAX implementation support as part of the base class library.

Next, there is the pull model that is designed to provide forward-only, read-only, non-cached access to XML data. The pull model allows you to read an XML document in a sequential but selective manner and thereby providing you with complete control over the parsing process. This is an interesting variant of the SAX model, which is non-selective in nature. There the parser will notify the client about each and every item that it encounters in the XML stream. See Figure 4-5

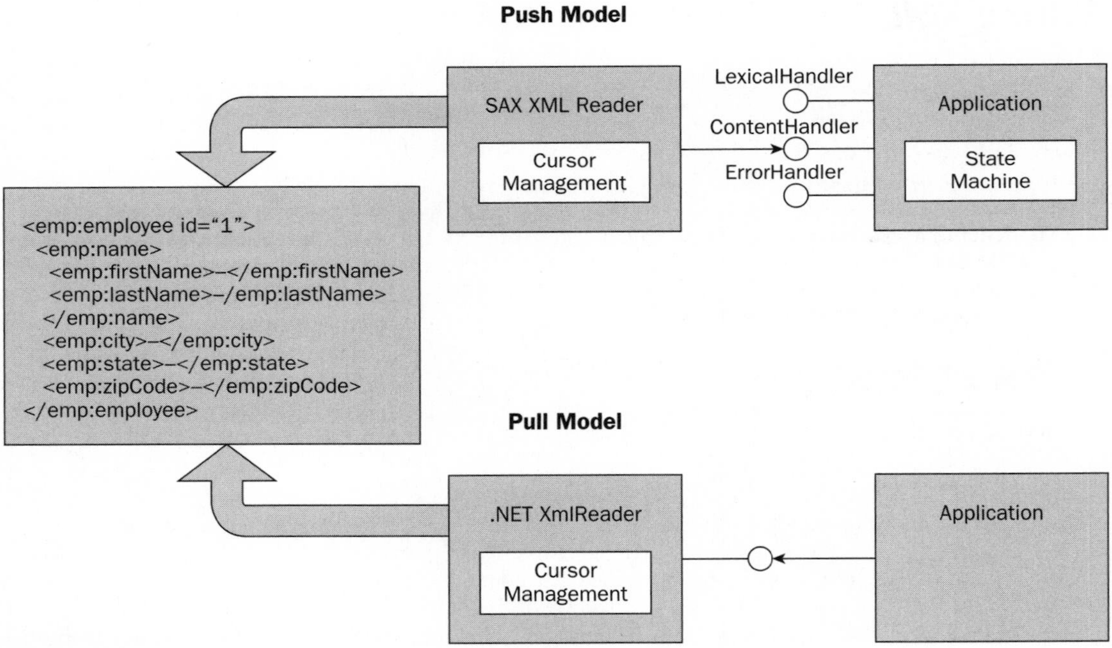

Push Model

Pull Model

Figure 4-5

> The XmlReader abstract class plays a very important role in implementing the new pull model. As part of the System.Xml tree, the primary objective of this class is to provide developers with a framework to implement this new model. If you're an adventurous developer, you can use this abstract class as the basis for your very own, custom-crafted XmlReader object.

Writing XML Data

At this point, you know all about reading and parsing XML files using the XmlReader object, and even checking if they're well-formed and valid. Take a step into more advanced territory with this expose of two objects that let you dynamically create well-formed XML documents in your ASP.NET applications on the fly.

Reading XML data is only half of the puzzle. What if you are a developer who gets an XML feed from a third-party vendor and needs to convert this data into a new XML file based on a custom DTD or XML schema? How do you accomplish this? Is it possible to write an XML file on-the-fly? Fortunately, just as there is a class for reading XML data using a read-only forward-only approach, the .NET framework comes with a class named XmlWriter for dynamically writing XML data in a fast, non-cached, forward-only manner. The XmlWriter object can best be considered as a counterpart to the XmlReader object, allowing you to perform the reverse function.

Writing XML Data with XmlWriter

If you've read about XML, you're probably aware that the XML 1.0 specification from W3C describes the serialized form of XML—the way that XML appears when rendered as text—complete with angle brackets, start tags and end tags, and namespace and XML declarations. If you've got some data that you want to write out as XML, it isn't hard to do it manually, but the .NET Framework provides you with the XmlWriter class to help with a lot of the formatting chores, such as keeping track of indentation and inserting namespace information everywhere it is needed. You can leverage the XmlWriter class to build XML documents that conform to the W3C Extensible Markup Language XML 1.0 Second Edition (www.w3 .org/TR/2000/REC-xml-20001006.html) recommendation and the XML Namespaces recommendation (www.w3.org/TR/REC-xml-names/). Table 4-6 outlines the important properties available through the XmlWriter object.

Table 4-6. Important Properties of the XmlWriter Class

Property	Description
Settings	Returns the XmlWriterSettings object used to create the instance of the XmlWriter object
WriteState	Returns the state of the writer in the form of an WriteState enumeration
XmlLang	Gets the current xml:lang scope; the xml:lang attribute gives authors a consistent way to identify the particular language contained within a particular element
XmlSpace	Gets the scope of the current xml:space in the form of an XmlSpace object; the xml:space attribute allows elements to declare to an application whether their white space is significant

Some of the more commonly used methods of the `XmlWriter` object are shown in Table 4-7.

Table 4-7. Important Methods of the XmlWriter Class

Method	Description
Close	Closes the current stream and the underlying stream
Create	Creates and returns an instance of the `XmlWriter` object
WriteAttributes	Writes out all the attributes found at the current position in the `XmlReader` object
WriteAttributeString	Writes and attribute with the specified value
WriteBase64	Encodes the specified binary bytes as base64 and writes out the resulting text
WriteCData	Writes out a `CData` section containing the specified text
WriteCharEntity	Writes out the Unicode character in hexadecimal character entity reference format
WriteChars	Used to write large amounts of text one buffer at a time
WriteComment	Writes out an `XmlComment` containing the specified text
WriteDocType	Writes out the `DOCTYPE` declaration with the specified name and optional attributes
WriteElementString	Writes an element containing specified string value
WriteEndAttribute	Closes the previous `WriteStartAttribute` method call initiated by the `XmlWriter`
WriteEndDocument	Closes all the open elements or attributes and puts the writer back in the start state
WriteEndElement	Closes the open element created using the `WriteStartElement` method of the `XmlWriter`; if the element contains no content, a short end tag "`/>`" is written; otherwise, a full end tag is written
WriteEntityRef	Writes out an entity reference
WriteFullEndElement	Closes the open element. The difference between this method and `WriteEndElement` is visible when it comes to writing empty elements. This method always closes the open tag by fully writing the end tag and is useful when writing tags such as script that is used for embedding HTML script blocks.
WriteName	Writes out the specified name
WriteNode	Copies everything from the source object to the current writer instance
WriteProcessingInstruction	Writes out a processing instruction with a space between the name and text

Method	Description
WriteQualifiedName	Writes out the namespace-qualified name by looking up the prefix that is in scope for the given namespace
WriteRaw	Writes out the raw markup manually without checking the contents
WriteStartAttribute	Writes the start of an attribute
WriteStartDocument	Writes the XML declaration
WriteStartElement	Writes out the specified start tag
WriteString	Writes out the supplied text content
WriteValue	Writes out the supplied value as a single typed value
WriteWhitespace	Writes out the given white space

As you can see from Table 4-7, to write elements, attributes, and documents, you need to call a WriteStartXXX and a WriteEndXXX function. When using XmlWriter, you don't simply write an element; you write the start tag, then write its content, and then write the end tag. Therefore, you have to keep track of where you are in the document to ensure that you call the correct end functions at the correct time.

In addition to providing methods for writing XML data, the XmlWriter also helps you to create valid XML. For example, the XmlWriter will not let you do things like write an attribute outside a tag. It will also make sure that you write elements in the correct order, such as placing the <?xml version="1.0"?> instruction before the <!DOCTYPE> statement, and so on. Note, however, that the XmlWriter will not perform any validation against a DTD or XML schema. To accomplish this, use the XmlWriter to write the document to a memory stream and then validate it using an XmlNodeReader object in conjunction with XmlWriterSettings object. The XmlWriter will also escape special characters in the output when necessary. For example, it will replace the &, <, and > characters with their corresponding Unicode entities: &, <, and >.

Starting and Ending a Document

The WriteStartDocument() and WriteEndDocument() functions are used to write the start and end of an XML document. The WriteStartDocument() function writes the opening <?xml version="1.0"?> statement that all XML documents should contain and takes a Boolean argument that indicates whether the document is a stand-alone XML document (all entity declarations required by the XML document are contained within the document). If this argument is true, standalone="yes" is added to the XML declaration.

> **The <?xml> declaration is technically optional, but the W3C XML specification recommends that you use it. You can find this specification at http://www.w3.org/xml.**

The `WriteEndDocument()` function closes any open attribute and element tags. Usually, you do this yourself by closing the elements and attributes as you go, but it is always a good idea to call this function when you get to the end of the document, just to make sure.

Writing Elements

Elements are written using pairs of `WriteStartElement()` and `WriteEndElement()` functions or by using the `WriteElementString()` function. The `WriteElementString()` function is the simplest because it allows you to write the name of an element and its content at the same time. The downside is that you cannot write any attributes onto the element when using this function.

For example, to write the XML element `<city>Seattle</city>`, you would simply use the following code:

```
writer.WriteElementString("city", "Seattle")
```

This is not always practical, however, because often you will want to write an element that contains attributes or other elements. To do this, your code needs to call `WriteStartElement()` followed by one or more of the other `XmlWriter` methods. For example, the following code snippet writes an element with another element nested inside it:

```
writer.WriteStartElement("name")
writer.WriteElementString("firstName","Nancy")
writer.WriteEndElement()
```

The XML fragment produced looks like this:

```
<name>
   <firstName>Nancy</firstName>
</name>
```

Writing Attributes

Attributes, like elements, can be written two ways. One way is with the `WriteAttributeString()` method, which writes an attribute and its value all at once. The other way is to use the `WriteStartAttribute()` and `WriteEndAttribute()` methods to add an attribute to an element. For example, the following code snippet uses the second way to add an attribute to an element:

```
writer.WriteStartElement("employee")
writer.WriteStartAttribute("id")
writer.WriteString("1")
writer.WriteEndAttribute()
writer.WriteEndElement()
```

This code produces an XML fragment that looks like this:

```
<employee id="1"/>
```

Writing Other Data

The XmlWriter class provides methods for writing other types of XML content to the output.

❑ The WriteString() method is very useful for writing string content to the XML file. It can be used to write the content of elements and attributes, and it will automatically replace the &, <, and > characters with their corresponding Unicode entities.

❑ The WriteCData() method writes a CDATA section to the XML file. CDATA sections are used to surround content that you do not want the XML parser to interpret as XML.

❑ The WriteComment() method inserts an XML comment into the file. XML comments are just like HTML comments: They are surrounded by <!-- and -->.

❑ The WriteRaw() method can be used to directly insert XML markup into the output. You should use this function with care, because it does not ensure that the markup is balanced or that special characters are converted to their corresponding Unicode entities.

As you utilize the various Write methods to write XML data, the XmlWriter object exhibits its state through the values set in the WriteState enumeration. Table 4-8 summarizes the allowable states for an XmlWriter. Values come from the WriteState enumeration type. An XmlWriter object is expected to properly and promptly update its WriteState property as various internal operations take place.

Table 4-8. Members of the WriteState **Enumeration**

State	Description
Attribute	The writer enters this state when an attribute is being written
Closed	When the Close method has been invoked and the writer is no longer available for writing operations
Content	The writer enters this state when the contents of a node is being written
Element	The writer enters this state when the start tag of an element is being written
Error	Signals an error in the writing operation that prevents the writer from proceeding forward
Prolog	The writer is writing the prolog (the section that declares the element names, attributes, and construction rules of valid markup for a data type) of a well-formed XML 1.0 document
Start	The writer is in an initial state, waiting for a write call to be issued

Now that you understand the base properties and methods of the XmlWriter class, it is time to move onto examples that leverage these properties and methods.

Writing a Simple XML File

This section demonstrates how to write a simple XML file utilizing the methods of the XmlWriter class from an ASP.NET page. Listing 4-6 shows the ASP.NET page used to perform this.

Listing 4-6: Writing a Simple XML File Using the XmlWriter **Class**

```
<%@ Page Language="C#" %>
<%@ Import Namespace="System.Xml" %>
<script runat="server">
void Page_Load(object sender, EventArgs e)
{
  string xmlFilePath = @"C:\Data\Employees.xml";
    try
    {
      using (XmlWriter writer = XmlWriter.Create(xmlFilePath))
      {
        //Start writing the XML document
        writer.WriteStartDocument(false);
        writer.WriteComment("This XML file represents the details of " +
          "an employee");
        //Start with the root element
        writer.WriteStartElement("employees");
          writer.WriteStartElement("employee");
          writer.WriteAttributeString("id", "1");
            writer.WriteStartElement("name");
              writer.WriteElementString("firstName", "Nancy");
              writer.WriteElementString("lastName", "lastName");
            writer.WriteEndElement();
            writer.WriteElementString("city", "Seattle");
            writer.WriteElementString("state", "WA");
            writer.WriteElementString("zipCode", "98122");
          writer.WriteEndElement();
        writer.WriteEndElement();
        writer.WriteEndDocument();
        //Flush the object and write the XML data to the file
        writer.Flush();
        lblResult.Text = "File is written successfully";
      }
    }
    catch (Exception ex)
    {
      lblResult.Text = "An Exception occurred: " + ex.Message;
    }
}
</script>
<html xmlns="http://www.w3.org/1999/xhtml" >
<head runat="server">
  <title>Writing XML File</title>
</head>
<body>
  <form id="form1" runat="server">
    <div>
      <asp:label id="lblResult" runat="server" />
    </div>
  </form>
</body>
</html>
```

Run this example in your browser, and you will see something like this:

An Exception occurred: Access to the path "C:\Data\Employees.xml" is denied.

This exception is due to the fact the ASPNET account used by the ASP.NET worker process does not have write permissions to the C:\Data directory. You can fix this by navigating to the C:\Data directory from Windows explorer and giving permissions to the ASPNET account to write to that directory. If you navigate to the page in the browser, you will see the message "File is written successfully." Navigate to the C:\Data directory from Windows explorer and look for a file called Employees.xml. This is what it should look like.

```xml
<?xml version="1.0" encoding="utf-8" standalone="no"?>
<!--This XML file represents the details of an employee-->
<employees>
  <employee id="1">
    <name>
      <firstName>Nancy</firstName>
      <lastName>lastName</lastName>
    </name>
    <city>Seattle</city>
    <state>WA</state>
    <zipCode>98122</zipCode>
  </employee>
</employees>
```

At first glance, this output is very unattractive to the naked eye. The next section shows you how to format this output using the XmlWriterSettings class. First, though, it's time for a step-by-step explanation of the code listing:

The first step in Listing 4-6 is to import all the classes required for the application. Within the Page_Load() function, there is a variable named xmlFilePath that holds the path to the XML file. It then declares a using block to create an XmlWriter object and passes the xmlFilePath as an argument. Next it begins the writing of XML document instance by invoking the WriteStartDocument() method. This writes the opening XML declaration to the file. It's obvious that the WriteComment() method is used to insert meaningful comments into the XML file. A good practice in general, this becomes a necessity if your XML file is widely distributed.

Next comes the process of building the XML document by adding elements to it one-by-one using the WriteStartElement() method. This method takes only one argument, the element name, and hence cannot be used to write elements that contain character data. The mirror image of the WriteStartElement() method is the WriteEndElement() method, which takes care of writing corresponding end elements to the XML document. Note that it is essential to get the order of method calls correct here, or your XML output will not be well-formed. Of course, writing elements without content may be a great deal of fun, but it isn't actually very useful, which is why there are also some methods that actually write data into the XML file.

First, the WriteElementString() method, which requires two parameters: the name of the element and the data to be contained within it. Note that you don't have to worry about closing elements written in this manner; the WriteElementString() method does all the work for you!

```
writer.WriteElementString("firstName", "Nancy");
```

The `XmlWriter` class also comes equipped with a handy `WriteAttributeString()` method for writing attributes. For example, the following code uses this method to add the id attribute to the `<employee>` element.

```
writer.WriteAttributeString("id", "1");
```

To wrap things up, the `Flush()` method actually writes the XML data stream that has been building in memory to a file. This is followed by a catch block to trap errors and gracefully exit the try block.

Formatting the Output of the XmlWriter

As you must have figured out by now, using the `XmlWriter` object is fairly easy. The introductory example demonstrated how you can write an XML file without much fuss using the `XmlWriter` class. In this section, you go much further by getting an understanding of how to format the output of the XML file through the methods of the `XmlWriterSettings` class. Before diving into an example, take a look at the properties and methods of the `XmlWriterSettings` class. Table 4-9 outlines the important properties of the `XmlWriterSettings` object.

Table 4-9. Important Properties of the `XmlWriterSettings` **Class**

Property	Description
CheckCharacters	Gets or sets a value that indicates if character checking is to be performed or not
Encoding	Gets or sets the text encoding to use in the form of Encoding object
Indent	Gets or sets a boolean value indicating whether to indent element
IndentChars	Gets or sets the character string to use when indenting
NewLineChars	Gets or sets the character string to use for line breaks
NewLineOnAttributes	Gets or sets a boolean value indicating if the attributes should be written in a new line
OmitXmlDeclaration	Gets or sets a boolean value indicating whether XML declarations should be written

In addition to the properties shown in Table 4-9, the `XmlWriterSettings` object also contains properties such as `ConformanceLevel` that are supported by the `XmlReaderSettings` object as well and these properties serve the same purpose. Listing 4-7 shows to how to take advantage of the `XmlWriterSettings` class to customize the output of the XML file created using the `XmlWriter` object.

Listing 4-7: Formatting the Output of the XML File through `XmlWriterSettings` **Class**

```
<%@ Page Language="C#" %>
<%@ Import Namespace="System.Xml" %>
<script runat="server">
  void Page_Load(object sender, EventArgs e)
  {
    string xmlFilePath = @"C:\Data\Employees.xml";
```

```
    try
    {
        XmlWriterSettings settings = new XmlWriterSettings();
        settings.Indent = true;
settings.ConformanceLevel = ConformanceLevel.Auto;
settings.IndentChars = "\t";
settings.OmitXmlDeclaration = false;
using (XmlWriter writer = XmlWriter.Create(xmlFilePath, settings))
{
  //Start writing the XML document
  writer.WriteStartDocument(false);
  //Start with the root element
  writer.WriteStartElement("employees");
    writer.WriteStartElement("employee");
    writer.WriteAttributeString("id", "1");
      writer.WriteStartElement("name");
        writer.WriteElementString("firstName", "Nancy");
        writer.WriteElementString("lastName", "lastName");
      writer.WriteEndElement();
      writer.WriteElementString("city", "Seattle");
      writer.WriteElementString("state", "WA");
      writer.WriteElementString("zipCode", "98122");
    writer.WriteEndElement();
  writer.WriteEndElement();
  writer.WriteEndDocument();
  //Flush the object and write the XML data to the file
  writer.Flush();
  lblResult.Text = "File is written successfully";
}
}
catch (Exception ex)
{
  lblResult.Text = "An Exception occurred: " + ex.Message;
}
    }
  </script>
  <html xmlns="http://www.w3.org/1999/xhtml" >
  <head runat="server">
    <title>Writing XML File with XmlWriterSettings</title>
  </head>
  <body>
    <form id="form1" runat="server">
      <div>
        <asp:label id="lblResult" runat="server" />
      </div>
    </form>
  </body>
  </html>
```

Here is the output generated by the code listing 4-7.

```
<?xml version="1.0" encoding="utf-8" standalone="no"?>
<employees>
<employee id="1">
<name>
```

```
<firstName>Nancy</firstName>
<lastName>lastName</lastName>
</name>
<city>Seattle</city>
<state>WA</state>
<zipCode>98122</zipCode>
</employee>
</employees>
```

Now take a close look at the changes that were made to the Listing 4-6 to bring about this amazing transformation. First up, an instance of the `XmlWriterSettings` object is created and then various properties such as `Indent`, `ConformanceLevel`, `IndentChars`, and `OmitXmlDeclaration` are set.

```
XmlWriterSettings settings = new XmlWriterSettings();
settings.Indent = true;
settings.ConformanceLevel = ConformanceLevel.Auto;
settings.IndentChars = "\t";
settings.OmitXmlDeclaration = false;
```

The `XmlWriterSettings` object is then passed as an argument to the `Create()` method of the `XmlWriter` object to apply the settings of the `XmlWriterSettings` object to the newly created `XmlWriter` object. That's all there is to utilizing the `XmlWriterSettings` object to control the output of the XML file created by the `XmlWriter` object.

XmlWriter Class's Namespace Support

In the `XmlWriter` class, all the methods available for writing element nodes and attributes have overloads to work with namespaces. You simply add a new argument to the call and specify the namespace prefix of choice. You insert a namespace declaration in the current node using the `xmlns` attribute. You can also optionally specify a namespace prefix. The prefix is a symbolic name that uniquely identifies the namespace.

> *A namespace is identified by a URN and is used to qualify both attribute and node names so that they belong to a particular domain of names.*

To declare a namespace, add a special attribute to the node that roots the target scope of the namespace, as shown here:

```
<node xmlns:prefix="namespace-urn">
```

You can write this XML text as raw text or use one of the methods of the writer object. Typically, you use one of the overloads of the WriteAttributeString method to accomplish this. The declaration of the WriteAttributeString method is as follows:

```
public void WriteAttributeString(string prefix, string attrName,
  string ns, string value);
```

The first two arguments specify the namespace and the local name of the attribute respectively. The third argument is expected to be the URN of the namespace for the attribute. In this case, however, the namespace prefix named xmlns points to the default XML namespace, so the ns argument must be set to null. Note that any attempt to set ns to a non-null value would result in an exception because the specified URN would not match the URN of the xmlns namespace prefix. The fourth and final argument, value, contains the URN of the namespace you are declaring. The following code shows how to declare a sample namespace rooted in the node <employees>:

```
writer.WriteStartElement("employees");
writer.WriteAttributeString("xmlns", "emp", null, "urn:employees-wrox");
```

This code produces the following output:

```
<employees xmlns:emp="urn:employees-wrox">
```

Listing 4-8 shows an example ASP.NET page that demonstrates how to add namespaces support to the elements of the Employees.xml file.

Listing 4-8: Adding Namespaces Support to the Employees XML File

```
<%@ Page Language="C#" %>
<%@ Import Namespace="System.Xml" %>
<script runat="server">
  void Page_Load(object sender, EventArgs e)
  {
    string xmlFilePath = @"C:\Data\Employees.xml";
    try
    {
      using (XmlWriter writer = XmlWriter.Create(xmlFilePath))
      {
        //Start writing the XML document
        writer.WriteStartDocument(false);
        //Start with the root element
        writer.WriteStartElement("employees");
        //Write the Namespace prefix for the root element
        writer.WriteAttributeString("xmlns", "emp", null, "urn:employees-wrox");
          writer.WriteStartElement("employee", "urn:employees-wrox");
          writer.WriteAttributeString("id", "1");
            writer.WriteStartElement("name", "urn:employees-wrox");
              writer.WriteElementString("firstName",
                "urn:employees-wrox", "Nancy");
              writer.WriteElementString("lastName",
                "urn:employees-wrox", "lastName");
            writer.WriteEndElement();
            writer.WriteElementString("city", "urn:employees-wrox", "Seattle");
            writer.WriteElementString("state", "urn:employees-wrox", "WA");
            writer.WriteElementString("zipCode", "urn:employees-wrox", "98122");
          writer.WriteEndElement();
        writer.WriteEndElement();
        writer.WriteEndDocument();
        //Flush the object and write the XML data to the file
        writer.Flush();
        lblResult.Text = "File is written successfully";
      }
    }
    catch (Exception ex)
    {
      lblResult.Text = "An Exception occurred: " + ex.Message;
```

```
      }
    }
  </script>
  <html xmlns="http://www.w3.org/1999/xhtml" >
  <head runat="server">
    <title>Writing XML File</title>
  </head>
  <body>
    <form id="form1" runat="server">
      <div>
        <asp:label id="lblResult" runat="server" />
      </div>
    </form>
  </body>
  </html>
```

Listing 4-8 uses "urn:employees-wrox" as the namespace and the namespace prefix used is "emp". If you navigate to the code Listing 4-8 in a browser, you will see the output shown in Figure 4-6.

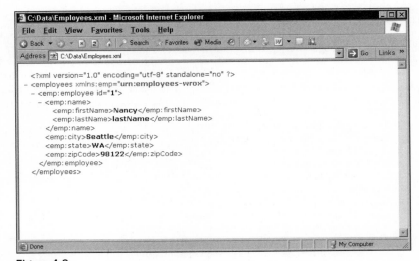

Figure 4-6

In Listing 4-8, you supplied the namespace as an argument to the WriteStartElement as shown in the following code.

```
writer.WriteStartElement("employee", "urn:employees-wrox");
```

You can also accomplish this effect using the following two lines of code as well.

```
string prefix = writer.LookupPrefix("urn:employees-wrox");
writer.WriteStartElement(prefix, "employee", null);
```

By leveraging the `LookupPrefix()` method, you can get reference to the namespace space prefix in a local variable and then supply it as an argument to methods such as `WriteStartElement()`. The advantage to this approach is that you don't have to supply the namespace to each of the creation methods; you simply supply the prefix obtained through the `LookupPrefix()` method to the creation methods.

Writing Images Using XmlWriter

The techniques described in the previous sections can also be used with any sort of binary data that can be expressed with an array of bytes, including images. This section provides you with an example and demonstrates how to embed a JPEG image in an XML document. The structure of the sample XML document is extremely simple. It consists of a single employee node, and inside that node there is an image node holding the binary image data plus an attribute containing the original file name. Code required for implementing this is shown in Listing 4-9.

Listing 4-9: Embedding an Image in an XML Document

```
<%@ Page Language="C#" %>
<%@ Import Namespace="System.Xml" %>
<%@ Import Namespace="System.IO" %>
<script runat="server">
  void Page_Load(object sender, EventArgs e)
  {
    string xmlFilePath = @"C:\Data\Employees.xml";
    string imageFileName = @"C:\Data\Employee.jpg";
    try
    {
      using (XmlWriter writer = XmlWriter.Create(xmlFilePath))
      {
        //Start writing the XML document
        writer.WriteStartDocument(false);
        writer.WriteStartElement("employee");
        writer.WriteAttributeString("id", "1");
          writer.WriteStartElement("image");
            writer.WriteAttributeString("fileName", imageFileName);
            //Get the size of the file
            FileInfo fi = new FileInfo(imageFileName);
            int size = (int)fi.Length;
            //Read the JPEG file
            byte[] imgBytes = new byte[size];
            FileStream stream = new FileStream(imageFileName, FileMode.Open);
            BinaryReader reader = new BinaryReader(stream);
            imgBytes = reader.ReadBytes(size);
            reader.Close();
            //Write the JPEG data
            writer.WriteBinHex(imgBytes, 0, size);
          writer.WriteEndElement();
        writer.WriteEndElement();
        writer.WriteEndDocument();
        //flush the object and write the XML data to the file
        writer.Flush();
        lblResult.Text = "File is written successfully";
      }
    }
    catch (Exception ex)
    {
```

```
        lblResult.Text = "An Exception occurred: " + ex.Message;
    }
  }
</script>
<html xmlns="http://www.w3.org/1999/xhtml" >
<head runat="server">
  <title>Writing Images using XmlWriter</title>
</head>
<body>
  <form id="form1" runat="server">
    <div>
       <asp:label id="lblResult" runat="server" />
    </div>
  </form>
</body>
</html>
```

Listing 4-9 uses the `FileInfo` class to determine the size of the JPEG file. `FileInfo` is a helper class in the `System.IO` namespace that allows you to retrieve information about individual files. The contents of the `employees.jpeg` file are extracted using the `ReadBytes` method of the .NET binary reader. The contents are then encoded as `BinHex` and written to the XML document. Figure 4-7 shows the output produced by the code.

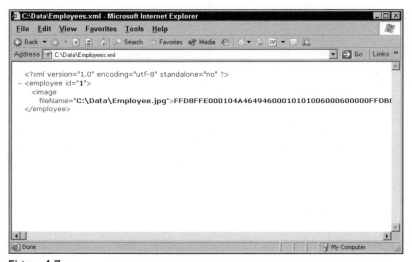

Figure 4-7

Summary

This chapter introduced you to .NET's XML-handling capabilities. The .NET architecture provides the most complete, integrated support platform for XML yet from Microsoft, and it makes many otherwise daunting tasks much easier to accomplish. This chapter introduced you to the SAX and DOM methods for processing XML, and showed you how the Microsoft approach attempts to marry these two approaches using a model that provides the benefits of both.

Specifically, you learned how to read XML using the XmlReader class, and how to use the XmlReaderSettings object in conjunction with the XmlReader object to customize the output of the XmlReader object. You learned how to use the XmlWriter class to write XML data files, which greatly reduces the amount of information that an application has to keep track of when writing XML. Finally, you learned how to use the XmlWriter object to create namespaces and embed images in an XML Document.

As you can see, after you know the basics of reading an XML file with the XmlReader, it's very easy to begin using its built-in constructs to extract and manipulate XML data to your precise needs. Hopefully this chapter gave you the motivation to start writing your own XML applications. XML is clearly going to play a large role in future Web development, and learning these skills is essential to the success of any Web application developer. As an exercise to better understand how this works, I recommend taking your own XML markup and writing a similar script to extract element and attribute values from it. After all, practice makes perfect!

5

XML Data Validation

In the previous chapters, you have seen all about reading XML files, and even checking if they are well-formed and valid. This chapter takes a step into more advanced territory by looking at how to perform validation of XML data at the time of reading XML data. This chapter discusses the different types of XML validation using the classes in the System.Xml namespace. This chapter also provides an in-depth discussion on the .NET Schema Object Model by providing examples on how to programmatically create and read XML schemas. Specifically, this chapter will cover:

- ❑ XML validation support provided by the .NET Framework 2.0

- ❑ How to validate an XML file using the XmlReaderSettings class in conjunction with the XmlReader class

- ❑ How to take advantage of the XmlSchemaSet class to cache XML schemas and then use them to validate XML files

- ❑ How to perform XML DOM validation through the XmlNodeReader class

- ❑ How to use inline schemas to validate XML data

- ❑ How to validate XML data using DTDs

- ❑ Visual Studio's support for creating XSD schemas

- ❑ How to programmatically read XSD schemas using XmlSchema

- ❑ How to programmatically create XSD schemas

- ❑ How to programmatically infer XSD schema from an XML file

The next section starts by reviewing the validation support provided by the .NET Framework 2.0.

XML Validation

Validation is the process of enforcing rules on the XML content either via a XSD schema or a DTD or a XDR schema. There are two ways to define a structure for an XML document, sometimes called a vocabulary: DTDs and XML schemas. Using an XML schema is a newer and somewhat more flexible technique than using a DTD, but both approaches are in common use. A DTD or schema may be embedded within an XML file, but more often it will be contained in a separate file. An XML processing program, called a parser, can check an XML document against its DTD or schema to see if it follows the rules; this process is called validation. An XML file that follows all the rules in its DTD or schema is said to be valid.

The XML schema file usually is an XML-Data Reduced (XDR) or XML Schema Definition language (XSD) file. XSD schema-based validation is the industry accepted standard and is the primary method of XML validation used in most of the applications. Although validation of XML data using DTDs is used only in legacy applications, this chapter provides you with an example on how to use DTDs for XML validation.

Validation Types Supported in .NET Framework 2.0

In .NET Framework, there are a number of ways you can perform validation of XML data. Before discussing those validation types, it is important to understand the key differences between the validation mechanisms (DTD, XDR, and XSD) supported by the .NET Framework.

❑ DTD — A text file whose syntax stems directly from the Standard Generalized Markup Language (SGML) — the ancestor of XML as we know it today. A DTD follows a custom, non-XML syntax to define the set of valid tags, the attributes each tag can support, and the dependencies between tags. A DTD allows you to specify the children for each tag, their cardinality, their attributes, and a few other properties for both tags and attributes. Cardinality specifies the number of occurrences of each child element.

❑ XDR — A schema language based on a proposal submitted by Microsoft to the W3C back in 1998. (For more information, see `http://www.w3.org/TR/1998/NOTE-XML-data-0105.`) XDRs are flexible and overcome some of the limitations of DTDs. Unlike DTDs, XDRs describe the structure of the document using the same syntax as the XML document. Additionally, in a DTD, all the data content is character data. XDR language schemas allow you to specify the data type of an element or an attribute. Note that XDR never reached the recommendation status.

❑ XSD — Defines the elements and attributes that form an XML document. Each element is strongly typed. Based on a W3C recommendation, XSD describes the structure of XML documents using another XML document. XSDs include an all-encompassing type system composed of primitive and derived types. The XSD type system is also at the foundation of the Simple Object Access Protocol (SOAP) and XML Web services.

As mentioned, XDR is an early hybrid specification that never reached the status of a W3C recommendation since it evolved into XSD. The .NET classes support XDR mostly for backward compatibility; however XDR is fully supported by the Component Object Model (COM)-based Microsoft XML Core Services (MSXML) parser.

> DTD was considered the cross-platform standard until a few years ago. The W3C then officialized a newer standard — XSD — which is, technically speaking, far superior to DTD. Today, XSD is supported by almost all parsers on all platforms. Although the support for DTD will not be deprecated anytime soon, you'll be better positioned if you start migrating to XSD or building new XML-driven applications based on XSD instead of DTD or XDR.

The .NET Framework provides a handy utility, named xsd.exe, that among other things can automatically convert an XDR schema to XSD. If you pass an XDR schema file (typically, an .xdr extension), xsd.exe converts the XDR schema to an XSD schema, as shown here:

```
xsd.exe Authors.xdr
```

The output file has the same name as the XDR schema, but with the .xsd extension.

XML Data Validation Using XSD Schemas

An XML document contains elements, attributes, and values of primitive data types. Throughout this chapter, I will use an XML document named Authors.xml, which is shown in Listing 5-1.

Listing 5-1: Authors.xml File

```xml
<?xml version="1.0"?>
<authors>
  <author>
    <au_id>172-32-1176</au_id>
    <au_lname>White</au_lname>
    <au_fname>Johnson</au_fname>
    <phone>408 496-7223</phone>
    <address>10932 Bigge Rd.</address>
    <city>Menlo Park</city>
    <state>CA</state>
    <zip>94025</zip>
    <contract>true</contract>
  </author>
  <author>
    <au_id>213-46-8915</au_id>
    <au_lname>Green</au_lname>
    <au_fname>Marjorie</au_fname>
    <phone>415 986-7020</phone>
    <address>309 63rd St. #411</address>
    <city>Oakland</city>
    <state>CA</state>
    <zip>94618</zip>
    <contract>true</contract>
  </author>
</authors>
```

XSD schema defines elements, attributes, and the relationship between them. It conforms to the W3C XML schema standards and recommendations. XSD schema for the Authors.xml document is Authors.xsd, and that is shown in Listing 5-2.

Listing 5-2: Authors.xsd File

```xml
<?xml version="1.0" encoding="utf-8"?>
<xs:schema attributeFormDefault="unqualified" elementFormDefault="qualified"
  xmlns:xs="http://www.w3.org/2001/XMLSchema">
  <xs:element name="authors">
    <xs:complexType>
      <xs:sequence>
        <xs:element maxOccurs="unbounded" name="author">
          <xs:complexType>
            <xs:sequence>
              <xs:element name="au_id" type="xs:string" />
              <xs:element name="au_lname" type="xs:string" />
              <xs:element name="au_fname" type="xs:string" />
              <xs:element name="phone" type="xs:string" />
              <xs:element name="address" type="xs:string" />
              <xs:element name="city" type="xs:string" />
              <xs:element name="state" type="xs:string" />
              <xs:element name="zip" type="xs:unsignedInt" />
              <xs:element name="contract" type="xs:boolean" />
            </xs:sequence>
          </xs:complexType>
        </xs:element>
      </xs:sequence>
    </xs:complexType>
  </xs:element>
</xs:schema>
```

.NET Framework 2.0 classes support the W3C XML schema recommendation. The classes that are commonly employed to validate the XML document are XmlReader, XmlReaderSettings, XmlSchemaSet, and XmlNodeReader. The sequence of steps to validate an XML document using an XSD schema is as follows.

Steps for Validating an XML Document

❑ A ValidationEventHandler event handler method is defined.

❑ An instance of the XmlReaderSettings object is created. XmlReaderSettings class allows you to specify a set of options that will be supported on the XmlReader object and these options will be in effect when parsing XML data. Note that the XmlReaderSettings renders the XmlValidatingReader class (used with .NET 1.x version) obsolete.

❑ The previously defined ValidationEventHandler method is associated with the XmlReaderSettings class.

❑ The ValidationType property of the XmlReaderSettings is set to ValidationType.Schema.

❑ An XSD schema is added to the XmlReaderSettings class through the Schemas property of the XmlReaderSettings class.

❑ The XmlReader class validates the XML document while parsing the XML data using the Read method.

Validation Event Handler

The `ValidationEventHandler` event is used to define an event handler for receiving the notification about XSD schema validation errors. The validation errors and warnings are reported through the `ValidationEventHandler` call-back function. Validation errors do not stop parsing and parsing only stops if the XML document is not well-formed. If you do not provide validation event handler callback function and a validation error occurs, however, an exception is thrown. This approach of using the validation event callback mechanism to trap all validation errors enables all validation errors to be discovered in a single pass.

Role of XmlReaderSettings Class in XML Validation

The `XmlReaderSettings` class is one of the most important classes along with the `XmlReader` class that provides the core foundation for validating XML data. Table 5-1 provides a brief recap of the validation related properties of the `XmlReaderSettings` class that will be utilized later in this chapter.

Table 5-1. Validation Related Properties and Events of XmlReaderSettings Class

Property	Description
ProhibitDtd	Indicates if the DTD validation is supported in the `XmlReaderSettings` class. The default value is true meaning that the DTD validation is not supported.
ValidationType	Specifies the type of validation supported on the `XmlReaderSettings` class. The permitted validation types are DTD, XSD, and None.
ValidationEventHandler	Specifies an event handler that will receive information about validation events.
ValidationFlags	Specifies additional validation settings such as use of inline schemas, identity constraints, and XML attributes that will be enforced when validating the XML data.
Schemas	Gets or sets the `XmlSchemaSet` object that represents the collection of schemas to be used for performing schema validation.

To validate XML data using the `XmlReaderSettings` class, you need to set the properties of the `XmlReaderSettings` class to appropriate values. This class does not operate on its own, but works in conjunction with an `XmlReader` or `XmlNodeReader` instance. You can use this class to validate against either a DTD or an XML schema.

An XML Validation Example

Now that you have a general understanding of the steps involved in validating XML data, it is time to look at an example to understand how it actually works. Listing 5-3 utilizes the `Authors.xsd` schema file to validate the `Authors.xml` file.

Listing 5-3: Validating XML Data Using XSD Schemas

```
<%@ Page Language="C#"%>
<%@ Import Namespace="System.Xml" %>
<%@ Import Namespace="System.Xml.Schema" %>
<script runat="server">
  private StringBuilder _builder = new StringBuilder();
  void Page_Load(object sender, EventArgs e)
  {
    string xmlPath = Request.PhysicalApplicationPath +
      @"\App_Data\Authors.xml";
    string xsdPath = Request.PhysicalApplicationPath +
      @"\App_Data\Authors.xsd";
    XmlReader reader = null;
    XmlReaderSettings settings = new XmlReaderSettings();
    settings.ValidationEventHandler += new
      ValidationEventHandler(this.ValidationEventHandler);
    settings.ValidationType = ValidationType.Schema;
    settings.Schemas.Add(null, XmlReader.Create(xsdPath));
    reader = XmlReader.Create(xmlPath, settings);
    while (reader.Read())
    {
    }
    if (_builder.ToString() == String.Empty)
      Response.Write("Validation completed successfully.");
    else
      Response.Write("Validation Failed. <br>" + _builder.ToString());
  }

  void ValidationEventHandler(object sender, ValidationEventArgs args)
  {
    _builder.Append("Validation error: " + args.Message + "<br>");
  }
</script>
<html xmlns="http://www.w3.org/1999/xhtml" >
<head runat="server">
  <title>XSD Validation</title>
</head>
<body>
  <form id="form1" runat="server">
    <div>
    </div>
  </form>
</body>
</html>
```

Before examining the code, Figure 5-1 shows the output produced by Listing 5-3.

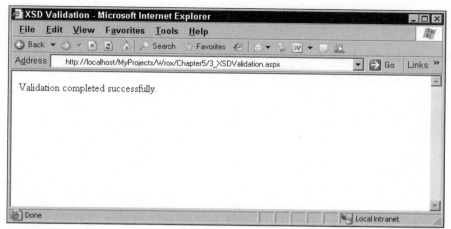

Figure 5-1

To start, Listing 5-3 declares variables that hold the path of the XML and XSD schema files. It then creates an instance of the XmlReaderSettings object and associates a validation event handler callback method to it.

```
XmlReaderSettings settings = new XmlReaderSettings();
settings.ValidationEventHandler += new
  ValidationEventHandler(this.ValidationEventHandler);
```

Then, it sets the ValidationType property of the XmlReaderSettings class to ValidationType.Schema signaling the XmlReader object to validate the XML data using the supplied XSD schema as it parses the XML data.

```
settings.ValidationType = ValidationType.Schema;
```

In addition to the schema, the ValidationType enumeration also supports other values that are shown in Table 5-2.

Table 5-2. ValidationType Enumeration Values

Value	Description
DTD	Indicates that the validation will be performed using DTD
None	No validation is performed and as a result no validation errors are thrown
Schema	Validates the XML document according to XML schemas, including inline XSD schemas

The code then adds the Authors.xsd file to the schemas collection of the XmlReaderSettings object. After that it invokes the static Create method of the XmlReader object passing in the path of the Authors.xml file and the XmlReaderSettings object. The Create method returns instance of the XmlReader object, which actually performs the validation using a DTD or an XML schema when parsing the document.

```
settings.Schemas.Add(null, XmlReader.Create(xsdPath));
reader = XmlReader.Create(xmlPath, settings);
```

Because the XmlReader objects are created with the Create method by passing in the XmlReaderSettings object, settings on the XmlReaderSettings will be supported on the XmlReader object. The Read method of the XmlReader object is then invoked in a While loop so that the entire XML file can be read and validated. The ValidationEventHandler method is invoked whenever a validation error occurs. Inside this method, a StringBuilder object keeps appending the contents of the validation error message to itself. If a validation event handler is not provided, an XmlSchemaException is thrown when a validation error occurs.

Handling Exceptions in XML Validation

In Listing 5-3, whenever an XML validation occurs, the control is automatically transferred to the ValidationEventHandler method that handles the exception by appending the validation error message (obtained through the Message property of the ValidationEventArgs object) to a StringBuilder object. And finally this error message is displayed to the user if the StringBuilder object contains any messages at all. Although this is sufficient for the purposes of this example, there are times when you may want to differentiate the different types of exceptions such as warnings or errors generated during the validation. To accomplish this, you check on the Severity property of the ValidationEventArgs object. This property returns an enumeration of type XmlSeverityType, which can be used to determine the type of the generated exception. This enumeration contains the values shown in Table 5-3.

Table 5-3. XmlSeverityType Enumeration Values

Value	Description
Error	Indicates that a validation error occurred when validating the instance document. This can be the result of validation using DTDs, and XSD schemas. If there is no validation event handler to handle this situation, an exception is thrown.
Warning	Indicates that a validating parser has run into a situation that is not an error but may be important enough to warn the user about. Warning differs from Error in that it doesn't result in an exception being thrown to the calling application.

For example, if you want to filter only the errors generated during the validation process, you can accomplish that by using the following line of code.

```
private void ValidationEventHandler(object sender, ValidationEventArgs args)
{
  if (args.Severity == XmlSeverityType.Error)
  {
    //Add code to handle the errors
  }
}
```

A Cache for Schemas

In the XmlReaderSettings class, the Schemas property represents a collection — that is, an instance of the XmlSchemaSet class that allows you to store one or more schemas that you plan to use later for validation. Using the schema collection improves overall performance because the various schemas are held in memory and don't need to be loaded each and every time validation occurs. You can add as many XSD schemas as you want, but bear in mind that the collection must be completed before the first Read call is made.

To add a new schema to the cache, you use the Add() method of the XmlSchemaSet object. The method has a few overloads, as follows:

```
public void Add(XmlSchemaSet);
public XmlSchema Add(XmlSchema);
public XmlSchema Add(string, string);
public XmlSchema Add(string, XmlReader);
```

The first overload populates the current collection with all the schemas defined in the given collection. The remaining three overloads build from different data and return an instance of the XmlSchema class — the .NET Framework class that contains the definition of an XSD schema.

Populating the Schema Collection

The schema collection actually consists of instances of the XmlSchema class — a kind of compiled version of the schema. The various overloads of the Add method allow you to create an XmlSchema object from a variety of input arguments. For example, consider the following method:

```
public XmlSchema Add(string ns, string url);
```

This method creates and adds a new schema object to the collection. The compiled schema object is created using the namespace URI associated with the schema and the URL of the source.

You can check whether a schema is already in the schema collection by using the Contains() method. The Contains() method can take either an XmlSchema object or a string representing the namespace URI associated with the schema. The former approach works only for XSD schemas. The latter covers both XSD and XDR schemas.

Validating XML Data Using XmlSchemaSet Class

The XmlSchemaSet class represents a cache of XML schemas. It allows you to compile multiple schemas for the same target namespace into a single logical schema.

> The XmlSchemaSet class replaces the XmlSchemaCollection class, which was the class of choice when caching schemas in .NET Framework 1.x. The new XmlSchemaSet class not only provides much better standards compliance but also increased performance.

Before taking a look at an example, I will provide a brief overview of the important properties and methods of the XmlSchemaSet class. Table 5-4 provides a listing of the important properties of the XmlSchemaSet class.

Table 5-4. Important Properties of the XmlSchemaSet Class

Property	Description
Count	Gets the count of logical XSD schemas contained in the XmlSchemaSet
GlobalAttributes	Gets reference to all the global attributes in all the XSD schemas contained in the XmlSchemaSet
GlobalElements	Gets reference to all the global elements in all the XSD schemas contained in the XmlSchemaSet
GlobalTypes	Gets all of the global simple and complex types in all the XSD schemas contained in the XmlSchemaSet
IsCompiled	Indicates if the XSD schemas in the XmlSchemaSet have been already compiled

Table 5-5 discusses the important methods of the XmlSchemaSet class.

Table 5-5. Important Methods of the XmlSchemaSet Class

Method	Description
Add	Adds the given XSD schema to the XmlSchemaSet
Compile	Compiles the XSD schemas added to the XmlSchemaSet class into a single logical schema that can then be used for validation purposes
Contains	Allows you to check if the supplied XSD schema is in the XmlSchemaSet
Remove	Removes the specified XSD schema from the XmlSchemaSet
Reprocess	Reprocesses an XSD schema that already exists in the XmlSchemaSet

Listing 5-4 shows you an example of how to utilize the XmlSchemaSet class for validating XML data.

Listing 5-4: Validating XML Data Using XmlSchemaSet Class

```
<%@ Page Language="C#"%>
<%@ Import Namespace="System.Xml" %>
<%@ Import Namespace="System.Xml.Schema" %>
<script runat="server">
  private StringBuilder _builder = new StringBuilder();
  void Page_Load(object sender, EventArgs e)
  {
    string xmlPath = Request.PhysicalApplicationPath +
      @"\App_Data\Authors.xml";
    string xsdPath = Request.PhysicalApplicationPath +
```

```
        @"\App_Data\Authors.xsd";
      XmlSchemaSet schemaSet = new XmlSchemaSet();
      schemaSet.Add(null, xsdPath);
      XmlReader reader = null;
      XmlReaderSettings settings = new XmlReaderSettings();
      settings.ValidationEventHandler += new
        ValidationEventHandler(this.ValidationEventHandler);
      settings.ValidationType = ValidationType.Schema;
      settings.Schemas = schemaSet;
      reader = XmlReader.Create(xmlPath, settings);
      while (reader.Read())
      {
      }
      if (_builder.ToString() == String.Empty)
        Response.Write("Validation completed successfully.");
      else
        Response.Write("Validation Failed. <br>" + _builder.ToString());
    }

    void ValidationEventHandler(object sender, ValidationEventArgs args)
    {
      _builder.Append("Validation error: " + args.Message + "<br>");
    }
</script>
<html xmlns="http://www.w3.org/1999/xhtml" >
<head runat="server">
  <title>XSD Validation using XmlSchemaSet</title>
</head>
<body>
  <form id="form1" runat="server">
    <div>
    </div>
  </form>
</body>
</html>
```

In Listing 5-4, after an instance of XmlSchemaSet class is created, its Add method is invoked to add the Authors.xsd schema to the XmlSchemaSet class.

```
      XmlSchemaSet schemaSet = new XmlSchemaSet();
      schemaSet.Add(null, xsdPath);
```

After the schema is added to the XmlSchemaSet, then you simply set the Schemas property of the XmlReaderSettings object to the XmlSchemaSet object.

```
      settings.Schemas = schemaSet;
```

You then invoke the Read method of the XmlReader object to parse the XML data in a loop. As similar to the previous example, the parser stops only if the XML data is not well-formed. By not stopping for validation errors, you are able to find all the validation errors in one pass without having to repeatedly parse the XML document. If you navigate to the page using a browser, you will see the same output as shown in Figure 5-1.

XML DOM Validation

Currently, if you have data stored in an `XmlDocument` object, the only type of validation you can perform is load-time validation. You do this by passing a validating reader object such as an `XmlReader` object into the `Load` method. If you make any changes, however, there is no way to ensure that the data still conforms to the schema. Using the `XmlNodeReader` class, which reads data stored in an `XmlNode` object, you can validate a DOM object by passing the `XmlNodeReader` to the `Create` method. Listing 5-5 shows you an example of how to accomplish this.

Listing 5-5: Performing XML DOM Validation

```
<%@ Page Language="C#"%>
<%@ Import Namespace="System.Xml" %>
<%@ Import Namespace="System.Xml.Schema" %>
<script runat="server">
  private StringBuilder _builder = new StringBuilder();
  void Page_Load(object sender, EventArgs e)
  {
    string xmlPath = Request.PhysicalApplicationPath +
      @"\App_Data\Authors.xml";
    string xsdPath = Request.PhysicalApplicationPath +
      @"\App_Data\Authors.xsd";
    XmlDocument xmlDoc = new XmlDocument();
    xmlDoc.Load(xmlPath);
    XmlElement authorElement = (XmlElement)
    xmlDoc.DocumentElement.SelectSingleNode
      ("//authors/author[au_id='172-32-1176']");
    authorElement.SetAttribute("test", "test");
    XmlNodeReader nodeReader = new XmlNodeReader(xmlDoc);
    XmlReader reader = null;
    XmlReaderSettings settings = new XmlReaderSettings();
    settings.ValidationEventHandler += new
      ValidationEventHandler(this.ValidationEventHandler);
    settings.ValidationType = ValidationType.Schema;
    settings.Schemas.Add(null, XmlReader.Create(xsdPath));
    reader = XmlReader.Create(nodeReader, settings);
    while (reader.Read())
    {
    }
    if (_builder.ToString() == String.Empty)
      Response.Write("Validation completed successfully.");
    else
      Response.Write("Validation Failed. <br>" + _builder.ToString());
  }

    void ValidationEventHandler(object sender, ValidationEventArgs args)
    {
      _builder.Append("Validation error: " + args.Message + "<br>");
    }
</script>
<html xmlns="http://www.w3.org/1999/xhtml" >
<head runat="server">
    <title>DOM Validation</title>
</head>
```

```
<body>
    <form id="form1" runat="server">
    <div>
    </div>
    </form>
</body>
</html>
```

Listing 5-5 illustrates how an XmlNodeReader object returned from the XmlDocument object (which in turn is loaded from the Authors.xml document) has XML schema validation support layered on top while reading.

Before reading the XmlDocument object into an XmlNodeReader object, the Authors.xml file is loaded into an XmlDocument and modified in-memory by adding an attribute called "test".

```
XmlDocument xmlDoc = new XmlDocument();
xmlDoc.Load(xmlPath);
XmlElement authorElement = (XmlElement)
xmlDoc.DocumentElement.SelectSingleNode
   ("//authors/author[au_id='172-32-1176']");
authorElement.SetAttribute("test", "test");
```

The XML document is then passed to an XmlNodeReader, which in turn is then passed to the factory-created XmlReader object.

```
reader = XmlReader.Create(nodeReader, settings);
```

When the validating reader parses the file, it can validate any changes made to the file. Because an invalid attribute is added to the XmlDocument object, the XSD schema will fail and you will see an output that is somewhat similar to Figure 5-2.

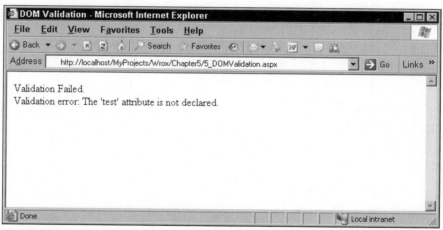

Figure 5-2

As you can see from Figure 5-2, the XML validation has failed because the modified XML data is not in compliance with the XSD schema.

XML Validation Using Inline Schemas

If you want, you can embed an XML schema at the top of an XML data file. This gives you a single XML file for transport that includes data and validation requirements. This is called an inline schema. An interesting phenomenon takes place when the XML schema is embedded in the same XML document being validated, as in the case of inline schemas. In this case, the schema appears as a constituent part of the source document. In particular, it is a direct child of the document root element.

The schema is an XML subtree that is logically placed at the same level as the document to validate. A well-formed XML document, though, cannot have two roots. Thus an all-encompassing root node must be created with two children: the schema and the document. You will see an example of this in Listing 5-6 that introduces a new XML element at the root called <root>. This code contains the XSD schema as well as the XML data to be validated as its children.

Listing 5-6: XML File That Contains the Inline XSD Schema

```
<?xml version="1.0"?>
<root xmlns:xs="http://www.w3.org/2001/XMLSchema" xmlns:x="urn:authors">
  <!-- Start of Schema -->
  <xs:schema targetNamespace="urn:authors">
    <xs:element name="authors">
      <xs:complexType>
        <xs:sequence>
          <xs:element maxOccurs="unbounded" name="author">
            <xs:complexType>
              <xs:sequence>
                <xs:element name="au_id" type="xs:string" />
                <xs:element name="au_lname" type="xs:string" />
                <xs:element name="au_fname" type="xs:string" />
                <xs:element name="phone" type="xs:string" />
                <xs:element name="address" type="xs:string" />
                <xs:element name="city" type="xs:string" />
                <xs:element name="state" type="xs:string" />
                <xs:element name="zip" type="xs:unsignedInt" />
                <xs:element name="contract" type="xs:boolean" />
              </xs:sequence>
            </xs:complexType>
          </xs:element>
        </xs:sequence>
      </xs:complexType>
    </xs:element>
  </xs:schema>
  <!-- End of Schema -->
  <x:authors>
    <author>
      <au_id>172-32-1176</au_id>
      <au_lname>White</au_lname>
      <au_fname>Johnson</au_fname>
      <phone>408 496-7223</phone>
      <address>10932 Bigge Rd.</address>
      <city>Menlo Park</city>
      <state>CA</state>
      <zip>94025</zip>
      <contract>true</contract>
    </author>
```

```
  <author>
    <au_id>213-46-8915</au_id>
    <au_lname>Green</au_lname>
    <au_fname>Marjorie</au_fname>
    <phone>415 986-7020</phone>
    <address>309 63rd St. #411</address>
    <city>Oakland</city>
    <state>CA</state>
    <zip>94618</zip>
    <contract>true</contract>
  </author>
  </x:authors>
</root>
```

Note that in Listing 5-6, the root element cannot be successfully validated because there is no schema information about it. When the `ValidationType` property is set to `ValidationType.Schema`, the `XmlReader` class throws a warning for the root element if an inline schema is detected. Be aware of this when you set up your validation code. A too strong filter for errors could signal as wrong a perfectly legal XML document if the XSD code is embedded. Listing 5-7 shows the code required to validate the inline XSD schema contained in the XML file.

Listing 5-7: Validating XML Data through Inline XSD Schema

```
<%@ Page Language="C#"%>
<%@ Import Namespace="System.Xml" %>
<%@ Import Namespace="System.Xml.Schema" %>
<script runat="server">
  private StringBuilder _builder = new StringBuilder();
  void Page_Load(object sender, EventArgs e)
  {
    string xmlPath = Request.PhysicalApplicationPath +
      @"\App_Data\Authors_InlineSchema.xml";
    XmlReader reader = null;
    XmlReaderSettings settings = new XmlReaderSettings();
    settings.ValidationType = ValidationType.Schema;
    settings.ValidationEventHandler += new
      ValidationEventHandler(this.ValidationEventHandler);
    settings.ValidationFlags &=
      XmlSchemaValidationFlags.ProcessInlineSchema;
    settings.ValidationFlags &=
      XmlSchemaValidationFlags.ReportValidationWarnings;
    reader = XmlReader.Create(xmlPath, settings);
    while (reader.Read())
    {
    }
    if (_builder.ToString() == String.Empty)
      Response.Write("Validation completed successfully.");
    else
      Response.Write("Validation Failed. <br>" + _builder.ToString());
  }

  void ValidationEventHandler(object sender, ValidationEventArgs args)
  {
    if (args.Severity == XmlSeverityType.Error)
    {
```

```
            _builder.Append("Validation error: " + args.Message + "<br>");
        }
    }
</script>
<html xmlns="http://www.w3.org/1999/xhtml" >
<head runat="server">
    <title>Inline XSD Schema Validation</title>
</head>
<body>
    <form id="form1" runat="server">
        <div>
        </div>
    </form>
</body>
</html>
```

The code that deselects the `ProcessInlineSchema` and `ReportValidationWarnings` is what differentiates this listing from the previous listings. To specify the schema options used by the `XmlReaderSettings` class, you assign the `ValidationFlags` property of the `XmlReaderSettings` class to one of the values of the `XmlSchemaValidationFlags` enumeration. The following lines of code accomplish this.

```
settings.ValidationFlags &= XmlSchemaValidationFlags.ProcessInlineSchema;
settings.ValidationFlags &= XmlSchemaValidationFlags.ReportValidationWarnings;
```

In addition to the values used in this example, the `XmlSchemaValidationFlags` enumeration also provides values shown in Table 5-6.

Table 5-6. XmlSchemaValidationFlags Enumeration Values

Value	Description
AllowXmlAttributes	Allows `xml` attributes even if they are not defined in the schema
None	The default validation options are utilized and no schema validation options are performed
ProcessIdentityConstraints	Processes identity constraints such as `xs:ID`, `xs:IDREF`, `xs:key`, `xs:keyref`, `xs:unique` that are encountered during validation
ProcessInlineSchema	Processes inline schemas that are encountered during validation
ProcessSchemaLocation	Processes schema location hints such as `xsi:schemaLocation`, `xsi:noNamespaceSchemaLocation` that are encountered during validation
ReportValidationWarnings	Reports schema validation warnings that are encountered during validation

Notice the use of the `XmlSeverityType` enumeration in the `ValidationEventHandler` to filter out the warnings generated by the parser. These warnings are caused by the fact that the root element that contains the inline schema is not considered as part of the validation.

```
if (args.Severity == XmlSeverityType.Error)
{
  _builder.Append("Validation error: " + args.Message + "<br>");
}
```

The check for `XmlSeverityType.Error` ensures that only errors are captured inside the validation event handler.

> *Although XML schema as a format is definitely a widely accepted specification, the same cannot be said for inline schema. The general guideline is to avoid inline XML schema whenever possible. This improves the bandwidth management (the schema is transferred at most once) and shields you from bad surprises. With the `XmlReaderSettings` object, you can preload the schemas in schema cache and use them when parsing the source XML data.*

Using DTDs

The DTD validation guarantees that the source document complies with the validity constraints defined in a separate file — the DTD. A DTD file uses a formal grammar to describe both the structure and the syntax of XML documents. XML authors use DTDs to narrow the set of tags and attributes allowed in their documents. Validating against a DTD ensures that processed documents conform to the specified structure. From a language perspective, a DTD defines a newer and stricter XML-based syntax and a new tagged language tailor-made for a related group of documents.

Historically speaking, the DTD was the first tool capable of defining the structure of a document. The DTD standard was developed a few decades ago to work side by side with SGML — a recognized ISO standard for defining markup languages. SGML is considered the ancestor of today's XML, which actually sprang to life in the late 1990s as a way to simplify the too-rigid architecture of SGML.

DTDs use a proprietary syntax to define the syntax of markup constructs as well as additional definitions such as numeric and character entities. You can correctly think of DTDs as an early form of an XML schema. Although doomed to obsolescence, DTD is today supported by virtually all XML parsers. An XML document is associated with a DTD file by using the `DOCTYPE` special tag. The validating parser (for example, the `XmlReader` class with the appropriate options set in the `XmlReaderSettings` class) recognizes this element and extracts from it the schema information. The `DOCTYPE` declaration can either point to an inline DTD or be a reference to an external DTD file.

Developing a DTD Grammar

To build a DTD, you normally start writing the file according to its syntax. In this case, however, you start from an XML file named `Authors_DTD.xml` that will actually be validated through a DTD file. The `Authors_DTD.xml` is shown in Listing 5-8.

Listing 5-8: Authors_DTD.xml File That Uses DTD Validation

```xml
<?xml version="1.0"?>
<!DOCTYPE authors SYSTEM "Authors.dtd">
<authors>
  <author>
    <au_id>172-32-1176</au_id>
    <au_lname>White</au_lname>
    <au_fname>Johnson</au_fname>
    <phone>408 496-7223</phone>
    <address>10932 Bigge Rd.</address>
    <city>Menlo Park</city>
    <state>CA</state>
    <zip>94025</zip>
    <contract>true</contract>
  </author>
  <author>
    <au_id>213-46-8915</au_id>
    <au_lname>Green</au_lname>
    <au_fname>Marjorie</au_fname>
    <phone>415 986-7020</phone>
    <address>309 63rd St. #411</address>
    <city>Oakland</city>
    <state>CA</state>
    <zip>94618</zip>
    <contract>true</contract>
  </author>
</authors>
```

Any XML document that must be validated against a given DTD file includes a DOCTYPE tag through which it simply links to the DTD of choice, as shown here:

```xml
<!DOCTYPE authors SYSTEM "Authors.dtd">
```

The word following DOCTYPE identifies the meta-language described by the DTD. This information is extremely important for the validation process. If the document type name does not match the root element of the DTD, a validation error is raised. The text following the SYSTEM attribute is the URL from which the DTD will actually be downloaded.

Listing 5-9 demonstrates a DTD that is tailor-made for the preceding XML document.

Listing 5-9: DTD for Validating the Authors_DTD.xml

```
<!ELEMENT authors (author+)>
<!ELEMENT author (au_id,au_lname,au_fname,phone,address,city,state,zip,contract)>
<!ELEMENT au_id (#PCDATA)>
<!ELEMENT au_lname (#PCDATA)>
<!ELEMENT au_fname (#PCDATA)>
<!ELEMENT phone (#PCDATA)>
<!ELEMENT address (#PCDATA)>
<!ELEMENT city (#PCDATA)>
<!ELEMENT state (#PCDATA)>
<!ELEMENT zip (#PCDATA)>
<!ELEMENT contract (#PCDATA)>
```

The ELEMENT tag identifies a node element. An element declaration has the following syntax:

```
<!ELEMENT element-name (element-content)>
```

Elements with only character data are declared with #PCDATA inside parenthesis. Elements with one or more children are defined with the name of the children elements inside parentheses. For example, an element that contains one child is declared as follows:

```
<!ELEMENT element-name (child-element-name)>
```

For an element that contains multiple children, it is declared as follows:

```
<!ELEMENT element-name (child1, child2,..... childn)>
```

After all the child elements are declared, you can then specify its data type using the element syntax shown previously.

Validating Against a DTD

The code snippet shown in Listing 5-10 creates an XmlReader object that works on the sample XML file Authors_DTD.xml discussed in Listing 5-8. The document is bound to a DTD file and is validated using the DTD validation type.

Listing 5-10: Validating an XML Document Against a DTD

```
<%@ Page Language="C#"%>
<%@ Import Namespace="System.Xml" %>
<%@ Import Namespace="System.Xml.Schema" %>
<script runat="server">
  private StringBuilder _builder = new StringBuilder();
  void Page_Load(object sender, EventArgs e)
  {
    string xmlPath = Request.PhysicalApplicationPath +
      @"\App_Data\Authors_DTD.xml";
    XmlReader reader = null;
    XmlReaderSettings settings = new XmlReaderSettings();
    settings.ValidationEventHandler += new
      ValidationEventHandler(this.ValidationEventHandler);
    settings.ValidationType = ValidationType.DTD;
    settings.ProhibitDtd = false;
    reader = XmlReader.Create(xmlPath, settings);
    while (reader.Read())
    {
    }
    if (_builder.ToString() == String.Empty)
      Response.Write("DTD Validation completed successfully.");
    else
      Response.Write("DTD Validation Failed. <br>" + _builder.ToString());
  }

  void ValidationEventHandler(object sender, ValidationEventArgs args)
  {
    _builder.Append("Validation error: " + args.Message + "<br>");
  }
</script>
```

```
<html xmlns="http://www.w3.org/1999/xhtml" >
<head runat="server">
  <title>DTD Validation</title>
</head>
<body>
  <form id="form1" runat="server">
    <div>
    </div>
  </form>
</body>
</html>
```

The following lines of code in Listing 5-10 warrant special attention.

```
settings.ValidationType = ValidationType.DTD;
settings.ProhibitDtd = false;
```

First, the ValidationType property of the XmlReaderSettings object is set to ValidationType.DTD to signal to the parser that a DTD is utilized for validation. When the validation mode is set to DTD, the validating parser returns a warning if the file has no link to any DTDs. If a DTD is correctly linked and accessible, the validation is performed, and in the process, entities are expanded. If the linked DTD file is not available, an exception is raised. What you'll get is not a schema exception but a simpler FileNotFoundException exception.

Next, you set the ProhibitDtd property to false to ensure that the DTDs are not prohibited. Note that this property is set to true, by default.

```
settings.ProhibitDtd = false;
```

If you navigate to the file using a browser, you see the output shown in Figure 5-3.

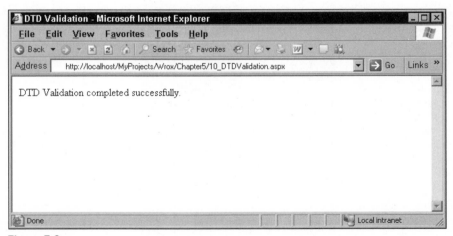

Figure 5-3

If you mistakenly use a DTD to validate an XML file with schema information, a schema exception is thrown, but with a low severity level. In practice, you get a warning informing you that no DTD has been found in the XML file.

Usage and Trade-Offs for DTDs

Unquestionably, the DTD validation format is an old one, although largely supported by virtually all available parsers. But if you are designing the validation layer for an XML-driven data exchange infrastructure today, XSDs should be the choice of validation mechanism. Because XSDs are more powerful than DTDs, you should consider using XSDs when possible.

> So when should you use DTDs instead of XSDs, and under what circumstances will DTDs be a better option? Compatibility and legacy code are the only possible answers to these questions. Especially if your application handles complex DTDs, porting them to an XSD can be costly and is in no way an easy task. There is no official and totally reliable tool to automatically convert DTDs to schemas. Converting DTDs to schemas is no simple matter — in some cases, it can be a daunting task on its own. For example, when converting DTDs to schemas, you should also consider rearchitecting tags into types and perhaps rearchitecting the way you expose data in light of the new features.

Certainly XSDs provide you with more functions than DTDs can. For one thing, schemas are all written in XML and don't require you to learn a new language. If you look at our basic DTD example in this context, you might not be scared by its unusual format. As you move from textbook examples and enter into the tough, real world, the complexity of an inflexible language such as DTD becomes more apparent. XSDs provide you with a finer level of control over the cardinality of the tags and the attribute types. In addition, XSDs can be used to set up a system of schema inheritance in which more complex types are built on top of existing ones much like the inheritance in Object Oriented Programming (OOP).

XSD schemas are the recommended approach to validating XML documents. There are times, however, where you might have used a lot of DTDs in your existing application for validation purposes and you will need to migrate them to XSD schemas at some point in time. With Visual Studio 2005, this migration is very simple and straightforward. You just need to select the Create Schema option from the XML menu in Visual Studio 2005 with the DTD document open in the XML editor.

Creating an XML Schema with Visual Studio 2005

With tools like Visual Studio available at your disposal, to create a schema for your XML files, you don't have to master the subtleties of XSD syntax. Visual Studio 2005 provides an impressive graphical designer that lets you point-and-click your way to success.

Making the Schema

Visual Studio provides a visual editor, the XML Editor for XSD files. Instead of handling yourself the intricacies of schema markup, you can simply edit XML files using the drag and drop features and shortcut menus provided by the editor. This section presents you with a walkthrough of the creation of the `Authors.xsd` file (that has been used throughout this chapter) using Visual Studio.

Go to the Solution Explorer window and add a new XML schema to your project. Name this new XML schema as `Authors_VS.xsd`. You will see a blank page as shown in Figure 5-4.

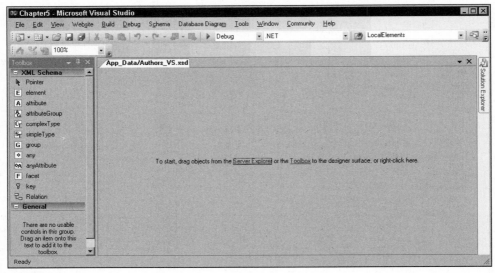

Figure 5-4

Drag and drop an element control from the toolbox onto your schema form. Name it `authors`. Click the cell right next to the authors and you will see a drop-down control. In the drop-down, select `Unnamed complexType`. Add a child element named `author` to the `authors` element by clicking the row right next to the `authors` and entering `author` as the element name. In alternative, you can also click the first cell in the row and choose element as the type from the drop-down and then name it `author`. For this `author` element, choose a type of `Unnamed complexType` in the cell next to it. This creates a `complexType` named `author` right next to the `authors` element, and also add the relationship to the `authors` element. To the `author complexType`, add the elements shown in Table 5-7 as its direct children.

Table 5-7. Elements to be Added to the Author Element

Element	Type
au_id	string
au_lname	string
au_fname	string
Phone	string
Address	string
City	string
State	string
Zip	unsignedint
Contract	boolean

120

After you have finished adding the elements, your schema form should look as similar to the Figure 5-5.

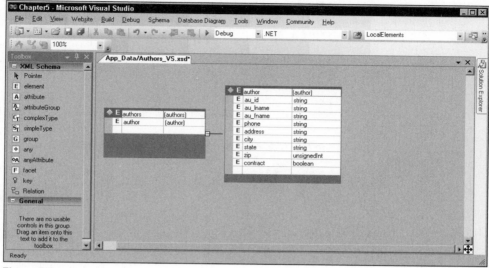

Figure 5-5

As you can see, Visual Studio provides an easy and effective way to create XSD schemas through a graphical editor.

Sometimes when you are creating schemas, you might want to build in sophisticated validation features into the schema itself. For example, you might want to make sure that the XML file you are checking actually has the values you are looking for. You might also want to make sure those values are unique in the XML file. You can do this by selecting the element and then bringing up the Properties window. Through the Properties window, you can perform most of the configurations specific to the selected element.

Creating XSD Schemas from an XML File

There are times where you might want to create an XSD schema based on the contents of the XML file. This section demonstrates the steps involved in accomplishing this. Start by adding the appropriate XML file to your project. You can then edit your XML data in one of two ways—in direct text view, which provides a color-coded display of the XML tags, or through a graphical editor that makes your XML content look like one or more database tables (see Figure 5-6). You can add new rows or change existing data with ease. To bring up this graphical editor, right-click on your XML file and select View Data Grid from the context menu.

To create the schema, open up the XML file and choose Create Schema from the XML menu. An XSD file with the same name as your XML file is generated automatically and added to your project.

> Visual Studio can also dynamically infer the schema from the currently displayed XML file. The task is actually accomplished by xsd.exe and can be easily repeated and controlled programmatically. You can also use the command line tool directly and generate XSD files, as shown here:
>
> ```
> xsd.exe Authors.xml
> ```

If you ask Visual Studio to infer the schema for the Authors.xml file, you will get an output file named Authors.xsd. The Authors.xsd schema file shown through the graphical designer is shown in Figure 5-6.

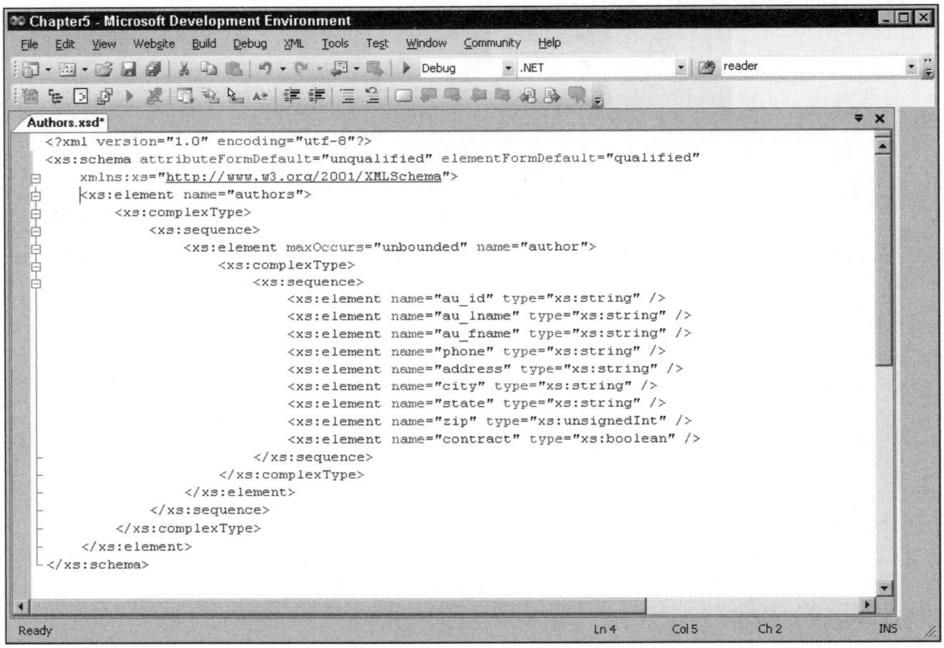

Figure 5-6

Figure 5-6 shows the schema that Visual Studio inferred from the Authors.xml document.

The .NET Schema Object Model (SOM)

In addition to Visual Studio 2005, there are other tools in the market that are capable of creating XML schemas in visual feature-rich graphical editors. XML Spy, for example, is another popular tool. The more powerful a tool is, however, the more details are hidden from the users. For an effective programmatic manipulation of an XML schema, you need an object model. An object model enables you to build and edit schema information in memory. It also gives you access to each element that forms the schema and that exposes read/write properties in compliance with the pre-schema-validation and post-schema-validation infoset specifications.

The .NET SOM comprises an extensive set of classes corresponding to the elements in a schema. For example, the `<xsd:schema>...</xsd:schema>` element maps to the `XmlSchema` class—all schema information that can possibly be contained within those tags can be represented using the `XmlSchema` class. Similarly `<xsd:element>...</xsd:element>` maps to `XmlSchemaElement`, `<xsd:attribute>...</xsd:attribute>` maps to `XmlSchemaAttribute` and so on. This mapping helps easy use of the API. For a complete listing of all the classes available in the `System.Xml.Schema` namespace, refer to the .NET Framework Class Library Reference.

The .NET Framework provides a hierarchy of classes under the `System.Xml.Schema` namespace to edit existing schemas or create new ones from the ground up. The root class of the hierarchy is `XmlSchema`. After your application holds an instance of this class, it can load an existing XSD file and populate the internal properties and collections with the contained information. By using the `XmlSchema` programming interface, you can then add or edit elements, attributes, and other schema components. Finally, the class exposes a `Write` method that allows you to persist the current contents of the schema onto a file using a valid stream object.

Reading a Schema from a File

You can create an instance of the `XmlSchema` class in two ways. You can use the default constructor, which returns a new, empty instance of the class, or you can use the static `Read` method.

The `Read()` method operates on schema information available through a stream, a text reader, or an XML reader. The schema returned is not yet compiled. The `Read()` method accepts a second argument— a validation event handler that will allow you to handle the exceptions thrown by the parser. You can set this argument to null, but in this case you won't be able to catch and handle validation errors. Listing 5-11 shows how to read and compile a schema using the .NET SOM by looping through all the root complex types contained in the `Authors.xsd` file.

Listing 5-11: Reading an XML Schema Using XmlSchema Class

```
<%@ Page Language="C#"%>
<%@ Import Namespace="System.IO" %>
<%@ Import Namespace="System.Reflection" %>
<%@ Import Namespace="System.Xml" %>
<%@ Import Namespace="System.Xml.Schema" %>
<script runat="server">
  private StringBuilder _builder = new StringBuilder();
  void Page_Load(object sender, EventArgs e)
  {
    string xsdPath = Request.PhysicalApplicationPath +
      @"\App_Data\Authors.xsd";
    XmlSchema schema = null;
    FileStream stream = new FileStream(xsdPath, FileMode.Open);
    schema = XmlSchema.Read(stream, new
      ValidationEventHandler(ValidationEventHandler));
    stream.Close();
    schema.Compile(new ValidationEventHandler(ValidationEventHandler));
    if (schema.IsCompiled)
```

```
      DisplaySchemaObjects(schema);
    else
      Response.Write("Schema Reading Failed. <br>" + _builder.ToString());
    }

    void DisplaySchemaObjects(XmlSchema schema)
    {
        foreach (XmlSchemaElement elem in schema.Elements.Values)
        {
            if (elem.ElementSchemaType is XmlSchemaComplexType)
            {
                Response.Write("Complex Element: " + elem.Name + "<br>");
                XmlSchemaComplexType ct =
                  (XmlSchemaComplexType)elem.ElementSchemaType;
                //Process the XmlSchemaComplexType
            }
        }
    }

    void ValidationEventHandler(object sender, ValidationEventArgs args)
    {
        _builder.Append("Validation error: " + args.Message + "<br>");
    }
</script>
<html xmlns="http://www.w3.org/1999/xhtml" >
<head runat="server">
  <title>Reading XSD Schema</title>
</head>
<body>
  <form id="form1" runat="server">
    <div>
    </div>
  </form>
</body>
</html>
```

In Listing 5-11, you get reference to the XmlSchema object using the following line of code.

```
schema = XmlSchema.Read(stream, new
  ValidationEventHandler(ValidationEventHandler));
```

After you read the schema into the XmlSchema object, you can then compile it by invoking the Compile() method of the XmlSchema object.

```
schema.Compile(new ValidationEventHandler(ValidationEventHandler));
```

If the compilation is successful, the IsCompiled() method of the XmlSchema will return true.

```
if (schema.IsCompiled)
  DisplaySchemaObjects(schema);
```

After the schema has been successfully compiled, you can then access the constituent elements of the schema, which is what the DisplaySchemaObjects() method is intended for.

To access the actual types in the schema, you use the `Elements` collection. After you have all the elements, you can then loop through them using a foreach loop.

```
foreach (XmlSchemaElement elem in schema.Elements.Values)
```

To determine if the current element is a complex type, you check the `ElementSchemaType` property of the `XmlSchemaElement` object as shown in the following code.

```
if (elem.ElementSchemaType is XmlSchemaComplexType)
{
  Response.Write("Complex Element: " + elem.Name + "<br>");
  XmlSchemaComplexType ct =
    (XmlSchemaComplexType)elem.ElementSchemaType;
  //Process the XmlSchemaComplexType
}
```

Finally the name of the complex element is displayed through the `Name` property of the `XmlSchemaElement` object.

Open up the page in the browser and you will see the output shown in Figure 5-7.

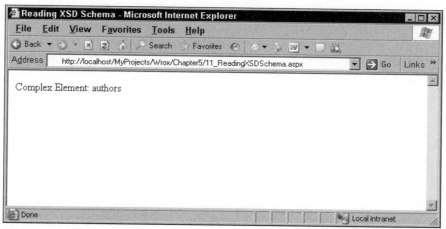

Figure 5-7

Creating a Schema Programmatically

After the schema has been read into memory, you can edit its child items by adding new elements and removing existing ones. When you have finished, you compile the schema and, if all went fine, save it to a disk. Compiling the schema prior to persisting changes is not strictly necessary to get a valid schema, but it helps to verify whether any errors were introduced during editing.

In addition to editing the schema, you can also create schemas from scratch on the fly. The code in Listing 5-12 creates the author schema in memory using the SOM API. The code uses a bottom-up approach in building the schema, meaning that it starts with constructing the child elements, attributes, and their corresponding types first, and then proceeds to build the top-level components.

Listing 5-12: Programmatically Creating the XSD Schema

```csharp
<%@ Page Language="C#"%>
<%@ Import Namespace="System.IO" %>
<%@ Import Namespace="System.Xml" %>
<%@ Import Namespace="System.Xml.Schema" %>
<script runat="server">
  private StringBuilder _builder = new StringBuilder();
  void Page_Load(object sender, EventArgs e)
  {
    string ns = "http://www.w3.org/2001/XMLSchema";
    string xsdPath = Request.PhysicalApplicationPath +
      @"\App_Data\NewAuthors.xsd";
    XmlSchema schema = new XmlSchema();
    //Create all the child elements
    XmlSchemaElement authorID = new XmlSchemaElement();
    authorID.Name = "au_id";
    authorID.SchemaTypeName = new XmlQualifiedName("string", ns );
    XmlSchemaElement authorLastName = new XmlSchemaElement();
    authorLastName.Name = "au_lname";
    authorLastName.SchemaTypeName = new XmlQualifiedName("string", ns);
    XmlSchemaElement authorFirstName = new XmlSchemaElement();
    authorFirstName.Name = "au_fname";
    authorFirstName.SchemaTypeName = new XmlQualifiedName("string", ns);
    XmlSchemaElement phone = new XmlSchemaElement();
    phone.Name = "phone";
    phone.SchemaTypeName = new XmlQualifiedName("string", ns);
    XmlSchemaElement address = new XmlSchemaElement();
    address.Name = "address";
    address.SchemaTypeName = new XmlQualifiedName("string", ns);
    XmlSchemaElement city = new XmlSchemaElement();
    city.Name = "city";
    city.SchemaTypeName = new XmlQualifiedName("string", ns);
    XmlSchemaElement state = new XmlSchemaElement();
    state.Name = "state";
    state.SchemaTypeName = new XmlQualifiedName("string", ns);
    XmlSchemaElement zip = new XmlSchemaElement();
    zip.Name = "zip";
    zip.SchemaTypeName = new XmlQualifiedName("unsignedInt", ns);
    XmlSchemaElement contract = new XmlSchemaElement();
    contract.Name = "contract";
    contract.SchemaTypeName = new XmlQualifiedName("boolean", ns);
    //Create the author element
    XmlSchemaElement authorElement = new XmlSchemaElement();
    authorElement.Name = "author";
    //Create an anonymous complex type for the author element
    XmlSchemaComplexType authorType = new XmlSchemaComplexType();
    XmlSchemaSequence authorSeq = new XmlSchemaSequence();
    //Add all the child elements to the sequence
    authorSeq.Items.Add(authorID);
    authorSeq.Items.Add(authorLastName);
    authorSeq.Items.Add(authorFirstName);
    authorSeq.Items.Add(phone);
    authorSeq.Items.Add(address);
    authorSeq.Items.Add(city);
```

```
        authorSeq.Items.Add(state);
        authorSeq.Items.Add(zip);
        authorSeq.Items.Add(contract);
        authorType.Particle = authorSeq;
        //Set the SchemaType of authors element to the complex type
        authorElement.SchemaType = authorType;
        //Add the root authors element to the schema
        schema.Items.Add(authorElement);
        //Compile the file to check for validation errors
        schema.Compile(new ValidationEventHandler(ValidationEventHandler));
        FileStream stream = new FileStream(xsdPath, FileMode.Create);
        //Write the file
        schema.Write(stream);
        stream.Close();
        if (_builder.ToString() == String.Empty)
          Response.Write("File written successfully");
        else
          Response.Write("Schema Creation Failed. <br>" + _builder.ToString());
        }

        void ValidationEventHandler(object sender, ValidationEventArgs args)
        {
          _builder.Append("Validation error: " + args.Message + "<br>");
        }
</script>
<html xmlns="http://www.w3.org/1999/xhtml" >
<head runat="server">
  <title>Writing XSD Schema</title>
</head>
<body>
  <form id="form1" runat="server">
    <div>
    </div>
  </form>
</body>
</html>
```

Listing 5-12 starts by creating an instance of the XmlSchema object; then it creates all the child elements of the author node using the following lines of code.

```
        XmlSchemaElement authorID = new XmlSchemaElement();
        authorID.Name = "au_id";
        authorID.SchemaTypeName = new XmlQualifiedName("string", ns );
        XmlSchemaElement authorLastName = new XmlSchemaElement();
        authorLastName.Name = "au_lname";
        authorLastName.SchemaTypeName = new XmlQualifiedName("string", ns);
        XmlSchemaElement authorFirstName = new XmlSchemaElement();
        authorFirstName.Name = "au_fname";
        authorFirstName.SchemaTypeName = new XmlQualifiedName("string", ns);
        XmlSchemaElement phone = new XmlSchemaElement();
        phone.Name = "phone";
        phone.SchemaTypeName = new XmlQualifiedName("string", ns);
        XmlSchemaElement address = new XmlSchemaElement();
        address.Name = "address";
        address.SchemaTypeName = new XmlQualifiedName("string", ns);
        XmlSchemaElement city = new XmlSchemaElement();
```

```
city.Name = "city";
city.SchemaTypeName = new XmlQualifiedName("string", ns);
XmlSchemaElement state = new XmlSchemaElement();
state.Name = "state";
state.SchemaTypeName = new XmlQualifiedName("string", ns);
XmlSchemaElement zip = new XmlSchemaElement();
zip.Name = "zip";
zip.SchemaTypeName = new XmlQualifiedName("unsignedInt", ns);
XmlSchemaElement contract = new XmlSchemaElement();
contract.Name = "contract";
contract.SchemaTypeName = new XmlQualifiedName("boolean", ns);
```

After all the elements are created, they can then be added to the author element. Before doing that, you need to create the author element and set its properties.

```
//Create the author element
XmlSchemaElement authorElement = new XmlSchemaElement();
authorElement.Name = "author";
//Create an anonymous complex type for the author element
XmlSchemaComplexType authorType = new XmlSchemaComplexType();
```

Now you create an XmlSchemaSequence object and then add all the child elements of the author element to it using the Add() method of the XmlSchemaObjectCollection.

```
XmlSchemaSequence authorSeq = new XmlSchemaSequence();
//Add all the child elements to the sequence
authorSeq.Items.Add(authorID);
authorSeq.Items.Add(authorLastName);
authorSeq.Items.Add(authorFirstName);
authorSeq.Items.Add(phone);
authorSeq.Items.Add(address);
authorSeq.Items.Add(city);
authorSeq.Items.Add(state);
authorSeq.Items.Add(zip);
authorSeq.Items.Add(contract);
```

The previously created XmlSchemaSequence object is then associated with the XmlSchemaComplexType object by setting the Particle property of the XmlSchemaComplexType object to the XmlSchemaSequence object. The XmlSchemaComplexType is tied to the author element by assigning the XmlSchemaComplexType object to the SchemaType property of the XmlSchemaElement object that represents the author element.

```
authorType.Particle = authorSeq;
//Set the SchemaType of authors element to the complex type
authorElement.SchemaType = authorType;
```

Now you add the author element to the XmlSchema object through the call to the Add() method.

```
//Add the root authors element to the schema
schema.Items.Add(authorElement);
```

Finally, the XmlSchema object is compiled and then written onto a file using the FileStream object. The Write() method the XmlSchema object is the one that writes out everything onto the file identified by the FileStream object.

```
//Compile the file to check for validation errors
schema.Compile(new ValidationEventHandler(ValidationEventHandler));
FileStream stream = new FileStream(xsdPath, FileMode.Create);
//Write the file
schema.Write(stream);
```

Now navigate to the previous page using the browser and you will see a message stating that the file has been successfully written. Open up the NewAuthors.xsd file and you will see the output shown in Listing 5-13.

Listing 5-13: XSD Schema Output

```xml
<?xml version="1.0"?>
<xs:schema xmlns:xs="http://www.w3.org/2001/XMLSchema">
  <xs:element name="author">
    <xs:complexType>
      <xs:sequence>
        <xs:element name="au_id" type="xs:string" />
        <xs:element name="au_lname" type="xs:string" />
        <xs:element name="au_fname" type="xs:string" />
        <xs:element name="phone" type="xs:string" />
        <xs:element name="address" type="xs:string" />
        <xs:element name="city" type="xs:string" />
        <xs:element name="state" type="xs:string" />
        <xs:element name="zip" type="xs:unsignedInt" />
        <xs:element name="contract" type="xs:boolean" />
      </xs:sequence>
    </xs:complexType>
  </xs:element>
</xs:schema>
```

Schema information is fundamental for letting client applications know about the structure of the XML data they get from servers. Especially in distributed applications, however, schema information is just an extra burden that takes up a portion of the bandwidth; however when the generation of XML documents is not completely controlled by the involved applications, schema information is a must even though it takes up a portion of bandwidth. In that case, you can optimize the use of the bandwidth by not sending the schema information along with the document. You have two options here.

❑ The first option is to let the client application store the schema locally and load it when needed to validate incoming documents. For .NET Framework applications, the Read() method of the XmlSchema object is just what you need to load existing schema files.

❑ The second option is to create and compile a schema object dynamically and then use it to validate documents. The code discussed in the previous section provides a concrete example of how .NET Framework applications can use the SOM to create schemas on the fly.

Programmatically Inferring XSD Schema from an XML File

In addition to creating an XSD schema programmatically, there are times where you might want to infer XSD schemas from XML files. To this end, the .NET Framework 2.0 introduces a class named XmlSchemaInference that provides this feature. The XmlSchemaInference class produces W3C XML and XML schemas compliant XSD schemas. The key method of XmlSchemaInference class that enables this is InferSchema(). Listing 5-14 shows an example ASP.NET page that demonstrates this.

Listing 5-14: Schema Inference Using XmlSchemaInference

```csharp
<%@ Page Language="C#"%>
<%@ Import Namespace="System.Xml" %>
<%@ Import Namespace="System.Xml.Schema" %>
<script runat="server">
  void Page_Load(object sender, EventArgs e)
  {
    Response.ContentType = "text/xml";
    string xmlPath = Request.PhysicalApplicationPath +
      @"\App_Data\Authors.xml";
    XmlReader reader = XmlReader.Create(xmlPath);
    XmlSchemaSet schemaSet = new XmlSchemaSet();
    XmlSchemaInference schema = new XmlSchemaInference();
    schemaSet = schema.InferSchema(reader);
    foreach (XmlSchema schemaObj in schemaSet.Schemas())
    {
      schemaObj.Write(Response.Output);
    }
  }
</script>
```

In Listing 5-14, you start by loading the `XmlReader` object with the `Authors.xml` file; then you create an instance of the `XmlSchemaInference` class and invoke its `InferSchema()` method passing in the `XmlReader` object as an argument. The `InferSchema()` method returns the corresponding XSD schema in the form of `XmlSchemaSet` object. You then simply loop through the `XmlSchemaSet` object and display the schema output onto the browser.

The ability to programmatically infer schemas is very powerful in that it enables exciting scenarios. For example, if you are exchanging XML documents with an external application and you want to ensure that the incoming XML document has the same structure as that of an existing XML document, the schema inference can be very beneficial in that scenario. In addition, you can also use the generated XSD schema to validate the same XML document that produced the XSD schema.

Summary

With XML schema, you have a standard way to describe the layout of the document in an extremely rigorous way that leaves nothing to the user's imagination. .NET Framework 2.0 provides excellent support for creating and consuming XSD schemas when it comes to validating XML data.

The .NET XML architecture provides the most complete, integrated support platform for XML validation thereby making many otherwise very difficult tasks much easier to accomplish. This chapter introduced you to the validation support offered by the .NET Framework, and showed you how to take advantage of those validation capabilities by providing examples. This chapter also spent a great deal of time focusing on the XSD schema-based validation and then providing a complete discussion on the programmatic creation and reading of XSD schemas. As you have seen here, the XML Schema Object Model enables you to take advantage of the schema support available in the .NET Framework by providing a programmatic API to create and read XSD schemas.

6

XML DOM Object Model

Over the years, XML has become an important technology because of its unrivalled capability to mark up content and make it more useful. Almost all modern development platforms now provide some kind of native support to read and parse XML documents. This includes .NET Framework, which comes with a set of DOM classes that enable XML document parsing. The DOM is a representation of the data in an XML document held in memory. It represents the document's tree-like hierarchy explicitly. In contrast, the XmlReader and XmlWriter classes discussed in Chapter 4 –provided a "Forward-Only XML" approach to process the document's nodes one at a time without storing information about the document's structure as a whole.

The DOM includes a collection of classes that represent various pieces of an XML document. For example, the XmlDocument class represents the XML document itself, and the XmlComment class represents a comment inside the document and so on. This chapter explores the DOM classes provided by .NET Framework 2.0. Using these classes your programs can build, load, modify, and save complicated XML documents quickly and easily. Specifically, this chapter explores the following areas.

- ❑ DOM classes provided by the .NET Framework 2.0 to parse XML data
- ❑ Loading an XML document into memory using XmlDocument class
- ❑ How to traverse a DOM tree using classes such as XmlNode and XmlAttribute
- ❑ How to query for specific nodes using XmlDocument class's methods
- ❑ How to use the XmlNodeReader object to process a subtree of an XML document
- ❑ How to create an XML document from scratch using the XmlDocument class
- ❑ How to append fragments of XML data onto an existing XmlDocument using XmlDocumentFragment
- ❑ How to execute XPath expressions through the various methods of the XmlDocument class

❏   How to select and navigate through a set of nodes using the XPathNavigator class

❏   How to leverage the new editing features of the XPathNavigator object to modify an XML document in memory

❏   How to take advantage of the new built-in validation support provided by the XmlDocument class

Exploring DOM Processing

The DOM is a specification for an API that lets programmers manipulates XML held in memory. The DOM specification is language-independent, and bindings are available for many programming languages, including C++. XmlDocument is based upon the DOM, with Microsoft extensions. Because it works with XML in memory, it has several advantages and disadvantages over the XmlReader forward-only approach.

One advantage is that, in reading the entire document and building a tree in memory, you have access to all the elements and can wander through the document at will. You can also edit the document, changing, adding, or deleting nodes, and write the changed document back to disk again. It is even possible to create an entire XML document from scratch in memory and write it out — serialize it — and this is a useful alternative to using XmlWriter.

The main disadvantage is that the whole of an XML document is held in memory at once, so the amount of memory needed by your program is going to be proportional to the size of the XML document you're working with. This means that if you're working with a very large XML document — or have limited memory — you might not be able to use XmlDocument. Another disadvantage is that the API for the XmlDocument is specified through the DOM model, limiting the options for implementing performance improvements behind the XmlDocument class.

XML Document Loaded in a DOM Tree

Working with an XmlDocument class is fundamentally different from working with the XmlReader and XmlWriter classes, although they share some similarities, such as the concept of nodes. When you use DOM processing, the entire XML document is loaded into a tree structure that matches the hierarchical structure of the document. The DOM provides a set of functions that examine the tree structure and manipulate the document's content. To see an example of this, consider the XML document shown in Listing 6-1 that contains a simple book store along with information about the various books that are part of the bookstore.

Listing 6-1: XML Document That Represents the Bookstore

```
<?xml version='1.0'?>
<!-- This file represents a fragment of a book store inventory database -->
<bookstore>
  <book genre="autobiography">
    <title>The Autobiography of Benjamin Franklin</title>
    <author>
      <first-name>Benjamin</first-name>
      <last-name>Franklin</last-name>
    </author>
```

```
      <price>8.99</price>
    </book>
    <book genre="novel">
      <title>The Confidence Man</title>
      <author>
        <first-name>Herman</first-name>
        <last-name>Melville</last-name>
      </author>
      <price>11.99</price>
    </book>
    <book genre="philosophy">
      <title>The Gorgias</title>
      <author>
        <name>Plato</name>
      </author>
      <price>9.99</price>
    </book>
  </bookstore>
```

Note that the books.xml file shown in Listing 6-1 is used throughout all the examples presented in this chapter. An XML document has a tree structure under the DOM, and each object in the tree is a node. This document, modeled using the DOM, would be represented as the tree structure shown in Figure 6-1.

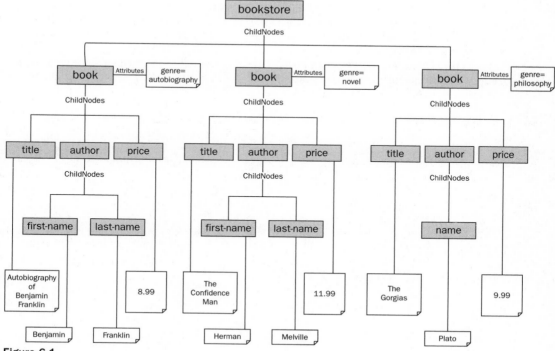

Figure 6-1

Each of the rectangles in this diagram is a node in the DOM structure. (Note that the genre attribute on the <book> tag is also a node, although attributes get special treatment in the DOM and are not actually a part of the document tree.) The class that represents nodes in .NET is XmlNode, and it provides methods for examining and modifying node information. The XmlDocument class, derived from XmlNode, adds more methods for creating new nodes and adding them to the document.

Each node's relationship to another node in the document is described with the terms parent, child, and sibling. In the example, the <book> node is a child of the <bookstore> node. The <book> node is a parent of <author>. The <author> node has child nodes of its own: <first-name> and <last-name>. These three nodes are siblings.

Programming with the XML Document Object Model

The XML DOM offers complete programmatic access to XML data. When working with the DOM, you approach your XML data as a tree of nodes, which starts from the root element and continues for as many levels of depth as your data structure requires. In this section, you learn about the classes of the DOM that enable you to navigate the DOM tree structure, read and change data, and also generate new XML structures in your application code.

There are two ways to navigate the XML document hierarchy. One option is to move through the node hierarchy from parent node to child nodes, for as many levels of nesting as the data contains. The other option is to use methods such as GetElementsByTagName, GetElementById, SelectNodes, or SelectSingleNode to directly locate one or many nodes that match selection criteria. SelectNodes and SelectSingleNode useXPath expressions to specify selection criteria. This is covered later in this chapter, in the section titled "XPath Support in XML DOM."

Each node in a document is one of the specialized types of nodes defined by the DOM. A node can represent the document itself, or an element, an attribute, text content, a processing instruction, a comment, or any of the other items that are valid in an XML file. The base class of XmlNode defines the basic set of properties and methods for all types of nodes. Each specialized type of node, which is a class derived from the XmlNode base class, has some additional properties and methods that are unique to that node type's characteristics. XmlNode is the abstract parent class of a handful of node-related classes that are available in the .NET Framework. Figure 6-2 shows the hierarchy of node classes.

Both XmlLinkedNode and XmlCharacterData are abstract classes that provide basic functionality for more specialized types of nodes. Linked nodes are nodes that you might find as constituent elements of an XML document just linked to a preceding or a following node. Character data nodes, on the other hand, are nodes that contain and manipulate only text.

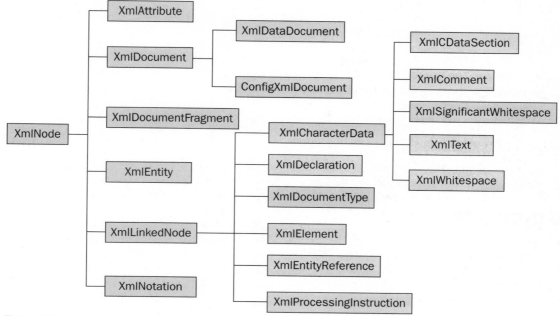

Figure 6-2

Document Classes

The important classes in the System.Xml namespace that deal with XML documents are XmlDocument, XmlDocumentFragment, and XmlDataDocument. An XmlDocument class represents an entire XML document, and the XmlDocumentFragment represents a fragment of document. The XmlDocumentFragment class is useful when you deal with a small fragment of a document. The XmlDataDocument class allows you to work with relational data using the DataSet. It not only provides functionality to store, retrieve, and manipulate data but also enables you to switch between relational and hierachical view of your data. The XmlDataDocument inherits from the XmlDocument class, which in turn inherits from the XmlNode class. An in-depth discussion of the XmlDataDocument class is provided in Chapter 8.

Besides the methods contained in XmlNode, the XmlDocument class implements a series of CreateXXX() methods to create a document's contents such as CreateComment(), CreateElement(), CreateText(), and so on. Each content type of an XML document has a corresponding class defined in this namespace. The classes are:

- ❑ XmlAttribute
- ❑ XmlCDataSection
- ❑ XmlComment
- ❑ XmlDeclaration
- ❑ XmlEntity
- ❑ XmlEntityReference

- ❑ `XmlProcessingInstruction`

- ❑ `XmlText`

- ❑ `XmlWhitespace`

All of these classes are self-explanatory. For example, the `XmlAttribute` and `XmlComment` classes represent an attribute and comments in a document, respectively. You see the usage of these classes in the examples presented later in this chapter.

Collection Classes

Also important in the XML DOM are two collection classes — the `XmlNodeList` collection class and the `XmlNamedNodeMap` collection class. The `XmlNodeList` collection class can be used to iterate through a set of related nodes. A set of related nodes can be based on the hierarchy — for example, all the child nodes of a selected element. An `XmlNodeList` collection can also consist of a set of nodes that match selection criteria, such as all nodes with a specific element tag name or matching value. The `XmlNodeList` collection can be navigated by index value in an ordered fashion. The `XmlNamedNodeMap` collection class is a collection of name/value pairs and is typically used to access sets of XML attributes. The .NET Framework has a class called `XmlAttributeCollection` that extends the base class `XmlNamedNodeMap`'s functionality.

The XmlDocument Class

The `XmlDocument` class implements the W3C DOM Level 1 Core and the Core DOM Level 2. When you work with XML DOM parsers, you mainly use the `XmlDocument` class. As shown in Figure 6-2, the `XmlDocument` class in turn derives from a base class, `XmlNode`, which provides all the core functions to navigate and create nodes. The `XmlDocument` class has a number of properties, and methods, the most important of which are summarized in Tables 6-1 and 6-2.

Table 6-1. Important Properties of the XmlDocument Class

Property	Description
Attributes	Returns the collection of attributes (in the form of an XmlAttributeCollection object) present in the current node
ChildNodes	Returns the child nodes of the current node in the form of an XmlNodeList object
DocumentElement	Get the root XmlElement for the document
DocumentType	Returns the node containing the DOCTYPE declaration
FirstChild	Returns the first child of the current node
HasChildNodes	Returns a boolean value that indicates if the current node has any child nodes
InnerText	Gets or sets the concatenated text values of the node and all its child nodes
InnerXml	Gets or sets the markup that represents the children of the current node

Property	Description
IsReadOnly	Returns a boolean indicating if the current node is read-only
Item	Gets the specified child element based on the supplied name and namespace URI
LastChild	Gets the last child of the current node
LocalName	Gets the local name of the node excluding the namespace prefix
Name	Gets the name of the node including the namespace prefix
NamespaceURI	Gets the namespace URI for this node
NextSibling	Gets the node immediately following the current node
NodeType	Gets the type of the current node
OuterXml	Gets the markup representing the current node and all of its child nodes
ParentNode	Gets the parent of the current node
Prefix	Gets or sets the namespace prefix for this code
PreserveWhitespace	Gets or sets a value that indicates whether to preserve white space in element content
PreviousSibling	Gets the node immediately preceding this node
Schemas	Gets or sets the XmlSchemaSet associated with this XmlDocument
Value	Gets or sets the value of the current node
XmlResolver	Sets the XmlResolver to use for resolving external resources

An important property of the XmlDocument class is DocumentElement, which returns a reference to the root element of the document. This is a common starting point for procedures that navigate the tree structure. Table 6-2 outlines the important methods of the XmlDocument class.

Table 6-2. Important Methods of the XmlDocument Class

Method	Description
AppendChild	Appends the specified node at the end of the list of child nodes
Clone	Creates a duplicate of the current node
CreateAttribute	Creates an XmlAttribute object with the specified name
CreateCDataSection	Creates an XmlCDataSection containing the specified data

Method	Description
CreateComment	Creates an XmlComment containing the specified data
CreateDocumentFragment	Creates an XmlDocument that represents a fragment of an XML document
CreateDocumentType	Creates a new XmlDocumentType object
CreateElement	Creates an XmlElement
CreateEntityReference	Creates an XmlEntityReference with the supplied name
CreateNode	Creates an XmlNode
CreateProcessingInstruction	Creates an XmlProcessingInstruction with the specified name and data
CreateSignificantWhitespace	Creates an XmlSignificantWhitespace node
CreateTextNode	Creates an XmlText with the specified text
CreateWhitespace	Creates an XmlWhitespace node
CreateXmlDeclaration	Creates an XmlDeclaration node with the supplied values
GetElementById	Returns the XmlElement with the supplied ID
GetElementsByTagName	Returns a collection of descendant elements (in the form of an XmlNodeList object) that match the specified name
GetEnumerator	Provides support for the for each style enumeration of nodes
ImportNode	Imports a node from another document to the current document
InsertAfter	Inserts the specified node immediately after the specified reference node
InsertBefore	Inserts the specific node immediately before the specified reference node
Load	Provides a number of overloaded methods that allow you to load the XML data from a Stream object, String, TextReader, or XmlReader
LoadXml	Loads the XML document from the specified string
PrependChild	Add the specified node to the beginning of the list of child nodes for this node
ReadNode	Creates an XmlNode object based on the information in the XmlReader
RemoveAll	Removes all the child nodes and attributes of the current node
RemoveChild	Removes the specified child node
ReplaceChild	Replaces one child node with the another child node

Method	Description
Save	Provides overloaded methods that allow you to save the XML document to a specified Steam, String, TextWriter, and XmlWriter objects
SelectNodes	Returns a list of matching nodes in the form of an XmlNodeList object based on the supplied XPath expression
SelectSingleNode	Selects the first XmlNode that matches the supplied XPath expression
Supports	Returns a boolean value depending on if the DOM supports a specific feature
Validate	Validates the XmlDocument against the XSD schemas contained in the XmlSchemaSet object that is set through the Schemas property
WriteContentTo	Saves all the children of the XmlDocument node to the specified XmlWriter
WriteTo	Saves the XmlDocument to the specified XmlWriter

As you can see from Table 6-2, the XmlDocument object provides methods such as CreateElement() and CreateAttribute() that allow you to programmatically create new sections of XML data that can be appended or inserted into the document's tree structure. Also important is the Load() method for populating your XmlDocument from a disk file or other object, and the LoadXml() method for populating your XmlDocument from a string. Now that you understand the properties and methods of the XmlDocument class, it is time to write code that interacts with the XmlDocument class.

Working with XmlDocument Class

To be fully accessible, an XML document must be entirely loaded in memory and its nodes and attributes mapped to relative objects derived from the XmlNode class. The process that builds the XML DOM is triggered when you call the Load() method. You can use a variety of sources to indicate the XML document to work on, including disk files and URLs and also streams and text readers. But before you load an XmlDocument, you need to first create an XML document, which is the topic of focus in the next section.

Creating an XmlDocument

To load an XML document into memory for full-access processing, you create a new instance of the XmlDocument class. The class features three public constructors, one of which is the default parameterless constructor, as shown here:

```
public XmlDocument();
public XmlDocument(XmlNameTable);
public XmlDocument(XmlImplementation);
```

The second overloaded constructor takes in an XmlNameTable object as an argument that allows the class to work faster with attribute and node names and optimize memory management. Just as the XmlReader class does, XmlDocument builds its own name table incrementally while processing the document. Passing a precompiled name table, however, can substantially speed up the overall execution. The third overloaded constructor allows you to initialize an XmlDocument class with the specified XmlImplementation class. The XmlImplementation class is a special class that allows you to define the context for a set of XmlDocument objects. This class provides methods for performing operations that are independent of any particular instance of the DOM.

> In the base implementation of the XmlImplementation class, the list of operations that various instances of XmlDocument classes can share is relatively short. These operations include creating new documents (through the CreateDocument() method), testing for supported features (through the HasFeature() method), and more important, sharing the same name table.

The following code snippet shows how to create two documents from the same implementation:

```
XmlImplementation xmlImpl = new XmlImplementation();
XmlDocument doc1 = xmlImpl.CreateDocument();
XmlDocument doc2 = xmlImpl.CreateDocument();
```

After you have an empty XmlDocument, you need to load it with XML data. The next section discusses how to perform this.

Loading XML Documents

Loading of an XML document is accomplished by calling the Load() method, which reads XML data and populates the document tree structure. There are four different versions of the Load() method, each of which uses a different source to read the data. Here are the various forms of the Load() method:

- ❑ Load(Stream): Loads the document from a Stream data source
- ❑ Load(string): Loads the document using the given file name string
- ❑ Load(TextReader): Loads the document using a TextReader as the data source
- ❑ Load(XmlReader): Loads the document using the given XmlReader as the data source

In addition to taking a Stream, TextReader, and XmlReader objects, the Load() method also takes in a file name as a string argument. Using this method, you can load an XML document from the specified URL. Apart from the overloaded Load() methods, there is also a method named LoadXml() that makes it possible to load the XML document from a string of data as its argument.

> Note that when you load a new XmlDocument object, the current instance of the XmlDocument object is cleared. This means that if you reuse the same instance of the XmlDocument class to load a second document, the existing contents are entirely removed and replaced with the contents of the second document.

Listing 6-2 shows two ways to load an XmlDocument: first from a disk file and then by using a string variable that you have created in your application code.

Listing 6-2: Loading XML Documents

```csharp
<%@ Page Language="C#" %>
<%@ Import Namespace="System.Xml" %>
<script runat="server">
  void Page_Load(object sender, EventArgs e)
  {
    string xmlPath = Request.PhysicalApplicationPath +
      @"\App_Data\Books.xml";
    XmlDocument booksDoc = new XmlDocument();
    XmlDocument empDoc = new XmlDocument();
    Response.ContentType = "text/xml";
    try
    {
      //Load the XML from the file
      booksDoc.PreserveWhitespace = true;
      booksDoc.Load(xmlPath);
      //Write the XML onto the browser
      Response.Write(booksDoc.InnerXml);
      //Load the XML from a String
      empDoc.LoadXml("<employees>" +
        "<employee id='1'>" +
        "<name><firstName>Nancy</firstName>" +
        "<lastName>Davolio</lastName>" +
        "</name><city>Seattle</city>" +
        "<state>WA</state><zipCode>98122</zipCode>" +
        "</employee></employees>");
      //Save the XML data onto a file
      empDoc.Save(@"C:\Data\Employees.xml");
    }
    catch (XmlException xmlEx)
    {
      Response.Write("XmlException: " + xmlEx.Message);
    }
    catch (Exception ex)
    {
      Response.Write("Exception: " + ex.Message);
    }
  }
</script>
```

In Listing 6-2, the Page_Load event starts by declaring a string variable that holds the path to the XML file. Then it creates two instances of XmlDocument object; one for loading an XML document from the file system and the other one for loading an XML document from a string variable. The ContentType property of the XmlDocument object is then set to text/xml to indicate to the browser that the rendered content is indeed an XML document.

```csharp
Response.ContentType = "text/xml";
```

Before loading the XML file, you also set the PreserveWhitespace property of the XmlDocument object to true to preserve the white spaces so that the document fidelity can be retained.

```csharp
booksDoc.PreserveWhitespace = true;
```

The code then loads the XML file by invoking the `Load()` method of the `XmlDocument` passing in the path to the XML file as an argument.

```
booksDoc.Load(xmlPath);
```

After that, the loaded XML content is displayed onto the browser through the `InnerXml` property of the `XmlDocument` object.

```
Response.Write(booksDoc.InnerXml);
```

The XML DOM programming interface also provides you with a `LoadXml()` method to build a DOM from a well-formed XML string. That XML is then persisted to a file named `Employees.xml` by calling the `Save()` method of the `XmlDocument` object. You see more on the `Save()` method in the "Creating XML Documents" section later in this chapter.

```
empDoc.Save(@"C:\Data\Employees.xml");
```

> When you load the XML through the `LoadXml()` method, you need to understand that this method neither supports validation nor preserves white spaces. Any context-specific information you might need (such as DTD, entities, namespaces) must necessarily be embedded in the string to be taken into account.

All these lines of code that load and save the XML are embedded within the scope of a `try..catch` block to ensure that the generated exceptions are caught and handled in a gracious manner. In this case, the exception message is displayed onto the browser. If everything goes well, navigating to the page using the browser results in the output shown in Figure 6-3.

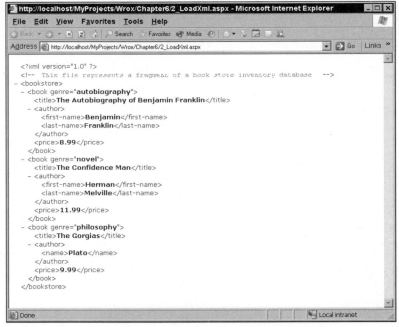

Figure 6-3

Parsing an XML Document Using XmlDocument Class

After the XmlDocument is loaded with data, you then need to be able to traverse the DOM tree. For this purpose, the XmlDocument exposes a number of methods. The best way to traverse a tree data structure is by recursion. Listing 6-3 shows how you can use recursion to traverse the XML DOM tree. As the code traverses the tree, it parses the contents of the XML document and outputs its element node including text and attributes to the browser.

Listing 6-3: Traversing DOM Tree Using XmlDocument Class

```csharp
<%@ Page Language="C#" %>
<%@ Import Namespace="System.Xml" %>
<script runat="server">
  void Page_Load(object sender, EventArgs e)
  {
    string xmlPath = Request.PhysicalApplicationPath +
      @"\App_Data\Books.xml";
    XmlDocument doc = new XmlDocument();
    doc.Load(xmlPath);
    XmlNode rootNode = doc.DocumentElement;
    DisplayNodes(rootNode);
  }

  void DisplayNodes(XmlNode node)
  {
    //Print the node type, node name and node value of the node
    if (node.NodeType == XmlNodeType.Text)
    {
      Response.Write("Type= [" + node.NodeType+ "] Value=" +
        node.Value + "<br>");
    }
    else
    {
      Response.Write("Type= [" + node.NodeType+"] Name=" +
        node.Name + "<br>");
    }
    //Print attributes of the node
    if (node.Attributes != null)
    {
      XmlAttributeCollection attrs = node.Attributes;
      foreach (XmlAttribute attr in attrs)
      {
        Response.Write("Attribute Name =" + attr.Name +
          "Attribute Value =" + attr.Value);
      }
    }
    //Print individual children of the node
    XmlNodeList children = node.ChildNodes;
    foreach (XmlNode child in children)
    {
      DisplayNodes(child);
    }
  }
</script>
<html xmlns="http://www.w3.org/1999/xhtml" >
<head runat="server">
```

```
      <title>Traversing the DOM Tree</title>
  </head>
  <body>
    <form id="form1" runat="server">
      <div>
      </div>
    </form>
  </body>
  </html>
```

As you can see from Listing 6-3, the core class that forms the root of this tree is the XmlDocument class. This code loads the XmlDocument with data from the books.xml file and uses that as the basis to traverse the document.

The XmlDocument is first instantiated, and a file URL is passed to it. The document loads the XML from the file and automatically generates the DOM tree.

```
XmlDocument doc = new XmlDocument();
doc.Load(xmlPath);
```

Next, you get a handle to the root node of the document tree:

```
XmlNode rootNode = doc.DocumentElement;
```

After the root node is obtained, the DisplayNodes() method is then invoked to recursively traverse through all the children of that node. DisplayNodes() is generic enough to print details of any node type. Remember that the DOM tree consists of nodes of different types (elements, attributes, processing instructions, comments, text nodes, and so on). This example just prints the generic information about the node (name, type); if it's a text node, it prints the value of the node as well.

```
if (node.NodeType == XmlNodeType.Text)
{
  Response.Write("Type= [" + node.NodeType+ "] Value=" +
  node.Value + "<br>");
}
else
{
  Response.Write("Type= [" + node.NodeType+"] Name=" +
    node.Name + "<br>");
}
```

Next, the code prints any attributes associated with the node.

```
    if (node.Attributes != null)
    {
      XmlAttributeCollection attrs = node.Attributes;
      foreach (XmlAttribute attr in attrs)
      {
        Response.Write("Attribute Name =" + attr.Name +
          "Attribute Value =" + attr.Value);
      }
    }
```

The last step gets all the children of the current node and calls `DisplayNodes()` on each of the children. Note that the `ChildNodes` method gets only the direct children of the node. To get all children of a node, you must use recursive code as follows.

```
XmlNodeList children = node.ChildNodes;
foreach (XmlNode child in children)
{
  DisplayNodes(child);
}
```

Navigate to the page from a browser and you should see something similar to Figure 6-4.

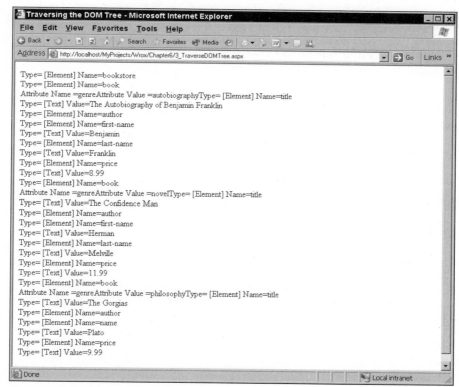

Figure 6-4

Finding Nodes

Using the `ChildNodes`, `FirstChild`, `LastChild`, `NextSibling`, `PreviousSibling`, `ParentNode`, and `OwnerDocument` properties of DOM, a program can navigate through a document hierarchy. You could use these methods to build a function that searches the hierarchy for specific nodes. Fortunately, the DOM provides several functions out of the box that obviates the need to write your own subroutines that search for nodes within an XML document. To this end, the DOM objects provide methods such as `GetElementsByTagName()`, `GetElementById()`, `SelectNodes()`, and `SelectSingleNode()` and for finding specific nodes. The following sections describe these methods in detail.

GetElementsByTagName

The GetElementsByTagName() method returns an XmlNodeList containing references to nodes that have a given name. Note that GetElementsByTagName() may return nodes at different levels of the subtree, and some nodes may be descendants of others. For example, if you have an XML document that defines a book node that contains two child nodes that are also named book. If a program searched this document for nodes named book, GetElementsByTagName() would return all three nodes. Depending on what you want to do with the nodes, you may need to be careful not to process a node more than once.

> Both the XmlDocument and XmlElement classes provide the GetElementsByTagName() method. The XmlDocument version searches the entire document for nodes with the given name. The XmlElement version of GetElementsByTagName() searches the document subtree rooted at the element.

The GetElementsByTagName() has two overloads.

```
public XmlNodeList GetElementsByTagName(string);
public XmlNodeList GetElementsByTagName(string, string);
```

The first method returns the list of all descendant elements that match the specified name. The second method also returns the same list of all descendant elements but based on criteria of the specified name as well as the namespace URI.

GetElementById

The GetElementById() method returns the first node it finds with a specified ID attribute. Similar to GetElementsByTagName(), this method searches for nodes that have a certain property. Unlike GetElementsByTagName(), however, this method only returns the first match it finds rather than an XmlNodeList containing all of the nodes that have the correct ID.

> GetElementById() returns only the first element with an ID attribute that has the value you specified. If you want to examine all matching nodes, you can use SelectNodes() to do something similar. For example, SelectNodes("//*[@Index='3']") returns an XmlNodeList containing all nodes that have Index attributes with value 3. Note that this statement does not verify that the attributes are marked with the ID type so it's not exactly the same as GetElementById. Although attributes of type ID can be defined in either XSD schemas or DTDs, the current implementation of the GetElementById only supports those defined in DTDs.

GetElementById() examines each node's attributes, looking for one that is marked as an ID. Simply naming the attribute ID is not enough. The XML document must identify the attribute as having type ID. After you find a node with a matching ID, you can use local navigation methods such as NextSibling, PreviousSibling, and Parent to move to different parts of the document.

SelectNodes

The SelectNodes() method returns an XmlNodeList containing references to nodes that match a specified XPath expression. An XPath expression gives a node's location within an XML document much as a file path describes a file's location on a disk. Although file paths are relatively simple, XPath allows you to specify a very complex set of node criteria to select nodes. You will see more on XPath and the use of SelectNodes() and SelectSingleNode() methods in a later section of this chapter.

SelectSingleNode

The SelectSingleNode() method is similar to SelectNodes() except it returns only the first node that matches an XPath expression instead of all of the nodes that match. After a program has located the matching node, it can use other document navigation methods such as NextSibling, PreviousSibling, and ParentNode to move through the document. In some cases this can be more efficient than using SelectNodes.

An Example on Finding Nodes

Listing 6-4 provides an example of how to find nodes in an XML document using the GetElementsByTagName() method.

Listing 6-4: Querying Nodes

```
<%@ Page Language="C#" %>
<%@ Import Namespace="System.Xml" %>
<script runat="server">
  void Page_Load(object sender, EventArgs e)
  {
    string xmlPath = Request.PhysicalApplicationPath +
      @"\App_Data\Books.xml";
    XmlDocument doc = new XmlDocument();
    doc.Load(xmlPath);
    //Get all job titles in the XML file
    XmlNodeList titleList = doc.GetElementsByTagName("title");
    Response.Write("Titles: " + "<br>");
    foreach (XmlNode node in titleList)
    {
      Response.Write("Title : " + node.FirstChild.Value + "<br>");
    }
    //Get reference to the first author node in the XML file
    XmlNode authorNode = doc.GetElementsByTagName("author")[0];
    foreach (XmlNode child in authorNode.ChildNodes)
    {
      if ((child.Name == "first-name") &&
        (child.NodeType == XmlNodeType.Element))
      {
        Response.Write("First Name : " + child.FirstChild.Value + "<br>");
      }
      if ((child.Name == "last-name") &&
        (child.NodeType == XmlNodeType.Element))
      {
        Response.Write("Last Name : " + child.FirstChild.Value + "<br>");
      }
    }
  }
</script>
<html xmlns="http://www.w3.org/1999/xhtml" >
<head runat="server">
  <title>Querying for specific nodes</title>
</head>
```

```
<body>
  <form id="form1" runat="server">
    <div>
    </div>
  </form>
</body>
</html>
```

In the code, you first get reference to all the title nodes in the form of an XmlNodeList object.

```
XmlNodeList titleList = doc.GetElementsByTagName("title");
```

You then loop through the XmlNodeList collection and display the value. Similarly you get reference to the first author node in the XML document using the same GetElementsByTagName() method.

```
XmlNode authorNode = doc.GetElementsByTagName("author")[0];
```

As you can see from the code, the first element in the XmlNodeList collection object is returned through the [0] prefix. You then loop though the child nodes of the author and display its contents using Response.Write() statements.

Selecting a DOM Subtree Using the XmlNodeReader Class

Suppose you have selected a node about which you need more information. To scan all the nodes that form the subtree using XML DOM, your only option is to use a recursive algorithm such as the one discussed with the previous example. The XmlNodeReader class gives you an effective, and ready-to-use, alternative by providing a reader over a given DOM node subtree. The following lines of code demonstrate this.

```
XmlDocument doc = new XmlDocument();
doc.Load(xmlPath);
//Get reference to the book node with the right genre attribute
XmlNode bookNode =
  doc.SelectSingleNode("/bookstore/book[@genre='autobiography']");
XmlNodeReader reader = new XmlNodeReader(bookNode);
while(reader.Read())
{
  //Display only the element names and values
  if (reader.NodeType == XmlNodeType.Element)
    lstOutput.Items.Add("Node Name:" + reader.Name);
  if (reader.NodeType == XmlNodeType.Text)
    lstOutput.Items.Add("Node Value:" + reader.Value);
}
```

The while loop visits all the nodes belonging to the specified XML DOM subtree. The node reader class is initialized using the XmlNode object that is one of the book nodes in the XML DOM subtree. After you have the node subtree in the form of an XmlNodeReader object, you can then easily loop through it using the Read() method.

> The XmlNodeReader **reads and returns nodes from the subtree, including entity reference nodes. The** XmlNodeReader **not only enforces the XML well-formedness rules, but also expands default attributes and entities, if DTD information is present in the** XmlDocument.

Programmatically Creating XML Documents

If your primary goal is analyzing the contents of an XML document, you will probably find the XML DOM parsing model much more effective than readers in spite of the larger memory footprint and set-up time it requires. A document loaded through XML DOM can be modified, extended, shrunk, and, more important, searched. The same can't be done with XML readers; XML readers solve a different type of problem.

To create an XML document using the XML DOM API, you must first create the document in memory, create nodes and then call the Save() method or one of its overloads. This approach gives you great flexibility because you can work with the in-memory document efficiently till you finally decide to save the document.

> In terms of the internal implementation, it is worth noting that the XML DOM's Save() **method makes use of an XML text writer to create the document. So unless the content to be generated is complex and subject to a lot of conditions, using an XML writer to create XML documents is much faster.**

The XmlDocument class provides a bunch of methods to create new nodes. These methods are named consistently with the writing methods of the XmlWriter class you encountered in Chapter 4. The next section reviews these methods in detail.

Creating and Appending Nodes

To add new nodes to the document, you must first use the XmlDocument class's factory methods for creating a new node and then add it somewhere in the document. They are called factory methods because they are responsible for creating a new node of a given type. These methods start with "Create" and end with the node type to create. For example, the method to create a new Text node is named CreateTextNode() and the method to create a new Element node is called CreateElement(). Also using the Create methods ensures that the created node will have the same namespace as the rest of the document. The following list reviews all the Create() methods and provides a brief description of their functionalities:

- ❑ CreateAttribute() — Creates an Attribute node with the given name
- ❑ CreateCDataSection() — Creates a CDATA section with the specified content
- ❑ CreateComment() — Creates a Comment node with the specified content
- ❑ CreateDocumentFragment() — Creates an empty DocumentFragment node
- ❑ CreateElement() — Creates an Element node with the given tag name

- ❑ `CreateEntityReference()` — Creates an `EntityReference` node
- ❑ `CreateProcessingInstruction()` — Creates a `ProcessingInstruction` node with the given content
- ❑ `CreateTextNode()` — Creates a new `Text` node with the specified content

For example, suppose you wanted to add another `<book>` element to the bookstore document. To do so, you would need to create nine new nodes to hold the information. Each of the four tags is a new node (`<title>`, `<first-name>`, `<last-name>`, and `<price>`), and the text that goes inside the nodes are also nodes. Finally, the genre attribute on the `<book>` tag is a new node.

> Note that XML DOM API in .NET Framework also provides the `InsertAfter()` method, which inserts a node after another node, but this method is not part of the standard W3C DOM API.

Now that you have a general understanding of the methods required for creating nodes, it is time to look at the basic steps to create an XML document on the fly. They are as follows:

- ❑ Create any necessary nodes
- ❑ Link the nodes to create a tree
- ❑ Append the tree to the in-memory XML document
- ❑ Optionally save the document

Before you create the necessary nodes, you should first create the standard XML declaration. The following code creates the XML prolog and appends to the `XmlDocument` instance the standard XML declaration and a comment node:

```
XmlDocument doc = new XmlDocument();
// Write and append the XML heading
XmlNode declarationNode = doc.CreateXmlDeclaration("1.0", "", "");
doc.AppendChild(declarationNode);
// Write and append some comment
XmlNode comment = doc.CreateComment("This file represents " +
  "a fragment of a book store inventory database");
doc.AppendChild(comment);
```

The `CreateXmlDeclaration()` method takes three arguments: the XML version, the required encoding, and a boolean value denoting whether the document can be considered stand-alone or has dependencies on other documents. All arguments are strings, including the encoding argument, as shown here:

```
<?xml version="1.0" standalone="yes" encoding="utf-8"?>
```

If specified, the encoding is written in the XML declaration and used by `Save()` to create the actual output stream. If the encoding is null or empty, no encoding attribute is set, and the default Unicode Universal Character Set Transformation Format, 8-bit form (UTF-8) encoding is used.

`CreateXmlDeclaration()` returns an `XmlDeclaration` node that you add as a child to the `XmlDocument` class. `CreateComment()`, on the other hand, creates an `XmlComment` node that represents an XML comment, as shown here:

```
<!-- This file represents a fragment of a book store inventory database -->
```

Element nodes are created using the `CreateElement()` method. The node is first configured with all of its expected child nodes and then added to the document. For example, to create an element named bookstore, you need to do the following.

```
XmlNode bookstoreNode = doc.CreateElement("bookstore");
```

Note that although all the `CreateXXX()` methods available in the `XmlDocument` class can create an XML node, that node is not automatically added to the XML DOM. You must do that explicitly using the `AppendChild()` method.

Appending Attributes

An attribute is simply a special type of node that you create using the `CreateAttribute()` method of the `XmlDocument` class. The return value of this method is an `XmlAttribute` object. The following code shows how to create a new attribute named genre and how to associate it with a parent book node:

```
XmlAttribute genreAttribute = doc.CreateAttribute("genre");
genreAttribute.Value = txtGenre.Text;
bookNode.Attributes.Append(genreAttribute);
```

Similar to `CreateElement()`, `CreateAttribute()` too allows you to qualify the name of the attribute using a namespace URI and optionally a prefix. The overloads for both methods have the same signature.

You set the value of an attribute using the `Value` property. At this point, however, the attribute node is not yet bound to an element node. To associate the attribute with a node, you must add the attribute to the node's `Attributes` collection. The `Append()` method of the `XmlAttributeCollection` class does this for you.

Persisting Changes

The final step in saving the XML document you have created is to save the document, as shown here:

```
doc.Save(xmPath);
```

To persist all the changes to storage medium, you call the `Save()` method, which contains four overloads, shown here:

- ❑ `Save(Stream)`: Saves the XML document to the specified stream
- ❑ `Save(string)`: Saves the XML document to the specified file
- ❑ `Save(TextWriter)`: Saves the XML document to the specified `TextWriter`
- ❑ `Save(XmlWriter)`: Saves the XML document to the specified `XmlWriter`

As you can see, you can save the XML document to a disk file as well as to an output stream, including network and compressed streams. You can also integrate the class that manages the document with other .NET Framework applications by using writers, and you can combine more XML documents using, in particular, XML writers. For example, the following code snippet saves the XML document to a string using a `StringWriter` object. (The `StringWriter` class is derived from `TextWriter`, which writes data to a string.)

```
StringWriter writer = new StringWriter();
//Load the XML from a String
empDoc.LoadXml("<?xml version='1.0'?><employees>" +
  "<employee id='1'>" +
  "<name><firstName>Nancy</firstName>" +
  "<lastName>Davolio</lastName>" +
  "</name><city>Seattle</city>" +
  "<state>WA</state><zipCode>98122</zipCode>" +
  "</employee></employees>");
//Save the XML data onto a file
empDoc.Save(writer);
txtResult.Text = writer.ToString();
```

Now that you understand the theory involved in creating an XML document from creating nodes to persisting the XML document, Listing 6-5 ties all these pieces together by providing a comprehensive example that demonstrates all of these concepts.

Listing 6-5: Creating an XML Document from Scratch

```
<%@ Page Language="C#" %>
<%@ Import Namespace="System.Xml" %>
<script runat="server">
  protected void btnSave_Click(object sender, EventArgs e)
  {
    string xmlPath = Request.PhysicalApplicationPath +
      @"\App_Data\NewBooks.xml";
    XmlDocument doc = new XmlDocument();
    //Check if the file already exists or not
    if (System.IO.File.Exists(xmlPath))
    {
      doc.Load(xmlPath);
      XmlNode bookNode = CreateBookNode(doc);
      //Get reference to the book node and append the book node to it
      XmlNode bookStoreNode = doc.SelectSingleNode("bookstore");
      bookStoreNode.AppendChild(bookNode);
      lblResult.Text = "XML Document has been successfully updated";
    }
    else
    {
      XmlNode declarationNode = doc.CreateXmlDeclaration("1.0", "", "");
      doc.AppendChild(declarationNode);
      XmlNode comment = doc.CreateComment("This file represents a " +
        "fragment of a book store inventory database");
      doc.AppendChild(comment);
      XmlNode bookstoreNode = doc.CreateElement("bookstore");
      XmlNode bookNode = CreateBookNode(doc);
      //Append the book node to the bookstore node
      bookstoreNode.AppendChild(bookNode);
      //Append the bookstore node to the document
      doc.AppendChild(bookstoreNode);
      lblResult.Text = "XML Document has been successfully created";
    }
    doc.Save(xmlPath);
  }

  XmlNode CreateBookNode(XmlDocument doc)
```

```
      {
        XmlNode bookNode = doc.CreateElement("book");
        //Add the genre attribute to the book node
        XmlAttribute genreAttribute = doc.CreateAttribute("genre");
        genreAttribute.Value = txtGenre.Text;
        bookNode.Attributes.Append(genreAttribute);
        //Add all the children of the book node
        XmlNode titleNode = doc.CreateElement("title");
        titleNode.InnerText = txtTitle.Text;
        bookNode.AppendChild(titleNode);
        //Create the author node and its children
        XmlNode authorNode = doc.CreateElement("author");
        XmlNode firstNameNode = doc.CreateElement("first-name");
        firstNameNode.InnerText = txtFirstName.Text;
        authorNode.AppendChild(firstNameNode);
        XmlNode lastNameNode = doc.CreateElement("last-name");
        lastNameNode.InnerText = txtLastName.Text;
        authorNode.AppendChild(lastNameNode);
        bookNode.AppendChild(authorNode);
        XmlNode priceNode = doc.CreateElement("price");
        priceNode.InnerText = txtPrice.Text;
        bookNode.AppendChild(priceNode);
        return bookNode;
      }
</script>
<html xmlns="http://www.w3.org/1999/xhtml" >
<head runat="server">
  <title>Creating an XmlDocument</title>
</head>
<body>
  <form id="form1" runat="server">
    <div>
      <table>
        <tr>
          <td colspan="2" style="width: 174px; height: 40px">
            <b>Book Details:</b>
          </td>
        </tr>
        <tr>
          <td style="width: 101px; height: 44px">
            Genre:
          </td>
          <td style="width: 204px; height: 44px">
            <asp:TextBox ID="txtGenre" runat="server" Width="201px">
            </asp:TextBox>
          </td>
        </tr>
        <tr>
          <td style="width: 101px; height: 44px">
            Title:
          </td>
          <td style="width: 204px; height: 44px">
            <asp:TextBox ID="txtTitle" runat="server" Width="201px">
            </asp:TextBox>
          </td>
        </tr>
```

```
      <tr>
        <td style="width: 101px; height: 41px">
          First Name:
        </td>
        <td style="width: 204px; height: 41px">
          <asp:TextBox ID="txtFirstName" runat="server"
            Width="201px">
          </asp:TextBox>
        </td>
      </tr>
      <tr>
        <td style="width: 101px; height: 41px">
          Last Name:
        </td>
        <td style="width: 204px; height: 41px">
          <asp:TextBox ID="txtLastName" runat="server"
            Width="201px">
          </asp:TextBox>
        </td>
      </tr>
      <tr>
        <td style="width: 101px; height: 41px">
          Price:
        </td>
        <td style="width: 204px; height: 41px">
          <asp:TextBox ID="txtPrice" runat="server" Width="201px">
          </asp:TextBox>
        </td>
      </tr>
      <tr>
        <td colspan="2" style="width: 101px; height: 41px">
          <asp:Button Text="Save" runat="server" ID="btnSave"
            Width="95px" OnClick="btnSave_Click"/>
        </td>
      </tr>
      <tr>
        <td colspan="2" style="width: 101px; height: 41px">
          <asp:Label runat="server" ID="lblResult"
            Width="295px"/>
        </td>
      </tr>
    </table>
  </div>
  </form>
</body>
</html>
```

Basically, Listing 6-5 provides a Web form where you can enter the details of a book. It captures the entered book details and saves them onto an XML file named NewBooks.xml. At the time of writing the file, it checks to see if the NewBooks.xml file is already available — if so, it appends the book details to the existing XML document; otherwise, it creates an XML document from scratch and adds the book details to that newly created document. Finally it saves the XML file using the Save() method.

It all starts with a check to see if the XML file is already available in the file system.

```
if (System.IO.File.Exists(xmlPath))
```

If the file is available, the file is loaded onto an XML document.

```
doc.Load(xmlPath);
```

As the name suggests, the `CreateBookNode()` method is a helper method that basically creates a book node that contains all the child nodes and the related attributes based on the details keyed in by the user.

```
XmlNode bookNode = CreateBookNode(doc);
```

After the book node is created, the next step is to append the book node to the root bookstore node. Before doing that, you need to get reference to the bookstore node.

```
XmlNode bookStoreNode = doc.SelectSingleNode("bookstore");
bookStoreNode.AppendChild(bookNode);
```

If the `NewBooks.xml` file is not present in the directory, you need to create that XML file from scratch. Start by creating the XML declaration and append that to the `XmlDocument` object.

```
XmlNode declarationNode = doc.CreateXmlDeclaration("1.0", "", "");
doc.AppendChild(declarationNode);
```

Add a comment indicating the purpose of the XML document by calling the `CreateComment()` method.

```
XmlNode comment = doc.CreateComment("This file represents a " +
    "fragment of a book store inventory database");
doc.AppendChild(comment);
```

After that, create the root bookstore node.

```
XmlNode bookstoreNode = doc.CreateElement("bookstore");
```

Again create the book node using the `CreateBookNode()` helper method and then append the returned book node to the root bookstore node.

```
XmlNode bookNode = CreateBookNode(doc);
//Append the book node to the bookstore node
bookstoreNode.AppendChild(bookNode);
//Append the bookstore node to the document
doc.AppendChild(bookstoreNode);
```

Finally, save the XML file.

```
doc.Save(xmlPath);
```

If you navigate to the above page using the browser, you see the output shown in Figure 6-5.

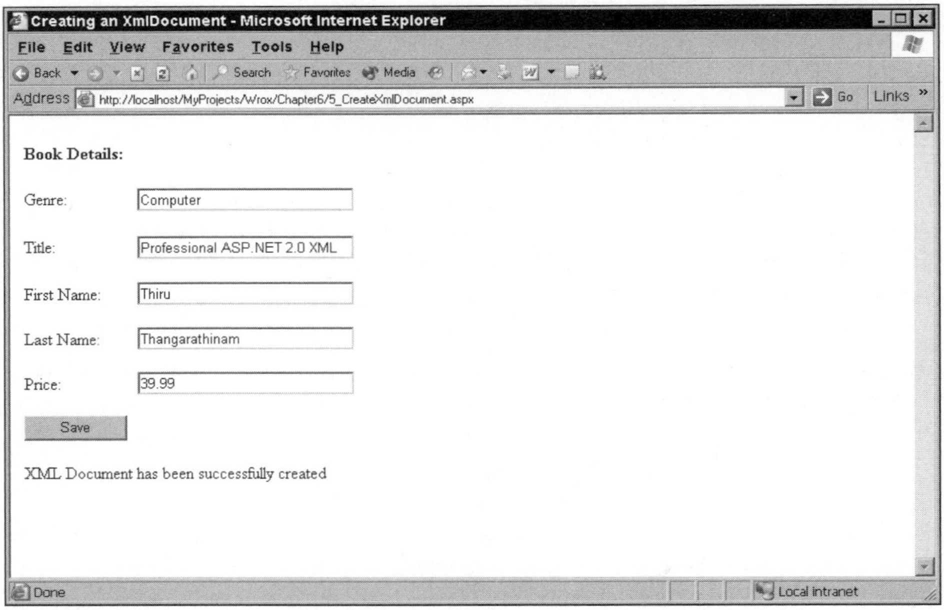

Figure 6-5

Figure 6-5 shows the output produced by the page after you enter the book details and save them. After saving the book details, navigate to the NewBooks.xml file through the browser, and you see the result as shown in Figure 6-6.

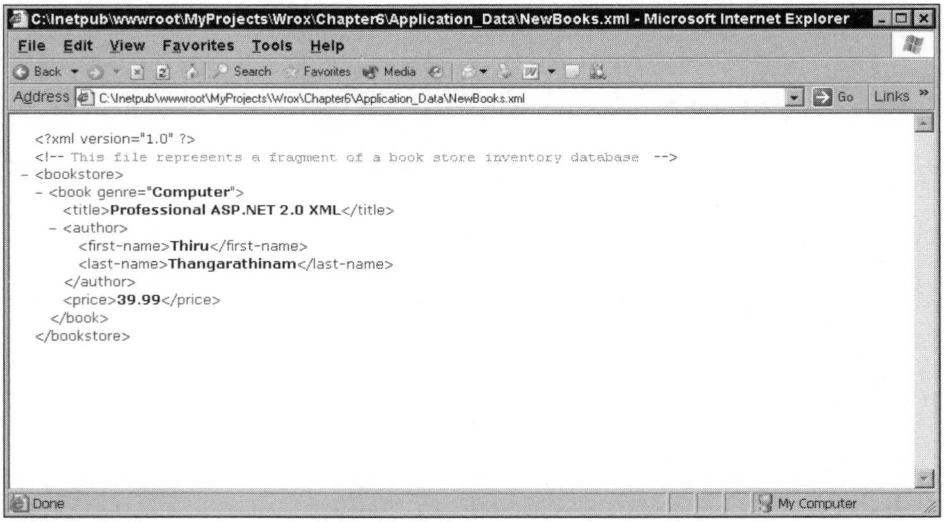

Figure 6-6

Changing Node Data

Node data can be changed after it has been created. For example, suppose that you want to change the price of a specific book after it has been released. To reflect this in the document, you would need to find the <title> node that contains the specific book and update its sibling <price> node with the new value. The following line of code shows how to do this using the Value property of the XmlNode class:

```
priceNode.FirstChild.Value = "10.99";
```

Deleting Nodes

To delete a node, simply remove it from the document. The RemoveChild() method of the XmlNode class accomplishes this. When called on an XmlNode object, the passed child node will be removed from its list of child nodes. For example, to delete the <title> node from the XML document, use the following code:

```
XmlDocument doc = new XmlDocument();
doc.LoadXml("<book genre=' autobiography''>" +
  "<title>The Autobiography of Benjamin Franklin</title>" +
  "</book>");
XmlNode root = doc.DocumentElement;
//Remove the title element.
root.RemoveChild(root.FirstChild);
```

In the example, the XmlDocument object is loaded from an XML string. After an XML document is loaded in memory, you get reference to the specific nodes that you want to remove from the XML document. After the reference to the specific node is obtained, invoke the RemoveChild() method, passing in the node to be removed.

Handling Events Raised by the XmlDocument

Before looking at the steps involved in handling the events raised by the XmlDocument, Table 6-3 briefly reviews the events raised by the XmlDocument class.

Table 6-3. Events of the XmlDocument Class

Event	Description
NodeChanged	Raised when the Value property of a node belonging to this document has been changed
NodeChanging	Raised when the Value property of a node belonging to this document is about to be changed
NodeInserted	Raised when a node belonging to this document has been inserted into another node
NodeInserting	Raised when a node belonging to this document is about to be inserted into another node
NodeRemoved	Raised when a node belonging to this document has been removed from its parent
NodeRemoving	Raised when a node belonging to this document is about to be removed from this document

All these events require the same delegate for the event handler, as follows:

```
public delegate void XmlNodeChangedEventHandler(
    object sender, XmlNodeChangedEventArgs e);
```

The XmlNodeChangedEventArgs structure contains the event data. The structure has six interesting properties:

❑   Node — Returns an XmlNode object that denotes the node that is being added, removed, or changed.

❑   OldParent — Returns an XmlNode object representing the parent of the node before the operation began.

❑   NewParent — Returns an XmlNode object representing the new parent of the node after the operation is complete. The property is set to null if the node is being removed. If the node is an attribute, the property returns the node to which the attribute refers.

❑   OldValue — Returns the original value of the node before the operation began

❑   NewValue — Returns the new value of the node

❑   Action — Contains a value indicating what type of change is occurring on the node by returning an enumeration of type XmlNodeChangedAction. Allowable values, listed in the XmlNodeChangedAction enumeration type are Insert, Remove, and Change.

Some of the actions you can take on an XML DOM are compound actions consisting of several steps, each of which could raise its own event. For example, be prepared to handle several events when you set the InnerXml property. In this case, multiple nodes could be created and appended, resulting in as many NodeInserting/NodeInserted pairs being raised. In some cases, the AppendChild() method of the XmlNode might fire a pair of NodeRemoving/NodeRemoved events prior to actually proceeding with the insertion. By design, to ensure XML well-formedness, AppendChild() checks whether the node you are adding already exists in the document. If it does, the existing node is first removed to avoid identical nodes in the same subtree. The following code shows how to set up a handler for the NodeInserted event.

```
//Add a new event handler.
XmlDocument doc = new XmlDocument();
doc.NodeInserted += new XmlNodeChangedEventHandler(
  NodeInsertedHandler);

//Define the event handler.
void NodeInsertedHandler(Object src, XmlNodeChangedEventArgs args)
{
    Response.Write("Node " + args.Node.Name + " inserted");
}
```

Inside the NodeInsertedHandler() method, the name of the node is retrieved from the XmlNodeChangedEventArgs object and displayed in the browser. As you can see, events provide with you with a flexible approach that can be used to synchronize changes between documents.

The XmlDocumentFragment Class

As you have seen in previous sections, after an XML document is loaded in memory, you can enter all the needed changes by simply accessing the property of interest and modifying the underlying value. For example, to change the value of an attribute, you proceed as follows:

```
// Retrieve a particular node and update an attribute
XmlNode node = doc.SelectSingleNode("book");
node.Attributes["genre"] = "novel";
```

To insert many nodes at the same time and in the same parent, you can take advantage of a little trick based on the concept of a document fragment. To this end, .NET Framework provides a class named XmlDocumentFragment that provides a lightweight object that is useful for tree operations. In essence, you concatenate all the necessary markup into a string and then create a document fragment, as shown here:

```
XmlDocumentFragment docFragment = doc.CreateDocumentFragment();
docFragment.InnerXml = "<book genre='novel'>...</book>";
parentNode.AppendChild(docFragment);
```

After creating an XmlDocumentFragment object, set its InnerXml property to the string value and add the XmlDocumentFragment to the parent node. The nodes defined in the body of the fragment are inserted one after the next. Listing 6-6 shows how the CreateBookNode() method in Listing 6-5 can be modified to take advantage of the XmlDocumentFragment object.

Listing 6-6: Creating Fragments of XML Using XmlDocumentFragment

```
XmlNode CreateBookNode(XmlDocument doc)
{
  XmlDocumentFragment docFragment = doc.CreateDocumentFragment();
  docFragment.InnerXml = "<book genre='" + txtGenre.Text + "'>" +
    "<title>" + txtTitle.Text +" </title>" +
    "<author><first-name>" + txtFirstName.Text + "</first-name>" +
    "<last-name>" + txtLastName.Text + "</last-name></author>" +
    "<price>" + txtPrice.Text + "</price></book>";
  return docFragment;
}
```

In general, when you set the InnerXml property on an XmlNode-based class, any detected markup text will be parsed, and the new contents will replace the existing contents. For this reason, if you want to simply add new children to a node, pass through the XmlDocumentFragment class, as described in the previous paragraph, and avoid using InnerXml directly on the target node.

XPath Support in XML DOM

The XPath language enables you to locate nodes in your XML data that match the specified criteria. An XPath expression can specify criteria by evaluating either the position of a node in the document hierarchy, data values of the node, or a combination of both. Basic XPath syntax uses a path such as notation. For example, the path /bookstore/book/author indicates an author element that is nested inside a book element, which, in turn, is nested in a root bookstore element. You can also use XPath to locate specific nodes. For example, this expression locates all book nodes:

```
//bookstore/book
```

But this expression matches only a node with the specific genre attribute value of novel:

```
//bookstore/book/[@genre='novel']/author
```

The XmlNode class defines two methods that perform XPath searches: `SelectNodes` and `SelectSingleNode`. These methods operate on all contained child nodes. Because the `XmlDocument` inherits from `XmlNode`, you can call `XmlDocument.SelectNodes()` to search an entire document.

XPath provides rich and powerful search syntax, and it's impossible to explain all of the variations you can use in a brief discussion. However, Table 6-4 outlines some of the key ingredients in more advanced XPath expressions and includes examples that show how they would work with the `books.xml` document.

Table 6-4. XPath Expression Syntax

Expression	Meaning
/	Starts an absolute path that selects from the root node. `/bookstore/book/title` selects all title elements that are children of the book element, which is itself a child of the root bookstore element.
//	Starts a relative path that selects nodes anywhere. `//book/title` selects all of the title elements that are children of a book element, regardless of where they appear in the document.
@	Selects an attribute of a node. `/book/@genre` selects the attribute named genre from the root book element.
*	Selects any element in the path. `/book/*` selects both title and author nodes because both are contained by a root book element.
|	Union operator that returns the union of the results of two paths. `/bookstore/book/title | bookstore/book/author` selects the title nodes used to describe a title and the author nodes used to describe an author.
.	Indicates the current default node.
..	Indicates the parent node. `//author/` selects any element that is parent to an author, which includes the book elements.
[ ]	Define selection criteria that can test a contained node or attribute value. `/book[@genre="autobiography"]` selects the book elements with the indicated attribute value.
starts-with	This function retrieves elements based on what text a contained element starts with. `/bookstore/book/author[starts-with(first-name, "B")]` finds all author elements that have a first-name element that starts with the letter B.

Expression	Meaning
position	This function retrieves elements based on position. /bookstore/book[position()=2] selects the second book element.
count	This function counts elements. You specify the name of the child element to count, or an asterisk (*) for all children. /bookstore/book/author[count(first-name) = 1] retrieves author elements that have exactly one nested first-name element.

Listing 6-7 shows an example that allows you to select an XPath expression from a drop-down list, apply that XPath to an XML document, and display the contents of the resultant object.

Listing 6-7: Evaluating XPath Expressions

```csharp
<%@ Page Language="C#" %>
<%@ Import Namespace="System.Xml" %>
<script runat="server">
  void Page_Load(object sender, EventArgs e)
  {
    if (!Page.IsPostBack)
    {
      ddlExpressions.Items.Add("//book/title");
      ddlExpressions.Items.Add("//book[@genre='novel']/title");
      ddlExpressions.Items.Add("//book/author/first-name");
      ddlExpressions.Items.Add("//book[@genre='philosophy']/title");
      ddlExpressions.Items.Add("//book/price");
      ddlExpressions.Items.Add("//book[3]/title");
      ddlExpressions.SelectedIndex = 0;
      //Set the default selection
      UpdateDisplay();
    }
  }

  void ddlExpressions_SelectedIndexChanged(object sender, EventArgs e)
  {
    //Display the value produced by evaluating the XPath Expression
    UpdateDisplay();
  }

  void UpdateDisplay()
  {
    lstOutput.Items.Clear();
    string xmlPath = Request.PhysicalApplicationPath +
      @"\App_Data\Books.xml";
    XmlDocument doc = new XmlDocument();
    doc.Load(xmlPath);
    XmlNodeList nodeList =
      doc.DocumentElement.SelectNodes(ddlExpressions.SelectedItem.Text);
    foreach (XmlNode child in nodeList)
    {
      lstOutput.Items.Add("Node Name:" + child.Name);
      lstOutput.Items.Add("Node Value:" + child.FirstChild.Value);
    }
```

```
    }
</script>
<html xmlns="http://www.w3.org/1999/xhtml" >
<head runat="server">
  <title>XPath Example</title>
</head>
<body>
  <form id="form1" runat="server">
    <div>
      Select the XPath Expression:
      <asp:DropDownList ID="ddlExpressions" AutoPostBack="true"
        runat="server" Width="410px"
        OnSelectedIndexChanged="ddlExpressions_SelectedIndexChanged">
      </asp:DropDownList>
      <br/><br/>
      <asp:ListBox ID="lstOutput" runat="server"
        Width="587px" Height="168px">
      </asp:ListBox>
    </div>
  </form>
</body>
</html>
```

The `Page_Load` event loads the drop-down list box with the set of predefined XPath expressions.

```
if (!Page.IsPostBack)
{
  ddlExpressions.Items.Add("//book/title");
  ddlExpressions.Items.Add("//book[@genre='novel']/title");
  ddlExpressions.Items.Add("//book/author/first-name");
  ddlExpressions.Items.Add("//book[@genre='philosophy']/title");
  ddlExpressions.Items.Add("//book/price");
  ddlExpressions.Items.Add("//book[3]/title");
  ddlExpressions.SelectedIndex = 0;
  //Set the default selection
  UpdateDisplay();
}
```

After loading all the values, a helper method named `UpdateDisplay()` is invoked. This method basically updates the display on a results list box based on the selected XPath expression. This method is also invoked from the `SelectedIndexChanged` event of the drop-down box to evaluate the selected XPath expression and display the results through the list box.

Code inside the `UpdateDisplay()` method is simple and straightforward. After loading the `XmlDocument` object with the contents of an XML file, it simply invokes the `SelectNodes()` method of the `XmlElement` object that is returned by invoking the `DocumentElement` property of the `XmlDocument` object. To the `SelectNodes()` method, the selected value in the drop-down list is supplied as an argument. The return value of the `SelectNodes()` method is an `XmlNodeList` object, which is then iterated through a for... each loop. Inside the for..each loop, the name and value of the node are added to the results list box.

```
XmlNodeList nodeList =
  doc.DocumentElement.SelectNodes(ddlExpressions.SelectedItem.Text);
foreach (XmlNode child in nodeList)
{
```

```
lstOutput.Items.Add("Node Name:" + child.Name);
lstOutput.Items.Add("Node Value:" + child.FirstChild.Value);
}
```

The output produced by the page looks similar to Figure 6-7.

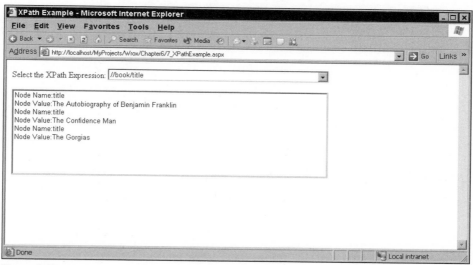

Figure 6-7

In Figure 6-7, selecting an XPath expression in the drop-down list results in that XPath expression being evaluated, and the output of that is displayed in the list box.

Performance Optimization with XPathNavigator

Another way to use XPath to query your XML data is to create and use an XPathNavigator object. The XPathNavigator class, in conjunction with the other classes in the System.Xml.XPath namespace such as XPathDocument, XPathExpression, and the XPathNodeIterator, enables you to optimize performance when working with XPath queries. The XPathNavigator class has methods such as Select, Compile, and Evaluate to perform queries on your XML data by using XPath expressions.

Among all the other things that you can do with an XPathNavigator object, keep in mind, is the use of XPathNavigator object to process the contents of an XML document in an efficient way. For example, if you are going to perform the same query a number of times, perhaps on a collection of documents, the query will execute significantly faster if you pre-compile the expression. You do this by calling the Compile() method on the navigator, passing in an XPath expression as a string, and getting back an instance of an XPathExpression object. You can pass that XPathExpression object to the Select method, and the execution of the Select method will be much quicker than if you passed in the XPath as a string every time.

By providing a cursor model, the XPathNavigator class enables you to navigate and edit XML information items as instances of the XQuery 1.0 and XPath 2.0 Data Model. An XPathNavigator object is created from a class that implements the IXPathNavigable interface such as the XPathDocument and XmlDocument classes. Table 6-5 lists the key methods of the XPathNavigator class.

Table 6-5. Key Methods of the XPathNavigator Class

Method	Description
AppendChild	Creates a new child node at the end of the list of child nodes of the current node
AppendChildElement	Creates a new child element node at the end of the list of child nodes of the current node using the namespace prefix, local name, and namespace URI specified with the value specified
CheckValidity	Verifies that the XML data in the XPathNavigator conforms to the supplied XSD schema
Clone	Creates a new XPathNavigator positioned at the same node as the current XPathNavigator
Compile	Compiles a string representing an XPath expression and returns the output in the form of an XPathExpression object
CreateAttribute	Creates an attribute node on the current element node
CreateAttributes	Returns an XmlWriter object used to create new attributes on the current element
DeleteSelf	Deletes the current node and all of its child nodes
GetAttribute	Gets the value of the attribute with the specified local name and namespace URI
GetNamespace	Returns the value of the namespace node corresponding to the specified local name
GetNamespacesInScope	Returns the in-scope namespaces of the current node
InsertAfter	Creates a new sibling node after the currently selected node
InsertBefore	Creates a new sibling node before the currently selected node
InsertElementAfter	Creates a new sibling element after the current node using the namespace prefix, local name, namespace URI, and the value specified
InsertElementBefore	Creates a new sibling element before the current node using the namespace prefix, local name, namespace URI, and the value specified
IsDescendant	Determines whether the specified XPathNavigator is a descendant of the current XPathNavigator
MoveToAttribute	Moves the XPathNavigator to the attribute with the matching local name and namespace URI
MoveToChild	Moves the XPathNavigator to the specified child node
MoveToFirst	Moves the XPathNavigator to the first sibling of the current node
MoveToFirstAttribute	Moves the XPathNavigator to the first attribute of the current node
MoveToFirstChild	Moves the XPathNavigator to the first child of the current node

Method	Description
MoveToFirstNamespace	Moves the XPathNavigator to the first namespace node of the current node
MoveToFollowing	Moves the XPathNavigator to the specified element
MoveToId	Moves the XPathNavigator to the attribute with the specified id that is indicated by the supplied string
MoveToNamespace	Moves the XPathNavigator to the namespace node with the specified namespace prefix
MoveToNext	Moves the XPathNavigator to the next sibling of the current node
MoveToNextAttribute	Moves the XPathNavigator to the next attribute
MoveToNextNamespace	Moves the XPathNavigator to the next namespace node
MoveToParent	Moves the XPathNavigator to the parent node of the current node
MoveToPrevious	Moves the XPathNavigator to the previous sibling of the current node
MoveToRoot	Moves the XPathNavigator to the root node that the current node belongs to
PrependChild	Creates a new child node at the beginning of the list of child nodes of the current node
PrependChildElement	Creates a new child element node at the beginning of the list of child nodes of the current node using the namespace prefix, local name, and namespace URI, and the value specified
ReadSubTree	Reads the current node and its child nodes into the supplied XmlReader object
ReplaceSelf	Replaces the current node with the content specified
Select	Selects a node set using the specified XPath expression and returns an object of type XPathNodeIterator
SelectAncestors	Selects all the ancestor nodes of the current node that match the selection criteria
SelectChildren	Selects all the child nodes of the current node that match the selection criteria
SelectDescendants	Selects all the descendant nodes of the current node matching the specified criteria
SelectSingleNode	Selects a single node in the XPathNavigator
SetTypedValue	Sets the typed value of the current node
SetValue	Sets the value of the current node
ValueAs	Returns the current node's value as the Type specified
WriteSubTree	Writes the current node and its child contents into the supplied XmlWriter object

As Table 6-5 points out, the `XPathNavigator` also has a set of `MoveToXXX()` methods such as `MoveToFirstChild()`, `MoveToNext()`, `MoveToParent()` — which give you the opportunity to explicitly position the `XPathNavigator` at a specific node. For example, you might use an XPath expression to locate a particular book node by matching the genre attribute value. After you have located the node you are interested in, you can use the `MoveToFirstChild` method to get to a particular data item.

> One of the new features introduced with `XPathNavigator` object in .NET Framework 2.0 is the ability to edit XML data using a cursor model. With .NET Framework 1.x, the `XPathNavigator` was only constrained to navigating XML data using a cursor model. To check if an `XPathNavigator` object is editable, invoke the `CanEdit` property of the `XPathNavigator` object that returns a Boolean value indicating if the `XPathNavigator` is editable.

Listing 6-8 shows how to create an `XPathDocument` and load data into it, compile an XPath expression string into an `XPathExpression` object, and use the `XPathNodeIterator` when your XPath expression returns an `XmlNodeList` collection.

Listing 6-8: An Example of Compiled XPath Expressions

```
<%@ Page Language="C#" %>
<%@ Import Namespace="System.Xml" %>
<%@ Import Namespace="System.Xml.XPath" %>
<script runat="server">
  void Page_Load(object sender, EventArgs e)
  {
    if (!Page.IsPostBack)
    {
      ddlExpressions.Items.Add("//book/title");
      ddlExpressions.Items.Add("//book[@genre='novel']/title");
      ddlExpressions.Items.Add("//book/author/first-name");
      ddlExpressions.Items.Add("//book[@genre='philosophy']/title");
      ddlExpressions.Items.Add("//book/price");
      ddlExpressions.Items.Add("//book[3]/title");
      ddlExpressions.SelectedIndex = 0;
      //Set the default selection
      UpdateDisplay();
    }
  }

  void ddlExpressions_SelectedIndexChanged(object sender, EventArgs e)
  {
    //Display the value produced by evaluating the XPath Expression
    UpdateDisplay();
  }

  void UpdateDisplay()
  {
    lstOutput.Items.Clear();
    string xmlPath = Request.PhysicalApplicationPath +
      @"\App_Data\Books.xml";
```

```
XPathDocument document = new XPathDocument(xmlPath);
XPathNavigator navigator = document.CreateNavigator();
//Compile the XPath expression
XPathExpression expr = navigator.Compile(
  ddlExpressions.SelectedItem.Text);
XPathNodeIterator nodes = navigator.Select(expr);
while (nodes.MoveNext())
{
  lstOutput.Items.Add("Name :" + nodes.Current.Name);
  lstOutput.Items.Add("Value : " + nodes.Current.Value);
}
}
</script>
<html xmlns="http://www.w3.org/1999/xhtml" >
<head runat="server">
  <title>XPathNavigator Selection Example</title>
</head>
<body>
  <form id="form1" runat="server">
    <div>
      Select the XPath Expression:
      <asp:DropDownList ID="ddlExpressions" AutoPostBack="true"
        runat="server" Width="410px"
        OnSelectedIndexChanged="ddlExpressions_SelectedIndexChanged">
      </asp:DropDownList>
      <br/><br/>
      <asp:ListBox ID="lstOutput" runat="server"
        Width="587px" Height="168px">
      </asp:ListBox>
    </div>
  </form>
</body>
</html>
```

The meat of the code in this example is contained in the UpdateDisplay() method. The implementations of Page_Load() and the SelectedIndexChanged events are similar to the previous code listing. The UpdateDisplay() method starts by creating an instance of the XPathDocument object passing in the path to the XML file.

```
XPathDocument document = new XPathDocument(xmlPath);
```

An XPathNavigator object is then instantiated by calling the CreateNavigator() method of the XPathDocument object.

```
XPathNavigator navigator = document.CreateNavigator();
```

The selected XPath expression is then compiled into an XPathExpression object through the invocation of the Compile() method of the XPathNavigator object.

```
XPathExpression expr = navigator.Compile(
  ddlExpressions.SelectedItem.Text);
```

You use an XPathExpression to identify all matching nodes in the XML file and then use an XPathNodeIterator to process each matching node.

```
XPathNodeIterator nodes = navigator.Select(expr);
while (nodes.MoveNext())
{
  lstOutput.Items.Add("Name :" + nodes.Current.Name);
  lstOutput.Items.Add("Value : " + nodes.Current.Value);
}
```

Save and test your work. When the application starts, you see a list of last names. These match the first item in the drop-down list. Try the other drop-down selections to see what data is returned.

> At this point, you might be wondering why the code in Listing 6-8 utilized an XPathDocument as opposed to using the XmlDocument as the tree model API for parsing the XML. It is mainly due to the fact that the XPathDocument class is optimized for use in XPath and XSLT and can also provide better performance when running XPath over an XML document or running XSLT over in-memory XML. In these scenarios, the XPathDocument should be preferred to the XmlDocument.

If you are evaluating an XPathExpression that will result in a value instead of a set of nodes, use the Evaluate() method instead of Select. Evaluate returns a value corresponding to the value that results from the evaluation of the XPath expression. It is important to keep in mind that the XPath expressions can result in a numeric, string, or Boolean value. The Evaluate method simply returns an object reference, so you have to cast the result to the appropriate type. The following lines of code show how to accomplish this.

```
XPathDocument document = new XPathDocument(xmlPath);
XPathNavigator navigator = document.CreateNavigator();
Double total = (double) navigator.Evaluate("sum(descendant::book/price)");
```

For numeric values, the return result comes into the .NET code as a double, so you have to cast appropriately there.

Updating an XPathNavigator Object

With the release of .NET 2.0 Framework, Microsoft has greatly increased the usefulness of the XPathNavigator by layering the ability to write XML data on top of the reading capabilities of the XPathNavigator object. Note, however, that the XPathNavigator objects created by XPathDocument objects are read-only while XPathNavigator objects created by XmlDocument objects can be edited. The CanEdit property of the XPathNavigator allows you to determine the read-only or edit status of the XPathNavigator object.

> With the ability to edit an XPathNavigator object in .NET Framework 2.0, you should consider using XPathNavigator as your primary programming model for working with XML data sources especially when you want a level of abstraction away from the underlying source.

Listing 6-9 demonstrates how to utilize an XPathNavigator object to edit an XML document. Specifically, the code listing adds a new discount attribute to each of the price nodes in the XML document. The discount is calculated by applying 10 percent of the value contained in the price node.

Listing 6-9: Using XPathNavigator to Update an XML Document

```csharp
<%@ Page Language="C#" %>
<%@ Import Namespace="System.Xml" %>
<%@ Import Namespace="System.Xml.XPath" %>
<script runat="server">
  void Page_Load(object sender, EventArgs e)
  {
    //Set the ContentType to XML to write XML values
    Response.ContentType = "text/xml";
    string xmlPath = Request.PhysicalApplicationPath +
      @"\App_Data\Books.xml";
    XmlDocument document = new XmlDocument();
    document.Load(xmlPath);
    XPathNavigator navigator = document.CreateNavigator();
    int count = navigator.Select("/bookstore/book").Count;
    //Navigate to the right nodes
    navigator.MoveToChild("bookstore", "");
    navigator.MoveToChild("book", "");
    //Loop through all the book nodes
    for(int i = 0; i < count; i++)
    {
      navigator.MoveToChild("price", "");
      //Calculate 10% discount on the price
      double discount = navigator.ValueAsDouble * (.1);
      navigator.CreateAttribute("", "discount", "",
        discount.ToString());
      //Move to the parent book element
      navigator.MoveToParent();
      //Move to the next sibling book element
      navigator.MoveToNext();
    }
    navigator.MoveToRoot();
    Response.Write (navigator.OuterXml);
  }
</script>
```

To start with, an instance of the XPathNavigator object is created by calling the CreateNavigator() method of the XmlDocument object. You then get the number of the book nodes contained in the books.xml file by using the following line.

Before looping through all the book nodes, you need to get to the first book node in the document. It is accomplished by making specific calls to the MoveToChild() method.

After you are on the book node, all you need to do is to get reference to the price node, retrieve its value, get 10 percent of its value, and create a new attribute with the calculated discount. The following lines of code accomplish this.

```csharp
for(int i = 0; i < count; i++)
{
  navigator.MoveToChild("price", "");
  //Calculate 10% discount on the price
  double discount = navigator.ValueAsDouble * (.1);
  navigator.CreateAttribute("", "discount", "",
  discount.ToString());
```

```
    //Move to the parent book element
    navigator.MoveToParent();
    //Move to the next sibling book element
    navigator.MoveToNext();
}
```

Note that after creating the code, there is a call to the `MoveToParent()` method, which ensures that the navigator is pointed to the parent book node. After you are at the parent book node, moving to the next book node is very easy — simply call the `MoveToNext()` method.

Now that you have added the discount attribute to all the price nodes, you are ready to display the modified XML document. But before doing that, position the navigator back to the root node by calling the `MoveToRoot()` method so that invoking `OuterXml` property will result in the entire XML document being displayed.

```
    navigator.MoveToRoot();
    Response.Write(navigator.OuterXml);
```

That's all there is to updating an XML document using the `XPathNavigator` object. Browse to the page using a browser.

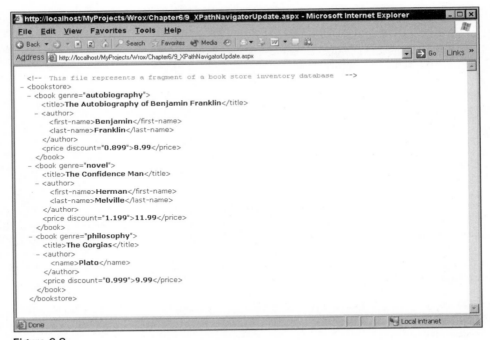

Figure 6-8

The output shown in Figure 6-8 is what you get when navigating to the page from a browser.

Validating XML in an XmlDocument

Chapter 5 provided a complete discussion of the validation features available for the XML reader classes. With the release of .NET Framework 2.0, Microsoft has built in the validation feature right into the XmlDocument itself. By using this feature, you can perform XML schema validation of the entire subtree or partial validation of nodes in the document. To this end, there is a new method named Validate() that is introduced with .NET Framework 2.0.

```
string xmlPath = Request.PhysicalApplicationPath +
  @"\App_Data\Books.xml";
string xsdPath = Request.PhysicalApplicationPath +
  @"\App_Data\Books.xsd";
XmlReaderSettings settings = new XmlReaderSettings();
settings.ValidationType = ValidationType.Schema;
settings.Schemas.Add(null, XmlReader.Create(xsdPath));
XmlReader reader = XmlReader.Create(xmlPath, settings);
XmlDocument doc = new XmlDocument();
doc.Load(reader);
ValidationEventHandler eventHandler = new
ValidationEventHandler(ValidationEventHandler);
doc.Validate(eventHandler);
```

As you can see, the validation process is initiated by the call to the Validate() method of the XmlDocument object.

Summary

This chapter introduced the basic concepts of XML DOM in .NET Framework and provided a concise overview of the .NET DOM classes available to read, store, and manipulate XML documents. The classes in the System.Xml namespaces contain probably the richest collection of XML-related functionalities available thus far in any other software development platform. XML DOM exposes a powerful object model that provides you with a rich set of methods and properties to manipulate the schema and contents of XML documents. The overall programming interface of the XmlDocument class might look familiar to those of you who have spent some time working with the COM-based MSXML library.

The XmlDocument class provides methods to load XML documents from a variety of sources, including XML readers and streams. To locate a node in the in-memory tree that represents the original XML document, you can proceed with a collection that returns only the first level of child nodes, or you can, more effectively, use an XPath query string to locate nodes by condition. Using the XmlDocument object, you can also create full-featured, rich XML documents from scratch. Creating new documents using XML DOM is not as efficient as using XML writers, but because the document is first built in memory, you have an unprecedented level of flexibility and can fine-tune your document before it is written to the output stream.

Editing an XML file as you are navigating through an XML document is made easier through the new editable XPathNavigator object. This feature makes the XPathNavigator object an ideal candidate for building applications that periodically build or examine documents, but still require a better performing navigator. Finally you now have the ability to perform validation of an XmlDocument object as you are building the XML DOM tree.

Transforming
XML Data with XSLT

In the last couple of chapters, you saw how parsers, XML schemas, and the DOM offer tremendous functionality. You can use XML schemas to add structure to your data and then publish them for others to consume. You can use the DOM from within your applications to access and modify your XML. This chapter focuses on XSLT (eXtensible Stylesheet Language Transformation), which you can use to transform XML and produce output that can be displayed on the Web. The W3C describes XSLT as "a language for transforming XML documents into other XML documents." But XSLT can do more than that. Perhaps a better definition of XSLT is that XSLT can be used to transform the content and structure of an XML document into some other form. While general and broad, this description hints at the power of XSLT. Another way to describe XSLT is to use an analogy: XSLT is to XML like SQL is to a database. Just as SQL can query and modify data, XSLT can query portions of an XML document and produce new content. This chapter explores the concepts of XSLT and demonstrates how XSLT can be used in conjunction with ASP.NET to construct data driven Web applications.

By the end of this chapter, you will have a good understanding of the following:

❑ What is XSLT?

❑ Structure of an XSLT document

❑ Applying XSL Style Sheets to XML documents to customize the output

❑ Support provided by the .NET Framework for transforming XML documents

❑ Using XSLT to build sophisticated ASP.NET pages

❑ Performing advanced XSLT operations in conjunction with .NET 2.0

❑ Debugging XSLT style sheets using Visual Studio 2005

This chapter also harnesses the XPath skills acquired from the previous chapter, and examines how to use transformations effectively in ASP.NET.

A Primer on XSLT

XSLT is a language that enables you to convert XML documents into other XML documents, into HTML documents, or into almost anything you like. When you specify a series of XSLT instructions for converting a class of XML documents, you do it by creating an "XSL style sheet." An XSL style sheet is an XML document that uses specialized XML elements and attributes to describe those changes you want made. The definition of these specialized elements and attributes comes from the W3C, the same standards body responsible for XML and HTML.

What Is XSLT, XSL, and XPath?

XSLT was originally part of XSL, the Extensible Stylesheet Language. In fact, it's still technically a part of it. The XSL specification describes XSL as a language with two parts: a language for transforming XML documents and an XML vocabulary for describing how to format document content. This vocabulary is a collection of specialized elements called "formatting objects" that specify page layout and other presentation-related details about the text marked up with these elements' tags: font family, font size, margins, line spacing, and other settings.

XSL transforms an XML document into another XML document by transforming each XML element into an (X)HTML element. XSLT can also add new elements into the output file, or remove elements. It can rearrange and sort elements, and test and make decisions about which elements to display, and a lot more.

One great feature of XSLT is its capability, while processing any part of a document, to grab information from any other part of that document. The mini-language developed as part of XSLT for specifying the path through the document tree from one part to another is called "XPath." XPath lets you say things like "get the `revisionDate` attribute value of the element before the current element's chapter ancestor element." This capability proved so valuable that the W3C also broke XPath out into its own specification so that other W3C specifications could incorporate this language.

How Does XSLT Work?

The transformation process needs two input files, the XML document, which makes up the source tree and the XSLT file, which consists of elements used to transform data to the required format. You can also use more than one XSLT file in the transformation process. The output file is a result tree, which can be an XML, HTML, or any other format. Several parsers are available for the transformation process using XSLT. Parsers are applications that validate an XML document and perform transformations to generate the required output. Figure 7-1 shows the transformation process.

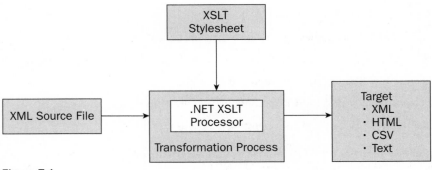

Figure 7-1

In the transformation process, XSLT uses XPath to define parts of the source document that match one or more predefined templates. When a match is found, XSLT transforms the matching part of the source document into the result document. The parts of the source document that do not match a template end up unmodified in the result document.

Need for XSLT

Before discussing the need for XSLT, you first need to remind yourself why XML has proved to be such a success and generated so much excitement. XML is a simple, standard way to interchange structured textual data between computer programs. Part of its success comes because it is also readable and writable by humans, using nothing more complicated than a text editor, but this doesn't alter the fact that it is primarily intended for communication between software systems. As such, XML satisfies two compelling requirements:

❑ Separating data from presentation: The need to separate information (such as a weather forecast) from details of the way it is to be presented on a particular device. The early motivation for this arose from the need to deliver information not only to the traditional PC-based Web browser (which itself comes in many flavors), but also to TV sets and WAP (Wireless Application Protocol) phones, not to mention the continuing need to produce print-on-paper. For many information providers, an even more important driver is the opportunity to syndicate content to other organizations that can republish it with their own look-and-feel.

❑ Transmitting data between applications: The need to transmit information (such as orders and invoices) from one organization to another without investing in software integration projects. As electronic commerce gathers pace, the amount of data exchanged between enterprises increases daily, and this need becomes ever more urgent.

Of course, these two ways of using XML are not mutually exclusive. An invoice can be presented onscreen as well as being input to a financial application package, and weather forecasts can be summarized, indexed, and aggregated by the recipient instead of being displayed directly. Another of the key benefits of XML is that it unifies the worlds of documents and data, providing a single way of representing structure regardless of whether the information is intended for human or machine consumption. The main point is that, whether the XML data is ultimately used by people or by a software application, it will very rarely be used directly in the form it arrives in: it first has to be transformed into something else such as another XML format or HTML format.

To communicate with a human reader, this something else might be a document that can be displayed or printed: for example, an HTML file, a PDF file, or even audible sound. Converting XML to HTML for display is the most common application of XSLT today, and it is the one that will be used in most of the examples in this chapter. After you have the data in HTML format, it can be displayed on any browser.

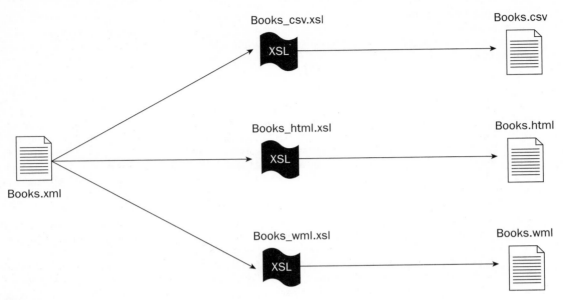

Figure 7-2

To transfer data between different applications, you need to be able to transform information from the data model used by one application to the model used by another. Figure 7-2 shows how an XML file can be converted into multiple formats using XSL style sheets. To load the data into an application, the required format might be a comma-separated-values file, an HTML file, a WML file, or a sequence of calls on a particular programming interface. Alternatively, it might be another XML file using a different vocabulary from the original. As XML-based electronic commerce becomes widespread, the role of XSLT in data conversion between applications also becomes ever more important. Just because everyone is using XML does not mean the need for data conversion will disappear. Because the XML used in those applications have a very different scope and purpose; but ultimately, it can handle the same content in a different form, and there is therefore a need for transformation when information is passed from one industry sector to the other.

XSLT Elements

If you've had the opportunity to work with HTML in the past, you're already aware of how elements are used to perform specific tasks. For example, the `<table>` element can be used along with the `<tr>` and `<td>` elements to construct a table for display in a browser. The `<img>` element can be used when an image needs to be displayed, and the `<form>` element can be used as a container for different form elements such as text boxes and radio buttons. Each of these elements has a specific purpose and when appropriate, can contain supporting child elements.

Similar to the HTML elements, the XSLT specification also lists several elements that can be used to transform XML documents. Table 7-1 contains a listing of important elements of the XSLT specification.

Table 7-1. XSLT Elements

Element	Description
xsl:apply-imports	Applies a template from an imported style sheet. Used in conjunction with imported style sheets to override templates within the source style sheet.
xsl:apply-templates	By default, applies a template rule to the current element or to the current element's child nodes. An XPath expression can be specified in the select attribute to direct the processor process a node set and match accordingly.
xsl:attribute	Represents an attribute node that is attached to an element that appears in the output structure.
xsl:attribute-set	Used when a commonly defined set of attributes will be applied to different elements in the style sheet. This is similar to named styles in CSS.
xsl:call-template	Used when processing is directed to a specific template. The template is identified by name.
xsl:choose	Used in conjunction with <when> and <otherwise> to express multiple conditional tests. Similar to using a switch statement in C# or Select Case statement in VB.NET.
xsl:comment	Creates a comment node in the result tree.
xsl:copy	Creates a copy of the current node (without child nodes and attributes).
xsl:copy-of	Creates a copy of the current node (with child nodes and attributes).
xsl:decimal-format	Defines the characters and symbols to be used when converting numbers into strings, with the format-number() function.
xsl:element	Creates an element with the specified name in the output structure.
xsl:fallback	Specifies an alternate code to run if the processor does not support an XSLT element. This element provides greater flexibility during transformations as new XSLT versions come out in the future.
xsl:for-each	Loops through each node in a specified node set.
xsl:if	Contains a template that will be applied only if a specified condition is true.
xsl:import	Imports the contents of one style sheet into another. Note an imported style sheet has lower precedence than the importing style sheet.
xsl:include	Includes the contents of one style sheet into another. Note an included style sheet has the same precedence as the including style sheet.

Element	Description
xsl:key	Declares a named key that can be used in the style sheet with the key() function.
xsl:message	Writes a message to the output (used to report errors).
xsl:namespace-alias	Replaces a namespace in the style sheet to a different namespace in the output.
xsl:number	Determines the integer position of the current node and formats a number.
xsl:otherwise	Used with the xsl:choose and xsl:when elements to perform conditional testing. Similar to using default in a switch statement.
xsl:output	Defines the format of the output document.
xsl:param	Used to declare a parameter with a local or global scope. Local parameters are scoped to the template in which they are declared.
xsl:preserve-space	Defines the elements for which white space should be preserved.
xsl:processing-instruction	Writes a processing instruction to the output.
xsl:sort	Used with xsl:for-each or xsl:apply-templates to specify sort criteria for selected node lists.
xsl:strip-space	Defines the elements for which white space should be removed.
xsl:stylesheet	Defines the root element of a style sheet. This element must be the outermost element in an XSLT document and must contain a namespace associated with the XSLT specification and a version attribute.
xsl:template	Defines a reusable template for producing output for nodes that match a particular pattern.
xsl:text	Writes literal text to the output.
xsl:transform	Defines the root element of a style sheet.
xsl:value-of	Writes out the value of the selected node to the result tree.
xsl:variable	Used to declare and assign variable values that can be either local or global in scope.
xsl:when	Used as a child element of xsl:choose to perform multiple conditional testing. Similar to using case in a switch or Select statement.
xsl:with-param	Used in passing a parameter to a template that is called via xsl:call-template.

Notice that each element shown in Table 7-1 is prefixed by the xsl namespace. These elements can be used in a variety of ways, including determining the output format, performing if/then type logic, looping, and writing out data within a node contained in the XML document to the result tree structure. An XSLT element is distinguished from other elements that may be within an XSLT document by its association with a namespace that defines a URI of `http://www.w3.org/1999/XSL/Transform`.

XSLT Functions

Now that you have seen the most important XSLT elements, it is time to examine the most important functions. In addition to the XPath core functions, XSLT has some functions of its own. Although the core XPath functions is available to XSLT, the XSLT defined functions are not available to XPath when it is used beyond the confines of XSLT. Table 7-2 provides a listing of the important XSLT functions.

Table 7-2. XSLT Functions

Function	Description
current()	Returns the current node
document()	Used to access the nodes in an XML document, allowing the possibility of accessing data from sources outside the initial data input stream
element-available()	Tests whether the specified element is supported by the XSLT processor
format-number()	Converts a number into a string
function-available()	Tests whether the specified function is supported by the XSLT processor
generate-id()	Returns a string value that uniquely identifies a specified node
key()	Returns a node-set using the index specified by an `<xsl:key>` element
system-property()	Returns the value of the system properties
unparsed-identity-uri()	Returns the URI of an unparsed entity

The names of these functions usually give away what they do and they do not require separate explanation. Now that you have an understanding of the XSLT functions and elements, it is time to examine how to apply those elements and functions for creating XSL style sheets.

Applying an XSL Style Sheet to an XML Document

Essentially, there are two ways to apply an XSLT style sheet to an XML document. You can either reference the style sheet in our XML document, or apply the style sheet programmatically. The first approach is considered static; the latter is more dynamic. You will see an example of the dynamic approach when looking at examples of using an XSL style sheet from an ASP.NET page. For reasons of brevity, the XSL style sheets are simply referred to as style sheets throughout this chapter.

Applying a Style Sheet Statically

To statically link a style sheet to an XML document, you add the `<?xml-stylesheet?>` processing directive to the start of the source XML. For instance, if the `books.xsl` and the `books.xml` files are in the same directory, you could add the following to the top of `books.xml`.

```
<?xml version="1.0" encoding="UTF-8" ?>
<?xml-stylesheet type="text/xsl" href="books.xsl" ?>
<!-- This file represents a fragment of a book store inventory database -->
<bookstore>
   <book genre="autobiography">
     . . .      . . .
     . . .      . . .
   </book>
<bookstore>
```

The type attribute specifies that it is an XSLT style sheet you want to apply, as you could also specify a cascading style sheet by setting this attribute to `"text/css"`. The `href` attribute supplies the location of the style sheet.

A Simple Example

This section provides you with a simple example that demonstrates the use of a style sheet to transform the contents of the XML file. Before looking at the style sheet, consider the XML document shown in Listing 7-1 that contains a simple book store that provides information about the various books that are part of the bookstore.

Listing 7-1: XML Document That Represents the Bookstore

```
<?xml version='1.0'?>
<?xml-stylesheet type="text/xsl" href="Books.xsl"?>
<!-- This file represents a fragment of a book store inventory database -->
<bookstore>
   <book genre="autobiography">
     <title>The Autobiography of Benjamin Franklin</title>
     <author>
       <first-name>Benjamin</first-name>
       <last-name>Franklin</last-name>
     </author>
     <price>8.99</price>
   </book>
   <book genre="novel">
     <title>The Confidence Man</title>
     <author>
       <first-name>Herman</first-name>
       <last-name>Melville</last-name>
     </author>
     <price>11.99</price>
   </book>
   <book genre="philosophy">
     <title>The Gorgias</title>
     <author>
       <name>Plato</name>
     </author>
     <price>9.99</price>
   </book>
</bookstore>
```

Note that the books.xml file shown in Listing 7-1 is used throughout all the examples presented in this chapter. Now that you have created the XML file, it is time to create the style sheet that transforms the XML into HTML. Listing 7-2 shows the declaration of the style sheet.

Listing 7-2: XSLT Style Sheet Used for Transforming the XML

```xml
<?xml version="1.0"?>
<xsl:stylesheet version="1.0" xmlns:xsl="http://www.w3.org/1999/XSL/Transform">
  <xsl:output method="html" />
  <xsl:template match="/">
    <html>
      <title>XSL Transformation</title>
      <body>
        <h2>My Book Collection</h2>
        <table border="1">
          <tr bgcolor="#9acd32">
            <th align="left">Title</th>
            <th align="left">Price</th>
          </tr>
          <xsl:for-each select="bookstore/book">
            <tr>
              <td>
                <xsl:value-of select="title"/>
              </td>
              <td>
                <xsl:value-of select="price"/>
              </td>
            </tr>
          </xsl:for-each>
        </table>
      </body>
    </html>
  </xsl:template>
</xsl:stylesheet>
```

If you have an XSLT compliant browser such as Internet Explorer, it will nicely transform your XML into HTML. Figure 7-3 shows the output in Internet Explorer.

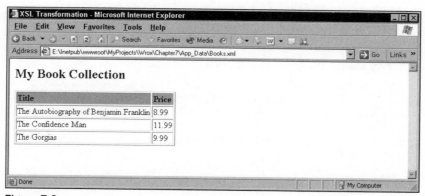

Figure 7-3

If you view the source for this page, you will see the source XML, not the XSLT output that produces the above display. Now that you have a general understanding of the transformation process, it is time to examine the XSL style sheet in depth.

Because the style sheet is an XML document itself, the document begins with an xml declaration:

```
<?xml version="1.0"?>
```

The <xsl:stylesheet> tag defines the start of the style sheet.

```
<xsl:stylesheet version="1.0" xmlns:xsl="http://www.w3.org/1999/XSL/Transform">
```

The <xsl:template> tag defines the start of a template. The match="/" attribute associates (matches) the template to the root (/) of the XML source document, which is the <bookstore> element in this case.

```
<xsl:template match="/">
```

The <xsl:for-each> element allows you to do looping in XSLT. In this case, the <xsl:for-each> element is used to select every XML element of a specified node set.

```
<xsl:for-each select="bookstore/book">
  <tr>
    <td>
      <xsl:value-of select="title"/>
    </td>
    <td>
      <xsl:value-of select="price"/>
    </td>
  </tr>
</xsl:for-each>
```

The <xsl:value-of> element can be used to select the value of an XML element and add it to the output stream of the transformation.

```
<xsl:value-of select="title"/>
```

Note the value of the required select attribute contains an XPath expression. It works like navigating a file system where a forward slash (/) selects subdirectories.

Sorting an XML File Using an XSL Style Sheet

To be able to sort the output of an XML document as it is being transformed through the XSL style sheet, use the <xsl:sort> element. For example, to transform the books.xml file to an HTML output, and sort it at the same time, simply add a sort element inside the <xsl:for-each> element in your XSL file.

```
<xsl:for-each select="bookstore/book">
  <xsl:sort select="title"/>
  <tr>
    <td>
      <xsl:value-of select="title"/>
    </td>
    <td>
```

```
      <xsl:value-of select="price"/>
    </td>
  </tr>
</xsl:for-each>
```

The select attribute in the `<xsl:sort>` element indicates what XML element to sort on.

Evaluating Conditions

The `<xsl:if>` element contains a template that will be applied only if a specified condition is true. To put a conditional if test against the content of the file, simply add an `<xsl:if>` element to your XSL document like this:

```
<xsl:if test="price &gt; 10">
  some output ...
</xsl:if>
```

The value of the required test attribute contains the expression to be evaluated.

```
<xsl:for-each select="bookstore/book">
  <xsl:if test="price &gt; 10">
    <tr>
      <td>
        <xsl:value-of select="title"/>
      </td>
      <td>
        <xsl:value-of select="price"/>
      </td>
    </tr>
  </xsl:if>
</xsl:for-each>
```

This code only selects the title and price if the price of the book is higher than 10.

The result of the transformation will look as shown in Figure 7-4.

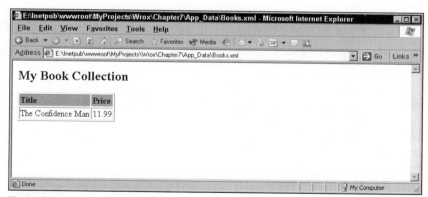

Figure 7-4

Evaluating Multiple Conditions

The `<xsl:choose>` element is used in conjunction with `<xsl:when>` and `<xsl:otherwise>` to express multiple conditional tests. To insert a conditional test against the content of the XML file, simply add the `<xsl:choose>`, `<xsl:when>`, and `<xsl:otherwise>` elements to your XSL document like this:

```
<xsl:choose>
    <xsl:when test="condition">
        ... some code ...
    </xsl:when>
    <xsl:otherwise>
        ... some code ....
    </xsl:otherwise>
</xsl:choose>
```

The following code uses the `<xsl:choose>` element to add appropriate background color to the `td` element in the table, depending on the price range of a book.

```
<xsl:choose>
    <xsl:when test="price &gt; 11">
        <td bgcolor="#ff00ff">
            <xsl:value-of select="price"/>
        </td>
    </xsl:when>
    <xsl:when test="price &gt; 9 and price &lt;= 11">
        <td bgcolor="#cccccc">
            <xsl:value-of select="price"/>
        </td>
    </xsl:when>
    <xsl:otherwise>
        <td>
            <xsl:value-of select="price"/>
        </td>
    </xsl:otherwise>
</xsl:choose>
```

The output produced by the above code is shown in Figure 7-5.

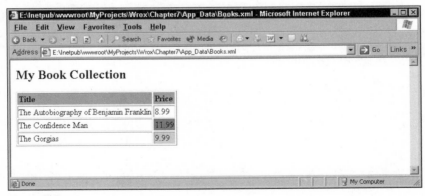

Figure 7-5

\<xsl:apply-templates\> Element

The `<xsl:apply-templates>` element applies a template rule to the current element or to the current element's child nodes. If you add a select attribute to the `<xsl:apply-templates>` element, it will process only the child element that matches the value of the attribute. You can use the select attribute to specify the order in which the child nodes are processed.

Look at the style sheet shown in Listing 7-3.

Listing 7-3: XSLT Style Sheet That Uses \<xsl:apply-templates\> Element

```
<?xml version="1.0"?>
<xsl:stylesheet version="1.0" xmlns:xsl="http://www.w3.org/1999/XSL/Transform">
  <xsl:output method="html" />
  <xsl:template match="/">
    <html>
      <body>
        <h2>My Book Collection</h2>
        <xsl:apply-templates/>
      </body>
    </html>
  </xsl:template>
  <xsl:template match="book">
    <p>
      <xsl:apply-templates select="title"/>
      <xsl:apply-templates select="price"/>
    </p>
  </xsl:template>
  <xsl:template match="title">
    Title:
    <span style="color:#ff0000">
      <xsl:value-of select="."/>
    </span>
    <br/>
  </xsl:template>
  <xsl:template match="price">
    Artist:
    <span style="color:#00ff00">
      <xsl:value-of select="."/>
    </span>
    <br />
  </xsl:template>
</xsl:stylesheet>
```

Although this style sheet uses `<xsl:apply-templates>` element to process the elements, it produces exactly the same result as that of the style sheet shown in Listing 7-2.

XSLT Variables

In XSLT, you can use `<xsl:variable>` to define an XSLT variable. A variable in XSLT functions similar to a named constant in traditional programming languages, such as C/C++. You can use a variable to store values that might be needed repeatedly. A variable is also useful for caching context-sensitive values or a temporary tree during the transformation.

```
<xsl:variable name="variable_name" select="variable_value" />
```

After defined, an XSLT variable cannot be changed until it falls out of its scope. To reference a defined variable, prefix the $ sign to the value of the name attribute of the <xsl:variable> element.

An XSLT variable is global if it is declared as an immediate child element of the <xsl:stylesheet> element. A global variable can be used anywhere in the style sheet. A variable is local if it is declared within a template rule. The scope of a local variable is only within the context in which it is defined.

XSLT Parameters

Parameters are useful in a variety of programming languages, with XSLT being no exception. Parameters can be used in XSLT documents in two basic ways. Parameter values can be passed in from an ASP.NET application. This allows data not found within the XML document or XSLT style sheet to be part of the transformation process. Also, parameter values can be passed between XSLT templates in much the same way that parameters can be passed between functions in C# or VB.NET.

> XSLT parameters differ from XSLT variables in that they can take a value passed in from outside its scope. For example, a global parameter can take a value passed in from a script in an HTML or ASP page. A local parameter can take a value passed in from the calling template rule.

An XSLT parameter is a parameterized XSLT variable. After defined, it cannot be changed until it falls out of its scope. An XSLT parameter is global if it is declared as an immediate child element of the <xsl:stylesheet> element. A global parameter can be used anywhere in the style sheet. A parameter is local if it is declared within a template rule. The scope of a local parameter is only within the context in which it *is* defined.

Declaring a parameter is similar to declaring a variable. Simply name the parameter and add an optional select attribute as follows:

```
<xsl:param name="param_name" select="param_value "/>
```

To reference a defined parameter, prefix the $ sign to the value of the name attribute of the <xsl:param> element.

.NET Classes Involved in XSL Transformation

Now that you've seen the different XSLT elements and functions that are at your disposal, it's time to learn about what classes in the .NET framework can be used in your ASP.NET applications when XSL transformations are necessary. After all, XSLT is simply a text-based language that is of little utility without an XSLT processor.

Several classes built in to the System.Xml assembly can be used when transforming XML into other structures via XSLT. In this section you learn more about these classes and a few others so that you are fully armed with everything you need to know to use XSLT in your ASP.NET applications. Table 7-3 shows the important .NET classes used for XSL transformations.

Table 7-3. .NET Classes Used in XSL Transformations

Class	Description
XslCompiledTransform	Core class that acts as the XSLT processor in .NET Framework 2.0. Used to transform XML data into other structures.
XsltArgumentList	Allows you to pass a variable number of parameters and extension objects to an XSL style sheet
XsltCompileException	This exception is thrown by the Load() method when an error is found in the XSLT style sheet
XsltException	Encapsulates the exception that is thrown when an error occurs while processing an XSLT style sheet
XsltSettings	Allows you to specify the XSLT features to support during execution of the XSLT style sheet
XmlDocument	As shown in Chapter 6, the XmlDocument class implements the IXPathNavigable interface and extends the XmlNode class; used as an input to the XSL transformation process
XmlDataDocument	Extends the XmlDataDocument class and can also be used an input to the XSL transformation process
XPathDocument	Implements the IXPathNavigable interface and provides high throughput when transforming XML via XSLT
XmlWriter	Provides forward-only writing capabilities and can be used to write the output of the transformation to a specific target such as a file, or a stream and so on
XmlReader	Provides forward-only reading capabilities that can be used an input to the transformation process

Because the XPathDocument class implements the IXPathNavigable interface, it is able to leverage features built in to the abstract XPathNavigator class (which, in turn, uses the XPathNodeIterator abstract class for iteration over node-sets) to provide cursor-style access to XML data, resulting in fast and efficient XSL transformations.

> Note that the XslTransform class used for XSL transformations in .NET Framework 1.x is now obsolete and replaced by the new XslCompiledTransform class. In addition to better compliance with the latest XSLT specification, the XslCompiledTransform also provides huge performance improvements over its predecessor. Starting from .NET Framework 2.0, the recommended approach to performing XSL transformations is through the XslCompiledTransform class. Because of the similarity in design to the XslTransform class, you can easily migrate your existing code to utilize the XslCompiledTransform class.

Loading an XslCompiledTransform Object

Before you can transform an XML document into the desired output format, you need to load the
XslCompiledTransform object with the right XSL style sheet. To this end, the XslCompiledTransform
object provides the following overloads:

```
public void Load(IXPathNavigable);
public void Load(string);
public void Load(XmlReader);
public void Load(IXPathNavigable, XsltSettings, XmlResolver);
public void Load(string, XsltSettings, XmlResolver);
public void Load(XmlReader, XsltSettings, XmlResover);
```

As you can see from the overloads, the source of the XSL file can be from either an IXPathNavigable
object, a string, or an XmlReader object. The XsltSettings class allows you to specify the XSLT features to support during the execution of the XSLT style sheet and the XmlResolver resolves any XSLT
import or include elements contained in the XSLT style sheet.

Similar to the Load() method, the Transform() method of the XslCompiledTransform class also provides a number of overloads.

```
public void Transform (IXPathNavigable, XmlWriter)
public void Transform (string, string)
public void Transform (string, XmlWriter)
public void Transform (XmlReader, XmlWriter)
public void Transform (IXPathNavigable, XsltArgumentList, Stream)
public void Transform (IXPathNavigable, XsltArgumentList, TextWriter)
public void Transform (IXPathNavigable, XsltArgumentList, XmlWriter)
public void Transform (string, XsltArgumentList, Stream)
public void Transform (string, XsltArgumentList, TextWriter)
public void Transform (string, XsltArgumentList, XmlWriter)
public void Transform (XmlReader, XsltArgumentList, Stream)
public void Transform (XmlReader, XsltArgumentList, TextWriter)
public void Transform (XmlReader, XsltArgumentList, XmlWriter)
public void Transform (XmlReader, XsltArgumentList, XmlWriter, XmlResolver)
```

The XML input to the Transform() method can be specified as an IXPathNavigable object, a string,
or an XmlReader object. The parameters and extension objects are passed to the XSL style sheet using
the XsltArgumentList object. The output produced by the transformation is captured in a Stream,
TextWriter, or an XmlWriter object. The last argument XmlResolver allows you to resolve the
document() function that is specified in the XSLT style sheet.

Simple XSL Transformation

Listing 7-4 shows the use of XslCompiledTransform class to transform the Books.xml into HTML format using the Books.xsl file.

Listing 7-4: Using the XslCompiledTransform Class

```
<%@ Page Language="C#" %>
<%@ Import Namespace="System.Xml" %>
<%@ Import Namespace="System.Xml.Xsl" %>
<%@ Import Namespace="System.Xml.XPath" %>
<script runat="server">
```

```
void Page_Load(object sender, System.EventArgs e)
{
  string xmlPath = Request.PhysicalApplicationPath +
    @"\App_Data\Books.xml";
  string xslPath = Request.PhysicalApplicationPath +
    @"\App_Data\Books.xsl";
  XPathDocument xpathDoc = new XPathDocument(xmlPath);
  XslCompiledTransform transform = new XslCompiledTransform();
  //Load the XSL stylesheet into the XslCompiledTransform object
  transform.Load(xslPath);
  transform.Transform(xpathDoc, null, Response.Output);
}
</script>
```

This code starts by declaring variables that hold the physical location of the Books.xml and Books.xsl files. You then create an instance of the XPathDocument object passing in the path of the XML file as an argument to it.

```
XPathDocument xpathDoc = new XPathDocument(xmlPath);
```

Now you create an instance of the XslCompiledTransform object and invoke its Load() method to load the style sheet.

```
XslCompiledTransform transform = new XslCompiledTransform();
transform.Load(xslPath);
```

Finally, you call the Transform() method to initiate the transformation process.

```
transform.Transform(xpathDoc, null, Response.Output);
```

Save the page, open up the browser, and navigate to the page. If everything goes fine, you will see the following output.

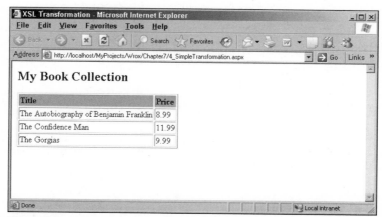

Figure 7-6

Figure 7-6 shows the output produced by the Listing 7-4.

> Note that in the example, I have used the XPathDocument object instead of the XmlDocument object to load the Books.xml file into the memory. This is because of the fact XPathDocument is optimized for processing XSLT and is of read-only mode. Consider using XmlDocument only when there is a need to update the XML document before transformation.

Passing Parameters to an XSL Style Sheet

Parameters or extension objects may also be passed to the style sheet. This is accomplished using the XsltArgumentList class. Passing a parameter to a style sheet gives the programmer the ability to initialize a globally scoped variable, which is defined as any xsl:variable that is a child of the xsl:style sheet and not contained inside an xsl:template. A parameter may be added to the XsltArgumentList class by calling the AddParam method providing a qualified name, the namespace URI, and value. If the parameter value is not a String, Boolean, Number, Node Fragment, or NodeSet, it will be forced to a double or string.

> XsltArgumentList class is a key class that enables you to create XSL reusable and maintainable style sheets by providing a mechanism to pass parameters to an XSL style sheet. It also provides you with the ability to associate a class with the namespace URI, using which you can call the methods of a class directly from a style sheet. These objects whose methods are invoked from the style sheet are called Extension objects.

Before looking at a code example involving the XsltArgumentList class, Table 7-4 shows the key methods of the XsltArgumentList class.

Table 7-4. Methods of the XsltArgumentList Class

Method	Description
AddExtensionObject	Adds a new object to the XsltArgumentList and associates it with the namespace URI
AddParam	Adds a parameter to the XsltArgumentList and associates it with the namespace qualified name
Clear	Removes all parameters and extension objects from the XsltArgumentList
GetExtensionObject	Gets the extension object associated with the given namespace
GetParam	Gets the parameter associated with the namespace qualified name
RemoveExtensionObject	Removes the object with the namespace URI from the XsltArgumentList
RemoveParam	Removes the parameter from the XsltArgumentList

To demonstrate the use of parameters and their use, Listing 7-5 builds on the previous example by adding the capability to calculate and display the discount for the books. The discount for each of the books is calculated by multiplying the discount percentage (which is passed in as a parameter to the style sheet) with the price of the book. To this end, Listing 7-5 declares a XSLT parameter named discount with a default value of .10.

Listing 7-5: XSL Style Sheet That Accepts Parameters

```
<?xml version="1.0"?>
<xsl:stylesheet version="1.0" xmlns:xsl="http://www.w3.org/1999/XSL/Transform">
<xsl:output method="html" />
<!-- Set the Discount parameter -->
<xsl:param name="discount" select=".10" />
  <xsl:template match="/">
    <html>
    <title>XSL Transformation</title>
    <body>
      <h2>My Book Collection</h2>
      <table border="1">
        <tr bgcolor="#9acd32">
          <th align="left">Title</th>
          <th align="left">Price</th>
          <th align="left">Calculated Discount</th>
        </tr>
        <xsl:for-each select="bookstore/book">
          <tr>
            <td>
              <xsl:value-of select="title"/>
            </td>
            <td>
              <xsl:value-of select="price"/>
            </td>
            <td>
              <xsl:value-of select="price * ($discount)"/>
            </td>
          </tr>
        </xsl:for-each>
      </table>
    </body>
    </html>
  </xsl:template>
</xsl:stylesheet>
```

After the declaration of the discount parameter, the code uses the discount parameter to calculate the discount by multiplying it with the value of the price element.

```
<xsl:value-of select="price * ($discount)"/>
```

Although the value of discount was hard-coded in the declaration using the<xsl:param> element, it could just as easily be passed from the calling ASP.NET page, as you see in the next listing. The ASP.NET calling page that passes parameters to the style sheet is shown in Listing 7-6.

Listing 7-6: Passing Parameters to an XSL Style Sheet

```
<%@ Page Language="C#" %>
<%@ Import Namespace="System.Xml" %>
<%@ Import Namespace="System.Xml.Xsl" %>
<%@ Import Namespace="System.Xml.XPath" %>
<script runat="server">
  void Page_Load(object sender, System.EventArgs e)
  {
    string xmlPath = Request.PhysicalApplicationPath +
      @"\App_Data\Books.xml";
    string xslPath = Request.PhysicalApplicationPath +
      @"\App_Data\Books_with_parameters.xsl";
    XPathDocument xpathDoc = new XPathDocument(xmlPath);
    XslCompiledTransform transform = new XslCompiledTransform();
    XsltArgumentList argsList = new XsltArgumentList();
    argsList.AddParam("discount", "", ".15");
    //Load the XSL stylsheet into the XslCompiledTransform object
    transform.Load(xslPath);
    transform.Transform(xpathDoc, argsList, Response.Output);
  }
</script>
```

To supply the discount parameter to the style sheet, you first create an instance of the XsltArgumentList class and invoke its AddParam() method, passing in the name of the parameter and its value as arguments.

```
XsltArgumentList argsList = new XsltArgumentList();
argsList.AddParam("discount", "", ".15");
```

Because the XsltArgumentList class relies on the HashTable class behind the scenes, multiple parameter name/value pairs can be added and stored.

After an XsltArgumentList class has been instantiated and filled with the proper name/value pairs, how do the parameters in the XSLT style sheet get updated with the proper values? The answer is to pass the XsltArgumentList into the XslCompiledTransform class's Transform() method, as follows.

```
transform.Transform(xpathDoc, argsList, Response.Output);
```

Because you have passed in the Response.Output object as an argument to the Transform, the output will be directly sent to the browser.

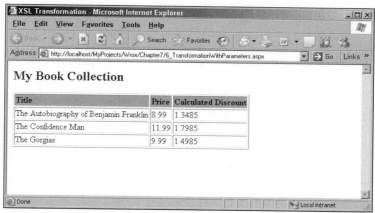

Figure 7-7

If you navigate to the above page from the browser, you will see the output shown in Figure 7-7.

User Defined Functions in an XSL Style Sheet

XSLT is a powerful language that can be used to transform XML into other formats such as HTML, flat-file, and even other forms of XML; however, XSLT does not contain all of the power found in languages such as C# or VB.NET. In situations where you need to perform functions that XSLT does not provide out of the box, you can resort to creating user-defined functions.

Some of the situations where you might need to resort to user-defined functions are:

❑   Call custom business logic

❑   Perform different actions depending on permissions

❑   Perform complex formatting for dates, strings, etc.

❑   Call a Web service

❑   Call methods of the classes in the .NET Framework class library

The `XslCompiledTransform` class provides two primary mechanisms for creating user defined functions. XSL style sheets can embed script functions written in C#, Visual Basic .NET or JScript.NET within `msxsl:script` elements, which can then be invoked from within the style sheet just as if they were regular XSLT functions. You see an example of this approach in the "Embedding Scripts Inside the XSL Style Sheet" section later in this chapter. Another approach is to use XSLT extension objects. Extension objects are regular objects whose public methods are accessible from a style sheet once the objects are added to the `XslCompiledTransform` class through the `AddExtensionObject()` method.

> **An important point of XSLT is that transformation should never provide side-effects. When loading an XSLT extension object, there are times where there might be a problem due to unloading of appdomains for assemblies used in extension objects. Because of this, it is recommended that you perform pre-processing instead of relying on a post-processing approach using extension objects.**

Extension Objects

You can think of an extension object as an external class that can be referenced and used within an XSL style sheet. Because of its powerful nature, extension objects can go a long way in increasing the functionality of style sheets. Extension objects are maintained by the `XsltArgumentList` class. The following are advantages to using an extension object rather than embedded script:

❑   Provides better encapsulation and reuse of classes

❑   Allows style sheets to be smaller and more maintainable

XSLT extension objects are added to the `XsltArgumentList` object using the `AddExtensionObject()` method. A qualified name and namespace URI are associated with the extension object at that time. To use an extension object, you need to go through the following steps:

1.   Create an `XsltArgumentList` object and add the extension object to the `XsltArgumentList` object using `AddExtensionObject()` method

2.   Pass the `XsltArgumentList` object to the `Transform()` method

3.   Call the extension object's methods from the style sheet

To see how this works in practice, the next code sample shown in Listing 7-8 replaces the parameter driven approach used (see Listing 7-5) for calculating the discount with the extension object-based approach. The next section demonstrates the code of the extension class that is used to calculate the discount.

Declaration of the Extension Class

Before looking at the XSL style sheet, take a look at the declaration of the `Discount` class shown in Listing 7-7. When creating the `Discount` class through Visual Studio, remember to place the class in the `App_Code` directory by saying "Yes" to the prompt that asks if you want to place the class in the `App_Code` directory. Placing the class in the `App_Code` directory ensures that the `Discount` class is automatically available to all the Web pages contained within the same virtual directory.

Listing 7-7: Declaration of the Discount Class

```
public class Discount
{
  public Discount()
  {
  }
  public string ReturnDiscount(string price)
  {
    decimal priceValue = Convert.ToDecimal(price);
    return (priceValue * 15/100).ToString();
  }
}
```

The `Discount` class contains only one method, named `ReturnDiscount()`, that calculates the discount and returns the calculated discount to the caller. Since the `ReturnDiscount()` method contains the necessary code to calculate the discount, the XSLT style sheet obviously needs to be able to reference the `Discount` object that is passed in and call its `ReturnDiscount()` method. This is accomplished by adding the proper namespace prefix and URI into the style sheet. Listing 7-8 shows the complete style sheet with the declaration of the namespace and shows how the `ReturnDiscount()` method is invoked.

Listing 7-8: XSL Style Sheet That Leverages the Extension Object

```
<?xml version="1.0"?>
<xsl:stylesheet version="1.0" xmlns:xsl="http://www.w3.org/1999/XSL/Transform"
   xmlns:myDiscount="urn:myDiscount">
  <xsl:output method="html" />
  <xsl:template match="/">
    <html>
    <title>XSL Transformation</title>
    <body>
      <h2>My Book Collection</h2>
      <table border="1">
        <tr bgcolor="#9acd32">
          <th align="left">Title</th>
          <th align="left">Price</th>
          <th align="left">Calculated Discount</th>
        </tr>
        <xsl:for-each select="bookstore/book">
          <tr>
            <td>
              <xsl:value-of select="title"/>
            </td>
            <td>
              <xsl:value-of select="price"/>
            </td>
            <td>
              <xsl:value-of select="myDiscount:ReturnDiscount(price)" />
            </td>
          </tr>
        </xsl:for-each>
      </table>
    </body>
    </html>
  </xsl:template>
</xsl:stylesheet>
```

At the top of the page is the namespace URI declaration of `urn:myDiscount` along with a namespace prefix of `myDiscount`.

```
<xsl:stylesheet version="1.0"
xmlns:xsl="http://www.w3.org/1999/XSL/Transform"
   xmlns:myDiscount="urn:myDiscount">
```

Any namespace URI can be used as long as it is consistent between the ASP.NET page and the style sheet. Listing 7-9 shows how this namespace URI is matched up with the ASP.NET page at the time of passing parameters to the style sheet. After you have the namespace prefix declared, it is then very easy to invoke the `ReturnDiscount()` method.

```
<td>
<xsl:value-of select="myDiscount:ReturnDiscount(price)" />
</td>
```

This line of code invokes the `ReturnDiscount()` method by passing in the value of the price element and simply writes out the returned value onto the browser. The last step in the use of extension objects is the step in which you supply the extension object as a parameter to the XSL style sheet using the `AddExtensionObject()` method of the `XsltArgumentList` object. Listing 7-9 shows how to accomplish this.

Listing 7-9: ASP.NET Page That Supplies the Extension Object to the XSL Style Sheet

```
<%@ Page Language="C#" %>
<%@ Import Namespace="System.Xml" %>
<%@ Import Namespace="System.Xml.Xsl" %>
<%@ Import Namespace="System.Xml.XPath" %>
<script runat="server">
  void Page_Load(object sender, System.EventArgs e)
  {
    string xmlPath = Request.PhysicalApplicationPath +
      @"\App_Data\Books.xml";
    string xslPath = Request.PhysicalApplicationPath +
      @"\App_Data\Books_with_extensions.xsl";
    XPathDocument xpathDoc = new XPathDocument(xmlPath);
    XslCompiledTransform transform = new XslCompiledTransform();
    XsltArgumentList argsList = new XsltArgumentList();
    Discount obj = new Discount();
    argsList.AddExtensionObject("urn:myDiscount", obj);
    //Load the XSL stylsheet into the XslCompiledTransform object
    transform.Load(xslPath);
    transform.Transform(xpathDoc, argsList, Response.Output);
  }
</script>
```

It is important to note that Listing 7-9 utilizes the `AddExtensionObject()` method of the `XsltArgumentList` object to supply the extension object to the style sheet.

```
Discount obj = new Discount();
argsList.AddExtensionObject("urn:myDiscount", obj);
```

These lines of code show how the `Discount` object is created and passed to the style sheet. Note how the namespace URI `"urn:myDiscount"` is associated with the `Discount` object. That's all there is to using an extension object from a style sheet.

Embedding Scripts Inside the XSL Style Sheet

In addition to using the extension objects, you can also embed scripts directly inside the XSL style sheet to execute custom logic. This is accomplished using the `msxsl:script` element. Listing 7-10 shows you an example of how to execute script code from within an XSL style sheet. This example recreates the same discount calculation functionality by using embedded scripts as opposed to using extension objects.

Listing 7-10: XSL Style Sheet That Utilizes the Script

```
<?xml version="1.0"?>
<xsl:stylesheet version="1.0" xmlns:xsl="http://www.w3.org/1999/XSL/Transform"
  xmlns:msxsl="urn:schemas-microsoft-com:xslt"
  xmlns:myDiscount="urn:myDiscount">
```

```
<msxsl:script language="C#" implements-prefix="myDiscount">
  <![CDATA[
  public string ReturnDiscount(string price)
  {
    decimal priceValue = Convert.ToDecimal(price);
    return (priceValue * 15/100).ToString();
  }
]]>
</msxsl:script>
<xsl:output method="html" />
<xsl:template match="/">
  <html>
  <title>XSL Transformation</title>
  <body>
    <h2>My Book Collection</h2>
    <table border="1">
      <tr bgcolor="#9acd32">
        <th align="left">Title</th>
        <th align="left">Price</th>
        <th align="left">Calculated Discount</th>
      </tr>
      <xsl:for-each select="bookstore/book">
        <tr>
          <td>
            <xsl:value-of select="title"/>
          </td>
          <td>
            <xsl:value-of select="price"/>
          </td>
          <td>
            <xsl:value-of select="myDiscount:ReturnDiscount(price)" />
          </td>
        </tr>
      </xsl:for-each>
    </table>
  </body>
  </html>
</xsl:template>
</xsl:stylesheet>
```

The prefix "msxsl" is assumed to be bound to the urn:schemas-microsoft-com:xslt namespace. Languages supported by the script tag include C#, VB.NET, and JScript.NET, which is the default language. An implements-prefix attribute that contains the prefix representing the namespace associated with the script block must also exist in the msxsl:script element. Multiple script blocks may exist in a style sheet, but only one language may be used per namespace. As you can see, the declaration of the ReturnDiscount() method is similar to the previous example that used an extension object to calculate the discount. Now that you have had a look at the XSL style sheet, Listing 7-11 examines the code of the ASP.NET page that leverages the XSL style sheet. Before that, it is important to examine the role of the new class named XsltSettings that allows you to configure the features of the XslCompiledTransform class.

The XsltSettings Class

This new class introduced with .NET Framework 2.0 allows you to specify the XSLT features to support during execution of the XSLT style sheet. For example, embedding script blocks and the use of XSLT `document()` function are optional features on the `XslCompiledTransform` class that are disabled by default. Enabling these features requires you to create an instance of the `XsltSettings` class, set appropriate properties of that object, and supply that as an input to the `Load()` method of the `XslCompiledTransform` object. Table 7-5 discusses the properties of the `XsltSettings` class.

Table 7-5. Properties of the XsltSettings Class

Property	Description
Default	The default setting disables support for the XSLT `document()` function and embedded script blocks and this is a static property
EnableDocumentFunction	Enables the use of XSLT `document()` function inside the XSLT style sheet
EnableScript	Enables you to place script inside the XSLT style sheet
TrustedXslt	This static property exposes an `XsltSettings` object that has support for the XSLT `document()` function and embedded script blocks

Because the XSL style sheet in code Listing 7-10 utilized embedded scripts inside the XSL style sheet, you supply an instance of the `XsltSettings` (with its properties set) to the `Load()` method of the `XslCompiledTransform` object.

Listing 7-11: Embedded Scripts Inside the XSL Style Sheet

```
<%@ Page Language="C#" %>
<%@ Import Namespace="System.Xml" %>
<%@ Import Namespace="System.Xml.Xsl" %>
<%@ Import Namespace="System.Xml.XPath" %>
<script runat="server">
  void Page_Load(object sender, System.EventArgs e)
  {
    string xmlPath = Request.PhysicalApplicationPath +
      @"\App_Data\Books.xml";
    string xslPath = Request.PhysicalApplicationPath +
      @"\App_Data\Books_with_script.xsl";
    XPathDocument xpathDoc = new XPathDocument(xmlPath);
    //Create the XsltSettings object with script enabled.
    XsltSettings settings = new XsltSettings(false, true)
    XslCompiledTransform transform = new XslCompiledTransform();
    //Load the XSL stylesheet into the XslCompiledTransform object
    transform.Load(xslPath, settings, null);
    transform.Transform(xpathDoc, null, Response.Output);
  }
</script>
```

The code shown in Listing 7-10 is similar to the previous transformation examples except for the difference that an `XsltSettings` object is used this time to enable the execution of scripts inside the style sheet. You indicate that you want to enable scripts by passing in appropriate values to the constructor of the `XsltSettings` class.

> `XsltSettings settings = new XsltSettings(false, true)`. **When compared to embedded script, extension objects provide a better alternative to reusing code because of the ability to decouple extension objects from a particular style sheet. Because of this decoupled nature, you can reuse an extension object from multiple XSL style sheets whereas you can't do this with scripts embedded in a XSL style sheet.**

A Complete Example

So far, you have seen the use of the XSLT related .NET classes such as `XslCompiledTransform`, `XsltArgumentList` for transforming an XML document into another format, passing parameters and extension objects to an XSL style sheet, and so on by looking at examples. In this section, you build on the concepts you have learned so far to build a complete solution that uses the combination of XML (which is retrieved from the products table in the `AdventureWorks` database in SQL Server) and XSL to create an ASP.NET page that displays products information (using paging approach) by passing in parameters to the XSL style sheet. It also categorizes the products that belong to a specific category by showing them in a specific background color. You see how to accomplish this functionality through the use of extension objects. Figure 7-8 shows the design of the solution.

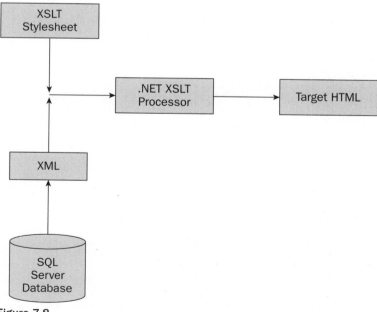

Figure 7-8

As shown in Figure 7-8, you perform the following steps.

❑ Pull products data from the AdventureWorks database in SQL Server in the form of an XML document fragment.

❑ Apply an external style sheet onto the XML data retrieved data from the SQL Server.

❑ At the time of transformation process, also supply the necessary parameters and extension objects to the style sheet.

❑ Write the resultant HTML (created due to the transformation) onto the client browser.

The next few sections provide you with a detailed explanation of the solution by looking at the implementation of the XSL style sheet, extension object, and finally the ASP.NET page.

Implementation of the XSL Style Sheet

To start with, take a look at the style sheet that is used for transformation purposes. Listing 7-12 shows the style sheet.

Listing 7-12: XSL Style Sheet That Displays Product Details

```
<?xml version="1.0" ?>
<xsl:stylesheet version="1.0"
  xmlns:xsl="http://www.w3.org/1999/XSL/Transform"
  xmlns:myColor="urn:myColor">
  <xsl:output method="html" />
<!--Set the paging characteristics - number of records per page, page number
  and the record count-->
<!-- Set the number of records per page-->
<xsl:param name="recordsPerPage" select="504" />
<!-- Page Number field -->
<xsl:param name="pageNumber" select="0" />
<!--Record Count Field-->
<xsl:param name="recordCount" select="504" />
<xsl:template match="/">
<HTML>
  <HEAD>
    <TITLE>Products Display</TITLE>
    </HEAD>
    <BODY>
      <span align="center" style="color:Blue;background-color:White;
        font-weight:bold;height:25px;width:634px;Z-INDEX: 102; LEFT: 203px;
        POSITION: absolute; TOP: 69px">
      Products Display
      </span>
      <table style="Z-INDEX: 101; LEFT: 171px; WIDTH: 501px;
        POSITION: absolute; TOP: 125px; HEIGHT: 322px" border="1"
        cellSpacing="1" cellPadding="1">
        <center>
          <xsl:for-each select="//Products">
            <!--this performs the output in table format - and shows only that many
              records passed in the recordcount parameter -->
            <xsl:if test="position() &gt; $recordsPerPage * number($pageNumber) and
              position() &lt;= number($recordsPerPage * number($pageNumber) +
```

```
          $recordsPerPage)">
          <!-- Each record on a seperate row -->
          <xsl:element name="tr">
            <xsl:attribute name="bgcolor">
              <xsl:value-of select="myColor:ReturnBGColor
                (ProductSubcategoryID)" />
            </xsl:attribute>
            <xsl:element name="td">
              <xsl:value-of select="ProductID" />
            </xsl:element>
            <xsl:element name="td">
              <xsl:value-of select="Name" />
            </xsl:element>
            <xsl:element name="td">
            <xsl:attribute name="align">center</xsl:attribute>
              <xsl:value-of select="ProductNumber" />
            </xsl:element>
            <xsl:element name="td">
              <xsl:attribute name="align">center</xsl:attribute>
              <xsl:value-of select="DaysToManufacture" />
            </xsl:element>
          </xsl:element>
        </xsl:if>
      </xsl:for-each>
    </center>
  </table>
  <!-- Start Of Show previous/next page links-->
  <!-- Show the previous page, only if pageNumber>0  -->
  <span style="Z-INDEX: 101; LEFT: 261px; WIDTH: 501px;
    POSITION: absolute; TOP: 500px; HEIGHT: 62px">
    <xsl:if test="$pageNumber &gt; 0">
      <xsl:element name="a">
        <xsl:attribute name="href">?pagenumber=<xsl:value-of
          select="number($pageNumber)-1" />
        </xsl:attribute>
        &lt;&lt; Previous Page
      </xsl:element>
             
    </xsl:if>
    <!-- Next page, do not show when at end() of listing -->
    <xsl:if test="($recordCount - ((1+number($pageNumber)) *
      $recordsPerPage))&gt; 0">
      <xsl:element name="a">
        <xsl:attribute name="href">?pagenumber=<xsl:value-of
          select="number($pageNumber)+1" />
        </xsl:attribute>
        Next Page &gt;&gt;
      </xsl:element>
    </xsl:if>
    <!-- End Of Show previous/next page links-->
  </span>
</BODY>
</HTML>
</xsl:template>
</xsl:stylesheet>
```

At the top of the `<xsl:stylesheet>` element, there is an attribute named `xmlns:myColor=`
`"urn:myColor"`. This attribute is used to associate a namespace URI for the extension object. The
following line of code creates the association.

```
<xsl:stylesheet version="1.0" xmlns:xsl="http://www.w3.org/1999/XSL/Transform"
  xmlns:myColor="urn:myColor">
```

After you have the association between the object and the namespace URI in place, you then can invoke
methods of the extension object from the style sheet as if it is part of the style sheet. For example, to
invoke the `ReturnBGColor` method, you qualify the name of the method with the namespace URI.

```
<xsl:value-of select="myColor:ReturnBGColor(ProductSubcategoryID)" />
```

As you can see, the `ReturnBGColor()` method takes in the value of the `ProductSubcategoryID`
element as an argument. You will see the implementation of the `ReturnBGColor` method in a moment.

After the declaration of the namespace URL, the style sheet has the following variables defined.

```
<xsl:param name="recordsPerPage" select="504" />
<!-- Page Number field -->
<xsl:param name="pageNumber" select="0" />
<!--Record Count Field-->
<xsl:param name="recordCount" select="504" />
```

These variables are used to define such characteristics as number of records to be shown in a page, the
current page number, and the total number of records contained in the `Product` table. Note that at the
time of defining the parameters, you also assign default values to them, which come into play if the caller
does not pass values to the style sheet.

After these variables are defined, you then use an `xsl:for-each` construct to loop through all the
elements found in the XML data.

```
<xsl:for-each select="//Products">
```

As you can see from the following, the style sheet also contains the necessary logic to display the
Previous Page and Next Page hyperlinks.

```
<xsl:if test="$pageNumber &gt; 0">
<xsl:element name="a">
    <xsl:attribute name="href">?pagenumber=<xsl:value-of
      select="number($pageNumber)-1" />
    </xsl:attribute>
    &lt;&lt; Previous Page
  </xsl:element>
         
</xsl:if>
<!-- Next Page, do not show when at end() of listing -->
<xsl:if test="($recordCount - ((1+number($pageNumber)) *
$recordsPerPage))&gt; 0">
<xsl:element name="a">
    <xsl:attribute name="href">?pagenumber=<xsl:value-of
      select="number($pageNumber)+1" />
    </xsl:attribute>
    Next Page &gt;&gt;
```

```
      </xsl:element>
    </xsl:if>
```

Products that belong to a specific category will show in the same background color. This means you need to be able to determine the background color specific to each of the categories that the products belong to. This is where the BGColor extension object comes into play.

Implementation of the BGColor Class

The BGColor contains a method named ReturnBGColor() that returns the specific background color to be used for a specific category id. The declaration of the BGColor is shown in Listing 7-13.

Listing 7-13: BGColor Class

```
public class BGColor
{
public BGColor()
{
}
public string ReturnBGColor(int categoryID)
{
  string bgColor = null;
    switch (categoryID)
    {
      case (1):
        bgColor = "#FFFFC0";
        break;
      case (2):
        bgColor = "#80FF80";
        break;
      case (3):
        bgColor = "#FFE0C0";
        break;
      case (4):
        bgColor = "#C0C0FF";
        break;
      case (5):
        bgColor = "#C0FFFF";
        break;
      case (6):
        bgColor = "#FFC0FF";
        break;
      case (7):
        bgColor = "#FFC0C0";
        break;
      case (8):
        bgColor = "#C0FFC0";
        break;
      default:
        bgColor = "#C0C0C0";
        break;

    }
   return (bgColor);
  }
}
```

Implementation of the `ReturnBGColor()` method is pretty straightforward. It simply returns an appropriate background color based on the passed category id. Now that you have seen how the `BGColor` class is defined, the next section examines the code of the ASP.NET page that ties the XSL style sheet and the extension objects together.

Implementation of the ASP.NET Page

The ASP.NET page is the one that ties everything together by loading the style sheet, retrieving the XML data from the `AdventureWorks` database, passing parameters and extension objects to the XSL style sheet, and initiating the transformation. Listing 7-14 shows the ASP.NET page.

Listing 7-14: Products Display Page

```csharp
<%@ Page Language="C#" %>
<%@ Import Namespace="System.Xml" %>
<%@ Import Namespace="System.Xml.Xsl" %>
<%@ Import Namespace="System.Xml.XPath" %>
<%@ Import Namespace="System.Data.SqlClient" %>
<%@ Import Namespace="System.Web.Configuration" %>
<script runat="server">
  void Page_Load(object sender, System.EventArgs e)
{
  string xslPath = Request.PhysicalApplicationPath +
    @"\App_Data\ProductsPaging.xsl";
  //Retrieve the connection string from the web.config file
  string connString = WebConfigurationManager.ConnectionStrings
    ["adventureWorks"].ConnectionString;
  SqlConnection sqlConn = new SqlConnection(connString);
  //Open the connection to the database
  sqlConn.Open();
  SqlCommand sqlCommand = new SqlCommand("Select ProductID, Name," +
    "ProductNumber, DaysToManufacture, IsNull(ProductSubcategoryID, 0) " +
    "as ProductSubcategoryID from Production.Product as Products " +
    "for xml auto, elements", sqlConn);
  XmlReader reader = sqlCommand.ExecuteXmlReader();
  //Associate the XmlReader object with the XPathDocument object
  XPathDocument xpathDoc = new XPathDocument(reader);
  //Close the connection to the database
  sqlConn.Close();
  XslCompiledTransform transform = new XslCompiledTransform();
  //Load the XSL stylsheet into the XslCompiledTransform object
  transform.Load(xslPath);
  XsltArgumentList argsList = new XsltArgumentList();
  //Retrieve the pageNumber from querystring
  int pageNumber = Convert.ToInt32(Request.QueryString["pagenumber"]);
  //Add the required parameters to the XmlArgumentList object
  argsList.AddParam("recordsPerPage", "", 10);
  argsList.AddParam("pageNumber", "", pageNumber);
  argsList.AddParam("recordCount", "", 504);
  //Instantiate the object to be added to the XmlArgumentList object
  BGColor obj = new BGColor();
  //Add the Extension object to XmlArgumentList object
  argsList.AddExtensionObject("urn:myColor",obj);
  transform.Transform(xpathDoc, argsList, Response.Output);
  }
</script>
```

In the previous code, you start by retrieving the connection string from the `web.config` file.

```
string connString = WebConfigurationManager.ConnectionStrings
  ["adventureWorks"].ConnectionString;
```

The connection string is stored in the `web.config` file as follows:

```
<connectionStrings>
<add name="adventureWorks" connectionString="server=localhost;
  integrated security=true;database=AdventureWorks"/>
</connectionStrings>
```

After you retrieve the connection string, you supply that as an argument to the constructor of the `SqlConnection` object and then open the connection to the database using the `Open()` method.

```
SqlConnection sqlConn = new SqlConnection(connString);
sqlConn.Open();
```

You then instantiate the SqlCommand object passing in the sql statement to be executed and the `SqlConnection` object as arguments to its constructor.

```
SqlCommand sqlCommand = new SqlCommand("Select ProductID, Name," +
  "ProductNumber, DaysToManufacture, IsNull(ProductSubcategoryID, 0) " +
  "as ProductSubcategoryID from Production.Product as Products " +
  "for xml auto, elements", sqlConn);
```

Next you execute the `sql` query and populate the `XmlReader` object with the results from the execution of the `sql` statement.

```
XmlReader reader = sqlCommand.ExecuteXmlReader();
```

Now that you have the required XML data in an `XmlReader` object, you can easily load it onto an `XPathDocument` object using the following line of code.

```
XPathDocument xpathDoc = new XPathDocument(reader);
```

In the following lines of code, you create an instance of the `XslCompiledTransform` object and then load the object with the XSL file by calling its `Load()` method.

```
XslCompiledTransform transform = new XslCompiledTransform();
transform.Load(xslPath);
```

After that, you create an instance of the `XsltArgumentList` object and then add all the required parameters using the `AddParam()` method calls.

```
XsltArgumentList argsList = new XsltArgumentList();
int pageNumber = Convert.ToInt32(Request.QueryString["pagenumber"]);
argsList.AddParam("recordsPerPage", "", 10);
argsList.AddParam("pageNumber", "", pageNumber);
argsList.AddParam("recordCount", "", 504);
```

In addition to adding the parameters, you also add the extension object using the `AddExtensionObject()` method of the `XsltArgumentList` object. Before that, you create an instance of the `BGColor` object.

```
BGColor obj = new BGColor();
argsList.AddExtensionObject("urn:myColor",obj);
```

After creating an instance of the object, the next step would be to add the instantiated object to the `XsltArgumentList` object. To this method, you pass the namespace to associate the object with and the actual object itself as arguments. In this case, because you want to associate the passed object with the namespace called `urn:myColor`, you pass that in the first argument.

```
argsList.AddExtensionObject("urn:myColor",obj);
```

Finally, you pass in the `XPathDocument` object, and the `XsltArgumentList` object (that consists of the extension object along with the rest of the parameters to the style sheet) to the `Transform()` method using the following line of code.

```
transform.Transform(xpathDoc, argsList, Response.Output);
```

Because the output of the transformation is written to the browser directly, requesting the previous page in a browser results in the following output.

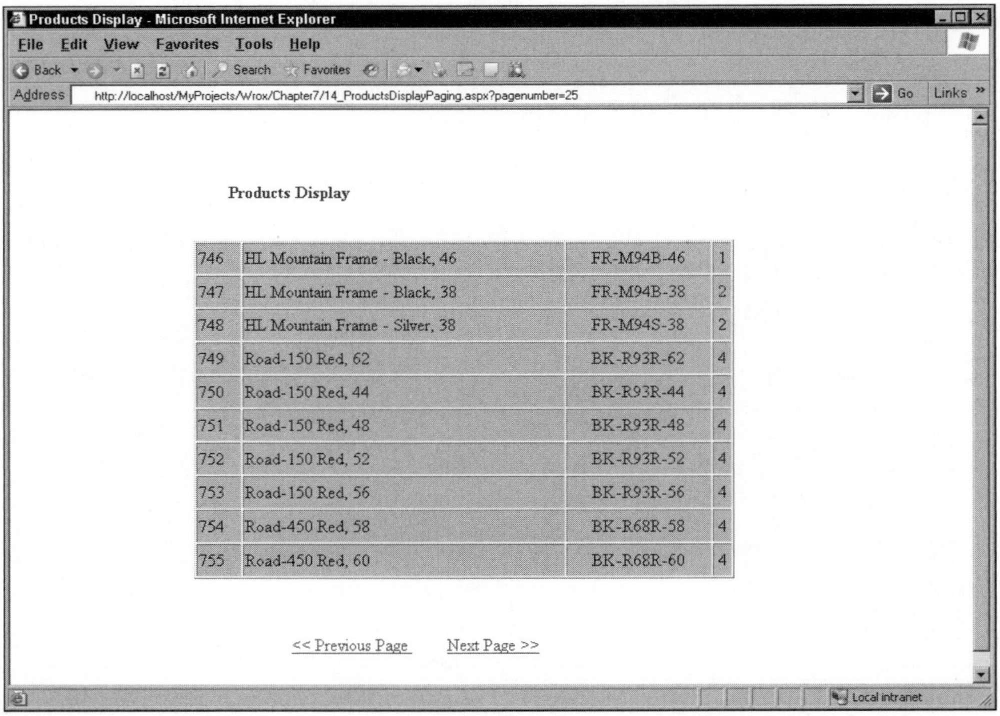

Figure 7-9

In Figure 7-9, you can click on the Next Page and Previous Page hyperlinks to display a specific set of the products in the products page. For reasons of simplicity, this example used hard-coded value for the number of records to be displayed per page as well as the total number of records in the page. But it is very easy to change the code to read those values from a control such as a text box or a drop-down list.

Advanced XSLT Operations

So far, you understand the basics of XSL transformations, passing parameters to an XSL style sheet, and so on. In this section, you see advanced XSLT operations that you can perform using XSLT in conjunction with .NET. To start with, look at how to pass a node-set as a parameter to an XSL style sheet.

Passing a NodeSet as a Parameter to an XSL Style Sheet

This example utilizes the Books.xml shown in Listing 7-1 as the input XML file. The XSL style sheet used for transformation is shown in Listing 7-15.

Listing 7-15: XSL Style Sheet That Accepts NodeSet as a Parameter

```xml
<?xml version="1.0"?>
<xsl:stylesheet version="1.0" xmlns:xsl="http://www.w3.org/1999/XSL/Transform">
  <xsl:output method="html" />
  <!-- Set the Discount parameter -->
  <xsl:param name="booklist" select="/.." />
  <xsl:template match="/">
    <html>
      <title>Passing a NodeSet as a Parameter</title>
      <body>
        <h2>My Book Collection</h2>
        <table border="1">
          <tr bgcolor="#9acd32">
            <th align="left">Title</th>
          </tr>
          <xsl:for-each select="$booklist">
            <tr>
              <td>
                <xsl:value-of select="title"/>
              </td>
            </tr>
          </xsl:for-each>
        </table>
      </body>
    </html>
  </xsl:template>
</xsl:stylesheet>
```

The important line of code to note in Listing 7-15 is the declaration of the parameter named booklist using <xsl:param> element.

```xml
<xsl:param name="booklist" select="/.." />
```

The booklist parameter is the one to which you supply a node set as an argument. Inside the <xsl:for-each> loop, this nodeset parameter is used as an input to loop through all the titles in the bookstore. Now that you have seen the XSL code, look at the code of the ASP.NET page that shows how to pass the nodeset parameter to the XSL style sheet.

Listing 7-16: Passing a NodeSet to an XSL Style Sheet from an ASP.NET Page

```
<%@ Page Language="C#" %>
<%@ Import Namespace="System.Xml" %>
<%@ Import Namespace="System.Xml.Xsl" %>
<%@ Import Namespace="System.Xml.XPath" %>
<script runat="server">
  void Page_Load(object sender, System.EventArgs e)
  {
    string xmlPath = Request.PhysicalApplicationPath + @"\App_Data\Books.xml";
    string xslPath = Request.PhysicalApplicationPath +
      @"\App_Data\Books_with_nodeset_parameter.xsl";
    XPathDocument xpathDoc = new XPathDocument(xmlPath);
    XslCompiledTransform transform = new XslCompiledTransform();
    XsltArgumentList argsList = new XsltArgumentList();
    XPathNavigator navigator = xpathDoc.CreateNavigator();
    XPathNodeIterator iterator = navigator.Select("/bookstore/book");
    argsList.AddParam("booklist", "", iterator);
    //Load the XSL stylsheet into the XslCompiledTransform object
    transform.Load(xslPath);
    transform.Transform(xpathDoc, argsList, Response.Output);
  }
</script>
```

Code shown in Listing 7-16 is similar to the previous examples except in this case, you pass in an `XPathNodeIterator` object as an argument to the XSL style sheet using the `XsltArgumentList` class.

You create the `XPathNodeIterator` object through the `XPathNavigator` object and supply the `XPathNodeIterator` object to the `AddParam()` method.

```
XPathNavigator navigator = xpathDoc.CreateNavigator();
XPathNodeIterator iterator = navigator.Select("/bookstore/book");
argsList.AddParam("booklist", "", iterator);
```

The XSL style sheet receives the booklist parameter and uses that to process the contents of the specific nodes of the XML file and displays the title of all the books in the browser.

Resolving External XSL Style Sheets Using XmlResolver

With the `document()` XSLT function, you can retrieve other XML resources from an XSL style sheet in addition to the initial data that the input stream provides. When using the `document()` function, you need an `XmlResolver` to resolve the `document()` function. The `XmlResolver` is used to resolve external XML resources, such as entities, document type definitions (DTDs), or schemas. `System.Xml.XmlUrlResolver` is a concrete implementation of `XmlResolver` and is the default resolver for all classes in the `System.Xml` namespace. The `XmlResolver` is very flexible in that it enables you to create your own resolver in addition to the default resolvers supplied with the .NET Framework.

Listing 7-17: ASP.NET Page that Resolves External Entities Using XmlSecureResolver

```
<%@ Page Language="C#" %>
<%@ Import Namespace="System.Net" %>
<%@ Import Namespace="System.Xml" %>
<%@ Import Namespace="System.Xml.Xsl" %>
<%@ Import Namespace="System.Xml.XPath" %>
```

```
<script runat="server">
  void Page_Load(object sender, System.EventArgs e)
  {
    string xmlPath = Request.PhysicalApplicationPath +
      @"\App_Data\Books.xml";
    XmlSecureResolver resolver = new XmlSecureResolver(new XmlUrlResolver(),
      "http://localhost");
    NetworkCredential cred = new NetworkCredential("username",
      "password","domain_name");
    resolver.Credentials = cred;
    XPathDocument xpathDoc = new XPathDocument(xmlPath);
    XslCompiledTransform transform = new XslCompiledTransform();
    XsltSettings settings = new XsltSettings();
    settings.EnableDocumentFunction = true;
    //Load the XSL stylsheet into the XslCompiledTransform object
    transform.Load("http://localhost/Books.xsl", settings, resolver);
    transform.Transform(xpathDoc, null, Response.Output);
  }
</script>
```

Listing 7-17 demonstrates the application of XmlSecureResolver class to resolve the Books.xsl, which is stored in http://localhost. Note that the System.Net.NetworkCredential class is leveraged to supply the network credentials to the XmlSecureResolver class.

```
NetworkCredential cred = new NetworkCredential("username",
  "password","domain_name");
resolver.Credentials = cred;
```

You also set the EnableDocumentFunction property of the XsltSettings class to true to indicate that the XSL style sheet uses document() function.

```
settings.EnableDocumentFunction = true;
```

If you navigate to the page shown in Listing 7-17 using the browser, you should see the list of books in the books.xml along with the price information.

Debugging XSLT Style Sheets

XSLT is a powerful technology for transforming XML documents. Depending on your application requirements, the XPath expressions used in XSL style sheets to match nodes in an XML document can be very complex. It can become difficult to debug what is happening in style sheet when the output is not what you expect. Also lack of debugging support from tools such as Visual Studio.NET 2003 did not help either; however, with the release of Visual Studio 2005, things have changed for the better.

> To aid in debugging problems in XSL style sheets, it is often helpful to develop the style sheet in small increments rather than creating the complete style sheet at one time. Write one rule at a time and run your transformation, verifying that the node list returned is what you expect. When you do encounter output that is not what you expect, you can be relatively sure the problem lies in the last rule you added. This can save you valuable time.

Visual Studio 2005 provides excellent built-in support for debugging XSL style sheets. You have all the rich familiar debugging features of Visual Studio such as Locals window, Immediate window, and so on available at your disposal for debugging an XSL style sheet. To debug an XSL style sheet using Visual Studio 2005, go through the following steps.

1. Set up break points in the style sheet.

2. Select Debug XSLT option from the XML menu.

To debug the `books.xsl`, open up the `books.xsl` file from the editor and set up break points in the XSL code. Figure 7-10 shows the Visual Studio editor with the break points set in the `books.xsl` file.

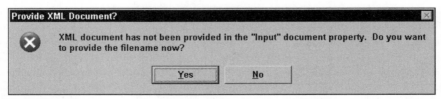

```
Chapter7 (2) - Microsoft Visual Studio
File  Edit  View  Website  Build  Debug  XML  Tools  Window  Community  Help

                                      Debug        .NET

App_Data/Books.xsl
    <?xml version="1.0"?>
    <xsl:stylesheet version="1.0" xmlns:xsl="http://www.w3.org/1999/XSL/Transform">
      <xsl:output method="html" />
      <xsl:template match="/">
        <html>
          <title>XSL Transformation</title>
          <body>
            <h2>My Book Collection</h2>
            <table border="1">
              <tr bgcolor="#9acd32">
                <th align="left">Title</th>
                <th align="left">Price</th>
              </tr>
              <xsl:for-each select="bookstore/book">
                <tr>
                  <td>
                    <xsl:value-of select="title"/>
                  </td>
                  <td>
                    <xsl:value-of select="price"/>
                  </td>
                </tr>
              </xsl:for-each>
            </table>
          </body>
        </html>
      </xsl:template>
    </xsl:stylesheet>

Ready                                    Ln 21     Col 20    Ch 20          INS
```

Figure 7-10

Now if you select the Debug XSLT option from the XML menu, you get a prompt asking you to provide an input XML document for the transformation process. This is shown in Figure 7-11.

```
Provide XML Document?                                               X

    X     XML document has not been provided in the "Input" document property.  Do you want
          to provide the filename now?

                        Yes                No
```

Figure 7-11

Say Yes to the prompt in Figure 7-11 and select the `Books.xml` file as the input XML document. This results in Visual Studio stopping in the break points provided in the `books.xsl`. Figure 7-12 shows the Visual Studio XSL Debugger in action.

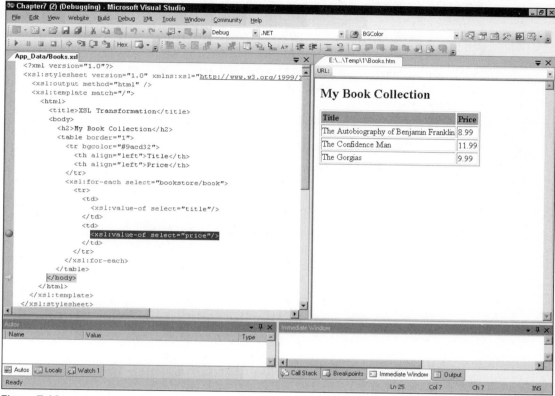

Figure 7-12

After you hit the break point, you will be able to leverage the rich debugging features of Visual Studio editor and perform operations such as looking at the values of the variables, modifying the value of a variable at runtime and so on. Figure 7-12 also shows how the page result window (shown on the right side of Visual Studio) within the Visual Studio editor can be used to examine the output of the transformation as you go through the debugging process.

Summary

XSLT provides a cross-platform, language-independent solution that can be used to transform XML documents into a variety of structures. Although XSLT is a large topic that can't possibly be covered in a single chapter, you have been exposed to some of the more important aspects of the language that will get you started transforming XML documents in ASP.NET applications. In this chapter, you learned the basics of XSLT and XSLT support in .NET Framework 2.0 through discussion and examples. In particular, you saw:

❑ How XSLT is a declarative language with procedural elements, matching XPath expressions to apply templates to nodes in the source tree, while including control flow elements to provide the procedural aspects

❑ A number of the elements used in XSLT, and how you can write useful style sheets with just this subset of the language

❑ A few of the functions built into the language, and how you can use these to give more control over your processing

❑ Different XSLT related classes provided by the .NET Framework such as `XslCompiledTransform`, `XPathDocument` that enable you to transform one XML data format into another XML format

❑ How to supply parameters to a style sheet from an ASP.NET page

❑ How to invoke the methods of an extension object from within a style sheet

❑ How to execute script code that is embedded inside the style sheet

❑ How to pass a node set as a parameter to an XSL style sheet

❑ How to resolve an external style sheet using `XmlResolver`

❑ How to debug an XSLT style sheet from within Visual Studio 2005

8

XML and ADO.NET

Despite the ubiquitous presence of relational databases as the powerhouses of most commercial environments today, the use of XML as a data format is growing steadily. The ease of transmission and storage of XML as a text document (or within a database table as text), and its inherent cross-platform nature make it ideal for many situations. In fact, within the .NET Framework, XML is actually the foundation for all data storage and serialization. One of the important areas where you can see this deep XML integration is the ADO.NET technology. In ADO.NET, XML is used to facilitate storing, manipulating, reorganizing, and sharing your data. Whenever requested, ADO.NET converts your data to or from XML on demand. Now with the release of .NET Framework 2.0, Microsoft has raised the bar to a great extent. A good example is the addition of XML-related features to the `DataTable` object. Using these features, your programs can retrieve relational data and load into an XML DOM object such as an `XmlDataDocument` and vice versa for easy navigation of data. In this chapter, you learn about the XML support provided by ADO.NET 2.0.

Specifically, this chapter explores the following areas.

- ❑ Built-in support provided by the `DataSet` object for XML data manipulation
- ❑ Loading an XML document and an XSD schema into a `DataSet`
- ❑ How to transform the contents of a DataSet to XML
- ❑ How to control the rendering behavior of the data columns inside a `DataSet`
- ❑ How to retrieve XML data in the form of a string from a `DataSet`
- ❑ How to generate a Typed `DataSet` using XSD schema
- ❑ Using annotations with a Typed `DataSet`
- ❑ Relationship between `XmlDataDocument` and `DataSet`
- ❑ How to switch between relational view and hierarchical views of the data using `XmlDataDocument` in conjunction with `DataSet`
- ❑ How to merge data with an `XmlDataDocument`
- ❑ New XML features of `DataTable`

Let's start by discussing the `DataSet` object and the XML support it offers.

ADO.NET and XML

One of the key objects in ADO.NET is the `DataSet`. A `System.Data.DataSet` object stores data in a hierarchical object model and hence is similar to a relational database in structure. Besides storing data in a disconnected cache, a `DataSet` also stores information such as the constraints and relationships that are defined for the `DataSet`. You use a `DataSet` to access data from the tables when disconnected from the data source. You can access the ADO.NET DataSet objects in two pathways regardless of the data source: the DataSet properties, methods, and events; and the XML DOM through the use of `XmlDataDocument` object. Both of these techniques have parallel access methods that permit you to follow sequential or hierarchical paths through your data.

ADO.NET supports the ability to construct `DataSet` objects from either XML streams or documents. These XML sources can include data or schema, or both. The schema is expressed as Extensible Schema Definition language (XSD) — another form of XML. You can also export data from a DataSet to an XML document, with or without the schema. This is handy when you have to send data through a firewall; in most situations, a firewall won't permit you to pass binary data.

> A `DataSet` can either be a typed DataSet or an untyped `DataSet`. A typed `DataSet` is a class derived from a `DataSet` class and has an associated XML Schema. On the other hand, an untyped `DataSet` does not have an associated XML Schema. You see more on typed `DataSets` later in this chapter.

Now that you have an understanding of the `DataSet`, the next section goes into more detail on how to populate a `DataSet` with XML data from an XML document and how to save the contents of a `DataSet` as XML.

Loading XML into a DataSet

There are several ways in which you can populate a `DataSet` with XML, but the most common is probably to use one of the eight different versions of the `DataSet.ReadXml()` method. Here are the first four.

- ❑ `ReadXml(Stream)`: This loads the `DataSet` with the XML in the stream object — that is, any object that inherits from `System.IO.Stream`, such as `System.IO.FileStream`; however, it could just as easily be a stream of data coming down from a Web site, and so on.

- ❑ `ReadXml(String)`: This loads the `DataSet` with the XML stored in the file whose name you provide.

- ❑ `ReadXml(TextReader)`: This loads the `DataSet` with the XML processed by the given text reader — that is, any object that inherits from `System.IO.TextReader`.

- ❑ `ReadXml(XmlReader)`: This loads the `DataSet` with the XML processed by the given XML reader. As you've seen, the `XmlValidatingReader` class inherits from `System.Xml.XmlReader`, so you can pass an `XmlValidatingReader` to this function.

The other four `ReadXml()` overloads correspond to the previous four, but with an additional parameter of type `XmlReadMode`, which is the focus in the next section.

XmlReadMode

The `System.Data.XmlReadMode` enumeration is used to determine the behavior of the XML parser when loading documents from various sources. Table 8-1 shows the members of the `XmlReadMode` enumeration, and the impact they have on the `DataSet` and how it loads the XML.

Table 8-1. Members of XmlReadMode Enumeration

Member	Description
Auto	This is the default. It attempts to select one of the other previous options automatically. If the data being loaded is a `DiffGram`, the `XmlReadMode` is set to `DiffGram`. If the `DataSet` has already been given a schema by some means, or the XML document has an inline schema defined, the `XmlReadMode` is set to `ReadSchema`. If the `DataSet` doesn't contain a schema, there is no inline schema defined and the XML document is not a `DiffGram`, the `XmlReadMode` is set to InferSchema. Because of this indirection, the `XmlReadMode.Auto` may be slower than using an explicit mode.
ReadSchema	This option loads any inline schema supplied by the `DataSet` and then load the data. If any schema information exists in the `DataSet` prior to this operation, the schema can be extended by the inline XML schema. If new table definitions exist in the inline schema that already exists in the `DataSet`, however, an exception will be thrown.
IgnoreSchema	Ignores any inline schema and loads the data into the existing `DataSet` schema. Any data that does not match the schema is discarded. If you are bulk loading data from existing XML sources, it might be useful to enable this option to get better performance.
InferSchema	This option forces the `DataSet` to infer the schema from the XML document, ignoring any inline schema in the document, and extending any schema already in place in the `DataSet`.
DiffGram	An XML representation of a "before" and "after" state for data. If you specify this argument, the `DataSet` loads a `DiffGram` and applies the changes it indicates to the `DataSet`.
Fragment	This option reads XML fragments like an XML document without a single root element. An example of this is the XML output generated by FOR XML queries. In this option, the default namespace is read as the inline schema.

> Depending on how much decision making needs to take place, using the default
> Auto mode may perform more slowly than explicitly setting the read mode. A good
> rule of thumb is to supply the read mode explicitly whenever you know what it will
> be ahead of time.

Now that you have some information on the `ReadXml()` method and how to process XML, load some
XML data into a `DataSet`. Before looking at the code, it is useful to examine the XML file (named
`Products.xml`) to be used. It is as follows:

```xml
<?xml version="1.0" standalone="yes"?>
<DocumentElement>
  <Products>
    <ProductID>1</ProductID>
    <ProductName>Chai</ProductName>
    <SupplierID>1</SupplierID>
    <CategoryID>1</CategoryID>
    <QuantityPerUnit>10 boxes x 20 bags</QuantityPerUnit>
    <UnitPrice>18.0000</UnitPrice>
    <UnitsInStock>39</UnitsInStock>
    <UnitsOnOrder>0</UnitsOnOrder>
    <ReorderLevel>10</ReorderLevel>
    <Discontinued>false</Discontinued>
  </Products>
  -----
  -----
</DocumentElement>
```

You can download the complete code of Products.xml from the Wrox Web site along with the support
material for this book. In Listing 8-1, you load the Products.xml file into a `DataSet` and then display that
information in a GridView control.

Listing 8-1: Reading XML into a DataSet Using ReadXml

```csharp
<%@ Page Language="C#" %>
<%@ Import Namespace="System.Configuration"%>
<%@ Import Namespace="System.Data"%>
<script runat="server">
void Page_Load(Object sender, EventArgs e)
{
    DataSet productsDataSet;
    string filePath = Server.MapPath("App_Data/Products.xml");
    productsDataSet = new DataSet();
    //Read the contents of the XML file into the DataSet
    productsDataSet.ReadXml(filePath);
    gridProducts.DataSource = productsDataSet.Tables[0].DefaultView;
    gridProducts.DataBind();
}
</script>
<html xmlns="http://www.w3.org/1999/xhtml" >
<head runat="server">
  <title>Reading XML Data into a DataSet object </title>
</head>
```

```
<body>
<form id="form1" runat="server">
    <div>
      <asp:GridView id="gridProducts" runat="server"
        AutoGenerateColumns="False" CellPadding="4"
        HeaderStyle-BackColor="blue" HeaderStyle-ForeColor="White"
        HeaderStyle-HorizontalAlign="Center" HeaderStyle-Font-Bold="True">
        <Columns>
          <asp:BoundField HeaderText="Product ID" DataField="ProductID" />
          <asp:BoundField HeaderText="Price"
            DataField="UnitPrice" ItemStyle-HorizontalAlign="Right" />
          <asp:BoundField HeaderText="Name" DataField="ProductName" />
          <asp:BoundField HeaderText="Description"
            DataField="QuantityPerUnit" />
        </Columns>
      </asp:GridView>
    </div>
  </form>
</body>
</html>
```

In Listing 8-1, you load an XML file into a DataSet using the ReadXml() method and then simply bind the DataSet onto a GridView control that renders the DataSet contents onto the browser. Navigate to the page and you should see an output similar to Figure 8-1.

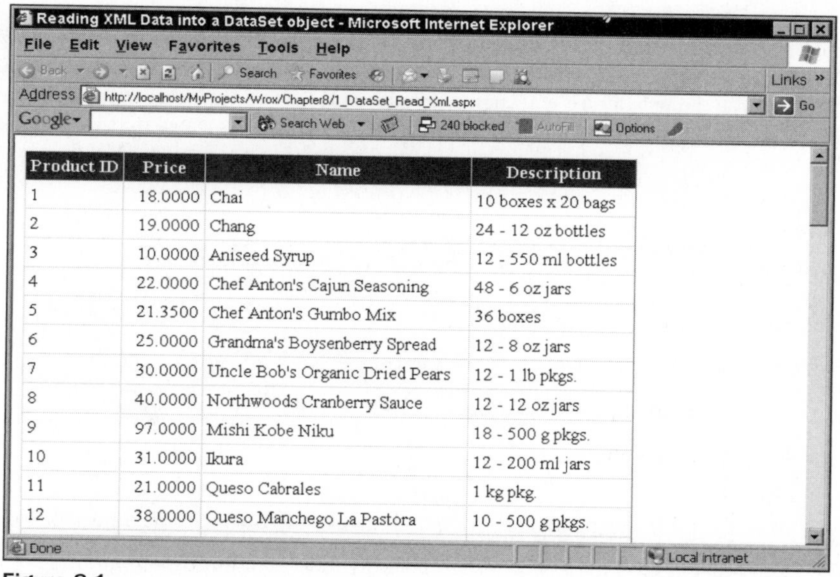

Figure 8-1

If you call ReadXml() to load a very large file, you may encounter slow performance. To ensure best performance for ReadXml(), on a large file, call the DataTable.BeginLoadData() method for each table in the DataSet and then call ReadXml(). Finally, call DataTable.EndLoadData() for each table in the DataSet as shown in the following example.

```
foreach (DataTable t in ds.Tables)

   t.BeginLoadData();

ds.ReadXml("file.xml");

foreach (DataTable t in ds.Tables)

   t.EndLoadData();
```

The `BeginLoadData()` *method turns off notifications, index maintenance, and constraints while loading data. The* `EndLoadData()` *method turns on notifications, index maintenance, and constraints after loading data.*

DataSet Schemas

In the previous section, you learned that you can load a `DataSet` with XML data by using the `ReadXml()` method of the DataSet object. But what do you do when you want to load a `DataSet` schema from an XML document?

You use either the `ReadXmlSchema()` or the `InferXmlSchema()` method of the `DataSet` to load `DataSet` schema information from an XML document. Before looking at these methods, it is important to understand what schema inference is.

Schema Inference

Schema inference is a process that's performed when a `DataSet` object without an existing data structure attempts to load data from an XML document. The `DataSet` will make an initial pass through the XML document to infer the data structure and then a second pass to load the `DataSet` with the information contained in the document. There is a set of rules for inferring `DataSet` schemas that is always followed. Therefore, you can accurately predict what the schema inferred from a given XML document will look like.

Inference Rules

When inferring a schema from an XML document, a `DataSet` follows these rules.

❑   Elements with attributes become tables.

❑   Elements with child elements become tables.

❑   Repeating elements become columns in a single table.

❑   Attributes become columns.

❑   If the document (root) element has no attributes and no child elements that can be inferred to be columns, it is inferred to be a `DataSet`; otherwise, the document element becomes a table.

❑   For elements inferred to be tables that have no child elements and contain text, a new column called `Tablename_Text` is created for the text of each of the elements. If an element with both child nodes and text is inferred to be a table, the text is ignored.

❑   For elements that are inferred to be tables nested within other elements inferred to be tables, a nested `DataRelation` is created between the two tables.

Inference Rules in Action

Consider a sample XML document to understand what kind of schema the `DataSet` will infer from that XML document.

```xml
<?xml version="1.0" standalone="yes"?>
<Products>
 <Product>
    <ProductID>1</ProductID>
    <ProductName>Chai</ProductName>
 </Product>
</Products>
```

If you load the XML into a `DataSet` object, you will notice that the `DataSet` automatically infers the schema; then, if you write the schema of the `DataSet` object to an XSD file using the `WriteXmlSchema()` method, you will see the output shown in Listing 8-2.

Listing 8-2: XSD Schema Produced through Schema Inference

```xml
<?xml version="1.0" standalone="yes"?>
<xs:schema id="Products" xmlns="" xmlns:xs="http://www.w3.org/2001/XMLSchema"
xmlns:msdata="urn:schemas-microsoft-com:xml-msdata">
<xs:element name="Products" msdata:IsDataSet="true"
  msdata:UseCurrentLocale="true">
    <xs:complexType>
      <xs:choice minOccurs="0" maxOccurs="unbounded">
        <xs:element name="Product">
          <xs:complexType>
            <xs:sequence>
              <xs:element name="ProductID" type="xs:string" minOccurs="0" />
              <xs:element name="ProductName" type="xs:string" minOccurs="0" />
            </xs:sequence>
          </xs:complexType>
        </xs:element>
      </xs:choice>
    </xs:complexType>
</xs:element>
</xs:schema>
```

As you can see from the XSD schema output, the schema inference process has automatically inferred a `DataSet` named Products, with a single table named Product. The most interesting aspect is that this provides a schema inference tool that can be used in other contexts. For example, you can utilize the schema inference tool to generate a schema that can be used to create a typed `DataSet` later in the chapter.

Supplied Schemas

Instead of allowing the `DataSet` to infer the schema, you can supply a schema to a `DataSet` explicitly. This is important because there are some limitations with the schema inference mechanism. For example, schema inference can only go so far before it deviates from how you would really like the data to be organized. It can't infer data types, and it won't infer existing column relationships — instead, it creates new columns and new relationships.

Because of the inherent problems related to schema inference, there are times you might want to explicitly supply a schema to your DataSet object. There are several ways you can accomplish this. Obviously, you can create one yourself by creating tables and columns in a DataSet object and by using the WriteXmlSchema() method as described previously. Alternatively, you can supply an XSD file (or an XmlSchema class) to the DataSet, or you can give the responsibility of generating the internal relational structure to a DataAdapter. When you supply a schema upfront, you can enforce constraints and richness of programming through Intellisense. The next section starts by looking at the last of those options first.

The FillSchema Method

The DataAdapter has a FillSchema() method that executes a query on the database to fill the schema information of table/tables into a DataSet. For an example of a situation in which this facility might be useful, imagine that you have an XML document whose data you would eventually like to add to a SQL Server database. As a first step toward doing that, you simply fill the DataSet with the schema of the ContactType table and then load the XML document with the DataSet's ReadXml() method. After that, you can easily use the DataSet to add to the SQL Server database. Before looking at the ASP.NET page, examine the ContactType.xml used for the purposes of this example.

```
<?xml version="1.0" standalone="yes"?>
<ContactType>
  <Table>
    <ContactTypeID>1</ContactTypeID>
    <Name>Accounting Manager</Name>
    <ModifiedDate>6/1/1998</ModifiedDate>
  </Table>
  <Table>
    <ContactTypeID>2</ContactTypeID>
    <Name>Assistant Sales Agent</Name>
    <ModifiedDate>6/1/1998</ModifiedDate>
  </Table>
</ContactType>
```

Now that you have looked at the XML file, Listing 8-3 shows the ASP.NET page in action.

Listing 8-3: Loading Schemas through FillSchema Method

```
<%@ Page Language="C#" %>
<%@ Import Namespace="System.Web.Configuration"%>
<%@ Import Namespace="System.Data"%>
<%@ Import Namespace="System.Data.SqlClient"%>
<script runat="server">
void Page_Load(Object sender, EventArgs e)
{
  string filePath = Server.MapPath("App_Data/ContactType.xml");
    string connString = WebConfigurationManager.
      ConnectionStrings["adventureWorks"].ConnectionString;
    string sql = "Select ContactTypeID, Name from Person.ContactType";
    DataSet contactsDataSet = new DataSet("ContactType");
    using (SqlConnection sqlConn = new SqlConnection(connString))
    {
      SqlDataAdapter adapter = new SqlDataAdapter(sql, sqlConn);
      adapter.FillSchema(contactsDataSet, SchemaType.Source);
    }
```

```
    contactsDataSet.ReadXml(filePath);
    DataTable table = contactsDataSet.Tables[0];
    int numCols = table.Columns.Count;
    foreach (DataRow row in table.Rows)
    {
        for (int i = 0; i < numCols; i++)
        {
            Response.Write(table.Columns[i].ColumnName +
                " = " + row[i].ToString() + "<br>");
        }
        Response.Write("<br>");
    }
}
</script>
<html xmlns="http://www.w3.org/1999/xhtml" >
<head runat="server">
    <title>Loading XML Schema using FillSchema method</title>
</head>
<body>
<form id="form1" runat="server">
    <div>
    </div>
    </form>
</body>
</html>
```

For the code to work, you need to ensure that the web.config file has the `<connectionStrings>` element present as follows:

```
<connectionStrings>
    <add name="adventureWorks" connectionString="server=localhost;integrated
    security=true;database=AdventureWorks;"/>
</connectionStrings>
```

After you have the connection string in the web.config file, you can then easily retrieve the connection string from within the ASP.NET page.

```
string connString = ConfigurationManager.
    ConnectionStrings["adventureWorks"].ConnectionString;
```

After you have loaded the required schema from the `ContactType` table through the `FillSchema()` method, you can then simply load the `ContactType.xml` document into the `DataSet` by calling the `ReadXml()` method.

Similar to loading the `DataSet` with the schema of the database table, you can also load a `DataTable` with the schema of the database table and then load that `DataTable` with XML data from an external XML document. This is made possible by the new XML support offered by the `DataTable`.

The ReadXmlSchema Method

You use the `ReadXmlSchema()` method when you want to load only `DataSet` schema information (and no data) from an XML document. This method loads a `DataSet` schema using the XSD schema. The `ReadXmlSchema()` method takes a stream, an `XmlReader`, or a file name as a parameter. In the event of absence of an inline schema in the XML document, the `ReadXmlSchema()` method interprets the schema from the elements in the XML document. When you use the ReadXmlSchema() method to load a DataSet that already contains a schema, the existing schema is extended, and new columns are added to the tables. Any tables that do not exist in the existing schema are also added. Note the ReadXmlSchema() method throws an exception if the types of the column in the DataSet and the column in the XML document are incompatible.

The InferXmlSchema Method

You can also use the InferXmlSchema() method to load the DataSet schema from an XML document. This method has the same functionality as that of the ReadXml() method that uses the XmlReadMode enumeration value set to InferSchema. The InferXmlSchema() method, besides enabling you to infer the schema from an XML document, enables you to specify the namespaces to be ignored when inferring the schema. This method takes two parameters. The first parameter is an XML document location, a stream, or an XmlReader; the second parameter is a string array of the namespaces that need to be ignored when inferring the schema.

Transforming DataSet to XML

You can easily fill a DataSet with data from an XML stream or document. The information supplied from the XML stream or document can be combined with existing data or schema information that is already present in the DataSet. On the other side, you can use the WriteXml() method of the DataSet object to serialize the XML representation of the DataSet to a file, a stream, an XmlWriter object, or a string. While serializing the contents, you can optionally include the schema information.

> Using ADO.NET, you can create an XML representation of a DataSet, with or without its schema, and transport the DataSet across HTTP for use by another application or XML-enabled platform. In an XML representation of a DataSet, the data is written in XML and the schema is written using the XML Schema definition language (XSD). Using industry standards such as XML and XML schema, you can seamlessly interact with XML-enabled applications that may be running in a completely different platform.

To control the actual behavior of the WriteXml() method, you set the XmlWriteMode enumeration to any of the values shown in Table 8-2. The values supplied to the XmlWriteMode enum determine the layout of the XML output. The DataSet representation includes tables, relations, and constraints definitions. The rows in the DataSet's tables are written in their current versions unless you choose to employ the DiffGram format. Table 8-2 summarizes the writing options available with XmlWriteMode.

Table 8-2. Members of XmlWriteMode Enumeration

Member	Description
DiffGram	Allows you to write the entire DataSet as a DiffGram, including original and current values
IgnoreSchema	Writes the contents of the DataSet as XML data, without an XSD schema
WriteSchema	Writes the contents of the DataSet as XML data with relational structure as inline XSD schema

As you can see, ADO.NET allows you to write XML data with or without the XML schema. When you write DataSet data as XML data, the current version of the DataSet rows is written; however, ADO.NET enables you to write the DataSet data as a DiffGram, which means that both original as well as current versions of the rows would be included. Before proceeding further with an example, it is important to understand what DiffGrams are.

DiffGrams

A DiffGram is in XML format and is used by the DataSet to store the contents. A DiffGram is used to discriminate between the original and current versions of data. When you write a DataSet as a DiffGram, the DiffGram is populated with all information that is required to re-create the contents of the dataset. These contents include the current and original values of the rows and the error information and order of the rows; however, the DiffGram format doesn't get populated with the information to re-create the XML schema. A DataSet also uses the DiffGram format to serialize data for transmission across the network.

> The DiffGram **format is used by default when you send and extract a** DataSet **from a Web service. In addition, you can explicitly specify that the dataset be read or written as a** DiffGram **when using the** ReadXml() **and** WriteXml() **methods.**

The DiffGram format consists of the following data blocks:

- ❏ <DataInstance> represents a row of the DataTable object or a dataset and contains the current version of data.

- ❏ <diffgr:before> contains the original version of the dataset or a row.

- ❏ <diffgr:errors> contains the information of the errors for a specific row in the <DataInstance> block.

Note the element or row that has been edited or modified is marked with the <diff:hasChanges> annotation in the current data section. Now that you have the basic knowledge of DiffGram, you will learn how you can write a dataset as XML data. If you want to write the XML representation of the DataSet to an XmlWriter, a stream, or a file, you need to use the WriteXml() method. The WriteXml() method takes two parameters. The first parameter is mandatory and is used to specify the destination of XML output. The second parameter is optional and is used to specify how the XML output would be written. The second parameter of the WriteXml() method is the XmlWriteMode enumeration to which you can pass in any of the values shown in Table 8-2.

Listing 8-4 shows you an example on how to serialize the DataSet to an XML file using the WriteXml() method of the DataSet. It also shows how easily you can cache the contents of the DataSet in a local XML file that obviates the need to retrieve the data from the database every time.

Listing 8-4: Serializing DataSet to XML Using WriteXml

```
<%@ Page Language="C#" %>
<%@ Import Namespace="System.Web.Configuration"%>
<%@ Import Namespace="System.Data"%>
<%@ Import Namespace="System.Data.SqlClient"%>
<%@ Import Namespace="System.IO"%>
<script runat="server">
```

```
void Page_Load(Object sender, EventArgs e)
{
    DataSet contactsDataSet;
    string filePath = Server.MapPath("App_Data/ContactType.xml");
    //Check if the file exists in the hard drive
    if (File.Exists(filePath))
    {
      contactsDataSet = new DataSet();
      //Read the contents of the XML file into the DataSet
      contactsDataSet.ReadXml(filePath);
    }
    else
    {
      contactsDataSet = GetContactTypes();
      //Write the contents of the DataSet to a local XML file
      contactsDataSet.WriteXml(filePath);
    }
    gridContacts.DataSource = contactsDataSet.Tables[0].DefaultView;
    gridContacts.DataBind();
}

DataSet GetContactTypes()
{
    string connString = WebConfigurationManager.
      ConnectionStrings["adventureWorks"].ConnectionString;
    string sql = "Select ContactTypeID, Name from Person.ContactType";
    DataSet contactsDataSet = new DataSet("ContactType");
    using (SqlConnection sqlConn = new SqlConnection(connString))
    {
      SqlDataAdapter adapter = new SqlDataAdapter(sql, sqlConn);
      adapter.Fill(contactsDataSet, "Contact");
    }
    return contactsDataSet;
  }
</script>
<html xmlns="http://www.w3.org/1999/xhtml" >
<head runat="server">
  <title>Serializing a DataSet object to XML</title>
</head>
<body>
  <form id="form1" runat="server">
    <div>
      <asp:GridView id="gridContacts" runat="server"
        AutoGenerateColumns="False" CellPadding="4"
        HeaderStyle-BackColor="blue" HeaderStyle-ForeColor="White"
        HeaderStyle-HorizontalAlign="Center" HeaderStyle-Font-Bold="True">
        <Columns>
          <asp:BoundField HeaderText="Contact Type ID" DataField="ContactTypeID"/>
          <asp:BoundField HeaderText="Name" DataField="Name"
            ItemStyle-HorizontalAlign="Right"/>
        </Columns>
      </asp:GridView>
    </div>
  </form>
</body>
</html>
```

The Page_Load event shown in Listing 8-4 starts by checking for the presence of an XML file named ContactType.xml. If the file is not present, it invokes a private helper method named GetContactTypes() that retrieves contract types from the database. After retrieving the contract types in the form of a DataSet, it then saves the contents of the DataSet into a local XML file named ContactType.xml. During subsequent requests, this local XML file is used to display the contact types information. Finally, the contents of the DataSet are displayed through a GridView control.

Controlling the Rendering Behavior of DataColumn Objects

When you serialize a DataSet object to XML, the contents in the DataSet are rendered either as elements or attributes. It is possible to control this rendering behavior by setting appropriate attributes at the DataColumn object level. The DataColumn object has a property called ColumnMapping that determines how columns are rendered in XML. The ColumnMapping property takes values from the MappingType enum. Table 8-3 summarizes the various values supported by the MappingType enum.

Table 8-3. Members of MappingType Enumeration

Member	Description
Element	Allows you to map a column to an element. This is the default behavior.
Attribute	Allows you to map a column to an attribute.
Hidden	Allows you to map a column to an internal structure.
SimpleContent	Allows you to map a column to an XmlText node.

The following code demonstrates the purpose of the MappingType enumeration by setting the ColumnMapping property for all the columns in the ContactType table to MappingType.Attribute.

```
for (int i = 0; i < contactsDataSet.Tables[0].Columns.Count; i++)
{
contactsDataSet.Tables[0].Columns[i].ColumnMapping =
  MappingType.Attribute;
}
```

This results in all the columns of the contact types table being rendered in the form of attributes when the DataSet is serialized to XML format.

Modifying the Table and Column Names

By default, when you use the DataAdapter to fill a DataSet, the column names that are used in the DataSet correspond to the column names defined in the data source. When you serialize the DataSet, the elements in the XML output exactly match the column names in the original DataSet. There are times where the default XML elements may not work for you and you might need the ability to tailor the XML elements. One way of solving this problem is to use some sort of mapping. With ADO.NET, there are two places that you can implement mapping: at the query level, or in the DataAdapter.

The SQL language provides a basic ability to change column names using the AS keyword. For example, the following query selects three columns from the `ContactType` table, and renames two of them.

```
SELECT ContactTypeID AS ID, Name AS ContactTypeName,
ModifiedDate FROM Person.ContactType
```

This technique is useful if you are following good design practices and placing your query in a view or stored procedure in the database. If column names change, you can simply update the corresponding view or stored procedure, and the client application will continue to work seamlessly.

The AS keyword isn't perfect, though. The most obvious drawback is that you can only use the AS keyword in a query. Another approach to changing the column names is using the column mapping technique in ADO.NET. The basic principle is to apply a list of column transformations to the `DataAdapter` object. When you fill a `DataSet` using the `DataAdapter`, it automatically renames the source columns and uses the names you have configured. Here's an example:

```
//Create the new mapping.
DataTableMapping map;
map = adapter.TableMappings.Add("ContactType", "ContactType");
//Define column mappings.
map.ColumnMappings.Add("ContactTypeID", "ID");
map.ColumnMappings.Add("Name", "ContactTypeName");
map.ColumnMappings.Add("Description", "Description");
//Fill the DataSet.
adapter.Fill(ds, "ContactType");
```

You may notice that the `DataAdapter` mappings also give you the opportunity to map table names. This isn't very useful in this context, however, because the table name is never drawn from the data source; instead, it is supplied as a parameter for the `Fill()` method. In the previous example, the table name "ContactType" is mapped to the `DataTable` named "ContactType"—in other words, the name is not changed. However, this step is still required. If no parameter is specified, the default name ("Table") is used. Note that this technique is useful if you are directly filling a `DataTable` and serializing it to XML.

Of course, nothing prevents you from using table mappings, if you want. In the following example, the `Fill()` method actually creates a table in the `DataSet` named `ContactTypeList`, not `ContactType`.

```
//Create the new mapping.
DataTableMapping map;
map = adapter.TableMappings.Add("ContactType", "ContactTypeList");
//Fill the DataSet.
adapter.Fill(ds, "ContactType");
```

One case in which table mapping can be useful is if you have a stored procedure or batch query that returns multiple result sets. In this case, a number is automatically added to the table name for each subsequent result set, as in `ContactType`, `ContactType1`, `ContactType2`, and so on. By adding a `DataTableMapping` object for each of these tables, you can correct this behavior:

```
// Create a mapping that returns a list of ContactTypes and a list of Contacts
DataTableMapping map;
adapter.TableMappings.Add("Results", "ContactType");
adapter.TableMappings.Add("Results1", "Contact");
//Fill the DataSet using a stored procedure that returns multiple result sets
adapter.Fill(ds, "Results");
```

The DataAdapter provides a special MissingMappingAction property that governs how it behaves if you do not supply column and table mappings. It takes one of the MissingMappingAction values described in Table 8-4.

Table 8-4. Values of MissingMappingAction Enumeration

Value	Description
Error	If there is any column that doesn't have a mapping, an exception is thrown
Ignore	All columns that do not have a mapping are ignored, and not added to the DataSet
Passthrough	If there is any column that doesn't have a mapping, the data source column name is used; this is the default

For example, to raise an error whenever there is a column that does not have mapping, set the MissingMappingAction property to MissingMappingAction.Error as shown here:

```
adapter.MissingMappingAction = MissingMappingAction.Error;
```

Getting XML as a String from a DataSet

It is also possible to serialize the contents of a DataSet into a string for use in your code. Although it is not a recommended technique for extracting XML from a DataSet, it can be useful in situations where you want to use the DataSet object as a string in your code. To accomplish this, use the GetXml() and GetXmlSchema() methods of the DataSet object. Listing 8-5 shows an example of how to retrieve XML data from a DataSet directly using GetXml() and GetXmlSchema() methods.

Listing 8-5: Retrieving XML as a String from a DataSet

```
<%@ Page Language="C#" %>
<%@ Import Namespace="System.Web.Configuration"%>
<%@ Import Namespace="System.Data"%>
<%@ Import Namespace="System.Data.SqlClient"%>
<%@ Import Namespace="System.IO"%>
<script runat="server">
void Page_Load(Object sender, EventArgs e)
{
    string connString = WebConfigurationManager.
      ConnectionStrings["adventureWorks"].ConnectionString;
    string sql = "Select TOP 2 * from Person.ContactType";
    DataSet contactsDataSet = new DataSet();
    using (SqlConnection sqlConn = new SqlConnection(connString))
    {
      SqlDataAdapter adapter = new SqlDataAdapter(sql, sqlConn);
      adapter.Fill(contactsDataSet);
    }
    //Assign the contents to literal controls
    ltlXmlData.Text = Server.HtmlEncode(contactsDataSet.GetXml());
    ltlXmlSchema.Text = Server.HtmlEncode(contactsDataSet.GetXmlSchema());
  }
</script>
```

```
<html xmlns="http://www.w3.org/1999/xhtml" >
<head runat="server">
  <title>Getting XML as a String from a DataSet</title>
</head>
<body>
<form id="form1" runat="server">
    <div>
     <asp:Literal runat="server" ID="ltlXmlData"></asp:Literal>
     <br/><br/><br/>
     <asp:Literal runat="server" ID="ltlXmlSchema"></asp:Literal>
    </div>
  </form>
</body>
</html>
```

The code shown in Listing 8-5 starts by retrieving `ContactType` details from AdventureWorks database into a `DataSet`. After retrieving the data in the form of a DataSet, it then retrieves XML data and its associated schema using `GetXml()` and `GetXmlSchema()` methods from the `DataSet` and displays them in literal controls.

Nesting XML Output from a DataSet

As you know, a `DataSet` can contain more than one table and also the relationships between these tables. In an ADO.NET dataset, `DataRelation` is used to implement the relationship between tables and work with the child rows from one table that are related to a specific row in the parent table. XML provides a hierarchical representation of data in which the parent entities contain nested child entities. The `DataRelation` object has a property named `Nested`. This property is false by default and has no effect when you are accessing the data using relational techniques. It does, however, affect the way the data is exported as XML when you save the contents of the `DataSet` using `WriteXml()` method.

> `DataRelation` **relates two** `DataTable` **objects by using** `DataColumn` **objects. These relationships are created between the matching records in the parent and child tables. The** `DataType` **value of these columns should be identical. The referential integrity between the tables is maintained by adding the** `ForeignKeyConstraint` **to** `ConstraintCollection` **of the** `DataTable` **object. Before a** `DataRelation` **is created, it first checks whether a relationship can be established. If a relationship can be established, a** `DataRelation` **is created and then added to the** `DataRelationCollection`. **You can then access the** `DataRelation` **objects from the** `DataRelationCollection` **by using the** `Relations` **property of the dataset and the** `ChildRelations` **and** `ParentRelations` **properties of the** `DataTable` **object.**

The code shown in Listing 8-6 demonstrates how to create nested XML output from a `DataSet` using an `XmlDataDocument` object.

Listing 8-6: Generating Nested XML Output from a DataSet

```
<%@ Page Language="C#" %>
<%@ Import Namespace="System.Web.Configuration"%>
<%@ Import Namespace="System.Data.SqlClient"%>
<%@ Import Namespace="System.Data"%>
<%@ Import Namespace="System.Xml"%>
```

```
<script runat="server">
void Page_Load(Object sender, EventArgs e)
{
    string filePath = Server.MapPath("NestedOutput.xml");
    //Get the values from the database
    DataSet prodCategoriesDataSet = GetCategoriesAndProducts();
    XmlDataDocument xmlDoc = new XmlDataDocument(prodCategoriesDataSet);
    //Write the dataset
    xmlDoc.DataSet.WriteXml(filePath);
    hlkDataSetOutput.NavigateUrl = "NestedOutput.xml";
}


DataSet GetCategoriesAndProducts()
{
    string connString = WebConfigurationManager.
      ConnectionStrings["adventureWorks"].ConnectionString;
    string sql = "Select * from Production.ProductSubCategory;" +
      "Select * from Production.Product";
    DataSet prodCategoriesDataSet = new DataSet();
    using (SqlConnection sqlConn = new SqlConnection(connString))
    {
      SqlDataAdapter adapter = new SqlDataAdapter(sql, sqlConn);
      adapter.Fill(prodCategoriesDataSet);
      //Name the DataTables properly
      prodCategoriesDataSet.Tables[0].TableName = "ProductSubCategories";
      prodCategoriesDataSet.Tables[1].TableName = "Products";
      prodCategoriesDataSet.Relations.Add(
        prodCategoriesDataSet.Tables[0].Columns["ProductSubCategoryID"],
        prodCategoriesDataSet.Tables[1].Columns["ProductSubCategoryID"]);
      prodCategoriesDataSet.Relations[0].Nested = true;
    }
    return prodCategoriesDataSet;
}
</script>
<html xmlns="http://www.w3.org/1999/xhtml" >
<head runat="server">
  <title>Nested XML Output from a DataSet Object</title>
</head>
<body>
        <form id="form1" runat="server">
          <div>
        <asp:HyperLink ID="hlkDataSetOutput" Runat="server">
          Click here to view the output of the Serialized DataSet Output
        </asp:HyperLink>
      </div>
    </form>
</body>
</html>
```

The key point to note in Listing 8-6 is the line of code where you set the Nested property of the DataRelation object to true.

```
prodCategoriesDataSet.Relations[0].Nested = true;
```

Opening up the XML file produced by the code in Listing 8-6 results in an output that is somewhat similar to Figure 8-2.

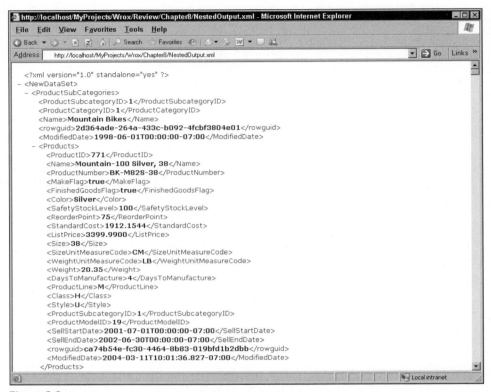

Figure 8-2

As you can see from the output, each `<ProductSubCategories>` element is a child of the document root, and the `<Products>` elements are nested within their respective `<ProductSubCategories>` elements.

Writing DataSet Schema

In addition to writing out XML data from a `DataSet`, you can also write out the schema of the `DataSet`. The `DataSet` enables you to write a `DataSet` schema through the `WriteXmlSchema()` method, facilitating the transportation of this schema in an XML document. This method takes one parameter, which specifies the location of the resulting XSD schema, and the location can be a file, an `XmlWriter`, or a `Stream`.

Typed DataSets

A typed `DataSet` is a subclass of `DataSet` class in which the tables that exist in the `DataSet` are derived by reading the XSD schema information. The difference between a typed `DataSet` and an ordinary `DataSet` is that the `DataRows`, `DataTables`, and other items are available as strong types; that is, rather than refer to `MyDataSet.Tables[0]` or `MyDataSet.Tables["customers"]`, you code against a strongly typed `DataTable` named, for example, `MyDataSet.Customers`. Typed `DataSets` have the advantage that the strongly typed variable names can be checked at compile time rather than causing errors at runtime.

Suppose you have a `DataSet` that contains a table named customers, which has a column named `CompanyName`. You can refer to the table and the column by ordinal or by name as shown here.

```
ds.Tables["Customers"].Rows[0].Columns["CompanyName"] = "XYZ Company";
```

As you can see, the data is loosely typed when referred to by ordinal or name, meaning that the compiler cannot guarantee that you have spelled the column name correctly or used the correct ordinal. The problem is that the error informing you of this occurs at runtime rather than at compile time. If the `DataSet` items were strongly typed, misspelling the column name or using the wrong ordinal would be prevented because the code simply would not compile. The following code shows you how to assign the same value to the same field but using a typed `DataSet`.

```
ds.Customers[0].CompanyName = "XYZ Company";
```

Now the table name and the field to be accessed are not treated as string literals, but instead are encased in an XML schema and a class that is generated from the `DataSet` class. When you create a typed `DataSet`, you are creating a class that implements the tables and fields based upon the schema used to generate the class. Basically, the schema is coded into the class.

As you compare the two examples, you see that a typed `DataSet` is easier to read and understand. It is less error-prone, and errors are realized at compile time as opposed to runtime.

Generating Typed DataSets

The easiest way to generate a typed `DataSet` is to use Visual Studio. In Visual Studio, just right-click on the existing table, stored procedure, SQL statement and select "Generate DataSet." The .NET Framework SDK also ships with a tool called XSD.exe that provides you with more control and options for generating the XML schema.

> The XML Schema Definition tool (`Xsd.exe`) is a utility that ships with .NET Framework SDK. This tool is designed primarily for two purposes:
>
> Allows you to generate either C# or Visual Basic class files that conform to a specific XML schema definition language (XSD) schema. The tool takes an XML schema as an argument and outputs a file that contains a number of classes. After you generate these classes and serialize them using XmlSerializer class, the output XML will be compliant with the XSD schema.
>
> Allows you to generate an XML schema document from a .dll file or .exe file. You can accomplish this by passing in the DLL or EXE as an argument to the tool, and you will get the XML schema as the output .Note that in this case, the XSD.exe tool is looking for `System.Xml.XmlSerializer` compatible types, meaning that it is looking for types with public fields, or public properties with both getter and setters.

Instead of using Visual Studio, you also have the option of generating the typed `DataSet` manually using the following steps.

1. Fill a `DataSet` with data from the database

2. Save the schema with `DataSet.WriteXmlSchema()`

3. Use the schema as input into `XSD.exe`

For example, generate a typed `DataSet` for the product table and see what you get.

```
SqlDataAdapter da = new SqlDataAdapter("select * from Production.Product " +
  " as Product",
"server=localhost;integrated security=true;database=AdventureWorks");
//Name the DataSet ProductsDataSet
DataSet ds = new DataSet("ProductsDataSet");
//Name the table ProductsTable
da.Fill(ds, "ProductsTable");
ds.WriteXmlSchema("Products.xsd");
```

After you have the `Products.xsd` file generated, you can then utilize the `XSD.exe` utility to generate the typed `DataSet`.

```
xsd /DataSet /language:CS C:\Data\Products.xsd
```

The previous command in the command prompt creates a typed `DataSet` called `ProductsDataSet` in the `Products.cs` file. Listing 8-7 shows a brief version of the `ProductsDataSet`.

Listing 8-7: Typed DataSet

```
[Serializable()]
[System.ComponentModel.DesignerCategoryAttribute("code")]
[System.ComponentModel.ToolboxItem(true)]
[System.Xml.Serialization.XmlSchemaProviderAttribute("GetTypedDataSetSchema")]
[System.Xml.Serialization.XmlRootAttribute("ProductsDataSet")]
[System.ComponentModel.Design.HelpKeywordAttribute("vs.data.DataSet")]
public partial class ProductsDataSet : System.Data.DataSet {
private ProductsTableDataTable tableProductsTable;
private System.Data.SchemaSerializationMode _schemaSerializationMode =
  System.Data.SchemaSerializationMode.IncludeSchema;
[System.Diagnostics.DebuggerNonUserCodeAttribute()]
public ProductsDataSet() {
    this.BeginInit();
    this.InitClass();
    System.ComponentModel.CollectionChangeEventHandler schemaChangedHandler =
      new System.ComponentModel.CollectionChangeEventHandler(
      this.SchemaChanged);
    base.Tables.CollectionChanged += schemaChangedHandler;
    base.Relations.CollectionChanged += schemaChangedHandler;
    this.EndInit();
}
    --------
    --------
    [System.Serializable()]
    [System.Xml.Serialization.XmlSchemaProviderAttribute("GetTypedTableSchema")]
    public partial class ProductsTableDataTable : System.Data.DataTable,
      System.Collections.IEnumerable {
      private System.Data.DataColumn columnProductID;
      private System.Data.DataColumn columnName;
      private System.Data.DataColumn columnProductNumber;
      private System.Data.DataColumn columnMakeFlag;
      --------
      --------
    }
```

```
        public partial class ProductsTableRow : System.Data.DataRow {
          private ProductsTableDataTable tableProductsTable;
          --------
          --------
        }
        public class ProductsTableRowChangeEvent : System.EventArgs {
          private ProductsTableRow eventRow;
          --------
          --------
        }
      }
```

The typed DataSet accomplishes strong typing by generating a class ProductsDataSet, which derives from DataSet class. The name of the subclass of the DataSet class is equal to DataSet.DataSetName in the original DataSet that produced the XML schema. As you can see from the previous code listing, four public nested classes are exposed:

❑   ProductsDataSet

❑   ProductsTableDataTable

❑   ProductsTableRow

❑   ProductsTableRowChangeEvent

A strongly typed DataSet can also contain more than one table. If you have tables with parent-child relationships — specified by the existence of a DataRelation in the DataSet's Relations collection — some additional information and methods are generated. When the DataSet contains a Relation, the following happens:

❑   The PrimaryKey property is added to DataColumn properties for the parent table.

❑   A ForeignKeyConstraint is added for the child table.

❑   DataRelation is added.

If the DataSet's Nested property was set in the original schema, it is preserved in the typed DataSet.

Using Typed DataSet

In most cases, you can use your Typed DataSet everywhere you would normally use a DataSet. Your Typed DataSet directly derives from DataSet so all the DataSet-related classes and methods will work. One of the distinct advantages of using a Typed DataSet is that elements of the DataSet are strongly typed and strongly named. The use of the new class is a little different than our old DataSet examples, as follows:

```
ProductsDataSet prodDS = new ProductsDataSet();
SqlDataAdapter adapter = new SqlDataAdapter("SELECT * FROM Production.Product " +
  " As Product",
"server=localhost;Integrated Security=true;Initial Catalog=AdventureWorks");
adapter.Fill(prodDS, "ProductsTable");
foreach (ProductsDataSet.ProductsTableRow row in prodDS.ProductsTable.Rows)
{
Response.Write(row.ProductID);
}
```

When filling the typed DataSet with data, you can expect the same behavior as that of the DataSet because the typed DataSet directly derives from the base DataSet class. As the previous code shows, after you fill it, you can use the typed accessors to get at rows and columns in a more direct way than with an untyped DataSet.

Using Annotations with a Typed DataSet

Although strongly typed DataSets are produced using the names in the schema, you can refine the naming process by using certain schema annotations. These attributes are specified on the element declaration that equates to the table. The annotations are as follows:

- ❑ typedName: Name of an object referring to a row
- ❑ typedPlural: Name of an object referring to a table
- ❑ typedParent: Name of a parent object in a parent-child relationship
- ❑ typedChild: Name of a child object in a parent-child relationship

There is also an annotation, nullValue, that refers to special handling in a strongly typed DataSet when the value in the underlying table is DBNull.

For example, consider the XSD schema.

```
<xs:element name="ProductsTable">
<xs:complexType>
    <xs:sequence>
      <xs:element name="ProductID" type="xs:int" minOccurs="0" />
    </xs:sequence>
</xs:complexType>
</xs:element>
```

The previous schema element for the ProductsTable that represents the Products table of the AdventureWorks database would result in a DataRow name of ProductsTableRow. In common scenarios, the object would be referred to without the Row identifier and instead would be simply referred to as a Product object. Similarly, you would want to refer to the collection of Products simply as Products. To accomplish this, you need to annotate the schema and identify new names for the DataRow and DataRowCollection objects. The following code shows the annotated schema that will produce the desired output.

```
<xs:element name="ProductsTable" codegen:typedName="Product"
  codegen:typedPlural="Products">
<xs:complexType>
    <xs:sequence>
      <xs:element name="ProductID" type="xs:int" minOccurs="0" />
    </xs:sequence>
  </xs:complexType>
</xs:element>
```

Now that you have set the codegen:typedName and codegen:typedPlural attributes to Product, Products respectively, if you regenerate the DataSet using XSD, you will find that the generated DataSet reflects the changes. Note that in the previous XML schema, there is a new prefix called codegen for which you need to add the following namespace declaration to the xsd:schema element.

```
xmlns:codegen="urn:schemas-microsoft-com:xml-msprop"
```

The following code shows how you can loop through the DataSet using the new DataRow and DataRowCollection object names.

```
ProductsDataSet prodDS = new ProductsDataSet();
SqlDataAdapter adapter = new SqlDataAdapter("SELECT * FROM Production.Product " +
  " as Product",
"server=localhost;Integrated Security=true;Initial Catalog=AdventureWorks");
adapter.Fill(prodDS, "ProductsTable");
foreach (ProductsDataSet.Product prod in prodDS.Products)
{
Response.Write(prod.ProductID);
}
```

Note that the previous code uses Product and Products to refer to the DataRow and DataRowCollection instances of the DataTable.

XmlDataDocument Object and DataSet

The key XML class that makes it possible to access both relational and hierarchical data in a consistent manner is the XmlDataDocument class. The XmlDataDocument class inherits from the base class XmlDocument and differs from it only in the ability to synchronize with DataSet objects. When synchronized, DataSet and XmlDataDocument classes work on the same collection of rows, and you can apply changes through both interfaces (nodes and relational tables) and make them immediately visible to both classes. Basically, DataSet and XmlDataDocument provide two sets of tools for the same data. As a result, you can apply XSLT transformations to relational data, query relational data through XPath expressions, and use SQL to select XML nodes. It can also be useful in situations when you want to retain the full fidelity of fairly unstructured XML and still use methods provided by the DataSet object.

Because the XmlDataDocument class is derived from the XmlDocument class, it supports all the properties and methods of the XmlDocument class. Additionally, the XmlDataDocument class has its own properties and methods for providing a relational view of the data contained in it. Table 8-5 discusses the properties and methods of the XmlDataDocument in this context.

Table 8-5. Important Properties and Methods of the XmlDataDocument Class

Property or Method	Description
DataSet	This property returns reference to the DataSet that provides a relational representation of the data in the XmlDataDocument
GetElementFromRow	This method retrieves the XmlElement associated with the specified DataRow
GetRowFromElement	This method returns reference to the DataRow associated with the specified XmlElement
Load	This method loads the XmlDataDocument using the specified data source and synchronizes the DataSet with the loaded data

Data can be loaded into an `XmlDataDocument` through either the `DataSet` interfaces or the `XmlDocument` interfaces. You can import the relational part of the XML document into `DataSet` by using an explicit or implied mapping schema. Whether changes are made through `DataSet` or through `XmlDataDocument`, the changed values are reflected in both objects. The full-fidelity XML is always available through the `XmlDataDocument`.

Associating an XmlDataDocument with a DataSet

There are a few ways to bind a `DataSet` object and `XmlDataDocument` object together. The first option is that you pass a non-empty `DataSet` object to the constructor of the `XmlDataDocument` class as follows.

```
XmlDataDocument xmlDoc = new XmlDataDocument(dataset);
```

Similar to its base class, `XmlDataDocument` provides a XML DOM approach to work with XML data. An alternate way of synchronizing the two objects is by creating a valid and non-empty `DataSet` object from a non-empty instance of the `XmlDataDocument` object. An example of this is illustrated here.

```
XmlDataDocument xmlDoc = new XmlDataDocument();
xmlDoc.Load(filePath);
DataSet dataset = xmlDoc.DataSet;
```

You can turn an `XmlDataDocument` into a `DataSet` object using the `XmlDataDocument`'s `DataSet` property. The property instantiates, populates, and returns a `DataSet` object. The `DataSet` is associated with the `XmlDataDocument` the first time you access the `DataSet` property. To view the XML data relationally, you must first specify a schema to use for data mapping. This can be done by calling the `ReadXmlSchema()` method on the same XML file. As an alternate approach, you can manually create the necessary tables and columns in the `DataSet`.

Keeping the two objects synchronized provides an unprecedented level of flexibility by allowing you to use two radically different types of navigation to move through records. In fact, you can use SQL-like queries on XML nodes, as well as XPath queries on relational rows. Keep in mind, however, that not all XML files can be successfully synchronized with a `DataSet`. For this to happen, XML documents must have a regular, tabular structure that can be mapped to a relational architecture where each row has the same number of columns. Also remember that when rendered as `DataSet` objects, XML documents lose any XML-specific information they may have and for which there isn't a relational counterpart. This information includes comments, declarations, and processing instructions.

Loading a DataSet through an XmlDataDocument

You can load a `DataSet` through either the `DataSet` interfaces or the `XmlDataDocument` interfaces. For example, you can import the relational part of the XML document into `DataSet` by using an explicit or implied mapping schema. One of the important advantages of this approach is that whether the changes are made through `DataSet` or through `XmlDataDocument`, the changed values are reflected in both objects. Moreover, you can obtain the full fidelity XML any time through the `XmlDataDocument`. Listing 8-8 illustrates the code required for loading a `DataSet` through an `XmlDataDocument`.

Listing 8-8: Using an XmlDataDocument to Load a DataSet

```
<%@ Page Language="C#" %>
<%@ Import Namespace="System.Web.Configuration"%>
<%@ Import Namespace="System.Data.SqlClient"%>
```

```
<%@ Import Namespace="System.Data"%>
<%@ Import Namespace="System.Xml"%>
<script runat="server">
void Page_Load(Object sender, EventArgs e)
{
    string xmlPath = Server.MapPath("App_Data/ContactType.xml");
    string xmlSchemaPath = Server.MapPath("App_Data/ContactType.xsd");
    SaveContacts(xmlPath, xmlSchemaPath);
    XmlDataDocument xmlDoc = new XmlDataDocument();
    xmlDoc.DataSet.ReadXmlSchema(xmlSchemaPath);
    xmlDoc.Load(xmlPath);
    DataSet contactsDataSet = xmlDoc.DataSet;
    //Bind the DataSet to the DataGrid object
    gridContacts.DataSource = contactsDataSet.Tables[0].DefaultView;
    gridContacts.DataBind();
}


void SaveContacts(string xmlPath, string xmlSchemaPath)
{
    string connString = WebConfigurationManager.
      ConnectionStrings["adventureWorks"].ConnectionString;
    string sql = "Select * from Person.ContactType";
    DataSet contactsDataSet = new DataSet("ContactTypes");
    using (SqlConnection sqlConn = new SqlConnection(connString))
    {
      SqlDataAdapter adapter = new SqlDataAdapter(sql, sqlConn);
      adapter.Fill(contactsDataSet);
    }
    contactsDataSet.WriteXml(xmlPath);
    contactsDataSet.WriteXmlSchema(xmlSchemaPath);
  }
</script>
<html xmlns="http://www.w3.org/1999/xhtml" >
<head runat="server">
  <title>Loading a DataSet through an XmlDataDocument</title>
</head>
<body>
<form id="form1" runat="server">
    <div>
      <asp:GridView id="gridContacts" runat="server"
        AutoGenerateColumns="False" CellPadding="4"
        HeaderStyle-BackColor="blue" HeaderStyle-ForeColor="White"
        HeaderStyle-HorizontalAlign="Center" HeaderStyle-Font-Bold="True">
        <Columns>
          <asp:BoundField HeaderText="Contact Type ID"
            DataField="ContactTypeID" />
          <asp:BoundField HeaderText="Name"
            DataField="Name"
            ItemStyle-HorizontalAlign="Right" />
        </Columns>
      </asp:GridView>
    </div>
  </form>
</body>
</html>
```

In the `Page_Load` event, an `XmlDataDocument` object is instantiated. After that, the `ReadXmlSchema()` method of the `DataSet` object is used to load the XML schema. After the schema is loaded, the actual XML data is then loaded using the `Load()` method of `XmlDataDocument` object. Now that the schema as well as the XML data is loaded into the `XmlDataDocument` object, you can now retrieve the `DataSet` using the `DataSet` property of the `XmlDataDocument` object. Finally, this `DataSet` object is bound to a `GridView` control. Navigate to the page using the browser, and you should see an output very similar to Figure 8-3.

Figure 8-3

Extracting XML Elements from a DataSet

When you are interacting with a `DataSet`, you may want to extract individual rows within a `DataSet` object as an XML element. To accomplish this, perform the following steps.

1. Create a `DataSet` object and fill it with the values from a database table.

2. Associate an `XmlDataDocument` object with the `DataSet` by passing in the `DataSet` object to the constructor of the `XmlDataDocument` object.

3. Invoke the `GetElementFromRow()` method of the `XmlDataDocument` object and pass in the `DataRow` object as an argument. The `GetElementFromRow()` method returns an XML representation of the `DataRow` object in the form of an `XmlElement` object.

Listing 8-9 shows an example of how to extract XML data using the `GetElementFromRow()` method of the `XmlDataDocument` object.

Listing 8-9: Extracting XML Elements from an XmlDataDocument Object

```
<%@ Page Language="C#" %>
<%@ Import Namespace="System.Web.Configuration"%>
<%@ Import Namespace="System.Data.SqlClient"%>
<%@ Import Namespace="System.Data"%>
<%@ Import Namespace="System.Xml"%>
```

```
<script runat="server">
void Page_Load(Object sender, EventArgs e)
{
    DataSet contactTypesDataSet = GetContactTypes();
    //Associate the DataSet with an XmlDataDocument object
    XmlDataDocument xmlDoc = new XmlDataDocument(contactTypesDataSet);
    //Loop through the DataTable and retrieve the XML Data
    DataTable table = xmlDoc.DataSet.Tables[0];
    StringBuilder builder = new StringBuilder();
    foreach (DataRow row in table.Rows)
    {
      builder.Append(xmlDoc.GetElementFromRow(row).OuterXml);
    }
    ltlXMLData.Text = Server.HtmlEncode(builder.ToString());
}

DataSet GetContactTypes()
{
    string connString = WebConfigurationManager.
      ConnectionStrings["adventureWorks"].ConnectionString;
    string sql = "Select * from Person.ContactType";
    DataSet contactTypesDataSet = new DataSet("ContactTypes");
    using (SqlConnection sqlConn = new SqlConnection(connString))
    {
      SqlDataAdapter adapter = new SqlDataAdapter(sql, sqlConn);
      adapter.Fill(contactTypesDataSet);
    }
    return contactTypesDataSet;
}
</script>
<html xmlns="http://www.w3.org/1999/xhtml" >
<head runat="server">
  <title>Retrieving XML Elements from a DataSet</title>
</head>
<body>
<form id="form1" runat="server">
    <div>
      <asp:Literal Runat="server" ID="ltlXMLData"></asp:Literal>
    </div>
  </form>
</body>
</html>
```

In this code, you start by retrieving contact types information from the AdventureWorks database into a DataSet. After retrieving the data, you associate the DataSet object with an XmlDataDocument object by passing the DataSet object to the constructor of the XmlDataDocument. You then retrieve the DataTable from the XmlDataDocument object via the DataSet property, and loop through all the rows in the DataTable object using a foreach construct. Inside the foreach loop, the GetElementFromRow() method of the XmlDataDocument object is used to get the XML representation of the DataRow. You get the XML representation of the data through the OuterXml property. Finally, the output from the StringBuilder object is displayed onto a literal control.

Similar to the `GetElementFromRow()` *method of the* `DataSet`, *there is also a mirror method named* `GetRowFromElement()` *of the* `XmlDataDocument` *object that exactly does the opposite. As the name suggests, this method takes in an* `XmlElement` *object as its parameter and returns a* `DataRow` *as its output. This method is useful in situations when you want to extract field information about the elements contained in the* `XmlElement` *object.*

Merging Data with XmlDataDocument

There are times when you may want to merge data from a relational database into an existing `XmlDataDocument` object. You can easily accomplish this by using the `Merge()` method of the `DataSet`. When you merge data into an `XmlDataDocument`'s `DataSet`, you need to ensure that the schema for both tables must be loaded when the original document is loaded; otherwise, this will result in an exception during `DataSet.Merge()`.

Listing 8-10: Merging Data in an XmlDataDocument with DataSet

```
<%@ Page Language="C#" %>
<%@ Import Namespace="System.Web.Configuration"%>
<%@ Import Namespace="System.Data.SqlClient"%>
<%@ Import Namespace="System.Data"%>
<%@ Import Namespace="System.Xml"%>
<script runat="server">
void Page_Load(Object sender, EventArgs e)
{
    DataSet contactTypesDataSet = GetContactTypes();
    XmlDataDocument xmlDoc = new XmlDataDocument();
    xmlDoc.DataSet.ReadXmlSchema(Server.MapPath("App_Data/ContactType.xsd"));
    xmlDoc.Load(Server.MapPath("App_Data/ContactType.xml"));
    //Merge two datasets
    contactTypesDataSet.Merge(xmlDoc.DataSet);
    //Bind the DataSet to the DataGrid object
    gridContactTypes.DataSource = contactTypesDataSet.Tables[0].DefaultView;
    gridContactTypes.DataBind();
}

DataSet GetContactTypes()
{
    string connString = WebConfigurationManager.
      ConnectionStrings["adventureWorks"].ConnectionString;
    string sql = "Select ContactTypeID, Name " +
      " from Person.ContactType";
    DataSet contactTypesDataSet = new DataSet("ContactTypes");
    using (SqlConnection sqlConn = new SqlConnection(connString))
    {
      SqlDataAdapter adapter = new SqlDataAdapter(sql, sqlConn);
      adapter.Fill(contactTypesDataSet);
    }
    return contactTypesDataSet;
  }
</script>
<html xmlns="http://www.w3.org/1999/xhtml" >
<head runat="server">
```

```
        <title>Merging a DataSet with an XmlDataDocument Object</title>
    </head>
    <body>
    <form id="form1" runat="server">
        <div>
            <asp:GridView id="gridContactTypes" runat="server"
                AutoGenerateColumns="False" CellPadding="4"
                HeaderStyle-BackColor="blue" HeaderStyle-ForeColor="White"
                HeaderStyle-HorizontalAlign="Center" HeaderStyle-Font-Bold="True">
                <Columns>
                    <asp:BoundField HeaderText="Contact Type ID"
                        DataField="ContactTypeID" />
                    <asp:BoundField HeaderText="Name"
                        DataField="Name" ItemStyle-HorizontalAlign="Right" />
                </Columns>
            </asp:GridView>
        </div>
    </form>
    </body>
    </html>
```

In Listing 8-10, the `Page_Load` event performs the core functionality. You first retrieve the contact types information from the AdventureWorks database in the form of a `DataSet`. After that, you merge that `Dataset` with another `DataSet` object that is created using the `XmlDataDocument` object. Finally, you display the merged contents onto the browser through a `GridView` control. Navigating to the page in a browser results in the following output.

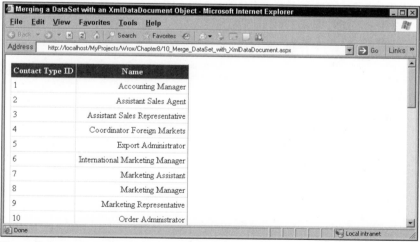

Figure 8-4

Relationship between XmlDataDocument and XPathNavigator

An additional advantage of using XmlDataDocument is that you can query the resulting object model using either the SQL-like syntax of DataView filters or the XPath query language. Using DataView filters, you can only filter sets of rows. But using a full-featured query language like XPath you can produce sets of nodes or scalar values that can be easily iterated through. You can use XPath directly via the SelectSingleNode and SelectNode methods that XmlDataDocument inherits from XmlDocument. The XPathNavigator class also lets you use precompiled XPath queries. Result sets from XPath queries are exposed as XPathNodeIterator objects that provide you with a mechanism for iterating over a set of selected nodes. You can also use XPathNavigator as an input to the XSLT transformation process exposed through the XslCompiledTransform class. Listing 8-11 demonstrates the use of XPathNavigator object by showing an example.

Listing 8-11: Navigating the Contents of an XmlDataDocument Using an XPathNavigator Object

```csharp
<%@ Page Language="C#" %>
<%@ Import Namespace="System.Web.Configuration"%>
<%@ Import Namespace="System.Data.SqlClient"%>
<%@ Import Namespace="System.Data"%>
<%@ Import Namespace="System.Xml"%>
<%@ Import Namespace="System.Xml.XPath"%>
<script runat="server">
void Page_Load(Object sender, EventArgs e)
{
    DataSet contactTypesDataSet = GetContactTypes();
    XmlDataDocument xmlDoc = new XmlDataDocument(contactTypesDataSet);
    XPathNavigator navigator = xmlDoc.CreateNavigator();
    XPathNodeIterator iterator = navigator.
      Select("/ContactTypes/ContactType/Name");
    Response.Write("The retrieved Contact Type Names are : <br>");
    while (iterator.MoveNext())
    {
      Response.Write(iterator.Current.Value + "<br>");
    }
}

DataSet GetContactTypes()
{
    string connString = WebConfigurationManager.
      ConnectionStrings["adventureWorks"].ConnectionString;
    string sql = "Select * from Person.ContactType";
    DataSet contactTypesDataSet = new DataSet("ContactTypes");
    using (SqlConnection sqlConn = new SqlConnection(connString))
    {
      SqlDataAdapter adapter = new SqlDataAdapter(sql, sqlConn);
      adapter.Fill(contactTypesDataSet, "ContactType");
    }
    return contactTypesDataSet;
  }
</script>
<html xmlns="http://www.w3.org/1999/xhtml" >
<head runat="server">
```

```
      <title>Navigating an XmlDataDocument through XPathNodeIterator</title>
   </head>
   <body>
   <form id="form1" runat="server">
       <div>
       </div>
     </form>
   </body>
   </html>
```

The code shown in Listing 8-11 starts by retrieving contact types information in the form of a DataSet from the AdventureWorks database. After that, it associates the DataSet to an XmlDataDocument object by passing the DataSet to the constructor of the XmlDataDocument. It then uses the CreateNavigator() method of the XmlDataDocument object to get reference to the XPathNavigator object. After it has reference to the XPathNavigator object, it then filters out a specific set of nodes by invoking the Select() method. Finally, it loops through all the selected nodes by repeatedly calling the MoveNext() method of the XPathNodeIterator class until the end of the XPathNavigator is reached.

> Note that Listing 8-11 uses the XmlDataDocument for loading the XML document into the memory. Because the XmlDataDocument is not optimized for XPath queries, this approach is not recommended and might result in negative performance impact to your application.

DataTable and XML

Now with ADO.NET 2.0, the DataTable is now a first class citizen and supports serialization along with other DataSet features. It is because of the fact the DataTable class now implements the IXmlSerializable interface. In addition, the DataTable class now supports the ReadXml/WriteXml methods that could only be emulated in .NET Framework 1.x. Table 8-6 outlines the important XML related methods supported by the DataTable class.

Table 8-6. DataTable's XML Methods

Method	Description
ReadXml	Reads XML and data into the DataTable from sources such as a Stream, XmlWriter, or a TextWriter
ReadXmlSchema	Reads an XML schema into the DataTable from a variety of sources like a Stream, XmlWriter, or a TextWriter
WriteXml	Allows you to write the current contents of the DataTable to a File, Stream, TextWriter, or an XmlWriter object
WriteXmlSchema	Allows you to write the schema of the DataTable object

Now that you have a general understanding of the XML related methods of the DataTable, Listing 8-12 shows you a code example that exercises some of these methods.

Listing 8-12 Serializing a DataTable to XML

```
<%@ Page Language="C#" %>
<%@ Import Namespace="System.Data" %>
<%@ Import Namespace="System.Data.SqlClient" %>
<%@ Import Namespace="System.IO" %>
<%@ Import Namespace="System.Xml" %>
<%@ Import Namespace="System.Web.Configuration" %>
<script runat="server">
void Page_Load(object sender, System.EventArgs e)
{
    string xmlFilePath = Server.MapPath("App_Data/ContactType.xml");
    string xmlSchemaFilePath = Server.MapPath("App_Data/ContactType.xsd");
    //Get the values from the database
    DataTable contactTypesTable = GetContactTypes();
    //Write the contents of the DataTable to a local XML file
    contactTypesTable.WriteXml(xmlFilePath);
    contactTypesTable.WriteXmlSchema(xmlSchemaFilePath);
    Response.Write("File is successfully written");
}

DataTable GetContactTypes()
{
    string connString = WebConfigurationManager.
      ConnectionStrings["adventureWorks"].ConnectionString;
    string sql = "Select * from Person.ContactType";
    DataTable contactTypesTable = new DataTable("ContactType");
    using (SqlConnection sqlConn = new SqlConnection(connString))
    {
      SqlDataAdapter adapter = new SqlDataAdapter(sql, sqlConn);
      adapter.Fill(contactTypesTable);
    }
    return contactTypesTable;
}
</script>
<html xmlns="http://www.w3.org/1999/xhtml" >
<head runat="server">
  <title>Writing XML data from a DataTable</title>
</head>
<body>
<form id="form1" runat="server">
    <div>
    </div>
  </form>
</body>
</html>
```

Listing 8-12 starts by retrieving the path of the ContactType.xml and ContactType.xsd files into local variables; then you invoke a helper method named GetContactTypes() that retrieves the contact types information from the AdventureWorks database and returns the output in the form of a DataTable to the caller. Finally, you write the XML and the XSD schema contents of the DataTable using the WriteXml() and WriteXmlSchema() methods, respectively.

Associating a DataReader with a DataTable

In ADO.NET 2.0, you can load a `DataReader` directly into a `DataTable` directly. A new method named `Load()` is available in `DataSet` and `DataTable`, by which you can load `DataReader` into `DataSet`/`DataTable`. Similarly, you can get a `DataReader` back from `DataSet` or `DataTable`.

> `DataTable` **object now provides a new method named** `CreateDataReader()` **that returns a** `DataTableReader` **object corresponding to the data contained in the** `DataTable`. **This method in addition to the** `WriteXml` **method enables you to easily switch between relational and hierarchical views of data when navigating through the data contained in the** `DataTable`. **Note that the** `DataTableReader` **is a new class introduced with .NET Framework 2.0 and this class provides forward-only read-only access to the data contained in the** `DataTable`. **The following code shows how to load XML data into a** `DataTable` **and then navigate through the contents of the** `DataTable` **using a** `DataTableReader` **object in a forward-only read-only fashion.**

```
DataTable contactTypesTable = new DataTable();
string sql = "Select * from Person.ContactType";
using (SqlConnection sqlConn = new SqlConnection(connString))
{
  SqlDataAdapter adapter = new SqlDataAdapter(sql, sqlConn);
  adapter.Fill(contactTypesTable);
}
DataTableReader reader = contactTypesTable.CreateDataReader();
while(reader.Read())
{
  //Do something with the DataTableReader contents
}
```

Summary

In ADO.NET, XML is much more than a simple output format for serializing data. You can use XML to streamline the entire contents of a DataSet, but you can also choose the actual XML schema and control the structure of the resulting XML document. There are several ways to persist a DataSet object's contents. By leveraging the integration features of DataSet with the XmlDataDocument, you can easily switch between relational and hierarchical representations of data thereby taking advantage of the features of both relational and hierarchical worlds. The DataTable object is now an independent object that you can query to get XML representation of your relational data.

XML Data Display

The last chapter demonstrated how the XML features of ADO.NET can be used to create rich data accessing functionality within your Web applications. You can use the XML features of ADO.NET to either directly retrieve XML data from your relational databases or convert relational data into XML data for further processing. Once you have the XML data, you then need to be able to transform that XML data using an XSL style sheet or supply that as an input to data source controls. This chapter focuses on the techniques of XML data display, which are useful in displaying the XML data in a meaningful manner to the users of your Web application. This chapter will explore the concepts of XML data display by looking at various data source controls, and server side controls that aid in transforming XML data before displaying them onto the browser. In addition, this chapter will also describe the caching techniques that you can use to cache XML data in the server side.

By the end of this chapter, you will have a good understanding of the following:

- ❑ What the ASP.NET Hierarchical data controls are
- ❑ Structure of a `web.sitemap` file and its role in describing the hierarchy of a Web site
- ❑ Codeless data binding and the controls that enable this
- ❑ Support provided by the `XmlDataSource` control for displaying XML data
- ❑ Applying an XSL style sheet to transform XML data using an `XmlDataSource` control
- ❑ Binding an `XmlDataSource` control to a `GridView` control
- ❑ Caching XML data in an `XmlDataSource` control
- ❑ Dynamic retrieval of XML data from the client side
- ❑ What Atlas technology is and its role in retrieving XML data

This chapter will also harness the XPath skills acquired from the previous chapter, and leverage it to select portions of XML data in an XML file.

ASP.NET 2.0 Hierarchical Data Controls

One of the most talked about features of .NET 2.0 is its code reduction feature, which can reduce the number of lines code required for an application by 70%. The new data source controls and the data-aware controls that ship with ASP.NET 2.0 are a major addition to this platform that can greatly contribute to this ambitious goal from Microsoft. One of the limitations of ASP.NET 1.x is that it did not provide a declarative model for binding data to data-aware controls such as `DataGrid`, `DataList`, and `Repeater`. Now in ASP.NET 2.0, you have a very powerful and easy-to-use declarative model for binding data directly from the database or from a middle tier object.

> Data source controls are controls that read the data from an external source such as a relational database table, or an XML file or from a middle tier object and make it readily available to data bound controls, which can read data from the data source controls (by using a declarative approach without involving any line of code) and then display the data in a meaningful manner to the users of the Web application.

The architecture of ASP.NET 2.0 controls for hierarchical data is very similar to the design of controls for tabular data. ASP.NET offers both hierarchical data source controls and hierarchical data-bound controls. In addition, there are some cases where you can use a tabular data-bound control.

- ❑ ASP.NET hierarchical Data Source Controls
  - ❑ `SiteMapDataSource`
  - ❑ `XmlDataSource`
- ❑ ASP.NET hierarchical Data Bound Controls
  - ❑ `TreeView`
  - ❑ `Menu`
  - ❑ Templated controls such as `DataList`

Because of the flexibility and common object model in the ASP.NET data story, there are some situations where you can use a data-bound control (that normally is for tabular data) for hierarchical data. For example, an XML file holding the names of states can be used as the source for a list box. A `GridView` can display hierarchical data in a grid, but it tends to get very flat grids. Throughout this chapter, I will demonstrate the applications of these controls in depth.

Site Navigation

In ASP.NET 2.0, you represent the navigation structures for a Web site through a file called `web.sitemap`. The `web.sitemap` file contains a single top-level `siteMap` element. Nested within the `siteMap` element is at least one `siteMapNode` element. The Site Navigation feature requires a single root `siteMapNode` to ensure that you will always converge on a single well-known node when walking up through the hierarchy of the nodes. You can nest as many `siteMapNode` elements beneath the root `siteMapNode` element as needed. Additionally, you can nest `siteMapNode` elements to any arbitrary depth.

The `siteMapNode` element usually contains the `Url`, `Title`, and `Description` attributes:

- ❏ The `Url` attribute indicates a virtual path that corresponds to a page in your application. It can also contain paths to pages in other applications, or URLs that point at completely different Web sites. You should use relative paths when specifying the `Url`s in the `web.sitemap` file.

- ❏ The `Title` attribute displays the textual content when rendering the UI for navigational data. For example, the `SiteMapPath` control uses the `Title` attribute to display the text of the hyperlinks in the control.

- ❏ If the `siteMapNode` contains a `Description` attribute, you use that information to display tool tips or ALT text.

Once you have the site navigation structure available in the web.sitemap file, you then can consume that information using a `SiteMapDataSource` control. `SiteMapDataSource` control allows you to bind hierarchical site map data with hierarchical Web server controls such as `SiteMapPath`, `TreeView`, `Menu`, and so on. To display the site navigation in data bound controls, you need to go through the following steps:

- ❏ Add a `SiteMapDataSource` control to your page. This control will automatically consume the contents of the `web.sitemap` file and make it readily available for the hierarchical data bound controls.

- ❏ Bind the data bound controls such as `SiteMapPath`, `TreeView`, and `Menu` to the `SiteMapDataSource` control and then display the site navigation information.

Now that you have an understanding of the procedures involved in displaying the site navigation information, it's time to briefly define the graphical site navigation controls:

- ❏ `SiteMapPath` — This is a breadcrumb control that retrieves the user's current page and displays the hierarchy of pages. Since the entire hierarchy is displayed through this control, it enables the users to navigate back to other pages in the hierarchy. `SiteMapPath` works exclusively with the `SiteMapDataSource` control.

- ❏ `TreeView` — This control provides a vertical user interface to expand and collapse selected nodes on a Web page, as well as providing check box functionality for selected items. By setting the `SiteMapDataSource` control as the data source for the `TreeView` control, you can leverage the automatic data binding capabilities of the `TreeView` control.

- ❏ `Menu` — This control provides a horizontal or vertical user interface that also can display additional sub-menus when a user hovers over an item. When you use the `SiteMapDataSource` control as the data source, data binding will be automatic.

Now that you have seen the different controls, let us go through few examples that exercise these controls.

In this example, you will use the `TreeView` control to display hierarchical information about the site structure using the contents of the web.sitemap file. In the `web.sitemap` file, you specify the list of nodes that specifies the navigation structure of the site, which can be completely independent of the site folder layout or other structure. Listing 9-1 shows an example `web.sitemap` file.

Listing 9-1: Web.sitemap File

```
<?xml version="1.0" encoding="utf-8" ?>
<siteMap>
  <siteMapNode title="Default" description="Home" url="Default.aspx" >
    <siteMapNode title="Members" description="Members"
      url="Members.aspx">
      <siteMapNode title="My Account" description="My Account"
        url="MyAccount.aspx" />
      <siteMapNode title="Products" description="Products"
        url="Products.aspx" />
    </siteMapNode>
    <siteMapNode title="Administration" description="Administration"
      url="~/Admin/Default.aspx">
      <siteMapNode title="Customer Admin" description="Customer Admin"
        url="~/Admin/Customer/default.aspx" />
      <siteMapNode title="Products Admin"
        description="Products Admin" url="~/Admin/ProductsAdmin.aspx" />
    </siteMapNode>
  </siteMapNode>
</siteMap>
```

Listing 9-2 shows how the SiteMapDataSource control can act as the data source control for a TreeView control.

Listing 9-2: Displaying Site Navigation Information

```
<%@ Page Language="C#" %>
<html xmlns="http://www.w3.org/1999/xhtml" >
<head>
  <title>Site Navigation Information through a SiteMapDataSource Control
  </title>
</head>
<body>
  <form id="form1" runat="server">
    <div>
      <asp:TreeView ID="TreeView1" Runat="server"
        DataSourceID="SiteMapDataSource1"
        ExpandDepth="2" ShowExpandCollapse="False" NodeIndent="10">
        <LevelStyles>
          <asp:TreeNodeStyle Font-Bold="True" Font-Underline="False"/>
          <asp:TreeNodeStyle Font-Italic="True" Font-Underline="False" />
          <asp:TreeNodeStyle Font-Size="X-Small"
            ImageUrl="~/Images/bullet.gif" Font-Underline="False" />
        </LevelStyles>
        <NodeStyle ChildNodesPadding="10" />
      </asp:TreeView>
      <asp:SiteMapDataSource ID="SiteMapDataSource1" Runat="server"/>
    </div>
  </form>
</html>
```

As you can see, the code has a SiteMapDataSource control in the page and the SiteMapDataSource control is used as the data source control for the treeview named TreeView1. This is accomplished by setting the DataSourceID property of the TreeView control to the ID of the SiteMapDataSource. The

`TreeView` control also defines the styles for the different node levels. In this example, because you have a `SiteMapDataSource` placed on the page, the `SiteMapDataSource` control will automatically look for a file with the name `web.sitemap`. It will read the contents of the web.sitemap file and make it readily available to data bound controls. Figure 9-1 shows the output produced by Listing 9-2.

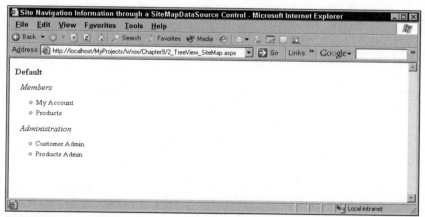

Figure 9-1

In addition to retrieving the contents of the web.sitemap file through the `SiteMapDataSource` control, it is also possible for you to programmatically retrieve site navigation data from within code. To this end, ASP.NET provides a new class named `SiteMap` that provides a number of static methods and properties. For example, you can invoke the `SiteMap.CurrentNode` property to reference a piece of navigation data matching the currently executing page.

XmlDataSource Control

The data controls supplied with ASP.NET support a variety of rich data-binding scenarios. By taking advantage of the new data source controls, you can bind to any data source without writing any code. One such control is `<asp:XmlDataSource>`. This control allows you to bind to XML data, which can come from a variety of sources, such as an external XML file, a DataSet object, and so on. Once the XML data is bound to the `XmlDataSource` control, this control can then act as a source of data for other data-bound controls such as `TreeView` and `Menu`. The `XmlDataSource` control can be bound to any of the following data controls:

- ❑ `<asp:TreeView>`
- ❑ `<asp:GridView>`
- ❑ `<asp:DataList>`
- ❑ `<asp:DropDownList>`
- ❑ `<asp:Repeater>`

The XmlDataSource control provides a rich set of properties and methods that can enable sophisticated data binding scenarios. Table 9-1 provides a brief overview of the important properties of the XmlDataSource control.

Table 9-1. Important Properties of the XmlDataSource Control

Property	Description
CacheDuration	Gets or sets the length of time the control caches data retrieved by the data source control.
CacheExpirationPolicy	Gets or sets the cache expiration behavior that describes the caching behavior of the data source control. Can be set to either Absolute or Sliding.
Data	Gets or sets a block of XML that data source control binds to.
DataFile	Specifies the name of an XML file that the data source control binds to.
Transform	Gets or sets a block of XSL that defines the XSLT transformation to be performed on the XML data.
TransformArgumentList	Provides a list of XSLT arguments that can be passed to the XSLT style sheet at runtime.
TransformFile	Specifies the file name of XSL file that defines the XSLT transformation to be performed on the XML data.
XPath	Specifies an XPath query to be applied to the XML data contained by the Data property or by the XML file indicated by the DataFile property.

You will employ most of these properties in Table 9-1 in the later sections of this chapter. Before looking at how to use XmlDataSource control, consider the XML document shown in Listing 9-3 that contains a simple bookstore that provides information about the various books that are part of the bookstore.

Listing 9-3: Bookstore.XML File

```
<bookstore>
<genre name="Fiction">
    <book ISBN="10-861003-324" Title="A Tale of Two Cities" Price="19.99">
      <chapter num="1" name="Introduction">
        Abstract...
      </chapter>
      <chapter num="2" name="Body">
        Abstract...
      </chapter>
      <chapter num="3" name="Conclusion">
        Abstract...
      </chapter>
    </book>
    <book ISBN="1-861001-57-5" Title="Pride And Prejudice" Price="24.95">
      <chapter num="1" name="Introduction">
        Abstract...
      </chapter>
```

```
        <chapter num="2" name="Body">
          Abstract...
        </chapter>
        <chapter num="3" name="Conclusion">
          Abstract...
        </chapter>
      </book>
    </genre>
    <genre name="NonFiction">
        <book ISBN="10-861003-324" Title="Statistics of Two Cities" Price="19.99">
          <chapter num="1" name="Introduction">
            Abstract...
          </chapter>
          <chapter num="2" name="Body">
            Abstract...
          </chapter>
          <chapter num="3" name="Conclusion">
            Abstract...
          </chapter>
        </book>
        <book ISBN="1-861001-57-6"
          Title="The Sea: becoming an Old Man and the Sea" Price="27.95">
          <chapter num="1" name="Introduction">
            Abstract...
          </chapter>
          <chapter num="2" name="Body">
            Abstract...
          </chapter>
          <chapter num="3" name="Conclusion">
            Abstract...
          </chapter>
        </book>
    </genre>
</bookstore>
```

Note that the books.xml file shown in Listing 9-3 will be used in most of the examples presented in this chapter. Now that you have created the XML file, it is time to create the style sheet that will transform the XML into HTML. Listing 9-4 shows the declaration of the XSL style sheet.

Listing 9-4: Bookstore.XSL File

```
<xsl:stylesheet version="1.0"
xmlns:xsl="http://www.w3.org/1999/XSL/Transform">
  <xsl:template match="bookstore">
    <bookstore>
      <xsl:apply-templates select="genre"/>
    </bookstore>
  </xsl:template>
  <xsl:template match="genre">
    <genre>
      <xsl:attribute name="name">
        <xsl:value-of select="@name"/>
      </xsl:attribute>
      <xsl:apply-templates select="book"/>
    </genre>
```

```
    </xsl:template>
    <xsl:template match="book">
      <book>
        <xsl:attribute name="ISBN">
          <xsl:value-of select="@ISBN"/>
        </xsl:attribute>
        <xsl:element name="title">
          <xsl:value-of select="title"/>
        </xsl:element>
        <xsl:element name="price">
          <xsl:value-of select="price"/>
        </xsl:element>
        <xsl:apply-templates select="chapters/chapter" />
      </book>
    </xsl:template>
    <xsl:template match="chapter">
      <chapter>
        <xsl:attribute name="num">
          <xsl:value-of select="@num"/>
        </xsl:attribute>
        <xsl:attribute name="name">
          <xsl:value-of select="@name"/>
        </xsl:attribute>
        <xsl:apply-templates/>
      </chapter>
    </xsl:template>
  </xsl:stylesheet>
```

Now that you have had a brief look at the XML and XSL files, the next section dives deep into the process of implementing data binding with the XmlDataSource control.

Data Binding with XmlDataSource Control

Typically, you will want to modify the display of the XML to provide more meaningful information. This section demonstrates how to bind the XmlDataSource control with a TreeView control. The TreeView control exposes bindings that let you specify how each node is rendered. For example, you can create a binding for the bookstore element that states that it should be rendered using the static text, Books. The TreeView also contains a number of built-in properties that let you easily customize its appearance. For example, you can set the ImageSet property to a specific value that will render with predefined graphics so that elements appear as folders. Listing 9-5 shows the code required for data binding an XmlDataSource control with a TreeView control.

Listing 9-5: Binding a TreeView Control to an XmlDataSource Control

```
<%@ Page Language="C#" %>
<html xmlns="http://www.w3.org/1999/xhtml" >
<head>
  <title>Binding XML Data from an XmlDataSource Control</title>
</head>
<body>
<form id="form1" runat="server">
  <div>
    <asp:TreeView ID="TreeView1" Runat="server"
```

```
        DataSourceID="XmlDataSource1">
        <DataBindings>
          <asp:TreeNodeBinding ImageUrl="~/Images/openbook.gif"
            TextField="Title" DataMember="book"></asp:TreeNodeBinding>
          <asp:TreeNodeBinding ImageUrl="~/Images/notepad.gif"
            TextField="name" DataMember="chapter"></asp:TreeNodeBinding>
        </DataBindings>
      </asp:TreeView>
    </div>
    <div>
      <asp:XmlDataSource ID="XmlDataSource1" Runat="server"
        DataFile="~/App_Data/Bookstore.xml"
        XPath="bookstore/genre[@name='Fiction']/book">
      </asp:XmlDataSource>
    </div>
  </form>
    XPath="bookstore/genre[@name='Fiction']/book"</body>
  </html>
```

In the above code, you have two controls on the page. The first, XmlDataSource, does all of the work, including reading the bookstore.xml and applying the XPath expression to the contents of the XML file. The second, the TreeView, takes that data and displays that information on the page. To bind the TreeView to the XmlDataSource source, you need to set the DataSourceID property of the TreeView control to the ID of the XmlDataSource control. With the preceding steps, you can see on your page a display of data from your XmlDataSource control. The output produced by the page is shown in Figure 9-2.

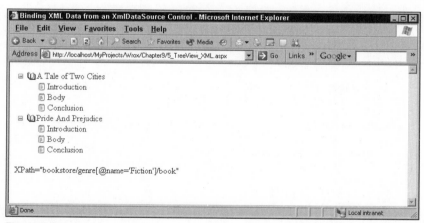

Figure 9-2

Data Binding an XmlDataSource Control with a GridView Control

Frequently, XML is the source of data in many cases. So you need a way to be able to display that XML data in other tabular controls apart from the TreeView control, which is hierarchical in nature. This section explores how to use an XmlDataSource control with a GridView control, and a DropDownList control.

> The GridView control is the successor to the DataGrid control that was part of
> ASP.NET 1.x versions. It is similar in functionality to the DataGrid control in that it
> is also used to display the contents from a data source. In a GridView control, each
> column represents a field, while each row represents a record. As you would expect,
> you can bind a GridView control to any data source controls, such as XmlDataSource,
> ObjectDataSource, and SqlDataSource, as well as any data source that implements
> the System.Collections.IEnumerable interface.

The code in Listing 9-6 uses an XmlDataSource control as the data source for a GridView control.

Listing 9-6: Binding a GridView and a ListBox Control to an XmlDataSource Control

```
<%@ Page Language="C#" %>
<%@ Import Namespace="System.Xml" %>
<html xmlns="http://www.w3.org/1999/xhtml" >
<head>
  <title>Displaying XML Data in a GridView and a ListBox</title>
</head>
<body>
  <form id="form1" runat="server">
    <div>
       
    </div>
    <div>
      <asp:ListBox ID="lstTitles" Runat="server"
        DataSourceID="XmlDataSource1" DataValueField="ISBN"
        DataTextField="Title"/>
    </div>
    <div>
      <asp:GridView ID="GridView1" Runat="server"
        DataSourceID="XmlDataSource1" AutoGenerateColumns="False">
        <Columns>
          <asp:BoundField HeaderText="ISBN" DataField="ISBN"
            SortExpression="ISBN"></asp:BoundField>
          <asp:BoundField HeaderText="Title" DataField="Title"
            SortExpression="Title"></asp:BoundField>
          <asp:BoundField HeaderText="Price" DataField="Price"
            SortExpression="Price"></asp:BoundField>
        </Columns>
      </asp:GridView>
    </div>
    <div>
      <asp:XmlDataSource ID="XmlDataSource1" Runat="server"
        DataFile="~/App_Data/Bookstore.xml"
        XPath="bookstore/genre[@name='Fiction']/book">
      </asp:XmlDataSource>
       
    </div>
    <div>
```

```
         
      </div>
    </form>
  </body>
</html>
```

In Listing 9-6, you have the `GridView` control named `GridView1` and its `DataSourceID` property is set to the ID of the `XmlDataSource` control. Once you have created that association, you can then bind the individual fields in the `XmlDataSource` control to the columns in the `GridView`. Note that `XmlDataSource` control has its `XPath` attribute set to a specific XPath expression, which will be evaluated at runtime. As part of the columns declaration, three columns are declared: `ISBN`, `Title`, and `Price`. Along with the columns declaration, you also set the `HeaderText`, `SortExpression`, and `DataField` properties to appropriate values. That's all there is to displaying data in a `GridView` control using `XmlDataSource` as the data source. Similarly, the `ListBox` control is also bound to the `XmlDataSource` through the `DataSourceID` property. Apart from setting the `DataSourceID` property, you also set the `DataValueField` and `DataTextField` properties to appropriate values. If you request the page from the browser, you should see the output shown in Figure 9-3.

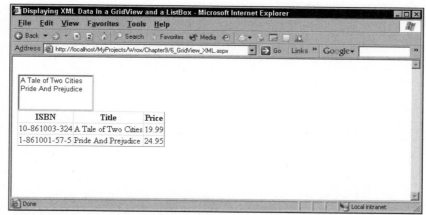

Figure 9-3

Inline XML Data with XmlDataSource Control

So far, you have seen how to utilize an external XML file to load the required data into the `XmlDataSource` control. However, if you have a relatively simple XML data and you know the XML contents at design time, you might then want to embed the XML data inline along with the `XmlDataSource` control declaration for reasons of simplicity. Listing 9-7 demonstrates how to use an `XmlDataSource` to display inline XML data contained by the `Data` property with a `TreeView` control.

Listing 9-7: Using Inline XML Data as the Input for the XmlDataSource Control

```
<%@ Page Language="C#" %>
<html xmlns="http://www.w3.org/1999/xhtml" >
<head>
  <title>Using Inline XML Data in an XmlDataSource Control</title>
</head>
```

```
<body>
  <form id="form1" runat="server">
    <div>
      <asp:TreeView ID="TreeView1" Runat="server"
        DataSourceID="XmlDataSource1">
        <DataBindings>
          <asp:TreeNodeBinding ImageUrl="~/Images/openbook.gif"
            TextField="Title" DataMember="book"></asp:TreeNodeBinding>
          <asp:TreeNodeBinding ImageUrl="~/Images/notepad.gif"
            TextField="name" DataMember="chapter"></asp:TreeNodeBinding>
        </DataBindings>
      </asp:TreeView>
    </div>
    <div>
      <asp:XmlDataSource ID="XmlDataSource1" Runat="server" XPath="bookstore/book">
        <Data>
          <bookstore>
            <book ISBN="10-861003-324" Title="A Tale of Two Cities" Price="19.99">
              <chapter num="1" name="Introduction">
                Abstract...
              </chapter>
              <chapter num="2" name="Body">
                Abstract...
              </chapter>
              <chapter num="3" name="Conclusion">
                Abstract...
              </chapter>
            </book>
            <book ISBN="1-861001-57-5" Title="Pride And Prejudice"
              Price="24.95">
              <chapter num="1" name="Introduction">
                Abstract...
              </chapter>
              <chapter num="2" name="Body">
                Abstract...
              </chapter>
              <chapter num="3" name="Conclusion">
                Abstract...
              </chapter>
            </book>
          </bookstore>
        </Data>
      </asp:XmlDataSource>
    </div>
  </form>
</body>
</html>
```

The above code is very similar to Listing 9-5 except for the difference that the XML data is embedded within the declaration of the XmlDataSource control in this case. In declarative scenarios such as the above one, the Data property is specified as a multiline inner property of the XmlDataSource object. An inner property is compatible with XML data, because it enables you to format the XML data in any way and ignore character adding issues, such as padding quote characters. Note that the value of the Data property is stored in view state.

Similar to the Data property, XmlDataSource *control also has a property named* Transform *that allows you to embed inline XSL style sheet as part of the* XmlDataSource *control declaration. This property defines an XSLT transformation to be performed on the XML data that is contained by the* Data *property or by the XML file indicated by the* DataFile *property. The default value is* System.String.Empty.

If both the DataFile and Data properties are set for an XmlDataSource control, the DataFile property takes precedence and the data in the XML file is used instead of the XML specified in the Data property.

XSL Transformations with XmlDataSource Control

XSLT is the most important part of the Extensible Stylesheet Language (XSL) Standards. As you have seen in Chapter 7, it is that part of XSL that is used to transform an XML document into another XML document, or another type of document that is recognized by a browser, such as HTML and XHTML. Traditionally performing XSL transformations in .NET Framework require you to use the XslCompiledTransform class and its methods. Fortunately with XmlDataSource control, you have an easy and effective way to perform XSL transformations by leveraging the built-in attributes of the XmlDataSource control. Listing 9-8 shows you an example of how to utilize XSL to format an XML document into another XML document.

Listing 9-8: Performing XSL Transformation on an XmlDataSource Control

```
<%@ Page Language="C#" %>
<html xmlns="http://www.w3.org/1999/xhtml" >
<head>
  <title>Applying XSL Transformation on an XmlDataSource Control</title>
</head>
<body>
<form id="form1" runat="server">
   <div>
     <asp:TreeView ID="TreeView1" Runat="server"
       DataSourceID="XmlDataSource1" />
     <asp:XmlDataSource ID="XmlDataSource1" Runat="server"
       DataFile="~/App_Data/Bookstore.xml"
       TransformFile="~/App_Data/Bookstore.xsl" />
   </div>
  </form>
</body>
</html>
```

You have two controls on the page. The first, XmlDataSource, does all of the work, including reading the Bookstore.xsl and loading of XML contents into its memory. Instead of directly using the XML from the XmlDataSource control, you transform the XML into another format. This is accomplished using the TransformFile property. In this case, you set the value of TransformFile property to Bookstore.xsl. The second control, the TreeView, takes that data and displays that information on the page. To bind the TreeView to the XmlDataSource source, you set the DataSourceID property of the TreeView control to the ID of the XmlDataSource control. Figure 9-4 shows the output of the page when requested through the browser.

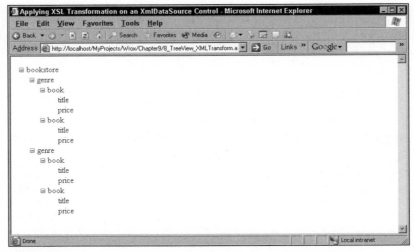

Figure 9-4

Nested DataList Controls with an XmlDataSource Control

The DataList control is used to display a repeated list of items that are bound to the control. However, the DataList control adds a table around the data items by default. The DataList control may be bound to a database table, an XML file, or another list of items. Code Listing 9-9 shows how to bind the XmlDataSource control to a DataList control.

Listing 9-9: XmlDataSource Control as a Data Source Control for Nested DataList Controls

```
<%@ Page Language="C#" %>
<html>
<head>
  <title>Displaying XML Data in Nested DataList Controls</title>
</head>
<body>
  <form runat="server">
    <h1>Bookstore: Fiction</h1>
    <asp:XmlDataSource id="MySource" DataFile="~/App_Data/Bookstore.xml"
      XPath="bookstore/genre[@name='Fiction']/book" runat="server"/>
    <asp:DataList id="DataList1" DataSourceId="MySource" runat="server">
      <ItemTemplate>
        <table>
          <tr>
            <td>
              <img src='<%# "images/" + XPath("@ISBN") + ".jpg" %>'>
            </td>
            <td>
              <h4><%# XPath("@Title") %></h4>
              <b>ISBN:</b> <%# XPath("@ISBN") %><br>
              <b>Price:</b> <%# XPath("@Price") %><br>
            </td>
          </tr>
        </table>
```

```
        <asp:DataList id="DataList2" DataSource='<%# XPathSelect("chapter")%>'
          runat="server">
          <ItemTemplate>
            <br>
            <u>
              Chapter <%# XPath("@num") %>: <%# XPath("@name") %>
            </u>
            <br>
              <%# XPath(".") %>
          </ItemTemplate>
        </asp:DataList>
      </ItemTemplate>
    </asp:DataList>
  </form>
</body>
</html>
```

In the above example, you have a DataList control named DataList1 and its DataSourceID property is set to the ID of the XmlDataSource control. In the DataList control, the ItemTemplate element is used to specify the data fields in the XmlDataSource control that will be displayed through the Label controls. As part of the label controls declaration, you use the XPath expression to identify the element in the XmlDataSource. To the XPath expression, you pass in the name of the data element as a parameter. Since the XmlDataSource contains elements such as ISBN, Title, and Price, you use them in the XPath expression. In addition to the outer DataList control, there is also an inner DataList control named DataList2 for which the outer data source control provides the source data. This is accomplished by setting the DataSource property of the DataList2 control to the output produced by the XPathSelect function.

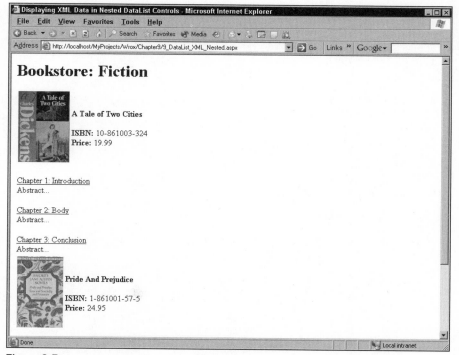

Figure 9-5

Output produced by the code in Listing 9-9 is shown in Figure 9-5.

Caching

Cache API in ASP.NET is one of the powerful features that can be immensely useful in increasing the performance of a Web application. The most dramatic way to improve the performance of a database-driven Web application is through caching. Retrieving data from a database is one of the slowest operations that you can perform in a Web site. If, however, you can cache the database data in memory, then you can avoid accessing the database with every page request, and dramatically increase your application's performance. Fortunately taking advantage of caching in ASP.NET is very simple and just requires a couple of attributes. There are two ways you can implement caching when it comes to caching XML output of a page.

❏   You can cache the entire page, which will result in the output of all the data source controls such as XmlDataSource control being cached in addition to the rest of the page.

❏   You can also cache just the output of the XmlDataSource control so that the rest of the page output will be generated dynamically every time.

The next two sections demonstrate both these types of caching.

Page Output Caching

Listing 9-10 shows the code required to perform page output caching. The OutputCache directive at the top of the page is used to specify the cache related attributes.

Listing 9-10: Page Output Caching

```
<%@ Page Language="C#" %>
<%@ OutputCache Duration="6000" VaryByParam="none" %>
<%@ Import Namespace="System.Xml" %>
<script runat="server">
  void Page_Load(object sender, EventArgs e)
  {
    lblCurrentTime.Text = "Current Time is : " +
      DateTime.Now.ToLongTimeString();
  }
</script>
<html xmlns="http://www.w3.org/1999/xhtml" >
<head>
  <title>Caching XML Data in an XmlDataSource Control</title>
</head>
<body>
  <form id="form1" runat="server">
    <div>
      <asp:Label Runat="server" ID="lblCurrentTime"></asp:Label>
    </div>
    <div>
      <asp:GridView ID="GridView1" Runat="server"
        DataSourceID="XmlDataSource1" AutoGenerateColumns="False">
        <Columns>
          <asp:BoundField HeaderText="ISBN" DataField="ISBN"
```

```
                SortExpression="ISBN"></asp:BoundField>
            <asp:BoundField HeaderText="Title" DataField="Title"
                SortExpression="Title"></asp:BoundField>
            <asp:BoundField HeaderText="Price" DataField="Price"
                SortExpression="Price"></asp:BoundField>
        </Columns>
      </asp:GridView>
      <asp:XmlDataSource ID="XmlDataSource1" Runat="server"
        DataFile="~/App_Data/Bookstore.xml"
        XPath="bookstore/genre[@name='Fiction']/book">
      </asp:XmlDataSource>
    </div>
  </form>
</body>
</html>
```

Because of the duration attribute value of 6000, the entire page is cached for 6000 seconds in the above example. To demonstrate the fact the page is cached for 6000 seconds, the Page_Load event populates a label control named lblCurrentTime with the current time of the server. This value should remain the same as long as you request the same page within the next 6000 seconds. The output produced by the page is shown in Figure 9-6.

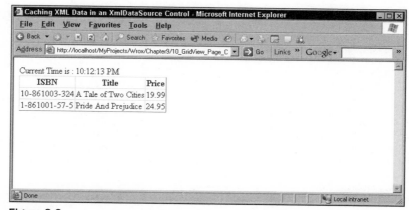

Figure 9-6

Implementing Caching with XmlDataSource Control

So far, you have seen how to take advantage of caching at the ASP.NET page output level. There are times where you might want to cache just parts of the page. For example, you might want to cache just the output of a data source control but still recreating the rest of the page every time the page is requested. The data source controls not only enable codeless data binding scenarios, but also make it easier for you to cache database data. This section explains how to implement caching with the XmlDataSource control.

Simply by setting a couple of properties on the XmlDataSource control, you can automatically cache the data represented by a data source control in memory. For example, if you want to cache the Bookstore.xml file in memory for 100 seconds, you can declare an XmlDataSource control like this.

```
<asp:XmlDataSource EnableCaching="true" CacheDuration="100"
  ID="XmlDataSource1" Runat="server"
  DataFile="~/App_Data/Bookstore.xml">
</asp:XmlDataSource>
```

Listing 9-11 shows the complete code of the page.

Listing 9-11: XmlDataSource Control Caching

```
<%@ Page Language="C#" %>
<%@ Import Namespace="System.Xml" %>
<script runat="server">
  void Page_Load(object sender, EventArgs e)
  {
    lblCurrentTime.Text = "Current Time is : " +
      DateTime.Now.ToLongTimeString();
  }
</script>
<html xmlns="http://www.w3.org/1999/xhtml" >
<head>
  <title>Caching XML Data in an XmlDataSource Control</title>
</head>
<body>
  <form id="form1" runat="server">
    <div>
      <asp:Label Runat="server" ID="lblCurrentTime"></asp:Label>
      <asp:GridView ID="GridView1" Runat="server"
        DataSourceID="XmlDataSource1" AutoGenerateColumns="False">
        <Columns>
          <asp:BoundField HeaderText="ISBN" DataField="ISBN"
            SortExpression="ISBN"></asp:BoundField>
          <asp:BoundField HeaderText="Title" DataField="Title"
            SortExpression="Title"></asp:BoundField>
          <asp:BoundField HeaderText="Price" DataField="Price"
            SortExpression="Price"></asp:BoundField>
        </Columns>
      </asp:GridView>
      <asp:XmlDataSource EnableCaching="true" CacheDuration="100"
        CacheExpirationPolicy="Absolute"
        ID="XmlDataSource1" Runat="server"
        DataFile="~/App_Data/Bookstore.xml"
        XPath="bookstore/genre[@name='Fiction']/book">
      </asp:XmlDataSource>
    </div>
  </form>
</body>
</html>
```

In Listing 9-11, the XmlDataSource control has its EnableCaching property to true. When the EnableCaching property is set to true, the XmlDataSource will automatically cache the XML data obtained by evaluating the XPath expression. The CacheDuration property enables you to specify, in seconds, how long the data should be cached before it is refreshed from the database. By default, the XmlDataSource will cache data using an absolute expiration policy, meaning that the data will be refreshed for every so many seconds that is specified in the CacheDuration property. You also have the option of enabling a sliding expiration policy. When the `XmlDataSource` is configured to use a sliding expiration policy, the data will not be dropped as long as it continues to be accessed. Employing a sliding expiration policy is useful whenever you have a large number of items that need to be cached, because this expiration policy enables you to keep only the most frequently accessed items in memory. In the preceding example, you cached the results of the XPath expression to 100 seconds by setting the `EnableCaching`, `CacheExpirationPolicy`, and `CacheDuration` attributes to `True`, `Absolute`, and `100`, respectively.

Xml Web Server Control

You can use the XML Web server control to write an XML document, or the results of an XSL Transformations (XSLT), into a Web page. The XML output appears in the Web page at the location of the control. The XML and the XSLT information can be in external documents, or you can include the XML inline. Table 9-2 shows the important properties of the `Xml` control.

Table 9-2. Xml Control's Properties

Property	Description
DocumentContent	Sets a string that contains the XML document to display in the Xml control
DocumentSource	Gets or sets the path to an XML document to display in the Xml control
Transform	Gets or sets the `XslTransform` object that formats the XML document before it is written to the output stream
TransformArgumentList	Gets or sets a `XsltArgumentList` object that enables you to pass parameters to the XSL style sheet
TransformSource	Gets or sets the path to an XSL style sheet that formats the XML document before it is written to the output stream

> Note that the `Document` property of the `Xml` control (used in .NET 1.x versions) that allows you to set or get the input XML data in the form of an `XmlDocument` object is now obsolete with .NET Framework 2.0.

There are three ways to load XML data into the XML Web server control.

- ❏ Provide a path to an external XML document, using the `DocumentSource` property
- ❏ Load the XML data in the form of a string using the `DocumentContent` property
- ❏ Include the XML content inline, between the opening and closing tags of the control

Before looking at how to use the `Xml` control, Listing 9-12 examines the XML file that will be used with the `Xml` server control.

Chapter 9

Listing 9-12: Menu.XML File

```xml
<?xml version='1.0'?>
<lunch-menu>
  <food>
    <name>Cheese Pizza</name>
    <price>$6.95</price>
    <description>Individual deep-dish pizza with lots of mozzarella
      Cheese
    </description>
    <calories>800</calories>
  </food>
  <food>
    <name>Pepperoni Pizza</name>
    <price>$7.95</price>
    <description>Individual deep-dish cheese pizza with thick-cut pepperoni
      slices
    </description>
    <calories>950</calories>
  </food>
  <food>
    <name>The "Everything" Pizza</name>
    <price>$9.95</price>
    <description>Individual deep-dish pizza with all our toppings. House
      specialty!
    </description>
    <calories>800</calories>
  </food>
  <food>
    <name>Hungarian Ghoulash</name>
    <price>$4.50</price>
    <description>Large serving in a sourdough bread bowl. A_local
      delight!
    </description>
    <calories>600</calories>
  </food>
  <food>
    <name>Maisey's Pork Sandwich</name>
    <price>$6.95</price>
    <description>A fresh pork fillet, deep-fried to perfection. Served with
  fries.</description>
    <calories>950</calories>
  </food>
</lunch-menu>
```

The above code provides a listing of menu details. The XSL style sheet that will be used to transform the menu.xml file is shown in Listing 9-13:

Listing 9-13: Menu.XSL File

```xml
<?xml version="1.0"?>
<xsl:stylesheet version="1.0" xmlns:xsl="http://www.w3.org/1999/XSL/Transform">
  <xsl:param name="calories">1500</xsl:param>
  <xsl:template match="/">
```

```
<HTML>
  <BODY STYLE="font-family:Arial, helvetica, sans-serif; font-size:12pt;
    background-color:#EEEEEE">
    <xsl:for-each select="lunch-menu/food[calories &lt;= $calories]">
      <DIV STYLE="background-color:blue; color:white; padding:4px">
        <SPAN STYLE="font-weight:bold; color:white">
          <xsl:value-of select="name"/>
        </SPAN>
          <xsl:value-of select="price"/>
      </DIV>
      <DIV STYLE="margin-left:20px; margin-bottom:1em; font-size:10pt">
        <xsl:value-of select="description"/>
        <SPAN STYLE="font-style:italic">
          (<xsl:value-of select="calories"/> calories per serving)
        </SPAN>
      </DIV>
    </xsl:for-each>
  </BODY>
</HTML>
</xsl:template>
</xsl:stylesheet>
```

Note that Listing 9-13 contains a parameter named calories that has a default value of 1500. This default value is overridden by passing parameters from the ASP.NET Web page. Listing 9-14 shows how to accomplish this.

Listing 9-14: Transforming and Displaying XML Data Using an Xml Control

```
<%@ Page Language="C#" %>
<%@ Import Namespace="System.Xml.Xsl" %>
<script runat="server">
  void Button1_Click(object sender, EventArgs e)
  {
    XsltArgumentList argsList = new XsltArgumentList();
    argsList.AddParam("calories", "", TextBox1.Text);
    Xml1.TransformArgumentList = argsList;
    Xml1.Visible = true;
  }
</script>
<html xmlns="http://www.w3.org/1999/xhtml" >
<head runat="server">
  <title>Transforming and Displaying XML Data using Xml Web Server
  Control
  </title>
</head>
<body>
  <form id="form1" runat="server">
    <div>
      <P>Maximum Calories:
        <asp:TextBox id="TextBox1" runat="server"></asp:TextBox>
        <asp:Button OnClick="Button1_Click" id="Button1" runat="server"
          Text="Filter Menu"></asp:Button>
      </P>
```

```
    <P>
      <asp:Xml id="Xml1" runat="server"
        DocumentSource="~/App_Data/Menu.xml"
        TransformSource="~/App_Data/Menu.xsl"></asp:Xml>
    </P>
  </div>
</form>
</body>
</html>
```

In code listing 9-14, the DocumentSource and TransformSource attributes of the Xml control are used to specify the XML and XSL files to use for display purposes. By default, the XSL calories parameter variable is populated with the value of 1500, which will result in the output shown in Figure 9-7.

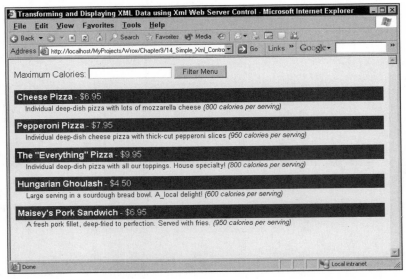

Figure 9-7

In the text box, specify a valid value for the calories and hit the Filter Menu button. This will result in the execution of the code in the Click event of the button, where you create an instance of the XsltArgumentList object and populate its parameter collection by invoking its AddParam() method. Finally, you set the TransformArgumentList property of the Xml control to the XsltArgumentList object.

```
XsltArgumentList argsList = new XsltArgumentList();
argsList.AddParam("calories", "", TextBox1.Text);
Xml1.TransformArgumentList = argsList;
```

If you enter 850 in the calories text box and click on the Filter Menu button, you should see an output that is somewhat similar to Figure 9-8.

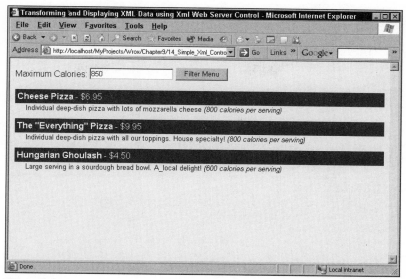

Figure 9-8

Programmatically Transforming Data Using Xml Control

The previous example demonstrated the steps involved in using static XML files and XSL files as an input to the Xml control. This section will provide an example that shows how easy it is to consume and display an RSS 2.0 feed with ASP.NET. Specifically the ASP.NET XML control will be used to transform an RSS feed into a presentable format on a Web page.

The RSS 2.0 XML File

First look at the structure of the RSS 2.0 XML file shown in Listing 9-15.

Listing 9-15: RSS.XML File

```
<?xml version="1.0"?>
<rss version="2.0">
<channel>
    <title>Channel title</title>
    <link>Link to channel page</link>
    <item>
      <title>First content item</title>
      <link>Link to first content item</link>
      <pubDate>First content item publication date</pubDate>
    </item>
    <item>
      <title>Second content item</title>
      <link>Link to second content item</link>
      <pubDate>Second content item publication date</pubDate>
```

```
      </item>
      <item>
        <title>nth content item</title>
        <link>Link to nth content item</link>
        <pubDate>nth content item publication date</pubDate>
      </item>
    </channel>
  </rss>
```

Although the RSS XML format includes some more elements, the code in Listing 9-15 highlights only the important ones for reasons of brevity. Now that you have the XML file, the next step is to define the XSL style sheet that defines a presentation template for the RSS feed. The XSL style sheet is shown in Listing 9-16.

Listing 9-16: RSS.XSL File

```
<?xml version="1.0" encoding="UTF-8"?>
<xsl:stylesheet version="1.0"
  xmlns:xsl="http://www.w3.org/1999/XSL/Transform">
  <xsl:template match="/">
    <xsl:apply-templates select="rss/channel" />
  </xsl:template>
  <xsl:template match="channel">
    <h2>
      <a href="{link}" target="_blank"><xsl:value-of select="title" /></a>
    </h2>
    <ul>
      <xsl:apply-templates select="item" />
    </ul>
  </xsl:template>
  <xsl:template match="item">
    <li>
      <a href="{link}" target="_blank">
        <xsl:value-of select="title" />
      </a>
        <xsl:value-of select="pubDate" />
      <br/>
      <xsl:value-of disable-output-escaping="yes" select="description" />
      <p/>
    </li>
  </xsl:template>
</xsl:stylesheet>
```

Now you are ready to write code to retrieve the remote RSS XML content. In order to do this, you create an XmlDocument object to load the RSS feed in the Page_Load event. The Load() method of the XmlDocument object reads the remote XML content into the object. Then you set the Document property of the Xml control to the XmlDocument object. Listing 9-17 shows the complete Web page with the implementation of the Page_Load event.

Listing 9-17: Programmatically Transforming XML Data using Xml Control

```
<%@ Page Language="C#" %>
<%@ Import Namespace="System.Xml" %>
<%@ Import Namespace="System.Xml.Xsl" %>
```

```
<script runat="server">
  private void Page_Load(object sender, EventArgs e)
  {
    XmlDocument doc = new XmlDocument();
    doc.Load("http://rss.news.yahoo.com/rss/topstories");
    Xml1.Document = doc;
    Xml1.TransformSource = "~/App_Data/RSS.xsl";
  }
</script>
<html xmlns="http://www.w3.org/1999/xhtml" >
<head runat="server">
  <title>Programmatically Displaying XML Data using Xml Web Server
    Control
  </title>
</head>
<body STYLE="font-family:Arial, helvetica, sans-serif; font-size:12pt;
  background-color:#EEEEEE">
  <form id="form1" runat="server">
    <div>
      <P>
        <asp:Xml id="Xml1" runat="server"></asp:Xml>
      </P>
    </div>
  </form>
</body>
</html>
```

Similar to the XmlDocument object, the XSL style sheet is also associated with the Xml control by using the TransformSource property. Requesting the above page from a browser should produce an output shown in Figure 9-9.

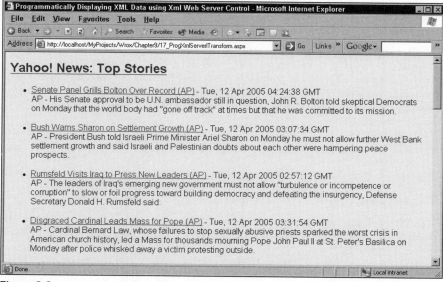

Figure 9-9

If you are displaying an RSS feed on a Web site, it may not be a good idea to retrieve the feed on every page load. In that case, you can cache the output of the page content thereby reducing the number of trips needed to retrieve the RSS feed. In addition to providing improved user experience, caching also results in lighter load on the serving Web site as well as the Web site syndicating its content.

Client-Side XML

So far, you have seen how to retrieve and process XML data from the server side. This section will demonstrate some of the XML processing techniques in the client side. One of the issues developers had when they first started to develop commercial Web sites was some of the limitations of using a browser as the interface. For instance, there were many cases where you wanted to retrieve information from the server after the user had performed some action, like entering an employee number in a Web page to retrieve the details of an employee. To accomplish this, you would post the current page to the server, retrieve the employee information from the database and refresh the page with the information retrieved from the server. Although this method of refreshing the whole page is very common today, it is inefficient because the Web page refreshes and re-renders the entire page of content, even if only a small percentage of the page has actually changed.

Fortunately ASP.NET 2.0 provides an efficient approach to invoke a remote function from a server page without refreshing the browser. This new feature is called ASP.NET 2.0 Script Callback, and it builds on the foundation of the `XmlHttp` object library. Using ASP.NET 2.0 script callback feature, you can emulate some of the behaviors of a traditional fat-client application in a Web-based application. It can be used to refresh individual controls, to validate controls, or even to process a form without having to post the whole page to the server. When you utilize script callback approach to retrieve data, you would typically transfer the data in the form of XML stream from the server side to the client and then load the XML data in a client-side XML DOM object to process the XML.

ASP.NET 2.0 Callback Feature

This section will consider an example wherein you retrieve the details of an employee based on the employee number entered in the Web page. To accomplish this, you will leverage the script callback feature and demonstrate how to retrieve the employee details from the AdventureWorks database without posting the page back to the server.

Before looking at the example, it is time to examine the steps involved in utilizing the callback feature.

❑ The client invokes a client-side method that will use the callback manager.

❑ The callback manager creates the request to a .aspx page on the server.

❑ The ASP.NET runtime on the server receives the request, processes the request by invoking a predefined sever-side function named `RaiseCallbackEvent` and passing in the client side argument to it. The `RaiseCallbackEvent` method stores the client-side arguments in a private variable for later use. After that, the ASP.NET invokes another method named `GetCallbackResult()`, which is responsible for returning the output of the server-side call to the client-side callback manager.

❑ The callback manager receives the server response and invokes a callback method located on the client-side. If there is an error during the server-side processing, the callback manager invokes a separate callback method.

❑ The client callback method processes the results of the server-side call.

Now that you have understood the steps, Listing 9-18 shows an example page that implements callback feature.

Listing 9-18: Retrieving XML Data Dynamically Using ASP.NET 2.0 Script Callback

```
<%@ Page language="C#" %>
<%@ Import Namespace="System.Data" %>
<%@ Import Namespace="System.Data.SqlClient" %>
<%@ Import Namespace="System.Xml" %>
<%@ Import Namespace="System.Web.Configuration" %>
<%@ implements interface="System.Web.UI.ICallbackEventHandler" %>
<script runat="server">
  private string _callbackArg;
  void ICallbackEventHandler.RaiseCallbackEvent(string eventArgument)
  {
    _callbackArg = eventArgument;
  }

  string ICallbackEventHandler.GetCallbackResult()
  {
    try
    {
      int value = Int32.Parse(_callbackArg);
      return GetEmployeeDetails(value);
    }
    catch (Exception ex)
    {
      throw new ApplicationException
        ("An Error has occurred during the processing " +
        " of your request. Error is :" + ex.Message);
    }
  }

  public string GetEmployeeDetails(int employeeID)
  {
    string connString = WebConfigurationManager.
      ConnectionStrings["adventureWorks"].ConnectionString;
    try
    {
      using(SqlConnection sqlConnection = new SqlConnection(connString))
      {
        DataSet employeeDataset = new DataSet("EmployeesRoot");
        //Pass in the name of the stored procedure to be executed and the
        //SqlConnection object as the argument
        SqlDataAdapter adapter = new SqlDataAdapter();
        SqlCommand command = new SqlCommand("Select EmployeeID, Title, "+
          "CAST(HireDate AS char(12)) AS HireDate, Gender, " +
```

```
                    "CAST(BirthDate AS char(12)) AS BirthDate from " +
                    "HumanResources.Employee Where EmployeeID =" + employeeID.ToString(),
                    sqlConnection);
                //Set the SqlCommand object properties
                command.CommandType = CommandType.Text;
                adapter.SelectCommand = command;
                //Fill the Dataset with the return value from the stored procedure
                adapter.Fill(employeeDataset,"Employees" );
                XmlDocument xmlDoc = new XmlDocument();
                return employeeDataset.GetXml();
            }
        }
        catch (Exception ex)
        {
            throw ex;
        }
    }

    public void Page_Load(object sender, EventArgs e)
    {
        if (!Request.Browser.SupportsCallback)
            throw new ApplicationException("This browser doesn't support " +
            "Client callbacks.");
        string src = Page.ClientScript.GetCallbackEventReference(this,
            "arg", "DisplayResultsCallback", "ctx", "DisplayErrorCallback", false);
        string mainSrc = @"function GetEmployeeDetailsUsingPostback(arg, ctx){ " +
            src + "; }";
        Page.ClientScript.RegisterClientScriptBlock(this.GetType(),
            "GetEmployeeDetailsUsingPostback", mainSrc, true);
    }
</script>
<html>
<head>
    <title>Retrieving XML Dynamically using ASP.NET 2.0 Script Callback</title>
    <script language="javascript">
    function GetEmployeeDetails()
    {
        var n = document.forms[0].txtEmployeeID.value;
        GetEmployeeDetailsUsingPostback(n, "txtNumber");
    }

    function DisplayResultsCallback( result, context )
    {
        var strXML,objXMLNode,objXMLDoc,objEmployee,strHTML;
        objXMLDoc = new ActiveXObject("Microsoft.XMLDOM");
        //Load the returned XML string into XMLDOM Object
        objXMLDoc.loadXML(result);
        //Get reference to the Employees Node
        objEmployee = objXMLDoc.selectSingleNode("EmployeesRoot").
            selectSingleNode("Employees");
```

```
        //Check if a valid employee reference is returned from the server
        strHTML = "<font color='#0000FF'>";
        if (objEmployee != null)
        {
          //Dynamically generate HTML and append the contents
          strHTML += "<br><br>Employee ID :<b>" +
            objEmployee.selectSingleNode("EmployeeID").text + "</b><br><br>";
          strHTML += "Title:<b>" +
            objEmployee.selectSingleNode("Title").text + "</b><br><br>";
          strHTML += "Hire Date :<b>" +
            objEmployee.selectSingleNode("HireDate").text + "</b><br><br>";
          strHTML += "Gender:<b>" +
            objEmployee.selectSingleNode("Gender").text + "</b><br><br>";
          strHTML += "Birth Date:<b>" +
            objEmployee.selectSingleNode("BirthDate").text + "</b><br><br>";
        }
        else
        {
          strHTML += "<br><br><b>Employee not found</b>";
        }
        strHTML += "</font>"
        //Assign the dynamically generated HTML into the div tag
        divContents.innerHTML = strHTML;
      }

      function DisplayErrorCallback( error, context )
      {
        alert("Employee Query Failed. " + error);
      }
    </script>
  </head>
<body>
  <form id="Form1" runat="server">
    <font color="#800080"><H1>Employee Details</H1></font>
    <br><br>
    <P align="left">
      <font color="#800080"><b>Enter the Employee ID:</b>
      </font>     
      <INPUT id="txtEmployeeID" name="txtEmployeeID"
        style="LEFT: 149px; TOP: 72px">
      <INPUT id="btnGetEmployee" type="button" value="Get Employee Details"
        name="btnGetEmployee" onclick="GetEmployeeDetails()">
    </P>
    <P></P>
    <div id="divContents">
    </div>
    <P></P>
  </form>
</body>
</html>
```

To understand the code better, consider the code listing as being made up of three different parts.

- ❏ Implementing the server-side event for callback
- ❏ Generating the client-side script for callback
- ❏ Implementing client callback method

Start by looking at the server-side event for callback.

Implementing the Server-Side Event for Callback

At the top of page, you import the required namespaces by using the Import directive. After that we use the implements directive to implement the ICallbackEventHandler interface. This interface has a method named RaiseCallbackEvent that must be implemented to make the callback work.

```
<%@ implements interface="System.Web.UI.ICallbackEventHandler" %>
```

The signature of the RaiseCallbackEvent method is as follows.

```
void ICallbackEventHandler.RaiseCallbackEvent(string eventArgs)
```

As you can see from the above, the RaiseCallbackEvent method takes an argument of type string. If you need to pass values to the server-side method, you should use this string argument. Inside the RaiseCallbackEvent method, you store the supplied event argument in a local private variable for future use.

```
void ICallbackEventHandler.RaiseCallbackEvent(string eventArgument)
{
  _callbackArg = eventArgument;
}
```

After that, you override the GetCallbackResult() method as shown below.

```
string ICallbackEventHandler.GetCallbackResult()
{
  int value = Int32.Parse(_callbackArg);
  return GetEmployeeDetails(value);
}
```

The GetCallbackResult() method is the one that is responsible for returning the output of the server-side execution to the client. Inside the GetCallbackResult() method, you first convert the supplied employee ID into an integer type and then invoke a function named GetEmployeeDetails passing in the employee ID as an argument.

```
int value = Int32.Parse(eventArgs);
return GetEmployeeDetails(value);
```

As the name suggests, the GetEmployeeDetails() method retrieves the details of the employee and returns that information in the form of an XML string. This method starts by retrieving the connection string from the web.config file by using the following line of code.

```
string connString = WebConfigurationManager.
  ConnectionStrings["adventureWorks"].ConnectionString;
```

The above line of code retrieves the connection string from the `connectionStrings` section of the `web.config` file. The connection string is stored in the `web.config` as follows.

```
<connectionStrings>
  <add name="adventureWorks"
    connectionString="server=localhost;Integrated Security=true;
    database=AdventureWorks"/>
</connectionStrings>
```

Once the connection string is retrieved, you then create an instance of the `SqlConnection` object passing in the connection string as an argument. Then you create instances of `DataSet`, `SqlDataAdapter`, and `SqlCommand` objects passing in the appropriate parameters to their constructors. Then you execute the sql query by invoking the `Fill()` method of the `SqlDataAdapter` object. Once the query is executed and the results available in the `DataSet` object, you then invoke the `GetXml()` method of the `DataSet` object to return the XML representation of the DataSet to the caller. The `GetCallbackResult()` method receives the output xml string and simply returns it back to the caller.

Generating the Client-Side Script for Callback

This section will look at the `Page_Load` event of the page. In the beginning of the `Page_Load` event, you check to see if the browser supports callback by examining the `SupportsCallback` property of the `HttpBrowserCapabilities` object.

```
if (!Request.Browser.SupportsCallback)
  throw new ApplicationException
```

Then you invoke the `Page.ClientScript.GetCallbackEventReference()` method to implement the callback in client-side. You can use this method to generate client-side code, which is required to initiate the asynchronous call to server.

```
string src = Page.ClientScript.GetCallbackEventReference(this, "arg",
  "DisplayResultsCallback", "ctx", "DisplayErrorCallback", false);
```

The arguments passed to the `GetCallbackEventReference` method are as follows:

- ❑ `this` — Control that implements `ICallbackEventHandler` (Current Page)
- ❑ `arg` — String to be passed to server-side as argument
- ❑ `DisplayResultsCallback` — Name of the client-side function that will receive the result from server-side event
- ❑ `ctx` — String to be passed from one client-side function to other client-side function through context parameter
- ❑ `DisplayErrorCallback` — Name of the client-side function that will be called if there is any error during the execution of the code
- ❑ `false` — Indicates that the server-side function to be invoked asynchronously

When you execute this page from the browser and view the HTML source code, you will see that the following callback code is generated due to the above `GetCallbackEventReference` method call.

```
WebForm_DoCallback('__Page', arg, DisplayResultsCallback,
  ctx,DisplayErrorCallback, false)
```

`WebForm_DoCallback` is a JavaScript function that in turn invokes the `XmlHttp` class methods to actually perform the callback. Then you embed the callback code inside a function by concatenating the callback generated code with a JavaScript function named `GetEmployeeDetailsUsingPostback` using the following line of code.

```
string mainSrc = @"function " +
  "GetEmployeeDetailsUsingPostback(arg, ctx)" + "{ " + src + "; }";
```

Finally you register the client script block through the `Page.ClientScript.RegisterClientScriptBlock()` method call. Note that in ASP.NET 2.0, the `Page.RegisterClientScriptBlock` and `Page.RegisterStartupScript` methods are obsolete. That's why you had to take the help of `Page.ClientScript` to render client-side script to client browser. `Page.ClientScript` property returns an object of type `ClientScriptManager` type, which is used for managing client scripts.

Implementing Client Callback Method

In the client side, you have a method named `GetEmployeeDetails`, which is invoked when the Get Employee Details command button is clicked.

```
function GetEmployeeDetails()
{
  var n = document.forms[0].txtEmployeeID.value;
  GetEmployeeDetailsUsingPostback(n, "txtNumber");
}
```

From within the `GetEmployeeDetails()` method, you invoke a method named `GetEmployeeDetailsUsingPostback()` and pass in the required parameters. Note that the definition of the `GetEmployeeDetailsUsingPostback()` method is added in the `Page_Load` event in the server side (through the `RegisterClientScriptBlock` method call). Once the server-side function is executed, the callback manager automatically calls the `DisplayResultsCallback()` method.

The code of the `DisplayResultsCallback()` method is shown below. In this example, because the value returned from the server-side page is an XML string, you load the returned XML into an XML-DOM parser and then parse its contents.

```
objXMLDoc = new ActiveXObject("Microsoft.XMLDOM");
//Load the returned XML string into XMLDOM Object
objXMLDoc.loadXML(strXML);
```

Then you get reference to the Employees node by invoking the `selectSingleNode` method of the MSXML DOM object.

```
objEmployee = objXMLDoc.selectSingleNode("EmployeesRoot").
  selectSingleNode("Employees");
```

If a valid `Employees` element is returned from the function call, you display its contents. You display this information in a `div` tag by setting the `innerHTML` property of the `div` element to the dynamically constructed HTML.

```
if (objEmployee != null)
{
  //Dynamically generate HTML and append the contents
  strHTML += "<br><br>Employee ID :<b>" +
    objEmployee.selectSingleNode("EmployeeID").text + "</b><br><br>";
  strHTML += "Title:<b>" +
    objEmployee.selectSingleNode("Title").text + "</b><br><br>";
  strHTML += "Hire Date :<b>" +
    objEmployee.selectSingleNode("HireDate").text + "</b><br><br>";
  strHTML += "Gender:<b>" +
    objEmployee.selectSingleNode("Gender").text + "</b><br><br>";
  strHTML += "Birth Date:<b>" +
    objEmployee.selectSingleNode("BirthDate").text + "</b><br><br>";
}
```

When you browse to Listing 9-18 using the browser and search for an employee with employee ID of 1, the page will display the employee attributes such as `title`, `hire date`, `gender`, and `birth date`.

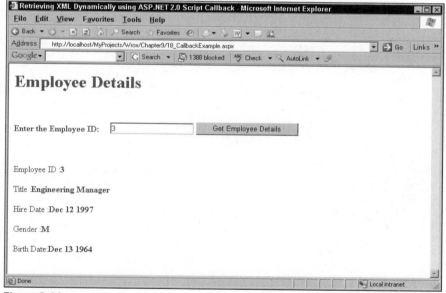

Figure 9-10

When you click on the `Get Employee Details` button in Figure 9-10, you will notice that the employee information is retrieved from the server and displayed in the browser; all without refreshing the page.

ASP.NET Atlas Technology

In the previous section, you have seen how to utilize the script callback feature to dynamically retrieve XML data from the client-side. Having introduced the script callback feature with ASP.NET2.0, the ASP.NET team immediately realized the need for a richer development framework for building interactive dynamic Web applications. To this end, the ASP.NET team has released the early community preview edition of a new technology named Atlas that provides a rich server-side and client-side libraries. Through this library, Atlas enables you to create rich Web applications that harness the power of the server and the browser. Moreover Atlas accomplishes all of this without the traditional need to post-back to the server.

> ASP.NET Atlas framework provides a suite of ASP.NET Server Controls, Web services, and JavaScript libraries. These simplify and enhance application creation by providing in-built controls and components that can be used in traditional JavaScript script and event or through ASP.NET Atlas script. Atlas script is a new construct that allows simple declarative definition of client-side controls, components, behaviors, and data binding that are tied to markup elements in the page.

Atlas Architecture

Figure 9-11 shows the architecture of Atlas in terms of the different client and server components and their interactions.

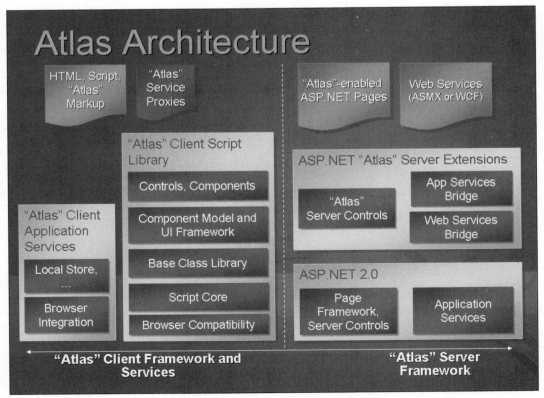

Figure 9-11

As you can see from the above picture, Atlas doesn't change or modify any core ASP.NET, .NET Framework or other binaries on your system. One of Atlas's goals has been to make it really easy for developers to leverage the rich browser features without having to install a whole bunch of software components. You can download the early preview edition of Atlas from the following link.

```
http://msdn.microsoft.com/asp.net/future/atlastemplate/default.aspx
```

Installing Atlas is very simple. You can download the msi from the above link. After completing the install, if you open up the Visual Studio 2005 New Project dialog box, you will see a new template for Atlas. If you don't want to run the install and you simply want to leverage the core functionalities, you can do that as well. All you need to do is to copy the assembly `Microsoft.Web.Atlas.dll` binary into your projects' `\bin` directory and copy the `Atlas\ScriptLibrary` directory of `.js` files into your project. The advantage of the msi installation is that it creates the ASP.NET Atlas Web Project template that you can use to create new Web sites.

Atlas is designed to be cross-browser. This first technology preview adds Ajax support to IE, FireFox and Safari browser clients. Our plan is to test and further expand browser support even more with subsequent builds. Note that all styling for Atlas-based controls are done purely through CSS.

> **Key Features of Atlas**
>
> Through a set of common UI building blocks, Atlas enables increased productivity by reducing the number of lines of code you need to write
>
> Atlas allows you to create code that is easier to author, debug, and maintain by providing a clean separation of content, style, behavior, and code
>
> Atlas is well integrated with design and development tools
>
> Atlas works with ASP.NET pages and server controls thereby providing access to ASP.NET hosted Web services and components
>
> Atlas works everywhere providing a cross-browser standards-based implementation

Retrieving Data from a Web Service Using Atlas

Now that you have had an understanding of the features of Atlas, it is time to look at an example. The code example shown in Listing 9-19 demonstrates the code of the Web service that simply returns the employee details as an array of `Employee` objects. Note that the Web service is just a standard `.asmx` file and does not contain any Atlas specific code.

Listing 9-19: Data Service that returns Employee Details

```
<%@ WebService Language="C#" Class="EmployeeService" %>
using System;
using System.Collections;
using System.Collections.Generic;
using System.Web.Services;
public class EmployeeService : System.Web.Services.WebService
{
    [WebMethod]
```

```
    public Employee[] GetAddresses()
    {
      List<Employee> data = new List<Employee>();
      data.Add(new Employee(0, "Thiru"));
      data.Add(new Employee(1, "Thamiya"));
      data.Add(new Employee(2, "Prabhu"));
      return data.ToArray();
    }
}
```

The Employee declaration is very simple and it just contains two properties: ID and Name. Listing 9-20 shows the implementation of the Employee class.

Listing 9-20: Declaration of Employee Class

```
using System;
public class Employee
{
  int _id;
  string _name;
  public Employee(){}
  public Employee(int id, string name)
  {
   _id = id;
   _name = name;
  }

  public int ID
  {
    set{_id = value;}
    get{return _id; }
  }

  public string Name
  {
    set{name = value; }
    get{return _name;}
  }
}
```

Now that the Web service is implemented, the next step is to invoke the Web service from an Atlas enabled Web page. Listing 9-21 shows the complete code of the Web page.

Listing 9-21: Using Atlas to Invoke a Remote Web Service

```
<%@ Page Language="C#" %>
<html xmlns="http://www.w3.org/1999/xhtml" xml:lang="en" lang="en">
<head>
  <title>Address Viewer</title>
  <atlas:ScriptManager ID="ScriptManager1" runat="server" />
  <script src="EmployeeService.asmx/js" type="text/javascript"></script>
  <script language="javascript" type="text/javascript">
```

```
        function btnAddress_onclick()
        {
          EmployeeService.GetAddresses(onSearchComplete);
        }

        function onSearchComplete(results)
        {
          var searchResults = document.getElementById("searchResults");
          searchResults.control.set_data(results);
        }
    </script>
</head>
<body>
    <form id="form1" runat="server">
        <div id="header">Get Addresses:
          <input id="btnAddress" type="button" value="Get"
            onclick="btnAddress_onclick();" />
        </div>
        <div id="content">
          <div class="left">
            <atlas:ListView id="searchResults" runat="server"
              ItemTemplateControlID="row">
              <LayoutTemplate>
                <ul id="Ul1" runat="server">
                  <li id="row" runat="server">
                    <atlas:Label id="id" runat="server">
                      <Bindings>
                        <atlas:Binding DataPath="ID" Property="text" />
                      </Bindings>
                    </atlas:Label>
                    ----
                    <atlas:Label ID="name" runat="server">
                      <Bindings>
                        <atlas:Binding DataPath="Name" Property="text" />
                      </Bindings>
                    </atlas:Label>
                  </li>
                </ul>
              </LayoutTemplate>
            </atlas:ListView>
          </div>
        </div>
    </form>
</body>
</html>
```

There are two important declarations in the above page: One is the reference to the Atlas script manager and the second one points to the EmployeeService.asmx with the /js flag specified at the end.

```
<atlas:ScriptManager ID="ScriptManager1" runat="server" />
<script src="EmployeeService.asmx/js" type="text/javascript"></script>
```

Once you have referenced the `EmployeeService` in this manner, you can then just call methods on the remote service and set up a callback event handler that will be invoked when the response is returned. You can then work with the data using the same object model (except for the difference that JavaScript will be used in this case) that was used on the server.

When you invoke the Web service, you obviously want to process the output returned by the Web service. In this case, the output is bound to a `ListView` control, which is one of the new controls in the Atlas suite of controls. With a couple of lines of declaration, you can easily bind the output returned by the Web service onto the `ListView` control.

```
<atlas:ListView id="searchResults" runat="server"
ItemTemplateControlID="row">
```

To perform data binding, there is a new element called `<atlas:Binding>` that allows you to specify the particular element to use as the bound field. In the below code, it is set to the `ID` property of the `Employee` object.

```
<atlas:Binding DataPath="ID" Property="text" />
```

On the JavaScript side, the Web service method invocation is initiated in the `Click` event of the `btnAddress` button.

```
function btnAddress_onclick()
{
   EmployeeService.GetAddresses(onSearchComplete);
}
```

To the Web service proxy method, you also supply the callback method name (in this example, it is `OnSearchComplete`) as an argument.

Inside the `OnSearchComplete()` method, you get reference to the `ListView` control and then bind the output of the Web service to the `ListView` using the `set_data()` method.

```
function onSearchComplete(results)
{
   var searchResults = document.getElementById("searchResults");
   searchResults.control.set_data(results);
}
```

Note that all Atlas-enabled ASP.NET Server Controls support both a client-side and server-side object model. This means you can write code against them both from client JavaScript and server code-behind file.

Summary

ASP.NET 2.0 provides excellent support for consuming and displaying XML data through a rich set of data source controls and server controls. Exploiting this bounty of features to build dynamic Web-based applications is simple and straightforward thanks to the codeless data binding features of the data source controls. In this chapter, you have learned the XML data display features of ASP.NET 2.0 through discussion and examples. In particular, you have seen:

❏ How `SiteMapDataSource` control can be used to describe the navigation structure of a Web site and can be subsequently bound to data bound controls such as `SiteMapPath`, `Menu`, and `TreeView`

❏ Using `XmlDataSource` control to display XML data by data binding a `TreeView` control with an `XmlDataSource` control

❏ How an `XmlDataSource` control can also be bound to controls such as `GridView`, and `DataList` that are non-hierarchical in nature

❏ How to implement caching using the caching features of the `XmlDataSource` control

❏ How to use the `<asp:Xml>` server control to rapidly display and transform XML data

❏ How to use the ASP.NET 2.0 script callback feature in conjunction with an XML transport to create rich user experience

❏ Use of Atlas feature for creating rich Web applications

10

SQL Server 2005 XML Integration

XML has become the standard format for transporting data over the Internet, and has also found its way into other application-design areas (such as data storage). XML standards simplify sharing data with various systems, regardless of platform or architecture. Another advantage is that XML is self-describing. Traditional binary data-storage formats require that you have an application that understands the format. But with XML, you actually describe and store the data in the XML format. And XML is a human-readable, data-storage format; you can open an XML file and understand the data. This readability is an advantage because it is not important to define exactly what data is in an XML file before you share the data.

Storing XML data in a relational database brings the benefits of data management and query processing. SQL Server provides powerful query and data modification capabilities over relational data, which has been extended with SQL Server 2005 to query and modify XML data. XML data can interoperate with existing relational data and SQL applications, so that XML can be introduced into the system as data modeling needs arise without disrupting existing applications. The database server also provides administrative functionality for managing XML data (for example, backup, recovery, and replication). These capabilities have motivated the need for native XML support within SQL Server 2005 to address increasing XML usage. This chapter gives you an overview of XML support in SQL Server 2005, describes some of the scenarios for XML usage, and goes into detailed discussions of the server-side and client-side XML feature sets.

By the end of this chapter, you will have a good understanding of the following:

❑   New XML Features in SQL Server 2005

❑   XQuery and the support provided by SQL Server 2005

❑   FOR XML clause and the new features

❑   How to execute FOR XML queries from ADO.NET

Chapter 10

❑ Asynchronous execution of FOR XML queries

❑ XML data type and the differences between Typed and Untyped XML columns

❑ Indexing XML data type columns

❑ How to work with XML data type columns from ADO.NET

❑ How to retrieve XSD schemas from SQL Server onto the client application

❑ How to leverage MARS for executing FOR XML queries

❑ How to work with OPENXML() from SQL Server 2005

New XML Features in SQL Server 2005

SQL Server 2000 enables you to store XML on the server by storing the XML text in a BLOB field, so you can't work with or reference the XML on the server. To work with the XML, you have to extract it to an application layer and then use a standard XML parser or DOM — a programming object for handling XML documents — to work with the data.

The SQL Server 2005 XML data type removes this limitation because it is implemented as a first-class native data type. The new data type lets the SQL Server engine understand XML data in the same way that it understands integer or string data. The XML data type lets you create tables that store only XML or store both XML and relational data. This flexibility enables you to make the best use of the relational model for structured data and enhance that data with XML's semi-structured data. When you store XML values natively in an XML data type column, you have two options.

❑ Typed column — XML data stored in this kind of column is validated using a collection of XML schemas.

❑ Untyped column — In this kind of column, you can insert any kind of XML data as long as the XML is well-formed.

> To help you get the most out of this combination of semi-structured and relational data, the native SQL Server 2005 XML data type supports several built-in methods that let you query and modify the XML data. These methods accept XQuery, an emerging W3C standard language, and include the navigational language XPath 2.0 along with a language for modifying XML data. You can combine query calls to the XML data type methods with standard T-SQL to create queries that return both relational and XML data.

In addition to the XML data type, FOR XML and OpenXML features have also been extended in SQL Server 2005. These features combined with the support for XQuery, SQL Server 2005 provides a powerful platform for developing rich applications for semi-structured and unstructured data management. With all the added functionality, the users have more design choices for their data storage and application development. To start with, look at the FOR XML feature in SQL Server 2005.

FOR XML in SQL Server 2005

SQL Server 2000 introduced the FOR XML clause to the SELECT statement and the FOR XML clause provided the ability to aggregate the relational rowset returned by the SELECT statement into XML. FOR XML on the server supports the following three modes; these modes provide different transformation semantics.

- ❑ RAW — The RAW mode generates single elements, which are named row, for each row returned.

- ❑ AUTO — This mode infers simple, one element name-per-level hierarchy based on the lineage information and the order of the data in a SELECT statement.

- ❑ EXPLICIT — This mode requires a specific rowset format that can be mapped into almost any XML shape, while still being formulated by a single SQL query.

All three modes are designed to generate the XML in a streamable way in order to be able to produce large documents efficiently. Although the EXPLICIT mode format is highly successful in achieving its goals, the SQL expression required to generate the rowset format is quite complex. Now with SQL Server 2005, the complexities associated with FOR XML modes have been simplified to a great extent. In addition to that, the FOR XML queries have also been integrated with the XML data type.

> *If you execute an XML query of any type (for example, "SELECT * FROM HumanResources .Employee FOR XML AUTO"), you will notice that the results shown in SQL Server Management Studio look similar to the XML results in SQL Server 2000 Query Analyzer except for the difference that the results are underlined, meaning that you can click them now. Clicking on them will result in a nice XML view for you to look at your XML results.*

The next few sections provide an overview of the new extensions added to FOR XML clause in SQL Server 2005.

Integration with XML Data Type

With the introduction of the XML data type, the FOR XML clause now provides the ability to generate an instance of XML directly using the new TYPE directive. For example,

```
SELECT * FROM HumanResources.Employee as Employee FOR XML AUTO, TYPE
```

returns the Employee elements as an XML data type instance, instead of the nvarchar(max) instance that would have been the case without the TYPE directive. This result is guaranteed to conform to the well-formedness constraints provided by the XML data type. Because the result is an XML data type instance, you can also use XQuery expressions to query and reshape the result. For example, the following expression retrieves the employee title into a new element.

```
SELECT (SELECT * FROM HumanResources.Employee as Employee
FOR XML AUTO, TYPE).query(
  '<Output>{
    for $c in /Employee
    return <Employee name="{data($c/@Title)}"/>
  }</Output>')
```

This query produces the following output.

```
<Output>
  <Employee name="Production Technician - WC60" />
  <Employee name="Marketing Assistant" />
  <Employee name="Engineering Manager" />
  ------
  ------
</Output>
```

Assigning FOR XML Results

Because FOR XML queries now return assignable values, the result of a FOR XML query can be assigned to an XML variable, or inserted into an XML column.

```
/* Assign the output of FOR XML to a variable */
DECLARE @Employee XML;
SET @Employee = (SELECT * FROM HumanResources.Employee FOR XML AUTO, TYPE)
CREATE TABLE Employee_New (EmployeeID int, XmlData XML)
/* Assign the output of FOR XML to a column*/
INSERT INTO Employee_New SELECT 1, @Employee
```

In these statements, you retrieve the results of the FOR XML query into an XML data typed variable, and utilize that variable to insert values into a table named Employee_New.

Executing FOR XML Queries from ADO.NET

To return an XML stream directly from SQL Server through the FOR XML query, you need to leverage the ExecuteXmlReader() method of the SqlCommand object. The ExecuteXmlReader() method returns an XmlReader object populated with the results of the query specified for a SqlCommand. Listing 10-1 shows you an example of ExecuteXmlReader in action by querying the DatabaseLog table in the AdventureWorks database.

Listing 10-1: Executing a FOR XML Query Using ExecuteXmlReader Method

```
<%@ Page Language="C#" ValidateRequest="false" %>
<%@ Import Namespace="System.Data" %>
<%@ Import Namespace="System.Data.SqlClient" %>
<%@ Import Namespace="System.Data.Sql" %>
<%@ Import Namespace="System.Xml" %>
<%@ Import Namespace="System.Web.Configuration" %>
<%@ Import Namespace="System.Data.SqlTypes" %>
<script runat="server">
  void btnReadXml_Click(object sender, EventArgs e)
  {
    int ID = Convert.ToInt32(txtID.Text);
    //Get the connection string from the web.config file
    string connString = WebConfigurationManager.ConnectionStrings
      ["adventureWorks"].ConnectionString;
    using (SqlConnection conn = new SqlConnection(connString))
    {
      System.Text.StringBuilder builder = new System.Text.StringBuilder();
      conn.Open();
```

```
            SqlCommand command = conn.CreateCommand();
            command.CommandText = "SELECT DatabaseLogID, XmlEvent FROM " +
               " DatabaseLog WHERE DatabaseLogID = " + ID.ToString() +
               " FOR XML AUTO, ROOT('DatabaseLogs'), ELEMENTS";
            XmlReader reader = command.ExecuteXmlReader();
            XmlDocument doc = new XmlDocument();
            //Load the XmlReader to an XmlDocument object
            doc.Load(reader);
            builder.Append("<b>Complete XML :</b>" +
               Server.HtmlEncode(doc.OuterXml) + "<br><br>");
            //Retrieve the DatabaseLogID and XmlEvent column values
            string idValue = doc.DocumentElement.SelectSingleNode
               ("DatabaseLog/DatabaseLogID").InnerText;
            builder.Append("<b>id :</b>" + Server.HtmlEncode(idValue) + "<br><br>");
            string xmlEventValue = doc.DocumentElement.SelectSingleNode
               ("DatabaseLog/XmlEvent").OuterXml;
            builder.Append("<b>XmlEvent :</b>" + Server.HtmlEncode(xmlEventValue) +
               "<br>");
            output.Text = builder.ToString();
         }
      }
   </script>
   <html xmlns="http://www.w3.org/1999/xhtml" >
   <head id="Head1" runat="server">
     <title>Executing a FOR XML Query from ADO.NET</title>
   </head>
   <body>
     <form id="form1" runat="server">
       <div>
         <asp:Label ID="lblID" Runat="server" Text="Enter ID:"
           Width="134px" Height="19px"></asp:Label>
         <asp:TextBox ID="txtID" Runat="server"></asp:TextBox>
         <asp:Button ID="btnReadXml" Runat="server" Text="Read Xml"
           Width="118px" Height="30px" OnClick="btnReadXml_Click" />
         <br/><br/><br/>
         <asp:Literal runat="server" ID="output" />
       </div>
     </form>
   </body>
   </html>
```

Listing 10-1 starts retrieving the connection string from the `web.config` file, and the connection string is stored in the `web.config` file as follows:

```
<connectionStrings>
  <add name="adventureWorks"
    connectionString="server=localhost;integrated
    security=true;database=AdventureWorks;"/>
</connectionStrings>
```

You then open the connection to the database passing in the connection string as an argument.

```
using (SqlConnection conn = new SqlConnection(connString))
```

After that, you create an instance of the `SqlCommand` object and set its properties.

```
SqlCommand command = conn.CreateCommand();
command.CommandText = "SELECT DatabaseLogID, XmlEvent FROM " +
  " DatabaseLog WHERE DatabaseLogID = " + ID.ToString() +
  " FOR XML AUTO, ROOT('DatabaseLogs'), ELEMENTS";
```

Now you execute the actual query by calling the `ExecuteXmlReader()` method on the `SqlCommand` object.

```
XmlReader reader = command.ExecuteXmlReader();
```

You then load the `XmlReader` object onto an `XmlDocument` for further processing.

```
XmlDocument doc = new XmlDocument();
//Load the XmlReader to an XmlDocument object
doc.Load(reader);
```

After the XML is loaded into an XmlDocument, the complete XML, DatabaseLogID, and XmlEvent column values are then displayed in a sequence. Figure 10-1 shows the resultant output.

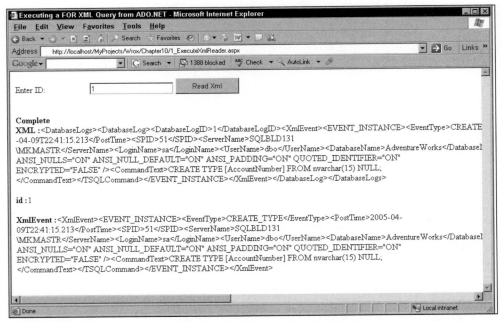

Figure 10-1

In Figure 10-1, the first line displays the entire XML output produced by the FOR XML query and the second and third lines display the values of the DatabaseLogID and XmlEvent columns, respectively. Because the XmlEvent column is a XML data typed column, you see the XML output directly being displayed by the XmlEvent column.

Asynchronous Execution of FOR XML Query

In the previous section, you saw how to synchronously execute a FOR XML query using the ExecuteXmlReader() method. Although this approach works, there are times where you might want to execute the query asynchronously for scalability and throughput reasons. Fortunately ADO.NET 2.0 comes shipped with a new feature that provides for asynchronous execution of SQL commands. Using this new feature, you can now asynchronously execute commands against a SQL Server database without waiting for the command execution to finish. This feature can be very handy in situations where you execute long-running database commands from a client application such as a Windows Forms application or an ASP.NET application. By doing this, you improve the overall performance and responsiveness of your application. The next section will explore the execution of FOR XML query using the asynchronous features of ADO.NET 2.0.

Synchronous versus Asynchronous Command Execution of Commands

Synchronous operations consist of component or function calls that operate in lockstep. A synchronous call blocks a process until the operation completes. Only then will the process execute the next line of code. Figure 10-2 details shows the steps involved in synchronously executing a command synchronously against the database.

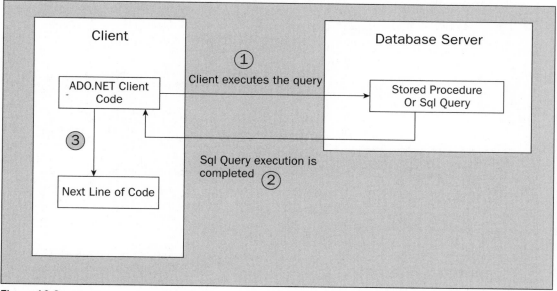

Synchronous Execution

Figure 10-2

As you can see from Figure 10-2, in a sequential execution, each command must complete before the next command begins executing.

❑   In Figure 10-2, the client application starts by creating a SqlCommand object and initializing various properties of the SqlCommand object with the appropriate values.

❑ Next, the client invokes any of the synchronous methods of the `SqlCommand` such as `ExecuteNonQuery()`, `ExecuteReader()`, and `ExecuteXmlReader()` through that `SqlCommand` object.

❑ Finally, the client waits until the database server either completes the query execution, or if there is no response for a given period of time the client times out, raising an error. Only after the method call returns is the client free to continue with its processing the next line of code.

Now that you have seen the steps involved in the executing synchronous execution of a command synchronously, contrast them with the steps involved in asynchronous execution. Figure 10-3 shows the steps involved in asynchronously executing a command against the database.

Asynchronous Execution

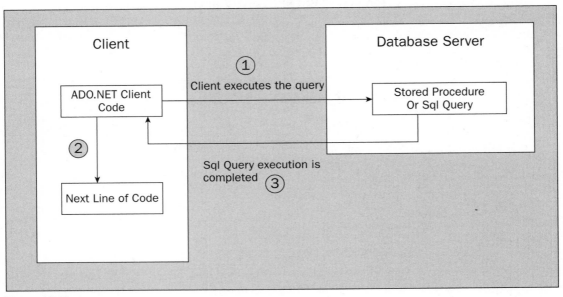

Figure 10-3

Although Figure 10-3 looks similar to Figure 10-2, it's worth walking through the differences.

❑ For an asynchronous operation, the client creates a `SqlCommand` object and initializes various properties of the `SqlCommand` object with the appropriate values. But in the asynchronous operation the client application also sets the `"async"` attribute in the connection string to `true`.

❑ Next, the client invokes any of the asynchronous methods such as `BeginExecuteNonQuery()`, `BeginExecuteReader()`, or `BeginExecuteXmlReader()` to start the asynchronous execution. Note that for this release of ADO.NET 2.0 these are the only asynchronous methods available for use.

❑ After invoking the SQL command, the client code immediately moves onto the next line of code without waiting for a response from the database. This means instead of waiting the client code can perform some other operations while the database server is executing the query, resulting in better utilization of resources.

The asynchronous execution requires that the corresponding method has both BeginXXX and EndXXX variations. The BeginXXX method initiates an asynchronous operation and returns immediately, returning a reference to an object that implements the IAsyncResult interface. Your client code needs to access that interface to monitor the progress of the asynchronous operation. When the asynchronous operation completes, you call the EndXXX method to obtain the result and clean up any supporting resources that were utilized to support the asynchronous call.

There are four common ways to use BeginXXX and EndXXX to make asynchronous calls. In all cases, you invoke BeginXXX to initiate the call. After that, you can do one of the following:

❑ Do some work and then call EndXXX. If the asynchronous operation is not finished, EndXXX will block until it completes.

❑ Using a WaitHandle obtained from the IAsyncResult.AsyncWaitHandle property, call the WaitOne() method to block until the operation completes; then call EndXXX.

❑ Poll the IAsynResult.IsCompleted property to determine when the asynchronous operation has completed; then call EndXXX.

❑ Pass a delegate for a callback function that you supply (of type IAsyncCallback) to BeginXXX. That callback function will execute when the asynchronous operation completes. Code in the callback function calls EndXXX to retrieve the result.

Listing 10-2 demonstrates the use of WaitHandle to retrieve the results of the asynchronous query execution.

Listing 10-2: Asynchronously Executing the FOR XML Query

```
<%@ Page Language="C#" ValidateRequest="false" %>
<%@ Import Namespace="System.Data" %>
<%@ Import Namespace="System.Data.SqlClient" %>
<%@ Import Namespace="System.Threading" %>
<%@ Import Namespace="System.Xml" %>
<%@ Import Namespace="System.Web.Configuration" %>
<%@ Import Namespace="System.Data.SqlTypes" %>
<script runat="server">
  void btnReadXml_Click(object sender, EventArgs e)
  {
    int ID = Convert.ToInt32(txtID.Text);
    //Note the new "async=true" attribute in the connection string
    string connString =
      "server=localhost;integrated security=true;" +
      "database=AdventureWorks;async=true";
    using (SqlConnection conn = new SqlConnection(connString))
    {
      conn.Open();
      SqlCommand command = conn.CreateCommand();
      command.CommandText = "SELECT DatabaseLogID, XmlEvent " +
        "FROM DatabaseLog WHERE DatabaseLogID = " + ID.ToString() +
        " FOR XML AUTO, ROOT('DatabaseLogs'), ELEMENTS";
      IAsyncResult asyncResult = command.BeginExecuteXmlReader();
      //Do some other processing here
      asyncResult.AsyncWaitHandle.WaitOne();
```

```
      XmlReader reader = command.EndExecuteXmlReader(asyncResult);
      XmlDocument doc = new XmlDocument();
      //Load the XmlReader to an XmlDocument object
      doc.Load(reader);
      output.Text = "XML : " + Server.HtmlEncode(doc.OuterXml);
    }
  }
</script>
<html xmlns="http://www.w3.org/1999/xhtml" >
<head id="Head1" runat="server">
  <title>
    Asynchronously executing a FOR XML Query using ExecuteXmlReader
  </title>
</head>
<body>
  <form id="form1" runat="server">
    <div>
      <asp:Label ID="lblID" Runat="server" Text="Enter ID:"
        Width="134px" Height="19px"></asp:Label>
      <asp:TextBox ID="txtID" Runat="server"></asp:TextBox>
      <asp:Button ID="btnSave" Runat="server" Text="Read Xml"
        Width="118px" Height="30px" OnClick="btnReadXml_Click" />
      <br/><br/><br/>
      <asp:Literal runat="server" ID="output" />
    </div>
  </form>
</body>
</html>
```

In Listing 10-2, you create instances of SqlConnection and SqlCommand objects and set its properties to appropriate values. After that, you invoke the BeginExecuteXmlReader() method of the SqlCommand objects and assign the returned IAsyncResult object to a local variable for later use.

```
IAsyncResult asyncResult = command.BeginExecuteXmlReader();
```

Next, you call the WaitOne() method of the WaitHandle object to wait for the query execution to finish. Note that before you invoke the WaitOne() method, you are free to do other processing.

```
//Do some other processing here
asyncResult.AsyncWaitHandle.WaitOne();
```

Note that the WaitOne() method is a blocking call meaning that it will not return until the query execution is complete. Finally you retrieve the results of the query by calling the EndExecuteXmlReader() method passing in the IAsyncResult object as an argument.

```
XmlReader reader = command.EndExecuteXmlReader(asyncResult);
```

Next you load the returned `XmlReader` into an `XmlDocument` object and display the output.

```
XmlDocument doc = new XmlDocument();
//Load the XmlReader to an XmlDocument object
doc.Load(reader);
output.Text = "XML : " + Server.HtmlEncode(doc.OuterXml);
```

The output produced by this page is shown in Figure 10-4.

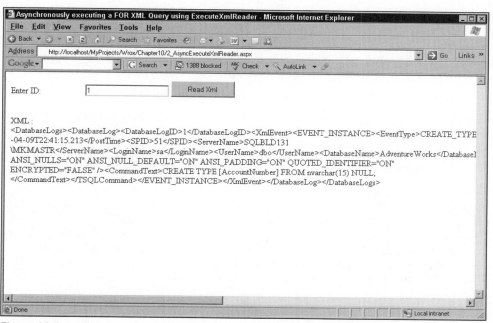

Figure 10-4

Listing 10-2 uses the `WaitHandle` object's `WaitOne()` method to wait for the command execution to complete. The `WaitHandle` class also contains other static methods such as `WaitAll()` and `WaitAny()`. These static methods take arrays of `WaitHandles` as parameters, and return when either all the calls have completed, or as soon as any of the calls have completed, depending on the method that you call. For example, if you are making three separate command execution calls, you can call each asynchronously; place the `WaitHandle` for each in an array and then call the `WaitAll` method until they are finished. Doing that allows all three commands to execute at the same time. It is also important to note that the `WaitOne()`, `WaitAll()`, and `WaitAny()` methods optionally accept a timeout parameter value. Using the timeout option, you can specify the amount of time that you want to wait for a command to return. If the methods time out, they will return a value of `False`.

XML Data Type in SQL Server 2005

The SQL Server 2005 XML data type implements the ISO SQL-2003 standard XML data type. In an XML data typed column, you can store both well-formed XML 1.0 documents as well as XML content fragments with text nodes. Moreover you can also store an arbitrary number of top-level elements in an untyped XML column. At the time of inserting the XML data, the system checks for the well-formedness of the data and rejects data that is not well-formed. The extent of the server-side validation is based on whether an XSD schema is associated with the XML data type column. Before looking at the XSD schemas and their role with an XML column, you need to understand the reasons for storing native XML data in an XML data type column. Storing XML data in an XML data type column can be extremely useful in the following situations:

❑ By storing XML data in the SQL Server, you have a straightforward way of storing your XML data at the server while preserving document order and document structure

❑ When you want the ability to query and modify your XML data

❑ When you want to exchange data with external systems without performing a lot of transformations

❑ When you have XML documents with a wide range of structures, or XML documents conforming to different or complex schemas that are too hard to map to relational structures

> SQL Server 2005 stores XML data as Unicode (UTF-16). XML data retrieved from the server comes out in UTF-16 encoding as well. If you want a different encoding, you need to perform the necessary conversion after retrieving the data either by casting or on the mid-tier. For example, you may cast your XML data to varchar type on the server, in which case the database engine serializes the XML with an encoding determined by the collation of the varchar.

Typed versus Untyped XML Column

For more structure or validation of XML data, SQL Server lets you associate schema with a particular XML column. This column is named typed XML column. If an XML schema is associated with an XML column, the schema validates the XML data at the time of inserting the XML data into the field. SQL Server 2005 supports many schemas grouped together in a schema collection, which lets you apply different schemas to an XML column. The server will validate all incoming XML against all the schemas. If the XML is valid for any of the collection's schemas, it can be stored in the XML field. Table 10-1 summarizes the differences between a typed XML column and an untyped XML column.

Table 10-1. Differences between a Typed and an Untyped XML Column

Characteristics	Untyped Column	Typed Column
Presence of Schema	No schema to validate your XML data	The typed column is associated with an XML schema
Validation Location	Because there is no schema on the server side, XML validation needs to be performed on the client side	Validation is automatically performed on the server at the time of inserting the XML data

Characteristics	Untyped Column	Typed Column
Query Optimization	Not possible because of lack of type information	Allows you to take advantage of storage and query optimizations based on type information
Constraint for one top-level element	Not possible	You can constrain a typed column to allow only one top-level element using the optional DOCUMENT keyword

In addition to typing an XML column, you can use relational (column or row) constraints on typed or untyped XML data type columns.

Untyped XML Columns

Untyped XML is useful when the schema is not known prior so that a mapping-based solution is not possible. It is also useful when the schema is known but mapping to relational data model is very complex and hard to maintain, or multiple schemas exist and are late bound to the data based on external requirements. The following statement creates a table called Employee in the AdventureWorks with an integer primary key id and an untyped XML column xml_data:

```
Use AdventureWorks
CREATE TABLE Employee( id int primary key, xml_data xml)
```

The Employee table that is created in the AdventureWorks database will be used throughout this chapter. To insert values into the previous table, use the following T-SQL statement.

```
INSERT INTO Employee values(2, '<employee id="2"><name>Joe</name></employee>')
```

Note that you can also create a table with more than one XML or relational columns with or without a primary key.

Typed XML Columns

If you have XML schemas in an XML schema collection describing your XML data, you can associate the XML schema collection with the XML column to yield typed XML. The XML schemas are used to validate the data, perform more precise type checks than untyped XML during compilation of query and data modification statements, and optimize storage and query processing.

XML Schema Collections

Support for typed XML columns is enabled by using XML schema collections in SQL Server. XML schema collections are defined like any other SQL Server object, and they are stored in SQL Server. An XML schema collection is created using CREATE XML SCHEMA COLLECTION T-SQL statement by providing one or more XML schemas. More XML schema components can be added to an existing XML schema, and more schemas can be added to an XML schema collection using ALTER XML SCHEMA COLLECTION syntax. XML schema collections can be secured like any SQL object using SQL Server 2005's security model. The syntax for the T-SQL DDL CREATE XML SCHEMA COLLECTION statement is as follows:

```
CREATE XML SCHEMA COLLECTION <Schema_Name>
AS
  -- Specify the schema contents here
GO
```

For example, to create a schema named `EmployeeSchema`, use the following command.

```
Create xml schema collection EmployeeSchema as
  N'<xs:schema xmlns:xs="http://www.w3.org/2001/XMLSchema"
  xmlns:company="http://www.wrox.com/books"
  targetNamespace="http://www.wrox.com/books"
  elementFormDefault="qualified">
  <xs:element name="employee">
    <xs:complexType>
      <xs:all>
        <xs:element name="name" type="xs:string" />
      </xs:all>
      <xs:attribute name="id" type="xs:int" />
    </xs:complexType>
  </xs:element>
</xs:schema>'
```

In addition to using the XML schema collection to type XML columns, you can also leverage that to type XML variables and parameters.

Associating Schemas with an XML Column

After the `EmployeeSchema` is created, you can easily associate that with the xml_data column of the Employee table by using the following syntax.

```
CREATE TABLE Employee( id int primary key,
  xml_data XML(EmployeeSchema))
```

Now when you insert values into the Employee table, the XML data for the xml_data column is validated against the `EmployeeSchema`.

```
Insert into Employee values(1, '<employee id="1"
xmlns="http://www.wrox.com/books"><name>Joe</name></employee>')
GO
Insert into Employee values(2, '<employee id="2"
xmlns="http://www.wrox.com/books"><name>Fred</name></employee>')
```

At the time of associating the schema to the XML column, you can use the DOCUMENT or CONTENT flags to specify whether XML trees or fragments can be stored in a typed column. For DOCUMENT, each XML instance specifies the target namespace of its top-level element in the instance, according to which it is validated and typed. For CONTENT, on the other hand, each top-level element can specify any one of the target namespaces in the schema collection. The XML instance is validated and typed according to all the target namespaces occurring in an instance. Execute the following sql statement that contains invalid namespace declaration.

```
Insert into Employee values(3, '<employee id="3"
xmlns="http://invalidnamespace/books"><name>InvalidData</name></employee>')
```

You should see an error message similar to the following as a result of the invalid namespace in the Insert statement.

```
Msg 6913, Level 16, State 1, Line 1
XML Validation: Declaration not found for element
'http://invalidnamespace/books:employee'. Location: /*:employee[1]
```

Inserting Data into an XML Column

Irrespective of whether the XML column is typed or not typed, you can supply the value for an XML column in the following ways.

❑ As a character or binary SQL type that is implicitly converted to XML data type.

❑ As the content of a file.

❑ As the output of the FOR XML with the TYPE directive that generates an XML data type instance.

The supplied value is checked for well-formedness and allows both XML documents and XML fragments to be stored. If the data fails the well-formedness check, it is rejected with an appropriate error message. For typed XML, the supplied value is checked for conformance to XML schemas registered with the XML schema collection typing the XML column. The XML instance is rejected if it fails this validation. Look at examples on the different ways of inserting values into an XML column.

To start with, the following statement inserts a new row into the Employee table with the value 1 for the integer column ID and an <employee> instance for the xml_data column. The <employee> data, supplied as a string, is implicitly converted to XML data type and checked for well-formedness during insertion.

```
INSERT INTO Employee values (2, '<employee id="2"><name>Joe</name></employee>')
```

It is also possible to utilize the contents of an XML file as an input to the Insert command. Consider the following XML document stored in a file called Employee.xml.

```
<employee id="6" xmlns="http://www.wrox.com/books">
   <name>Dave</name>
</employee>
```

Now if you execute the following T-SQL command, you will see the contents of the Employee.xml file being loaded into the xml_data column.

```
INSERT INTO Employee SELECT 7, xml_value FROM
  (SELECT * FROM OPENROWSET (BULK 'C:\Data\Employee.xml',
  SINGLE_BLOB) AS xml_value) AS R(xml_value)
```

The third option is to utilize the output of the FOR XML with the TYPE directive as an input to the insert command. With SQL Server 2005 FOR XML has been enhanced with a TYPE directive to generate the result as an XML data type instance. The resulting XML can be assigned to an XML column, variable, or parameter. In the following statement, the XML instance generated using FOR XML TYPE is assigned to an XML data type variable @var. Then the variable is used in the insert statement.

```
DECLARE @var xml
SET @var = (SELECT xml_data FROM Employee FOR XML AUTO,TYPE)
--Insert the value of the variable into a new table named EmployeeOutput
CREATE TABLE EmployeeOutput (xml_data xml)
INSERT INTO EmployeeOutput (xml_data) VALUES (@var)
```

XML Data Type Methods

Although the XML data type is a built-in data type, it also functions like a user-defined data type (UDT) by providing several methods that let you query and update data stored in an XML variable or column. You can use these methods to query, obtain scalar values from, and modify an XML document that's stored in a variable, column, or parameter. Table 10-2 lists the XML data type methods.

Table 10-2. Methods Supported by the XML Data Type

Method	Description
query	Allows you to specify an XQuery against an instance of the XML data type. The method returns an instance of untyped XML and the result type is XML.
value	Allows you to execute an XQuery against the XML and returns a value of sql type that is supplied in the second parameter. This method returns a scalar value.
exist	This method allows you to determine if a query returns a nonempty resultset.
modify	Allows you to execute XML DML (Data Manipulation Language) statements against an XML data type column.
nodes	Allows you to shred an XML into multiple rows to propagate parts of XML documents into rowsets.

What Is XQuery?

XQuery is a query language that lets you retrieve data items from XML formatted documents. The language is not "complete"—it is still a work in progress under the auspices of the W3C's XML Query working group. The current implementation of XQuery in SQL Server 2005 is based on the June 2004 working drafts of the W3C XQuery language. Because the W3C specifications may undergo future revisions before becoming a W3C recommendation, the SQL Server 2005 implementation may differ from the final recommendation.

Indexing XML Columns

XML indexes can be created on XML data type columns. It indexes all tags, values, and paths over the XML instances in the column and can result in improved query performance. XML indexing can be very useful in the following scenarios.

❑ When there is a need to frequently execute queries on XML columns.

❑ When the values you retrieve from XML values are relatively small compared to the size of the XML column itself. By indexing that XML column, you can avoid parsing the whole data at run-time and be benefited by index lookups for efficient query processing.

There are two types of indexes that can be created on an XML column. They are primary XML index and secondary XML index. As the name suggests, the first index on an XML column is the primary XML index. Using it, three types of secondary XML indexes can be created on the XML column to speed up common classes of queries.

Primary XML Index

This indexes all tags, values, and paths within the XML instances in an XML column. The base table (that is, the table in which the XML column occurs) must have a clustered index on the primary key of the table. The primary key is used to correlate index rows with the rows in the base table. The following statement creates a primary XML index called `idx_xml_data` on the XML column xml_data of the table Employee:

```
CREATE PRIMARY XML INDEX idx_xml_data on Employee (xml_data)
```

Secondary XML Indexes

After the primary XML index has been created, you may want to create secondary XML indexes to speed up different classes of queries within your workload. There are three types of secondary XML indexes named PATH, PROPERTY, and VALUE that can benefit path-based queries, custom property management scenarios, and value-based queries, respectively.

The PATH index builds a B+-tree on the (path, value) pair of each XML node in document order over all XML instances in the column. The PROPERTY index creates a B+-tree clustered on the (PK, path, value) pair within each XML instance, where PK is the primary key of the base table. Finally, the VALUE index creates a B+-tree on the (value, path) pair of each node in document order across all XML instances in the XML column.

> If your workload uses path expressions heavily on XML columns, the PATH secondary XML index is likely to speed up your workload. If your workload retrieves multiple values from individual XML instances using path expressions, clustering paths within each XML instance in the PROPERTY index may be helpful. If your workload involves querying for values within XML instances without knowing the element or attribute names that contain those values, you may want to create the VALUE index.

To create a PATH index on the xml_data column, use the following command.

```
CREATE XML INDEX idx_xml_data_path on Employee (xml_data)
   USING XML INDEX idx_xml_data FOR PATH
```

Working with XML Data Type Columns from ADO.NET

You get your first indication that XML is now a first class relational database type by referencing the relational data type enumerations in ADO.NET 2.0. System.Data.DbType and System.Data.SqlDbType contain additional values for DbType.Xml and SqlDbType.Xml, respectively. There is also a new class called SqlXml that is contained in the System.Data.SqlTypes namespace, and this class acts as a factory class for creating XmlReader instances on top of the XML type value.

You can access the XML columns either using in-proc access from within SQL Server 2005 itself or using ADO.NET from your client applications. To start with, look at the in-proc access.

In-Process Access to the XML Data Type Column

Before looking at an example, it is important to understand the CLR integration features of SQL Server 2005. One of the excellent features of SQL Server 2005 is the integration with the .NET CLR (Common Language Runtime). The integration of CLR with SQL Server 2005 extends the capability of SQL Server in several important ways. In previous versions of SQL Server, database programmers were limited to using T-SQL when writing code on the server side. With CLR integration, database developers can now perform tasks that were impossible or difficult to achieve with Transact-SQL alone. Both Visual Basic .NET and C# are modern programming languages offering full support for arrays, structured exception handling, and collections. Developers can leverage CLR integration to write code that has more complex logic and is more suited for computation tasks using languages such as VB.NET and C#. Both VB.NET and C# offer object-oriented capabilities such as encapsulation, inheritance, and polymorphism.

Advantages of CLR Integration

Managed code is better suited than Transact-SQL for number crunching and complicated execution logic, and features extensive support for many complex tasks, including string handling and regular expressions. With the functionality found in the .NET Framework Base Class Library (BCL), database developers now have access to thousands of pre-built classes and routines which can be easily accessed from any stored procedure, trigger, or user-defined function. The BCL includes classes that provide functionality for improved string functioning, advanced math operations, file access, cryptography, and more. Although many of these classes are available for use from within SQL CLR code, those that are not appropriate for server-side use (for example, windowing classes) are not available.

Another benefit of managed code is type safety. Before managed code is executed, the CLR verifies that the code is safe. This process is known as "verification." During verification, the CLR performs several checks to ensure that the code is safe to run. For example, the code is checked to ensure that no memory is read that has not been written to. The CLR will also prevent buffer overflows. By default, both Visual Basic .NET and C# always produce safe code; however, C# programmers have the option of using the unsafe keyword to produce unsafe code that, for example, directly accesses memory.

For the purposes of this example, consider the

Employee table that has been used in the previous examples.

```
CREATE TABLE Employee (id int primary key, xml_data xml( EmployeeSchema))
```

Listing 10-3 illustrates how the XML data type can be accessed from the in-proc provider. The context connection allows you to execute SQL statements in the same context that the CLR code was invoked. For out-of-proc access, a new connection to the database must be established.

Listing 10-3: Accessing an XML Data Type Column Using In-Proc

```
using System;
using System.Data;
using System.Data.SqlClient;
```

```
using System.Data.SqlTypes;
using Microsoft.SqlServer.Server;

public partial class StoredProcedures
{
  [Microsoft.SqlServer.Server.SqlProcedure]
  public static void GetEmployeeNameByID(int id)
  {
    string retValue = "";
    using (SqlConnection conn = new
      SqlConnection("context connection=true"))
    {
      conn.Open();
      //Prepare query to select xml data
      SqlCommand cmd = conn.CreateCommand();
      string sql = "SELECT xml_data.query " +
        "('declare namespace ns=\"http://www.wrox.com/books\";" +
        " <Employee Name=\"{/ns:employee/ns:name}\"/>') as Result " +
        " FROM Employee WHERE id = " + id.ToString();
      cmd.CommandText = sql;
      //Execute query and retrieve incoming data
      SqlDataReader reader = cmd.ExecuteReader();
      if (reader.Read())
      {
        //Get the XML value as string
        retValue = (string)reader.GetValue(0);
      }
      else
        retValue = "No Value";
    }
    //Send the output XML back to the caller
    SqlContext.Pipe.Send(retValue);
  }
};
```

The in-proc provider is optimized for working with data inside the SQL Server process. Using the classes and methods of the in-process managed provider, you can easily submit queries to the database, execute DML and DDL statements, and return result sets and messages to client applications. The `Microsoft` `.Data.SqlServer` namespace groups the types that make up the in-proc provider. This namespace shares many similarities and interfaces with ADO.NET's SqlClient namespace, which is used by developers accessing SQL Server data from managed client and middle-tier applications. Because of this similarity, you can easily migrate code from client applications to server libraries and back again.

There are three important classes in the `Microsoft.SqlServer.Server` namespace that are specific to the in-proc provider:

- ❑ `SqlContext` — This class encapsulates the other extensions. In addition it provides the transaction and database connection, which are part of the environment in which the routine executes

- ❑ `SqlPipe` — This class enables routines to send tabular results and messages to the client. This class is conceptually similar to the Response class found in ASP.NET in that it can be used to send messages to the callers.

Now that you have an understanding of the important classes, walk through the code of Listing 10-3.

To start with, you import the `Microsoft.SqlServer.Server` namespace so that you can access the types in the in-proc provider. Next, the function is decorated with the `[SqlProcedure]` custom attribute, which is found in the `Microsoft.SqlServer.Server` namespace. On the next line, the stored procedure is declared as a public static method.

```
[Microsoft.SqlServer.Server.SqlProcedure]
public static void GetEmployeeNameByID(int id)
```

You then establish connection to the database by creating an instance of the `SqlConnection` object passing in the appropriate connection string. Note that the connection string passed to the constructor of the `SqlConnection` object is set to `"context connection=true"` meaning that you want to use the context of the logged on user to open the connection to the database.

```
using (SqlConnection conn = new
    SqlConnection("context connection=true"))
```

You then create an instance of the `SqlCommand` object and set its properties appropriately.

```
SqlCommand cmd = conn.CreateCommand();
string sql = "SELECT xml_data.query " +
    "('declare namespace ns=\"http://www.wrox.com/books\";" +
    " <Employee Name=\"{/ns:employee/ns:name}\"/>') as Result " +
    " FROM Employee WHERE id = " + id.ToString();
cmd.CommandText = sql;
```

You then execute the `sql` statement by calling the `ExecuteReader()` method of the `SqlCommand` object and then return the output of the sql statement directly to the caller.

```
SqlContext.Pipe.Send(retValue);
```

If you are creating the above stored procedure using Visual Studio 2005, you can deploy it with the click of a button. To this end, first build the solution using the Build→Build Solution menu. After that, deploy the stored procedure onto SQL Server 2005 using Build→Deploy Solution menu option.

Before executing the stored procedure, you need to enable CLR execution in your SQL Server if it is not enabled already. To do this, execute the following code.

```
sp_configure 'clr enabled', 1
GO
RECONFIGURE
GO
```

Now if you execute the stored procedure using the following command in SQL Server Management Studio.

```
exec dbo.GetEmployeeNameByID 2
```

You should see the following output.

```
<Employee Name="Fred" />
```

Choosing between Transact-SQL and Managed Code

When writing stored procedures, triggers, and user-defined functions, one decision programmers will now have to make is whether to use traditional Transact-SQL, or a .NET language such as Visual Basic .NET or C#. The answer depends upon the particular situation involved. In some situations, you'll want to use Transact-SQL; in other situations, you will want to use managed code.

T-SQL is best used in situations where the code will mostly perform data access with little or no procedural logic. Managed code is best suited for CPU intensive functions and procedures that feature complex logic, or where you want to leverage the .NET Framework's Base Class Library. Code placement is another important factor to consider. Both Transact-SQL and in-process managed code can be run on the server. This functionality places code and data close together, and allows you to take advantage of the processing power of the server machine. On the other hand, you may want to avoid placing processor intensive tasks on your database server. Most client machines today are very powerful, and you may want to take advantage of this processing power by placing as much code as possible on the client. Although Transact-SQL code cannot run on a client machine, the SQL Server in-process provider was designed to be as similar as possible to client-side managed ADO.NET, enhancing the portability of code between server and client.

Retrieving the XML Data Type Column from Client

This section focuses on the out-of-process access to the XML data type from a client ASP.NET page. There are different ways to retrieve an XML data typed column using a `SqlDataReader` object. Using the methods of the `SqlDataReader` class, you can retrieve the XML data either as a string or as an `SqlXml` object. The next section starts by exploring the steps involved in retrieving the contents of an XML column as a string.

Retrieving the XML Data Type Column as a String

Listing 10-4 retrieves the contents of the XML column as a string value from a client ASP.NET page. To this end, it executes a simple select statement to retrieve the contents of the xml_data column based on the supplied `id` value. Finally it displays the retrieved XML data as a string value in a text box.

Listing 10-4: Retrieving an XML Data Type Column as a String

```
<%@ Page Language="C#" ValidateRequest="false" %>
<%@ Import Namespace="System.Data" %>
<%@ Import Namespace="System.Data.SqlClient" %>
<%@ Import Namespace="System.Data.Sql" %>
<%@ Import Namespace="System.Web.Configuration" %>
<script runat="server">
  void btnReadXml_Click(object sender, EventArgs e)
  {
    int ID = Convert.ToInt32(txtID.Text);
    //Get the connection string from the web.config file
```

```
      string connString = WebConfigurationManager.ConnectionStrings
        ["adventureWorks"].ConnectionString;
      using (SqlConnection conn = new SqlConnection(connString))
      {
        conn.Open();
        SqlCommand command = conn.CreateCommand();
        command.CommandText = "SELECT xml_data FROM Employee WHERE id = " +
          ID.ToString();
        SqlDataReader reader = command.ExecuteReader();
        if (reader.Read())
        {
          //Get the XML value as string
          string xmlValue = (string)reader.GetValue(0);
          txtXmlData.Text = xmlValue;
        }
        else
          txtXmlData.Text = "No Value";
      }
    }
</script>
<html xmlns="http://www.w3.org/1999/xhtml" >
<head id="Head1" runat="server">
  <title>Retrieving an XML data type column as a String</title>
</head>
<body>
  <form id="form1" runat="server">
    <div>
      <asp:Label ID="lblID" Runat="server" Text="ID:" Width="134px"
        Weight="19px"></asp:Label>
      <asp:TextBox ID="txtID" Runat="server"></asp:TextBox>
      <asp:Button ID="btnReadXml" Runat="server" Text="Read Xml"
        Width="118px" Height="30px" OnClick="btnReadXml_Click" />
      <br/><br/><br/>
      <asp:Label ID="lblXmlData" Runat="server" Text="XML:"
        Width="134px" Height="19px"></asp:Label>
      <asp:TextBox ID="txtXmlData" Runat="server" Width="398px"
        Height="123px" TextMode="MultiLine"></asp:TextBox>
    </div>
  </form>
</body>
</html>
```

In this example, you execute the simple select query through a call to the `ExecuteReader()` method. After the results are available in the `SqlDataReader` object, you then retrieve the XML column value as a string using the `GetValue()`. Figure 10-5 shows the output produced by requesting the page from the browser.

Now that you have understood how easy it is to extract the contents of an XML data type column as a string value, the next section focuses on the steps required for extracting the output as an `SqlXml` object.

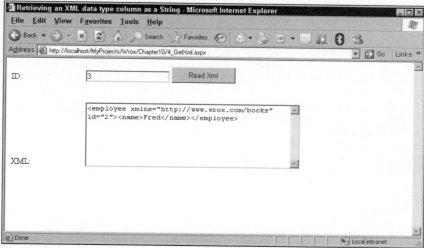

Figure 10-5

Retrieving XML Data Type Column as an SqlXml object

Before looking at the use of SqlXml object, it is important to get an overview of the properties and methods supported by the SqlXml object. The SqlXml class is a new class introduced with ADO.NET 2.0 and it represents the XML data retrieved from a database server. The SqlXml class is exposed by the System.Data.SqlTypes namespace. Table 10-3 discusses the properties of the SqlXml class that you are going to have to most likely work with.

Table 10-3. Properties of SqlXml Class

Property	Description
IsNull	Returns a Boolean indicating if this instance represents a null SqlXml value
Null	Represents a null instance of the SqlXml type
Value	Returns the string representation of the XML content contained in the SqlXml instance

Table 10-4 discusses the methods of the SqlXml class.

Table 10-4. Methods of SqlXml

Method	Description
CreateReader	Factory method that gets the value of the XML content of the SqlXml object as an XmlReader
GetXsdType	Static method that returns a string that indicates the XSD of the specified XmlSchemaSet

Now that you have a brief overview of the `SqlXml` class, it is time to demonstrate an example. Listing 10-5 shows how the `GetSqlXml()` method of the `SqlDataReader` can be used to get reference to an `SqlXml` object. Subsequently it also discusses how to create an instance of the `XmlReader` object using the `CreateReader()` method of the `SqlXml` class.

Listing 10-5: Accessing an XML Data Type Column as an SqlXml Object

```
<%@ Page Language="C#" ValidateRequest="false" %>
<%@ Import Namespace="System.Data" %>
<%@ Import Namespace="System.Data.SqlClient" %>
<%@ Import Namespace="System.Data.Sql" %>
<%@ Import Namespace="System.Xml" %>
<%@ Import Namespace="System.Web.Configuration" %>
<%@ Import Namespace="System.Data.SqlTypes" %>
<script runat="server">
  void btnGetXml_Click(object sender, EventArgs e)
  {
    int ID = Convert.ToInt32(txtID.Text);
    //Get the connection string from the web.config file
    string connString = WebConfigurationManager.ConnectionStrings
      ["adventureWorks"].ConnectionString;
    using (SqlConnection conn = new SqlConnection(connString))
    {
      conn.Open();
      SqlCommand command = conn.CreateCommand();
      command.CommandText = "SELECT xml_data FROM Employee WHERE ID = " +
        ID.ToString();
      SqlDataReader reader = command.ExecuteReader();
      if (reader.Read())
      {
        SqlXml sqlXmlValue = reader.GetSqlXml(0);
        XmlReader xmlReader = sqlXmlValue.CreateReader();
        if (xmlReader.Read())
          output.Text = Server.HtmlEncode(xmlReader.ReadOuterXml());
      }
      else
        output.Text = "No Value";
    }
  }
</script>
<html xmlns="http://www.w3.org/1999/xhtml" >
<head id="Head1" runat="server">
  <title>Accessing an XML data type column as an SqlXml object</title>
</head>
<body>
  <form id="form1" runat="server">
    <div>
      <asp:Label ID="lblID" Runat="server" Text="Enter ID:"
        Width="134px" Height="19px"></asp:Label>
      <asp:TextBox ID="txtID" Runat="server"></asp:TextBox>
      <asp:Button ID="btnReadXml" Runat="server" Text="Read Xml"
        Width="118px" Height="30px" OnClick="btnGetXml_Click" />
      <br/><br/><br/>
```

```
        <asp:Literal runat="server" ID="output"/>
      </div>
    </form>
  </body>
</html>
```

As similar to the previous example, this example also utilizes the `ExecuteReader()` method of the `SqlDataReader` object to execute the select query. After executing the query, the code invokes the `GetSqlXml()` method of the `SqlDataReader` object to obtain reference to the `SqlXml` object.

```
SqlXml sqlXmlValue = reader.GetSqlXml(0);
```

The code then invokes the factory method named `CreateReader()` to get an `XmlReader` object from the `SqlXml` object.

```
XmlReader xmlReader = sqlXmlValue.CreateReader();
```

Finally the `ReadOuterXml()` method of the `XmlReader` object is invoked to display the results onto the browser.

```
    if (xmlReader.Read())
      output.Text = Server.HtmlEncode(xmlReader.ReadOuterXml());
```

Navigate to this page using the browser, enter in an appropriate id, and hit the command button. You should see an output similar to Figure 10-6.

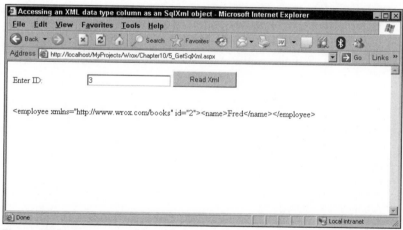

Figure 10-6

Passing Parameters to an XML Data Type Column

So far, you have seen how to retrieve an XML data type column from the client ASP.NET page. This section focuses on how to pass parameters to an XML data type column. As similar to the retrieval, here also you have two options in terms of choosing the appropriate parameter data type.

- ❑ Use NVarChar as the SqlDbType and rely on the automatic conversion wherein SQL Server automatically typecasts the parameter to XML data type

- ❑ Use SqlXml object

The next few sections examine both of these approaches in detail.

Passing NVarChar as a Parameter Type to an XML Data Type Column

The classes in the System.Data.SqlClient namespace provide symmetric functionality for XML parameters meaning that you can also use the String data type with these. Being able to pass in a string (NVARCHAR) where an XML type is expected relies on the fact that SQL Server provides automatic conversion of VARCHAR or NVARCHAR to the XML data type. Listing 10-6 shows you an example of this in action.

Listing 10-6: Automatic Conversion of NVarChar to XML Data Type

```
<%@ Page Language="C#" ValidateRequest="false" %>
<%@ Import Namespace="System.Data" %>
<%@ Import Namespace="System.Web.Configuration" %>
<%@ Import Namespace="System.Data.SqlClient" %>
<%@ Import Namespace="System.Xml" %>
<script runat="server">
  void btnSave_Click(object sender, EventArgs e)
  {
    int ID = Convert.ToInt32(txtID.Text);
    string xmlValue = txtXmlData.Text;
    //Get the connection string from the web.config file
    string connString = WebConfigurationManager.ConnectionStrings
      ["adventureWorks"].ConnectionString;
    try
    {
      using (SqlConnection conn = new SqlConnection(connString))
      {
        conn.Open();
        SqlCommand cmd = conn.CreateCommand();
        cmd.CommandText = "Insert Employee(id, xml_data) " +
          "Values(@id, @xml_data)";
        //Set value of parameters
        SqlParameter idParameter = cmd.Parameters.Add("@id",
          SqlDbType.Int);
        idParameter.Value = ID;
        SqlParameter xmlDataParameter = cmd.Parameters.Add("@xml_data",
          SqlDbType.NVarChar);
        xmlDataParameter.Value = xmlValue;
        //Execute and close connection
        cmd.ExecuteNonQuery();
      }
      output.Text = "Successfully Saved";
    }
    catch (Exception ex)
    {
      output.Text = "Exception : " + ex.Message;
    }
  }
```

```
    </script>
    <html xmlns="http://www.w3.org/1999/xhtml" >
    <head id="Head1" runat="server">
      <title>Passing value to an XML data type column as a String</title>
    </head>
    <body>
      <form id="form1" runat="server">
        <div>
          <asp:Label ID="lblID" Runat="server" Text="ID:"
            Width="134px" Height="19px"></asp:Label>
          <asp:TextBox ID="txtID" Runat="server"></asp:TextBox>
          <br/><br/><br/>
          <asp:Label ID="lblXmlData" Runat="server" Text="XML:"
            Width="134px" Height="19px"></asp:Label>
          <asp:TextBox ID="txtXmlData" Runat="server" Width="447px"
            Height="153px" TextMode="MultiLine"></asp:TextBox>
          <br/><br/><br/><br/> 
          <asp:Button ID="btnSave" Runat="server" Text="Save Values"
            Width="118px" Height="30px" OnClick="btnSave_Click" />
          <br/><br/><br/><br/> 
          <asp:Literal runat="server" ID="output" />
        </div>
      </form>
    </body>
    </html>
```

The lines of interest in this code are where you actually pass in the parameter to the xml_data column. As you can see from the following, you supply the `SqlDbType.NVarChar` as the second argument to the `Add` method and rely on the automatic conversion provided by SQL Server 2005.

```
SqlParameter xmlDataParameter = cmd.Parameters.Add("@xml_data",
  SqlDbType.NVarChar);
xmlDataParameter.Value = xmlValue;
```

Fire up the page in a browser, enter all the details including the id and the XML data, and click on the `Save` button. If everything goes well, you will get a message indicating that the data has been successfully saved. One interesting point to note is that you cannot insert an XML document that is not well-formed.

Passing SqlXml Object to an XML Data Type Column

This section demonstrates how to utilize an `SqlXml` object to pass parameter. To this end, Listing 10-7 creates an object of type `SqlXml` and assigns that to the Value property of the `SqlParameter` object that represents the `@xml_data` parameter.

Listing 10-7: Passing SqlXml Object as a Parameter to an XML Column

```
<%@ Page Language="C#" ValidateRequest="false" %>
<%@ Import Namespace="System.Web.Configuration" %>
<%@ Import Namespace="System.Data.SqlClient" %>
<%@ Import Namespace="System.Data.SqlTypes" %>
<%@ Import Namespace="System.Data" %>
```

```
<%@ Import Namespace="System.Xml" %>
<script runat="server">
  void btnSave_Click(object sender, EventArgs e)
  {
    int ID = Convert.ToInt32(txtID.Text);
    string xmlValue = txtXmlData.Text;
    //Get the connection string from the web.config file
    string connString = WebConfigurationManager.ConnectionStrings
      ["adventureWorks"].ConnectionString;
    try
    {
      using (SqlConnection conn = new SqlConnection(connString))
      {
        conn.Open();
        SqlCommand cmd = conn.CreateCommand();
        cmd.CommandText = "Insert Employee(id, xml_data) Values(@id, @xml_data)";
        //Set value of parameters
        SqlParameter idParameter = cmd.Parameters.Add("@id", SqlDbType.Int);
        idParameter.Value = ID;
        SqlParameter xmlDataParameter = cmd.Parameters.Add("@xml_data",
          SqlDbType.Xml);
        xmlDataParameter.Value = new SqlXml(new XmlTextReader(xmlValue,
          XmlNodeType.Document, null));
        //Execute and close connection
        cmd.ExecuteNonQuery();
      }
      output.Text = "Successfully Saved";
    }
    catch (Exception ex)
    {
      output.Text = "Exception:" + ex.Message;
    }
  }
</script>
<html xmlns="http://www.w3.org/1999/xhtml" >
<head id="Head1" runat="server">
  <title>Passing value to an XML data type column as a SqlXml</title>
</head>
<body>
  <form id="form1" runat="server">
    <div>
      <asp:Label ID="lblID" Runat="server" Text="ID:"
        Width="134px" Height="19px"></asp:Label>
      <asp:TextBox ID="txtID" Runat="server"></asp:TextBox>
      <br/><br/><br/>
      <asp:Label ID="lblXmlData" Runat="server" Text="XML:"
        Width="134px" Height="19px"></asp:Label>
      <asp:TextBox ID="txtXmlData" Runat="server" Width="308px"
        Height="82px" TextMode="MultiLine"></asp:TextBox>
      <br/><br/><br/><br/> 
      <asp:Button ID="btnSave" Runat="server" Text="Save Values"
        Width="118px" Height="30px" OnClick="btnSave_Click" />
```

```
    <asp:Literal runat="server" id="output" />
  </div>
  </form>
</body>
</html>
```

There are two important things that you need to note in the previous code listing. You first supply the SqlDbType.Xml value to the second parameter of the SqlParameter's Add method.

```
SqlParameter xmlDataParameter = cmd.Parameters.Add("@xml_data",
SqlDbType.Xml);
```

Next, you assign an object of type SqlXml to the Value property of the SqlParameter object.

```
xmlDataParameter.Value = new SqlXml(new XmlTextReader(xmlValue,
    XmlNodeType.Document, null));
```

Navigate to this page using the browser. Now enter the ID value of 6 and the following XML as an input argument and hit the Save Values button.

```
<employee xmlns="http://www.wrox.com/books" id="6">
  <name>Thiru</name>
</employee>
```

You should get a confirmation message saying "Successfully Saved." So far, you have used the XML data entered by the user in the text box as an input to the XML data type column. There are times where you might want to utilize an external XML file as an input to the XML data type column. Listing 10-8 shows you how to accomplish this.

Listing 10-8: XML File Contents as a Parameter to the XML Column

```
<%@ Page Language="C#" ValidateRequest="false" %>
<%@ Import Namespace="System.Data" %>
<%@ Import Namespace="System.Web.Configuration" %>
<%@ Import Namespace="System.Data.SqlClient" %>
<%@ Import Namespace="System.IO" %>
<%@ Import Namespace="System.Xml" %>
<%@ Import Namespace="System.Data.SqlTypes" %>
<script runat="server">
  void btnSave_Click(object sender, EventArgs e)
  {
    int ID = Convert.ToInt32(txtID.Text);
    //Get the connection string from the web.config file
    string connString = WebConfigurationManager.ConnectionStrings
      ["adventureWorks"].ConnectionString;
    try
    {
      using (SqlConnection conn = new SqlConnection(connString))
      {
        conn.Open();
        SqlCommand cmd = conn.CreateCommand();
        cmd.CommandText = "Insert Employee(id, xml_data) " +
```

```
                "Values(@id, @xml_data)";
            //Set value of parameters
            SqlParameter idParameter = cmd.Parameters.Add("@id", SqlDbType.Int);
            idParameter.Value = ID;
            SqlParameter xmlDataParameter = cmd.Parameters.Add("@xml_data",
              SqlDbType.Xml);
            string xmlFile = @"C:\Data\Employee.xml";
            XmlReader reader = XmlReader.Create(xmlFile);
            xmlDataParameter.Value = new SqlXml(reader);
            //Execute Insert and close connection
            cmd.ExecuteNonQuery();
        }
        output.Text = "Successfully Saved";
    }
    catch (Exception ex)
    {
        output.Text = "Exception: " + ex.Message;
    }
}
</script>
<html xmlns="http://www.w3.org/1999/xhtml" >
<head id="Head1" runat="server">
  <title>XML File input as a parameter to the XML column</title>
</head>
<body>
  <form id="form1" runat="server">
    <div>
      <asp:Label ID="lblID" Runat="server" Text="ID:"
        Width="134px" Height="19px"></asp:Label>
      <asp:TextBox ID="txtID" Runat="server"></asp:TextBox>
      <br/><br/><br/>
      <asp:Button ID="btnSave" Runat="server" Text="Save Values"
        Width="118px" Height="30px" OnClick="btnSave_Click" />
      <br/><br/><br/>
      <asp:Literal runat="server" ID="output" />
    </div>
  </form>
</body>
</html>
```

Listing 10-8 is similar to Listing 10-7 except for the following lines of code.

```
string xmlFile = @"C:\Data\Employee.xml";
XmlReader reader = XmlReader.Create(xmlFile);
xmlDataParameter.Value = new SqlXml(reader);
```

As you can see from this example, the input to the parameter is provided from an external XML file named Employee.xml. Note that the worker process account needs to have the necessary permissions to access the external file. This input is supplied to the constructor of the SqlXml object in the form of an XmlReader object.

Using XML Schema on the Client

When you use strongly typed XML data inside SQL Server 2005 from the client, validation is done on the server, not on the client. As an example, if you update the value of the xml_data column, the data is sent across the network to SQL Server before validation occurs; however, with little work, it is possible to retrieve the XML schemas from the schema collections of the SQL Server and temporarily store them on the client side to accomplish client side validation. This can save some round trips by preventing a user or Web service from sending schema-invalid XML to your client for SQL Server storage.

> Note that there are two caveats that must be considered before temporarily storing schemas on the client side. Relying on XML schema information fetched from SQL Server is like relying on any cached client-side metadata. It is possible that someone may have altered the schema collection using the ALTER XML SCHEMA statement, or even dropped the schema collection and re-created it, rendering your client-side checking useless. Fortunately the new Event notification feature of SQL Server 2005 allows you to guard yourself against surprises by leveraging the event notification feature in conjunction with CREATE/ALTER/DROP/ XML SCHEMA DDL statements.

Before looking at the steps involved in retrieving the XML schemas, examine the metadata of an XML data type column. Listing 10-9 displays the metadata of the xml_data column in the Employee table.

Listing 10-9: Retrieving Metadata of an XML Data Type Column

```csharp
<%@ Page Language="C#" ValidateRequest="false" %>
<%@ Import Namespace="System.Data" %>
<%@ Import Namespace="System.Data.SqlClient" %>
<%@ Import Namespace="System.Web.Configuration" %>
<script runat="server">
  void Page_Load(object sender, EventArgs e)
  {
       //Get the connection string from the web.config file
    string connString = WebConfigurationManager.ConnectionStrings
      ["adventureWorks"].ConnectionString;
    using (SqlConnection conn = new SqlConnection(connString))
    {
      conn.Open();
      SqlCommand command = conn.CreateCommand();
      command.CommandText = "SELECT TOP 0 xml_data FROM Employee ";
      System.Text.StringBuilder builder = new System.Text.StringBuilder();
      SqlDataReader reader = command.ExecuteReader();
      DataTable table = reader.GetSchemaTable();
      //Display specific columns
      builder.Append("ColumnName: " + table.Rows[0]["ColumnName"] + "<br>");
      builder.Append("DataType: " +  table.Rows[0]["DataType"] + "<br>");
      builder.Append("ProviderSpecificDataType: " +
        table.Rows[0]["ProviderSpecificDataType"] + "<br>");
      builder.Append("XmlSchemaCollectionDatabase: " +
        table.Rows[0]["XmlSchemaCollectionDatabase"] + "<br>");
```

```
          builder.Append("XmlSchemaCollectionOwningSchema: " +
             table.Rows[0]["XmlSchemaCollectionOwningSchema"] + "<br>");
          builder.Append("XmlSchemaCollectionName: " +
             table.Rows[0]["XmlSchemaCollectionName"] + "<br>");
          output.Text = builder.ToString();
       }
    }
</script>
<html xmlns="http://www.w3.org/1999/xhtml" >
<head id="Head1" runat="server">
  <title>Metadata about XML data type column</title>
</head>
<body>
  <form id="form1" runat="server">
    <div>

      <asp:Literal ID="output" runat="server" />
    </div>
  </form>
</body>
</html>
```

In Listing 10-9, you execute a select statement against the Employee table specifying the xml_data as the only output column in the select statement. You then execute the query by calling the ExecuteReader() method of the SqlDataReader object.

```
SqlDataReader reader = command.ExecuteReader();
```

After that, you call the GetSchemaTable() method of the SqlDataReader object to retrieve the metadata about the xml_data column.

```
DataTable table = reader.GetSchemaTable();
```

You then display specific column values in the browser. Output produced by the code is shown in Figure 10-7.

As shown in the output, you can get complete details such as XmlSchemaCollectionDatabase, XmlSchemaCollectionOwningSchema, and XmlSchemaCollectionName about the XML schema used by the xml_data column. This information is valuable when you want to dynamically query the database for the available XML schemas and retrieve them for client-side validations.

Retrieving XSD Schemas from a Client Application

To do client-side XML Schema validation, the first thing you need to do is to retrieve the SQL Server XML SCHEMA COLLECTION by using the T-SQL function xml_schema_namespace(). This requires an XML schema collection name and database schema name because XML schema collections are database schema scoped. After you have figured out which XML schema collection to retrieve, you can use the T-SQL function to retrieve it into a client-side XmlSchemaSet.

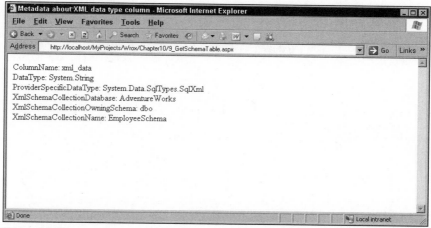

Figure 10-7

Note that for reasons of brevity, I have simply hard-coded the XSD schema information in the following code. In a real-world application, you would retrieve this information using the GetSchemaTable() method of the SqlDataReader (as shown in Listing 10-9).

Listing 10-10: Retrieving XSD Schemas Stored in SQL Server 2005

```
<%@ Page Language="C#" ValidateRequest="false" %>
<%@ Import Namespace="System.Data" %>
<%@ Import Namespace="System.Xml" %>
<%@ Import Namespace="System.Xml.Schema" %>
<%@ Import Namespace="System.Data.SqlClient" %>
<%@ Import Namespace="System.Web.Configuration" %>
<script runat="server">
  void btnRetrieve_Click(object sender, EventArgs e)
  {
    //Get the connection string from the web.config file
    string connString = WebConfigurationManager.ConnectionStrings
      ["adventureWorks"].ConnectionString;
    using (SqlConnection conn = new SqlConnection(connString))
    {
      conn.Open();
      SqlCommand command = conn.CreateCommand();
      command.CommandText = "SELECT xml_schema_namespace " +
        "(N'dbo',N'EmployeeSchema')";
      XmlSchemaSet schemaSet = new XmlSchemaSet();
      SqlDataReader sqlReader = command.ExecuteReader();
      sqlReader.Read();
      XmlReader reader = sqlReader.GetSqlXml(0).CreateReader();
      //Add the schemas to the XmlSchemaSet
      do
      {
```

```
          schemaSet.Add(XmlSchema.Read(reader, null));
          reader.Read();
        }
        while (reader.NodeType == XmlNodeType.Element);
        output.Text = "Schemas Count : " + schemaSet.Schemas().Count.ToString();
      }
    }
</script>
<html xmlns="http://www.w3.org/1999/xhtml" >
<head id="Head1" runat="server">
  <title>Retrieving XML Schemas stored in SQL Server 2005</title>
</head>
<body>
  <form id="form1" runat="server">
    <div>
      <asp:Button ID="btnRetrieve" Runat="server" Text="Retrieve XML Schemas"
        Width="170px" Height="30px" OnClick="btnRetrieve_Click" />
      <br/><br/><br/>
      <asp:Literal runat="server" ID="output" />
    </div>
  </form>
</body>
</html>
```

To retrieve the XML schemas, you use the xml_schema_namespace T-SQL function as follows.

```
command.CommandText = "SELECT xml_schema_namespace " +
  "(N'dbo',N'EmployeeSchema')";
```

After you execute the query, you retrieve the resultset into an XmlReader object.

```
XmlReader reader = sqlReader.GetSqlXml(0).CreateReader();
```

Now you loop through all the nodes in the XmlReader and add the schemas to an XmlSchemaSet object.

```
      do
      {
        schemaSet.Add(XmlSchema.Read(reader, null));
        reader.Read();
      }
      while (reader.NodeType == XmlNodeType.Element);
```

The output of the page shows the number of schemas in the schemas collection.

Performing Client Side Validation Using SQL Server XSD Schemas

Now that you know how to retrieve the XSD schemas from SQL Server, performing validation using schemas is a very simple process. Listing 10-11 shows you how to accomplish this.

Listing 10-11: Performing Client Side Validations Using SQL Server XSD Schemas

```csharp
<%@ Page Language="C#" ValidateRequest="false" %>
<%@ Import Namespace="System.Data" %>
<%@ Import Namespace="System.Xml" %>
<%@ Import Namespace="System.Xml.Schema" %>
<%@ Import Namespace="System.Data.SqlClient" %>
<%@ Import Namespace="System.Web.Configuration" %>
<%@ Import Namespace="System.Data.SqlTypes" %>
<script runat="server">
  private StringBuilder _builder = new StringBuilder();
  void btnSaveXml_Click(object sender, EventArgs e)
  {
    int ID = Convert.ToInt32(txtID.Text);
    string connString = WebConfigurationManager.ConnectionStrings
      ["adventureWorks"].ConnectionString;
    XmlSchemaSet schemaSet = GetSchemas(connString);
    try
    {
      using (SqlConnection conn = new SqlConnection(connString))
      {
        conn.Open();
        //Associate the XmlSchemaSet with the XmlReader
        XmlReaderSettings settings = new XmlReaderSettings();
        settings.ValidationEventHandler += new
          ValidationEventHandler(this.ValidationEventHandler);
        settings.ValidationType = ValidationType.Schema;
        settings.Schemas = schemaSet;
        XmlReader reader = XmlReader.Create(@"c:/Data/Employee.xml",
          settings);
        while (reader.Read()){}
        SqlCommand cmd = conn.CreateCommand();
        cmd.CommandText = "Insert Employee(id, xml_data) " +
          "Values(@ID, @xml_data)";
        //Set value of parameters
        cmd.Parameters.AddWithValue("@ID", ID);
        cmd.Parameters.AddWithValue("@xml_data", new SqlXml(reader));
        //Execute Insert and close connection
        cmd.ExecuteNonQuery();
        output.Text = "Successfully Saved";
      }
    }
    catch (Exception ex)
    {
      output.Text = "Exception : " + ex.Message;
    }
  }

  XmlSchemaSet GetSchemas(string connString)
  {
    XmlSchemaSet schemaSet = new XmlSchemaSet();
```

```
        using (SqlConnection conn = new SqlConnection(connString))
        {
          conn.Open();
          SqlCommand command = conn.CreateCommand();
          command.CommandText = "SELECT xml_schema_namespace " +
            "(N'dbo',N'EmployeeSchema')";
          SqlDataReader sqlReader = command.ExecuteReader();
          sqlReader.Read();
          XmlReader reader = sqlReader.GetSqlXml(0).CreateReader();
          do
          {
            schemaSet.Add(XmlSchema.Read(reader, null));
            reader.Read();
          }
          while (reader.NodeType == XmlNodeType.Element);
        }
        return schemaSet;
      }

      void ValidationEventHandler(object sender, ValidationEventArgs args)
      {
        _builder.Append("Validation error: " + args.Message + "<br>");
      }
</script>
<html xmlns="http://www.w3.org/1999/xhtml" >
<head id="Head1" runat="server">
  <title>Client side XML validation using XSD Schemas in SQL Server</title>
</head>
<body>
  <form id="form1" runat="server">
    <div>
      <asp:Label ID="lblID" Runat="server" Text="Enter ID:"
        Width="134px" Height="19px"></asp:Label>
      <asp:TextBox ID="txtID" Runat="server"></asp:TextBox>
      <asp:Button ID="btnSave" Runat="server" Text="Save Xml"
        Width="118px" Height="30px" OnClick="btnSaveXml_Click" />
      <br/><br/><br/>
      <asp:Literal runat="server" ID="output" />
    </div>
  </form>
</body>
</html>
```

In this code, the GetSchemas() helper method retrieves the EmployeeSchema from the database. This schema is ultimately tied to the XmlReader object through the XmlReaderSettings object using the following lines of code.

```
XmlReaderSettings settings = new XmlReaderSettings();
settings.Schemas = schemaSet;
```

```
XmlReader reader = XmlReader.Create(@"c:/Data/Employee.xml",
    settings);
```

After the association is performed, the following line of code ensures that the supplied XML data is in compliance with the XSD schema. If the XML data is not compliant, it raises an exception.

```
cmd.Parameters.AddWithValue("@xml_data", new SqlXml(reader));
```

Consider the following data in the `Employee.xml`.

```
<employee xmlns="http://www.wrox.com/books" id="10">
    <name>Dave</name>
</employee>
```

Request the page in a browser and if everything goes fine, you will see a message indicating that the data is successfully saved to the database.

Multiple Active Result Sets (MARS) in ADO.NET

In the previous sections, you have seen how to execute a single FOR XML query through the ExecuteXmlReader() method using a single connection using ADO.NET. The fact that you could execute only one query at any given time is a restriction with ADO.NET 1.x versions and SQL Server 2000. With the release of ADO.NET 2.0 and SQL Server 2005, however, this is no longer valid. Using a new feature named MARS, you can execute multiple queries or stored procedures on a single connection resulting in multiple forward-only read-only result sets.

If you have ever seen the dreaded error message "There is already an open DataReader associated with this Connection which must be closed first" while using SqlDataReader or XmlReader in your applications, you will love the MARS feature. MARS solves this problem by allowing you to open multiple SqlDataReader or XmlReader objects on a single connection. MARS allows an application to have more than one SqlDataReader or XmlReader open on a connection when each instance of SqlDataReader is started from a separate command. As you add each SqlCommand object, an additional session is added to the connection.

Now that you have had an introduction to MARS, look at and understand the steps involved in using MARS from ADO.NET 2.0:

1. Create a SqlConnection object and initialize it with the appropriate connection string.

2. Open the Connection by using the Open() method of the SqlConnection object.

3. Create individual SqlCommand objects with the required parameters to execute the query. While creating the SqlCommand objects, remember to associate the SqlCommand objects with the previously created SqlConnection object.

4. After you have the SqlConnection object, you then invoke the ExecuteReader method of the SqlCommand object to execute the queries.

5. Finally, close the SqlConnection object by executing the Close() method.

> By default, MARS is available only on MARS-enabled hosts. SQL Server 2005 is the
> first SQL Server version to support MARS. By default, MARS is enabled whenever
> you use the classes in the System.Data.SqlClient namespace to connect to SQL
> Server; however you can also explicitly control this feature by using a keyword pair
> in your connection string. To explicitly enable MARS, you add a new attribute
> named MultipleActiveResultSets that is set to True as follows.
>
> ```
> "Server=localhost;Database=AdventureWorks;"Trusted_Connection=True;
> MultipleActiveResultSets=True"
> ```

To better understand how MARS works, look at an example wherein you display the categories and
products information from the AdventureWorks database using parent child relationship. For each category
gory that is retrieved from the categories table, a query to the products table is made to return all the
products that belong in that category. Listing 10-12 shows you the code required to implement this.

Listing 10-12: Executing Multiple FOR XML Queries Using MARS

```csharp
<%@ Page Language="C#" ValidateRequest="false" %>
<%@ Import Namespace="System.Data" %>
<%@ Import Namespace="System.Data.SqlClient" %>
<%@ Import Namespace="System.Data.Sql" %>
<%@ Import Namespace="System.Xml" %>
<%@ Import Namespace="System.Web.Configuration" %>
<%@ Import Namespace="System.Data.SqlTypes" %>
<script runat="server">
  void Page_Load(object sender, EventArgs e)
  {
    string connectionString = WebConfigurationManager.ConnectionStrings
      ["adventureWorks"].ConnectionString;
    int categoryID = 0;
    string categorySql = "SELECT ProductSubcategoryID, Name FROM " +
      "Production.ProductSubCategory As Categories " +
      "FOR XML AUTO, ROOT('Root'), ELEMENTS";
    string productSql = "SELECT ProductID, Name FROM " +
      "Production.Product As Products WHERE " +
      "ProductSubcategoryID = @ProductSubcategoryID " +
      "FOR XML AUTO, ROOT('Root'), ELEMENTS";
    using (SqlConnection conn = new
      SqlConnection(connectionString))
    {
      conn.Open();
      //Check if the SQL Server supports MARS
      if (conn.ServerVersion.StartsWith("09"))
      {
        SqlCommand categoryCommand = new SqlCommand(categorySql, conn);
        SqlCommand productCommand = new SqlCommand(productSql, conn);
        productCommand.Parameters.Add("@ProductSubcategoryID", SqlDbType.Int);
        //Execute the first XML query
        using (XmlReader categoryReader = categoryCommand.ExecuteXmlReader())
        {
          //Load the XmlReader into an XmlDocument object
          XmlDocument doc = new XmlDocument();
```

```
            doc.Load(categoryReader);
            XmlNodeList list =
              doc.DocumentElement.SelectNodes("//Categories");
            foreach (XmlNode node in list)
            {
              categoryID= Convert.ToInt32(node.SelectSingleNode
                ("ProductSubcategoryID").InnerText);
              string categoryName = node.SelectSingleNode
                ("Name").InnerText;
              output.Controls.Add(new LiteralControl("<b>Category: " +
                categoryName + "</b><br>"));
              productCommand.Parameters["@ProductSubcategoryID"].Value = categoryID;
              //Execute the next query using the same connection
              using (XmlReader productReader = productCommand.ExecuteXmlReader())
              {
                while (productReader.Read())
                {
                  if (productReader.NodeType == XmlNodeType.Element)
                  {
                    if (productReader.Name == "ProductID")
                      output.Controls.Add(new
                        LiteralControl(productReader.ReadString() + "  "));
                    if (productReader.Name == "Name")
                      output.Controls.Add(new
                        LiteralControl(productReader.ReadString() + "<br>"));
                  }
                }
              }
              output.Controls.Add(new LiteralControl("<br>"));
            }
          }
        else
          Response.Write("MARS is not supported");
        }
      }
</script>
<html xmlns="http://www.w3.org/1999/xhtml" >
<head id="Head1" runat="server">
  <title>Executing multiple queries using MARS</title>
</head>
<body>
  <form id="form1" runat="server">
    <div>
      <asp:PlaceHolder ID="output" Runat="Server"></asp:PlaceHolder>
    </div>
    </form>
</body>
</html>
```

In Listing 10-12, you start by initializing the `categorySql`, and `productSql` variables with appropriate sql statements. After that, you create an instance of the `SqlConnection` object and establish the connection to the database by calling the `Open()` method of the `SqlConnection` object; then check the `ServerVersion` property of the `SqlConnection` to see if the SQL Server supports MARS. If the major version returned by the ServerVersion property is "09, it is safe to assume that MARS is supported in SQL Server.

You then create two instances of the SqlCommand object and assign them to categoryCommand and productCommand variables, respectively. Next, add the ProductSubcategoryID parameter to the productCommand variable. Now you execute the query contained in the categoryCommand object by invoking the ExecuteXmlReader() method of the categoryCommand object. You capture the results of the sql query execution in an XmlReader variable, load the XmlReader object into an XmlDocument object, and get reference to the <Categories> elements in the form of an XmlNodeList object. For each node in the XmlNodeList collection, you execute the sql command contained in the productCommand object. Finally, you loop through the productReader object that contains the products resultset and display that information through a PlaceHolder control.

If you browse to the Web form using the browser, you will see the output shown in Figure 10-8.

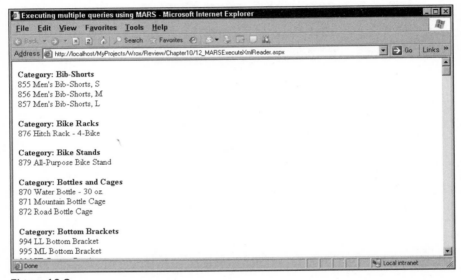

Figure 10-8

XML Data Type and a DataSet

In addition to the SqlDataReader object, the DataSet object has also been enhanced with the ability to read XML data typed columns from SQL Server 2005; however, by default, a DataAdapter does not populate a DataSet with columns of type XML. When it encounters an XML column in the rowset coming from the database (as returned by the SelectCommand that the DataAdapter is using), it creates a column in the DataSet of type String, and places the incoming XML content into that column as a String value. This maintains backward compatibility with existing code.

To generate an XML column in the DataSet, you set the ReturnProviderSpecificTypes property of the DataAdapter to true before calling the Fill() method. Listing 10-13 demonstrates how to retrieve the XML data type column value as a string.

Listing 10-13: Retrieving XML Column as a String from a DataSet

```
<%@ Page Language="C#" ValidateRequest="false" %>
<%@ Import Namespace="System.Data" %>
<%@ Import Namespace="System.Data.SqlClient" %>
<%@ Import Namespace="System.Data.Sql" %>
<%@ Import Namespace="System.Xml" %>
<%@ Import Namespace="System.Web.Configuration" %>
<script runat="server">
  void btnRetrieveXml_Click(object sender, EventArgs e)
  {
    int ID = Convert.ToInt32(txtID.Text);
    //Get the connection string from the web.config file
    string connString = WebConfigurationManager.ConnectionStrings
      ["adventureWorks"].ConnectionString;
    using (SqlConnection conn = new SqlConnection(connString))
    {
      SqlCommand command = conn.CreateCommand();
      command.CommandText = "SELECT xml_data FROM Employee " +
        "WHERE id = " + ID.ToString();
      SqlDataAdapter adapter = new SqlDataAdapter(command);
      DataSet empDataSet = new DataSet();
      adapter.Fill(empDataSet);
      //Get the XML value as string
      if (empDataSet.Tables[0].Rows.Count > 0)
      {
        string xml = empDataSet.Tables[0].Rows[0]["xml_data"].ToString();
        XmlDocument doc = new XmlDocument();
        doc.LoadXml(xml);
        output.Text = Server.HtmlEncode("Output : " +  doc.OuterXml);
      }
      else
        output.Text = "No value";
    }
  }
</script>
<html xmlns="http://www.w3.org/1999/xhtml" >
<head id="Head1" runat="server">
  <title>Retrieving an XML column through a DataSet </title>
</head>
<body>
  <form id="form1" runat="server">
    <div>
      <asp:Label ID="lblID" Runat="server" Text="Enter ID:" Width="134px"
        Height="19px"></asp:Label>
      <asp:TextBox ID="txtID" Runat="server"></asp:TextBox>
      <asp:Button ID="btnRetrieveXml" Runat="server" Text="Retrieve XML"
        Width="118px" Height="30px" OnClick="btnRetrieveXml_Click" />
      <br/><br/><br/>
      <asp:Literal ID="output" runat="Server"/>
    </div>
  </form>
</body>
</html>
```

In this code, you retrieve the XML data type column using the following line of code.

```
string xml = empDataSet.Tables[0].Rows[0]["xml_data"].ToString();
```

Figure 10-9 shows the resultant output.

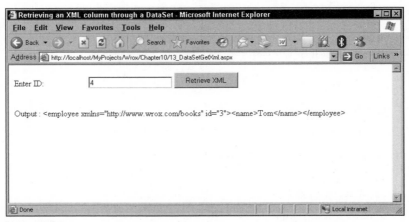

Figure 10-9

As you know, when you use a `SqlDataReader` to access a rowset containing a XML data type column, the XML content is returned in the rowset as a `SqlXml` type. You can call the `CreateReader()` method on this to get an `XmlReader`, or get the value as a `String` from the `Value` property (or just call `ToString()` on it). Based on the same concept, the `DataSet` should also support `SqlXml` types in the future, however there are backward compatibility issues to be resolved. Listing 10-14 shows the pseudo code of this capability.

Listing 10-14: Retrieving XML Column as a SqlXml from a DataSet

```
<%@ Page Language="C#" ValidateRequest="false" %>
<%@ Import Namespace="System.Data" %>
<%@ Import Namespace="System.Data.SqlClient" %>
<%@ Import Namespace="System.Data.Sql" %>
<%@ Import Namespace="System.Xml" %>
<%@ Import Namespace="System.Web.Configuration" %>
<%@ Import Namespace="System.Data.SqlTypes" %>
  <script runat="server">
  void btnRetrieveXml_Click(object sender, EventArgs e)
  {
    int ID = Convert.ToInt32(txtID.Text);
    //Get the connection string from the web.config file
    string connString = WebConfigurationManager.ConnectionStrings
      ["adventureWorks"].ConnectionString;
    using (SqlConnection conn = new SqlConnection(connString))
    {
      SqlCommand command = conn.CreateCommand();
      command.CommandText = "SELECT xml_data FROM Employee WHERE id = " +
        ID.ToString();
```

```
            SqlDataAdapter adapter = new SqlDataAdapter(command);
            adapter.ReturnProviderSpecificTypes = true;
            DataSet empDataSet = new DataSet();
            adapter.Fill(empDataSet);
            SqlXml xml = (SqlXml)empDataSet.Tables[0].Rows[0]["xml_data"];
            output.Text = xml.Value;
        }
    }
</script>
<html xmlns="http://www.w3.org/1999/xhtml" >
<head id="Head1" runat="server">
  <title>Retrieving an XML column as a SqlXml</title>
</head>
<body>
<form id="form1" runat="server">
    <div>
        <asp:Label ID="lblID" Runat="server" Text="Enter ID:"
          Width="134px" Height="19px"></asp:Label>
        <asp:TextBox ID="txtID" Runat="server"></asp:TextBox>
        <asp:Button ID="btnRetrieveXml" Runat="server" Text="Retrieve XML"
          Width="118px" Height="30px" OnClick="btnRetrieveXml_Click" />
        <br/><br/><br/>
        <asp:Literal ID="output" runat="server" />
    </div>
  </form>
</body>
</html>
```

After you have the results in a `DataSet` object, you typecast the xml_data column value into a `SqlXml` object.

```
SqlXml xml = (SqlXml)empDataSet.Tables[0].Rows[0]["xml_data"];
```

Finally, you invoke the `Value` property of the `SqlXml` object and display its value in a `Literal` control.

```
output.Text = xml.Value;
```

OPENXML()

SQL Server 2000 introduced the OPENXML function that can be used to shred XML document into relational rowset. In other words, it can be used to convert hierarchical XML data into relational table, rows, and columns.

With SQL Server 2005, you can still use OPENXML to convert XML into relational rowset, but the preferred approach is to use nodes() method on the XML data type.

XML is one of the easiest ways to exchange data between applications. When XML first became available, many developers attempted to write their own XML parsers in the language of their choice. Indeed, because XML consists of tags, writing such a parser in T-SQL isn't very difficult; however, going though thousands of lines of XML can quickly degrade performance. That's why it is nice to have the OPENXML function, which does the parsing work for you fairly efficiently.

The OPENXML function must be used with two system stored procedures: sp_xml_preparedocument and sp_xml_removedocument. As the names of these procedures suggest, the former prepares an internal representation of the XML document in memory, and the latter removes such representation to free up resources. sp_xml_preparedocument has two parameters: the XML document, which is accepted as an input parameter, and an output parameter with the integer type. After the document is prepared with sp_xml_preparedocument, OPENXML can translate it into a row set.

When you invoke the sp_xml_preparedocument procedure, the procedure performs the following steps:

1. **Reads the XML text provided as input.**

2. **Parses the text using the XML parser.**

3. **Provides the parsed document, which is in tree form containing various nodes (elements, attributes, text, comments, and so on) in the XML document.**

4. **It returns a handle that can be used to access the newly created internal representation of the XML document. This handle is valid until the connection is reset, or until the execution of sp_xml_removedocument.**

Before looking at the example, consider a table named Authors whose declaration is as follows:

```
Create Table Authors(au_id VARCHAR(11), au_lname VARCHAR(20),
  au_fname VARCHAR(30), phone VARCHAR(12),
  address VARCHAR(50), city VARCHAR(20),
  state CHAR(2), zip CHAR(5), contract BIT)
```

Consider the simple example shown in Listing 10-15 to understand the OPENXML function:

Listing 10-15: Using OPENXML

```
DECLARE @xml_text VARCHAR(4000), @i INT
SELECT @xml_text = '
  <root>
    <authors  au_id="172-32-1176" au_lname="White" au_fname="Johnson"
      phone="408 496-7223"  address="10932 Bigge Rd."  city="Menlo Park"
      state="CA" zip="94025" contract="1"/>
    <authors au_id="213-46-8915" au_lname="Green" au_fname="Marjorie"
      phone="415 986-7020" address="309 63rd St. #411" city="Oakland"
      state="CA" zip="94618" contract="1"/>
    <authors au_id="238-95-7766" au_lname="Carson" au_fname="Cheryl"
      phone="415 548-7723" address="589 Darwin Ln." city="Berkeley"
      state="CA" zip="94705" contract="1"/>
</root>'
EXEC sp_xml_preparedocument @i OUTPUT, @xml_text
SELECT * FROM OPENXML(@i, '/root/authors') WITH authors
EXEC sp_xml_removedocument @i
```

Running these statements results in the output shown in Figure 10-10.

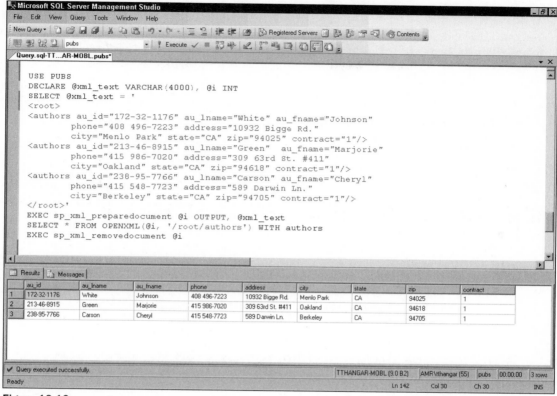

Figure 10-10

In Listing 10-15, because the structure of XML document passed to the OPENXML function was identical to the authors structure, I simply specified the WITH authors clause at the end of OPENXML. Alternatively, you could specify the structure of the parsed document for OPENXML as follows:

```
SELECT * FROM OPENXML(@i, '/root/authors')
  WITH (au_id VARCHAR(11), au_lname VARCHAR(20),
au_fname VARCHAR(30), phone VARCHAR(12),
address VARCHAR(50), city VARCHAR(20),
  state CHAR(2), zip CHAR(5), contract BIT)
```

The output would be the exactly the same as in the first example. The advantage of specifying the structure in this case is that it makes code more readable; however, if the parsed XML does not match any of the user table's structure, you have no choice but to provide the document structure for OPENXML.

SQL Server 2000 essentially treated the FOR XML clause and the OPENXML rowset function as inverse companions. That is, with FOR XML you can retrieve relational data as XML; with OPENXML you can turn XML into relational data, against which you can set up SQL joins or execute queries. SQL Server 2005 enhances the functionality of OPENXML. In addition to the XML data type, support for several new data types is provided, such as user-defined types (UDTs). You can use these in the OPENXML WITH clause, and you can also pass an XML data type instance to sp_preparedocument.

Other XML Features

You can utilize the new SET SHOWPLAN_XML T-SQL command to obtain query execution plan information for a specific sql query as a well-formed XML document. To test this out, execute the following command to turn on the XML-based show plan.

```
SET SHOWPLAN_XML ON
```

After that, execute a simple query like the following.

```
Use AdventureWorks
Select * from Person.ContactType
```

As a result of this command, you should see the following query execution plan displayed in XML format.

Listing 10-16: Output Produced through XML-based Show Plan

```xml
<ShowPlanXML xmlns="http://schemas.microsoft.com/sqlserver/2004/07/showplan"
  Version="0.5" Build="9.00.1116">
  <BatchSequence>
    <Batch>
      <Statements>
        <StmtSimple StatementText="&#xD;&#xA;Select * from Person.ContactType"
          StatementId="1" StatementCompId="1" StatementType="SELECT"
          StatementSubTreeCost="0.0032952" StatementEstRows="12"
          StatementOptmLevel="TRIVIAL">
          <StatementSetOptions QUOTED_IDENTIFIER="true" ARITHABORT="true"
            CONCAT_NULL_YIELDS_NULL="true" ANSI_NULLS="true" ANSI_PADDING="true"
            ANSI_WARNINGS="true" NUMERIC_ROUNDABORT="false" />
          <QueryPlan CachedPlanSize="8">
            <RelOp NodeId="0" PhysicalOp="Clustered Index Scan"
              LogicalOp="Clustered Index Scan" EstimateRows="12"
              EstimateIO="0.003125" EstimateCPU="0.0001702" AvgRowSize="4027"
              EstimatedTotalSubtreeCost="0.0032952" Parallel="0"
              EstimateRebinds="0" EstimateRewinds="0">
              <OutputList>
                <ColumnReference Database="[AdventureWorks]" Schema="[Person]"
                  Table="[ContactType]" Column="ContactTypeID" />
                <ColumnReference Database="[AdventureWorks]" Schema="[Person]"
                  Table="[ContactType]" Column="Name" />
                <ColumnReference Database="[AdventureWorks]" Schema="[Person]"
                  Table="[ContactType]" Column="ModifiedDate" />
              </OutputList>
              <IndexScan Ordered="0" ForcedIndex="0" NoExpandHint="0">
                <DefinedValues>
                  <DefinedValue>
                    <ColumnReference Database="[AdventureWorks]" Schema="[Person]"
                      Table="[ContactType]" Column="ContactTypeID" />
                  </DefinedValue>
                  <DefinedValue>
                    <ColumnReference Database="[AdventureWorks]" Schema="[Person]"
                      Table="[ContactType]" Column="Name" />
                  </DefinedValue>
```

```
          <DefinedValue>
            <ColumnReference Database="[AdventureWorks]" Schema="[Person]"
              Table="[ContactType]" Column="ModifiedDate" />
          </DefinedValue>
        </DefinedValues>
        <Object Database="[AdventureWorks]" Schema="[Person]"
          Table="[ContactType]" Index="PK_ContactType_ContactTypeID" />
      </IndexScan>
    </RelOp>
  </QueryPlan>
  </StmtSimple>
 </Statements>
 </Batch>
 </BatchSequence>
</ShowPlanXML>
```

The beauty of an XML output like this is that you can load up this XML using an XML parser, and parse the XML to perform query optimizations.

Summary

In this chapter, you saw the XML technologies in SQL Server 2005. On the server side, you have seen features such as native implementation for XML storage, indexing, and query processing. In addition to the new native XML storage, existing features such as FOR XML and OPENXML have also been enhanced. XML data type preserves document order and is useful for applications such as document management. It can also handle recursive XML schemas. You can store two types of XML (typed XML, and untyped XML) in an XML data typed column. For a typed column, you use an XML schema to define the structure of the XML data stored, and the schemas optimize storage and query processing besides providing data validation. On the client side, there are enhancements to ADO.NET 2.0 to support the XML data type and the FOR XML enhancements.

11

Building an Airline Reservation System Using ASP.NET 2.0 and SQL Server 2005

So far in this book, you have learned about XML DOM, XML support in ADO.NET, XSLT features in .NET, XML data display, and XML support in SQL Server 2005. This chapter focuses on incorporating these features in a real-world Web site. This case study not only discusses the application of these features in a Web site but also demonstrates the best practices of using these features. Toward this end, this chapter discusses and showcases the following features:

❑   How to design and develop an N-tier Web site using the XML features of ASP.NET 2.0 and SQL Server 2005. To support this design, this chapter discusses how to encapsulate the data access logic in the form of reusable components.

❑   How to work with an XML data type column by persisting data in it using ADO.NET

❑   How to utilize the XSD schemas support provided by SQL Server 2005 to validate XML data

❑   How to transform the XML data into HTML using the XSLT features of .NET 2.0

❑   How to display the XML data using an `XmlDataSource` control with a `GridView` control

❑   How to read and write XML data using `XmlReader` and `XmlWriter` classes

❑   How to validate XML data using XSD schemas

Overview of the Case Study

For this case study, consider an airline reservations system. This airline system provides the basic features of an online reservation system. Some of the features include searching for flights based on specific search criteria and booking tickets for a particular flight. It also provides for the users to have membership in the site by registering themselves with the site.

Architecture of System

Figure 11-1 illustrates the proposed architecture of the online reservation system.

Architecture of Online Reservation Web Site

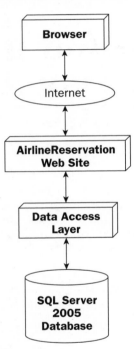

Figure 11-1

As shown in Figure 11-1, the Web site primarily depends on the middle tier .NET component (AirlineReservationsLib) for all of its functionalities. When the user comes to the site and performs operations such as searching for flights, the Web site invokes the methods of the .NET component to carry out those tasks. Before looking at the implementation of the architecture, it is important to examine the business processes supported by the ShoppingAssistant.

Business Processes

Although the scope of the case study is to show how to effectively utilize XML features of ASP.NET 2.0 and SQL Server 2005 to build a Web site, it is imperative that you review the business processes before choosing the best approach. The business processes that the online reservation system is going to have to enable are as follows:

❑   Login process — The login system allows the users to identify themselves to the system. The user must provide a valid user id and a valid password to be able to log onto the system. After logged in, the user can carry out tasks such as searching for flights and booking tickets.

❑   New user registration process — If you are a new user, you have the opportunity to become a member of the site by filling out the online forms and selecting the desired preferences. In this step, the user is asked to create a unique user id, which is used to identify the user in the system. The user is also required to choose a password of his choice to protect their membership and prevent someone else from using their account. And the user also can fill out relevant details like name, address, and so on. After the user enters all the details, the user's profile is stored in the database for later retrieval.

❑   Search flights process — As the name suggests, this process allows the user to search for flights.

❑   Book tickets process — In this process, the user can book the tickets for a specified flight.

❑   Logout process — Allows the user to log out of the site, thereby terminating the session.

Limitations

This case study is not aimed at demonstrating how to build and deploy a real-world online reservation system. The intended purpose is to show how to tie different XML features of ASP.NET together. For that reason, many issues are not addressed in this example, including:

❑   Security — No regard is taken to security in the implementation of the Web services in this example.

❑   Payment — Obviously in this example no real bookings are made and none of the issues concerned with payment are handled.

Implementation

Now that you have understood the business processes involved, examine the individual building blocks that are required for implementing this solution. For the purposes of this example, the discussion of the remaining part of the case study will be split into the following sections.

❑   Database design

❑   Implementation of .NET component (AirlineReservationsLib)

❑   Implementation of Web site

To start with, consider the database design that is required to support the Web site.

Database Design

The database, called AirlineReservation, used in this case study has minimum number of tables required to implement this solution. The AirlineReservation database consists of six tables. The entity relationship diagram for the database is as follows:

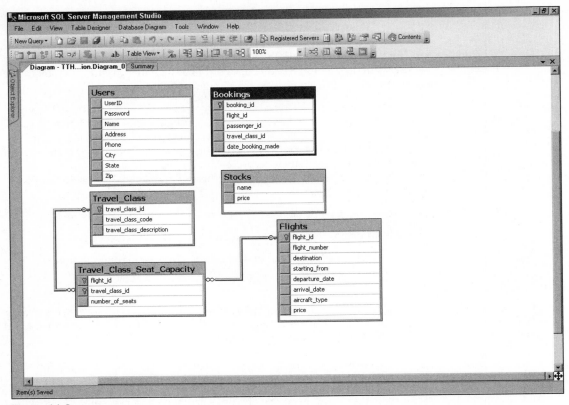

Figure 11-2

The structure of these tables is shown in Table 11-1, starting with Flights table.

Table 11-1. Structure of Flights Table

Name	Data Type	Length	AllowNull	Description
flight_id	int	4	No	Represents the flight id
flight_number	char	10	No	Represents the flight number
destination	varchar	50	No	Destination location
starting_from	varchar	50	No	Starting location
departure_date	Datetime	8	No	Departure date
arrival_date	Datetime	8	No	Arrival date
aircraft_type	varchar	50	Yes	Type of the air craft
price	money	8	Yes	Price

The Travel_Class table is defined in Table 11-2.

Table 11-2. Structure of Travel_Class Table

Name	Data Type	Length	AllowNull	Description
travel_class_id	int	4	No	Represents the travel class id
travel_class_code	char	1	No	Represents the different travel class codes
travel_class_ description	varchar	50	No	Provides a description of the travel class

The stored procedure named SearchFlight is used to search for flights based on the following parameters: starting location, destination, arrival date, departure date, and the type of travel class.

```
CREATE Procedure dbo.SearchFlight
@startingFrom varchar(50), @destination varchar(50),
@arrivalDate datetime, @departureDate datetime,
@travelClassID int
As
Begin
  set nocount on
  select F.*,TC.travel_class_id
  from flights F inner join travel_class_seat_capacity TCSC
  on TCSC.flight_id = F.flight_id inner join travel_class TC
  on TC.travel_class_id = TCSC.travel_class_id
  where F.starting_from = @startingFrom and F.destination = @destination
  and F.arrival_date = @arrivalDate and F.departure_date = @departureDate
  and TC.travel_class_id = @travelClassID and TCSC.number_of_seats > 0
End
```

Table 11-3 describes the structure of the Travel_Class_Capacity table.

Table 11-3. Structure of Travel_Class_Capacity Table

Name	Data Type	Length	AllowNull	Description
flight_id	int	4	No	Represents the flight id
travel_class_id	int	4	No	Represents the travel class id
number_of_seats	Int	4	No	Number of seats available in a particular flight

The Bookings table is defined as follows in Table 11-4.

Table 11-4. Structure of Bookings Table

Name	Data Type	Length	AllowNull	Description
booking_id	int	4	No	Represents the booking id
flight_id	int	4	No	Represents the flight id
passenger_id	int	4	No	Specifies the passenger id
travel_class_id	int	4	No	Specifies the travel class id
date_booking_made	datetime	8	No	Specifies the date of booking

To create a new booking in the bookings table, a stored procedure named InsertBooking is utilized.

```
CREATE procedure dbo.InsertBooking
@flightID int, @passengerID varchar(20),
@travelClassID int, @bookingID int output
As
Begin
  Set nocount on
  Insert into Bookings(flight_id,passenger_id,travel_class_id)
  Values(@flightID,@passengerID,@travelClassID)
  Select @bookingID = @@identity
End
```

The definition of Stocks table is shown in Table 11-5.

Table 11-5 Structure of Stocks Table

Name	Data Type	Length	AllowNull	Description
name	Char	4	No	Represents the company symbol
price	Varchar	10	No	Represents the stock price

The stored procedure GetStockQuote retrieves the stock quote based on the supplied symbol.

```
Create procedure GetStockQuote
@Name char(4)
As
Begin
  set nocount on
  select * from Stocks where Name = @Name FOR XML AUTO, Elements
End
```

The Users table that is meant for storing the details of the logged on users is shown in Table 11-6.

Table 11-6. Structure of Users Table

Name	Data Type	Length	AllowNull	Description
UserID	varchar	20	No	Represents the User ID
Password	varchar	10	No	Represents the password assigned to a user
Name	varchar	128	No	Represents the name of the logged on user
Address	varchar	128	Yes	Represents the address of the user
Phone	xml	N/A	Yes	Typed XML column that represents the phone numbers XML format
City	varchar	50	Yes	Represents the city
State	char	2	Yes	Represents the state
Zip	char	9	Yes	Represents the zip code

As you can see from Table 11-6, the Phone column is a typed column that has an XML schema associated with it. The DDL for creating the schema used by this column is as follows:

```
CREATE XML Schema collection PhoneSchema as
N'<xs:schema attributeFormDefault="unqualified"
elementFormDefault="qualified" xmlns:xs="http://www.w3.org/2001/XMLSchema">
<xs:element name="phone">
    <xs:complexType>
      <xs:sequence>
        <xs:element name="homePhone" type="xs:string" />
        <xs:element name="cellPhone" type="xs:string" />
        <xs:element name="officePhone" type="xs:string" />
      </xs:sequence>
    </xs:complexType>
</xs:element>
</xs:schema>'
GO
```

After the schema is created, you can associate the schema with the Phone column using the Alter Table statement.

```
Alter table Users Alter Column Phone XML(PhoneSchema)
```

To insert rows into the Users table, the InsertUser stored procedure is utilized.

```
CREATE Procedure InsertUser
  (@UserID char(20), @Password char(10), @Name varchar(128),
   @Address varchar(128), @Phone xml, @City varchar(50),
   @State char(2), @Zip char(5))
As
Begin
Insert into Users(UserID,Password,Name,Address,Phone, City,State,Zip)
Values(@UserID,@Password,@Name,@Address,@Phone,@City,@State,@Zip)
End
```

In addition to storing the user details, you also need a way to be able to verify the credentials of a user that is trying to log onto the site. To this end, the CheckUserLogin is used.

```
CREATE Procedure CheckUserLogin
(
@UserID varchar(20), @Password varchar(10),    @RetValue int OUTPUT
)
As
Begin
SELECT * FROM Users WHERE UserID = @UserID AND Password = @Password
IF @@Rowcount < 1
    SELECT @RetValue = -1
ELSE
    SELECT @RetValue = 1
End
```

Now that you have implemented the stored procedures, the next step is to implement the middle tier component that will consume the stored procedures.

Implementation of AirlineReservationsLib Component

In this section, you learn the implementation of the C# class library AirlineReservationsLib. This component contains all the necessary classes and methods that provide the core functionalities for the online reservations system. To start, create a new Visual C# Class library project named AirlineReservationsLib using Visual Studio 2005. After the project is created, change the name of the default class from Class1 to UserInfo. The UserInfo class simply acts as a container for holding user-related data, and its implementation is shown in Listing 11-1.

Listing 11-1: Declaration of the UserInfo Class

```
using System;
namespace AirlineReservationsLib
{
[Serializable]
public class UserInfo
{
    protected string userID;
    protected string passWord;
    protected string name;
    protected string address;
    protected string phone;
    protected string city;
    protected string state;
    protected string zip;

    public string UserID
    {
      get{return userID;}
      set{userID = value;}
    }
    public string PassWord
    {
```

```
      get{return passWord;}
      set{passWord = value;}
    }
    public string Name
    {
      get{return name;}
      set{name = value;}
    }
    public string Address
    {
      get{return address;}
      set{address = value;}
    }
    public string Phone
    {
      get{return phone;}
      set{phone = value;}
    }
    public string City
    {
      get{return city;}
      set{city = value;}
    }
    public string State
    {
      get{return state;}
      set{state = value;}
    }
    public string Zip
    {
      get{return zip;}
      set{zip = value;}
    }
  }
}
```

As you can see from this code, the UserInfo class simply exposes a bunch of properties that act as the container for user-related data.

Implementation of Data Access Layer Methods

So far, you have seen the container class for holding user-related data. That is only part of the story, and you need a data access layer class for persisting that data and retrieving that data from the Users table. This is where the UserDB class comes into play. Implementation of the UserDB class is illustrated in Listing 11-2.

Listing 11-2: Implementation of UserDB Class

```
using System;
using System.Collections.Generic;
using System.Data;
using System.Data.SqlClient;
using System.Text;
```

```
namespace AirlineReservationsLib
{
 public class UserDB
 {
     public bool CheckUserLogIn(string userName, string passWord)
     {
       try
       {
         using (SqlConnection conn = new SqlConnection())
         {
           string connString = System.Web.Configuration.WebConfigurationManager.
             ConnectionStrings["airlines"].ConnectionString;
           conn.ConnectionString = connString;
           conn.Open();
           SqlCommand command = new SqlCommand("CheckUserLogIn", conn);
           command.CommandType = CommandType.StoredProcedure;
           SqlParameter paramUserName = new SqlParameter("@UserID",
             SqlDbType.VarChar, 20);
           paramUserName.Value = userName;
           command.Parameters.Add(paramUserName);
           SqlParameter paramPassWord = new SqlParameter("@Password",
             SqlDbType.VarChar, 10);
           paramPassWord.Value = passWord;
           command.Parameters.Add(paramPassWord);
           SqlParameter paramRetValue = new SqlParameter("@RetValue",
             SqlDbType.Int, 4);
           paramRetValue.Direction = ParameterDirection.Output;
           command.Parameters.Add(paramRetValue);
           command.ExecuteNonQuery();
           //Obtain the return value of the stored procedure into a variable
           int retValue = (int)paramRetValue.Value;
           if (retValue == -1)
           {
             throw new InValidLoginException("Invalid Login");
           }
           else
           {
             return true;
           }
         }
       }
       catch (Exception ex)
       {
         throw ex;
       }
     }

     public bool InsertUserInfo(UserInfo userInfo)
     {
       try
       {
         using (SqlConnection conn = new SqlConnection())
```

```
        {
            string connString = System.Web.Configuration.WebConfigurationManager.
                ConnectionStrings["airlines"].ConnectionString;
            conn.ConnectionString = connString;
            conn.Open();
            SqlCommand command = new SqlCommand("InsertUser", conn);
            command.CommandType = CommandType.StoredProcedure;
            SqlParameter paramUserName = new SqlParameter("@UserID",
                SqlDbType.VarChar, 20);
            paramUserName.Value = userInfo.UserID;
            command.Parameters.Add(paramUserName);
            SqlParameter paramPassWord = new SqlParameter("@Password",
                SqlDbType.VarChar, 10);
            paramPassWord.Value = userInfo.PassWord;
            command.Parameters.Add(paramPassWord);
            SqlParameter paramName = new SqlParameter("@Name",
                SqlDbType.VarChar, 128);
            paramName.Value = userInfo.Name;
            command.Parameters.Add(paramName);
            SqlParameter paramAddress = new SqlParameter("@Address",
                SqlDbType.VarChar, 128);
            paramAddress.Value = userInfo.Address;
            command.Parameters.Add(paramAddress);
            SqlParameter paramPhone = new SqlParameter("@Phone", SqlDbType.Xml);
            paramPhone.Value = new SqlXml(new XmlTextReader(userInfo.Phone,
                XmlNodeType.Document, null));
            command.Parameters.Add(paramPhone);
            SqlParameter paramCity = new SqlParameter("@City",
                SqlDbType.VarChar, 50);
            paramCity.Value = userInfo.City;
            command.Parameters.Add(paramCity);
            SqlParameter paramState = new SqlParameter("@State",
                SqlDbType.Char, 2);
            paramState.Value = userInfo.State;
            command.Parameters.Add(paramState);
            SqlParameter paramZip = new SqlParameter("@Zip", SqlDbType.Char, 5);
            paramZip.Value = userInfo.Zip;
            command.Parameters.Add(paramZip);
            command.ExecuteNonQuery();
            return true;
        }
    }
    catch (Exception ex)
    {
        throw ex;
    }
    }
  }
}
```

The UserDB class contains two methods: CheckUserLogIn() and InsertUserInfo().The
CheckUserLogIn() method authenticates a customer's user name and password against the
AirlineReservation database. Under the hood, CheckUserLogIn() method invokes the stored procedure
CheckUserLogIn. The CheckUserLogIn stored procedure returns 1, if a record with the specified user

name and password is found, else returns –1. Depending on the value returned by the stored procedure, the CheckUserLogIn method either returns true or raises an exception of type InValidLoginException. The declaration of the InvalidLoginException is as follows:

```
public class InValidLoginException : Exception
{
  public InValidLoginException(string exceptionMessage) :
    base(exceptionMessage)
  {
  }
}
```

> User-defined exceptions allow you to notify the clients when a particular business logic violation occurs or when a specific condition is reached. They also allow you to implement custom exception processing mechanisms such as logging the errors to event log, and sending emails to an administrator and so on.

The InsertUserInfo() method persists the details of the user in the Users table. It takes the UserInfo object as an argument, parses its contents, executes a stored procedure, and returns true or false, depending on the result of its execution. Note how the phone column (which is of type XML) is added to the Parameters collection of the SqlCommand object.

```
SqlParameter paramPhone = new SqlParameter("@Phone", SqlDbType.Xml);
paramPhone.Value = new SqlXml(new XmlTextReader(userInfo.Phone,
  XmlNodeType.Document, null));
command.Parameters.Add(paramPhone);
```

You specify the type of the column as XML by passing in the enumeration SqlDbType.Xml to the second parameter of the SqlParameter's constructor. You then assign an object of type System.Data .SqlTypes.SqlXml object to the Value property of the SqlParameter object. Now that you have had a look at the UserDB class, focus on the FlightDB class that is specifically focused on searching of flights and booking of flights.

Implementation of FlightDB Class

One of the methods exposed by the FlightDB class is SearchFlight() that allows you to search for flights based on a specific set of search criteria. Listing 11-3 shows the code of the FlightDB class.

Listing 11-3: Implementation of FlightDB Class

```
using System;
using System.Data;
using System.Data.SqlClient;
namespace AirlineReservationsLib
{
public class FlightDB
{
    public DataSet SearchFlight(string startPlace, string destinationPlace,
      DateTime departureDate, DateTime arrivalDate,int travelClassID)
    {
```

```
      try
      {
        using (SqlConnection conn = new SqlConnection())
        {
          string connString = System.Web.Configuration.WebConfigurationManager.
            ConnectionStrings["airlines"].ConnectionString;
          conn.ConnectionString = connString;
          DataSet flight = new DataSet("Flights");
          SqlDataAdapter adapter = new SqlDataAdapter("SearchFlight", conn);
          adapter.SelectCommand.CommandType = CommandType.StoredProcedure;
          SqlParameter paramStartPlace = new SqlParameter("@startingFrom",
            SqlDbType.VarChar, 50);
          paramStartPlace.Value = startPlace;
          adapter.SelectCommand.Parameters.Add(paramStartPlace);
          SqlParameter paramDestination = new SqlParameter("@destination",
            SqlDbType.VarChar, 50);
          paramDestination.Value = destinationPlace;
          adapter.SelectCommand.Parameters.Add(paramDestination);
          SqlParameter paramArrivalDate = new SqlParameter("@arrivalDate",
            SqlDbType.DateTime);
          paramArrivalDate.Value = arrivalDate;
          adapter.SelectCommand.Parameters.Add(paramArrivalDate);
          SqlParameter paramDepartureDate = new SqlParameter("@departureDate",
            SqlDbType.DateTime);
          paramDepartureDate.Value = departureDate;
          adapter.SelectCommand.Parameters.Add(paramDepartureDate);
          SqlParameter paramTravelClassID = new SqlParameter("@travelClassID",
            SqlDbType.Int);
          paramTravelClassID.Value = travelClassID;
          adapter.SelectCommand.Parameters.Add(paramTravelClassID);
          adapter.Fill(flight, "Flight");
          return flight;
        }
      }
      catch (Exception ex)
      {
        throw ex;
      }
    }

    public int InsertBooking(int flightID, string passengerID,
      int travelClassID)
    {
      try
      {
        using (SqlConnection conn = new SqlConnection())
        {
          string connString = System.Web.Configuration.WebConfigurationManager.
            ConnectionStrings["airlines"].ConnectionString;
          conn.ConnectionString = connString;
          conn.Open();
          SqlCommand command = new SqlCommand("InsertBooking", conn);
          command.CommandType = CommandType.StoredProcedure;
          SqlParameter paramFlightID = new SqlParameter("@flightID",
            SqlDbType.Int);
```

```
                paramFlightID.Value = flightID;
                command.Parameters.Add(paramFlightID);
                SqlParameter paramPassengerID = new SqlParameter("@passengerID",
                  SqlDbType.VarChar, 20);
                paramPassengerID.Value = passengerID;
                command.Parameters.Add(paramPassengerID);
                SqlParameter paramTravelClassID = new SqlParameter("@travelClassID",
                  SqlDbType.Int);
                paramTravelClassID.Value = travelClassID;
                command.Parameters.Add(paramTravelClassID);
                SqlParameter paramBookingID = new SqlParameter("@bookingID",
                  SqlDbType.Int);
                paramBookingID.Direction = ParameterDirection.Output;
                command.Parameters.Add(paramBookingID);
                command.ExecuteNonQuery();
                int bookingID = Convert.ToInt32(
                  command.Parameters["@bookingID"].Value);
                return bookingID;
            }
        }
        catch (Exception ex)
        {
            throw ex;
        }
        }
    }
}
```

In addition to the SearchFlight() method, the FlightDB class also contains a method named InsertBooking() that persists the details of the booking onto the database. For reasons of brevity, the implementation of these methods will not be discussed in detail; however, you can download the complete code of the case study from the Wrox Web site.

Implementation of StockDB Class

As the name suggests, the StockDB class provides methods specifically for working with the Stocks table. It exposes a method named GetStockQuote() that returns the stock quote based on the supplied symbol. Listing 11-4 illustrates the code of the StockDB class.

Listing 11-4: Implementation of StockDB Class

```
using System;
using System.Data;
using System.Data.SqlClient;
namespace AirlineReservationsLib
{
public class StockDB
{
    public XmlDocument GetStockQuote(string name)
    {
```

```
        try
        {
          using (SqlConnection conn = new SqlConnection())
          {
            //Retrieve the connection string from the configuration file
            string connString = System.Web.Configuration.WebConfigurationManager.
              ConnectionStrings["airlines"].ConnectionString;
            conn.ConnectionString = connString;
            conn.Open();
            SqlCommand command = conn.CreateCommand();
            command.CommandText = "GetStockQuote";
            command.CommandType = CommandType.StoredProcedure;
            SqlParameter paramName = new SqlParameter("@Name",
              SqlDbType.Char, 4);
            paramName.Value = name;
            command.Parameters.Add(paramName);
            XmlReader reader = command.ExecuteXmlReader();
            XmlDocument doc = new XmlDocument();
            //Load the XmlReader to an XmlDocument object
            doc.Load(reader);
            return doc;
          }
        }
        catch (Exception ex)
        {
          throw ex;
        }
      }
    }
  }
```

The GetStockQuote() method simply retrieves the stock quote by executing a stored procedure named GetStockQuote that accepts the stock ticker company as an argument and returns the XML output in the form of an XmlReader object. This XmlReader object is then loaded into an XmlDocument object and is finally returned back to the caller.

Implementation of Web Site

This section focuses on the implementation of the ASP.NET Web site. The code of the Web site is discussed by considering the different processes involved. Before getting into that discussion, go over the code of the master page that is used throughout the Web site.

A Look at Master Pages

A professional Web site has a standardized look across all pages. For example, one of the commonly used layouts has its navigation menu on the left side of the page, a copyright on the bottom, and content in the middle. It can be difficult to maintain a standard look if you start duplicating the common logic and look and feel in every Web page you build. In ASP.NET 2.0, Master Pages will make the job easier. You will need to write the common pieces only once in the Master Page. A Master Page can serve as a template for one or more Web pages. Each ASPX Web page only needs to define the content unique to itself, and this content will plug into specified areas of the Master Page layout.

A Master Page looks similar to an ASPX file, except a Master Page will have a .master file extension instead of an .aspx extension, and uses an @ Master directive instead of an @ Page directive at the top. Master Pages will define the <html>, <head>, <body >, and <form> tags. A new control, the ContentPlaceHolder *control, also appears in the Master Page. You can have one or more* ContentPlaceHolder *controls in a Master Page.* ContentPlaceHolder *controls are where you want the ASPX Web pages to place their content. A Web page associated with a Master Page is called a content page. A content page may only contain markup inside of content controls. If you try to place any markup or controls outside of the content controls, you will receive a compiler error. Each Content control in a content page maps to exactly one of the* ContentPlaceHolder *controls in the Master Page.*

Listing 11-5 shows the code of the Master Page that will be used in the online reservations Web site.

Listing 11-5: Master Page That Provides Consistent Look and Feel

```
<%@ Master Language="C#" %>
<%@ Import Namespace="System.IO" %>
<%@ Import Namespace="System.Xml" %>
<%@ Import Namespace="AirlineReservationsLib" %>
<script runat="server">
  void Page_Load(object sender, EventArgs e)
  {
    string path = Server.MapPath("App_Data/Stocks.xml");
    if (!File.Exists(path))
    {
      //Create the XML file for the first time
      CreateXmlFile(path);
    }
    else
    {
      //Check to make sure that the file is not more than 20 minutes old
      TimeSpan elapsedTimespan =
        DateTime.Now.Subtract(File.GetLastWriteTime(path));
      if (elapsedTimespan.Minutes > 20)
      //Refresh the contents of the XML file
      CreateXmlFile(path);
    }
  }

  void CreateXmlFile(string path)
  {
    StockDB stock = new StockDB();
    XmlDocument doc = stock.GetStockQuote("WOTS");
    doc.Save(path);
  }
</script>
<html xmlns="http://www.w3.org/1999/xhtml" >
<head runat="server">
  <title>Master Page</title>
</head>
<body>
  <form id="form1" runat="server">
    <div>
```

```
        <asp:Table id="tblTop" BackColor="Red" runat="server" Width="819px"
          Height="108px" ForeColor="blue">
          <asp:TableRow runat="server">
            <asp:TableCell  runat="server">
              <img src="Images/logo.gif">
            </asp:TableCell>
            <asp:TableCell runat="server">
              <img align="right" src="Images/head.gif">
            </asp:TableCell>
          </asp:TableRow>
          <asp:TableRow  runat="server" HorizontalAlign="Center">
            <asp:TableCell  runat="server" ColumnSpan="2">
              <asp:Label id="Label1" runat="server" ForeColor="White"
                Font-Size="medium">Online Reservation System
              </asp:Label>
            </asp:TableCell>
          </asp:TableRow>
        <asp:TableRow  runat="server" HorizontalAlign="Center">
          <asp:TableCell  runat="server" ColumnSpan="2" ForeColor="White">
            <asp:XmlDataSource runat="server" DataFile="~/App_Data/Stocks.xml"
              ID="XmlDataSource1" XPath="Stocks" />
            <asp:GridView BorderWidth=0 BorderStyle=Ridge Font-Bold="true"
              Font-Size=Small ShowHeader=false runat="server" ID="stockoutput"
              AutoGenerateColumns="false" DataSourceID="XmlDataSource1">
              <Columns>
                <asp:HyperLinkField Text="WOTS:"
                  NavigateUrl="http://finance.yahoo.com/q?s=WOTS"/>
                <asp:BoundField HeaderText="Price" DataField="price"
                  SortExpression="price"></asp:BoundField>
              </Columns>
            </asp:GridView>
          </asp:TableCell>
        </asp:TableRow>
        <asp:TableRow runat="server" HorizontalAlign="Right">
          <asp:TableCell runat="server" ColumnSpan="2">
            <asp:HyperLink runat="server" ForeColor="White" Text="Logout"
              NavigateUrl="Logout.aspx" />
          </asp:TableCell>
        </asp:TableRow>
      </asp:Table>
      <asp:contentplaceholder id="ContentPlaceHolder1" runat="server">
      </asp:contentplaceholder>
    </div>
  </form>
  </body>
  </html>
```

The Master Page encapsulates the header information for all the pages of the Web site. The header also contains the stock quote details that are displayed through a combination of an XmlDataSource control and a GridView control. The XmlDataSource control acts as the source of data for the GridView control that actually displays the stock quote.

```
<asp:XmlDataSource runat="server" DataFile="~/App_Data/Stocks.xml"
  ID="XmlDataSource1" XPath="Stocks" />
```

The `XmlDataSource` control utilizes a local XML file `Stocks.xml` as the source of XML data. The `Stocks.xml` file is very simple, and it just contains only one line of code.

```
<?xml version="1.0" ?>
<Stocks name="WOTS" price="96"/>
```

The contents of the `Stocks.xml` are updated periodically (specifically only in 20 minutes) through the logic contained in the `Page_Load` event. Let us focus on the `Page_Load` event.

In the `Page_Load`, you first check to see if an XML file named `Stocks.xml` file is available.

```
if (!File.Exists(path))
{
//Create the XML file for the first time
CreateXmlFile(path);
}
```

If the XML file is not available, it invokes a local method named `CreateXml()` to create the XML file by calling the `GetStockQuote()` method of the `StockDB` class.

```
void CreateXmlFile(string path)
{
   StockDB stock = new StockDB();
   XmlDocument doc = stock.GetStockQuote("WOTS");
   doc.Save(path);
}
```

The XmlDocument returned by the `GetStockQuote()` method is directly saved to the `Stocks.xml` file.

If the `Stocks.xml` file is available locally, the `Page_Load` method then checks to make sure that the file is not more than 20 minutes old. If the file is more than 20 minutes old, it invokes the `CreateXml()` method to refresh the contents of the XML file with the latest quote from the database.

```
else
{
//Check to make sure that the file is not more than 20 minutes old
TimeSpan elapsedTimespan = DateTime.Now.Subtract
   (File.GetLastWriteTime(path));
if (elapsedTimespan.Minutes > 20)
   //Refresh the contents of the XML file
   CreateXmlFile(path);
}
```

Now that you have had a look at the Master Page, examine the content pages that provide the core functionality. To start with, consider the login process.

Login Process

In the Web site, the user must be logged in to perform tasks such as searching for the flights and booking the tickets. The login page authenticates the customer's user name and password against the Users table in the AirlineReservation database. After validation, the user is redirected to the search flights page. If the user does not have a valid login, they can opt to create one by clicking the hyperlink New Users

`Click Here` in the login page. Clicking this hyperlink takes the user to the registration page where the user provides all the necessary details for completing the registration.

The login feature of the Web site is implemented using a forms-based authentication mechanism. To enable forms-based authentication for the Web site, add the following entry in the web.config file directly under the `<system.web>` element.

```
<authentication mode="Forms">
<forms name="OnlineReservationAuth" loginUrl="Login.aspx" protection="All"
   path="/">
</forms>
</authentication>
```

The loginUrl attribute in the `<forms>` element specifies the name of the login page that you want the users to be redirected to, any time they access a page or resource that does not allow anonymous access. For every Web page that you want to secure using the forms based authentication mechanism, you need to add an entry to the web.config file. For example, to set the restrictions of authenticated user access for a page called `SearchFlights.aspx`, set the following entry directly under the `<configuration>` element of the web.config file.

```
<location path="SearchFlights.aspx">
<system.web>
    <authorization>
      <deny users="?" />
    </authorization>
</system.web>
</location>
```

When a user attempts to access the `SearchFlights.aspx` page, the ASP.NET forms-based security system will automatically redirect the user to the `Login.aspx` page, and will continue to prevent them from accessing it until they have successfully validated their user name and password credentials to the application. Similarly you protect the other secured pages using similar entries in the web.config file.

> The forms-based authentication technology depends on cookies to store the authentication information for the currently logged in user. After the user is authenticated, cookies are used to store and maintain session information enabling the users to identify themselves to the Web site.

Now that you have a general understanding of the forms-based authentication, you are ready to examine the `Login.aspx` page. The `Login.aspx` page is discussed in Listing 11-6.

Listing 11-6: Implementation of Login Page That Derives from the Master Page

```
<%@ Page Language="C#" MasterPageFile="~/Common.master" Title="Login Page" %>
<%@ Import Namespace="AirlineReservationsLib" %>
<script runat="server">
void btnLogin_Click(object sender, System.EventArgs e)
{
    try
```

```
      {
        UserDB user = new UserDB();
        if (user.CheckUserLogIn(txtUserName.Text, txtPassword.Text) == true)
        {
          FormsAuthentication.SetAuthCookie(txtUserName.Text, true);
          Session["UserID"] = txtUserName.Text;
          Response.Redirect("SearchFlights.aspx");
        }
      }
      catch (InValidLoginException ex)
      {
        lblMessage.Visible = true;
        lblMessage.Text = ex.Message;
      }
    }
</script>
<asp:Content ID="Content1" ContentPlaceHolderID="ContentPlaceHolder1"
  Runat="Server">
<table align=center>
<tr>
    <td colspan=2 align=center>
      <asp:Label id="lblHeading" runat="server" ForeColor="Black" Height="27px"
        Width="154px" BackColor="Transparent" BorderStyle="Ridge"> Login
      </asp:Label>
    </td>
</tr>
<tr height="60">
    <td>
      <asp:Label id="lblUserName" tabIndex="5" runat="server" Height="19px"
        Width="131px" Font-Bold="True">User Name:</asp:Label>
    </td>
    <td>
      <asp:TextBox id="txtUserName" tabIndex="1" runat="server"></asp:TextBox>
      <asp:RequiredFieldValidator id="RequiredFieldValidator1" tabIndex="10"
        runat="server" ControlToValidate="txtUserName" ErrorMessage="*"
        Enabled="True"></asp:RequiredFieldValidator>
    </td>
</tr>
<tr height="40">
    <td>
      <asp:Label id="lblPassWord" tabIndex="6" runat="server" Height="19px"
        Width="121px" Font-Bold="True">Password:</asp:Label>
    </td>
    <td>
      <asp:TextBox TextMode="Password" id="txtPassword" tabIndex="2"
        runat="server"></asp:TextBox>
      <asp:RequiredFieldValidator id="RequiredFieldValidator2" tabIndex="11"
        runat="server" ControlToValidate="txtPassword" ErrorMessage="*"
        Enabled="True"></asp:RequiredFieldValidator>
    </td>
</tr>
<tr height="40">
```

```
        <td colspan=2 align=center>
          <asp:Label id="lblMessage" tabIndex="8" runat="server" Height="19px"
            Width="203px" Visible="False"></asp:Label>
        </td>
    </tr>
    <tr height="40">
        <td colspan=2 align=center>
          <asp:Button id="btnLogin" OnClick="btnLogin_Click" tabIndex="3"
            runat="server" Height="29px" Width="105px" Text="Login">
          </asp:Button>
        </td>
    </tr>
    <tr height="40">
        <td colspan=2 align=center>
          <asp:HyperLink id="lnkUserRegistration" tabIndex="4" runat="server"
            Height="28px" Width="176px" Font-Bold="True"
            NavigateUrl="Registration.aspx">New Users Click here</asp:HyperLink>
        </td>
    </tr>
</table>
</asp:Content>
```

After the user enters the user name and password and hits the Login button, you invoke the
CheckUserLogIn() method of the UserDB class to validate the user.

```
UserDB user = new UserDB();
if (user.CheckUserLogIn(txtUserName.Text, txtPassword.Text) == true)
{
FormsAuthentication.SetAuthCookie(txtUserName.Text, true);
Session["UserID"] = txtUserName.Text;
Response.Redirect("SearchFlights.aspx");
}
```

If the login is successful, you invoke the SetAuthCookie() method to generate an authentication ticket for
the authenticated user name and password and attach it to the cookies collection of the outgoing response.
After the cookie is generated, it is used to maintain information about the session information for every
user that logs in to our site. You also store the logged on user id in a session variable for later use.

Whenever the exception InValidLoginException occurs, you catch that in the catch block and display
the exception message in the label control lblMessage.

```
catch (InValidLoginException ex)
{
lblMessage.Visible = true;
lblMessage.Text = ex.Message;
}
```

Figure 11-3 shows the login page in action.

In this case study, since I utilized custom tables to store user details, I need to validate the user credentials against those custom tables. With ASP.NET 2.0, however, you can utilize the membership store to
store user details and also leverage the built-in security mechanisms to validate the user. An example
implementation of this approach is discussed in Chapter 15.

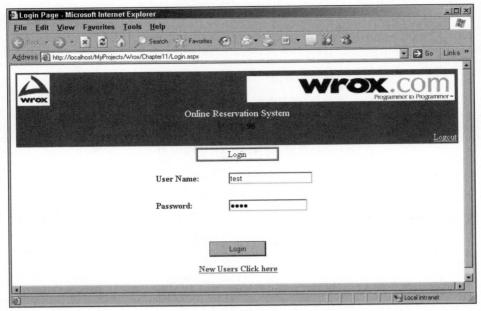

Figure 11-3

New User Registration Process

The registration page allows users wanting to take advantage of online reservation system to register themselves as members. Implementation of the registration page is discussed in Listing 11-7.

Listing 11-7: New User Registration Page

```csharp
<%@ Page Language="C#" MasterPageFile="~/Common.master" Title="New User
  Registration Page" %>
<%@ Import Namespace="System.Xml" %>
<%@ Import Namespace="AirlineReservationsLib" %>
<script runat="server">
void btnSave_Click(object sender, EventArgs e)
{
    UserInfo user = new UserInfo();
    user.UserID = txtUserName.Text;
    user.PassWord = txtPassWord.Text;
    user.Name = txtName.Text;
    user.Address = txtAddress.Text;
    string xml = CreateXml();
    user.Phone = xml;
    user.City = txtCity.Text;
    user.State = txtState.Text;
    user.Zip = txtZip.Text;
    UserDB userDB = new UserDB();
    userDB.InsertUserInfo(user);
    //Redirect the user to the Confirmation page
    Server.Transfer("Confirmation.aspx");
```

```
    }

    string CreateXml()
    {
        System.Text.StringBuilder output = new System.Text.StringBuilder();
        XmlWriter writer = XmlWriter.Create(output);
        writer.WriteStartDocument(false);
        writer.WriteStartElement("phone");
        writer.WriteElementString("homePhone", txtHomePhone.Text);
        writer.WriteElementString("cellPhone", txtCellPhone.Text);
        writer.WriteElementString("officePhone", txtOfficePhone.Text);
        writer.WriteEndElement();
        writer.WriteEndDocument();
        writer.Flush();
        return output.ToString();
    }
</script>
<asp:Content ID="Content1" ContentPlaceHolderID="ContentPlaceHolder1"
Runat="Server">
<table align=center>
    <tr>
      <td colspan=2 align=center>
        <asp:Label id="lblHeading" runat="server" ForeColor="Black"
          Height="27px" Width="154px" BackColor="Transparent"
          BorderStyle="Ridge"> New User Registration</asp:Label>
      </td>
    </tr>
    <tr height="32">
      <td>
        <asp:Label id="lblUserName" runat="server" Height="19px" Width="93px"
          Font-Bold="True">User Name:</asp:Label>
      </td>
      <td>
        <asp:TextBox id="txtUserName" tabIndex="1" runat="server"
          MaxLength="8"></asp:TextBox>
        <asp:RequiredFieldValidator id="RequiredFieldValidator1" runat="server"
          ControlToValidate="txtUserName" ErrorMessage="*">
        </asp:RequiredFieldValidator>
      </td>
    </tr>
    <tr height="32">
      <td>
        <asp:Label id="lblPassWord" runat="server" Height="19px" Width="93px"
          Font-Bold="True">Password:</asp:Label>
      </td>
      <td>
        <asp:TextBox id="txtPassWord" TextMode="Password" tabIndex="2"
          runat="server" MaxLength="8"></asp:TextBox>
        <asp:RequiredFieldValidator id="RequiredFieldValidator2" runat="server"
          ControlToValidate="txtPassWord" ErrorMessage="*">
        </asp:RequiredFieldValidator>
      </td>
    </tr>
    <tr height="32">
```

```
      <td>
        <asp:Label id="lblConfirmPassWord" runat="server" Height="24px"
          Width="103px" Font-Bold="True">Confirm Password:</asp:Label>
      </td>
      <td>
        <asp:TextBox id="txtConfirmPassword" TextMode="Password" tabIndex="3"
          runat="server" MaxLength="8"></asp:TextBox>
        <asp:RequiredFieldValidator id="RequiredFieldValidator3" runat="server"
          ControlToValidate="txtConfirmPassword" ErrorMessage="*">
        </asp:RequiredFieldValidator>
        <asp:CompareValidator id="CompareValidator1" style="Z-INDEX: 105; LEFT:
          648px; POSITION: absolute; TOP: 259px" runat="server" Height="20px"
          Width="203px" ControlToValidate="txtPassWord" ErrorMessage="Please
          enter same value for Password and Confirm Password"
          ControlToCompare="txtConfirmPassword"></asp:CompareValidator>
      </td>
    </tr>
    <tr height="32">
      <td>
        <asp:Label id="lblName" runat="server" Height="25px" Width="39px"
          Font-Bold="True">Name:</asp:Label>
      </td>
      <td>
        <asp:TextBox id="txtName" tabIndex="4" runat="server" MaxLength="50">
        </asp:TextBox>
        <asp:RequiredFieldValidator id="RequiredFieldValidator4" runat="server"
          ControlToValidate="txtName" ErrorMessage="*">
        </asp:RequiredFieldValidator>
      </td>
    </tr>
    <tr height="32">
      <td>
        <asp:Label id="lblAddress" runat="server" Height="25px" Width="62px"
          Font-Bold="True">Address:</asp:Label>
      </td>
      <td>
        <asp:TextBox id="txtAddress" tabIndex="5" runat="server"
          MaxLength="60"></asp:TextBox>
        <asp:RequiredFieldValidator id="RequiredFieldValidator5" runat="server"
          ControlToValidate="txtAddress" ErrorMessage="*">
        </asp:RequiredFieldValidator>
      </td>
    </tr>
    <tr height="32">
      <td>
        <asp:Label id="lblHomePhone" runat="server" Height="25px" Width="116px"
          Font-Bold="True">Home Phone:</asp:Label>
      </td>
      <td>
        <asp:TextBox id="txtHomePhone" tabIndex="5" runat="server"
          MaxLength="60"></asp:TextBox>
        <asp:RequiredFieldValidator id="RequiredFieldValidator9" runat="server"
          ControlToValidate="txtHomePhone" ErrorMessage="*">
```

```
        </asp:RequiredFieldValidator>
      </td>
  </tr>
  <tr height="32">
    <td>
      <asp:Label id="lblOfficePhone" runat="server" Height="25px"
        Width="126px" Font-Bold="True">Office Phone:</asp:Label>
    </td>
    <td>
      <asp:TextBox id="txtOfficePhone" tabIndex="5" runat="server"
        MaxLength="60"></asp:TextBox>
      <asp:RequiredFieldValidator id="RequiredFieldValidator10" runat="server"
        ControlToValidate="txtOfficePhone" ErrorMessage="*">
      </asp:RequiredFieldValidator>
    </td>
  </tr>
  <tr height="32">
    <td>
      <asp:Label id="lblCellPhone" runat="server" Height="25px" Width="136px"
        Font-Bold="True">Cell Phone:</asp:Label>
    </td>
    <td>
      <asp:TextBox id="txtCellPhone" tabIndex="5" runat="server"
        MaxLength="60"></asp:TextBox>
      <asp:RequiredFieldValidator id="RequiredFieldValidator11" runat="server"
        ControlToValidate="txtCellPhone" ErrorMessage="*">
      </asp:RequiredFieldValidator>
    </td>
  </tr>
  <tr height="32">
    <td>
      <asp:Label id="lblCity" runat="server" Height="25px" Width="44px"
        Font-Bold="True">City:</asp:Label>
    </td>
    <td>
      <asp:TextBox id="txtCity" tabIndex="6" runat="server"
        MaxLength="25"></asp:TextBox>
      <asp:RequiredFieldValidator id="RequiredFieldValidator6" runat="server"
        ControlToValidate="txtCity" ErrorMessage="*">
      </asp:RequiredFieldValidator>
    </td>
  </tr>
  <tr height="32">
    <td>
      <asp:Label id="lblState" runat="server" Height="20px" Width="52px"
        Font-Bold="True">State:</asp:Label>
    </td>
    <td>
      <asp:TextBox id="txtState" tabIndex="7" runat="server"
        MaxLength="2"></asp:TextBox>
      <asp:RequiredFieldValidator id="RequiredFieldValidator7" runat="server"
        ControlToValidate="txtState" ErrorMessage="*">
      </asp:RequiredFieldValidator>
```

```
            </td>
          </tr>
          <tr height="32">
            <td>
              <asp:Label id="lblZip" runat="server" Height="20px" Width="52px"
                Font-Bold="True">Zip:</asp:Label>
            </td>
            <td>
              <asp:TextBox id="txtZip" tabIndex="8" runat="server"
                MaxLength="9"></asp:TextBox>
              <asp:RequiredFieldValidator id="RequiredFieldValidator8" runat="server"
                ControlToValidate="txtZip" ErrorMessage="*">
              </asp:RequiredFieldValidator>
            </td>
          </tr>
          <tr height="32">
            <td colspan=2 align=center>
              <asp:Button id="btnSave" OnClick="btnSave_Click" tabIndex="9"
                runat="server" Height="24px" Width="100px" Text="Save Details">
              </asp:Button>
            </td>
          </tr>
        </table>
    </asp:Content>
```

The registration page contains a number of input controls and for each of the mandatory fields, server-side validation controls are leveraged to validate their data. After the user fills out all the mandatory fields and hits the Save Details button, you create an instance of the UserInfo object, populate the object with the information entered by the user and then invoke the InsertUserInfo() method of the UserDB class. The population of the UserInfo object with the values from the form is a very simple exercise except for the fact that you need to create an XML string for the Phone property of the UserInfo object.

```
string xml = CreateXml();
user.Phone = xml;
```

The creation of an XML structure for the phone details is accomplished through a helper method named CreateXml(), which simply creates an XML string on the fly dynamically using the methods of the XmlWriter object.

Figure 11-4 shows the registration page when requested from the browser.

After the registration is completed, the Web site redirects the user to the SearchFlights.aspx page through a call to the Server.Transfer() method.

Logout Process

All you need to do to log out of the site is to click on the Logout hyperlink on the header. When you click on that link, the user is redirected to the Logout.aspx page shown in Listing 11-8.

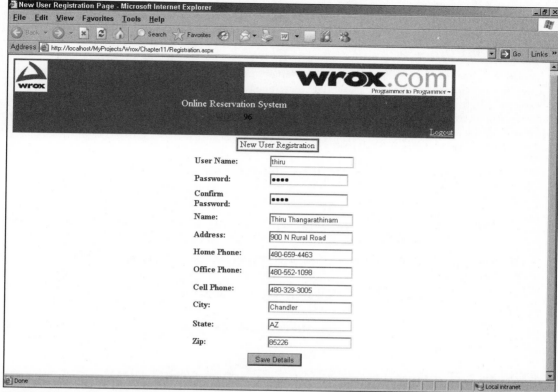

Figure 11-4

Listing 11-8: Implementation of Logout Functionality

```
<%@ Page Language="C#" MasterPageFile="~/Common.master" Title="Logout Page" %>
<%@ Import Namespace="AirlineReservationsLib" %>
<script runat="server">
void Page_Load(object sender, System.EventArgs e)
{
    FormsAuthentication.SignOut();
  }
</script>
<asp:Content ID="Content1" ContentPlaceHolderID="ContentPlaceHolder1"
Runat="Server">
<asp:Label id="lblMessage" style="Z-INDEX: 101; LEFT: 170px; POSITION: absolute;
  TOP: 161px" runat="server" Width="409px" Height="59px" Font-Size="Medium">
  You have been logged out of the system. Thank you for using Online Reservation
    System
</asp:Label>
</asp:Content>
```

As Listing 11-8 shows, the logout implementation requires just one line of code. You simply call the SignOut() method of the System.Web.Security.FormsAuthentication class. That clears all the cookies (used for authentication purposes) in the client machine and the user will be automatically redirected to the login page.

Search Flight Process

This involves searching for flights based on parameters such as arrival date, start date, and starting from, destination, and travel class code. The search page is an important page in that it showcases the various XML features of .NET. One of the important features of the search page is that it retrieves the search results from the server side without even posting back to the server. Figure 11-5 clearly outlines the flow of the page as it relates to the communication from the client side to the server side as well as the different XML features used during those steps.

The XML features utilized in the search page are as follows:

❏   XSD validation of input XML search criteria

❏   Use of ASP.NET 2.0 Script Callback to asynchronously retrieve XML data from the client side without refreshing the browser

❏   Use of the XML features of DataSet object to convert the DataSet object contents into an XML representation

❏   Transformation of XML to HTML using XSL transformation

SearchFlights Page Flow

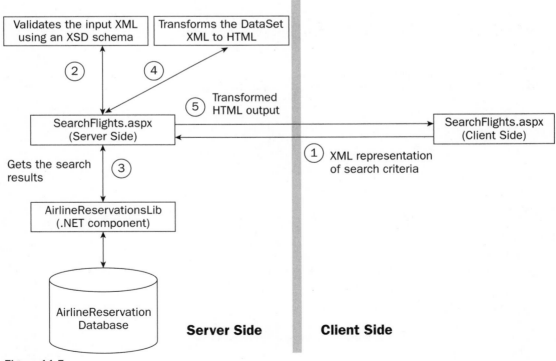

Figure 11-5

Listing 11-9 discusses the code of the `SearchFlights.aspx` page.

Listing 11-9: Implementation of Search Functionality

```
<%@ Page Language="C#" MasterPageFile="~/Common.master"
  Title="Search Flights" %>
<%@ Import Namespace="System.Data" %>
<%@ Import Namespace="System.Data.SqlClient" %>
<%@ Import Namespace="System.IO" %>
<%@ Import Namespace="System.Xml" %>
<%@ Import Namespace="System.Xml.Schema" %>
<%@ Import Namespace="System.Xml.Xsl" %>
<%@ Import Namespace="AirlineReservationsLib" %>
<%@ implements interface="System.Web.UI.ICallbackEventHandler" %>
<script runat="server">
  private StringBuilder _builder = new StringBuilder();
  private string _callbackArg;
  void ICallbackEventHandler.RaiseCallbackEvent(string eventArgument)
  {
    _callbackArg = eventArgument;
  }

  string ICallbackEventHandler.GetCallbackResult()
  {
    try
    {
      return GetSearchResults(_callbackArg);
    }
    catch (Exception ex)
    {
      throw new ApplicationException("An Error has occurred during the " +
        "processing of your request. Error is :" + ex.Message);
    }
  }

string GetSearchResults(string input)
{
    XmlDocument inputDoc = new XmlDocument();
    if (IsInputXmlValid(input))
    {
      inputDoc.LoadXml(input);
      string startingFrom = inputDoc.DocumentElement.SelectSingleNode
        ("startingFrom").InnerText;
      string destination = inputDoc.DocumentElement.SelectSingleNode
        ("destination").InnerText;
      DateTime departureDate = Convert.ToDateTime(inputDoc.DocumentElement.
        SelectSingleNode("departureDate").InnerText);
      DateTime arrivalDate = Convert.ToDateTime(inputDoc.DocumentElement.
        SelectSingleNode("arrivalDate").InnerText);
      int travelClassCode = Convert.ToInt32(inputDoc.DocumentElement.
        SelectSingleNode("travelClassCode").InnerText);
      //Assign the TravelClassID to a session variable for future use
      Session["TravelClassID"] = travelClassCode;
      FlightDB flightObj = new FlightDB();
```

```
            DataSet flights = flightObj.SearchFlight(startingFrom,
               destination, departureDate, arrivalDate, 1);
            return TransformXmltoHtml(flights.GetXml());
        }
        else
        {
            throw new ApplicationException("Input XML is Invalid");
        }
    }

string TransformXmltoHtml(string xml)
{
    XmlDocument xmlDoc = new XmlDocument();
    xmlDoc.LoadXml(xml);
    string xslPath = Request.PhysicalApplicationPath +
      @"\App_Data\SearchOutput.xsl";
    XslCompiledTransform transform = new XslCompiledTransform();
    //Load the XSL stylsheet into the XslCompiledTransform object
    transform.Load(xslPath);
    StringWriter writer = new StringWriter();
    transform.Transform(xmlDoc, null, writer);
    return writer.ToString();
}

bool IsInputXmlValid(string xml)
{
    TextReader textReader = new StringReader(xml);
    string xsdPath = Request.PhysicalApplicationPath +
      @"\App_Data\SearchInput.xsd";
    XmlReader reader = null;
    XmlReaderSettings settings = new XmlReaderSettings();
    settings.ValidationEventHandler += new
      ValidationEventHandler(this.ValidationEventHandler);
    settings.ValidationType = ValidationType.Schema;
    settings.Schemas.Add(null, XmlReader.Create(xsdPath));
    reader = XmlReader.Create(textReader, settings);
    while (reader.Read())
    {}
    bool success;
    if (_builder.ToString() == String.Empty)
      success = true;
    else
      success = false;
    return success;
}

void ValidationEventHandler(object sender, ValidationEventArgs args)
{
    _builder.Append("Validation error: " + args.Message + "<br>");
}

public void Page_Load(object sender, EventArgs e)
{
```

```
            if (!Request.Browser.SupportsCallback)
              throw new ApplicationException("Browser doesn't support callbacks.");
            string src = Page.ClientScript.GetCallbackEventReference(this, "arg",
              "DisplayResultsCallback","ctx", "DisplayErrorCallback", false);
            string mainSrc = @"function GetSearchDetailsUsingPostback(arg, ctx)
              { " + src + "; }";
            Page.ClientScript.RegisterClientScriptBlock(this.GetType(),
              "GetSearchDetailsUsingPostback", mainSrc, true);
        }
  </script>
  <asp:Content ID="Content1" ContentPlaceHolderID="ContentPlaceHolder1"
    Runat="Server">
  <script language="javascript">
  function GetSearchDetails()
  {
      var inputXML ="<input>" +
        "<startingFrom>" + document.all.<%=lstStartingFrom.ClientID%>.value +
        "</startingFrom>" + "<destination>" +
        document.all.<%=lstDestination.ClientID%>.value + "</destination>" +
        "<departureDate>" + document.all.<%=txtDepartureDate.ClientID%>.value +
        "</departureDate>" + "<arrivalDate>" +
        document.all.<%=txtArrivalDate.ClientID%>.value + "</arrivalDate>" +
        "<travelClassCode>" + document.all.<%=lstTravelClassCode.ClientID%>.value +
        "</travelClassCode>" + "</input>";
      GetSearchDetailsUsingPostback(inputXML, "Input");
  }


  function DisplayResultsCallback( result, context )
  {
      divSearchOutput.innerHTML = result;
  }


  function DisplayErrorCallback( error, context )
  {
      alert("Search Failed. " + error);
    }
  </script>
  <table align=center>
  <tr>
    <asp:XmlDataSource ID="CitiesSource" Runat="server"
      DataFile="~/App_Data/Cities.xml" XPath="cities/city">
    </asp:XmlDataSource>
      <td colspan=2 align=center>
        <asp:Label id="lblHeading" runat="server" ForeColor="Black" Height="27px"
          Width="154px" BackColor="Transparent" BorderStyle="Ridge"> Search for
          lights</asp:Label>
      </td>
  </tr>
  <tr height="40">
      <td>
        <asp:Label id="lblStartingFrom" runat="server" Width="112px"
          Height="19px">Starting From:</asp:Label>
      </td>
      <td>
        <asp:DropDownList id="lstStartingFrom" runat="server" Width="176px"
```

```
                      Height="22px" tabIndex="1" DataSourceID="CitiesSource"
                      DataTextField="name" DataValueField="name"/>
            </td>
        </tr>
        <tr height="40">
            <td>
              <asp:Label id="lblDestination" runat="server" Width="112px"
                Height="19px">Destination:</asp:Label>
            </td>
            <td>

              <asp:DropDownList id="lstDestination" runat="server" Width="176px"
                Height="22px" tabIndex="2" DataSourceID="CitiesSource"
                DataTextField="name" DataValueField="name"/>
            </td>
        </tr>
        <tr height="40">
            <td><asp:Label id="lblDepartureDate" runat="server" Width="112px"
                Height="19px">Departure Date:</asp:Label>
            </td>
            <td>
              <asp:TextBox id="txtDepartureDate" runat="server" Width="169px"
                Height="26px" tabIndex="3"></asp:TextBox>
              <asp:RequiredFieldValidator id="RequiredFieldValidator1" runat="server"
                ControlToValidate="txtDepartureDate"
                ErrorMessage="*">
              </asp:RequiredFieldValidator>
            </td>
        </tr>
        <tr height="40">
            <td>
              <asp:Label id="lblArrivalDate" runat="server" Width="112px"
                Height="19px">Arrival Date:</asp:Label>
            </td>
            <td>
              <asp:TextBox id="txtArrivalDate" runat="server" Width="169px"
                Height="26px" tabIndex="4"></asp:TextBox>
              <asp:RequiredFieldValidator id="RequiredFieldValidator2" runat="server"
                ControlToValidate="txtArrivalDate"
                ErrorMessage="*"></asp:RequiredFieldValidator>
            </td>
        </tr>
        <tr height="40">
            <td>
              <asp:Label id="lblTravelClassCode" runat="server" Width="125px"
                Height="38px">Travel Class Code:</asp:Label>
            </td>
            <td>
              <asp:DropDownList id="lstTravelClassCode" runat="server" Width="176px"
                Height="38px" tabIndex="5">
                <asp:ListItem Value="1">A</asp:ListItem>
```

```
              <asp:ListItem Value="2">B</asp:ListItem>
              <asp:ListItem Value="3">C</asp:ListItem>
              <asp:ListItem Value="4">D</asp:ListItem>
          </asp:DropDownList>
      </td>
  </tr>
  <tr height="40">
      <td colspan=2 align=center>
        <input type="button" id="btnSearch" value="Search"
        onclick="GetSearchDetails()"/>
      </td>
  </tr>
  </table>
  <div id="divSearchOutput">
  </div>
  </asp:Content>
```

Note that the cities name is retrieved from an XML file named Cities.xml using the XmlDataSource control as the data source control. The Cities.xml file is defined as follows:

```
<?xml version="1.0" encoding="utf-8" ?>
<cities>
  <city name="Phoenix"/>
  <city name="Chennai"/>
  <city name="Los Angeles"/>
  <city name="London"/>
  <city name="Chicago"/>
  <city name="New York"/>
  <city name="SanFrancisco"/>
  <city name="Philadelphia"/>
  <city name="Delhi"/>
</cities>
```

The Cities.xml file acts as the data source for the DropDownList controls lstStartingFrom and lstDestination. As you can see, the search page is complex and utilizes a variety of features to provide the complete functionality. For reasons of brevity, the implementation of the search page is discussed in the following sections.

ASP.NET 2.0 Script Callback

The script callback is the core feature that provides you with the ability to retrieve the search results returned by the server-side method call without refreshing the page. The search page uses this feature to search for flights from the client side.

> ASP.NET 2.0 script callback is a new feature introduced with ASP.NET 2.0 that enables you to invoke a remote function from the server side of a Web page without refreshing the browser. This new feature builds on the foundation of the XmlHttp object library. Using the ASP.NET 2.0 script callback feature, you can emulate some of the behaviors of a traditional rich client application in a Web-based application. It can be used to refresh individual controls, to validate controls, or even to process a form without having to post the whole page to the server.

At the top of the page, you use the implements directive to implement the `ICallbackEventHandler` interface, which has two methods named `RaiseCallbackEvent()` and `GetCallbackResult()` that must be implemented to make the callback work.

```
<%@ implements interface="System.Web.UI.ICallbackEventHandler" %>
```

The signature of the `RaiseCallbackEvent()` method is as follows:

```
void ICallbackEventHandler.RaiseCallbackEvent(string eventArgument)
```

The `RaiseCallbackEvent` method takes an argument of type string. This argument allows you to pass values to the server-side method. Inside the `RaiseCallbackEvent` method, you simply assign the supplied argument to a private variable for further processing.

```
_callbackArg = eventArgument;
```

After invoking the `RaiseCallbackEvent()` method, the ASP.NET runtime invokes the `GetCallbackResult()` method wherein you can perform the actual server-side processing and render out the results back to the client application.

```
string ICallbackEventHandler.GetCallbackResult()
{
try
{
    return GetSearchResults(_callbackArg);
}
catch (Exception ex)
{
    throw new ApplicationException("An Error has occurred during the " +
      "processing of your request. Error is :" + ex.Message);
  }
}
```

The `GetSearchResults()` method is the one that does the majority of the work. It starts out by invoking another method named `IsInputXmlValid()` to check the validity of the input XML. You see more on the `IsInputXmlValid()` method in the XSD Validation section.

```
if (IsInputXmlValid(input))
{
inputDoc.LoadXml(input);
string startingFrom = inputDoc.DocumentElement.SelectSingleNode
    ("startingFrom").InnerText;
string destination = inputDoc.DocumentElement.SelectSingleNode
    ("destination").InnerText;
DateTime departureDate = Convert.ToDateTime(inputDoc.DocumentElement.
    SelectSingleNode("departureDate").InnerText);
DateTime arrivalDate = Convert.ToDateTime(inputDoc.DocumentElement.
    SelectSingleNode("arrivalDate").InnerText);
int travelClassCode = Convert.ToInt32(inputDoc.DocumentElement.
    SelectSingleNode("travelClassCode").InnerText);
//Assign the TravelClassID to a session variable for future use
```

```
Session["TravelClassID"] = travelClassCode;
FlightDB flightObj = new FlightDB();
DataSet flights = flightObj.SearchFlight(startingFrom,
    destination, departureDate, arrivalDate, 1);
return TransformXmltoHtml(flights.GetXml());
}
```

If the input XML is valid, you then parse the contents of the XML into local variables and pass them as arguments to the `SearchFlight()` method of the FlightDB class. The `SearchFlight()` method returns a `DataSet` object, which is then converted to an XML format and passed to a helper method named `TransformXmlToHtml()`. The `TransformXmlToHtml()` method is discussed in detail in the Transforming XML to HTML section later in this chapter.

In addition to the implementing the `ICallbackEventHandler` interface on the server side, the ASP.NET 2.0 script callback also requires you to generate appropriate hooks on the client side to enable the server-side method to be called. To this end, the `Page_Load` method uses the `Page.ClientScript.GetCallbackEventReference()` method.

```
string src = Page.ClientScript.GetCallbackEventReference(this, "arg",
    "DisplayResultsCallback","ctx", "DisplayErrorCallback", false);
```

The `GetCallbackEventReference()` method generates the client-side code which is required to initiate the asynchronous call to server.

You then embed the callback code inside a function by concatenating the generated code with a JavaScript function named `GetSearchDetailsUsingPostback` using the following line of code.

```
string mainSrc = @"function GetSearchDetailsUsingPostback(arg, ctx)
    { " + src + "; }";
```

Finally, you register the client script block through the `Page.ClientScript.RegisterClientScriptBlock()` method call.

```
Page.ClientScript.RegisterClientScriptBlock(this.GetType(),
    "GetSearchDetailsUsingPostback", mainSrc, true);
```

XML Formatted Search Criteria

After the user has entered all the search details, you need a way to be able to pass in the search criteria to the server side. Because you can only send in a string value to the server side using the ASP.NET 2.0 script callback, you create an XML string on the client side and send in the XML string to the server. This is shown as follows.

```
function GetSearchDetails()
{
var inputXML ="<input>" +
    "<startingFrom>" + document.all.<%=lstStartingFrom.ClientID%>.value +
    "</startingFrom>" + "<destination>" +
    document.all.<%=lstDestination.ClientID%>.value + "</destination>" +
```

```
"<departureDate>" + document.all.<%=txtDepartureDate.ClientID%>.value +
"</departureDate>" + "<arrivalDate>" +
document.all.<%=txtArrivalDate.ClientID%>.value + "</arrivalDate>" +
"<travelClassCode>" + document.all.<%=lstTravelClassCode.ClientID%>.value +
"</travelClassCode>" + "</input>";
GetSearchDetailsUsingPostback(inputXML, "Input");
}
```

Because all the input controls are placed inside `<asp:Content>` control, you need to utilize the `<Control_Name>.ClientID` property to reference them in the client side.

XSD Validation

As you have already seen, the client generates an XML on the fly and sends that XML over as an input to the `SearchFlight()` method. In a Service Oriented world, you should never trust the input, especially when the input is coming directly from a browser. To ensure that the input XML is valid and does not contain malicious data, the server side validates the XML data using a helper method named `IsInputXmlValid()`. Before looking at the `IsInputXmlValid()` method, briefly review the XSD file that actually contains the schema.

Listing 11-10: XSD Schema Used for Validating Input XML Data

```
<?xml version="1.0" encoding="utf-8"?>
<xs:schema attributeFormDefault="unqualified" elementFormDefault="qualified"
xmlns:xs="http://www.w3.org/2001/XMLSchema">
<xs:element name="input">
    <xs:complexType>
      <xs:sequence>
        <xs:element name="startingFrom" type="xs:string" />
        <xs:element name="destination" type="xs:string" />
        <xs:element name="departureDate" type="xs:string" />
        <xs:element name="arrivalDate" type="xs:string" />
        <xs:element name="travelClassCode" type="xs:unsignedByte" />
      </xs:sequence>
    </xs:complexType>
</xs:element>
</xs:schema>
```

Now that you have looked at the schema itself, it is time to examine the `IsInputXmlValid()` method.

The `IsInputXmlValid()` method starts out by loading the XML into a `StringReader` object.

```
TextReader textReader = new StringReader(xml);
```

It then uses an `XmlReaderSettings` object to set the validation type, validation event handler as well as the XSD schema used for validation.

```
string xsdPath = Request.PhysicalApplicationPath +
@"\App_Data\SearchInput.xsd";
XmlReader reader = null;
XmlReaderSettings settings = new XmlReaderSettings();
```

```
settings.ValidationEventHandler += new
ValidationEventHandler(this.ValidationEventHandler);
settings.ValidationType = ValidationType.Schema;
settings.Schemas.Add(null, XmlReader.Create(xsdPath));
reader = XmlReader.Create(textReader, settings);
```

The Read() method of the XmlReader object is then invoked in a While loop so that the entire XML file can be read and validated. The ValidationEventHandler() method will be invoked whenever a validation error occurs. Inside this method, a StringBuilder object keeps appending the contents of the validation error message to itself.

```
while (reader.Read())
{}
bool success;
if (_builder.ToString() == String.Empty)
  success = true;
else
  success = false;
```

At the end of the method, you examine the StringBuilder object to verify if the validation is successful.

Transforming XML to HTML

After you invoke the SearchFlight() method of the FlightDB class and have the results in the form of a DataSet object, there are two ways which you can send it to the client.

❑   DataSet contents in XML format and also send in an XSL file and let the client transform the XML to the required HTML format

❑   Convert the XML output of the DataSet to HTML using XSL transformation and send in the converted HTML

For the purposes of this example, consider the second approach and perform the XML->HTML transformation on the server side. Before looking at the code required for this, Listing 11-1 examines the code of the XSL file.

Listing 11-11: XSL File for Transforming the XML Search Result to HTML

```
<?xml version="1.0" ?>
<xsl:stylesheet version="1.0" xmlns:xsl="http://www.w3.org/1999/XSL/Transform"
  xmlns:ms="urn:schemas-microsoft-com:xslt"
xmlns:dt="urn:schemas-microsoft-com:datatypes">
<xsl:output method="html" />
<xsl:template match="/">
    <table border="1" cellSpacing="1" cellPadding="1" align="center">
      <center>
        <tr bgcolor="#00AAAA" height="40">
          <td>Flight Number</td>
          <td>Destination</td>
          <td>Departure Date</td>
          <td>Arrival Date</td>
          <td>Price</td>
```

```
            <td>Book Tickets</td>
        </tr>
        <xsl:for-each select="/Flights/Flight">
          <xsl:element name="tr">
            <xsl:attribute name="style">background-color:buttonface;
            </xsl:attribute>
            <xsl:attribute name="height">40</xsl:attribute>
            <xsl:element name="td">
              <xsl:value-of select="flight_number" />
            </xsl:element>
            <xsl:element name="td">
              <xsl:attribute name="align">center</xsl:attribute>
              <xsl:value-of select="destination" />
            </xsl:element>
            <xsl:element name="td">
              <xsl:attribute name="align">center</xsl:attribute>
              <xsl:value-of select="ms:format-date
                (departure_date,'MMM dd,yyyy')"/>
            </xsl:element>
            <xsl:element name="td">
              <xsl:attribute name="align">center</xsl:attribute>
              <xsl:value-of select="ms:format-date
                (arrival_date, 'MMM dd, yyyy')" />
            </xsl:element>
            <xsl:element name="td">
              <xsl:attribute name="align">center</xsl:attribute>
              <xsl:value-of select='format-number(price, "#.00")' />
            </xsl:element>
            <xsl:element name="td">
              <xsl:attribute name="align">center</xsl:attribute>
              <a>
                <xsl:attribute name="href">BookTickets.aspx?FlightID=
                  <xsl:value-of select="flight_id" />
                </xsl:attribute>
                Click here to book the ticket
              </a>
            </xsl:element>
          </xsl:element>
        </xsl:for-each>
      </center>
    </table>
  </xsl:template>
</xsl:stylesheet>
```

Now that you have had a look at the XSL file, turn your focus to the .NET code that actually performs the transformation. The transformation logic is embedded inside the TransformXmlToHtml() method.

```
string TransformXmltoHtml(string xml)
{
XmlDocument xmlDoc = new XmlDocument();
xmlDoc.LoadXml(xml);
```

```
string xslPath = Request.PhysicalApplicationPath +
    @"\App_Data\SearchOutput.xsl";
XslCompiledTransform transform = new XslCompiledTransform();
//Load the XSL stylsheet into the XslCompiledTransform object
transform.Load(xslPath);
StringWriter writer = new StringWriter();
transform.Transform(xmlDoc, null, writer);
return writer.ToString();
}
```

The `XslCompiledTransform` class encapsulates the XSLT processor engine and does the actual transformation. The transformation is initiated through the call to the `Transform()` method. In this example, the output of the transformation is placed inside a `StringWriter` object.

When the user performs a search after entering all the search criteria, the page produces an output very similar to Figure 11-6.

From the search output, the user can choose to book a particular flight by following the hyperlink Click here to book the ticket. This hyperlink transfers the user to the confirmation page, which is the topic of discussion in the next section.

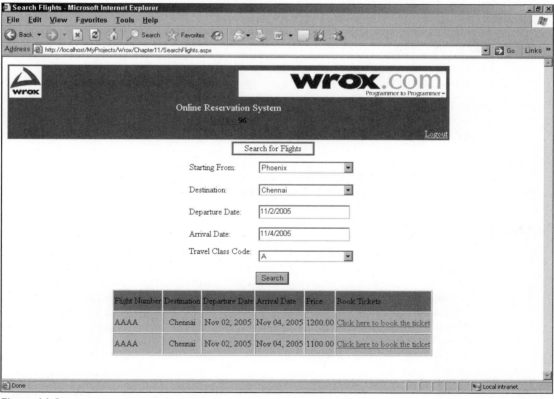

Figure 11-6

Implementation of Confirmation Page

When the user clicks the link to book the ticket in the search results page, they are redirected to the BookTickets.aspx page. The code of the BookTickets.aspx page is shown in Listing 11-12.

Listing 11-12: Implementation of Confirmation Page

```
<%@ Page Language="C#" MasterPageFile="~/Common.master"
Title="Confirmation Page" %>
<%@ Import Namespace="AirlineReservationsLib" %>
<script runat="server">
void Page_Load(object sender, EventArgs e)
{
    if (!Page.IsPostBack)
    {
        int flightID = Convert.ToInt32(Request.QueryString["flightid"]);
        string userID = Session["UserID"].ToString();
        int travelClassID = Convert.ToInt32(Session["TravelClassID"]);
        FlightDB flight = new FlightDB();
        int bookingID = flight.InsertBooking(flightID, userID, travelClassID);
        lblConfirmationNumber.Text = bookingID.ToString();
    }
}
</script>
<asp:Content ID="Content1" ContentPlaceHolderID="ContentPlaceHolder1"
Runat="Server">
<asp:Label id="lblTitle" style="Z-INDEX: 100; LEFT: 262px; POSITION: absolute;
  TOP: 266px" runat="server" Width="225px" Height="46px" Font-Bold="True">
  Your ticket has been booked. Your confirmation number is :</asp:Label>
<asp:Label id="lblConfirmationNumber" style="Z-INDEX: 101; LEFT: 528px;
  POSITION: absolute; TOP: 268px" runat="server" Height="29px" Width="168px"
  Font-Bold="True"></asp:Label>
</asp:Content>
```

The Page_Load method retrieves the required parameters and simply sends them onto the InsertBooking() method of the FlightDB class to save the booking. The InsertBooking() method also returns a confirmation number that is displayed in a label control.

Putting It All Together

Now that you have constructed the different parts of the application, test it by navigating to the login page of your site. If you enter a valid user id and password and click "Login", you will be directed to the search flights page where you are presented with a Web form that allows you to search for flights. If you enter all the details and click Search, an asynchronous search is initiated through the script callback. The search results are then sent to the client side in the form of HTML. From the search results list, you can opt to book a ticket for a particular flight by clicking the link Click here to book the ticket. This will take you to the confirmation page wherein you are given the confirmation message and the booking number. If you are a new user and would like to create a new account, you can get to the new user page using the hyperlink in the login page.

Summary

This case study has discussed the following features:

- ❏ How to work with a typed XML column in the SQL Server 2005 database
- ❏ How to validate XML data using XSD schemas
- ❏ How to transform XML to HTML using the XSLT support provided by the .NET Framework
- ❏ How to generate XML output from a `DataSet` object
- ❏ How to create rich ASP.NET Web pages using the new script callback feature

12

XML Serialization

XML was designed to be a technology for data exchange across heterogeneous systems. You can easily transmit XML between distributed components because of its platform independence and its simple, text-based, self-describing format, yet these features hardly form the basis for a solid programming platform. Text-based data does not enforce type-safety rules. Programmers are much more enticed by object-oriented programming models because each object is of a certain type, so the compiler can warn of potential type problems, and data encapsulated by an object can be easily accessed. The ideal programming environment would use an object-oriented model to build the software but leverage the benefits of XML to communicate between distributed components, over the Internet or Message Queues, for example. This is where XML serialization plays an important role by providing you with the bridge that enables you to seamlessly transform an object to XML and vice versa.

XML serialization is the process of translating a collection of data into a stream of information. Deserialization is the reverse: translating a stream of information back into the data that originally produced it. Sometimes these processes are called dehydration and rehydration. The `System.Xml.Serialization` namespace contains classes to create an XML representation for an object or initialize an object directly from XML. Using XML serialization will reduce the amount of code you have to develop for an XML-based data exchange application. You no longer have to parse XML to initialize objects, neither do you have to develop code for objects to persist themselves to XML. After you define what the XML format you use to exchange data looks like, you can quickly develop classes that can automatically store their data to the XML format or objects can be automatically created from XML.

This chapter focuses on the serialization features of .NET framework that are used to serialize objects to an XML-based representation and then deserializing the XML back into objects. You also learn how to customize the output generated by the serialization of objects so their XML representation will map to a given XML format. By the end of this chapter, you will have a good understanding of the following:

❑   XML serialization

❑   How to serialize an object into an XML format

Chapter 12

❑   Serializing object graphs using the `XmlSerializer` class

❑   Customizing the serialization output by using design time attributes

❑   Customizing the serialization output by using `XmlAttributeOverrides` class at runtime

❑   Handling namespaces during XML serialization

❑   How to deserialize an XML representation back into an object

❑   Serializing and deserializing generics types using the `XmlSerializer` class

❑   Improving serialization performance by pregenerating assemblies using the new XML Serializer Generator tool

This chapter also harnesses the XPath skills acquired from the previous chapter and examines how to use transformations effectively in ASP.NET.

A Primer on Serialization

Serialization is the runtime process that converts an object, or a graph of objects, to a linear sequence of bytes. You can then use the resultant block of memory either for storage or for transmission over the network on top of a particular protocol. In the Microsoft .NET Framework, object serialization can have three different output forms. They are:

❑   Binary — Formats objects into binary format

❑   Simple Object Access Protocol (SOAP) — Formats objects into SOAP format

❑   XML — Formats objects into XML format that can then be transmitted to another application

Runtime object serialization (for example, binary and SOAP) and XML serialization are significantly different technologies with different implementations and, more important, different goals. Nevertheless, both forms of serialization do just one key thing: they save the contents and the state of living objects out to memory, and from there to any other storage media.

> *The formatter namespaces and classes contained in the* `System.Runtime.Serialization` *namespace provide support for binary and SOAP serializations. The XML serialization is primarily supported by the* `XmlSerializer` *class in* `System.Xml.Serialization` *namespace.*

Serialization is useful for transporting or storing complex data in a simple format. For example, an application might build a complicated data structure consisting of dozens of objects and serialize it into a text string. It could then transmit the string to another program across the network. The receiving program would deserialize the text to create a duplicate of the original data structure. Serialization need not translate objects into text. It could represent the objects as a stream of binary data. It also need not transmit the data across a network. For example, it could copy the serialization into a file or database for later re-creation. The thing all of these uses of serialization have in common is they convert a possibly complex data structure into a simple serial representation and then translate it back again.

Now that you have an understanding of the different serialization techniques, the remainder of this chapter focuses on the XML serialization.

The XmlSerializer Class

The central element in the XML serialization architecture is the XmlSerializer class, which belongs to the System.Xml.Serialization namespace. The XML serialization process can be used to quickly develop an XML-driven application and get the best of both worlds — objects for programming and XML for data transfer or storage. The XmlSerializer does the transformations from one representation to the other. To accomplish its functionalities, the XmlSerializer class exposes the methods shown in Table 12-1.

Table 12-1. Methods of the XmlSerializer Class

Method	Description
CanDeserialize	Indicates if the XmlSerializer object can deserialize a specified XML document
Deserialize	Deserializes an XML document that is read from a stream, text, or an XML reader
FromMappings	Static method that returns an instance of the XmlSerializer class from the specified mappings that are created through the XmlTypeMapping object
FromTypes	Static method that returns an array of XmlSerializer objects created from an array of types; useful for speeding operations when you need to create multiple serializers for different types
GenerateSerializer	Static method that returns an XML serialization assembly that contains typed serializers; the returned assembly is one that is created through the tool XML serializer generator (sgen.exe)
GetXmlSerializerAssemblyName	Static method that returns the name of the assembly that contains one or more versions of the XmlSerializer that is specifically created to serialize or deserialize specific types
Serialize	Serializes an object into an XML document

The Serialize() method has a number of overloads. The first parameter to the Serialize method is overridden so that it can serialize XML to a Stream, a TextWriter, or an XmlWriter. When serializing to Stream, TextWriter, or XmlWriter a third parameter to the Serialize method is permissible. This third parameter is of type XmlSerializerNamespaces and is used to specify a list of namespaces that qualify the names in the XML-generated document. The permissible overrides of the Serialize method are:

```
void Serialize(Stream, Object);
void Serialize(TextWriter, Object);
void Serialize(XmlWriter, Object);
void Serialize(Stream, Object, XmlSerializerNamespaces);
void Serialize(TextWriter, Object, XmlSerializerNamespaces);
void Serialize(XmlWriter, Object, XmlSerializerNamespaces);
void Serialize (XmlWriter, Object, XmlSerializerNamespaces, String)
void Serialize (XmlWriter, Object, XmlSerializerNamespaces, String, String)
```

The fourth and fifth parameters allow you to specify the encoding style and the id used for generating SOAP encoded messages respectively. Now that you have a general understanding of the XmlSerializer class, the next section discusses an example that exercises these concepts.

Serializing Objects

The first and foremost step to use serialization is to create the class that will be serialized through the XmlSerializer class. Listing 12-1 shows the implementation of the Category class.

Listing 12-1: Category Class

```
using System;
[Serializable]
public class Category
{
  public long CategoryID;
  public string CategoryName;
  public string Description;
}
```

As you can see from the code listing, the Category class contains three public properties that represent the details of a category. As you are creating the Category class, remember to place the Category class inside the App_Code directory so that the class is made available automatically to all the ASP.NET Web pages in the Web site. Now that the Category class is available for use, you can now serialize it and convert it into an XML format. Listing 12-2 shows the code required to perform this.

Listing 12-2: Serializing the Category Class

```
<%@ Page Language="C#" %>
<%@ Import Namespace="System.IO" %>
<%@ Import Namespace="System.Xml.Serialization" %>
<script runat="server">
  void Page_Load(object sender, System.EventArgs e)
  {
    string xmlFilePath = @"C:\Data\Category.xml";
    Category categoryObj = new Category();
    categoryObj.CategoryID = 1;
    categoryObj.CategoryName = "Beverages";
    categoryObj.Description = "Soft drinks, coffees, teas, beers, and ales";
    XmlSerializer serializer = new XmlSerializer(typeof(Category));
    TextWriter writer = new StreamWriter(xmlFilePath);
    //Serialize the Category and close the TextWriter
    serializer.Serialize(writer, categoryObj);
    writer.Close();
    Response.Write("File written successfully");
  }
</script>
<html xmlns="http://www.w3.org/1999/xhtml" >
<head runat="server">
  <title>Simple XML Serialization</title>
</head>
<body>
  <form id="form1" runat="server">
```

```
        <div>
        </div>
      </form>
    </body>
  </html>
```

Listing 12-2 starts by defining the variable that is used to hold the path to the XML file.

```
string xmlFilePath = @"C:\Data\Category.xml";
```

You then create an instance of the `Category` class and set its properties to appropriate values.

```
Category categoryObj = new Category();
categoryObj.CategoryID = 1;
categoryObj.CategoryName = "Beverages";
categoryObj.Description = "Soft drinks, coffees, teas, beers, and ales";
```

The `XmlSerializer` class also has several constructors, the simplest of which takes a `System.Type`. You can then use the `XmlSerializer` object to create XML documents that comprise serialized instances of this type by passing the type to the constructor.

```
XmlSerializer serializer = new XmlSerializer(typeof(Category));
```

After that, you create an instance of the `StreamWriter` object and supply the path of the XML file as an argument to its constructor.

```
TextWriter writer = new StreamWriter(xmlFilePath);
```

You then call the `Serialize()` method with the writer object and the object to serialize.

```
serializer.Serialize(writer, categoryObj);
```

The `StreamWriter` controls where and how the output of the method is written. If you open up the `Category.xml` file in the `C:\Data directory`, you will see the output shown in Listing 12-3.

Listing 12-3: Serialized XML Output

```
<?xml version="1.0" encoding="utf-8" ?>
<Category xmlns:xsi="http://www.w3.org/2001/XMLSchema-instance"
  xmlns:xsd="http://www.w3.org/2001/XMLSchema">
  <CategoryID>1</CategoryID>
  <CategoryName>Beverages</CategoryName>
  <Description>Soft drinks, coffees, teas, beers, and ales</Description>
</Category>
```

As Listing 12-3 shows, all the public fields of the `Category` class are serialized into XML elements with the same name as the field name in the class declaration. All these elements are contained in a root `Category` element that maps back to the name of the class, which is `Category` in this example. Imagine how easy to build applications that exchange XML when you can transform your application objects into XML with two lines of code. The `Serialize()` method makes use of the pluggable architecture allowing you to supply any classes derived from `System.IO.Stream`, `System.Xml.XmlWriter`, or `System.IO.TextWriter`, thus allowing a great deal of flexibility in terms of the location where the objects are persisted to.

The Category *class shown in the previous example exposes the public fields directly to the client application. This might be a cause for concern because this approach breaks encapsulation that you are all used to with the traditional object-oriented programming. The good news is that you do not necessarily have to expose public fields to the serializer. XML serialization also works with properties as long as they provide read and write accessor methods. It will not process read- or write-only properties because the* XmlSerializer *makes sure it only processes properties that can be transformed both ways; however, if the order of the serialized elements matters, as it does when your class maps to certain XML schema types, your class must not mix properties and fields. The* XmlSerializer *does not maintain the order of which fields and properties appear in the class definition. It first maps all the properties to the XML document, then all the fields.*

Handling Object Graphs

The examples shown so far have been simple, inasmuch as the objects being serialized have been small and straightforward; however, you can serialize entire graphs of related objects using the same mechanism. For example, the Category class can encapsulate all the products (that belong to the same category) as a nested element. To demonstrate this, declare the Product class as shown in Listing 12-4.

Listing 12-4: Product Class

```
using System;
public class Product
{
  public long ProductID;
  public string ProductName;
  public string QuantityPerUnit;
  public string UnitPrice;
  public int UnitsInStock;
}
```

Similar to the Category class, the Product class also consists of a few public properties. Add the following line of code to the Category class shown in Listing 12-1.

```
public Product[] Products;
```

Now if you serialize the Category class, it will also result in the Products array being serialized. Listing 12-5 shows the code of the ASP.NET page.

Listing 12-5: Nesting Objects During Serialization

```
<%@ Page Language="C#" %>
<%@ Import Namespace="System.IO" %>
<%@ Import Namespace="System.Xml.Serialization" %>
<script runat="server">
  void Page_Load(object sender, System.EventArgs e)
  {
    string xmlFilePath = @"C:\Data\Category.xml";
    Category categoryObj = new Category();
    categoryObj.CategoryID = 1;
    categoryObj.CategoryName = "Beverages";
    categoryObj.Description = "Soft drinks, coffees, teas, beers, and ales";
    //Populate the products array
    Product prodObj = new Product();
```

```
        prodObj.ProductID = 1;
        prodObj.ProductName = "Chai";
        prodObj.QuantityPerUnit = "10 boxes x 20 bags";
        prodObj.UnitPrice = "18";
        prodObj.UnitsInStock = 39;
        //Insert the item into the array
        Product[] products = {prodObj};
        categoryObj.Products = products;
        XmlSerializer serializer = new XmlSerializer(typeof(Category));
        TextWriter writer = new StreamWriter(xmlFilePath);
        //Serialize the Category and close the TextWriter
        serializer.Serialize(writer, categoryObj);
        writer.Close();
        Response.Write("File written successfully");
    }
</script>
<html xmlns="http://www.w3.org/1999/xhtml" >
<head runat="server">
  <title>Nesting Objects during XML Serialization</title>
</head>
<body>
  <form id="form1" runat="server">
    <div>
    </div>
  </form>
</body>
</html>
```

As similar to the previous serialization example, this code listing also starts by defining a `Category` class and then populating the `Category` object with the appropriate values. Then the code creates an array of `Product` objects and populates the first product object in the array with appropriate values. After that, the `Products` property of the `Category` object is set to the populated products array.

```
        categoryObj.Products = products;
```

The rest of the code resembles the previous code example wherein you invoke the `Serialize()` method of the `XmlSerializer` to serialize the object into XML format and then close the writer object. If you request this page in the browser, it should result in a file named `Category.xml`, whose contents are shown in Listing 12-6.

Listing 12-6: Serialized XML Output

```
<?xml version="1.0" encoding="utf-8"?>
<Category xmlns:xsi="http://www.w3.org/2001/XMLSchema-instance"
  xmlns:xsd="http://www.w3.org/2001/XMLSchema">
  <CategoryID>1</CategoryID>
  <CategoryName>Beverages</CategoryName>
  <Description>Soft drinks, coffees, teas, beers, and ales</Description>
  <Products>
    <Product>
      <ProductID>1</ProductID>
      <ProductName>Chai</ProductName>
      <QuantityPerUnit>10 boxes x 20 bags</QuantityPerUnit>
```

```
        <UnitPrice>18</UnitPrice>
        <UnitsInStock>39</UnitsInStock>
      </Product>
    </Products>
  </Category>
```

This example placed only one `Product` object in the Products array and that's why you see only one `<Product>` element inside the `<Products>` element. If the array contains multiple product objects, all of them will be embedded under the single root `<Products>` element.

The XML Schema Definition Tool

Installed as part of the .NET Framework SDK, the XML Schema Definition Tool (`xsd.exe`) has several purposes. When it comes to XML serialization, the tool is helpful in a couple of scenarios. For example, you can use xsd.exe to generate source class files that are the C# or Microsoft Visual Basic .NET counterpart of existing XSD schemas. In addition, you can make the tool scan the public interface exposed by managed executables (`DLL` or `EXE`) and extrapolate an XML schema for any of the contained classes.

In the first case, the tool automatically generates the source code of a .NET Framework class that is conformant to the specified XML schema. This feature is extremely handy when you are in the process of writing an application that must cope with a flow of XML data described by a fixed schema. In a matter of seconds, the tool provides you with either C# or Visual Basic source files containing a number of classes that, when serialized through `XmlSerializer`, conform to the schema.

> **Another common situation in which xsd.exe can help considerably is when you don't have the source code for the classes your code manages. In this case, the tool can generate an XML schema document from any public class implemented in a `DLL` or an `EXE`.**

In addition to using the XSD utility, you can also use Visual Studio 2005 to generate an XSD schema for an XML file. To generate the XSD schema, add the XML file to a project, display it, and choose Create Schema from the XML menu.

Advanced Serialization

In the previous examples, the public fields of the class are simply mapped to XML elements in the output XML document. Although this one-to-one mapping approach works for simple serialization scenarios, there are times where you would want to customize the generated output. Fortunately XML serialization enables you to customize the final output of the XML data being created. Although the code of the class is not directly involved in the generation of the output, the .NET Framework provides the programmers with a couple of tools to significantly influence the serialization process. They are as follows:

❑   In this approach, you decorate the various members of the class to be serialized with attributes that control the serialization process. This approach is static and allows you to render a given member as an attribute, an element, or plain text, or completely ignore it depending on the attribute set.

❑ The second approach is more dynamic and, more importantly, does not require the availability of the class source code. This approach is particularly effective and can be used in a wide variety of situations.

The next few sections discuss both of these approaches in detail.

XML Serialization Attributes

The XmlAttributes class represents a collection of .NET Framework attributes that let you exercise complete control over how the XmlSerializer class processes an object.

> The XmlAttributes **class is similar to the** SoapAttributes **class except for the difference that the** XmlAttributes **class outputs to XML, whereas the SoapAttributes class returns SOAP-encoded messages with type information.**

Each property of the XmlAttributes class corresponds to an attribute class. Table 12-2 lists the available properties of the XmlAttributes class.

Table 12-2. Properties of the XmlAttributes Class

Property	Description
XmlAnyAttribute	Corresponds to the XmlAnyAttributeAttribute attribute and applies to properties that return an array of XmlAttribute objects.
XmlAnyElements	Corresponds to the collection of XmlAnyElementAttribute attributes and applies to properties that return an array of XmlElement objects.
XmlArray	Corresponds to the XmlArrayAttribute attribute and applies to all properties that return an array of user-defined objects. This attribute causes the contents of the property to be rendered as an XML array.
XmlArrayItems	Corresponds to the XmlArrayItemAttribute attribute and applies to all properties that return an array of objects.
XmlAttribute	Corresponds to the XmlAttributeAttribute attribute and applies to public properties, causing the serializer to render them as attributes. By default, if no attribute is applied to a public read/write property, it will be serialized as an XML element.
XmlChoiceIdentifier	This attribute lets you express the choice of which data member to consider for serialization and this attribute corresponds to the XmlChoiceIdentifierAttribute attribute and implements the xsi:choice XSD data structure.
XmlDefaultValue	Corresponds to the XmlDefaultValueAttribute attribute and gets or sets the default value of an XML element or attribute.
XmlElements	Corresponds to the collection of XmlElementAttribute attributes and forces the serializer to render a given public field as an XML element.

Property	Description
XmlEnum	Corresponds to the XmlEnumAttribute attribute and specifies the way in which an enumeration member is serialized.
XmlIgnore	Corresponds to the XmlIgnoreAttribute attribute and specifies whether a given property should be ignored and skipped or serialized to XML as the type dictates.
Xmlns	Gets or sets a value that specifies whether to keep all namespace declarations when an object containing a member that returns an XmlSerializerNamespaces object is overridden.
XmlRoot	Corresponds to the XmlRootAttribute attribute and overrides any current settings for the root node of the XML serialization output, replacing it with the specified element.
XmlText	Corresponds to the XmlTextAttribute attribute and instructs the XmlSerializer class to serialize a public property as XML text. The property to which this attribute is applied must return primitive and enumeration types, including an array of strings or objects.
XmlType	Corresponds to the XmlTypeAttribute attribute and can be used to control how a type is serialized. When a type is serialized, the XmlSerializer class uses the class name as the XML element name. The TypeName property of the XmlTypeAttribute class lets you change the XML element name.

In the attributes shown in Table 12-2, the XmlRootAttribute allows you to identify a class as forming the root element of an XML document, which is useful primarily if you're defining classes that contain non-primitive public members, effectively defining a data hierarchy. The class at the top of the hierarchy can be tagged with XmlRoot attribute, and you can specify a namespace and an element name.

One of the advantages of XML serialization is that it enables you to control the structure of the XML document that will be generated. You can do so by applying special attributes (shown in Table 12-2) to the members of the class. Listing 12-7 shows the Category class decorated with the XML serialization attributes.

Listing 12-7: Category Class with XML Serialization Attributes

```
using System;
using System.Xml;
using System.Xml.Serialization;
[XmlRoot("CategoryRoot", Namespace = "http://www.wrox.com",
  IsNullable = false)]
public class Category
{
  [XmlAttribute("ID")]
  public long CategoryID;

  [XmlAttribute("Name")]
```

```
    public string CategoryName;

    [XmlElementAttribute(IsNullable = false)]
    public string Description;
}
```

With these changes made to the `Category` class, if you request the ASP.NET page shown in Listing 12-2 from the browser, you will get a message indicating that the file is written successfully. Now if you open up the `Category.xml` file, it should look somewhat similar to the following.

```
<?xml version="1.0" encoding="utf-8"?>
<CategoryRoot xmlns:xsi="http://www.w3.org/2001/XMLSchema-instance"
  xmlns:xsd="http://www.w3.org/2001/XMLSchema" xmlns="http://www.wrox.com"
  ID="1" Name="Beverages">
  <Description>Soft drinks, coffees, teas, beers, and ales</Description>
</CategoryRoot>
```

As you can see from this output, the root element is renamed to `CategoryRoot` using the `XmlRoot` attribute class. As part of the XmlRoot attribute, you also specify values for the `Namespace` and the `IsNullable` properties. The `CategoryID`, `CategoryName` elements are then renamed to `ID` and `Name`, respectively, and both of them are created as attributes.

Controlling Output Using XmlAttributeOverrides

In the previous section, you have seen how to override the XML elements by means of hard-coded XML serialization attributes.

> The ability to override the XML elements at runtime is very powerful and can enable a number of powerful scenarios. Imagine your application sends updates about the categories to interested parties in an XML format. For some reason there is one client who needs the data in a slightly different format. Instead of writing an entire different set of classes to produce the custom format, you can simply customize the existing ones using the `XmlAttributeOverrides` class.

For the purposes of this example, you use the `Category` class shown in Listing 12-1. But during serialization, you rename the `CategoryID` field in the `Category` class to `ID` and also add it as an XML attribute instead of an XML element. Here are the steps required to accomplish using the `XmlAttributeOverrides` object.

1. Create an instance of the `XmlAttributeAttribute` class.

2. Set the AttributeName of the `XmlAttributeAttribute` to `"ID"`.

3. Create an instance of the `XmlAttributes` class.

4. Set the `XmlAttribute` property of the `XmlAttributes` object to the `XmlAttributeAttribute`.

5. Create an instance of the `XmlAttributeOverrides` class.

6. Add the `XmlAttributes` to the `XmlAttributeOverrides`, passing the type of the object to override and the name of the member being overridden.

7. Create an instance of the `XmlSerializer` class with `XmlAttributeOverrides`.

8. Create an instance of the `Category` class, and serialize or deserialize it.

Listing 12-8 shows the complete code in action.

Listing 12-8: Using XmlAttributeOverrides to Customize XML Output

```
<%@ Page Language="C#" %>
<%@ Import Namespace="System.IO" %>
<%@ Import Namespace="System.Xml.Serialization" %>
<script runat="server">
  void Page_Load(object sender, System.EventArgs e)
  {
    string xmlFilePath = @"C:\Data\Category.xml";
    Category categoryObj = new Category();
    categoryObj.CategoryID = 1;
    categoryObj.CategoryName = "Beverages";
    categoryObj.Description = "Soft drinks, coffees, teas, beers, and ales";
    //Rename the CategoryID to ID and add it as an attribute
    XmlAttributeAttribute categoryIDAttribute = new XmlAttributeAttribute();
    categoryIDAttribute.AttributeName = "ID";
    XmlAttributes attributesIdCol = new XmlAttributes();
    attributesIdCol.XmlAttribute = categoryIDAttribute;
    XmlAttributeOverrides attrOverrides = new XmlAttributeOverrides();
    attrOverrides.Add(typeof(Category),"CategoryID", attributesIdCol);
    //Rename the CategoryName to Name and add it as an element
    XmlElementAttribute categoryNameElement = new XmlElementAttribute();
    categoryNameElement.ElementName = "Name";
    XmlAttributes attributesNameCol = new XmlAttributes();
    attributesNameCol.XmlElements.Add(categoryNameElement);
    attrOverrides.Add(typeof(Category), "CategoryName", attributesNameCol);
    XmlSerializer serializer = new XmlSerializer(typeof(Category),
      attrOverrides);
    TextWriter writer = new StreamWriter(xmlFilePath);
    //Serialize the Category and close the TextWriter
    serializer.Serialize(writer, categoryObj);
    writer.Close();
    Response.Write("File written successfully");
  }
</script>
<html xmlns="http://www.w3.org/1999/xhtml" >
<head runat="server">
  <title>
    Customizing XML Output at runtime using XmlAttributeOverrides
  </title>
</head>
<body>
  <form id="form1" runat="server">
    <div>
    </div>
  </form>
</body>
</html>
```

The `XmlAttributes` object collects all the overrides you want to enter for a given element. In this case, after creating a new `XmlAttributeAttribute` object, you change the attribute name and store the resultant object in the `XmlAttribute` property of the overrides container.

```
XmlAttributeAttribute categoryIDAttribute = new XmlAttributeAttribute();
categoryIDAttribute.AttributeName = "ID";
XmlAttributes attributesIdCol = new XmlAttributes();
attributesIdCol.XmlAttribute = categoryIDAttribute;
```

When the overrides are for a specific element, you use a particular overload of the `XmlAttributeOverrides` class's `Add` method. In this case, you specify a third argument — the name of the element being overridden.

```
attrOverrides.Add(typeof(Category), "CategoryName",
   attributesNameCol);
```

You then create the `XmlSerializer` object passing in the type of the object being serialized as well as the `XmlAttributeOverrides` object as arguments to its constructor.

```
XmlSerializer serializer = new XmlSerializer(typeof(Category),
   attrOverrides);
```

Now if you request the page in a browser, it should result in an XML file named `Category.xml` file being created, which should appear as follows:

```
<?xml version="1.0" encoding="utf-8"?>
<Category xmlns:xsi="http://www.w3.org/2001/XMLSchema-instance"
  xmlns:xsd="http://www.w3.org/2001/XMLSchema" ID="1">
  <Name>Beverages</Name>
  <Description>Soft drinks, coffees, teas, beers, and ales</Description>
</Category>
```

Note that you need a distinct `XmlAttributes` object for each element you want to override. This means if you are trying to override two elements, you need to create two distinct `XmlAttributes` object and add it to the `XmlAttributeOverrides` object.

Generating Qualified Names Using Namespaces

Often applications need to add new information to existing XML documents or combine existing XML documents. To avoid naming conflicts in these scenarios, the WC3 consortium standardized XML namespaces. You can think of a namespace as a last name for elements and attributes. Calling for somebody in a crowd just by their first name might cause many people to respond, but if you call for somebody by their first and last name you can address the right person. XML namespaces work the same way: the first name is an XML element or attribute; the last name is the namespace URI. Using both, you can uniquely identify attributes and elements in an XML document.

The default namespaces added to the XML generated by the XmlSerializer are `xmlns:xsd` (http://www.w3.org/2001/XMLSchema) and `xmlns:xsi` (http://www.w3.org/2001/XMLSchema-instance). You can override this behavior by creating an `XmlSerializerNamespaces` object and populating it with a list of namespaces and aliases. To attach the namespace `http://northwind.com/` category to the XML output and give it the alias cate, you would create the following `System.Xml.Serialization.XmlSerializerNamespaces` object:

```
XmlSerializerNamespaces namespaces = new XmlSerializerNamespaces();
nameSpaces.Add("cate", "http://northwind.com/category ");
```

An `XmlSerializerNamespaces` can contain a list of several namespaces. The `Add` method simply appends a namespace to the list it holds. To emit the namespace information when the XML is generated, you must invoke a variant of the `Serialize` method:

```
serializer.Serialize(stream, category, namespaces);
```

This overloaded method of the `Serialize()` method takes a third argument, specifically an `XmlSerializerNamespaces` object which is normally used as a container for a collection of namespaces and prefixes to use in the serialization of the object.

Listing 12-9 creates an `XmlSerializerNamespaces` object, and adds a namespace pair to it. The example then passes the `XmlSerializerNamespaces` to the `Serialize()` method, which serializes a Category object into an XML document. Using the `XmlSerializerNamespaces` object, the `Serialize()` method qualifies each XML element and attribute with the namespace.

Listing 12-9: Using XmlSerializerNamespaces Class to Generate Qualified Names

```
<%@ Page Language="C#" %>
<%@ Import Namespace="System.IO" %>
<%@ Import Namespace="System.Xml" %>
<%@ Import Namespace="System.Xml.Serialization" %>
<script runat="server">
  void Page_Load(object sender, System.EventArgs e)
  {
    string xmlFilePath = @"C:\Data\Category.xml";
    Category categoryObj = new Category();
    categoryObj.CategoryID = 1;
    categoryObj.CategoryName = "Beverages";
    categoryObj.Description = "Soft drinks, coffees, teas, beers, and ales";
    XmlSerializerNamespaces namespaces = new XmlSerializerNamespaces();
    namespaces.Add("cate", "http://northwind.com/category");
    XmlSerializer serializer = new XmlSerializer(typeof(Category));
    TextWriter writer = new StreamWriter(xmlFilePath);
    //Serialize the Category and close the TextWriter
    serializer.Serialize(writer, categoryObj, namespaces);
    writer.Close();
    Response.Write("File written successfully");
  }
</script>
<html xmlns="http://www.w3.org/1999/xhtml" >
<head runat="server">
  <title>
    Using XmlSerializerNamespaces class to generate Qualified Names
  </title>
</head>
<body>
  <form id="form1" runat="server">
    <div>
```

```
      </div>
    </form>
  </body>
</html>
```

Listing 12-9 uses the Category class, whose declaration is shown next.

```
[XmlRoot(Namespace="http://northwind.com/category")]
public class Category
{
  public long CategoryID;
  public string CategoryName;
  public string Description;
}
```

The Category class consists of an XmlRoot attribute that is used to specify the namespace value "http://northwind.com/category". Listing 12-9 creates an instance of the XmlSerializerNamespaces object and then invoke its Add method to add the namespace to the XmlSerializerNamespaces object.

```
XmlSerializerNamespaces namespaces = new XmlSerializerNamespaces();
namespaces.Add("cate", "http://northwind.com/category");
```

After you have the XmlSerializerNamespaces object with all the namespaces, you can then supply it as the third parameter to the Serialize() method. XML Output produced by the page is shown in Figure 12-1.

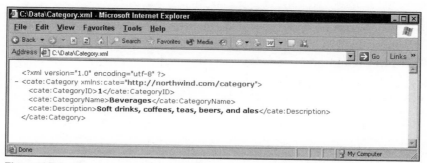

Figure 12-1

Removing the xsd and xsi Declarations

If you have ever done any serialization before, you will know that when you use the XmlSerializer to serialize a class you get a number of namespace declarations as part of the resultant xml, something along the lines of the following output.

```
<Category xmlns:xsi="http://www.w3.org/2001/XMLSchema-instance"
    xmlns:xsd="http://www.w3.org/2001/XMLSchema">
```

As you can see, the xsd and xsi namespace declarations are placed in the resultant output by the serializer. To remove the xsi and xsd namespace declarations, you need to create an empty

XmlSerializerNamespaces class and add a single entry, specifying an empty namespace prefix and namespace uri as follows.

```
XmlSerializerNamespaces namespaces = new XmlSerializerNamespaces();
namespaces.Add("", "");
```

Serializing Collections

Collection classes are similar to arrays but don't require a fixed size, can hold unrelated types, and are optimized for different usage scenarios. The .NET Framework provides a number of collection classes ready to use in the System.Collections namespace, for example an ArrayList, a Dictionary, or a Hashtable just to name a few.

You can also serialize graphs of multiple objects, such as the list of Category classes discussed earlier in this chapter, using the XmlSerializer class. To serialize a collection or array, you must also supply information to the XmlSerializer object about the type of the collection and the type or types of the contents. For example, consider the situation where the object being serialized is an ArrayList and the contents are Category and Product objects. The XmlSerializer class supplies a constructor for just such an eventuality — it expects the type of the containing class and an array of types describing the classes comprising the contents:

```
Type[] extraTypes = new Type[2];
extraTypes[0] = Type.GetType("Category");
extraTypes[1] = Type.GetType("Product");
XmlSerializer serializer = new
  XmlSerializer(typeof(ArrayList), extraTypes);
```

You can then create a stream and serialize to that stream, much as before.

Serializing Custom Collections

The XmlSerializer can also process custom collection objects as long as they implement one of the .NET framework's collection interfaces: IEnumerable or ICollection. All collections provided by the .NET framework implement these interfaces, so you can serialize or deserialize these collections without much additional work.

> The contents of a container object, such as a collection (an object that implements the ICollection interface), will be serialized automatically as long as some conditions are met; the Add method must take a single parameter, and the Item method must take a single integer parameter. In addition to selecting an appropriate collection type, you must of course ensure that the contents of the collection themselves meet the XML serialization requirements, which are as follows: Each class must supply a default constructor, and you should provide a means of accessing the contents of the class through publicly available members or properties.

Listing 12-10 gives an example for a strongly typed collection based on an ArrayList with a default accessor.

Listing 12-10: Implementation of the CategoriesList Class

```csharp
using System;
using System.Collections;
using System.Xml.Serialization;
public class CategoriesList
{
  private ArrayList _categoriesList;
  public CategoriesList()
  {
    _categoriesList = new ArrayList();
  }
  public Category[] Categories
  {
    get
    {
      Category[] categories = new Category[_categoriesList.Count];
      _categoriesList.CopyTo(categories);
      return categories;
    }
    set
    {
      if (value == null)
        return;
      Category[] categories = (Category[])value;
      _categoriesList.Clear();
      foreach (Category cate in categories)
        _categoriesList.Add(cate);
    }
  }
  public int AddCategory(Category cate)
  {
    return _categoriesList.Add(cate);
  }
}
```

Now that you have had a look at the code of the collection object, Listing 12-11 examines the code of the ASP.NET page that populates this collection object and then serializes its contents into an XML file.

Listing 12-11: Serializing CategoriesList Object

```aspx
<%@ Page Language="C#" %>
<%@ Import Namespace="System.Collections" %>
<%@ Import Namespace="System.IO" %>
<%@ Import Namespace="System.Xml.Serialization" %>
<script runat="server">
  void Page_Load(object sender, System.EventArgs e)
  {
    string xmlFilePath = @"C:\Data\Categories.xml";
    Category category1 = new Category();
    category1.CategoryID = 1;
    category1.CategoryName = "Beverages";
    category1.Description = "Soft drinks, coffees, teas, beers, and ales";
```

```
        Category category2 = new Category();
        category2.CategoryID = 2;
        category2.CategoryName = "Condiments";
        category2.Description = "Sweet and savory sauces, relishes," +
          " spreads, and seasonings";
        CategoriesList list = new CategoriesList();
        list.AddCategory(category1);
        list.AddCategory(category2);
        XmlSerializer serializer = new XmlSerializer(typeof(CategoriesList));
        TextWriter writer = new StreamWriter(xmlFilePath);
        //Serialize the Category and close the TextWriter
        serializer.Serialize(writer, list);
        writer.Close();
        Response.Write("File written successfully");
    }
</script>
<html xmlns="http://www.w3.org/1999/xhtml" >
<head runat="server">
  <title> Serializing a Collection Object</title>
</head>
<body>
  <form id="form1" runat="server">
    <div>
    </div>
  </form>
</body>
</html>
```

In this code, two instances of the Category class are created and populated with appropriate values. They are then added to the CategoriesList collection object. After that, the collection object is passed to the constructor of the XmlSerializer object as follows.

```
    XmlSerializer serializer = new XmlSerializer(typeof(CategoriesList));
```

Figure 12-2 shows the resultant XML produced by the page.

Deserializing XML

The XmlSerializer class provides a Deserialize() method that you can invoke to read an XML stream and use to create and populate objects. You can deserialize from a generic stream, a TextReader, or an XmlReader. The overloads for Deserialize are:

```
Object Deserialize(Stream);
Object Deserialize(TextReader) ;
Object Deserialize(XmlReader);
Object Deserialize(XmlReader, String);
Object Deserialize(XmlReader, XmlDeserializationEvents);
Object Deserialize(XmlReader, String, XmlDeserializationEvents);
```

The remaining parameters allow you to pass the encoding style and the XmlDeserializationEvents object to the deserialization process.

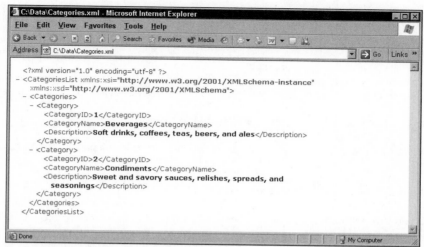

Figure 12-2

To deserialize a Category object from the file Category.xml (created in the previous example), you can simply open a file stream, instantiate an XmlSerializer, and call Deserialize. The complete code is shown in Listing 12-12.

Listing 12-12: Deserializing an XML File into an Object

```csharp
<%@ Page Language="C#" %>
<%@ Import Namespace="System.IO" %>
<%@ Import Namespace="System.Xml.Serialization" %>
<script runat="server">
  void Page_Load(object sender, System.EventArgs e)
  {
    string xmlFilePath = @"C:\Data\Category.xml";
    XmlSerializer serializer = new XmlSerializer(typeof(Category));
    TextReader reader = new StreamReader(xmlFilePath);
    //Deserialize the Category and close the TextReader
    Category categoryObj = (Category)serializer.Deserialize(reader);
    reader.Close();
    Response.Write("CategoryID: " + categoryObj.CategoryID + "<br>");
    Response.Write("Category Name: " + categoryObj.CategoryName + "<br>");
    Response.Write("Category Description: " +
      categoryObj.Description + "<br>");
  }
</script>
<html xmlns="http://www.w3.org/1999/xhtml" >
<head runat="server">
  <title>Simple XML Deserialization</title>
</head>
<body>
  <form id="form1" runat="server">
    <div>
```

```
      </div>
    </form>
  </body>
</html>
```

As with serialization using the Serialize() method, the deserialization also requires that the XmlSerializer object be constructed using the type of the object that is being deserialized.

```
XmlSerializer serializer = new XmlSerializer(typeof(Category));
```

You then create an instance of the StreamReader object passing in the path to the XML file as an argument.

```
TextReader reader = new StreamReader(xmlFilePath);
```

After that, you invoke the Deserialize() method with the StreamReader object as an argument.

```
Category categoryObj = (Category)serializer.Deserialize(reader);
```

Note that the return value of the Deserialize method is of type Object and it needs to be typecast into Category object. After you have the Category object populated with the values, you can display them onto the browser using the Response.Write statements.

Handling Events Raised by the XmlSerializer

If the input stream does not match what is expected, the deserialization process will attempt to recover as best it can, but as a result one or more objects might be set to null when the procedure has completed. To help you handle these situations, the XmlSerializer class publishes four events that you can trap. These events are raised when certain conditions arise. Table 12-3 lists the events that the XmlSerializer class triggers during the deserialization process.

Table 12-3. Events of the XmlSerializer Class

Event	Description
UnknownAttribute	Fires when the XmlSerializer encounters an XML attribute of unknown type during deserialization
UnknownElement	Fires when the XmlSerializer encounters an XML element of unknown type during deserialization
UnknownNode	Fires when the XmlSerializer encounters any XML node, including Attribute and Element during deserialization
UnreferencedObject	Fires when the XmlSerializer encounters a recognized type that is not used during deserialization; occurs during the deserialization of a SOAP-encoded XML stream

You can catch these events by creating an appropriate delegate and referencing a method to be executed when the event is raised. The System.Xml.Serialization namespace supplies a delegate for each of these events:

- ❑ XmlAttributeEventHandler
- ❑ XmlElementEventHandler
- ❑ XmlNodeEventHandler
- ❑ UnreferencedObjectEventHandler

You subscribe to an event by hooking up the delegate for the UnknownElement event with the XmlSerializer object. The following code shows how to set up the event handler for the UnknownElement method:

```
serializer.UnknownElement += new
  XmlElementEventHandler(XmlSerializer_UnknownElement);
```

After you have an event handler registered, you can declare the event handler.

```
void XmlSerializer_UnknownElement(object sender, XmlElementEventArgs e)
{
  //logic
}
```

> The EventArgs parameter passed to the event handler contains information about the unexpected element and the position in the input stream at which it occurred. For example, when the XmlSerializer fires for an unmapped attribute in the XML stream, it passes a reference to itself and an XmlAttributeEventArgs object to the registered event handler. The arguments object contains the line number and position of the attribute within the deserialized XML document, as well as the attribute itself. You can use this information to take some corrective action or record the fact that some unexpected input was received.

Listing 12-13 shows how to set up event handlers to log the event details about nodes the XmlSerializer could not map to any class members to the browser.

Listing 12-13: Handling Events Raised by the XmlSerializer Class

```
<%@ Page Language="C#" %>
<%@ Import Namespace="System.IO" %>
<%@ Import Namespace="System.Xml" %>
<%@ Import Namespace="System.Xml.Serialization" %>
<script runat="server">
  void Page_Load(object sender, System.EventArgs e)
  {
    string xmlFilePath = @"C:\Data\Category.xml";
    XmlSerializer serializer = new XmlSerializer(typeof(Category));
    serializer.UnknownElement += new
```

```
      XmlElementEventHandler(XmlSerializer_UnknownElement);
   TextReader reader = new StreamReader(xmlFilePath);
   //Deserialize the Category and close the TextReader
   Category categoryObj = (Category)serializer.Deserialize(reader);
   reader.Close();
   Response.Write("<b>Result of Deserialization:" + "</b><br>");
   Response.Write("CategoryID: " + categoryObj.CategoryID + "<br>");
   Response.Write("Category Name: " + categoryObj.CategoryName + "<br>");
}

void XmlSerializer_UnknownElement(object sender, XmlElementEventArgs e)
{
   Response.Write("<b>Unknown Element:" + "</b><br>");
   Response.Write("Unknown Element Name: " + e.Element.Name + "<br>");
   Response.Write("Unknown Element Value: " + e.Element.InnerText + "<br><br>");
}
</script>
<html xmlns="http://www.w3.org/1999/xhtml" >
<head runat="server">
   <title>Handling Events Raised by XmlSerializer </title>
</head>
<body>
   <form id="form1" runat="server">
      <div>
      </div>
   </form>
</body>
</html>
```

This code assumes the following declaration of the Category class.

```
public class Category
{
   public long CategoryID;
   public string CategoryName;
}
```

As you can see, the Category class is missing the Description field that was used in the previous examples. The contents of the XML file used as an input XML document to the Listing 12-13 are as follows:

```
<?xml version="1.0" encoding="utf-8"?>
<Category xmlns:xsi="http://www.w3.org/2001/XMLSchema-instance"
   xmlns:xsd="http://www.w3.org/2001/XMLSchema">
   <CategoryID>1</CategoryID>
   <CategoryName>Beverages</CategoryName>
   <Description>Soft drinks, coffees, teas, beers, and ales</Description>
</Category>
```

By comparing the Category class and the contents of the XML file, you can see that the Description node in the XML file does not have a matching field in the Category class. When you request the code in Listing 12-13 in a browser, you will see the output shown in Figure 12-3.

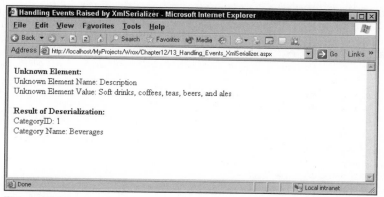

Figure 12-3

During the deserialization, when the `Description` node is encountered, the `XmlSerializer_UnknownElement` event handler is invoked wherein you display information about the unexpected node in the browser.

```
void XmlSerializer_UnknownElement(object sender, XmlElementEventArgs e)
{
    Response.Write("<b>Unknown Element:" + "</b><br>");
    Response.Write("Unknown Element Name: " + e.Element.Name + "<br>");
    Response.Write("Unknown Element Value: " + e.Element.InnerText
        + "<br><br>");
}
```

Note that the `XmlElementEventArgs` object exposes a property named `ObjectBeingSerialized` that enables you to get reference to the `Category` object during the deserialization. This can be very useful when you want to execute some logic based on the contents of the object being populated.

Mapping SQL Server Data Using Deserialization

When you get it right, XML deserialization is almost trivial, but getting it right relies on you having a valid XML data and making sure that the class or classes you're attempting to deserialize into are compatible with the contents of that file. This is a common issue when you are trying to map the results of a sql query onto an object using SQL Server's XML support and XML serialization.

As you have seen in the previous chapters, SQL Server can return the results of a query in XML format. The XML document describing the result of a query corresponds to the serialized version of a custom document and, if you can create a class that matches the schema of the XML document, you will be able to deserialize SQL Server's XML response into an instance of the custom class. This section describes a technique for moving data out of SQL Server and into an instance of a custom class, without using DataSets. The custom object is an object that represents a customer.

> The advantage of this approach, as compared to a straight ADO.NET approach based on DataSets, is that you don't have to worry about related tables and accessing related rows in `DataTable` objects. This approach also drastically reduces the amount of code required to consume data retrieved from a database.

For the purposes of this example, you use the following sql query that queries the `Person.Contact` table in the `AdventureWorks` database and returns the results in the form of an XML document.

```
Select ContactID, FirstName, MiddleName, LastName, EMailAddress from
Person.Contact as Contacts where ContactID = 2 for xml auto, elements
```

The last clause of the statement instructs SQL Server to return the result of the query in XML format. The result of this query is an XML document with the following structure:

```
<Contacts>
  <ContactID>2</ContactID>
  <FirstName>Catherine</FirstName>
  <MiddleName>R.</MiddleName>
  <LastName>Abel</LastName>
  <EMailAddress>catherine0@adventure-works.com</EMailAddress>
</Contacts>
```

At this point, you can write a class with public fields that reflect the hierarchy of the XML document returned by the query.

> Although it's fairly straightforward to build this class manually, you can use the XSD command line tool to automate the generation of the class. To use this tool, copy the XML document returned by the query, paste it into a new text document, and save the document in a file with a short path with extension XML. You can save it as `Contacts.xml` in the root path; then open a Command Prompt window and switch to the `<DriveName>\Program Files\Microsoft Visual Studio 8\SDK\v2.0\Bin` folder. There you can execute the following statement to extract an XML schema from the document:
>
> `xsd c:\Contacts.xml`
>
> The XSD utility will process the XML file and will generate a new file with the document's XSD schema. The XSD file will be saved in the current folder. Run again the XSD utility, this time specifying the name of the XSD file and two options: the `/classes` option (to generate the classes that correspond to the specified schema) and the `/language` option (to generate C# code):
>
> `xsd Contacts.xsd /classes /language:cs`
>
> This command will generate a new file, the `Contacts.cs` file, which contains a serializable class that has the same structure as the XML document.

For the purposes of this example, you manually create the `Contact` class as shown in Listing 12-14.

Listing 12-14: Contact Class

```
[XmlRoot("Contacts")]
public class Contact
{
  public string ID;
  public string FirstName;
  public string MiddleName;
  public string LastName;
}
```

If you compare the Contacts class declaration with the XML output returned by the sql query, you will see the following anomalies.

❑ The class name is declared as Contact whereas the XML output contains <Contacts> node as the root node. To properly map the <Contacts> element back to the class, the Contact class is decorated with an XmlRoot attribute that specifies the name to be used for deserialization purposes. This ensures proper mapping between the SQL Server data and the Contact class.

❑ There is an element named <ContactID> in the XML output whereas the same element is declared as ID in the Contact class declaration. The deserialization code handles this using the XmlAttributeOverrides class that enables you to override an element name at runtime. This is shown in Listing 12-14.

❑ There is an element named <EMailAddress> in the XML output, and the Customer class does not have a corresponding field to hold that value. Listing 12-14 handles this situation by wiring up an UnknownElement event handler with the XmlSerializer object.

Now that you have an understanding of the features to implement, take a look at Listing 12-15.

Listing 12-15: Mapping Contacts Data in AdventureWorks Database with the Contact Object

```
<%@ Page Language="C#" %>
<%@ Import Namespace="System.Collections" %>
<%@ Import Namespace="System.Web.Configuration" %>
<%@ Import Namespace="System.Data.SqlClient" %>
<%@ Import Namespace="System.IO" %>
<%@ Import Namespace="System.Xml" %>
<%@ Import Namespace="System.Xml.Serialization" %>
<script runat="server">
  void Page_Load(object sender, System.EventArgs e)
  {
    Contact cont;
    //Rename the ContactID to ID element and add it as an attribute
    XmlElementAttribute contIDElement = new XmlElementAttribute();
    contIDElement.ElementName = "ContactID";
    XmlAttributes attributesIdCol = new XmlAttributes();
    attributesIdCol.XmlElements.Add(contIDElement);
    XmlAttributeOverrides attrOverrides = new XmlAttributeOverrides();
    attrOverrides.Add(typeof(Contact), "ID", attributesIdCol);
    string connString =
      WebConfigurationManager.ConnectionStrings["adventureWorks"].
      ConnectionString;
    SqlConnection sqlConn = new SqlConnection(connString);
    sqlConn.Open();
    //Instantiate the SqlCommand object and pass the query to be executed
    SqlCommand sqlCommand = new SqlCommand("Select ContactID," +
      "FirstName, MiddleName, LastName, EMailAddress from Person.Contact " +
      "as Contacts where ContactID = 2 for xml auto, elements", sqlConn);
    XmlReader reader = sqlCommand.ExecuteXmlReader();
    XmlSerializer serializer = new XmlSerializer(typeof(Contact),
      attrOverrides);
    serializer.UnknownElement += new
      XmlElementEventHandler(XmlSerializer_UnknownElement);
```

```
      if (serializer.CanDeserialize(reader))
      {
        cont = (Contact)serializer.Deserialize(reader);
        Response.Write("<b>Result of Deserialization:" + "</b><br>");
        Response.Write("ID: " + cont.ID + "<br>");
        Response.Write("First Name: " + cont.FirstName + "<br>");
        Response.Write("Middle Name: " + cont.MiddleName + "<br>");
        Response.Write("Last Name: " + cont.LastName + "<br>");
      }
      else
        Response.Write("Cannot serialize data");
    }

    void XmlSerializer_UnknownElement(object sender, XmlElementEventArgs e)
    {
      Response.Write("<b>Unknown Element:" + "</b><br>");
      Response.Write("Unknown Element Name: " + e.Element.Name + "<br>");
      Response.Write("Unknown Element Value: " + e.Element.InnerText +
        "<br><br>");
    }
</script>
<html xmlns="http://www.w3.org/1999/xhtml" >
<head runat="server">
  <title>
    Mapping Contacts Data in AdventureWorks Database with the Customer
      Object
  </title>
</head>
<body>
  <form id="form1" runat="server">
    <div>
    </div>
  </form>
</body>
</html>
```

Before examining the code in details, the output produced by Listing 12-14 is shown in Figure 12-4.

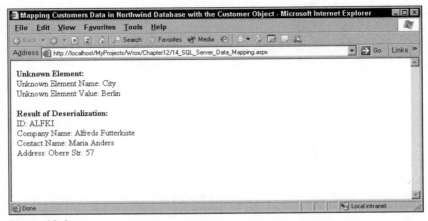

Figure 12-4

Listing 12-14 starts by mapping the `<ContactID>` element in the XML output to the ID field in the `Contact` class through the `XmlAttributeOverrides` class. After that, it executes the sql query and retrieves the XML output of the query onto an `XmlReader` object. This `XmlReader` object is supplied as an input to the `Deserialize()` method. Before invoking the `Deserialize()` method, the code also sets up an event handler to handle the `UnknownElement` event that will be raised when the serializer encounters an unexpected node in the input XML.

Generics and XML Serialization

With the release of .NET Framework 2.0, the CLR gets a huge addition in expressive power in that Generic types get added with full support in the runtime. XML serialization has been extended to support generic types for serialization and deserialization.

What Are Generics?

Generics are used to help make the code in your software components much more reusable. They are a type of data structure that contains code that remains the same; however, the data type of the parameters can change with each use. Additionally, the usage within the data structure adapts to the different data type of the passed variables. In summary, a generic is a code template that can be applied to use the same code repeatedly. Each time the generic is used, it can be customized for different data types without needing to rewrite any of the internal code. Generics also allow you to avoid the messy and intensive conversions from reference types to native types. Additionally, you can create routines that are much more type-safe.

A generic is defined using a slightly different notation. The following is the basic code for a generic named `Compare` that can compare two items of the same type and return the larger or smaller value, depending on which method is called:

```
public class Compare<ItemType, ItemType>

{
  public ItemType ReturnLarger(ItemType data, ItemType data2)
  {
    // logic...
  }
}
```

This generic could be used with any data type, ranging from basic data types such as integers to complex classes and structures. When you use the generic, you identify what data type you are using with it. For example, to use an integer with the previous `Compare` generic, you would write code similar to the following:

```
Compare<int, int> compare = new Compare<int, int>;
int result = compare.ReturnLarger(3, 5);
```

Because of the built-in support for generics, you can take advantage of XML serialization to serialize and deserialize particular specializations of the generics type by using the following code.

```
XmlSerializer serializer = new XmlSerializer
  (typeof(NameValue<int, string>));
```

Before looking at the code required to serialize or deserialize a generic type, Listing 12-16 examines the code of the generic type.

Listing 12-16: NameValue Class

```
using System;
using System.Collections;
using System.Xml.Serialization;

[XmlRoot("NameValuePair")]
public class NameValue<KeyType, ValueType>
{
  private KeyType _key;
  private ValueType _value;
  public NameValue()
  {
  }

  public ValueType Value
  {
    get
    {
      return _value;
    }
    set
    {
      _value = value;
    }
  }

  public KeyType Key
  {
    get
    {
      return _key;
    }
    set
    {
      _key = value;
    }
  }
}
```

In this code, you declare a class named NameValue that accepts two runtime types — one for the key element, and another one for the value element. As part of the class declaration, there is also an XmlRoot attribute that ensures the root element of the XML document is named as NameValuePair. The code then contains two public properties named Value and Key that simply set or get values from the private variables _value and _key respectively. Now that you understand the implementation of the NameValue class, Listing 12-17 discusses the code required to serialize or deserialize the NameValue class using XML serialization.

Listing 12-17: Performing Serialization and Deserialization with Generics

```
<%@ Page Language="C#" %>
<%@ Import Namespace="System.IO" %>
<%@ Import Namespace="System.Xml.Serialization" %>
<script runat="server">
  private string _xmlFilePath = @"C:\Data\NameValue.xml";
  void Serialize(object sender, EventArgs e)
  {
    NameValue<int, string> nameVal = new NameValue<int, string>();
    nameVal.Key = 1;
    nameVal.Value = "Manufacturing";
    XmlSerializer serializer = new XmlSerializer
      (typeof(NameValue<int, string>));
    TextWriter writer = new StreamWriter(_xmlFilePath);
    //Serialize the NameValue object and close the TextWriter
    serializer.Serialize(writer, nameVal);
    writer.Close();
    lblResult.Text = "File written successfully";
  }

  void Deserialize(object sender, EventArgs e)
  {
    XmlSerializer serializer = new XmlSerializer
      (typeof(NameValue<int, string>));
    TextReader reader = new StreamReader(_xmlFilePath);
    //Deserialize the Category and close the TextReader
    NameValue<int, string> nameVal = (NameValue<int, string>)
      serializer.Deserialize(reader);
    reader.Close();
    lblResult.Text = "Key : " + nameVal.Key + "<br>";
    lblResult.Text += "Value: " + nameVal.Value;
  }
</script>
<html xmlns="http://www.w3.org/1999/xhtml" >
<head runat="server">
  <title>Using Generics for Serialization and Deserialization</title>
</head>
<body>
  <form id="form1" runat="server">
    <div>
      <asp:Button runat="Server" ID="btnSerialize"
        OnClick="Serialize" Text="Serialize" />
      <asp:Button runat="Server" ID="btnDeserialize"
        OnClick="Deserialize" Text="Deserialize" />
      <br/><br/>
      <asp:Label runat="Server" ID="lblResult" Height="21px" Width="351px"/>
    </div>
  </form>
</body>
</html>
```

Listing 12-17 contains two methods named `Serialize()` and `Deserialize()`. The `Serialize()` method starts by declaring a `NameValue` object with the type parameters set to `int` and `string`, respectively.

```
NameValue<int, string> nameVal = new NameValue<int, string>();
```

The code then invokes the `Key` and `Value` properties of the `NameValue` object and sets its values appropriately.

```
nameVal.Key = 1;
nameVal.Value = "Manufacturing";
```

You supply the `NameValue` object as a parameter to the constructor of the `XmlSerializer` object, indicating the typed parameters.

```
XmlSerializer serializer = new XmlSerializer
   (typeof(NameValue<int, string>));
```

That's all there is to serializing a generic type. The rest of the code is similar to the previous code examples. The `Deserialize()` method also works along the same lines passing in the typed parameters to the constructor of the `XmlSerializer` and then finally invoking the `Deserialize()` method to deserialize the XML data into an instance of the `NameValue` object.

Serializing Generics Collections

In addition to creating simple generic types, you can also create strongly typed generic collections that provide better type safety and performance than non-generic strongly typed collections. The `System .Collections.Generic` namespace contains a number of interfaces and classes that allow you to define generic collections. Consider the following code to understand how to create a strongly typed categories collection object using the `List` class.

```
List<Category> list = new List<Category>();
```

Serializing this collection is simple and straightforward. All you need to do is to pass in the type of the collection to the constructor of the `XmlSerializer` class.

```
XmlSerializer serializer = new XmlSerializer(typeof(List<Category>));
```

After you indicate the type of the collection, you can simply invoke the `Serialize()` method to serialize the contents of the `List` collection object onto an XML file indicated through the `TextWriter` object.

```
serializer.Serialize(writer, list);
```

Output produced by serializing the strongly typed category collection object is shown in Figure 12-5.

By overriding the attribute overrides, it is also possible to rename the root XML element name `"ArrayOfCategory"` to a different value.

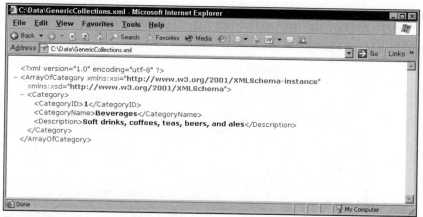

Figure 12-5

Pregenerating Serialization Assemblies

The XML serializer is a powerful tool that can transform a fair number of .NET Framework classes into portable XML code. The key thing to note is that the serializer behaves similar to a compiler. It first imports type information from the class and then serializes it to the output stream. It also works the other way around. The serializer reads XML data and maps elements to the target class members. Because each of these classes is unique in certain way, it is impossible for a generic tool to work efficiently on all possible classes. That's why when you try to serialize a type for the first time, there can be an unexpected performance hit that can have a negative impact on your application.

Now with .NET Framework 2.0, there is a new tool named XML Serializer Generator (Sgen.exe) that allows you to pregenerate those assemblies and deploy them along with your application. The XML Serializer Generator creates an XML serialization assembly for types in a specified assembly that can go a long way in improving the startup performance of an XmlSerializer.

> By default (without using the XML Serializer Generator), an XmlSerializer generates serialization code and a serialization assembly for each type every time an application is run. To avoid this performance hit, it is recommended that you use the Sgen.exe tool to generate those assemblies in advance. The SGen.exe generates serialization code for all the types contained in the assembly or executable specified by file name.

You can find the sgen.exe in the following path.

```
<Drive Name>:\Program Files\Microsoft Visual Studio 8\SDK\v2.0\Bin
```

Navigate to the above path in the command prompt and enter the following command.

```
sgen.exe <Name of the Assembly that contains the types to be serialized>
```

If the assembly containing the type to serialize is named `SerializationAssembly.dll`, the associated serialization assembly will be named `SerializationAssembly.XmlSerializers.dll`. Output produced by the serializer generator is shown in Figure 12-6.

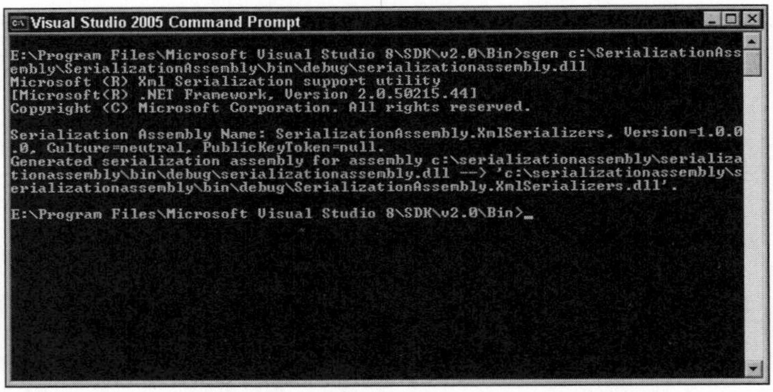

Figure 12-6

For more options on using sgen, type in `sgen /?` from the command prompt.

After the assembly is generated, you can simply deploy it in the bin directory of the application so that the CLR can automatically locate the assembly and use it at runtime.

Handling Exceptions

The `XmlSerializer` throws exceptions to indicate all sorts of problems. In most cases, the `Serialize()` or `Deserialize()` methods will throw a `System.InvalidOperationException`, which makes the `StackTrace` property useless because it does not offer any more insight into the root cause of the exception. To make matters worse, the exception's `Message` property only yields very generic information. For example, if you are trying to serialize an undeclared type for example, the `Serialize()` method would throw a `System.InvalidOperationException` with the following message: "There was an error generating the XML document."

This message is annoying, at best, because you already know that much when the exception is thrown and this does not provide any help when it comes to troubleshooting the problem. The trick to get to the real exception information about the problem is to examine the exception's `InnerException` property, which contains very detailed information about the problem and where it occurred.

> **The `InnerException`'s message is usually descriptive and provides everything you need to know the about the exception. It not only pinpoints the problem but in some cases it also offers a possible solution.**

Listing 12-18 demonstrates how to set up the exception handler and how to access the `InnerException` property.

Listing 12-18: Handling Exceptions Generated by XmlSerializer

```
void Page_Load(object sender, EventArgs e)
{
  try
  {
    string xmlFilePath = @"C:\Data\Collections.xml";
    List<Category> list = new List<Category>();
    Category categoryObj = new Category();
    categoryObj.CategoryID = 1;
    categoryObj.CategoryName = "Beverages";
    list.Add(categoryObj);
    XmlSerializer serializer = new XmlSerializer(typeof(List<Category>));
    TextWriter writer = new StreamWriter(xmlFilePath);
    serializer.Serialize(writer, list, namespaces);
    writer.Close();
    Response.Write("File written successfully");
  }
  catch (Exception ex)
  {
    if (ex.InnerException != null)
      ProcessException(ex.InnerException);
  }
}
void ProcessException(Exception ex)
{
  Response.Write("Exception : " + ex.Message);
}
```

In this listing, the exception generated during serialization is handled using the try.catch block. Within the catch block, you examine the `InnerException` property of the `Exception` object to check if it contains a valid reference to the `Exception` object. If it does, you pass that exception reference to another private method named `ProcessException()`, wherein you display the exception message onto the browser.

Summary

This chapter provided insight into how to use the serialization and deserialization features of the .NET Framework to construct representations of objects that can be transported in a portable manner. XML serialization is one of the major new components of .NET and it's used heavily throughout the Framework. The `XmlSerializer` class allows you to easily serialize and deserialize classes, arrays, and hierarchical data structures built from linked objects. The XML serialization is simple and is relatively easy to understand. The XML serialization mechanisms are convenient and quick and can also be tailored by applying the various XML attribute classes. For example, by placing attributes on an object's public variables and property procedures, a program can map values into XML attributes and change their names. Also with the addition of new features such as generics support, ability to pregenerate serialization assemblies, XML serialization definitely deserves a serious consideration whenever XML transport mechanism is required between two object-oriented systems.

13

XML Web Services

Web services are objects and methods that can be invoked from any client over HTTP. Web services are built on the Simple Object Access Protocol (SOAP). Unlike the Distributed Component Object Model (DCOM) and Common Object Request Broker Architecture (CORBA), SOAP enables messaging over HTTP on port 80 (for most Web servers) and uses a standard means of describing data. SOAP makes it possible to send data and structure easily over the Web. Web services capitalize on this protocol to implement object and method messaging. Web services function primarily through XML in order to pass information back and forth through the Hypertext Transfer Protocol (HTTP). Web services are a vital part of what the .NET Framework offers to programmers. In this chapter, you get a thorough understanding of the XML Web service by discussing XML Web services created using .NET Framework 2.0. After the initial discussion, this chapter goes on to discuss advanced Web service concepts such as SOAP headers, SOAP extensions, XML serialization customization, schema importer extensions, asynchronous Web service methods, and asynchronous invocation of Web methods.

By the end of this chapter, you will have a good understanding of the following:

- ❑ XML Web service
- ❑ How to build an ASP.NET XML Web service
- ❑ Creating a `Proxy` class for the Web service
- ❑ How to return complex types from a Web service
- ❑ How to utilize SOAP headers
- ❑ How to create SOAP extensions and use that with a Web Service Method
- ❑ How to asynchronously invoke a Web service from an ASP.NET page
- ❑ How to asynchronously invoke a Web service from IE browser
- ❑ How to control XML serialization of custom types using `IXmlSerializable`
- ❑ How to use Schema Importer extensions

XML Web Service

XML Web service in ASP.NET is a new model of exposing application logic. The entire .NET Framework has been built around the Web services concept, and there are a number of tools and hidden functionality that make it quite simple to build and consume XML Web services in .NET.

> **One way to think of an XML Web service is that when you use a Web service, you are calling a function over Hyper Text Transfer Protocol (HTTP) or by a URL. This model of Web services is quite different from what was available in the past, but similar to some models that you are already familiar with. For example, the classic Active Server Pages model was based upon the client/server technologies. The client made a request over the Internet or HTTP; and the response, if there was one, was sent back by the same means. On the receiving end of the request, application logic or registration was applied and, in most cases, a response was sent back.**

Working with XML Web services basically follows the same model as that of a regular ASP.NET page, except that you are not using ASP.NET to build an interface to activate requests and receive responses over HTTP. There are many situations where you might want to expose the logic or information in a database, but you might not want to build a visual interface to that logic or information. Look at an example of this situation. Say that you are a large wholesaler of a wide variety of widgets, and you have a number of customers that depend upon your current inventory status to allow their customers to place appropriate orders. The entire widget inventory is stored in a SQL Server database, and you want to give your customers access to this database. You could build a Web interface to this database in ASP.NET that would enable a client to log onto your system and gather the information that it needs. What if the customer doesn't want that, but instead wants to put this information in its own Web site or extranet for its own customers? This is where you can expose your widget information by providing it as an XML Web service. Doing this enables the end user to utilize this information in whatever fashion it chooses. Now within its own Web page, the customer can make a call to your XML Web service and get the information in an XML format to use as it sees fit. So instead of building separate Web interfaces for different clients to access this data, you can just provide the application logic to the end users and let them deal with it in their own way.

It is true there are component technologies, already available for some time, that perform similar functions; however, these technologies, such as Distributed Component Object Model (DCOM), Remote Method Invocation (RMI), Common Object Request Broker Architecture (CORBA), and Internet Inter-ORB Protocol (IIOP) are accessed via object-model–specific protocols. The main difference between XML Web services and these component technologies is that XML Web services are accessed via standard Internet protocols such as HTTP and XML. This enables these services to be called across multiple platforms, regardless of the platform compatibility of the calling system.

The outstanding thing about using XML Web services is that it does not matter what system the end user employs to make this request. This is not a Microsoft-proprietary message format that is being sent to the end user. Instead, everything is being sent over standard protocols. What is happening is that this message is being sent over HTTP using SOAP, a flavor of XML. So any system that is able to consume XML over HTTP can use this model.

Building an ASP.NET Web Service

A Web service is an ordinary class with public and protected methods. The `WebService` class is normally placed in a source file that is saved with an `.asmx` extension. Web service files must contain the

@ WebService directive that informs the ASP.NET runtime about the nature of the file, the language in use throughout, and the main class that implements the service, as shown here:

```
<%@ WebService Language="C#" Class="MyWebService" %>
```

The Language attribute can be set to C#, VB, or JS. The main class must match the name declared in the Class attribute and must be public. A complete Web service example is shown in Listing 13-1.

Listing 13-1: A Simple Web Service

```csharp
<%@ WebService Language="C#" Class="MyWebService"%>
using System.Web;
using System.Web.Services;
using System.Web.Services.Protocols;

[WebService(Name="My Web Service", Description="Sample Web Service",
  Namespace="http://www.wrox.com/books/ProASPNETXML")]
[WebServiceBinding(ConformsTo = WsiProfiles.BasicProfile1_1)]
public class MyWebService: System.Web.Services.WebService
{
  public MyWebService()
  {
  }

  [WebMethod(CacheDuration=60,Description="Returns a simple string",
    EnableSession=false)]
  public string HelloWorld()
  {
    return "Hello World";
  }
}
```

Indicating the base class for a .NET Framework Web service is not mandatory. A Web service can also be architected starting from the ground up using a new class. Inheriting the behavior of the WebService class has some advantages, however. A Web service based on the System.Web.Services.WebService class has direct access to common ASP.NET objects, including Application, Request, Cache, Session, and Server. These objects are packed into an HttpContext object, which also includes the time when the request was made. If you do not have any need to access the ASP.NET object model, you can do without the WebService class and simply implement the Web service as a class with public methods. With the WebService base class, however, a Web service also has access to the ASP.NET User object in the server side, which can be used to verify the credentials of the current user executing the method.

> Similar to ASP.NET pages, you can also have code-behind for AS.NET Web services as well. To this end, you just add the CodeBehind attribute to the WebService attribute.
>
> CodeBehind="~/App_Code/MyWebService.cs"
>
> The CodeBehind specifies the source file that contains the class implementing the Web service when the class is neither located in the same file nor resident in a separate assembly. And then create the MyWebService.cs file to the appropriate location (in this case, the App_Code directory). Throughout this chapter, you create Web services that have the actual class embedded inside a separate code behind.

The `Class` attribute is normally set to a class residing in the same file as the @ `WebService` directive, but nothing prevents you from specifying a class within a separate assembly. In such cases, the entire Web service file consists of a single line of code:

```
<%@ WebService Language="C#" Class="MyAssembly.MyWebService" %>
```

The actual implementation is contained in the specified class, and the assembly that contains the class must be placed in the bin subdirectory of the virtual folder where the Web service resides. The @ `WebService` directive also supports another attribute named `Debug` that indicates whether the Web service should be compiled with debug symbols.

The next few sections go through each of the attributes discussed in Listing 13-1.

The WebService Attribute

The `WebService` attribute is optional and does not affect the activity of the `WebService` class in terms of what is published and executed. The `WebService` attribute is represented by an instance of the `WebServiceAttribute` class and enables you to change three default settings for the Web service: the namespace, the name, and the description.

The syntax for configuring the `WebService` attribute is declarative and somewhat self-explanatory. Within the body of the `WebService` attribute, you simply insert a comma-separated list of names and values, as shown in the following code. The keyword `Description` identifies the description of the Web service, whereas `Name` points to the official name of the Web service.

```
[WebService(Name="My Web Service", Description="Sample Web Service",
  Namespace="http://www.wrox.com/books/ProASPNETXML")]
public class MyWebService : WebService
{
//Add the code here
}
```

Changing the name and description of the Web service is mostly a matter of consistency. The .NET Framework assumes that the name of the implementing class is also the name of the Web service; no default description is provided. The `Name` attribute is used to identify the service in the WSDL text that explains the behavior of the service to prospective clients. The description is not used in the companion WSDL text; it is retrieved and displayed by the IIS default page only for URLs with an `.asmx` extension.

Each Web service should have a unique namespace that makes it clearly distinguishable from other services. By default, the .NET Framework gives each new Web service the same default namespace: `http://tempuri.org`. This namespace comes with the strong recommendation to change it as soon as possible and certainly prior to publishing the service on the Web. Using a temporary name does not affect the overall functionality, but it will affect consistency and violate Web service naming conventions. Although most namespace names out there look like URLs, you don't need to use real URLs. A name that you're reasonably certain is unique will suffice.

The only way to change the default namespace of a .NET Framework Web service is by setting the Namespace property of the WebService attribute, as shown in following code.

```
[WebService(Name="My Web Service", Description="Sample Web Service",
   Namespace="http://www.wrox.com/books/ProASPNETXML")]
   public class MyWebService : WebService
```

This example uses a namespace named "http://www.wrox.com.books/ProASPNETXML" for the MyWebService.

The WebServiceBinding Attribute

With the .NET 1.x release, you can build services that conform to the Basic Profile today by following the guidance in Building Interoperable Web Services; however .NET 2.0 makes it even easier to build Web services that conform to the Basic Profile 1.0. To accomplish this, you need to add the WebServiceBinding attribute that allows you to build a WS-I Basic Profile conformant Web service. Setting WebServiceBinding.ConformsTo to WsiProfiles.BasicProfile1_1 makes the SOAP 1.1 port exposed by this service conforms to the WS-I Basic Profile 1. As you can see from the following code, by default, new Web services created by Visual Studio are Basic Profile conformant.

```
[WebServiceBinding(ConformsTo = WsiProfiles.BasicProfile1_1)]
```

Note that there are some important service features that would break Basic Profile conformance and would cause an exception when you invoke the Web service or request its WSDL. For example, if you use SOAP encoding (by using SoapRpcService or SoapRpcMethod attributes), your service no longer conforms to the Basic Profile. To use these non-conforming features, you simply need to indicate that your service does not conform to the Basic Profile by setting the WebServiceBindingAttribute.ConformsTo property to WsiProfiles.None.

When consuming any Web service, wsdl.exe will check the service's WSDL for Basic Profile conformance and will display warnings if it finds the service to be non-conformant. These warnings let you know upfront any conformance issues with the service's WSDL without preventing you from consuming the service.

The WebMethod Attribute

Unlike the .NET Framework remoting classes, the public methods of a Web service class are not automatically exposed to the public. To be effectively exposed over the Web, a Web service method requires a special attribute in addition to being declared as public. Only methods marked with the WebMethod attribute gain the level of visibility sufficient to make them available over the Web.

In practice, the WebMethod attribute represents a member modifier similar to public, protected, or internal. Only public methods are affected by WebMethod, and the attribute is effective only to callers invoking the class over the Web. This characteristic increases the overall flexibility of the class design. A software component allowed to instantiate the Web service class sees all the public methods and does not necessarily recognize the service as a Web service; however, when the same component is invoked as part of a Web service, the IIS and ASP.NET infrastructure ensure that external callers can see only methods marked with the WebMethod attribute. Any attempt to invoke untagged methods via a URL results in a failure. The WebMethod attribute features several properties that you can use to adjust the behavior of the method. Table 13-1 lists the properties.

Table 13-1. Properties of the WebMethod Attribute

Property	Description
BufferResponse	Indicates that the IIS runtime should buffer the method's entire response before sending it to the client. This property is set to true, by default. Even if set to `false`, the response is partially buffered; however, in this case, the size of the buffer is limited to 16 KB.
CacheDuration	Specifies the number of seconds that the IIS runtime should cache the response of the method. This information is useful when your Web method needs to handle several calls in a short period of time.
Description	Provides the description for the method. The value of the property is then embedded into the WSDL description of the service.
EnableSession	This property makes available the Session object of the ASP.NET environment to the Web method. Depending on how Session is configured, using this property might require cookie support on the client or a Microsoft SQL Server support on the server.
MessageName	Allows you to provide a publicly callable name for the method. You can use this property to give distinct names to overloaded methods in the event that you use the same class as part of the middle tier and a Web service.
TransactionOption	Specifies the level of transactional support you want for the method. A Web service method can have only two behaviors, regardless of the value assigned to the standard `TransactionOption` enumeration you select— either it does not require a transaction or it must be the root of a new transaction.

The following code snippet shows how to set a few method attributes:

```
[WebMethod(CacheDuration=60,Description="Returns a simple string",
   EnableSession=false)]
public string HelloWorld()
{
   return "Hello World";
}
```

This code sets the `CacheDuration`, `Description`, and `EnableSession` attributes of the `WebMethodAttribute` class.

Creating a Proxy Class for the Web Service

After you have created the Web service, the next step is for the clients to access the Web service and invoke its methods. To accomplish this, you need to create a proxy class that acts as an intermediary between the Web service and the client. After the proxy is created and referenced from the client application, whenever the client invokes any of the Web methods, it is the proxy class that receives all of the requests. The proxy is responsible for communicating with the Web service over the network by processing the SOAP messages sent to and from the XML Web service. There are two ways you can create a proxy class for the Web Service.

❑ Using the WSDL utility

❑ Using the Add Web Reference option in Visual Studio

Each of these methods is covered in the following sections.

Using the WSDL Utility to Generate Proxy Code

The ASP.NET page framework provides a set of classes and tools that greatly simplifies interacting with a Web service. The set of classes provides a base set of functionality for creating Web service proxies. One of the tools is a utility called WSDL.exe that consumes the WSDL for a Web service and then automatically generates proxy code for you.

> WSDL.exe *ships with the .NET Framework. You can use it to create a strongly typed proxy for accessing the targeted Web service. Just as ASP.NET will map a large number of .NET data types to their XML counterparts,* WSDL.exe *will map XML data types described within the Web service's WSDL document to their .NET equivalents.*

To create a proxy for a Web service located at http://localhost/MyProjects/Wrox/Chapter13/WebService/MyWebService.asmx, use the following command from the .NET Framework SDK command prompt.

```
WSDL http://localhost/MyProjects/Wrox/Chapter13/WebService/MyWebService.asmx?wsdl
```

The command will parse the WSDL document and generate MyWebService.cs, which contains C# code you can compile to form a strongly typed .NET MyWebService proxy class that exposes the functionality of the MyWebService. By default, WSDL.exe will generate C# code that targets the SOAP implementation of the Web service interface.

Similar to ASP.NET Web services, WSDL.exe can create proxies only for the HTTP protocol; however, WSDL.exe-generated proxies can use one of three bindings: SOAP, HTTP GET, or HTTP POST. You can use optional command line parameters to set the type of binding as well as other configurations such as the language in which the auto-generated code will be written. Table 13-2 lists the command line switches that you can specify when you use WSDL.exe to generate a proxy for a Web service.

Table 13-2. Command Line Switches for WSDL.exe

Switch	Description
/<url or path>	Specifies the URL or path to a WSDL contract, an XSD schema, or .discomap document.
/nologo	Suppresses the banner containing the version and copyright information.
/language:[CS | VB | JS] or /l:[CS | VB | JS]	Specifies the language in which the proxy code should be generated. The default is CS.
/sharetypes	Turns on type sharing feature. This new feature allows you to create one code file with a single type definition for identical types shared between different services.

Table continued on following page

Table 13-2. *(continued)*

Switch	Description
/verbose or /v	Displays extra information when the /sharetypes switch is specified.
/fields or /f	Specifies that fields should be generated instead of properties.
/order	Generates explicit order identifiers on particle members.
/enableDataBinding or /edb	Implements INotifyPropertyChanged interface on all generated types to enable data binding.
/namespace:[namespace] or /n:[namespace]	Specifies the .NET namespace in which the proxy code will reside.
/out:[filename] or /o:[filename]	Specifies the name of the file that will contain the generated code.
/protocol:[SOAP | HttpPost | HttpGet]	Specifies the binding the generated proxy code should target. The default is SOAP.
/username:[username] or /u:[username] /password:[password] or /p:[password] /domain:[domain] or /d:[domain]	Specifies the credentials that should be passed when connecting to a Web server that requires authentication. The supported authentication types include Basic Authentication and Windows NT Challenge/ Response.
/proxy:[url]	The URL of the proxy server. The default is to use the settings defined within the system's Internet Options.
/proxyusername:[username] or /pu:[username] /proxypassword:[password] or /pp:[password] /proxydomain:[domain] or /pd:[domain]	Specifies the credentials that should be used to log into the proxy server. The supported authentication types include Basic Authentication and Windows NT Challenge/ Response.
/appsettingurlkey:[key] or /urlkey:[key]	Generates code that sets the URL property of the proxy object to the value of the application setting with the specified key in the configuration file. If the application setting is not found, the value will be set to the URL that was originally targeted by WSDL.exe.
/appsettingbaseurl:[url] or /baseurl:[url]	Generates code that sets the URL property of the proxy object to the concatenation of the specified URL and the value of the application setting specified by the /appsettingurlkey switch.
/parsableerrors	Prints errors in a format similar to those reported by compilers.
/serverinterface	Generates an abstract class for an XML Web service implementation using ASP.NET based on the contracts.

If you use WSDL.exe to generate proxy code that will be deployed to production, you will most likely end up using at least the following command line parameters to generate the proxy:

❑ /language—The proxy code should be created using the programming language standardized for the project

❑ /namespace—The proxy classes should reside within a namespace to prevent collisions with other data type definitions

❑ /appsettingurlkey—The target URL for the Web service should be stored in the configuration file and not hard coded within the proxy. If the Web service is relocated, you do not need to recompile your code

Using the Add Web Reference Option in Visual Studio

If you do not want to go through the complexities of using a command prompt to create a proxy class, you will be glad to know that the functionality of WSDL.exe is integrated within Visual Studio itself. The Add Web Reference option in Visual Studio internally uses WSDL.exe to create proxies. To add a Web reference using Visual Studio, follow these steps:

1. On the Web site menu, choose Add Web Reference.

2. In the URL box of the Add Web Reference dialog box, type the URL to obtain the service description of the XML Web service you want to access, such as http://localhost/MyProjects/Wrox/Chapter13/WebService/MyWebService.asmx. Then click the Go button to retrieve information about the XML Web service. This is shown in Figure 13-1. If the XML Web service exists on the local machine, click the Web services on the local machine link in the browser pane; then click the link for the MyWebService from the list provided to retrieve information about the XML Web service.

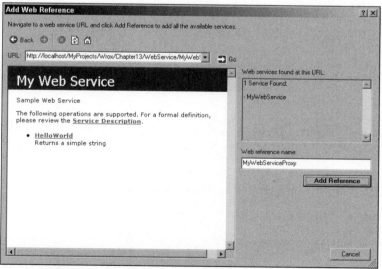

Figure 13-1

3. In the Web reference name box, rename the Web reference to `MyWebServiceProxy`, which is the namespace you will use for this Web reference.

4. Click Add Reference to add a Web reference for the target XML Web service.

Visual Studio downloads the service description and generates a proxy class to interface between your application and the XML Web service.

> Note that the Add Web Reference wizard is not as configurable as `WSDL.exe`. If you are looking for finer level of control over the proxy generation process, you will find the `WSDL.exe` utility very helpful.

As a result of adding Web reference, Visual Studio automatically stores the location of the Web service in the `web.config` file as follows:

```
<add key="MyWebServieProxy.MyWebService"
    value="http://localhost/MyProjects/Wrox/Chapter13/WebService/
    MyWebService.asmx"/>
```

By storing the configuration settings in the web.config file, you can react to the change in Web service URL by simply changing the location in web.config without having to change any code.

Returning Complex Types

So far, you have seen a simple HelloWorld Web service that returns a simple string value. This section discusses how you can return more complex data types from a Web Service. Specifically, you look at how you can pass:

❑ A DataSet

❑ A `Custom` object

❑ An `XmlDocument` object

The ability to pass complex data types enables interesting scenarios. For example, by returning a DataSet from a Web service, you can use data binding and bind user interface elements to the DataSet. The `XmlSerializer` that is part of ASP.NET runtime is the core component that enables the serialization and deserialization of these complex types. To start with, let us look at how to return a DataSet object from a Web service.

Returning a DataSet Object from the Web Service

As you learned in Chapter 8, the DataSet object is an integral component of the ADO.NET architecture. A DataSet can either contain a single table or several tables. In addition, the DataSet is also capable of holding the relationship between tables. In that respect it is sort of a mini-database in memory. When serialized and transported, the DataSet is represented as XML. DataSets are powerful. You can bind user interface elements such as a data grid to a DataSet. A DataSet also keeps track of changes made to it so that you can have changes updated back in the database.

For the purposes of this example, you learn how to return the contents of the categories table in the Adventureworks database in the form of a DataSet object.

Listing 13-2: Categories Web Service That Returns a DataSet Object

```csharp
using System;
using System.Web.Configuration;
using System.Data;
using System.Data.SqlClient;
using System.Diagnostics;
using System.Web;
using System.Web.Services;
using System.Web.Services.Protocols;

[WebService(Namespace = "http://tempuri.org/")]
[WebServiceBinding(ConformsTo = WsiProfiles.BasicProfile1_1)]
public class CategoriesService : System.Web.Services.WebService
{
  public CategoriesService()
  {
  }

  [WebMethod]
  public DataSet GetCategoriesAsDataSet()
  {
    try
    {
      using (SqlConnection conn = new SqlConnection())
      {
        string connectionString = WebConfigurationManager.ConnectionStrings
          ["adventureWorks"].ConnectionString;
        conn.ConnectionString = connectionString;
        SqlCommand command = new SqlCommand("Select * from " +
          "Production.ProductCategory", conn);
        command.CommandType = CommandType.Text;
        SqlDataAdapter adapter = new SqlDataAdapter(command);
        DataSet categories = new DataSet("Categories");
        adapter.Fill(categories);
        return categories;
      }
    }
    catch (Exception ex)
    {
      EventLog.WriteEntry("Application", ex.Message);
      throw ex;
    }
  }
}
```

The GetCategoriesAsDataSet() method returns a DataSet. No special code is needed to return a DataSet. The XmlSerializer is able to serialize a DataSet into XML. Similar to the examples in previous chapters, the connection string is retrieved from the <connectionStrings> section of the web.config file.

```
<connectionStrings>
  <add name="adventureWorks"
    connectionString="server=localhost;integrated
    security=true;database=AdventureWorks;"/>
</connectionStrings>
```

When you are developing a Web service, you might need a quick and dirty way of testing the Web service without having to write a client application. Fortunately, ASP.NET provides a default test harness (that is customizable) for testing the Web service. For example, if you request the CategoriesService.asmx Web service from a browser, you will see the test harness shown in Figure 13-2 that allows you to test the Web service.

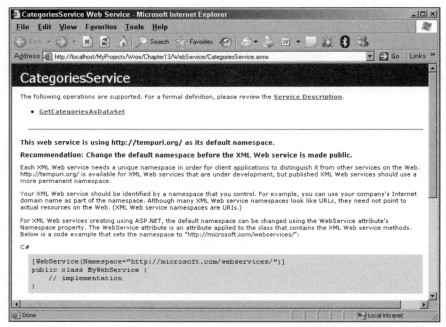

Figure 13-2

Note that the test harness uses HTTP GET to invoke the Web service.

Implementing Data Binding with the Output of a Web Service from an ASP.NET Page

One of the advantages of returning a DataSet object from a Web service is that you can grab the output of the Web service and directly bind that to a data bound control such as `GridView` control without writing a lot of code. Before invoking the Web service methods, remember to add reference to the Web service. For the purposes of this example, a proxy named `CategoriesProxy` that talks to the `CategoriesService` through the Add Web Reference menu option has already been created. Listing 13-3 illustrates how to call a Web service method and bind the result of the call to a `GridView` control.

Listing 13-3: Implementing Data Binding with the Output of a Web Service

```
<%@ Page Language="C#" %>
<script runat="server">
  void Page_Load(object sender, EventArgs e)
  {
    CategoriesProxy.CategoriesService obj = new
      CategoriesProxy.CategoriesService();
    output.DataSource = obj.GetCategoriesAsDataSet();
    output.DataBind();
  }
</script>
<html xmlns="http://www.w3.org/1999/xhtml" >
<head runat="server">
  <title>Performing Data Binding with the DataSet returned from a Web
    Service
  </title>
</head>
<body>
  <form id="form1" runat="server">
    <div>
      <asp:GridView runat="server" ID="output" />
    </div>
  </form>
</body>
</html>
```

As Listing 13-3 shows, invoking the Web service method is very simple and straightforward. All you need to do is create an instance of the proxy class and invoke the appropriate methods on the Web service.

```
CategoriesProxy.CategoriesService obj = new
  CategoriesProxy.CategoriesService();
```

Next, you call the `GetCategoriesAsDataSet()` method of the Web service and simply bind the results of the method to the `GridView` control.

```
output.DataSource = obj.GetCategoriesAsDataSet();
output.DataBind();
```

That's all there is to consuming the Web service method from an ASP.NET page. Requesting the page using the browser should result in an output similar to Figure 13-3.

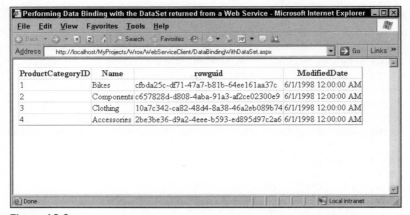

Figure 13-3

Figure 13-3 displays all the categories that are retrieved from the GetCategoriesAsDataSet() Web service method.

Returning a Custom Object from a Web Service

Similar to the DataSet, you can also return a custom class from a Web service method. The XML serializer built with ASP.NET runtime automatically handles the serialization and deserialization aspects of a custom class. Before discussing an example on how to return a custom class from a Web service, let us look at the declaration of the class itself. To this end, Listing 13-4 shows the declaration of a class named Address that will be used as the return value.

Listing 13-4: Declaration of Address Class

```
using System;
public class Address
{
  public string Street;
  public string City;
  public int ZIP;
  public string Country;
  // Default constructor needed by XmlSerializer
  public Address()
  {
  }
  public Address(string _Street, string _City, int _ZIP, string _Country)
  {
    this.Street = _Street;
    this.City = _City;
    this.ZIP = _ZIP;
    this.Country = _Country;
  }
}
```

The `Address` class exposes few public properties named `Street`, `City`, `Zip`, and `Country`. In addition to the default parameter-less constructor required by the XML serializer, it also provides another constructor that takes in values for the properties. Now that you understand the implementation of the `Address` class, look at the Web service method that uses the `Address` class. Listing 13-5 illustrates how a collection of `Address` objects can be returned from a Web service method in the form of an `ArrayList` object.

Listing 13-5: Returning Address Object from the Web Service

```
using System;
using System.Web;
using System.Collections;
using System.Web.Services;
using System.Web.Services.Protocols;
using System.Xml.Serialization;

[WebService(Namespace = "http://tempuri.org/")]
[WebServiceBinding(ConformsTo = WsiProfiles.BasicProfile1_1)]
public class CustomObjectService : System.Web.Services.WebService
{
  public CustomObjectService ()
  {
  }

  [WebMethodAttribute]
  [XmlInclude(typeof(Address))]
  public ArrayList GetArrayList()
  {
    ArrayList list = new ArrayList();
    Address add1 = new Address("900, N Rural Road", "Chandler", 85226, "US");
    Address add2 = new Address("2644, E Remington Place", "Chandler", 85249, "US");
    Address add3 = new Address("5000, W Chandler Blvd ", "Chandler", 85226, "US");
    list.Add(add1);
    list.Add(add2);
    list.Add(add3);
    return list;
  }
}
```

The `CustomObjectService` has only one method named `GetArrayList()` that returns an object of type `ArrayList`. The `ArrayList` object is made up of a collection of `Address` objects that are created on the fly. Now you are ready to consume the Web service, which is the topic of focus in the next section.

Implementing Data Binding with the Complex Object Returned from the Web Service

In the previous section, you learned how to bind a DataSet returned from a Web service to a `GridView` control. Although this was possible in earlier versions (such as .NET 1.x), the earlier versions did not provide a way to bind a collection of objects returned from a Web service to a data bound control. Now with the release of .NET Framework 2.0, this is no longer an issue. .NET Framework 2.0 enables this scenario by generating properties on client proxy types rather than fields making auto-generated proxy types suitable for data binding by default. Listing 13-6 illustrates the steps involved in accomplishing this.

Listing 13-6: Consuming the Custom Object Returned from the Web Service

```
<%@ Page Language="C#" %>
<script runat="server">
  void Page_Load(object sender, EventArgs e)
  {
    CustomObjectProxy.CustomObjectService obj = new
      CustomObjectProxy.CustomObjectService();
    output.DataSource = obj.GetArrayList();
    output.DataBind();
  }
</script>
<html xmlns="http://www.w3.org/1999/xhtml" >
<head runat="server">
  <title>Consuming the Custom object returned from a Web Service</title>
</head>
<body>
  <form id="form1" runat="server">
    <div>
      <asp:GridView runat="server" ID="output" />
    </div>
  </form>
</body>
</html>
```

If you see the return type of the GetArrayList() by looking at the generated proxy class, you notice that it is an array of type object. This object array is directly bound to the GridView control. The output produced by the page is shown in Figure 13-4.

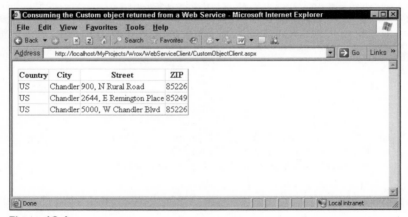

Figure 13-4

The ability to bind the collection output of a Web service is very powerful in that it not only enables interesting data binding scenarios but also makes the Web service client developers' life easy.

Handling and Throwing Exceptions in a Web Service

Exceptions can be thrown when an XML Web service is processing a request SOAP message or building a response SOAP message. When an exception is thrown in an XML Web service, the error message is sent back inside the SOAP <fault> message according to SOAP specifications. The SOAP <fault> XML element contains details such as the exception string and the source of the exception.

If a SoapException error is thrown by a Web method, the ASP.NET runtime will serialize the information into a SOAP fault message that will be sent back to the client. In order to throw a SOAP exception in your XML Web service, you first import the System.Web.Services.Protocols namespace. In your code that throws the SoapException, you must use the following structure and include at least some of the enclosed attributes.

```
throw new SoapException([message], [code], [actor], [detail]);
```

The SoapException class exposes a number of read-only properties to provide the exception information. Because the properties are read-only, the SoapException class has numerous overloaded constructors that enable the properties to be set. Table 13-3 lists the properties that can be set via an overloaded constructor.

Table 13-3. Properties of the SoapException Class

Property	Description
Actor	Gets the piece of the code that caused the exception and it represents the information contained in the <faultactor> element of the SOAP fault message. A possible value to use is Context.Request.Url.AbsoluteUri.
Code	Gets the type of the fault code that indicates the cause of the exception (client or server) and it represents the information contained in the <faultcode> element.
Detail	Gets an XmlNode that represents the specific application specific error information details and it this information is contained in the <faultdetail> element.
Message	Gets a message that describes the exception and it represents the information contained in the <faultstring> element.
Node	Gets a URI including the name of the Web service method that caused the exception.
SubCode	Gets the optional error information contained in the <subcode> XML element of a SOAP fault message. You can use this optional code to return user-defined error codes specific to the application.

> If an exception is thrown by the Web method that is not of type `SoapException`, the ASP.NET runtime will serialize it into the body of the SOAP `<fault>` element. The `faultcode` element will be set to Server, and the `faultstring` element will be set to the output of the `ToString()` method of the `Exception` object. The output usually contains the call stack and other information that would be useful for the Web service developer but not the client.

Listing 13-7 shows an example of how to raise a SOAP exception from a Web service.

Listing 13-7: Raising SOAP Exceptions from a Web Service

```
using System;
using System.Xml;
using System.Web;
using System.Collections;
using System.Web.Services;
using System.Web.Services.Protocols;

[WebService(Namespace = "http://wrox.com/quotes")]
[WebServiceBinding(ConformsTo = WsiProfiles.BasicProfile1_1)]
public class QuotesService : System.Web.Services.WebService
{
  [WebMethod(Description = "Returns real time quote for a given stock symbol")]
  public double GetStockPrice(string symbol)
  {
    double price = 0;
    switch (symbol.ToUpper())
    {
      case "INTC":
        price = 70.75;
        break;
      case "MSFT":
        price = 50;
        break;
      case "DELL":
        price = 42.25;
        break;
      default:
        throw new SoapException("Invalid Symbol", SoapException.ClientFaultCode,
          "http://wrox.com/quotes/GetStockPrice");
    }
    return price;
  }
}
```

Listing 13-7 exposes a Web method named `GetStockPrice()` that returns the real-time quote for a given stock symbol. If the supplied stock symbol is not present in the list, you throw a `SoapException` using the below statement.

```
throw new SoapException("Invalid Symbol", SoapException.ClientFaultCode,
  "http://localhost/MyProjects/Wrox/Chapter12/WebService/" +
  "QuotesService/GetStockPrice");
```

This results in a SOAP fault element being sent to the client. Now that you have seen the Web service implementation, examine the client code that shows how to handle the SoapException. Listing 13-8 shows the complete client code.

Listing 13-8: Handling SOAP Exceptions Raised from a Web Service

```
<%@ Page Language="C#" %>
<%@ Import Namespace="System.Web.Services.Protocols" %>
<script runat="server">
  void btnGetQuote_Click(object sender, EventArgs e)
  {
    try
    {
      QuotesProxy.QuotesService obj = new QuotesProxy.QuotesService();
      output.Text = obj.GetStockPrice(txtSymbol.Text).ToString();
    }
    catch (SoapException soapEx)
    {
      output.Text = "Actor: " + soapEx.Actor + "<br><br>";
      output.Text += "Code: " + soapEx.Code + "<br><br>";
      output.Text += "Message: " + soapEx.Message + "<br><br>";
      output.Text += "Node: " + soapEx.Node;
    }
    catch (Exception ex)
    {
      output.Text = "Exception is : " + ex.Message;
    }
  }
</script>
<html xmlns="http://www.w3.org/1999/xhtml" >
<head id="Head1" runat="server">
  <title>Handling Exceptions returned from a Web Service</title>
</head>
<body>
  <form id="form1" runat="server">
    <div>
      Enter Stock Symbol: <asp:TextBox runat="server" ID="txtSymbol" />
      <asp:Button Text="Get Quote" runat="server" ID="btnGetQuote"
        OnClick="btnGetQuote_Click" />
      <br /><br /><br />
      <asp:Label Font-Bold=true runat="server" ID="output" />
    </div>
  </form>
</body>
</html>
```

In the try.catch block, there is a separate catch block that specifically deals with SOAP exceptions.

```
catch (SoapException soapEx)
```

You then write out the values contained in the properties of the SoapException using a label control.

```
output.Text = "Actor: " + soapEx.Actor + "<br><br>";
output.Text += "Code: " + soapEx.Code + "<br><br>";
output.Text += "Message: " + soapEx.Message + "<br><br>";
output.Text += "Node: " + soapEx.Node;
```

Another catch block handles all the other exceptions generated during Web service execution.

Request the page using the browser and enter an invalid stock symbol, you should get an output shown in Figure 13-5.

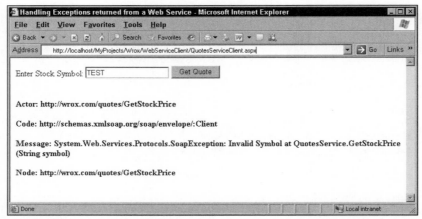

Figure 13-5

As you can see from Figure 13-5, the Web service method populates the SoapException object with the appropriate values.

Advantages of Using SoapException

There are a number of advantages to using SoapException class to convey the exception information back to the consumers of the Web service. They are as follows:

- ❑ Allows you to handle exceptional conditions in a consistent fashion

- ❑ Because its implementation is based on the SOAP specification, it allows the client applications to handle the exceptions in a standardized and consistent manner

- ❑ By explicitly raising the SoapException, you can communicate more information about the exception such as the reason for the exception, URL of the Web service method and so on using properties such as Actor, Code, Detail

- ❑ You can use the FaultCode enum to clearly convey the root cause for the exception: client or server

Using SOAP Headers

When you communicate with a Web service using SOAP, the SOAP message that is sent to the Web service follows a standard format. The XML document inside the SOAP message is structured into two main parts: the optional headers and the mandatory body. The `Body` element comprises the data specific to the message. The optional `Header` element can contain additional information not directly related to the particular message. Each child element of the `Header` element is called a SOAP header.

> SOAP headers are also a good place to put optional information, and a good means to supporting evolving interfaces. For example, imagine your bank allows you to manage multiple accounts with one ATM card. If you use your bank's ATM, you now have to specify if you want the withdrawal to be made from my primary, secondary, or tertiary account. If you use an ATM from another bank that isn't affiliated with you bank, you do not get asked that question. So the account identifier is clearly an optional parameter, with a reasonable default.

ASP.NET provides a mechanism for defining and processing SOAP headers. You can define a new SOAP header by deriving from the `SoapHeader` class. After you define a SOAP header, you can then associate the header with a particular endpoint within the Web service by using the `SoapHeader` attribute. Table 13-4 lists the properties exposed by the `SoapHeader` class.

Table 13-4. Properties of the SoapHeader Class

Property	Description
`Actor`	Indicates the intended recipient of the header.
`DidUnderstand`	Indicates whether a header whose `mustUnderstand` attribute is `true` was understood and processed by the recipient.
`EncodedMustUnderstand`	Indicates whether a header whose `mustUnderstand` attribute is `true` and whose value is encoded was understood and processed by the recipient. This property is used when communicating with the SOAP 1.1 version.
`EncodedMustUnderstand12`	Very similar to `EncodedMustUnderstand` except that it is used in conjunction with SOAP 1.2 version.
`MustUnderstand`	Indicates whether the header must be understood and processed by the recipient.
`Relay`	Indicates if the SOAP header is to be relayed to the next SOAP node if the current node does not understand the header.
`Role`	Indicates the recipient of the SOAP header.

By default, the name of the class derived from `SoapHeader` will become the name of the root header element, and any public fields or properties exposed by the class will define elements within the header. SOAP headers are defined by classes derived from the `SoapHeader` class. Elements within the header are defined by public fields or read/writable properties.

Implementing a SOAP Header Class

Imagine you want to modify the QuotesService used in the previous examples to accept a SOAP header that contains the payment information. Listing 13-9 illustrates the definition of the Payment header.

Listing 13-9: SOAP Header Declaration

```
using System;
using System.Xml;
using System.Xml.Serialization;
using System.Web.Services.Protocols;

public class SoapPaymentHeader : SoapHeader
{
  private string nameOnCard;
  private string creditCardNumber;
  private CardType creditCardType;
  private DateTime expirationDate;
  public string NameOnCard
  {
    get { return nameOnCard; }
    set { nameOnCard = value; }
  }
  public string CreditCardNumber
  {
    get { return creditCardNumber; }
    set { creditCardNumber = value; }
  }
  public CardType CreditCardType
  {
    get { return creditCardType; }
    set { creditCardType = value; }
  }
  public DateTime ExpirationDate
  {
    get { return expirationDate; }
    set { expirationDate = value; }
  }
}
```

The preceding class definition defines a SOAP header named `SoapPaymentHeader` with four child elements: `NameOnCard`, `CreditCardNumber`, `CreditCardType`, and `ExpirationDate`.

This code uses an enum named `CardType` that is declared as follows:

```
public enum CardType
{
  VISA,
  MASTERCARD,
  AMX,
  DISCOVER
}
```

After you define the headers, the next step is to associate them with the actual Web service method.

Processing the SOAP Header from a Web Service

The SoapHeader attribute is used to associate a SOAP header with a Web method. A public member variable is added to the `WebService` class to hold an instance of the class derived from the `SoapHeader` class. The name of the member variable is then communicated to the ASP.NET runtime via the SoapHeader attribute. Listing 13-10 shows the modified `QuotesService` class definition that is now capable of processing the `SoapPaymentHeader`.

Listing 13-10: Web Service Method That Processes the SOAP Header

```
using System;
using System.Xml;
using System.Web;
using System.Collections;
using System.Web.Services;
using System.Web.Services.Protocols;

[WebService(Namespace = "http://tempuri.org/")]
[WebServiceBinding(ConformsTo = WsiProfiles.BasicProfile1_1)]
public class QuotesService : System.Web.Services.WebService
{
  public SoapPaymentHeader paymentHeader;
  [WebMethod(Description = "Returns real time quote for a given stock ticker")]
  [SoapHeader("paymentHeader", Direction = SoapHeaderDirection.In)]
  public double GetStockPriceWithPayment(string symbol)
  {
    //Process the SOAP header
    if (paymentHeader != null)
    {
      string nameOnCard = paymentHeader.NameOnCard;
      string creditCardNumber = paymentHeader.CreditCardNumber;
      CardType type = paymentHeader.CreditCardType;
      DateTime ExpirationDate = paymentHeader.ExpirationDate;
      //Process the payment details
      //.........
      ///End Processing
    }
    else
      throw new SoapHeaderException("Invalid information in SOAP Header",
        SoapException.ClientFaultCode);
    double price;
```

```
      switch (symbol.ToUpper())
      {
        case "INTC":
          price = 70.75;
          break;
        case "MSFT":
          price = 50;
          break;
        case "DELL":
          price = 42.25;
          break;
        default:
          throw new SoapException("Invalid Symbol", SoapException.ClientFaultCode,
            "http://wrox.com/quotes/GetStockPriceWithPayment");
      }
      return price;
  }
}
```

Listing 13-10 declares a member variable named paymentHeader to hold the data contained in the payment SOAP header.

```
    public SoapPaymentHeader paymentHeader;
```

Note that you do not create an instance of the SoapPaymentHeader class because the ASP.NET runtime is responsible for creating this object and populating its properties with the data contained within the payment header received from the client.

Next, you add two SoapHeader attributes to declare that the headers should formally be described as part of the Web method. The constructor of the SoapHeader attribute takes a string that contains the name of the public member variable that should be associated with the SOAP header.

```
    [SoapHeader("paymentHeader", Direction = SoapHeaderDirection.In)]
```

You set the Direction property to SoapHeaderDirection.In. The Direction property indicates whether the client or the server is supposed to send the header. In this case, because the payment header is received from the client, you set the Direction property to SoapHeaderDirection.In. If a SOAP header is received from the client and then also sent back to the client, the value of the Direction property should be set to SoapHeaderDirection.InOut.

Next, the code processes the contents of the SOAP payment header. If the payment header information is not passed in, you throw a SoapHeaderException back to the callers.

```
    throw new SoapHeaderException("Invalid information in SOAP Header",
      SoapException.ClientFaultCode);
```

The rest of the implementation is similar to the previous example.

Now that you have associated the payment header with the Web method, the next task is to send the payment SOAP header from the client. Listing 13-11 shows the ASP.NET pages that creates an instance of the SOAP payment header and sends that as part of the SOAP request that is sent to the server.

Listing 13-11: Passing SOAP Header Information to a Web Service Method

```csharp
<%@ Page Language="C#" %>
<%@ Import Namespace="System.Web.Services.Protocols" %>
<script runat="server">
  void btnGetQuote_Click(object sender, EventArgs e)
  {
    try
    {
      QuotesProxy.SoapPaymentHeader header = new
        QuotesProxy.SoapPaymentHeader();
      header.CreditCardNumber = "xxxxxxxxxxxxxxxx";
      header.CreditCardType = QuotesProxy.CardType.VISA;
      header.NameOnCard = "XXXXXX";
      header.ExpirationDate = DateTime.Today.AddDays(365);
      QuotesProxy.QuotesService obj = new QuotesProxy.QuotesService();
      obj.SoapPaymentHeaderValue = header;
      output.Text = obj.GetStockPriceWithPayment(txtSymbol.Text).ToString();
    }
    catch (SoapHeaderException soapEx)
    {
      output.Text = "Actor : " + soapEx.Actor + "<br><br>";
      output.Text += "Code  : " + soapEx.Code + "<br><br>";
      output.Text += "Message: " + soapEx.Message + "<br><br>";
      output.Text += "Detail: " + Server.HtmlEncode(soapEx.Detail.OuterXml);
    }
    catch (Exception ex)
    {
      output.Text = "Exception is : " + ex.Message;
    }
  }
</script>
<html xmlns="http://www.w3.org/1999/xhtml" >
<head id="Head1" runat="server">
  <title>Passing SOAP Headers to a Web Service Method</title>
</head>
<body>
  <form id="form1" runat="server">
    <div>
      Enter Stock Symbol: <asp:TextBox runat="server" ID="txtSymbol" />
      <asp:Button Text="Get Quote" runat="server" ID="btnGetQuote"
        OnClick="btnGetQuote_Click" />
      <br /><br /><br />
      <asp:Label Font-Bold=true runat="server" ID="output" />
    </div>
  </form>
</body>
</html>
```

To start with, Listing 13-11 creates an instance of the `SoapPaymentHeader` object and sets its properties to appropriate values. It then sets the `SoapPaymentHeaderValue` property of the proxy object to the `SoapHeader` object.

```
obj.SoapPaymentHeaderValue = header;
```

After you set the `SoapPaymentHeaderValue` property, the contents of the SOAP header will be automatically transferred as part of the SOAP message. Next you also handle any errors thrown by the Web service using two catch blocks: `SoapHeaderException` block and a generic `Exception` block.

Using SOAP Extensions

SOAP extensions provide a way of creating encapsulated reusable functionality that you can apply declaratively to your Web service. The SOAP extensions framework allows you to intercept SOAP messages exchanged between the client and the Web service. You can inspect or modify a message at various points during the processing of the message. You can apply a SOAP extension to either the server or the client.

A SOAP extension is composed of a class derived from the `SoapExtension` class. It contains the implementation details that are generally used to examine or modify the contents of a SOAP message. After you have defined the SOAP extension class, you can then define an attribute derived from `SoapExtensionAttribute` that associates the SOAP extension with a particular Web method or a class.

Creating the SOAP Extension Class

A SOAP extension derives from the `SoapExtension` class. The ASP.NET runtime invokes methods exposed by the SOAP extension class at various points during the processing of the request. These methods can be overridden by the SOAP extension to provide custom implementation. Table 13-5 describes the methods that can be overridden by a custom SOAP extension.

Table 13-5. Methods of the SoapExtension Class

Method	Description
ChainStream	Provides a means of accessing the memory buffer containing the SOAP request or response message.
GetInitializer	Used to perform initialization that is specific to the Web service method. This method is overloaded to provide a separate initializer for a single method or for all methods exposed by a type.
Initialize	Used to receive the data that was returned from `GetInitializer`.
ProcessMessage	Provides a means of allowing the SOAP extension to inspect and modify the SOAP messages at each stage of processing the request and response messages.

The SOAP extension framework provides two methods of accessing the contents of the message. One way is through a stream object received by the `ChainStream` method that contains the raw contents of the message. The other way is through the properties and methods exposed by the instance of the `SoapMessage` object passed to the `ProcessMessage` method. For the `PaymentAuthExtension` class, you use the `ProcessMessage` method.

For the purposes of this example, you modify the payment processing functionality of the `QuotesService` and implement that as a SOAP extension. So in this case, the `PaymentAuthExtension` class will process the payment header on behalf of the Web method. The advantage of using this approach is that you can ensure the integrity of the payment information passed in the SOAP headers without adding that verification code in each of the Web service methods. Listing 13-12 shows the implementation of the SOAP extension that processes the payment header information.

Listing 13-12: SOAP Extension Class for Processing the Payment Header

```
using System;
using System.Data;
using System.Configuration;
using System.Web;
using System.Web.Services.Protocols;
public class PaymentAuthExtension : SoapExtension
{
  public override void ProcessMessage(SoapMessage message)
  {
    if (message.Stage == SoapMessageStage.AfterDeserialize)
    {
      //Check for an SoapPaymentHeader containing valid credit card information
      foreach (SoapHeader header in message.Headers)
      {
        if (header is SoapPaymentHeader)
        {
          SoapPaymentHeader paymentHeader = (SoapPaymentHeader)header;
          if (paymentHeader.CreditCardNumber.Length != 0 &&
            paymentHeader.NameOnCard.Length != 0)
            return; // Allow call to execute
            break;
        }
      }
      //Throw an exception if we get here
      throw new SoapException("Invalid credit card information",
        SoapException.ClientFaultCode);
    }
  }

  public override Object GetInitializer(Type type)
  {
    return GetType();
  }

  public override Object GetInitializer(LogicalMethodInfo info,
```

```
    SoapExtensionAttribute attribute)
  {
    return null;
  }

  public override void Initialize(Object initializer)
  {
  }
}
```

If multiple extensions are associated with a Web method, every extension will be called during each stage in the order of priority. The `Initialize` method performs any initialization that is specific to the method invocation. In the case of the `PaymentAuthExtension` extension, no initialization needs to be accomplished.

The `ProcessMessage()` method contains the implementation for processing the request message received from the client and the response message sent by the Web service. `ProcessMessage()` is called by the ASP.NET runtime at four points. It is called twice during the process of deserializing the request message, once before the message is deserialized and once after. The `ProcessMessage()` method is also called twice during the process of serializing the response message, once before serialization and once after. Each time the `ProcessMessage()` method is called, it is passed an instance of the `SoapMessage` class. During the `BeforeSerialize` and `AfterSerialize` stages, the object is initialized with the data contained within the SOAP message.

The code to process the payment header accesses the header information via the message parameter. The message object is populated with the data contained within the SOAP request message only after the message has been deserialized. Therefore, the code to process the payment information is placed within the `SoapMessageStage.AfterDeserialize` case block.

```
if (message.Stage == SoapMessageStage.AfterDeserialize)
{
```

The `SoapMessage` object exposes the `Headers` property, which is of type `SoapHeaderCollection`. You obtain the payment header by looping through the `SoapHeaderCollection` and checking for the type of the object. If the object is of type `SoapPaymentHeader`, you process the object by checking for the length of the `CreditCardNumber` and `NameOnCard` properties.

```
foreach (SoapHeader header in message.Headers)
{
  if (header is SoapPaymentHeader)
  {
    SoapPaymentHeader paymentHeader = (SoapPaymentHeader)header;
    if (paymentHeader.CreditCardNumber.Length != 0 &&
      paymentHeader.NameOnCard.Length != 0)
      return; // Allow call to execute
    break;
  }
}
```

If the payment header information is not found, you throw an exception using the following line of code.

```
//Throw an exception if we get here
throw new SoapException("Invalid credit card information",
  SoapException.ClientFaultCode);
```

> Another way to access the data contained within a SOAP message is using the
> ChainStream() method. This method is used by the extension to receive a raw
> stream containing the contents of the message and to pass the modified version of
> the stream back to the ASP.NET runtime.

Creating a Custom SOAP Extension Attribute for Use with Web Service Methods

To configure your Web methods to run with a SOAP extension, you need to decorate the Web method
with a custom attribute derived from the SoapExtensionAttribute class. Listing 13-13 shows an
example of a SOAP extension attribute for use with the PaymentAuthExtension.

Listing 13-13: Custom SOAP Extension Attribute

```
using System;
using System.Data;
using System.Configuration;
using System.Web;
using System.Web.Services.Protocols;

[AttributeUsage(AttributeTargets.Method)]
public class PaymentAuthExtensionAttribute : SoapExtensionAttribute
{
  int _priority = 1;
  public override int Priority
  {
    get { return _priority; }
    set { _priority = value; }
  }

  public override Type ExtensionType
  {
    get { return typeof(PaymentAuthExtension); }
  }
}
```

In this code, ASP.NET learns what kind of extension to use by querying the ExtensionType() method
that returns the type of extension to load.

All SOAP extension attributes must override the Priority property. This property specifies the priority
in which the SOAP extension will be executed with respect to other SOAP extensions. The priority of the
SOAP extension is used by ASP.NET to determine when it should be called in relation to other SOAP
extensions. The higher the priority, the closer the SOAP extension is to the actual message being sent
by the client and the response sent by the server. For example, a SOAP extension that compresses
the body and the header of a SOAP message should have a high priority. On the other hand, the
PaymentAuthExtension SOAP extension does not need to have a high priority because it can function
properly after other SOAP extensions have processed.

Applying SOAP Extension to a Web Method

To associate the SOAP extension with a particular Web method, you need to add the `PaymentAuth Extension` as an attribute to the Web method. Listing 13-14 illustrates the technique of decorating a Web method with a SOAP extension.

Listing 13-14: Applying SOAP Extension to a Web Method

```
using System;
using System.Xml;
using System.Web;
using System.Collections;
using System.Web.Services;
using System.Web.Services.Protocols;

[WebService(Namespace = "http://tempuri.org/")]
[WebServiceBinding(ConformsTo = WsiProfiles.BasicProfile1_1)]
public class QuotesService : System.Web.Services.WebService
{
  public SoapPaymentHeader paymentHeader;

  [PaymentAuthExtension]
  [WebMethod(Description = "Returns real time quote for a given stock ticker")]
  [SoapHeader("paymentHeader", Direction = SoapHeaderDirection.In)]
  public double GetStockPriceWithSoapExtension(string symbol)
  {
    double price;
    switch (symbol.ToUpper())
    {
      case "INTC":
        price = 70.75;
        break;
      case "MSFT":
        price = 50;
        break;
      case "DELL":
        price = 42.25;
        break;
      default:
        throw new SoapException("Invalid Symbol", SoapException.ClientFaultCode,
          "http://wrox.com/quotes/GetStockPriceWithSoapExtension");
    }
    return price;
  }
}
```

In Listing 13-14, the line of code that is of interest is where you apply the SOAP extension to the Web method.

```
[PaymentAuthExtension]
[WebMethod(Description = "Returns real time quote for a given stock ticker")]
[SoapHeader("paymentHeader", Direction = SoapHeaderDirection.In)]
public double GetStockPriceWithSoapExtension(string symbol)
```

The attribute `PaymentAuthExtension` will ensure that the `PaymentAuthExtension` is invoked before the `GetStockPriceWithSoapExtension()` method is invoked.

> In addition to using the custom SOAP extension attribute class in each of the Web methods, you can also apply the SOAP extension globally for all the Web methods in a Web service using the following settings in the `Web.config` file.
>
> ```
> <system.web>
>   <webServices>
>     <soapExtensionTypes>
>       <add type="PaymentAuthExtension, App_Code"
>         priority="1" group="0" />
>     </soapExtensionTypes>
>   </webServices>
> </system.web>
> ```
>
> In this example, the `PaymentAuthExtension` class was placed in the `App_Code` folder. For reasons of increased reusability, it might be a good idea to place the SOAP extensions in a separate assembly so that they can be shared across multiple applications or even by the client applications.

Now that you have understood the SOAP extension and configured the Web service method to use the SOAP extension, the next step is to the Web method from the ASP.NET page. Listing 13-15 shows the code required to perform this.

Listing 13-15: Invoking the SOAP Extension Configured Web Service Method

```csharp
<%@ Page Language="C#" %>
<%@ Import Namespace="System.Web.Services.Protocols" %>
<script runat="server">
  void btnGetQuote_Click(object sender, EventArgs e)
  {
    try
    {
      QuotesProxy.SoapPaymentHeader header = new
        QuotesProxy.SoapPaymentHeader();
      header.CreditCardNumber = "";
      header.CreditCardType = QuotesProxy.CardType.VISA;
      header.NameOnCard = "";
      header.ExpirationDate = DateTime.Today.AddDays(365);
      QuotesProxy.QuotesService obj = new QuotesProxy.QuotesService();
      obj.SoapPaymentHeaderValue =  header;
      output.Text = obj.GetStockPriceWithSoapExtension(txtSymbol.Text).ToString();
    }
    catch (SoapHeaderException soapEx)
    {
      output.Text = "Actor : " + soapEx.Actor + "<br><br>";
      output.Text += "Code   : " + soapEx.Code + "<br><br>";
      output.Text += "Message: " + soapEx.Message + "<br><br>";
      output.Text += "Detail: " + Server.HtmlEncode(soapEx.Detail.OuterXml);
    }
    catch (Exception ex)
```

```
      {
         output.Text = "Exception is : " + ex.Message;
      }
   }
</script>
<html xmlns="http://www.w3.org/1999/xhtml" >
<head id="Head1" runat="server">
  <title>Invoking SOAP Extensions on the server side</title>
</head>
<body>
  <form id="form1" runat="server">
    <div>
       Enter Stock Symbol: <asp:TextBox runat="server" ID="txtSymbol" />
       <asp:Button Text="Get Quote" runat="server" ID="btnGetQuote"
         OnClick="btnGetQuote_Click" />
       <br /><br /><br />
       <asp:Label Font-Bold=true runat="server" ID="output" />
    </div>
  </form>
</body>
</html>
```

From the ASP.NET perspective, there is no change in the code when compared to the previous SOAP header client page except that in this case, you are calling the GetStockPriceWithSoapExtension() method. To exercise the SOAP extension on the server side, set the CreditCardNumber and NameOnCard properties to empty values and invoke the Web service method. You will see the output shown in Figure 13-6.

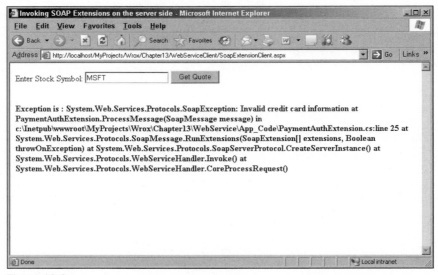

Figure 13-6

Figure 13-6 shows the exception raised by the SOAP extension when you supply insufficient payment information.

SOAP Extensions on the Client

A SOAP extension isn't just for the server. If you consider an extension that decrypts a request and encrypts a response, you will realize that there is not much point in placing it on the server if it does not also exist on the client where it will encrypt requests and decrypt responses. Fortunately, you can incorporate a targetable SOAP extension into your client by using the following steps:

1.   Generate a proxy class to the Web service for your client project.

2.   Add the class files for your extension and its attribute to your client project.

3.   Open the class file for your proxy class and tag the methods that need processing by your extension with its attribute.

4.   Save the proxy class and build your client as you normally would.

5.   Compile and run the extension.

By and large, an extension written for the server will work as expected on the client without any code modifications. This is because the four message stages in ProcessMessage are in a different order on the client. ProcessMessage generates a request and receives a response in this order:

❑   BeforeSerialize

❑   AfterSerialize

❑   BeforeDeserialize

❑   AfterDeserialize

If the extension really needs to know whether it is existing on the client or the server, however, you can find out in ProcessMessage() by calling typeof on its SoapMessage parameter. The typeof operator will return SoapServerMessage if the extension is on the server, and it will return SoapClientMessage if the extension is on the client. Both these classes inherit from SoapMessage.

Asynchronous Invocation of Web Services from a Client Application

.NET Framework provides excellent support for asynchronous programming by providing a rich plumbing for performing lengthy operations asynchronously. Asynchronous programming can be defined as the ability of a method to return immediately without waiting (or without blocking on the calling thread) for the called method to finish its execution. When the called method has finished its execution, it notifies the caller by invoking the callback function that was specified at the time of invoking the method asynchronously.

Asynchronous call provides a lot of flexibility when compared to synchronous approach wherein the calling thread is blocked and has to wait until the called function completes. Asynchronous call also provides for more parallelism. Applications built with asynchronous mechanism also allow for network efficiency that can be used to optimize bandwidth and enable occasionally connected functionality. It also protects the users from network inefficiencies since they are not forced to wait for the Web service to return, thereby greatly enhancing the user experience.

The need for asynchronous processing becomes significant in the development of distributed applications, which typically depend on different independent and remote entities such as Web services to perform its operations. Also remember that the Web services you are trying to invoke can be present anywhere in the Internet. To make matters worse, you do not have any control over the public networks on which your request has to travel as well as over the machines on which the Web services reside.

Asynchronous Programming in .NET

Invoking Web Services asynchronously from within a .NET client application follows the same design pattern used by the .NET framework for invoking asynchronous processes. The design pattern dictates that, for each synchronous method implemented, there should be two asynchronous methods: a Begin and an End asynchronous method. The Begin method takes input from the client and kicks off the asynchronous operation. The End method supplies the results of the asynchronous operation back to the client.

In addition to accepting the input parameters required by the asynchronous operation, the Begin method also takes an AsyncCallback delegate to be called when the asynchronous operation is completed. The AsyncCallback delegate will serve as a pointer to a function that the client application will implement to retrieve the results from the method call. The return value of the Begin method is an object that implements the IAsyncResult interface. This object is used by the client to determine the status of the asynchronous operation. The client application will then use the End method to obtain the results of the asynchronous operation by supplying the AsyncResult object.

When calling the Begin method to kick-off an asynchronous call, there are two options available to the client for initiating the operation:

❑   Supply the AsyncCallback delegate when beginning the asynchronous operation. This will provide a mechanism for the server to notify the client application that the method call has completed

❑   Don't supply the AsyncCallback delegate when beginning the asynchronous operation. The callback delegate is not required if the client application chooses to poll for completion instead, or if the return value of the function being called is not needed

The client application also has a number of options available for completing asynchronous operations:

❑   Poll the returned IAsyncResult.IsCompleted property periodically for completion. Note that this does add processing overhead due to the constant polling.

❑   Attempt to complete the operation prematurely by calling the End method, which blocks the calling thread until the operation completes.

❑   Wait on the IAsyncResult object. The difference between this and the previous option is that the client can use timeouts to wake up periodically.

❑   Wait for the callback to occur and complete the operation inside the AsyncCallback routine.

If you make an asynchronous Web service call from within an ASP.NET page and then you return immediately within your code, you may not have the opportunity to include the data from the Web service call in the data returned to the user. You can overcome this shortcoming, however, by not releasing the thread that is currently executing. To accomplish this, you need to use the WaitHandle object. With WaitHandle you can do some processing after your Web service call has been made and then block until the Web service call has completed. Listing 13-16 shows the code required for the asynchronous invocation of Web services.

Listing 13-16: Invoking a Web Service Asynchronously from an ASP.NET Page

```
<%@ Page Language="C#" %>
<%@ Import Namespace="System.Data" %>
<script runat="server">
  void btnInvoke_Click(object sender, EventArgs e)
  {
    CategoriesProxy.CategoriesService obj = new
      CategoriesProxy.CategoriesService();
    IAsyncResult result;
    result = obj.BeginGetCategoriesAsDataSet(null, null);
    //Do some dummy processing.
    //     ...
    //Completed processing.  Wait for completion.
    result.AsyncWaitHandle.WaitOne();
    DataSet categoriesDataSet = obj.EndGetCategoriesAsDataSet(result);
    output.DataSource = categoriesDataSet.Tables[0];
    output.DataBind();
  }
</script>
<html xmlns="http://www.w3.org/1999/xhtml" >
<head runat="server">
  <title>Asynchronous Invocation of Web Services</title>
</head>
<body>
  <form id="form1" runat="server">
    <div>
      <asp:Button runat="server" Text="Invoke Web Service"
        OnClick="btnInvoke_Click" ID="btnInvoke" />
      <br/><br/>
      <asp:GridView runat="server" ID="output" />
    </div>
  </form>
</body>
</html>
```

Listing 13-16 starts by creating an instance of the `CategoriesService` and then invokes the asynchronous version of `GetCategoriesAsDataSet` (named `BeginGetCategoriesAsDataSet`) method to initiate the Web service method call.

```
result = obj.BeginGetCategoriesAsDataSet(null, null);
```

> When you create a proxy for a Web service using the `WSDL.exe` utility or using the Add Web reference option in Visual Studio, you will find that the created proxy contains the `Begin<MethodName>` and `End<MethodName>` methods for each of the Web methods contained in the Web service. These two methods provide a way for you to asynchronously invoke the Web service.

After initiating the Web service call, you now have an opportunity to perform custom processing. When you are done with your custom processing, you need to ensure that the Web service execution is finished before you can retrieve the results returned by the Web service. This is where the `WaitOne()` method comes into play.

```
result.AsyncWaitHandle.WaitOne();
```

After that, you invoke the `EndGetCategoriesAsDataSet()` method to retrieve the results returned by the Web service method.

```
DataSet categoriesDataSet = obj.EndGetCategoriesAsDataSet(result);
```

You then bind the returned DataSet object directly to a `GridView` control.

```
output.DataSource = categoriesDataSet.Tables[0];
output.DataBind();
```

The `WaitHandle` class also contains other static methods such as `WaitAll()` and `WaitAny()`. These two static methods take arrays of `WaitHandle` as parameters, and return either when all the calls have completed, or as soon as any of the calls have completed, depending on the method that you call. For example, if you are calling three separate Web services, you can call each asynchronously; place the `WaitHandle` for each in an array, then call the `WaitAll()` method until they are finished. This allows all the three Web service calls to execute at the same time. It is also important to note that the `WaitOne()`, `WaitAll()`, and `WaitAny()` methods all have the option of taking a timeout as a parameter. Using the timeout option, you can specify the amount of time that you want to wait for a Web service call to return. If the methods timeout, you will get a return value of false.

Using Async Pages to Asynchronously Invoke Web Services

ASP.NET 2.0 introduces a new concept known as asynchronous (known as "async") pages. With async pages, it is now possible to write a page that is serviced asynchronous with respect to the request thread. Here are the steps required for creating async pages.

1. Set the `Async="true"` in the `Page` directive.

2. Register two event handlers (`BeginEventHandler` and `EndEventHandler`) with the `AddOnPreRenderCompleteAsync()` method.

With these steps completed, when the ASP.NET internal method executes, it will execute up to the `PreRender` and then invoke the `BeginEventHandler` if you have registered one. When the `IAsyncResult` returned from the `BeginEventHandler` is signaled that the asynchronous operation is complete, it completes the page lifecycle by invoking the `EndEventHandler` method and then finally unloads the page. Listing 13-17 shows you how to leverage the async feature to invoke a Web service asynchronously.

Listing 13-17: Using the Async Pages Feature to Asynchronously Invoke a Web Service

```
<%@ Page Language="C#" Async="true" %>
<%@ Import Namespace="System.Data" %>
<script runat="server">
  CategoriesProxy.CategoriesService obj = new
```

```
          CategoriesProxy.CategoriesService();

      void Page_Load(object sender, EventArgs e)
      {
        BeginEventHandler begin = new BeginEventHandler(this.BeginGetAsyncData);
        EndEventHandler end = new EndEventHandler(this.EndGetAsyncData);
        AddOnPreRenderCompleteAsync(begin, end);
      }

      IAsyncResult BeginGetAsyncData(Object src, EventArgs args,
        AsyncCallback cb, Object state)
      {
        return obj.BeginGetCategoriesAsDataSet(cb, state);
      }

      void EndGetAsyncData(IAsyncResult ar)
      {
        DataSet categoriesDataSet = obj.EndGetCategoriesAsDataSet(ar);
        output.DataSource = categoriesDataSet.Tables[0];
        output.DataBind();
      }
</script>
<html xmlns="http://www.w3.org/1999/xhtml" >
<head runat="server">
  <title>
    Asynchronous Invocation of a Web Service using Asynchronous Pages
  </title>
</head>
<body>
  <form id="form1" runat="server">
    <div>
      <asp:GridView runat="server" ID="output" />
    </div>
  </form>
</body>
</html>
```

In the `BeginGetAsyncData()` method, you initiate the asynchronous invocation of the Web service method.

```
    return obj.BeginGetCategoriesAsDataSet(cb, state);
```

In the `EndGetAsyncData()` method, you simply call the `EndGetCategoriesAsDataSet()` method to retrieve the results of the Web method call and then display the output onto a `GridView` control.

```
  DataSet categoriesDataSet = obj.EndGetCategoriesAsDataSet(ar);
  output.DataSource = categoriesDataSet.Tables[0];
  output.DataBind();
```

The main advantage of the async page approach is that it allows you to write your page as you normally would, and just spin off and perform an asynchronous operation before the page is rendered and the response is returned. This approach also allows you to free up the request thread to service other requests while you await the return of the Web service invocation.

Asynchronous Invocation of Web Services from a Browser Using IE Web Service Behavior

In addition to invoking the Web services asynchronously on the ASP.NET side, you can also do that from a browser client. You can accomplish this using the IE Web service behavior that enables client-side script to invoke remote Web Service methods using SOAP over HTTP. This behavior makes it possible for you to use and leverage SOAP, without requiring expert knowledge of its implementation. Furthermore, Web service behavior can go a long way in improving the usability of Web applications by providing you with the ability to execute a remote Web service method without even having to refresh the page.

The Web service behavior is implemented with an HTML Component (HTC) file as an attached behavior, and it can be used in Internet Explorer 5 and later versions. Basically the Web service behavior simplifies the remote invocation of Web services by handling the communication of the SOAP data packets between the browser and the Web services. This obviates the need for you to write code for assembling and disassembling SOAP messages. All the SOAP-specific handling code is encapsulated inside the behavior, simplifying the client-side script in the main Web page.

> The Web service behavior is a JavaScript file named `WebService.htc` embedded in a Web page using specific IE behavior syntax. By exposing properties and methods to client-side scripts, the Web service behavior performs assembling messages as well as disassembling responses that are sent back by the Web services. The objects that are exposed by the behavior not only enable a cleaner error handling approach but also provide easy access to the returned data.

How the IE Web Service Behavior Works

The Web service behavior receives method calls from the client-side script and sends the requests to the Web service using SOAP messages. The results are returned to the client script and processing continues. The Web page can then use the information in whatever context is required, such as updating some portion of the page, sending error messages, and so on. A key feature of the Web service behavior is that it enables client-side script to access a Web service without requiring navigation to another URL. The following listing details the important methods supported by the Web service behavior:

❑ `createUseOptions` — Allows you to preserve authentication information across remote method invocations. Can be very useful when using SSL to communicate with the remote Web service.

❑ `callService` — Allows you to invoke the remote Web service method.

❑ `useService` — Allows you to establish a friendly name for the Web service that can be used while invoking the Web service.

> To be able to use the behavior in a Web page in IE5.0 and above, you will need to download the `Webservice.htc` behavior file and save it in the same folder as that of your Web page.

Now that you have a general understanding of the Web service behavior, look at an example to demonstrate the usage of Web service behavior in an ASP.NET page. Before creating the Web page, you need to first create the Web service. For this example, a Web service named `EmployeeService` is shown that returns the employee details based on the supplied employee id. Listing 13-18 shows the implementation of the Web service.

Listing 13-18: Implementation of Employee Service That Returns an XmlDocument Object

```
using System;
using System.Data;
using System.Data.SqlClient;
using System.Web;
using System.Web.Configuration;
using System.Web.Services;
using System.Web.Services.Protocols;
using System.Xml;

[WebService(Namespace = "http://tempuri.org/")]
[WebServiceBinding(ConformsTo = WsiProfiles.BasicProfile1_1)]
public class EmployeeService : System.Web.Services.WebService
{
  public EmployeeService ()
  {
  }

  [WebMethod]
  public XmlDocument GetEmpDetailsByEmpID(int employeeID)
  {
    try
    {
      string connString = WebConfigurationManager.ConnectionStrings
        ["adventureWorks"].ConnectionString;
      using (SqlConnection sqlConnection = new SqlConnection(connString))
      {
        DataSet employeeDataset = new DataSet("EmployeesRoot");
        SqlDataAdapter adapter = new SqlDataAdapter();
        SqlCommand command = new SqlCommand
          ("Select EmployeeID, Title, CAST(BirthDate AS char(12)) " +
          "AS BirthDate, MaritalStatus from HumanResources.Employee " +
          "as Employees Where EmployeeID =" + employeeID.ToString(),
          sqlConnection);
        command.CommandType = CommandType.Text;
        adapter.SelectCommand = command;
        //Fill the Dataset with the return value from the stored procedure
        adapter.Fill(employeeDataset, "Employees");
        XmlDocument xmlDoc = new XmlDocument();
        xmlDoc.LoadXml(employeeDataset.GetXml());
        return xmlDoc;
      }
    }
    catch (Exception ex)
    {
      throw ex;
    }
  }
}
```

Chapter 13

Listing 13-18 starts by retrieving the connection string from the `web.config` file. After that, it creates a `SqlConnection` object passing in the connection string as an argument. You then create a DataSet object passing in the name of the DataSet to its constructor.

```
DataSet employeeDataset = new DataSet("EmployeesRoot");
```

When you create an XML representation of a DataSet, the DataSet name becomes the root of the XML document.

You then create instances of the `SqlDataAdapter` and `SqlCommand` objects and set its properties to appropriate values. After that, you fill the DataSet with the results of the query execution through the call to the `Fill()` method of the `SqlDataAdapter` object. To the `Fill()` method, you also supply the name of the DataTable besides the DataSet object.

```
adapter.Fill(employeeDataset, "Employees");
```

Load an `XmlDocument` object named `xmlDoc` with the contents of the DataSet using the `LoadXml()` method.

```
xmlDoc.LoadXml(employeeDataset.GetXml());
```

The `GetXml()` method of the DataSet object returns the XML representation of the DataSet as a string. This XML is then passed to the `LoadXml()` method of the `XmlDocument` object. Finally, you return the `XmlDocument` object back to the caller.

```
return xmlDoc;
```

Now that you have created the Web service, the next step is to create the ASP.NET page.

Using the Web Service Behavior to Invoke the Web Service

The first thing that must be done to use the Web service behavior in a Web page is to embed it using syntax similar to this:

```
<div id="service" style="BEHAVIOR:url(webservice.htc)"></div>
```

This code relies on the behavior functionality built into IE 5 (and higher) to identify the location of the JavaScript file that will be used to call Web services. As discussed previously, the `Webservice.htc` file should be available on the same folder as that of the Web page. It is important to note that the loading of the behavior file occurs on the client rather than on the server.

After embedded, the behavior can be invoked and linked to a WSDL 1.1-compliant Web service using JavaScript code. This is accomplished by referencing the embedded behavior id and calling its `useService()` method:

```
service.useService
("http://localhost/MyProjects/Wrox/Chapter13/WebService/EmployeeService.asmx?WSDL",
"svcEmployee");
```

The `useService()` method accepts the following arguments.

- ❑ Path to the WSDL file for the Web service.

- ❑ A friendly name that can be later used to reference the Web service. You can use this friendly name to reference the Web methods in the `EmployeeService`.

You then invoke the `useService()` method in the onload event handler for the page to ensure that the Web service is properly mapped before any methods are invoked on the Web service.

Now that the Web service is setup for access, you can asynchronously invoke the Web service method using a two-step approach. In the first step, invoke the Web method and supply a callback function as an argument. As a second step, the call back function gets automatically invoked when the Web service returns after executing the method.

Listing 13-19 shows the complete code of the ASP.NET page.

Listing 13-19: Invoking the Employee Service Asynchronously from a Browser Using IE Web Service Behavior

```
<%@ Page Language="C#" %>
<html xmlns="http://www.w3.org/1999/xhtml" >
<head runat="server">
  <title>
    IE Web Service Behavior for asynchronously invoking the Web Service
  </title>
  <script language="JScript">
    //Declare a module level variable to capture the event id
    var iCallID ;
    function GetEmployeeDetails()
    {
      //Call the GetEmployeeDetails method on the svcEmployee web service
      iCallID = service.svcEmployee.callService
        (DisplayResults,"GetEmpDetailsByEmpID", txtEmployeeID.value);
    }

    function DisplayResults(result)
    {
      var strXML,objXMLNode,objXMLDoc,objEmployee,strHTML;
      //Check if the event id is the same
      if (iCallID != result.id)
        return;
      if(result.error)
      {
        //Pull the error information from the errorDetail property
        var faultCode   = result.errorDetail.code;
        var faultString = result.errorDetail.string;
        alert("ERROR: Code = " + faultCode + ", Fault String=" + faultString);
      }
      else
      {
        //Get the resultant value into a local variable
        objXMLNode = result.value;
```

```
        objXMLDoc = new ActiveXObject("Microsoft.XMLDOM");
        //Load the returned XML string into XMLDOM Object
        objXMLDoc.loadXML(objXMLNode.xml);
        //Get reference to the Employees Node
        objEmployee = objXMLDoc.selectSingleNode ("GetEmpDetailsByEmpIDResult").
          selectSingleNode("EmployeesRoot").selectSingleNode("Employees");
        //Check if a valid employee reference is returned from the server
        strHTML = "<font color='#0000FF'>";
        if (objEmployee != null)
        {
           strHTML += "<br><br>Employee ID :<b>" +
             objEmployee.selectSingleNode("EmployeeID").text + "</b><br><br>";
           strHTML += "Title :<b>" + objEmployee.selectSingleNode("Title").text +
             "</b><br><br>";
           strHTML += "Birth Date :<b>" +
             objEmployee.selectSingleNode("BirthDate").text + "</b><br><br>";
           strHTML += "Marital Status :<b>" +
             objEmployee.selectSingleNode("MaritalStatus").text + "</b><br><br>";
        }
        else
        {
           strHTML += "<br><br><b>Employee not found</b>";
        }
        strHTML += "</font>"
        //Assign the dynamically generated HTML into the div tag
        divContents.innerHTML = strHTML;
      }
    }

    function init()
    {
       //Create an instance of the web service and call it svcEmployee
       service.useService
("http://localhost/MyProjects/Wrox/Chapter13/WebService/EmployeeService.asmx?WSDL",
"svcEmployee");
    }
  </script>
</head>
<body onload="init()">
  <div id="service" style="BEHAVIOR: url(webservice.htc)"></div>
  <H1 align="center">Employee Details</H1>
  <br><br>
  <P align="left"><b>Enter the Employee ID:</b>
         
    <INPUT id="txtEmployeeID" name="txtEmployeeID"
      style="LEFT: 149px; TOP: 72px">
   <INPUT id="btnAdd" type="button" value="Get Employee Details"
      name="btnGetEmployee" onclick="return GetEmployeeDetails()">
  </P>
```

```
  <P></P>
  <div id="divContents">
  </div>
  <P></P>
 </body>
</html>
```

In the `GetEmployeeDetails()` JavaScript method, you invoke the Web service method passing in the callback method name and the Web service input parameters as arguments. This is accomplished through the call to the `callService()` method.

```
function GetEmployeeDetails()
{
  //Call the GetEmployeeDetails method on the svcEmployee web service
  iCallID = service.svcEmployee.callService
    (DisplayResults,"GetEmpDetailsByEmpID", txtEmployeeID.value);
}
```

The `callService()` method returns a unique identifier that can later be used to identify the Web service call. This is required if you are making multiple Web service calls asynchronously and then assemble the returned results together in the client browser itself. In that case, you match this returned ID with the ID that is available as a property of the result object. This matching is done in the callback function, which is covered later in this chapter.

At the time of invoking the Web service, because you specified the `DisplayResults()` function as the callback function, the `DisplayResults` method will automatically get invoked, after the Web service has finished its execution. In the `DisplayResults()` function, you match the id of the result object with the id that was already returned by the callService method.

```
if (iCallID != result.id)
   return;
```

Check the error property to check if there was any error during the execution of the Web service. If an error occurred, you then display the error information in a message box.

```
if(result.error)
{
  //Pull the error information
  var faultCode   = result.errorDetail.code;
  var faultString = result.errorDetail.string;
  alert("ERROR: Code = " + faultCode + ", Fault String=" + faultString);
}
```

If there is no error, process the returned results and display them in a HTML <DIV> tag.

In the employee text box, enter a valid Employee ID and then click on the Get Employee Details button to invoke the remote Web service. This will result in an asynchronous invocation of the Web service, and the result from the Web service will be displayed in the <DIV> element of the Web page. The output produced by this page is shown in Figure 13-7.

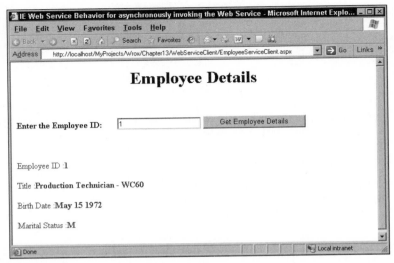

Figure 13-7

Asynchronous Web Service Methods

The previous section discussed how to call Web services asynchronously over HTTP using the client-side capabilities of the .NET Framework. This approach is an extremely useful way to make calls to a Web service without locking up your application or spawning a bunch of background threads. This section discusses asynchronous Web service methods that provide similar capabilities on the server side.

When you invoke a normal, synchronous ASP.NET Web service method, the response for a synchronous Web method is sent when you return from the method. If it takes a relatively long period of time for a request to complete, then the thread that is processing the request will be in use until the method call is done. Unfortunately, most lengthy calls are due to something like a long database query, or perhaps a call to another Web service. For instance, if you make a Web service call across the Internet, the current thread waits for the Web service call to complete. The thread has to simply wait around doing nothing until it hears back from the Web service. In this case, if you can free up the thread to do other work while waiting for the Web service, you can increase the throughput of your application.

> Waiting threads can impact the performance of a Web service because they don't do anything productive, such as servicing other requests. To overcome this problem, you need a way to be able to start a lengthy background process on a server, but return the current thread to the ASP.NET process pool. When the lengthy background process completes, you would like to have a callback function invoked so that you can finish processing the request and somehow signal the completion of the request to ASP.NET. This is exactly what ASP.NET offers through asynchronous Web methods.

How Asynchronous Web Methods Work

When you write a typical ASP.NET Web service using Web methods, Visual Studio simply compiles your code to create the assembly that will be called when requests for its Web methods are received. When your application is first launched, the ASMX handler reflects over your assembly to determine which Web methods are exposed. For normal, synchronous requests, it is simply a matter of finding which methods have a WebMethod attribute associated with them, and setting up the logic to call the right method based on the SOAPAction HTTP header.

For asynchronous requests, during reflection the Web service handler looks for Web methods with a specific signature that differentiates the method as being asynchronous. In particular, it looks for a pair of methods that have the following rules:

- ❑ There is a `BeginXXX` and `EndXXX` Web method where `XXX` is any string that represents the name of the method you want to expose.

- ❑ The `BeginXXX` function returns an `IAsyncResult` interface and takes an `AsyncCallback`, and an object as its last two parameters, respectively.

- ❑ The `EndXXX` function takes as its only parameter an `IAsyncResult` interface.

- ❑ Both `BeginXXX` and `EndXXX` methods must be flagged with the `WebMethod` attribute.

If the Web service handler finds two methods that meet all these requirements, it will expose the method `XXX` in its WSDL as if it were a normal Web method. The method will accept the parameters defined before the AsyncCallback parameter in the signature for `BeginXXX` as input, and it will return what is returned by the `EndXXX` function. So if you have a Web method whose synchronous declaration looks like the following:

```
[WebMethod]
public string SleepForSpecificDuration(int milliseconds)
{...}
```

An asynchronous declaration will look like the following:

```
[WebMethod]
public IAsyncResult BeginSleepForSpecificDuration (
  int milliseconds,  AsyncCallback callback, object s)
{...}

[WebMethod]
public string EndSleepForSpecificDuration (IAsyncResult call)
{...}
```

The WSDL for both synchronous and asynchronous methods will be the same.

After the Web service handler reflects on an assembly and detects an asynchronous Web method, it must handle requests for that method differently than it handles synchronous requests. Instead of calling a simple method, it calls the `BeginXXX` method. It deserializes the incoming request into the parameters to be passed to the function—as it does for synchronous requests—but it also passes the pointer to an internal callback function as the `AsyncCallback` parameter to the `BeginXXX` method.

Now that you have a general understanding of the asynchronous Web methods, Listing 13-20 shows an example implementation.

Listing 13-20: Creating Asynchronous Web Service Methods

```
using System;
using System.Web;
using System.Collections;
using System.Web.Services;
using System.Web.Services.Protocols;

[WebService(Namespace = "http://tempuri.org/")]
[WebServiceBinding(ConformsTo = WsiProfiles.BasicProfile1_1)]
public class AsyncWebService : System.Web.Services.WebService
{
  public delegate string SleepForSpecificDurationAsyncStub(int milliseconds);

  public string SleepForSpecificDuration(int milliseconds)
  {
    System.Threading.Thread.Sleep(milliseconds);
    return "Completed";
  }

  public class WebServiceState
  {
    public object PreviousState;
    public SleepForSpecificDurationAsyncStub AsyncStub;
  }

  [WebMethod]
  public IAsyncResult BeginSleepForSpecificDuration(int milliseconds,
    AsyncCallback callback, object s)
  {
    SleepForSpecificDurationAsyncStub stub = new
        SleepForSpecificDurationAsyncStub(SleepForSpecificDuration);
    WebServiceState state = new WebServiceState();
    state.PreviousState = s;
    state.AsyncStub = stub;
    return stub.BeginInvoke(milliseconds, callback, state);
  }

  [System.Web.Services.WebMethod]
  public string EndSleepForSpecificDuration(IAsyncResult call)
  {
    WebServiceState state = (WebServiceState)call.AsyncState;
    return state.AsyncStub.EndInvoke(call);
  }
}
```

In Listing 13-20, after the Web service handler calls the `BeginSleepForSpecificDuration()` method, it will return the thread to the process thread pool so it can handle any other requests that are received. The `HttpContext` for the request will not be released yet. The ASMX handler will wait until the callback function that it passed to the `BeginSleepForSpecificDuration()` function is called for it to finish processing the request. After the callback function is called, the ASMX handler will call the `EndSleep`

`ForSpecificDuration()` function so that your Web method can complete any processing it needs to perform, and the return data can be supplied that will be serialized into the SOAP response. Only when the response is sent after the `EndSleepForSpecificDuration()` function returns will the `HttpContext` for the request be released.

Controlling XML Serialization Using IXmlSerializable

In .NET V1.x, you had only limited control over how types were serialized using the `XmlSerializer`. You could attribute types at design time and you could also override those attributes with new values at runtime, but it was based on attributes and you never really had complete control over the serialization process. Now with the release of .NET 2.0, this is no longer true. The `IXmlSerializable` interface, which has been present in the .NET Framework since version 1.x (but meant only for internal use), is now available for general use, thereby providing you with the ability to have more control over the generated schema and wire format.

One change that has been introduced with the `IXmlSerializable` interface is that the `GetSchema()` method should no longer be used. Instead you should use a new attribute named `XmlSchemaProvider` to specify the static method that generates and inserts the schema in the `XmlSchemaSet` for the Web service. The `ReadXml()` method controls reading the serialized format and is handed an `XmlReader` to read from the stream and populate the type. The `WriteXml()` method controls writing the serialized format and is handed an `XmlWriter` to write out the data to the stream.

> An example where you might need this type of control is when streaming large amounts of data. To enable streaming of data, you have to turn off response buffering and then chunk the data into discrete blocks of data demarcated with XML elements. `IXmlSerializable` lets you control the schema for this chunking format and control the reading and writing of this data to the stream with the `ReadXml()` and `WriteXml()` methods.

Listing 13-21 shows the `Customer` class implementing the `IXmlSerializable` interface.

Listing 13-21: Implementing IXmlSerializable Interface to Customize XML Serialization

```
using System;
using System.Xml;
using System.Xml.Schema;
using System.Xml.Serialization;

[XmlSchemaProvider("CreateCustomerSchema")]
public class Customer : IXmlSerializable
{
  private string _firstName;
  private string _lastName;
  private string _address;

  public Customer()
  {
```

```
  }

  public Customer(string firstName, string lastName, string address)
  {
    _firstName = firstName;
    _lastName = lastName;
    _address = address;
  }

  public static XmlQualifiedName CreateCustomerSchema(XmlSchemaSet set)
  {
    XmlSchema schema = new XmlSchema();
    schema.Id = "Test";
    schema.TargetNamespace = "urn:types-wrox-com";
    XmlSchemaComplexType type = new XmlSchemaComplexType();
    type.Name = "customerType";
    XmlSchemaAttribute firstNameAttr = new XmlSchemaAttribute();
    firstNameAttr.Name = "firstName";
    type.Attributes.Add(firstNameAttr);
    XmlSchemaAttribute lastNameAttr = new XmlSchemaAttribute();
    lastNameAttr.Name = "lastName";
    type.Attributes.Add(lastNameAttr);
    XmlSchemaAttribute addressAttr = new XmlSchemaAttribute();
    addressAttr.Name = "address";
    type.Attributes.Add(addressAttr);
    XmlSchemaElement customerElement = new XmlSchemaElement();
    customerElement.Name = "customer";
    XmlQualifiedName name = new XmlQualifiedName("customerType",
      "urn:types-wrox-com");
    customerElement.SchemaTypeName = name;
    schema.Items.Add(type);
    schema.Items.Add(customerElement);
    set.Add(schema);
    return name;
  }

  public XmlSchema GetSchema()
  {
    return (null);
  }

  public void WriteXml(XmlWriter writer)
  {
    writer.WriteStartElement("customer", "urn:wrox-com");
    writer.WriteAttributeString("firstName", _firstName);
    writer.WriteAttributeString("lastName", _lastName);
    writer.WriteAttributeString("address", _address);
    writer.WriteEndElement();
  }

  public void ReadXml(XmlReader reader)
  {
```

```
        XmlNodeType type = reader.MoveToContent();
        if ((type == XmlNodeType.Element) && (reader.LocalName == "customer"))
        {
          _firstName = reader["firstName"];
          _lastName = reader["lastName"];
          _address = reader["address"];
        }
      }

    public override string ToString()
    {
      return (string.Format("Person [{0} {1}]"));
    }
  }
```

In Listing 13-21, the Customer class implements the IXmlSerializable interface and the read/write is implemented in ReadXml() and WriteXml() methods, respectively. Note that the Customer class is decorated with an XmlSchemaProvider attribute which states that the schema for the serialized form of Customer class will be provided by the CreateCustomerSchema() method. In the CreateCustomer Schema() method, you make up a schema each time and provide it back to the framework.

With the Customer class in place, you should be able to use that class from a Web service as shown in Listing 13-22.

Listing 13-22: Utilizing the Customer Class from a Web Service Method

```
using System;
using System.Web.Services;
using System.Web.Services.Protocols;

[WebService(Namespace = "http://tempuri.org/")]
[WebServiceBinding(ConformsTo = WsiProfiles.BasicProfile1_1)]
public class CustomerService : System.Web.Services.WebService
{
  public CustomerService ()
  {
  }

  [WebMethod]
  public Customer GetCustomer()
  {
    Customer cust = new Customer("Thiru", "Thangarathinam",
      "900 N Rural Road, Chandler, AZ");
    return cust;
  }
}
```

In Listing 13-22, the GetCustomer() method simply creates an instance of the Customer object and returns it back to the caller. If you test this Web service method using the default Web service test harness, you should see an output similar to Figure 13-8.

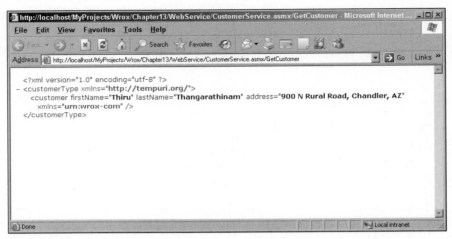

Figure 13-8

Using Schema Importer Extensions

In the .NET Framework 2.0, there is a new namespace named System.Xml.Serialization.Advanced that supports advanced XML serialization and schema generation scenarios. Currently, this namespace contains the following types:

❑   SchemaImporterExtension — Allows you to customize the code generated from a WSDL document

❑   SchemaImporterExtensionCollection — Represents the collection of SchemaImporterExtension objects

Schema importation occurs whenever a Web service proxy is produced through a tool such as the Add Web Reference dialog box found in Visual Studio, or by using the WSDL.exe. Schema importation also occurs when using the XML Schema Definition Tool (Xsd.exe) to generate code from a specific XSD document.

The SchemaImporterExtension Class

The SchemaImporterExtension class allows you to modify the code generated when using any of the automated tools. For example, you may have an existing class that processes book orders on a system and you have an existing XSD document that supplies your orders. Using the SchemaImporter Extension class, you can instruct the automated tools to generate code that uses your class. To control the generation of the code, you must use the classes found in the System.CodeDom namespace.

You need to go through the following steps to enable the proxy generation tools to use your extensions.

1.   Create an implementation of the SchemaImporterExtension class.

2.   Use the ImportSchemaType method to write code for the code generator. The method contains parameters that allow you to examine the intercepted XSD type and create CodeDOM objects that are used to generate the new CLR code.

3. Optionally, use the `ImportAnyElement()` method to handle `<xsd:any>` elements found in the XSD document.

4. Optionally, use the `ImportDefaultValue()` method to examine default values found in the XSD document and return a different default value.

5. Compile your extension into a library.

6. Sign the assembly.

7. Install the assembly in the Global Assembly Cache (GAC).

8. Modify the `machine.config` file to include the extension.

Now that you understand the steps, the next section examines the creation of a schema importer extension class.

Creating a Schema Importer Extension Class

Creating a schema importer extension is pretty easy. You simply derive from `SchemaImporterExtension` and override the appropriate methods. In most cases, you will override the `ImportSchemaType()` method, which perform most of the heavy lifting. Listing 13-23 shows an example in action.

Listing 13-23: Custom Schema Importer Extension for the Customer Class

```
using System;
using System.CodeDom;
using System.CodeDom.Compiler;
using System.Collections;
using System.Xml;
using System.Xml.Schema;
using System.Xml.Serialization;
using System.Xml.Serialization.Advanced;

namespace SchemaImporterExtensionsLib
{
  public sealed class CustomerSchemaImporterExtension : SchemaImporterExtension
  {
    public override string ImportSchemaType(string name, string ns,
      XmlSchemaObject context, XmlSchemas schemas, XmlSchemaImporter importer,
      CodeCompileUnit compileUnit, CodeNamespace mainNamespace,
      CodeGenerationOptions options, CodeDomProvider codeProvider)
    {
      if (name.Equals("Customer") && ns.Equals("urn:wrox-com"))
      {
        CodeTypeDeclaration customer = new CodeTypeDeclaration("Customer");
        mainNamespace.Types.Add(customer);
        CodeMemberField firstNameField = new CodeMemberField(
          new CodeTypeReference(typeof(string)),"_firstName");
        customer.Members.Add(firstNameField);
        CodeMemberProperty firstNameProperty = new CodeMemberProperty();
        firstNameProperty.Attributes = MemberAttributes.Public |
          MemberAttributes.Final;
        firstNameProperty.GetStatements.Add(new CodeMethodReturnStatement(
          new CodeFieldReferenceExpression(new
```

```
                    CodeThisReferenceExpression(), "_firstName")));
            firstNameProperty.Name = "FirstName";
            firstNameProperty.SetStatements.Add(new CodeAssignStatement(
              new CodeFieldReferenceExpression(new
              CodeThisReferenceExpression(),"_firstName"),
              new CodePropertySetValueReferenceExpression()));
            firstNameProperty.Type = new CodeTypeReference(typeof(string));
            customer.Members.Add(firstNameProperty);
              CodeMemberField lastNameField = new CodeMemberField(
              new CodeTypeReference(typeof(string)),"_lastName");
            customer.Members.Add(lastNameField);
            CodeMemberProperty lastNameProperty = new CodeMemberProperty();
            lastNameProperty.Attributes = MemberAttributes.Public |
              MemberAttributes.Final;
            lastNameProperty.GetStatements.Add(new CodeMethodReturnStatement(
              new CodeFieldReferenceExpression(new
              CodeThisReferenceExpression(),"_lastName")));
            lastNameProperty.Name = "LastName";
            lastNameProperty.SetStatements.Add(new CodeAssignStatement(
              new CodeFieldReferenceExpression(new
              CodeThisReferenceExpression(),"_lastName"),
              new CodePropertySetValueReferenceExpression()));
            lastNameProperty.Type = new CodeTypeReference(typeof(string));
            customer.Members.Add(lastNameProperty);
            return "Customer";
        }
        return null;
      }
    }
  }
```

In this code example, you can see that the only type this extension can process is the element named Customer that resides in the namespace, "urn:wrox-com". This means that whenever this schema importer extension finds a type it is responsible for generating custom code, it does so via the Code DOM provided by the .NET Framework.

Changes to the machine.config File

When a proxy generation tool is used to import a XML Schema, it uses the System.Xml.Serialization .XmlSchemaImporter class internally to process the schema elements found in the XML Schema document. When created, the XmlSchemaImporter class loads any schema importer extensions defined in the underlying configuration. In this instance, by default, all the schema importer extensions are registered in the machine.config file. The following declaration shows how a schema importer extension is registered in machine.config.

```
<configuration>
  --------
  --------
  <system.xml.serialization>
    <schemaImporterExtensions>
      <add name="CustomerSchemaExtension"
        type="SchemaImporterExtensionsLib.CustomerSchemaImporterExtension,
```

```
            SchemaImporterExtensionsLib, Version=1.0.0.0,
            Culture=neutral,PublicKeyToken=2489eb64bbbf6741" />
      </schemaImporterExtensions>
    </system.xml.serialization>
  </configuration>
```

After the extension is registered in the machine.config file, whenever a proxy generation tool encounters the type urn:wrox-com:Customer, the custom code (through the ImportSchemaType() method) will be added to the generated class file.

> Custom schema importer extension is useful when the client of a Web service has custom types that are much richer than those generated by wsdl.exe. Prior to the .NET Framework 2.0, this was possible only by modifying the generated proxy. But the problem with this approach was that the changes were lost when the proxy was regenerated. Schema Importer Extensions can now be developed and registered to map schema type to the custom type every time the proxy is generated.

Miscellaneous Web Service Features in .NET Framework 2.0

.NET Framework 2.0 provides a number of new features for the Web service developers. Some, which you have already seen, are the support for WS-I Basic Profile, custom XML serialization through IXmlSerializable interface, and schema importer extensions. In addition to these features, there are a couple of minor but important features that deserve a mention. The next few sections give you a rundown of these features.

Enabling Decompression in a Web Service Client

Now with .NET 2.0, enabling decompression on the client side just requires one line of code. All you need to do is to set the EnableDecompression property on an instance of a client proxy class to true, as follows.

```
CategoriesService obj = new CategoriesService();
obj.EnableDecompression = true;
```

This gives the Web clients the capability to interoperate with services that support compression. To disable decompression, set EnableDecompression to false. Setting this property to false enables the server to know that decompression is not supported on the client side.

Type Sharing across Proxies

ASP.NET Web services now support proxy type sharing. This feature allows you to share identical types from different Web services within the client-side proxy class. For example, you can take a type instance returned from one Web service and pass it to another, and vice versa.

In many real-world scenarios, you may want to factor your application's functionality into individual services that group methods that logically fit together. This typically leads to sharing one or more data types between those Web services. For example, you may have an Order Entry service that returns an Order object and an Order Status service that takes in an Order object. In this scenario, you can leverage the new type sharing feature of .NET 2.0 and provide the client with one Order class that is shared by the two service proxies. This feature is exposed on wsdl.exe with the /sharetypes switch. When using this switch you supply the URLs of two or more WSDL documents on the command line. For example:

```
wsdl.exe /sharetypes http://localhost/OrderService.asmx?wsdl
http://localhost/OrderStatusService.asmx?wsdl
```

The code generation engine recognizes when types are equivalent based on their names and name-spaces, and by comparing their schema definition.

Support for W3C SOAP 1.2

Version 2.0 of the .NET Framework includes support for the W3C SOAP version 1.2 protocol in addition to the existing SOAP version 1.1 protocol. On the server side, SOAP 1.2 is on by default and can be turned off via configuration settings in machine.config or web.config:

```
<system.web>
  <webServices>
    <protocols>
      <remove name="HttpSoap12"/>
    </protocols>
  </webServices>
</system.web>
```

With both SOAP 1.1 and SOAP 1.2 enabled on the server side, each Web service will support both proto-cols, allowing the client to choose one of the two protocols. This increases the reach of your Web ser-vices. On the client side, you can select SOAP 1.1 or 1.2 by setting the SoapVersion property of the proxy class. For example:

```
proxy.SoapVersion = System.Web.Services.Protocols.SoapProtocolVersion.Soap12;
```

When using wsdl.exe to consume a Web service that supports both SOAP 1.1 and 1.2, you can specify /protocol:SOAP12 on the command line to generate a proxy class that has its SoapVersion property set to SoapProtocolVersion.Soap12. After you set this property, when you invoke the service you will be using SOAP 1.2.

Summary

This chapter exposed you to the core building blocks of .NET Web services. The chapter began by exam-ining the creation of a simple Web service and discussed the different attributes used with a Web service. As you learned, Web services developed using the .NET platform require little more than applying the WebMethod attribute to each member you want to expose from the XML Web service type. After you have created any number of WebMethod-enabled members, you can interact with a Web service through an intervening proxy. You can either use the WSDL.exe utility or the Add Web Reference option to gener-ate such a proxy, which can then be used by a Web service client. You can use this proxy to syn-chronously and asynchronously invoke a Web service method.

With the extensibility features built into the .NET Framework, you also have the option of leveraging sophisticated features such as SOAP headers, SOAP extensions, custom XML serialization, and schema importer extensions while building Web services. Finally, the .NET Framework 2.0 also offers new fea-tures such as enable decompression, type sharing across proxies, and support for SOAP 1.2.

14

ASP.NET 2.0 Configuration

When ASP.NET 1.0 was first released, it was lauded for the comprehensive feature set with which it shipped. The long list of new features included object-oriented programming model, caching, rich server controls, declarative programming model, and so on; however ASP.NET 1.0 provided only basic support for configuration management, leaving Notepad pretty much the tool of choice for configuration management. But now with the release of ASP.NET 2.0, things have dramatically changed with the suite of new configuration improvements that Web developers and administrators can take advantage of. As part of this, ASP.NET 2.0 ships with a new configuration management API that enables users to programmatically build programs or scripts that create, read, and update `web .config` and `machine.config` configuration files. In addition, ASP.NET 2.0 also provides a new comprehensive admin tool that plugs into the existing IIS Administration MMC, enabling an administrator to graphically read or change any setting within our XML configuration files. This chapter focuses on the new configuration management API by demonstrating the classes, properties, and methods of the new API and examples of how to use them from within your ASP.NET applications.

By the end of this chapter, you will have a good understanding of the following:

- ❑ New configuration sections introduced with ASP.NET 2.0
- ❑ How to store and retrieve application settings from predefined ASP.NET sections
- ❑ How to utilize the web.config file settings to write database independent code
- ❑ How to encrypt and decrypt configuration settings
- ❑ How to enumerate configuration sections
- ❑ How to read contents of the configuration section using strongly typed API
- ❑ How to read contents of the configuration section using raw XML
- ❑ How to create a custom configuration section and persist its contents onto a `web.config` file
- ❑ Built-in management tools supplied with ASP.NET 2.0 and Visual Studio 2005

The next section starts by exploring the ASP.NET configuration architecture.

ASP.NET Configuration

A web.config file is an XML-based text file that can contain standard XML document elements, including well-formed tags, comments, text, cdata, and so on. The file may be ANSI, UTF-8, or Unicode; the system automatically detects the encoding. The root element of a web.config file is always a `<configuration>` tag. ASP.NET end-user settings are then encapsulated within the tag, as follows:

```
<configuration>
  <!- Configuration settings would go here. -->
</configuration>
```

ASP.NET configuration settings are represented within configuration tag sections, also nested within a `<configuration>` tag (and, optionally, within section group tags). For example, in the following sample, the tag `<pages>` is the configuration section that defines configuration settings for the ASP.NET page compiler. Configuration section groups allow hierarchical grouping of sections for organizational purposes. For example, all built-in ASP.NET sections belong in the `<system.web>` section group. Section groups may appear inside other section groups.

In the following example, the configuration file contains configuration settings for the built-in `<pages>` ASP.NET section. This section is contained within the built in section group called `<system.web>`.

```
<configuration>
  <system.web>
    <pages enableSessionState="true" />
  </system.web>
</configuration>
```

> Note tag names in a configuration file are case-sensitive and must be typed exactly as shown. Various attributes and settings for ASP.NET are also case-sensitive and will not be examined by the configuration runtime if the case does not match.

Configuration Hierarchy

ASP.NET configuration model inherits settings from server to application through a hierarchical model. With a hierarchical model, you can specify settings in the machine.config or web.config file of a parent application, and those settings will propagate to any child applications. Child applications can inherit from parent applications, and all applications inherit from the machine.config file. You can specify settings for an entire server, single or multiple applications, single or multiple directories, or even a single file. The following rules apply to the inheritance of configuration settings.

- ❑ Applications first inherit their settings from the machine.config file of the server, then from the web.config file of any parent applications, and finally from their own web.config file.

- ❑ The settings in each web.config file override the settings from the machine.config and web.config files before it.

- ❑   Inheritance follows the URL of the requested resource and not necessarily the physical structure of the files.

- ❑   The web.config file is a subset of machine.config, written according to the same XML schema.

- ❑   The settings in the machine.config file or a parent application's web.config file can prevent settings from being overridden.

- ❑   The settings can be targeted to a specific directory, application, or file using the location setting.

An application can override most of the default values stored in the machine.config file by creating one or more web.config files. At a minimum, an application creates a web.config file in its root folder. Although web.config allows you to override some of the default settings, you cannot override all settings defined in machine.config. In particular, the information about the ASP.NET process model can be defined only in a machine-wide manner using the machine.config file.

> If the application contains child directories, it can define a web.config file for each folder. The scope of each configuration file is determined in a hierarchical, top-down manner. The settings actually applied to an application and thus its Web pages are determined by the sum of the changes that the various web.config files in the hierarchy of the application carry. Along this path, any of those web.config files can extend, restrict, and override any type of settings defined at an upper level, including the machine level, unless the setting is restricted to a certain level (such as process model). If no configuration file exists in an application folder, the settings valid at the upper level are applied.

ASP.NET 1.x Way of Accessing Configuration Sections

In ASP.NET 1.x, there was only one view of configuration: runtime. That view is implemented by an object call System.Configuration.ConfigurationSettings returns configuration sections through calls to a static method named GetConfig that takes in the sectionName as an argument. The sectionName you passed into GetConfig checks to see that the sectionName itself is valid before any config files are opened.

Things have changed for the better in ASP.NET 2.0. ASP.NET 2.0 ships with a comprehensive management API for reading, editing, and creating web.config file settings. The root class for programmatic access to the configuration infrastructure is Configuration. Using the static methods of this class, you can access the machine.config file and any web.config file defined in the context of the application. The next section starts by looking at the new configuration sections introduced with ASP.NET 2.0.

ASP.NET 2.0 Configuration Management

Now that you have a general understanding of the ASP.NET configuration architecture, the remainder of this chapter covers the configuration management functionalities of ASP.NET 2.0. The next section looks at the new configuration sections introduced with ASP.NET 2.0.

New Configuration Sections in ASP.NET 2.0

ASP.NET has added a number of new configuration sections to support the new features of ASP.NET 2.0. Table 14-1 lists the important ones that you are most likely going to have to work with.

Table 14-1. New Configuration Sections

Section	Description
<anonymousIdentification>	Configures the built-in mechanism for configuring the ID assigned to the anonymous user.
<connectionStrings>	Declares the connection strings used by the application. Each connection string is identified by a unique name, which is used to reference the connection string from the code.
<healthMonitoring>	Allows you to configure the health monitoring API, which provides a set of tools designed to trace the performance of running applications.
<membership>	Allows you to configure providers that are registered to store and retrieve membership data.
<profile>	Allows you to configure how a user profile is persisted. This section lets you define the schema of the class that represents the user profile.
<roleManager>	Allows you to configure how role information about the current user will be stored.
<siteMap>	Allows you to register the providers supported for storing site layout. By default, the site map information is stored in a file called web.sitemap.
<urlMappings>	Allows you to map virtual URLs to physical URLs by providing a declarative way to transform a physical page into multiple logical pages.
<webParts>	Allows you to configure the settings required for Web parts.

Note that Table 14-1 simply highlights the important newly added configuration sections and it does not provide an exhaustive list of changes to the configuration schema. In addition to the newly added sections, the existing ASP.NET 1.x sections such as <pages>, <compilation>, <httpHandlers>, <httpModules>, and <sessionState> have also undergone major revisions. For more details, refer to the .NET Framework documentation.

Classes Mapped to ASP.NET Configuration Sections

ASP.NET 2.0 also provides a number of public configuration classes (one per predefined section) that expose the contents of the .config file sections through properties and methods. These classes are all derived from the System.Web.InternalSection class, which in turn is derived from the System .Configuration.ConfigurationSection class. Table 14-2 provides a representation of these classes that provide one-to-one mapping with the actual configuration sections in the web.config file. Note that all of these classes are contained in the System.Web.Configuration namespace.

Table 14-2. Configuration Section Classes in web.config File

Class	Description
AnonymousIdentificationSection	Configures anonymous identification for users that are not authenticated and represents the `<anonymousIdentification>` section in the `web.config` file.
AuthenticationSection	Configures the authentication for a Web application and provides a representation of the `<authentication>` section in the `web.config` file.
AuthorizationSection	Allows you to configure the authorization-related settings for a Web application and provides a mapping with the `<authorization>` section in the `web.config` file.
CacheSection	Allows you to configure the cache settings for the entire Web application and provides a mapping with the `<cache>` section in the `web.config` file.
CompilationSection	Responsible for all the compilation settings used by ASP.NET and provides a mapping with the `<compilation>` section in the `web.config` file.
CustomErrorsSection	Allows you to configure the ASP.NET custom errors and provides a mapping with the `<customErrors>` section in the `web.config` file.
GlobalizationSection	Allows you to define the configuration settings that are used to support the globalization infrastructure of Web applications. This class provides a mapping with the `<globalization>` section in the `web.config` file.
HealthMonitoringSection	Allows you to configure ASP.NET profiles that determine how health monitoring events are sent to event providers. This class provides a mapping with the `<healthmonitoring>` section in the `web.config` file.
HostingEnvironmentSection	Responsible for hosting the server environment that hosts ASP.NET applications. This class provides a mapping with the `<hosting Environment>` section in the `web.config` file.
HttpCookiesSection	Responsible for configuring cookie-related properties for the Web application and provides a mapping with the `<httpCookies>` section in the `web.config` file.

Class	Description
HttpModulesSection	Responsible for configuring HTTP modules within an application and provides a mapping with the <httpModules> section in the web.config file.
HttpHandlersSection	Responsible for mapping incoming URL to handler classes that are derived from the IHttpHandler class. This class provides a mapping with the <httpHandlers> section in the web.config file.
HttpRuntimeSection	Allows you to configure the ASP.NET HTTP runtime by providing a mapping with the <httpRuntime> section in the web.config file.
IdentitySection	Responsible for configuring the Windows identity used to run a Web application. This class provides a mapping with the <identity> section in the web.config file.
MachineKeySection	Responsible for configuring the encryption key used to encrypt secrets such as forms authentication tickets and so on. This class provides a mapping with the <machineKey> section in the web.config file.
MembershipSection	Responsible for configuring settings and providers for the ASP.NET membership system. This class provides a mapping with the <membership> section in the web.config file.
PagesSection	Responsible for individual ASP.NET page settings. This class provides a mapping with the <pages> section in the web.config file.
ProcessModelSection	Responsible for configuring ASP.NET process model settings. This class provides a mapping with the <processModel> section in the web.config file.
ProfileSection	Responsible for configuring settings and providers for the ASP.NET role manager. This class provides a mapping with the <profile> section in the web.config file.
SessionPageStateSection	Responsible for configuring how session state can be used to save page viewstate for small devices. This class provides a mapping with the <sessionPageState> section in the web.config file.

Class	Description
SessionStateSection	Responsible for configuring the HTTP session state module, and this class provides a mapping with the `<sessionState>` section in the `web.config` file.
SiteMapSection	Allows you to define the configuration settings that are used to support the navigation infrastructure for configuring, storing, and rendering site navigation. This class provides a mapping with the `<siteMap>` section in the `web.config` file.
TraceSection	Responsible for configuring the ASP.NET trace service. This class provides a mapping with the `<trace>` element in the `web.config` file.
TrustSection	Allows you to configure the code access security that is applied to an application. This class provides a mapping with the `<trust>` section in the `web.config` file.
UrlMappingsSection	Responsible for configuring URL mappings used by the ASP.NET site navigation system. This class provides a mapping with the `<urlMappings>` section in the `web.config` file.
WebPartsSection	Responsible for configuring the settings used by ASP.NET Web parts. This class provides a mapping with the `<webParts>` section in the `web.config` file.
XhtmlConformanceSection	Responsible for XHTML conformance settings of ASP.NET controls. This class provides a mapping with the `<xhtmlConformance>` section in the `web.config` file.

These classes expose the attributes of the corresponding section as typed properties, making it easy for you to read or edit values.

WebConfigurationManager Class

One of the important configuration-related classes is the WebConfigurationManager class that provides programmatic access to configuration files and configuration sections. This class is contained in the System.Web.Configuration namespace and is specifically used for retrieving and updating configuration settings from a web.config file. Table 14-3 discusses the properties of the WebConfigurationManager class.

Table 14-3. Properties of the WebConfigurationManager Class

Property	Description
AppSettings	Allows you to retrieve the configuration settings stored in the `<appSettings>` section of the `web.config` file
ConnectionStrings	Allows you to retrieve the configuration settings stored in the `<connectionStrings>` section of the `web.config` file

Table 14-4 lists the methods of the `WebConfigurationManager` class. Note all these methods are static.

Table 14-4. Methods of the WebConfigurationManager Class

Method	Description
GetWebApplicationSection	Allows you to retrieve the specified configuration section for the current Web application's default configuration
OpenMachineConfiguration	Allows you to get reference to the `machine.config` file in the form of a Configuration object
OpenMappedMachineConfiguration	Allows you to get reference to the `machine.config` file in the form of a Configuration object using the specified file mapping
OpenMappedWebConfiguration	Allows you to get reference to the web.config file in the form of a Configuration object using the specified file mapping
OpenWebConfiguration	Allows you to get reference to the `web.config` file in the form of a Configuration object

> Note that in .NET 2.0, there are two main classes used for managing configuration settings. They are `ConfigurationManager` and the `WebConfigurationManager`. You should use the `ConfigurationManager` if you want to update or add sections to the `app.config` file. You should use the `WebConfigurationManager` class if you want to update or add sections to the `web.config` file.

The major functionality provided by the `WebConfigurationManager` class falls into three categories.

❑ Easy and effective access to the `appSettings` and `connectionStrings` sections of the current application's `web.config` file. This is made possible through the introduction of new properties such as `AppSettings` and `ConnectionStrings`.

❏   Ability to access a specific configuration section from the current application's `web.config` file using methods such as `GetSection()`, and `GetWebApplicationSection()`.

❏   Ability to open a configuration file for updating configuration settings. To this end, the `WebConfigurationManager` class exposes methods such as `OpenMachineConfiguration()`, `OpenMappedMachineConfiguration()`, `OpenWebConfiguration()`, and `OpenMappedWebConfiguration()`.

This chapter discusses most of these properties and methods in detail in the next few sections.

> *Note that for the examples shown in this chapter, the ASP.NET process account needs sufficient permissions to be able to read and write into the configuration file. For reasons of simplicity, Integrated Windows authentication for Web site is enabled through IIS and also turned on impersonation for the Web site using the following configuration settings under the `<system.web>` element in the `web.config` file.*
>
> `<identity impersonate="true"/>`
>
> *Because of these settings, the ASP.NET code will execute using the credentials of logged on user's account instead of using the default ASP.NET (if you are running Windows XP) account. Note that in production applications, it is recommended that you run your ASP.NET code using a domain account that has the minimum set of permissions on the server to execute code.*

The next section discusses the use of `WebConfigurationManager` class in retrieving connection strings from a `web.config` file.

Retrieving Configuration from Predefined Sections

To retrieve configuration settings from within an ASP.NET application, you use the `WebConfigurationManager` class. ASP.NET by default provides two predefined sections that can be used to store configuration information for later retrieval. These sections are as follows:

❏   `<appSettings>` — Primarily used for storing application settings such as path to an XML Web Service and so on

❏   `<connectionStrings>` — As the name suggests, this section is used for storing connection strings information

In the next few sections, you see how to retrieve values stored in these sections.

Using Application Settings

Configuration files are perfectly suited for storing custom application settings, such as database file paths, or remote XML Web service URLs. ASP.NET, by default, supports a section named `<appSettings>` that can store these settings as name/value pairs. The following example shows how to retrieve the share location path from an `<appSettings>` section.

Listing 14-1: Using WebConfigurationManager Class to Retrieve Application Settings

```
<%@ Import Namespace="System.Web.Configuration" %>
<script runat=server language=C# >
void Page_Load(object source, EventArgs e)
{
  string shareLocationFromConfig =
      WebConfigurationManager.AppSettings["shareLocation"];
    Response.Write("Retrieved value : " + shareLocationFromConfig);
    //Code to connect to the share for file processing
  }
</script>
<html xmlns="http://www.w3.org/1999/xhtml">
<head>
<title>
  Retrieving Configuration Settings from appSettings section
  </title>
</head>
<body>
<form id="form1" runat="server">
    <div>
    </div>
  </form>
</body>
</html>
```

This code is simple and straightforward. By making a call to the AppSettings property of the WebConfigurationManager class, the code retrieves the value of the shareLocation key from the web.config file. Place the following <appSettings> element inside the web.config file.

```
<appSettings>
<add key="shareLocation" value="\\dev-server\share"/>
</appSettings>
```

If you navigate to the page from the browser, you should see the value of the appSettings element identified by the key shareLocation displayed in the browser.

Using Connection Strings

Similar to general application settings, ASP.NET provides a configuration section specifically for storing database connection strings, used by ADO.NET. This configuration section is called <connectionStrings> and it allows for secure storage and retrieval of database connection strings through the Configuration API. It is important to note that this is not under the <appSettings> section. The following example shows a <connectionStrings> configuration section for an application that uses the AdventureWorks sample database.

```
<configuration>
  <connectionStrings>
          <add name="adventureWorks" connectionString="server=localhost;integrated
```

```
        security=true;database=AdventureWorks;"/>
    </connectionStrings>
    ----------
    ----------
    <configuration>
```

After you have the connection string stored in this fashion, you just need one line of code to retrieve that connection string. Listing 14-2 shows you how to accomplish this.

Listing 14-2: Using WebConfigurationManager Class to Retrieve Connection Strings

```csharp
<%@ Import Namespace="System.Data" %>
<%@ Import Namespace="System.Data.SqlClient" %>
<%@ Import Namespace="System.Web.Configuration" %>
<script runat=server language=C# >
void Page_Load(object source, EventArgs e)
{
    string connString = WebConfigurationManager.
      ConnectionStrings["adventureWorks"].ConnectionString;
      using (SqlConnection conn = new SqlConnection(connString))
      {
        conn.Open();
        SqlCommand command = new SqlCommand("Select * from Person.ContactType",
          conn);
        command.CommandType = CommandType.Text;
        SqlDataReader reader = command.ExecuteReader();
        contactTypeView.DataSource = reader;
        contactTypeView.DataBind();
      }
  }
</script>
<html xmlns="http://www.w3.org/1999/xhtml">
<head>
  <title>Retrieving Connection Strings from connectionStrings section</title>
</head>
<body>
  <form id="form1" runat="server">
    <div>
      <asp:GridView runat="server" ID="contactTypeView"/>
    </div>
  </form>
</body>
</html>
```

The code retrieves the connection string from the web.config file using the ConnectionStrings property of the WebConfigurationManager class; then, it opens up a connection to the AdventureWorks database and executes a query against ContactType table. It simply displays the output of the query execution in a GridView control. The output produced by Listing 14-2 is shown in Figure 14-1.

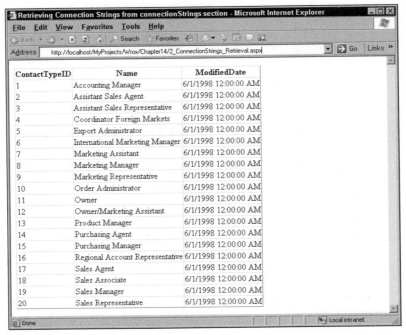

Figure 14-1

Use of Expression Builders

Listing 14-2 utilized the `WebConfigurationManager` to programmatically retrieve the connection string. In addition to the programmatic approach, ASP.NET 2.0 also provides a new declarative approach to retrieve configuration settings using "$" expressions. These expressions are new in ASP.NET 2.0, and they allow you to load connection strings, resources, and other items using a declarative approach. For example, you can retrieve the same adventureWorks connection string using the syntax `<%$ConnectionStrings:adventureWorks%>`. The following is the code that uses the adventureWorks connection string to retrieve contact type information through a `SqlDataSource` control and then displays the same through a `GridView` control.

```
<asp:SqlDataSource ID="contactTypeSource" runat="server"
 ConnectionString="<%$ConnectionStrings:adventureWorks%>"
 SelectCommand="Select * from Person.ContactType">
</asp:SqlDataSource>

<asp:GridView runat="server" ID="authorsView"
 DataSourceID="contactTypeSource">
</asp:GridView>
```

Writing Database Provider Independent Code Using web.config Settings

In addition to storing the actual connection string, you can also store the `providerName` in the web.config file and use that as a foundation for creating database independent code. For example, modify the connection string section of the web.config file to look as follows:

```
<connectionStrings>
        <add name="adventureWorks" connectionString="server=localhost;integrated
    security=true;database=AdventureWorks;"
    providerName="System.Data.SqlClient"/>
</connectionStrings>
```

You can use the `providerName` attribute value to identify the database provider to use. Listing 14-3 demonstrates the use of the `ProviderName` property of `ConnectionStringSettings` class to create provider independent code.

Listing 14-3: Using providerName Setting to Create Provider Independent Data Access Code

```csharp
<%@ Import Namespace="System.Web.Configuration" %>
<%@ Import Namespace="System.Data" %>
<%@ Import Namespace="System.Data.Common" %>
<script runat="server" language="C#" >
void Page_Load(object source, EventArgs e)
{
    string providerName = WebConfigurationManager.
      ConnectionStrings["adventureWorks"].ProviderName;
    DbProviderFactory factory=DbProviderFactories.GetFactory(providerName);
    using (DbConnection conn = factory.CreateConnection())
    {
        string connString = WebConfigurationManager.
          ConnectionStrings["AdventureWorks"].ConnectionString;
        conn.ConnectionString = connString;
        using (DbDataAdapter adapter = factory.CreateDataAdapter())
        {
          adapter.SelectCommand = conn.CreateCommand();
          adapter.SelectCommand.CommandText = "SELECT * FROM Person.ContactType";
          DataTable table = new DataTable("ContactType");
          adapter.Fill(table);
          contactTypeView.DataSource = table;
          contactTypeView.DataBind();
        }
    }
}
</script>
<html xmlns="http://www.w3.org/1999/xhtml">
<head>
<title>
  Creating DB provider independant code using providerName setting
</title>
</head>
<body>
<form id="form1" runat="server">
    <div>
```

```
          <asp:GridView runat="server" ID="contactTypeView"></asp:GridView>
      </div>
    </form>
  </body>
</html>
```

In Listing 14-3, by setting the providerName property of the connection string, you connect to the database generically using ADO.NET provider factories, rather than using code specific to the type of ADO.NET provider. You retrieve the providerName by using the following line of code.

```
string providerName = WebConfigurationManager.
  ConnectionStrings["adventureWorks"].ProviderName;
```

Use the provider name as an argument to the GetFactory() method of the DbProviderFactories class.

```
DbProviderFactory factory = DbProviderFactories.GetFactory(providerName);
```

After you have a DbProviderFactory object that is specific to the database you are connecting to, you can use that object to create instances of the DbConnection, and DbDataAdapter objects that are specific to the database you are connecting to. These objects are then utilized to open connection to the database, execute the sql query against the contact type table in the AdventureWorks database, and finally bind the output of the query execution to the database.

> .NET Framework 2.0 has new factory classes that make it easier to write data access code independent of the database. This is made possible by the introduction of database-independent factory class named DbProviderFactory that allows you to create database specific DbConnection and DbDataAdapter objects to work with specific databases. The provider to use at runtime is obtained by calling the GetFactory() static method of the DbProviderFactories class passing in a string uniquely representing that provider. This string is called Provider Invariant Name and is registered by each provider in machine.config. For example, for ODBC provider, it is System.Data.Odbc. The advantage of this methodology is that it gives you the option of seamlessly working with multiple providers like OleDb and ODBC without having to lock onto a specific implementation like SqlClient.

Encrypting and Decrypting Configuration Sections

A powerful feature of the ASP.NET 2.0 Configuration API is its support for encryption. Using this encryption API, you can almost encrypt and decrypt almost all sections of your configuration files, including any user-defined sections. There are some exceptions, such as the <httpRuntime> section, that needs to be accessed outside of ASP.NET by some IIS ISAPI code and therefore cannot be encrypted.

The encryption API is extremely useful when you are dealing with sensitive data such as usernames and passwords from within your Web applications. Although ASP.NET configures IIS to prevent browser access to web.config files, it is nevertheless a good practice to never store such data as plain text in a configuration file. Once you encrypt specific sections using the configuration API, those encrypted values are virtually impossible to read using a text editor.

> By default, ASP.NET supports two protected configuration providers: RSA and DPAPI. The DPAPI provider uses a machine-specific key, so you must physically encrypt the configuration settings on each machine. The RSA provider, which is used by default, allows you the option to create an RSA key and install it on other machines, so that you can copy the same configuration file between these machines, thereby deploying the ASP.NET applications using XCOPY.

Calls to the configuration API can transparently work with encrypted sections because the API automatically handles encryption and decryption. To programmatically set a configuration section to be encrypted, you call the `ConfigurationSection.SectionInformation` property to get the `SectionInformation` object, and then call the `ProtectSection()` method on the `SectionInformation` object. To decrypt the encrypted section, call the `UnprotectSection()` method of the `SectionInformation` object. The following example shows how sections can be programmatically encrypted and decrypted, and how the configuration API automatically handles encrypted sections. Listing 14-4 uses two command buttons named `btnEncrypt` and `btnDecrypt` that are used to encrypt or decrypt the `connectionStrings` section of the `web.config` file, respectively.

Listing 14-4: Encrypting and Decrypting a Configuration Section

```csharp
<%@ Import Namespace="System.Configuration" %>
<%@ Import Namespace="System.Web.Configuration" %>
<script runat="server" language="C#" >
const string PROVIDER = "DataProtectionConfigurationProvider";
protected void btnEncrypt_Click(object sender, EventArgs e)
{
    try
    {
      Configuration config = WebConfigurationManager.
        OpenWebConfiguration(Request.ApplicationPath);
      ConnectionStringsSection sect = config.ConnectionStrings;
      sect.SectionInformation.ProtectSection(PROVIDER);
      config.Save();
      lblResult.Text = "Connection string section is now " +
        "encrypted in web.config file<br>";
    }
    catch (Exception ex)
    {
      lblResult.Text = "Exception: " + ex.Message;
    }
    //Note when you read the encrypted connection string,
    //it is automatically decrypted for you
    lblResult.Text += "Connection String is:" +
      WebConfigurationManager.ConnectionStrings["adventureWorks"].
      ConnectionString;
    }

protected void btnDecrypt_Click(object sender, EventArgs e)
{
    try
    {
      Configuration config = WebConfigurationManager.
```

```
        OpenWebConfiguration (Request.ApplicationPath);
      ConnectionStringsSection sect = config.ConnectionStrings;
      if (sect.SectionInformation.IsProtected)
      {
        sect.SectionInformation.UnprotectSection();
        config.Save();
      }
      lblResult.Text = "Connection string is now decrypted in " +
        "web.config file";
    }
    catch (Exception ex)
    {
      lblResult.Text = "Exception: " + ex.Message;
    }
  }
}
</script>
<html xmlns="http://www.w3.org/1999/xhtml">
<head>
  <title>Encrypting and Decrypting Connection Strings</title>
</head>
<body>
<form id="form1" runat="server">
    <div>
       
      <asp:Button ID="btnEncrypt" Runat="server" Text="Encrypt"
        Width="96px" Height="35px" OnClick="btnEncrypt_Click" />
      <asp:Button ID="btnDecrypt" Runat="server" Text="Decrypt"
        Width="102px" Height="35px" OnClick="btnDecrypt_Click" />
      <br/><br/><br/>
      <asp:Label ID="lblResult" runat="server" Height="19px"
        Width="435px"></asp:Label>
    </div>
  </form>
</body>
</html>
```

At the top of the page, the code declares a constant named PROVIDER that indicates the type of provider to use. You then get reference to the connectionStrings section of the web.config file by calling the ConnectionStrings property of the Configuration object.

```
ConnectionStringsSection sect = config.ConnectionStrings;
```

After that, you invoke the ProtectSection() method of the SectionInformation object passing in the provider to use for encryption.

```
sect.SectionInformation.ProtectSection(PROVIDER);
```

Finally, you call the Save() method of the Configuration object to persist the changes back to the web.config file.

```
config.Save();
```

Now the connection string is read back from the web.config file using the
WebConfigurationManager.ConnectionStrings property.

```
lblResult.Text += "Connection String is:" +
    WebConfigurationManager.ConnectionStrings["adventureWorks"].ConnectionString;
```

When you read the encrypted connection string from within the code, you will notice that the encrypted
value is automatically decrypted for you.

In the Click event of the btnDecrypt button, check to see if the section is encrypted by invoking the
IsProtected property of the SectionInformation object. If it is encrypted, you simply call the
UnprotectSection() method to decrypt the section. After it is decrypted, you simply persist the
changes back to the web.config file through a call to the Save() method.

```
if (sect.SectionInformation.IsProtected)
{
sect.SectionInformation.UnprotectSection();
config.Save();
}
```

Before navigating to the page from the browser, ensure you have the following connection strings section in the web.config file.

```
<connectionStrings>
  <add name="adventureWorks" connectionString="server=localhost;integrated
    security=true;database=AdventureWorks;"/>
</connectionStrings>
```

Now request the page from the browser and click the Encrypt button. The connection strings section in
the web.config file will be encrypted as follows:

```
<protectedData>
  <protectedDataSections>
    <add name="connectionStrings"
      provider="DataProtectionConfigurationProvider"
      inheritedByChildren="false" />
</protectedDataSections>
</protectedData>
<connectionStrings>
<EncryptedData>
    <CipherData>
      <CipherValue>
        AQAAANCMnd8BFdERjHoAwE--------
      </CipherValue>
    </CipherData>
</EncryptedData>
</connectionStrings>
```

Clicking on the Decrypt button will result in decrypting of the above encrypted value. The configuration
API provides a seamless way to encrypt or decrypt sections from the configuration file with very few
lines of code.

For the code shown in Listing 14-4 to work, you need to ensure that the ASP.NET worker process
account has sufficient permissions to modify the web.config file.

Enumerating Configuration Sections

So far, you have seen how to store and retrieve connection strings as well as the steps involved in encrypting or decrypting connection strings. In this section, you learn how to enumerate the contents of a specific section in the `web.config` file. For the purposes of this example, you learn how to enumerate the built-in sections by looping through the `ConfigurationSectionCollection` object. This type of enumeration is useful if you are building a user interface editor that will enable the users to edit the configuration settings.

Listing 14-5: Enumerating All the Configuration Sections

```csharp
<%@ Import Namespace="System.Configuration" %>
<%@ Import Namespace="System.Web.Configuration" %>
<script runat=server language=C# >
public void Page_Load(object source, EventArgs e)
{
    string path = Request.CurrentExecutionFilePath;
    path = path.Substring(0, path.LastIndexOf('/'));
    Configuration config = WebConfigurationManager.OpenWebConfiguration(path);
    //Enumerate the configuration sections and display them
    Response.Write("<b>Configuration sections in the web.config:</b><br>");
    foreach (ConfigurationSection section in config.Sections)
    {
      Response.Write("Name: " + section.SectionInformation.Name + "<br>");
      Response.Write("IsProtected:" +
        section.SectionInformation.IsProtected.ToString() + "<br><br>");
    }
}
</script>
<html xmlns="http://www.w3.org/1999/xhtml">
<head>
  <title>Enumerating Configuration Sections</title>
</head>
<body>
<form id="form1" runat="server">
    <div>
    </div>
  </form>
</body>
</html>
```

As similar to the previous examples, this example also utilizes the `OpenWebConfiguration()` method of the `WebConfigurationManager` class to get reference to the configuration section in the `web.config` file. After you have done that, you can easily get reference to all the sections through the Sections property of the Configuration object. Inside each loop, you loop through all the sections and write their name as well as their encryption status onto a browser one at a time. Figure 14-2 shows the output of the page.

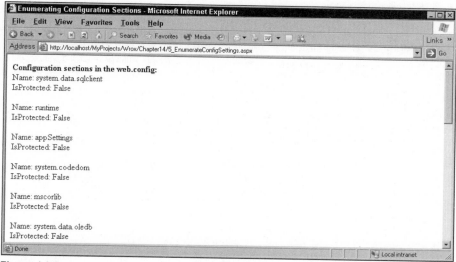

Figure 14-2

Reading Configuration Sections

The Configuration object contains a hierarchy of configuration sections and configuration section groups, corresponding to the hierarchy of sections and groups in the configuration file. To obtain the root of this hierarchy, you can call the `Configuration.RootSectionGroup` property. From this object, you can navigate the Sections collection, which contains all sections that are direct children of the section group, or the SectionGroups collection, which contain all section groups that are direct children.

You can also access a section directly by calling the `Configuration.GetSection ()`, passing in the path to the section required. Configuration sections are represented by the `ConfigurationSection` type meaning that they all inherit from the `ConfigurationSection` class. After you have reference to the section, there are two ways you can process the contents of the section.

❑ Because each section returned is typically a strongly typed object (that inherits from the `ConfigurationSection` class), you can simply call the properties of the object to access the values.

❑ You can also access the contents of the section as a raw XML. The ability to process the contents of the section as a raw XML is particularly useful for legacy ASP.NET 1.x sections that do not support a strongly typed management API. Note that the raw XML returned is for the current level only, and does not automatically reflect inherited settings.

For the purposes of this chapter, you learn how to retrieve the settings from the <customErrors> element using the above approaches.

Retrieving Configuration Settings Using Strongly Typed API

In this section, you learn how to use the strongly typed object named `CustomErrorsSection` to process the settings from the `<customErrors>` element. Listing 14-6 shows the code required to accomplish this.

Listing 14-6: Using Strongly Typed API to Retrieve <customErrors> Section Settings

```
<%@ Import Namespace="System.Configuration" %>
<%@ Import Namespace="System.Web.Configuration" %>
<script runat=server language=C# >
void Page_Load(object source, EventArgs e)
{
    string path = Request.CurrentExecutionFilePath;
    path = path.Substring(0, path.LastIndexOf('/'));
    Configuration config = WebConfigurationManager.
      OpenWebConfiguration(path);
    CustomErrorsSection sect = config.GetSection
      ("system.web/customErrors") as CustomErrorsSection;
    Response.Write("Mode : " + sect.Mode.ToString() + "<br>");
    Response.Write("DefaultRedirect : " + sect.DefaultRedirect + "<br><br>");
    Response.Write("Status Code =====>  Redirect URLs<br>");
    foreach (CustomError error in sect.Errors)
    {
      Response.Write("Status Code:" + error.StatusCode.ToString() +
        "======>Redirect:" + error.Redirect.ToString() + "<br>");
    }
  }
</script>
<html xmlns="http://www.w3.org/1999/xhtml">
<head>
<title>
  Retrieving Configuration Settings using Strongly Typed API
</title>
</head>
<body>
<form id="form1" runat="server">
    <div>
    </div>
  </form>
</body>
</html>
```

Similar to the previous examples, you start by getting reference to the Configuration object through the call to the `OpenWebConfiguration()` method. You then make a call to the `GetSection()` method of the Configuration object passing in the name of the section.

```
CustomErrorsSection sect = config.GetSection
("system.web/customErrors") as CustomErrorsSection;
```

You typecast the returned value of the `GetSection()` method to `CustomErrorsSection` object and store it in a local variable. After that, write out the mode and defaultRedirect attributes of the `<customErrors>` element by calling the `Mode` and `DefaultRedirect` properties, respectively.

```
Response.Write("Mode : " + sect.Mode.ToString() + "<br>");
Response.Write("DefaultRedirect : " + sect.DefaultRedirect + "<br><br>");
```

Loop through all the `<customError>` elements inside the `<customErrors>` by looping through the `CustomErrorCollection` object.

```
foreach (CustomError error in sect.Errors)
{
  Response.Write("Status Code:" + error.StatusCode.ToString() +
    "======>Redirect:" + error.Redirect.ToString() + "<br>");
}
```

As the code shows, the resultant listing is neat and simple to understand. Before testing the page from the browser, place the following `customErrors` section in your `web.config` file.

```
<customErrors defaultRedirect="Error.aspx" mode="RemoteOnly">
<error statusCode="401" redirect="Unauthorized.aspx" />
<error statusCode="404" redirect="NotFound.aspx" />
</customErrors>
```

Now requesting the page from the browser should produce an output that is somewhat similar to Figure 14-3.

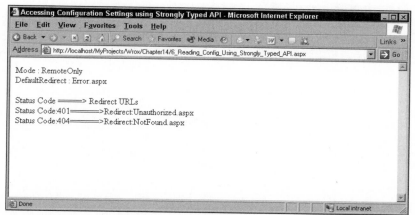

Figure 14-3

Note that the output produced by the strongly typed configuration section object will normally show all the inherited values, not just the contents of the current web.config file.

In addition to retrieving the contents of the configuration section, you can also update the contents of the configuration section by directly setting its properties of the strongly typed configuration section object (such as CustomErrorsSection object) and then calling the Save() method of the Configuration object.

Retrieving Configuration Sections Using Raw XML

All configuration sections also allow you to read and write their configuration settings using raw XML. This is useful particularly for legacy ASP.NET 1.x sections that do not support a strongly typed configuration API. Note that the raw XML returned is for the current level only, and does not automatically reflect inherited settings. Listing 14-7 implements the same functionality discussed in Listing 14-6 but with using raw XML instead of strongly typed API.

Listing 14-7: Using Raw XML to Retrieve <customErrors> Section Settings

```
<%@ Import Namespace="System.Configuration" %>
<%@ Import Namespace="System.Web.Configuration" %>
<%@ Import Namespace="System.Xml" %>
<script runat=server language=C# >
void Page_Load(object source, EventArgs e)
{
    string path = Request.CurrentExecutionFilePath;
    path = path.Substring(0, path.LastIndexOf('/'));
    Configuration config = WebConfigurationManager.
      OpenWebConfiguration(path);
    CustomErrorsSection sect = config.GetSection
      ("system.web/customErrors") as CustomErrorsSection;
    XmlDocument xmlDoc = new XmlDocument();
    xmlDoc.LoadXml(sect.SectionInformation.GetRawXml());
    Response.Write("Mode : " +
      xmlDoc.DocumentElement.Attributes["mode"].Value + "<br>");
    Response.Write("DefaultRedirect : " +
      xmlDoc.DocumentElement.Attributes["defaultRedirect"].Value +
      "<br><br>");
    Response.Write("Status Code =====>  Redirect URLs <br>");
    foreach (XmlNode node in xmlDoc.DocumentElement.ChildNodes)
    {
        Response.Write("Status Code:" + node.Attributes["statusCode"].Value +
          "======>Redirect:" + node.Attributes["redirect"].Value + "<br>");
    }
  }
</script>
<html xmlns="http://www.w3.org/1999/xhtml">
<head>
  <title>Retrieving Configuration Settings using Raw XML</title>
</head>
<body>
<form id="form1" runat="server">
    <div>
    </div>
  </form>
</body>
</html>
```

In this code, you get reference to the contents of the <customErrors> element by calling the GetRawXml() method of the SectionInformation object. Load that raw XML into an XmlDocument object for further processing. From that point onwards, process the raw XML through the properties and methods of the XmlDocument object.

In addition to reading the configuration settings in the form of raw XML, you can also update the configuration settings by invoking the SetRawXml() method of the SectionInformation object. To this method, you supply the new XML string value as an argument.

For reasons of maintainability, ASP.NET applications should never modify the `machine.config` file, and you should carefully consider any updates to `web.config`. You should try to save custom settings (that need to be modified at runtime) to a separate external file. For example, you can use an external XML file linked to the `<appSettings>` section:

```
<configuration>
 <appSettings file="externalFile.config" />
</configuration>
```

The custom `.config` file must have the same schema as standard configuration files. Using an external file offers a number of benefits. It simplifies the management of the parameters. Also, you don't need to touch a system file. Notice that any modifications to a `.config` file cause the affected pages (which might include the whole application) to recompile. If you need to save custom settings, using a distinct file saves you from such side effects.

Creating a Custom Configuration Section

There are times where you may have to create a custom configuration section and add it to a configuration file at runtime. For example, if you are creating a Windows installer for deploying a Web application and you need to create sections of the web.config file dynamically, you need to be able to create and persist a custom section at runtime. With ASP.NET 2.0, you now have an easy and effective way to accomplish this. You accomplish this by going through the following steps:

1. Create a custom object (that derives from the `ConfigurationSection` class). This class represents a specific custom section in the configuration file.

2. Populate that object with the right values.

3. Add the custom object to the `ConfigurationSectionCollection` using the `Add()` method.

4. Finally persist the contents by calling the `Save()` method of the Configuration class.

Listing 14-8 shows the implementation of the custom class.

Listing 14-8: Declaration of the FontSettingSection Class

```
using System.Configuration;
using System.Web.Configuration;
public class FontSettingSection : ConfigurationSection
{
//Specify the attribute names
private const string fontType = "fontType";
private const string fontSize = "fontSize";
private const string fontBold = "fontBold";

[ConfigurationProperty(FontSettingSection.fontType,
  DefaultValue = "Arial")]
public string FontType
```

```
{
    get
    {
        return (string)base[FontSettingSection.fontType];
    }
    set
    {
        base[FontSettingSection.fontType] = value;
    }
}

[ConfigurationProperty(FontSettingSection.fontSize,
  DefaultValue = "10")]
public int FontSize
{
    get
    {
        return (int)base[FontSettingSection.fontSize];
    }
    set
    {
        base[FontSettingSection.fontSize] = value;
    }
}

[ConfigurationProperty(FontSettingSection.fontBold,
  DefaultValue = "false")]
public bool FontBold
{
    get
    {
        return (bool)base[FontSettingSection.fontBold];
    }
    set
    {
        base[FontSettingSection.fontBold] = value;
    }
}
}
```

As you can see from Listing 14-8, the implementation of the custom class is simple and straightforward. The custom class inherits from the ConfigurationSection class and exposes three properties named FontType, FontSize, and FontBold. These properties are decorated with an attribute named ConfigurationProperty. The ConfigurationProperty class represents a configuration property, attribute, or child element contained within an element of a configuration file. To the constructor of the ConfigurationProperty class, you supply the name of the attribute as an argument as well as a default value for that attribute. Now that you understand the FontSettingSection class, Listing 14-9 shows the code required to persist that class into a web.config file.

Listing 14-9: Reading and Writing a Custom Configuration Section

```csharp
<%@ Import Namespace="System.Configuration" %>
<%@ Import Namespace="System.Web.Configuration" %>
<%@ Import Namespace="System.Text" %>
<script runat=server language=C# >
void btnSave_Click(object sender, EventArgs e)
{
    try
    {
      Configuration config = WebConfigurationManager.OpenWebConfiguration
        (Request.ApplicationPath);
      FontSettingSection fontSettingSection = new FontSettingSection();
      fontSettingSection.FontType = txtFontType.Text;
      fontSettingSection.FontSize = Convert.ToInt32(txtFontSize.Text);
      fontSettingSection.FontBold = Convert.ToBoolean(txtFontBold.Text);
      config.Sections.Clear();
      config.Sections.Add("fontSettingSection", fontSettingSection);
      config.Save();
      lblResult.Text = "Successfully saved";
    }
    catch (System.Exception ex)
    {
      lblResult.Text = ex.Message;
    }
}


void btnRetrieve_Click(object sender, EventArgs e)
{
    try
    {
      Configuration config = WebConfigurationManager.OpenWebConfiguration
        (Request.ApplicationPath);
      foreach (string key in config.Sections.Keys)
      {
        if (key.Equals("fontSettingSection"))
        {
          lblResult.Text = "Custom section is found";
          FontSettingSection sect =
            (FontSettingSection)WebConfigurationManager.
            GetWebApplicationSection("fontSettingSection");
          txtFontType.Text = sect.FontType;
          txtFontSize.Text = sect.FontSize.ToString();
          txtFontBold.Text = sect.FontBold.ToString();
        }
      }
    }
    catch (System.Exception ex)
    {
      lblResult.Text = ex.Message;
    }
  }
</script>
```

```
<html xmlns="http://www.w3.org/1999/xhtml">
<head>
  <title>Serializing a custom section into a Configuration File</title>
</head>
<body>
<form id="form1" runat="server">
    <div>
      <asp:Label ID="lblFontType" runat="server" Text="Font Type"/>
      <asp:TextBox ID="txtFontType" runat="server" Width="208px"/ >
      <br/><br/>
      <asp:Label ID="lblFontSize" runat="server" Text="Font Size"/>
      <asp:TextBox ID="txtFontSize" runat="server" Width="208px"/>
      <br/><br/>
      <asp:Label ID="lblFontBold" runat="server" Text="Font Bold"/>
       
      <asp:TextBox ID="txtFontBold" runat="server" Width="208px"/>
      <br/><br/>
      <asp:label ID="lblResult" Runat="server"/>
      <br/><br/>
      <asp:Button ID="btnSave" runat="server" Text="Save"
        OnClick="btnSave_Click"/>
      <asp:Button ID="btnRetrieve" runat="server" Text="Retrieve"
        OnClick="btnRetrieve_Click" />
    </div>
  </form>
</body>
</html>
```

In the Click event of the btnSave control, you start by obtaining reference to the web.config file. Create an instance of the FontSettingSection class. After an instance of the FontSettingSection class is created, set its properties to appropriate values. After that, clear all the custom sections in the configuration file by invoking the Clear() method. To persist the newly added section, you then invoke the Save() method. That's all there is to creating a custom class and serializing its contents into a section in a web.config file. Now open up your web.config file and you should see an output as similar to the following.

```
<configuration>
  <configSections>
    <section name="fontSettingSection"
      type="FontSettingSection, App_Code" />
  </configSections>
  <fontSettingSection fontType="Verdana" fontSize="12"
    fontBold="true" />
  ------
  ------
</configuration>
```

The rest of the code in Listing 14-9 is executed when the Click event of the btnRetrieve is invoked. In the Click event, you get reference to all the keys in the ConfigurationSectionCollection to verify if the newly added section is actually present in the configuration file or not. To accomplish this, loop through all the sections by using the Keys property. While looping through the collection, if a section named "FontSettingSection" is found, it simply displays a message indicating that the section is found in the configuration file. It then retrieves the values from the FontSettingSection object and displays the property values in the appropriate text box controls. Figure 14-4 shows the output of the page when the Retrieve button is clicked.

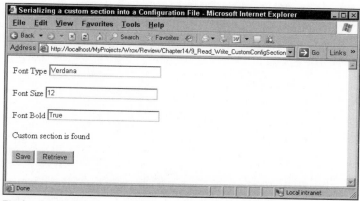

Figure 14-4

Built-in Configuration Management Tools

So far, you have seen how to take advantage of the rich ASP.NET object model for storing and retrieving configuration settings from the configuration file. In addition to the programmatic API, ASP.NET 2.0 also provides a suite of configuration management tools that you can use to configure settings for your Web applications. These tools can be categorized as follows:

❑ GUI Tools — These tools are seamlessly integrated with the IIS (Internet Information Services) MMC and Visual Studio 2005.

❑ Command line tools — These command line tools allow you to configure common ASP.NET settings from a command line.

The next couple of sections provide you with a walkthrough of these tools and show how to use them.

GUI Tools

In this category, there are two tools.

❑ ASP.NET MMC (Microsoft Management Console) Snapin

❑ Web Site Administration Tool

Both of these tools are covered in the following sections.

ASP.NET MMC Snapin

In addition to full programmatic access to the configuration settings, ASP.NET 2.0 provides an interactive tool for administering the environment. The tool integrates with the IIS Microsoft Management Console (MMC) snapin. As a result, a new property page (named ASP.NET) is added to each virtual directory node. To bring up the ASP.NET MMC snapin, open IIS Manager through Start→Programs→ Administrative Tools menu. After within IIS, navigate to the virtual directory of interest, and right-click on that virtual directory and select Properties from the context menu. Click the ASP.NET tab from the Properties dialog box. You will see the output shown in Figure 14-5.

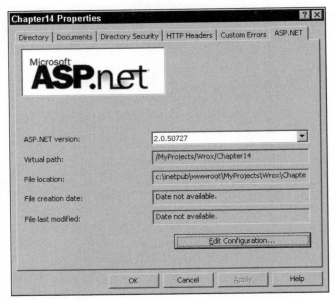

Figure 14-5

In the ASP.NET tab (shown in Figure 14-5), you can review or change the ASP.NET version used for the current application. Any change you make to this setting applies to all child applications. Now click the Edit Configuration button to bring up the ASP.NET Configuration Settings MMC snapin. Figure 14-6 shows the ASP.NET MMC snapin.

As the Figure 14-6 shows, you can use the ASP.NET MMC snapin to configure settings such as application settings, custom errors configuration, authorization, authentication, page settings, state management, and so on. Note that the code behind the ASP.NET administrative tool leverages the underlying configuration API.

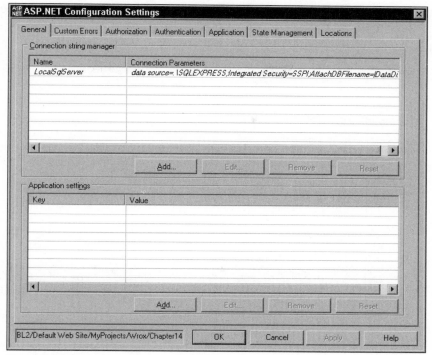

Figure 14-6

Web Site Administration Tool

Another excellent addition to Visual Studio 2005 is a graphical administration tool named Web Site Administration Tool that allows you to configure common application and security settings for your Web sites. Using the Web Site Administration Tool, you can now make changes to your site configuration without having to manually edit the web.config file.

> When you use Web Site Administration Tool to administer a Web site that does not have an associated web.config file, the tool will automatically create a web.config at the root directory of the Web site. For most settings, changes made through the Web site administration Tool take effect immediately, and are reflected in the web.config file.

To open the Web Site Administration Tool, select ASP.NET Configuration from the Web site menu in Visual Studio 2005. This will open up the Web Site Administration Tool as shown in Figure 14-7.

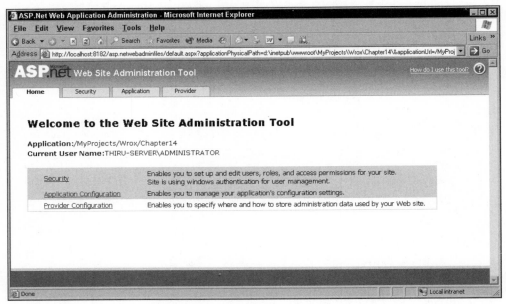

Figure 14-7

As the Figure 14-7 shows, the Web Site Administration Tool consists of a tabbed interface that has four tabs.

❑   Home — Provides link to other tabs.

❑   Security — Allows you to manage access rules for specific resources within your Web site. The tab also enables you to manage user accounts and roles.

❑   Application — Allows you to manage application settings (name/value pairs stored in the appSettings section of the web.config file), SMTP settings, application status (online or offline), and debugging settings.

❑   Provider — Allows you to manage providers. Providers are nothing but classes that are used to store application data, such as users and roles.

Figure 14-8 shows the Application tab in action.

The Web Site Administration Tool is available with all versions of Visual Studio 2005.

> *Because the changes you make through the Web Site Administration Tool take effect immediately, this will require the Web site to be restarted. This might result in all the active sessions being lost. So it is recommended that you exercise caution before making changes to the Web site through the Web Site Administration Tool.*

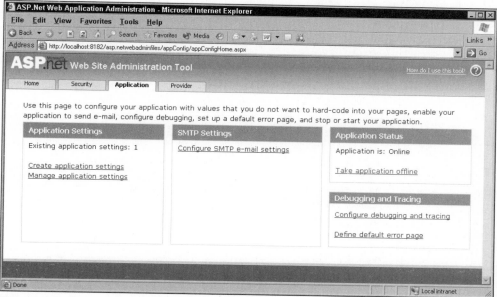

Figure 14-8

Command Line Tools

ASP.NET 2.0 provides two command line tools that can be used to configure application services and manage encryption of your configuration settings. These tools are as follows:

❑ ASPNET_REGSQL — This tool allows you to manage the ASP.NET application services such as session state, membership, roles, user profilers, personalization, and SQL cache invalidation and provide you with the ability to store these application service-related configurations in a SQL Server database.

❑ ASPNET_REGIIS — In addition to configuring the Web site to use a particular version of ASP.NET, you can also use this tool to manage configuration-related encryption features.

Summary

ASP.NET 2.0 contains many architectural enhancements designed to improve manageability aspects of a deployed ASP.NET application. Not only has the configuration schema been improved to support new elements, the programmatic access to those elements has also been greatly enhanced, thereby making the management of a .NET application a breezy experience. In this chapter, you learned the configuration improvements of ASP.NET 2.0 through discussion and examples.

Building a ShoppingAssistant Using XML Web Services

In previous chapters, you learned the new Web service features of .NET Framework 2.0 and understood how to create ASP.NET Web services using .NET Framework 2.0. Now that you have learned these features, it is time to implement them in a real-world application. This chapter is based on a case study named ShoppingAssistant that provides one-stop shopping for consumers that want to find out information such as the products that are on sale, availability of products in different stores, comparison of the price of the product across different stores, and so on. It also provides consumers with details of a specific product. This case study introduces you to a few advanced features and concepts related to building Web services by using asynchronous Web service invocation capabilities in conjunction with other features such as XML Serialization, FileSystemWatcher, and Timer component.

ShoppingAssistant Case Study

This case study is based on a fictitious application named ShoppingAssistant that supplies the consumers with an online guide that provides the product information and the best possible values. The business model of ShoppingAssistant Web site rallies around the following two main requirements.

❑   Need to seamlessly get information from their partners through industry standard approaches. Although the information displayed in the site is not that time-sensitive, it still requires you to update that information once in a while (maybe once in a day), if not real-time updates

❑   Need to generate reporting data for example, which is the most popular product in the site, for their business partners

Currently, ShoppingAssistant gets all the required information from its content provider partners as XML feeds. It is done by making a HTTP request to an .aspx file or any other server-side scripting file, receiving the response in XML format and converting that response back to a form that is usable in the site. Although this approach works and meets the current needs, it is obvious that this approach requires a lot of plumbing and infrastructure code to accomplish the desired function-alities. And also due to the tightly coupled nature of the design, even minor changes in the logic that is used to generate the XML document ends up breaking the client-side implementation of the application.

Having realized the need to come up with the better and effective automated solution for getting the XML information feed, ShoppingAssistant started looking around for content providers who can sat-isfy their need. Luckily they found a company called ContentPublisher that exposes the information required by ShoppingAssistant in the form of Web services. Because of the inherent benefits of XML-based Web services, ShoppingAssistant decided to take advantage of the Web services capability exposed by the ContentPublisher.

The main focus of this case study is how ShoppingAssistant consumes the Web services from ContentPublisher and optimizations they have to perform to increase the throughput of their Web site without compromising the needs of their business. Obviously this approach requires an iterative approach from an implementation perspective that necessitates constant evolution of the site.

Architecture of ShoppingAssistant

Figure 15-1 illustrates the proposed architecture of the ShoppingAssistant using the Web services exposed by the ContentPublisher.

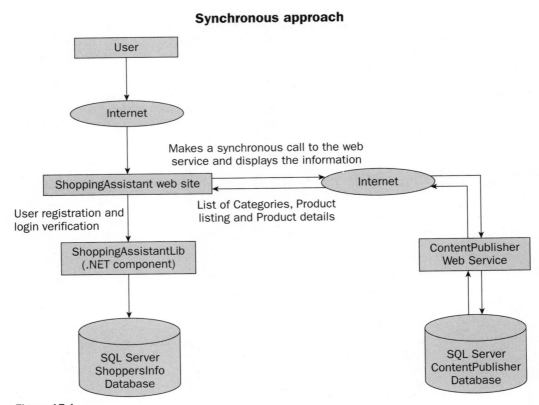

Figure 15-1

As shown in Figure 15-1, the ShoppingAssistant Web site incorporates the functionality implemented by the .NET component (ShoppingAssistantLib) and the ContentPublisher Web service into its Web site. When the user comes to the site and performs operations such as reporting data collection, the ShoppingAssistant invokes the methods of the .NET component ShoppingAssistantLib to carry out those tasks. The ShoppingAssistant Web application connects to the ContentPublisher Web service across the Internet to fetch information whenever the user performs any of the following actions.

- ❑ Browsing the categories page
- ❑ Browsing the product listing page
- ❑ Navigating to the product details page

Before looking at the implementation of the architecture shown in Figure 15-1, it is important to examine the business processes supported by the ShoppingAssistant.

Business Processes

Although the scope of the case study is to show how to effectively consume Web services from within an ASP.NET Web site, it is imperative that you review the business processes before choosing the best approach. The business processes that ShoppingAssistant is going to have to enable are as follows:

- ❑ Login process — Registered users are given the option to log in to ShoppingAssistant site so that they can review other information in the site. The user must provide an existing user id and a valid password to be allowed to enter the system.

- ❑ New user registration process — New users are given the opportunity to become members of the site by filling out an online form. In this step, the user is asked to create a unique user id, which is used to identify the user in the system. The user can also fill out details such as email, and security question that can then be used by the system administrator to contact the user when necessary. After the user has entered all the details and the data has been validated, the user's profile is stored in the database for later retrieval.

- ❑ Catalog browsing process — Users can browse through the list of categories available in the site.

- ❑ Products listing process — In this process, the list of products available in a particular category is shown with a hyperlink that takes the users to a page that displays detailed information about a product.

- ❑ Product details process — When the user clicks on the hyperlink of a particular product, the user is taken to the page where detailed explanation about that product is shown.

- ❑ Logout process — Allows the user to log out of the site.

- ❑ Reporting data gathering process — In this step, before showing the products information on the Web site, you store the product details in a separate table, which can, later, be used for reporting purposes.

To better organize the solution, this case study is split into the following parts.

- ❑ In the first part, you create a Web service named ContentPublisherService whose primary purpose is to expose information related to various categories and products that are available on sales to other Web sites. The consumers of the Web service can then consume this information in any fashion they like in their site.

❑   In the second part, you create an ASP.NET Web site that consumes the information exposed by the `ContentPublisher` Web service. After implementing the solution, you will learn about the performance implications that you have to incur due to the synchronous and blocking Web service method calls that are employed to get the required information.

❑   After you identify the shortcomings of a synchronous approach, this chapter covers an alternative approach to address this issue. To this end, you create a solution that uses a Windows Service (with a `System.Threading.Timer` component on it) to asynchronously invoke the Web service. By invoking the Web services at the specified time intervals set by the timer component, you get the latest information from the Web service and store that in local XML files for the `ShoppingAssistant` Web site to make use of.

❑   In this part, you see how to incorporate effective data collection capabilities into the `ShoppingAssistant` Web site. This data collection activity is mainly surrounding the number of times a particular product has been viewed by the customers. As the page is rendered, you need a way to collect this data and store this information without compromising on the response time of the site. To reduce the impact on the page, you implement this functionality using a combination of both synchronous and asynchronous approaches. Before drawing on the page, you create an XML string dynamically based on the displayed product information and then store that XML string in an XML file. After the information is persisted in the directory, the calling ASP.NET application immediately returns and continues with the task of drawing the page, thereby minimizing the amount of processor cycles spent for collecting this information. Because this directory is being monitored by a `FileSystemWatcher` component (that is hosted in a Windows service), this file will be automatically read and its contents stored in the database.

Implementation

Now that you understand the business processes involved, it is time to examine the individual building blocks that are required for implementing this solution. For the purposes of this example, the discussion of the remaining part of the case study is divided into the following sections.

❑   Database Design

❑   Implementation of `ContentPublisher` Web Service

❑   Implementation of .NET component (`ShoppingAssistantLib`)

❑   Implementation of `ShoppingAssistant` Web Site

❑   Implementation of Asynchronous Invocation of Web Services using a Windows Service

❑   Implementation of Data Collection Capabilities using a Windows Service and `FileSystemWatcher` Component

To start, consider the database design that is required to support the `ShoppingAssistant`.

Database Design

Because the main aim of the case study is to lay emphasis on .NET Web services, the databases you design and implement in this chapter have minimum number of tables required to implement this solution. As you can see from the architecture of the system, two data stores are used to store and provide information to ShoppingAssistant.

First, consider the design of the ShoppersInfo database.

ShoppersInfo Database Design

This database is basically used to store and retrieve reporting related information that will be used to track the categories and products visited by the users. The ShoppersInfo database has only one table named ReportInfo, whose structure is depicted in Table 15-1.

Table 15-1. Structure of ReportInfo Table

Name	Data Type	Length	AllowNull	Description
ProductID	Int	4	No	Represents the product id
CategoryID	Int	4	No	Represents the category id
Browser	Varchar	256	Yes	Name of the browser
RequestType	Varchar	256	Yes	Request type of the browser
Authenticated	Varchar	50	Yes	Type of authentication

The population of ReportInfo table is handled by a stored procedure named InsertReportInfo whose declaration is shown as follows. The InsertReportInfo stored procedure simply adds a record to the ReportInfo table using the supplied parameters.

```
Create Proc InsertReportInfo
(
@ProductID int, @CategoryID int, @Browser varchar(256),
@RequestType Varchar(256), @Authenticated varchar(50)
)
As
   Insert into ReportInfo(ProductID,CategoryID,Browser,RequestType,Authenticated)
   Values(@ProductID,@CategoryID,@Browser,@RequestType,@Authenticated)
```

ContentPublisher Database Design

The ContentPublisher database consists of two tables: Categories and Products. The entity relationship diagram for the ContentPublisher is shown in Figure 15-2.

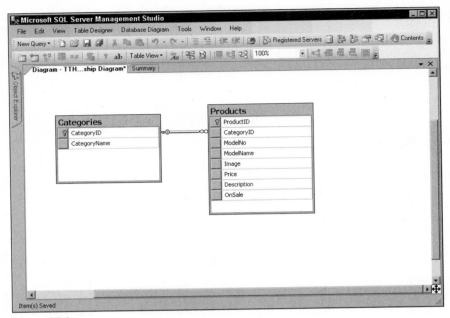

Figure 15-2

Figure 15-2 shows that the ProductID column acts as the primary key for the Products table and CategoryID column is used as the primary key for the Categories table. It also shows the presence of the referential integrity constraint between the Products and Categories tables through the CategoryID column. Table 15-2 shows the design of the Categories table.

Table 15-2. Structure of Categories Table

Name	Data Type	Length	AllowNull	Description
CategoryID	int	4	No	Indicates the category id
CategoryName	varchar	50	No	Represents the category name

Table 15-3 shows the design of the Products table.

Table 15-3. Structure of Products Table

Name	Data Type	Length	AllowNull	Description
ProductID	int	4	No	Represents the product id
CategoryID	int	4	No	Represents the category id
ModelNo	varchar	50	Yes	Model number of the product
Image	varchar	50	Yes	Image file name of the product

Name	Data Type	Length	AllowNull	Description
Price	money	8	No	Price of the product
Description	varchar	2000	Yes	Description of the product
OnSale	char	1	No	Specifies whether the product is on sale

Now that you have had a look at the design of the ContentPublisher database, look at the stored procedures required for the ContentPublisher Web service. The GetCategories stored procedure simply returns all the categories available in the database.

```
CREATE Procedure GetCategories
As
   SELECT *  FROM Categories
```

As the name suggests, the GetProducts stored procedure returns all the available products in the database.

```
CREATE Procedure GetProducts
As
   SELECT *  FROM Products WHERE CategoryID = @CategoryID
```

The GetProductsByCategoryID stored procedure returns all the products that belong to a particular category.

```
CREATE Procedure GetProductsByCategoryID
(
@CategoryID int
)
As
   SELECT *  FROM Products WHERE CategoryID = @CategoryID
```

As the name suggests, GetProductDetails procedure returns the details of a particular product based on the passed product id.

```
CREATE Procedure GetProductDetails
(
@ProductID int
)
As
   SELECT *  FROM Products  WHERE ProductID = @ProductID
```

Now that you have implemented the stored procedures, the next step is to implement the Web services that will, in turn, consume the stored procedures.

Implementation of ContentPublisher Web Service

In this section, you create a Web service project called ContentPublisherService that contains Web service classes to expose categories and products information to the consumers. To start with, create a new Visual C# Web Service project named ContentPublisherService using Visual Studio 2005. After the project is created, add a new Web service named `CategoriesService.asmx` to the project; then, modify the code in the `CategoriesService.asmx` to look as shown in Listing 15-1.

Listing 15-1: Implementation of CategoriesService

```csharp
<%@ WebService Language="C#" Class="CategoriesService" %>
using System;
using System.Collections.Generic;
using System.Data;
using System.Data.SqlClient;
using System.Web;
using System.Web.Configuration;
using System.Web.Services;
using System.Web.Services.Protocols;

[WebService(Namespace = "http://www.wrox.com/Books/ProASPNET20XML/")]
[WebServiceBinding(ConformsTo = WsiProfiles.BasicProfile1_1)]
public class CategoriesService  : System.Web.Services.WebService
{
[WebMethod(Description = "This method allows a remote client to retrieve all the
    categories available in the site.", EnableSession = false)]
public List<Category> GetCategories()
{
  List<Category> list = new List<Category>();
    using (SqlConnection conn = new SqlConnection())
    {
      string connString = WebConfigurationManager.ConnectionStrings
        ["contentPublisher"].ConnectionString;
      conn.ConnectionString = connString;
      SqlCommand command = new SqlCommand("GetCategories", conn);
      command.CommandType = CommandType.StoredProcedure;
      conn.Open();
      using (SqlDataReader reader = command.ExecuteReader())
      {
        while (reader.Read())
        {
          Category cate = new Category();
          cate.CategoryID = Convert.ToInt32(reader["CategoryID"]);
          cate.CategoryName = reader["CategoryName"].ToString();
          list.Add(cate);
        }
      }
    }
    return list;
    }
}
```

The Web service starts by importing the required namespaces.

```csharp
using System;
using System.Collections.Generic;
using System.Data;
using System.Data.SqlClient;
using System.Web;
```

```
using System.Web.Configuration;
using System.Web.Services;
using System.Web.Services.Protocols;
```

The `CategoriesService` class is derived from the `System.Web.Services.WebService` class. Because of this inheritance, the `CategoriesService` class will have access to the built-in ASP.NET objects such as Application, Session, User, and Context.

```
public class CategoriesService   : System.Web.Services.WebService
```

In the following code, the attribute `WebMethod` indicates that the method is to be exposed as Web callable method. Because of the `WebMethod` attribute, when the Web service is deployed, the ASP.NET runtime provides all the plumbing required to make this method callable across the Internet using XML and SOAP protocols.

```
[WebMethod(Description = "This method allows a remote client to retrieve all the
    categories available in the site.", EnableSession = false)]
```

To the constructor of the `WebMethod` attribute, you also supply a brief description of the Web service using the named parameter `Description`. In this case, since there is no need to store session state — it is set to false. Explicitly setting the `EnableSession` to false allows you to indicate to the ASP.NET runtime that you do not want the session specific data to be stored thereby eliminating the performance overheads that may be caused due to the amount of resources required for storing the session state.

As the signature of the `GetCategories()` method shows, the return value of the `GetCategories()` method is of type generic collection `List<Product>`.

```
public List<Category> GetCategories()
```

Inside the `GetCategories()` method, you first create an instance of the `List<Product>` object.

```
List<Category> list = new List<Category>();
```

Create an instance of the `SqlConnection` object, retrieve the connection string from the `web.config` file, and set the `ConnectionString` property of the `SqlConnection` object.

```
using (SqlConnection conn = new SqlConnection())
{
string connString = WebConfigurationManager.ConnectionStrings
    ["contentPublisher"].ConnectionString;
  conn.ConnectionString = connString;
```

In these lines of code, the connection string is retrieved from the `<connectionStrings>` section of the `web.config` file using the `ConnectionString` property. To be able to dynamically retrieve the connection string, you need to have the connection string defined in the `web.config` file as shown below.

```
<configuration>
  <connectionStrings>
  <add name="contentPublisher"
    connectionString="server=localhost;uid=sa;pwd=thiru;
    database=ContentPublisher"/>
  </connectionStrings>
</configuration>
```

The nice feature of storing configuration settings in the web.config file is that you can dynamically change the configuration settings without even having to touch the application code.

Next, create an instance of SqlCommand object passing to its constructor the name of the stored procedure to be executed as well as the SqlConnection object as arguments.

```
SqlCommand command = new SqlCommand("GetCategories", conn);
```

You then open the connection to the database by calling the Open() method of the SqlConnection object.

```
conn.Open();
```

Now you the stored procedure through the ExecuteReader() method of the SqlCommand object.

```
using (SqlDataReader reader = command.ExecuteReader())
```

After you have the results in the SqlDataReader object, loop through the SqlDataReader object using the Read() method.

```
while (reader.Read())
{
   Category cate = new Category();
   cate.CategoryID = Convert.ToInt32(reader["CategoryID"]);
   cate.CategoryName = reader["CategoryName"].ToString();
list.Add(cate);
}
```

Inside the While loop, you read the contents of the corresponding row of the SqlDataReader object and load that into a Category object. After that, the Category object is added to the previously created generic collection.

Finally, return the generic collection back to the caller using the return keyword.

```
return list;
```

The GetCategories() method returns a generic collection of object type Category whose declaration is shown in Listing 15-2.

Listing 15-2: Implementation of the Category Class

```
using System;
[Serializable]
public class Category
{
   protected int _categoryID;
protected string _categoryName;
public int CategoryID
{
   get{return _categoryID;}
     set{_categoryID = value;}
}
```

```
public string CategoryName
{
  get{return _categoryName;}
    set{_categoryName = value;}
  }
}
```

The `Category` class contains protected member variables that are used to hold information about a specific category. The protected variables are exposed as public properties. This will give you greater degree of control over the values that can be assigned to the member variables. It also enables you to easily enforce the data validation rules.

To test the Web service, right-click on the `CategoriesService` in Visual Studio 2005 and select View in Browser from the context menu. Follow through the steps to invoke the Web service and finally you should see the output shown in Figure 15-3.

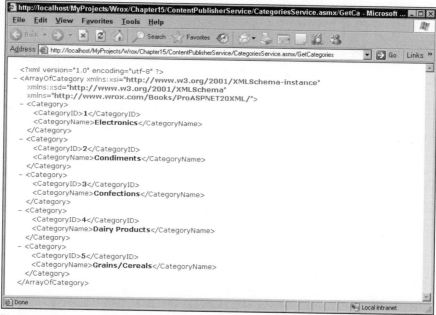

Figure 15-3

As the output shows, the generic collection return value (of type List<Product>) manifests itself as an array of `Category` objects when the output of the Web service is serialized.

Implementation of ProductsService

In this section, you learn the implementation of the `ProductsService` that specifically deals with the retrieval of `Products` information from the `ContentPublisher` database. Before that, you need to get an understanding of the `Product` class's implementation, which is used to represent a single instance of a product in our site. Listing 15-3 illustrates the declaration of the `Product` class.

Listing 15-3: Declaration of the Product Class

```
using System;
[Serializable]
public class Product
{
protected int _productID;
protected int _categoryID;
protected string _modelNo;
protected string _modelName;
protected string _image;
protected string _price;
protected string _description;
protected string _onSale;
public int ProductID
{
  get{return _productID;}
  set{_productID = value;}
}
public int CategoryID
{
  get{return _categoryID;}
    set{_categoryID = value;}
}
public string ModelNo
{
  get{return _modelNo;}
    set{_modelNo = value;}
}
public string ModelName
{
  get{return _modelName;}
  set{_modelName = value;}
}
public string Image
{
  get{return _image;}
  set{_image = value;}
}
public string Price
{
  get{return _price;}
    set{_price = value;}
}
public string Description
{
  get{return _description;
    set{_description = value;}
}
public string OnSale
{
  get{return _onSale;}
    set{_onSale = value;}
  }
}
```

As you can see, the `Product` class is similar to the `Category` class except it exposes a different set of properties. Now that you have implemented the `Product` class, it is time to focus on the `ProductsService` class whose methods have the `Product` generic collection as their return value. Listing 15-4 illustrates the different methods exposed by the `ProductsService`.

Listing 15-4: Implementation of ProductsService

```csharp
<%@ WebService Language="C#" Class="ProductsService" %>
using System;
using System.Collections.Generic;
using System.Data;
using System.Data.SqlClient;
using System.Web.Configuration;
using System.Web;
using System.Web.Services;
using System.Web.Services.Protocols;

[WebService(Namespace = "http://www.wrox.com/Books/ProASPNET20XML/")]
[WebServiceBinding(ConformsTo = WsiProfiles.BasicProfile1_1)]
public class ProductsService  : System.Web.Services.WebService
{
[WebMethod(Description = "This method allows a remote client to retrieve all
   the products available in the site.", EnableSession = false)]
public List<Product> GetProducts()
{
  List<Product> list = new List<Product>();
    using (SqlConnection conn = new SqlConnection())
    {
      string connString = WebConfigurationManager.ConnectionStrings
        ["contentPublisher"].ConnectionString;
      conn.ConnectionString = connString;
      SqlCommand command = new SqlCommand("GetProducts", conn);
      command.CommandType = CommandType.StoredProcedure;
      conn.Open();
      using (SqlDataReader reader = command.ExecuteReader())
      {
        while (reader.Read())
        {
          Product prod = ConvertReaderToProduct(reader);
          list.Add(prod);
        }
      }
    }
    return list;
}

[WebMethod(Description = "This method allows a remote client to retrieve all
   the products based on the category id", EnableSession = false)]
public List<Product> GetProductsByCategoryID(int categoryID)
{
    List<Product> list = new List<Product>();
    using (SqlConnection conn = new SqlConnection())
    {
      string connString = WebConfigurationManager.ConnectionStrings
```

```
        ["contentPublisher"].ConnectionString;
      conn.ConnectionString = connString;
      conn.Open();
      SqlCommand command = new SqlCommand("GetProductsByCategoryID", conn);
      command.CommandType = CommandType.StoredProcedure;
      command.Parameters.Add(new SqlParameter("@CategoryID", SqlDbType.Int));
      command.Parameters["@CategoryID"].Value = categoryID;
      using (SqlDataReader reader = command.ExecuteReader())
      {
        while (reader.Read())
        {
          Product prod = ConvertReaderToProduct(reader);
          list.Add(prod);
        }
      }
    }
    return list;
}

[WebMethod(Description = "The ProductDetailsGetObject method allows a remote
  client to retrieve the details of a product based on the product id in the
  form of a ProductDetails object.", EnableSession = false)]
public List<Product> GetProductDetails(int productID)
{
  List<Product> list = new List<Product>();
    using (SqlConnection conn = new SqlConnection())
    {
      string connString = WebConfigurationManager.ConnectionStrings
        ["contentPublisher"].ConnectionString;
      conn.ConnectionString = connString;
      conn.Open();
      SqlCommand command = new SqlCommand("GetProductDetails", conn);
      command.CommandType = CommandType.StoredProcedure;
      Product prod = new Product();
      command.Parameters.Add(new SqlParameter("@ProductID", SqlDbType.Int));
      command.Parameters["@ProductID"].Value = productID;
      SqlDataReader reader = command.ExecuteReader();
      Product prod = null;
      while (reader.Read())
      {
        prod = ConvertReaderToProduct(reader);
      }
      //This will be a collection with just one object
      list.Add(prod);
    }
    return list;
  }
}

public Product ConvertReaderToProduct(SqlDataReader reader)
{
  Product prod = new Product();
```

```
         //Assign the column values to the Product object
         prod.ProductID = Convert.ToInt32(reader["ProductID"].ToString());
         prod.CategoryID = Convert.ToInt32(reader["CategoryID"].ToString());
         prod.ModelNo = reader["ModelNo"].ToString();
         prod.ModelName = reader["ModelName"].ToString();
         prod.Image = reader["Image"].ToString();
         prod.Price = reader["Price"].ToString();
         prod.Description = reader["Description"].ToString();
         return prod;
     }
```

All the Web methods of the `ProductsService` have a similar pattern in that they all execute a stored procedure in the `ContentPublisher` database, transform the contents of the `SqlDataReader` object into a List<Product> collection using a helper method named `ConvertReaderToProduct()`, and finally return the generic collection back to the caller. The implementation of these methods will not be discussed in detail; however, you can download the complete code of the case study from the Wrox Web site.

Now that you have had a brief look at the Web service methods, it is time to shift focus to the implementation of the .NET component `ShoppingAssistantLib`, which provides such functionalities as collecting the details of the product viewed by the users for reporting purposes.

Implementation of ShoppingAssistantLib Component

Create a new Visual C# Class library project named `ShoppingAssistantLib` using Visual Studio 2005. After the project is created, change the name of the default class from Class1 to `ReportInfo`. The `ReportInfo` class simply acts as a container for holding report-related data, and its implementation is shown in Listing 15-5.

Listing 15-5: ReportInfo Class That Acts as a Container for Holding Reporting Data

```
using System;
using System.Collections.Generic;
using System.Text;
namespace ShoppingAssistantLib
{
[Serializable]
public class ReportInfo
{
    protected int _productID;
    protected int _categoryID;
    protected string _browser;
    protected string _requestType;
    protected string _authenticated;
    public int ProductID
    {
      get{return _productID;}
      set{_productID = value;}
    }
    public int CategoryID
    {
      get{return _categoryID;}
```

```
        set{_categoryID = value;}
      }
      public string Browser
      {
        get{return _browser;}
        set{_browser = value;}
      }
      public string RequestType
      {
        get{return _requestType;}
        set{_requestType = value;}
      }
      public string Authenticated
      {
        get{return _authenticated;}
        set{_authenticated = value;}
      }
    }
  }
}
```

The `ReportInfo` class provides the data structure for storing the report related data. An instance of this class will represent a record in the `ReportInfo` table of the `ShoppersInfo` database.

Implementation of Data Access Layer Methods

So far, you have seen the container class used for holding reporting data. That is only part of the story and you need a data access layer class for persisting that data into the `ReportInfo` table. This is where the `ReportDB` class comes into play. Implementation of the `ReportDB` class is illustrated in Listing 15-6.

Listing 15-6: Data Access Layer for Interacting with the ReportInfo Table

```
using System;
using System.Data;
using System.Data.SqlClient;
using System.Collections.Generic;
using System.Text;
using System.Web.Configuration;

namespace ShoppingAssistantLib
{
public class ReportDB
{
    public bool InsertReportInfo(ReportInfo report)
    {
      string connString = WebConfigurationManager.ConnectionStrings
        ["shoppersInfo"].ConnectionString;
      using (SqlConnection conn = new SqlConnection(connString))
      {
```

```
            conn.Open();
            SqlCommand command = new SqlCommand("InsertReportInfo", conn);
            command.CommandType = CommandType.StoredProcedure;
            //Add all the parameters
            command.Parameters.Add(new SqlParameter("@ProductID", SqlDbType.Int));
            command.Parameters["@ProductID"].Value = report.ProductID;
            command.Parameters.Add(new SqlParameter("@CategoryID", SqlDbType.Int));
            command.Parameters["@CategoryID"].Value = report.CategoryID;
            command.Parameters.Add(new SqlParameter("@Browser",
              SqlDbType.VarChar, 256));
            command.Parameters["@Browser"].Value = report.Browser;
            command.Parameters.Add(new SqlParameter("@RequestType",
              SqlDbType.VarChar, 256));
            command.Parameters["@RequestType"].Value = report.RequestType;
            command.Parameters.Add(new SqlParameter("@Authenticated",
              SqlDbType.VarChar, 50));
            command.Parameters["@Authenticated"].Value = report.Authenticated;
            command.ExecuteNonQuery();
            return true;
          }
        }
      }
    }
```

As you can see from Listing 15-6, the main purpose of the `ReportDB` class is to expose methods that allow you to add reporting related information to the database. The `InsertReportInfo()` method accepts a `ReportInfo` object as an argument and uses the `ReportInfo` object's properties to assign values to the stored procedure parameters. The `InsertReportInfo` stored procedure is finally executed by calling the `ExecuteNonQuery()` method of the `SqlCommand` object.

Implementation of ShoppingAssistant Web Application

In this part of the case study, you learn the implementation of the `ShoppingAssistant` Web site that uses the following building blocks that were already created in the previous sections.

- ❏   `ContentPublisherService` — Consists of ASP.NET Web services: `CategoriesService` and `ProductsService`. These Web services provide information such as list of categories available, products present in each category, and the details of the product. To add reference to a Web service, use the Add Web Reference option.

- ❏   `ShoppingAssistantLib` — C# Class library that allows you to track the reporting related information in the database. You add reference to this library through the Add Reference option.

Create a new Visual C# Web Site named `ShoppingAssistant`. After the Web site is created, add a master page named `CommonMaster.master` to the Web page. Through a Master Page, you can easily provide a consistent look and feel for all the pages in your Web site.

What Is a Master Page?

As you learned in a previous chapter, ASP.NET 2.0 introduced a new concept known as Master Pages, in which a common base master file is created to provide a consistent layout for all the pages in a Web site. Master Pages allow you to isolate the look and feel and standard behavior for all the pages in your application to a centralized Master Page. In that page, you add placeholders (known as `ContentPlaceHolder`) for the content (or child pages) to add their custom content. When users request a content page, the output of the content pages is merged with the output of the Master Page, resulting in an output that combines the layout of the Master Page with the output of the content page.

For the `ShoppingAssistant` Web site, the `CommonMaster.master` page provides the standard heading and left navigation for all the pages. The code of the `CommonMaster.master` is shown in Listing 15-7.

Listing 15-7: CommonMaster.master Page for Consistent Look and Feel

```
<%@ Master Language="C#" %>
<html xmlns="http://www.w3.org/1999/xhtml" >
<head runat="server">
  <title>Common Master Page</title>
</head>
<body>
<form id="form1" runat="server">
    <div>
        <asp:Table BorderStyle=Double id="tblTop" runat="server" Width="100%"
          Height="105px" ForeColor="Black">
        <asp:TableRow>
          <asp:TableCell>
            <img src="Images/wrox_logo.gif">
          </asp:TableCell>
          <asp:TableCell>
            <font size=30>Shopping Assistant</font>
          </asp:TableCell>
        </asp:TableRow>
        <asp:TableFooterRow>
          <asp:TableCell ColumnSpan="2"><br /></asp:TableCell>
        </asp:TableFooterRow>
      </asp:Table>
      <asp:Table BorderStyle=Double id="bodyTable" runat="server"
        Width="100%" Height="100%" ForeColor="Black">
        <asp:TableRow VerticalAlign=Top>
          <asp:TableCell>
            <asp:Table BackColor=LightSteelBlue runat="server" Height="100%"
              Width="135px" ID="leftTable">
            <asp:TableRow Height="75">
              <asp:TableCell VerticalAlign=Top>
                <asp:HyperLink Font-Bold=true
                  NavigateUrl="~/CategoriesListing.aspx" runat="server"
                  ID="categoriesListingLink" Text="Categories Listing">
                </asp:HyperLink>
                <br/><br/><br/>
```

```
<asp:HyperLink Font-Bold=true NavigateUrl="~/CreateUser.aspx"
    runat="server" ID="createNewLink" Text="Create New User">
</asp:HyperLink><br/><br/><br/>
<asp:HyperLink Font-Bold=true NavigateUrl="~/Login.aspx"
    runat="server" ID="loginLink" Text="Login">
</asp:HyperLink><br/><br/><br/>
<asp:HyperLink Font-Bold=true NavigateUrl="~/Logout.aspx"
    runat="server" ID="logoutLink" Text="Logout">
</asp:HyperLink><br/><br/><br/>
            </asp:TableCell>
        </asp:TableRow>
    </asp:Table>
</asp:TableCell>
<asp:TableCell HorizontalAlign=Left>
    <asp:contentplaceholder id="BodyContent" runat="server">
    </asp:contentplaceholder>
</asp:TableCell>
        </asp:TableRow>
    </asp:Table>
</div>
</form>
</body>
</html>
```

The Master Page contains a header that displays the Wrox logo and the name of the Web site. It also contains a left navigation bar that facilitates easy navigation of the pages in the ShoppingAssistant Web site. Inside the Master Page, there is a ContentPlaceHolder control that allows the content pages (also know as child or inherited pages) to substitute their content.

How Master Pages Work?

The Master Page defines content areas using the ContentPlaceHolder control, and the content pages place their content in the areas identified by the ContentPlaceHolder control in the Master Page. Pages that use a Master Page to define the layout can place content only in the areas defined by the ContentPlaceHolder, thus enabling a consistent site design. Master Pages are saved with the file extension .master and they contain the Master directive at the top of the page instead of the Page directive that is used by the traditional ASP.NET pages. In addition to hosting all the contents that are required for defining the standard look and feel of the application, the Master Pages also contain all the top-level HTML elements for a page, such as <html>, <head>, and <form>. The Master Pages also contain one or more content placeholders that are used to define regions that will be rendered through the content pages.

Login Process

In the ShoppingAssistant Web site, the user must be logged in to browse through the different pages of the site. To this end, create a new ASP.NET page named Login.aspx that allows the user to log into the site. The login page authenticates the user's username and password against the Membership store provided by ASP.NET. Before looking at the code of the Login.aspx page, it is useful to briefly examine the underlying authentication technology used by the ShoppingAssistant.

The login feature of the Web site is implemented using forms-based authentication mechanism. The forms-based authentication technology depends on cookies to store the authentication information for the currently logged in user. After the user is authenticated, cookies are used to store and maintain session information enabling the users to identify themselves to the Web site. To enable forms-based authentication for the ShoppingAssistant Web site, add the following entry in the web.config file directly under the <system.web> element.

```
<authentication mode="Forms">
<forms name=".ASPXSHOPPINGASSISTANT" loginUrl="Login.aspx" protection="All"
  timeout="30" path="/">
</forms>
</authentication>
```

The loginUrl attribute in the <forms> element specifies the name of the login page that you want the users to be redirected to, any time they access a page or resource that does not allow anonymous access. For every Web form that you want to secure using the forms-based authentication mechanism, you need to add an entry to the web.config file. For example, to set the restrictions of authenticated user access for a page called CategoriesListing.aspx, set the following entry directly under the <configuration> element of the web.config file.

```
<location path="CategoriesListing.aspx">
<system.web>
    <authorization>
        <deny users="?" />
    </authorization>
</system.web>
</location>
```

When a user attempts to access the CategoriesListing.aspx page, the ASP.NET forms-based security system will automatically redirect the user to the Login.aspx page, and will continue to prevent them from accessing it until they have successfully validated their user name and password credentials to the ShoppingAssistant application. Similarly you protect the ProductsListing.aspx and ProductDetail.aspx pages also using similar entries in the web.config file.

Now that you have a general understanding of the forms-based authentication, you are ready to examine the Login.aspx page. The Login.aspx page is implemented in Listing 15-8.

Listing 15-8: Login Page Using <asp:Login> Server Control

```
<%@ Page Language="C#" MasterPageFile="~/CommonMaster.master" Title="Login" %>
<asp:Content ID="Content1" ContentPlaceHolderID="BodyContent" Runat="Server">
  <asp:login ID="Login1" runat="server" createuserurl="CreateUser.aspx"
    DestinationPageUrl="~/CategoriesListing.aspx"
    createusertext="Create a New Account" />
</asp:Content>
```

If you have ever implemented forms authentication by hand, you will appreciate the <asp:Login> control. In the past, an equivalent implementation to perform a database lookup would have required a couple of hundred lines of more code. The Login control shown in Listing 15-8 not only provides you with the interface, but also provides the underlying validation by leveraging the default membership provider. When you submit your username and password by using the Login control, your credentials are automatically validated by the configured membership provider.

Security Features in ASP.NET 2.0

New security features are an important improvement in ASP.NET 2.0. These features include membership services that manage a database of user accounts, hashed passwords, a role manager for managing role membership for users, and new security-related server-side controls that make implementing forms authentication much easier. ASP.NET 2.0 also offers a provider model that gives you complete control over the implementation of the Membership and Role services and cookieless forms authentication.

In addition to the extensible provider model, ASP.NET 2.0 also provides a suite of server controls that interact with the membership and role stores. The Login control provides a daunting list of properties. The vast majority of these properties simply enable you to control different aspects of the appearance of the login interface. For example, you can use the FailureText property to control the content of the text that is displayed when a login attempt fails. Additionally, you can use the CreateUserUrl and PasswordRecoveryUrl properties to create links to a registration page and password recovery page.

In the login page, try logging in with an invalid username or password, and notice that an appropriate default error message appears. It is all handled automatically for you. Figure 15-4 shows the output of the Login.aspx page.

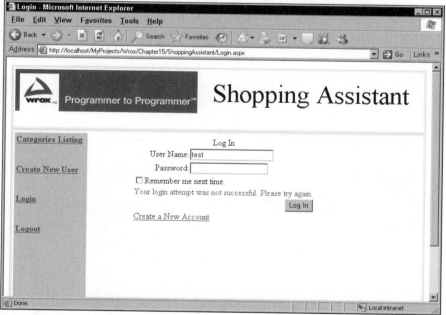

Figure 15-4

Before using the login feature, you need to register some users with the membership service to get started, so the first page you will be writing is one that allows you to add users. For this purpose, create a new page named `CreateUser.aspx`. If the user does not have a valid account, they can get to the `CreateUser.aspx` page using the Create New Account hyperlink on the `Login.aspx` page or by clicking the Create New User hyperlink in the left navigation. Performing any of these operations directs the user to the `CreateUser.aspx` page, whose implementation is shown in Listing 15-9.

Listing 15-9: Creating New User using <asp:CreateUserWizard> Server Control

```
<%@ Page Language="C#" MasterPageFile="~/CommonMaster.master"
Title="Create User" %>
<asp:Content ID="Content1" ContentPlaceHolderID="BodyContent" Runat="Server">
<asp:CreateUserWizard ID="CreateUserWizard1" runat="server"
  continuedestinationpageurl="CategoriesListing.aspx" />
</asp:Content>
```

Listing 15-9 produces the output shown in Figure 15-5.

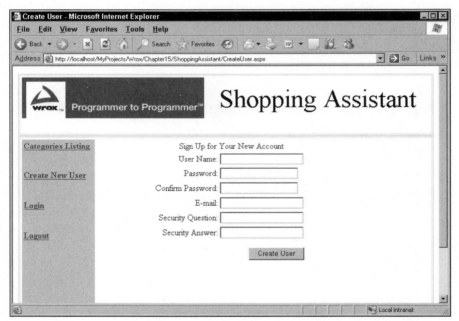

Figure 15-5

After you create an account using the page shown in Figure 15-5, if you click the Continue button, you will be redirected to the `CategoriesListing.aspx` page. This is because of the value set in the `ContinueDestinationPageUrl` attribute of the `<asp:CreateUserWizard>` control.

After you are finished adding users, take a close look at your virtual directory. You should see a new subdirectory called "App_Data" that has a SQL Server 2005 Express database named ASPNETDB.MDF inside. This is where the membership and role services store their data by default, but you can also override the default storage mechanism to use SQL Server database or your own custom data repository.

The `CreateUserWizard` control enables you to create a standard user registration page. Simply by adding the following tag to a page, you can enable new users to register at your Web site.

```
<asp:CreateUserWizard ID="CreateUserWizard1" Runat="server" />
```

The `CreateUserWizard` control is powerful in that you can configure the control to send email messages by assigning values to the control's `MailDefinition` property. The `MailDefinition` property represents an instance of the `MailDefinition` class that contains all of the properties required for defining an email message. For example, the following `CreateUserWizard` control will send the contents of the `Registration.txt` file as the body of the registration email message whenever someone completes the registration wizard.

```
<asp:CreateUserWizard ID="CreateUserWizard1" Runat="server">

<MailDefinition BodyFileName="~/Registration.txt"

  From="YourName@YourDomain.com" Subject="Thanks for registering">

</MailDefinition>

</asp:CreateUserWizard>
```

The `CreateUserWizard` control's email functionality also can be useful in more complicated registration scenarios in which you need to validate a user's email address before you provide the user with access to your Web application. If you enable the `CreateUserWizard` control's `AutoGeneratePassword` property, the control will randomly generate a password for a user. By taking advantage of the `CreateUserWizard` control's email functionality, you can automatically send the randomly generated password to the user. If the user subsequently authenticates against your Web application using the sent password, you know that the user must have supplied a valid email address.

Logout Process

All you need to do to log out of the site is to click the `Logout` hyperlink on the left navigation. When you click that link, the user is redirected to the `Logout.aspx` page shown in Listing 15-10.

Listing 15-10: Implementation of Logout Functionality

```
<%@ Page Language="C#" MasterPageFile="~/CommonMaster.master" Title="Logout" %>
<%@ Import Namespace="System.Web.Security" %>
<script runat="server">
void Page_Load(object sender, EventArgs e)
{
    FormsAuthentication.SignOut();
    Response.Redirect("Login.aspx");
}
</script>
<asp:Content ID="Content1" ContentPlaceHolderID="BodyContent" Runat="Server">
</asp:Content>
```

As Listing 15-10 shows, the logout implementation requires just one line of code. You simply call the `SignOut()` method of the `System.Web.Security.FormsAuthentication` class. That will clear all the cookies (used for authentication purposes) in the client machine. Then you simply redirect the users to the `Login.aspx` page.

Categories Listing Process

All the categories present in the site are displayed through the `CategoriesListing.aspx` page. In the categories listing page, you use an `<asp:GridView>` Web control to display the categories. You bind the `GridView` control directly to the List<Category> returned by the Web service in the `Page_Load` event.

To add the Web reference, right-click on the project in the Solution explorer and select Add Web Reference in the context menu. In the Add Web Reference dialog box, enter the path of the `.asmx` file of the Web service. When you add a Web reference of a Web service to your project, Visual Studio 2005 automatically generates a proxy class that not only interfaces with the Web service but also provides a local representation of the Web service.

Listing 15-11 illustrates the code of the `CategoriesListing.aspx` page.

Listing 15-11: Categories Listing Page that Uses CategoriesService

```
<%@ Page Language="C#" MasterPageFile="~/CommonMaster.master"
  Title="Categories Listing" %>
<%@ Import Namespace="CategoriesProxy" %>
<script runat="server">
void Page_Load(object sender, EventArgs e)
{
    CategoriesProxy.CategoriesService obj = new
      CategoriesProxy.CategoriesService();
    gridCategories.DataSource = obj.GetCategories();
    gridCategories.DataBind();
}
</script>
<asp:Content ID="Content1" ContentPlaceHolderID="BodyContent" Runat="Server">
<asp:GridView id="gridCategories" style="Z-INDEX: 101; LEFT: 162px; POSITION:
  absolute; TOP: 147px" runat="server" Height="321px" width="529px"
  BorderColor="Black" cellpadding="4" Font-Names="Verdana" Font-Size="8pt"
  AutoGenerateColumns="False" ShowFooter="True">
    <FooterStyle ForeColor="Control" BackColor="ActiveCaptionText"></FooterStyle>
    <HeaderStyle BackColor="Gray"></HeaderStyle>
    <RowStyle BackColor="Control"></RowStyle>
    <Columns>
      <asp:BoundField DataField="CategoryName" HeaderText="Category Name"/>
      <asp:HyperLinkField Text="Show all products"
        DataNavigateUrlFields="CategoryID"
        DataNavigateUrlFormatString="ProductsListing.aspx?CategoryID={0}"
        HeaderText="All products in the Category"></asp:HyperLinkField>
    </Columns>
  </asp:GridView>
</asp:Content>
```

The GetCategories() method of the CategoriesService returns an array of Category objects that is directly bound to the GridView control. When called from browser, the Categories listing page looks like the output shown in Figure 15-6.

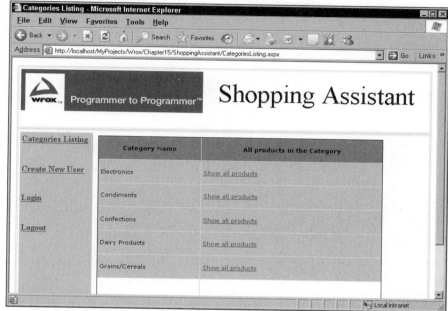

Figure 15-6

Products Listing Process

As the name suggests, the ProductListing.aspx page shows the list of products available on the site and the list of products shown is based on the category the user has selected in the categories listing page. The Page_Load event handler contains the code to invoke the ProductsService Web service, retrieve data from it, and then display its contents into a GridView control. The code of the ProductsListing.aspx page is shown in Listing 15-12.

Listing 15-12: Products Listing Page That Uses ProductsService

```
<%@ Page Language="C#" MasterPageFile="~/CommonMaster.master"
  Title="Products Listing" %>
<%@ Import Namespace="ProductsProxy" %>

<script runat="server">
void Page_Load(object sender, EventArgs e)
{
    /* Synchronous Web Service Call approach */
    ProductsProxy.ProductsService obj = new ProductsProxy.ProductsService();
    int categoryID = Convert.ToInt32(Request.QueryString["CategoryID"]);
    //Bind the Web service return value to Products GridView
```

```
      gridProducts.DataSource = obj.GetProductsByCategoryID(categoryID);
      gridProducts.DataBind();
   }
</script>
<asp:Content ID="Content1" ContentPlaceHolderID="BodyContent" Runat="Server">
<asp:GridView id="gridProducts" style="Z-INDEX: 101; LEFT: 162px; POSITION:
   absolute; TOP: 147px" runat="server" Height="321px" width="529px"
   BorderColor="Black" cellpadding="4" Font-Names="Verdana" Font-Size="8pt"
   AutoGenerateColumns="False" ShowFooter="True">
      <FooterStyle ForeColor="Control" BackColor="ActiveCaptionText"/>
      <HeaderStyle BackColor="Gray"></HeaderStyle>
      <RowStyle BackColor="Control"></RowStyle>
      <Columns>
        <asp:BoundField DataField="ModelNo" HeaderText="ModelNumber"/>
        <asp:BoundField DataField="ModelName" HeaderText="ModelName"/>
        <asp:BoundField DataField="Description" HeaderText="Description"/>
        <asp:BoundField DataField="Price" HeaderText="Price"/>
        <asp:HyperLinkField Text="Product Details" DataNavigateUrlFields="ProductID"
          DataNavigateUrlFormatString="productdetails.aspx?ProductID={0}"
          HeaderText="Show Details"/>
      </Columns>
   </asp:GridView>
</asp:Content>
```

In the `Page_Load` event, you retrieve the `CategoryID` passed in the query string and supply it as a parameter when invoking the Web service method `GetProductsByCategoryID()`. Navigating to the page in the browser results in the output as similar to Figure 15-7.

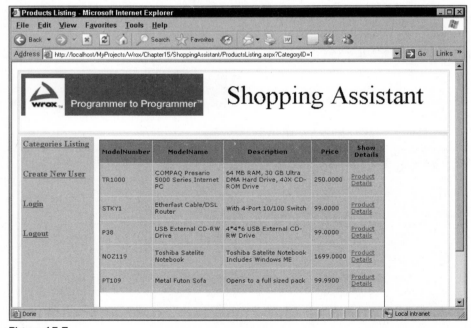

Figure 15-7

Figure 15-7 displays the products that belong to the category that was selected in the categories listing page.

Product Details Listing Process

When the user selects a particular product from the list of products, the user is taken to the product details page where details about the product are shown. For showing the product details, you will create a Web page named `ProductDetails.aspx` that encapsulates all the code required for retrieving the details of the product from the Web service. The code of the `ProductDetails.aspx` page is shown in Listing 15-13.

Listing 15-13: Product Details Page That Uses ProductsService

```
<%@ Page Language="C#" MasterPageFile="~/CommonMaster.master"
  Title="Product Details" %>
<%@ Import Namespace="ProductsProxy" %>
<script runat="server">
void Page_Load(object sender, EventArgs e)
{
    /* Synchronous Web Service Call approach */
    ProductsProxy.ProductsService obj = new ProductsProxy.ProductsService();
    int productID = Convert.ToInt32(Request.QueryString["ProductID"]);
    formProductDetails.DataSource = obj.GetProductDetails(productID);
    formProductDetails.DataBind();
}
</script>
<asp:Content ID="Content1" ContentPlaceHolderID="BodyContent" Runat="Server">
<table width="95%" cellpadding="0" cellspacing="0" border="0">
  <tr>
      <td>
        <asp:FormView ID="formProductDetails" runat="server">
          <HeaderTemplate>
            <tr>
              <td height="40" align="center" colspan="2">
                <asp:Label runat="server" Font-Bold="true" ForeColor="Brown"
                   ID="heading">Product Details</asp:Label>
              </td>
            </tr>
          </HeaderTemplate>
          <ItemTemplate>
            <tr>
              <td height="60" width="30%" bgcolor="buttonface">
                <asp:label Font-Bold=true Text="Model Number : " runat="server"
                   ID="lblModelNumber" />
                <br>
              </td>
              <td height="60" bgcolor="buttonface">
                <asp:label Text='<%#Eval("ModelNo")%>' runat="server"
                   ID="lblModelNumberValue" />
                <br>
              </td>
            </tr>
            <tr>
              <td height="60" width="30%" bgcolor="buttonface">
                <asp:label Font-Bold=true Text="Model Name : " runat="server"
```

```
            ID="lblModelName" />
        <br>
      </td>
      <td height="60" bgcolor="buttonface">
        <asp:label Text='<%#Eval("ModelName")%>' runat="server"
          ID="lblModelNameValue" />
        <br>
      </td>
    </tr>
    <tr>
      <td height="60" width="30%" bgcolor="buttonface">
        <asp:label Font-Bold=true Text="Description : " runat="server"
          ID="lblDescription" />
        <br>
      </td>
      <td height="60" bgcolor="buttonface">
        <asp:label Text='<%#Eval("Description")%>' runat="server"
          ID="lblDescriptionValue"/>
        <br>
      </td>
    </tr>
    <tr>
      <td height="60" width="30%" bgcolor="buttonface">
        <asp:label Font-Bold=true Text="Price : " runat="server"
          ID="lblPrice" />
        <br>
      </td>
      <td height="60" bgcolor=buttonface>
        <asp:label Text='<%#Eval("Price")%>' runat="server"
          ID="lblPriceValue" />
        <br>
      </td>
    </tr>
  </ItemTemplate>
</asp:FormView>
      </td>
    </tr>
  </table>
</asp:Content>
```

In Listing 15-13, the `<asp:FormView>` control is used to display information about a specific product in the Web page.

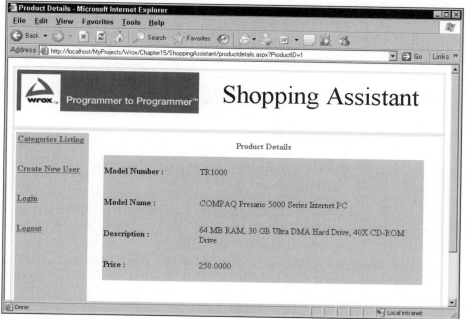

Figure 15-8

The FormView control lays out the product details page and performs data binding with the results of the `GetProductDetails()` method of the `ProductsService`.

Testing the ShoppingAssistant Application

Now that you have constructed the different parts of the application, it is time to test it by navigating to the login page of the Web site. If you enter a valid user id and password and click login, you will be directed to the categories listing page where all the categories in the site are displayed. Clicking the Show all Products hyperlink (displayed next to the category name) takes you to the product listing page where you can see all the products that belong to the selected category. If you click the hyperlink Product Details in the product listing page, you should be able to see the details of the specific product.

There is one disadvantage to this approach. Due to the synchronous approach, every time a request is made, you go across the Internet to retrieve the details from the Web service. Obviously, the response time is severely impacted due to the network trip that is made. Because the network loads can be unpredictable, systems can become backlogged or unable to process requests in a timely manner. This may lead to system failure as services time out or become unavailable. When this occurs, consumers of synchronous Web services may lock critical resources while waiting for a result that may never come.

To overcome this, you implement an asynchronous approach wherein you implement a combination of Windows service and a `System.Threading.Timer` component to asynchronously invoke the Web service. The result of this asynchronous Web service execution is then saved into a local XML file, which will then be used by the `ShoppingAssistant` Web site.

Using Asynchronous Invocation of Web Services and Windows Service

This section discusses how to substitute the synchronous Web service invocation approach with the asynchronous approach that would greatly improve the throughput of the pages. The idea here is to get the data from the remote Web services in asynchronous manner and then store that information as XML files in a local folder. After the information is available in the XML files, the ShoppingAssistant Web pages can retrieve the required information from local XML files for display purposes. To enable this asynchronous invocation of Web services at periodic intervals, you use the System.Threading.Timer component running inside a Windows Service application. Here is how the different pieces are tied together.

❑   Windows service application that has the Timer component invokes the remote Web service in asynchronous fashion. Although invoking the Web service, it also utilizes the new event based asynchronous programming model of Web services to specify the name of the callback function that will be automatically invoked when the Web service has finished its execution. This callback function then writes the returned result into a local XML file for the ShoppingAssistant Web application to make use of.

❑   Due to the presence of the Timer component (that fires a specific method at periodic intervals), you execute the action defined in the previous step for every pre-determined amount of time. This ensures that you have the latest information from the Web service in the local XML file. The frequency with which the Web service is invoked is determined by the value passed to the constructor of the Timer object.

❑   The ShoppingAssistant Web forms application then reads the information to be displayed on the site from the local XML file instead of making blocking synchronous calls to the remote Web service.

Windows Service

There are times where you may want to have your code always running on your server. If you have ever done any work in MSMQ, you might have created an application that polls the message queue for every predefined amount of time and checks for new messages. In that case, the application that checks the queue for messages should always be running as a Windows NT Service to be able to have the ability to poll the message queue frequently. These windows services do not have any user interface and you can configure windows services in such a way that they can be automatically started when the computer starts or they can be paused and restarted at any time.

Prior to Visual Studio.NET, if you want to write a windows service application either you have to use the template provided by ATL (Active Template Library that exposes a set of classes used for COM programming in the Windows environment) or if you are a VB programmer, you have to embed custom NT service controls in VB to achieve the same functionality. But with Visual Studio.Net, you can easily create an application that has the capability to run as a Service. Visual Studio.Net is supplied with a new project template called Windows Service that provides all the plumbing required for creating the application that can run as a Service. When you create a Visual Studio.Net project as a Service, you can write code to respond to the actions like what should happen when the service is started, paused, resumed, and stopped. After you create the service, it has to be installed using either InstallUtil.exe (Command line utility) or Setup and Deployment Project template. After you install the service, you can start, stop, pause, and resume it using the Service Control Manager.

To start, consider the implementation of Windows service application.

> **Through the property pages of the** PollingService, **you can set properties such as** CanStop **and** CanShutdown **to either true or false. These settings determine what methods can be called on your service at runtime. For example, when the** CanStop **property is set to true, the** OnStop() **method will be automatically called when the service is stopped through the Service Control Manager.**

Implementation of Windows Service Application

Create Visual C# Windows Service application named WinInformationPollingService. After the project is created, rename the service class from Service1 to PollingService.

The PollingService class inherits from the System.ServiceProcess.ServiceBase class. The ServiceBase class exposes the following lifecycle methods that you can override to indicate what happens when the state of the service is changed (such as starting, stopping, and so on) in the Services Control Manager. The lifecycle events fired by the service are:

- ❑ OnStart — Invoked when the service is started
- ❑ OnPause — Invoked when the service is paused
- ❑ OnStop — Invoked when the service stops running
- ❑ OnContinue — To decide the behavior that should happen when the service resumes normal functioning after being paused for a while
- ❑ OnShutDown — To indicate what should happen just prior to system shutdown, if the service is running at that time

Because the Windows service needs to be able to invoke the methods of the ContentPublisherService to get the information, you need to add reference the Categories and Products services that were created in the previous step. Listing 15-14 shows the complete code of the PollingService.

Listing 15-14: PollingService That Asynchronously Invokes ContentPublisher Web Service

```csharp
using System;
using System.Collections.Generic;
using System.ComponentModel;
using System.Data;
using System.IO;
using System.Diagnostics;
using System.ServiceProcess;
using System.Threading;
using System.Xml;
using System.Xml.Serialization;
using ShoppingAssistantLib;
using WinInformationPollingService.CategoriesProxy;
using WinInformationPollingService.ProductsProxy;

namespace WinInformationPollingService
```

```
{
partial class PollingService : ServiceBase
{
    private CategoriesService _categoriesService;
    private ProductsService _productsService;
    Timer stateTimer;

    public PollingService()
    {
        InitializeComponent();
    }

    protected override void OnStart(string[] args)
    {
        //Create the delegate that invokes methods for the timer
        AutoResetEvent autoEvent = new AutoResetEvent(false);
        TimerCallback timerDelegate = new TimerCallback(GetData);
        //Create a timer that signals the delegate to invoke GetData method
        //immediately, and every 10 seconds thereafter
        stateTimer = new Timer(timerDelegate, autoEvent, 0, 10000);
    }

    private void GetData(Object stateInfo)
    {
        _categoriesService = new CategoriesService();
        _categoriesService.GetCategoriesCompleted += new
          GetCategoriesCompletedEventHandler(this.GetCategoriesCompleted);
        _categoriesService.GetCategoriesAsync();
        _productsService = new ProductsService();
        _productsService.GetProductsCompleted += new
          GetProductsCompletedEventHandler(this.GetProductsCompleted);
        _productsService.GetProductsAsync();
    }

    void GetCategoriesCompleted(object sender,
      GetCategoriesCompletedEventArgs args)
    {
        string xmlFilePath = @"C:\Projects\Wrox\Categories.xml";
        Category[] categoryArray = args.Result;
        XmlSerializer serializer = new XmlSerializer(typeof(Category[]));
        TextWriter writer = new StreamWriter(xmlFilePath);
        //Serialize the Category array and close the TextWriter
        serializer.Serialize(writer, categoryArray);
        writer.Close();
    }

    void GetProductsCompleted(object sender,
      GetProductsCompletedEventArgs args)
```

```
        {
            string xmlFilePath = @"C:\Projects\Wrox\Products.xml";
            Product[] productArray = args.Result;
            XmlSerializer serializer = new XmlSerializer(typeof(Product[]));
            TextWriter writer = new StreamWriter(xmlFilePath);
            //Serialize the Product array and close the TextWriter
            serializer.Serialize(writer, productArray);
            writer.Close();
        }
    }
}
```

The OnStart event creates a new TimerCallback and passes that to the constructor of the System.Threading.Timer object.

```
stateTimer = new Timer(timerDelegate, autoEvent, 0, 10000);
```

To the constructor, you also supply the start and frequency of the timer event as arguments as 0 and 10000, respectively. This will result in the immediate firing of GetData() method and after that it will fire for every 10,000 milliseconds. Inside the GetData() method, you invoke the GetCategoriesAsync() method of the CategoriesService. Before invoking the GetCategoriesAsync() method, you set the GetCategoriesCompleted event handler to a local method named GetCategoriesCompleted(). This means after the asynchronous version of the GetCategories() method (called as GetCategoriesAsync()) is done with its execution, it will call back the GetCategoriesCompleted() method passing in the results of the Web service execution. Similar is the case with the asynchronous invocation of the ProductsService using its GetProductsAsync() method.

In the GetCategoriesCompleted() method, you retrieve the results of the Web service method call, load that into an array.

```
Category[] categoryArray = args.Result;
```

Serialize the contents of the Category array into an XML file named Categories.xml through Serialize() method of the XmlSerializer object.

```
serializer.Serialize(writer, categoryArray);
```

Similarly the GetProductsCompleted() method retrieves the results of the Web service call and serializes that result into an XML file named Products.xml.

.NET Framework 2.0 provides a new event-based asynchronous programming model for asynchronous invocation of Web services. This approach greatly simplifies the task of asynchronously invoking a Web service by introducing a new paradigm based on event handlers and arguments that are based on the name of the Web service method itself.

With this new approach, if you have a Web service method named MethodXXX, you call the <MethodName>**Async** to asynchronously invoke the Web service. For example, if you have a Web service method named GetCategories and you want to leverage asynchronous invocation framework, you need to do two things:

1. **Create an event handler for the** GetCategoriesCompleted **method and hook it up to a local method that can process the results returned by the Web service. One of the arguments passed to this method is of type** GetCategoriesCompletedEventArgs**, whose Result property contains the return value of the Web service method.**

2. **Invoke the Web service method by calling the** GetCategoriesAsync() **method through the Web service proxy.**

Another important benefit of this approach is that it also takes care of thread synchronization automatically so that event handlers are invoked on the same thread that made the asynchronous call.

Now that you have created a fully functional Windows service application that asynchronously calls the Web service and ensures that the latest categories and products information are available locally, you can modify the Web forms to retrieve data from the local .xml files, instead of calling out to the remote Web service every time the Web form is drawn.

Deploying the Windows Service

The next step is to add the installers that are required for installing the Windows service application onto the target machine. There are two ways you can do this.

- ❏ Using the InstallUtil Command line utility
- ❏ Using Windows installers created through the Setup and Deployment Project template

For the purposes of this case study, you use the set up and deployment project to create the Windows installer. Before adding the setup and deployment project, add installers to the PollingService by right-clicking on the design window of the PollingService and selecting Add Installer from the context menu. This will result in an installer named ProjectInstaller.cs being added to the project. If you open up the ProjectInstaller.cs file, there will be two components in the design surface. These components are represented by the System.ServiceProcess.ServiceProcessInstaller and System.ServiceProcess.ServiceInstaller classes respectively. Select the component named serviceProcessInstaller1 that represents the ServiceProcessInstaller class and bring up its properties window by pressing F4. In the properties window, change the value of the Account property to LocalSystem so that the PollingService runs using the credentials of the local system account.

Now add a new Setup and Deployment project named `WinInformationPollingServiceSetup` to the solution. After the setup project is created, add the Project Output of the `WinInformationPolling Service` to the setup project. Right-click on the `WinInformationPollingServiceSetup` project from the Solution Explorer and select Add->Project Output from the context menu. In the Add Project Output Group dialog box, ensure `WinInformationPollingService` project is selected in the Project drop-down list, select Primary Output, and click OK. Now that you have added the output of the `WinInformation PollingService` project to the setup project, add the installer that you created earlier in the `WinInformationPollingService` project as a custom action. To do this, select the `WinInformation PollingServiceSetup` project from the Solution Explorer and select View->Editor->Custom Actions from the menu. In the Custom Actions editor, right-click on the Custom Actions folder and select Add Custom Action from the context menu; then select the Primary Output of the `WinInformationPollingService` project from the dialog box. Now build the `WinInformationPollingServiceSetup` project, and it should result in a Windows installer named `WinInformationPollingServiceSetup.msi` file being created. Run the installer file.

Start the `PollingService` by opening up the Service Control Manager, right-clicking on the `PollingService`, and selecting Start from the context menu. After the service is started, it will keep polling the Web service and refresh the contents of the local XML files with the latest information retrieved from the Web service.

Modifying the ShoppingAssistant Web Pages to Consume XML Files

In the previous implementation of `ShoppingAssistant` Web site, the Web pages depended on synchronous Web service call to get categories and products information. But now with the availability of local XML files, the Web pages can just read the required information from the local XML files instead of making remote Web service calls. To illustrate the modification that needs to be done, consider the `CategoriesListing.aspx` page. Listing 15-15 shows the modified `Page_Load` event of the `CategoriesListing.aspx` page.

Listing 15-15: Page_Load Event of CategoriesListing.aspx Page That Uses XML File as the Data Store

```
void Page_Load(object sender, EventArgs e)
{
/* Asynchronous Web Service Call through the XML file generated
by the Windows Service */
string xmlFilePath = @"C:\Projects\Wrox\Categories.xml";
XmlSerializer serializer = new XmlSerializer(typeof(Category[]));
TextReader reader = new StreamReader(xmlFilePath);
//Deserialize the Category and close the TextReader
gridCategories.DataSource = (Category[])serializer.Deserialize(reader);
gridCategories.DataBind();
reader.Close();
}
```

The `Deserialize()` method of the `XmlSerializer` object is utilized to convert the `Categories.xml` file contents into a `Category` array that can then be directly bound to the `gridCategories`.

```
gridCategories.DataSource = (Category[])serializer.Deserialize(reader);
```

You need to perform the same modification to all the other Web pages as well to take advantage of the information that is available in the local XML files; however, with the `ProductsListing.aspx` and `ProductDetails.aspx` pages, there is a challenge. As you might remember, the Windows service populated all the products returned by the Web service into an XML file named `Products.xml`. Now in the `ProductsListing.aspx` page, you need to be able to display only those products that belong to the selected category. Listing 15-16 shows how this is implemented by looping through the `Product` array and filtering out the unwanted products.

Listing 15-16: Performing Data Binding with the Local XML File

```
void Page_Load(object sender, EventArgs e)
{
int categoryID = Convert.ToInt32(Request.QueryString["CategoryID"]);
List<Product> prodList = new List<Product>();
string xmlFilePath = @"C:\Projects\Wrox\Products.xml";
XmlSerializer serializer = new XmlSerializer(typeof(Product[]));
TextReader reader = new StreamReader(xmlFilePath);
Product[] prodArray = (Product[])serializer.Deserialize(reader);
  //Loop through the array and store the products with the matching category id
for (int i = 0; i < prodArray.Length; i++)
{
    Product temp = prodArray[i];
    //Only add the matching products to the new collection
    if (temp.CategoryID == categoryID)
      prodList.Add(temp);
}
reader.Close();
gridProducts.DataSource = prodList;
gridProducts.DataBind();
}
```

Similar to the Categories Listing page, the Products Listing is also modified to retrieve the products information from a local XML file named `Products.xml`. After the products information is loaded into a local array variable, loop through the array and filter the products with the matching category id into a generic collection variable named list. Bind the generic collection to the `gridProducts` control.

If you go back to the `ShoppingAssistant` Web site and navigate through the pages, you will find that the performance and throughput of the site has vastly improved due to the change in the way you obtain the data for display.

Implementation of FileSystemWatcher to Facilitate Reporting Data Collection

Now you have a working Web site that shows all the information related to categories and products available in the site. Imagine, for example, one of the partners of `ShoppingAssistant` site wants to find out the number of times a particular product has been viewed by the users. To accomplish this, you need to be able to store the details of all the products that are displayed on the product details page. If you were to handle this process of storing data in a synchronous way (such as making a database call whenever a product related page is requested), the user would have to wait till this information is stored in the database because the control will not be returned to the caller application until the changes are saved. This might result in an increase in the response time for the product details page to be rendered on the user's browser. It would be nice if you could perform this data collection operation in an asynchronous manner without impacting the throughput of the Web site. To enable this approach, add some more elements to the existing architecture. Figure 15-9 shows the new architecture.

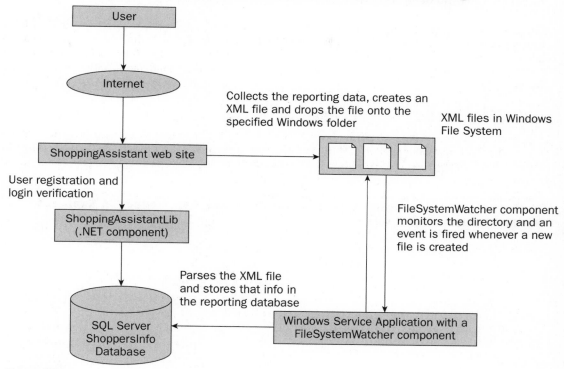

Asynchronous Data Collection Framework for Reporting

Figure 15-9

When the user navigates to the `Products` page, perform a number of independently running operations to ensure that the data relevant for reporting purposes is collected and stored in the database.

- ❑ When the user navigates to the ASP.NET Web page that displays the product details, take the products information, convert that information into an XML file, and store it in a specified `Drop` directory.

- ❑ This specified directory is already monitored for creation of new files by a `FileSystemWatcher` component, which is placed in a Windows service that always runs in the background as a service.

- ❑ When an XML file is created in the `Drop` directory, an event is automatically raised to the Windows Service that reads the contents of the xml file into an object named `ReportInfo`, and passes the `ReportInfo` object to the `InsertReportInfo()` method of the `ReportDB` class that is present in the `ShoppingAssistantLib` class library.

- ❑ The `InsertReportInfo()` method simply inserts the details into a table named `ReportInfo` through the `InsertReportInfo` procedure.

By carrying out the reporting data collection operation in an asynchronous fashion, you allow the control to return to the application as soon as the reporting information is captured in an XML file (as opposed to storing that information in a database through an expensive network call). After that, a separate set of operations are executed in a separate thread to save the reporting details to the database. This asynchronous approach not only helps in increasing the performance, but also provides the users with the best possible browsing experience.

For reasons of manageability, this section of the implementation is split into two sections. In the first section, you modify the Products Web page to store the details of the products information into an XML file before displaying the details of a specific product to the user. The second section discusses the steps for setting up the FileSystemWatcher component on the Windows service to monitor the directory for the creation of files.

Modification to the Products Page

This section focuses on the changes that need to be made to the ProductDetails.aspx page to gather the product information into a local XML file for reporting purposes. Because the changes are only on the server-side code, Listing 15-17 shows the modified server-side code of the ProductDetails.aspx page.

Listing 15-17: Implementing Asynchronous Reporting Data Collection Support in Product Details Display Page

```
<%@ Page Language="C#" MasterPageFile="~/CommonMaster.master"
  Title="Product Details" %>
<%@ Import Namespace="System.Collections.Generic" %>
<%@ Import Namespace="System.IO" %>
<%@ Import Namespace="System.Xml" %>
<%@ Import Namespace="System.Xml.Serialization" %>
<%@ Import Namespace="ProductsProxy" %>
<script runat="server">
void Page_Load(object sender, EventArgs e)
{
    int categoryID = 0;
    int productID = Convert.ToInt32(Request.QueryString["ProductID"]);
    List<Product> prodList = new List<Product>();
    string xmlFilePath = @"C:\Projects\Wrox\Products.xml";
    XmlSerializer serializer = new XmlSerializer(typeof(Product[]));
    TextReader reader = new StreamReader(xmlFilePath);
    Product[] prodArray = (Product[])serializer.Deserialize(reader);
    //Loop through the array and retrieve products with the matching product id
    for (int i = 0; i < prodArray.Length; i++)
    {
      Product temp = prodArray[i];
      //Only add the matching products to the new collection
      if (temp.ProductID == productID)
      {
        prodList.Add(temp);
        categoryID = temp.CategoryID;
      }
    }
    reader.Close();
```

```
        formProductDetails.DataSource = prodList;
        formProductDetails.DataBind();
        //Store the parameters related to the Request into local variables
        string browser = Request.UserAgent.ToString();
        string requestType = Request.RequestType.ToString();
        string authenticated = Request.IsAuthenticated.ToString();
        CreateXMLDocument(browser, requestType, authenticated,
           categoryID, productID);
    }

    public bool CreateXMLDocument(string browser, string requestType,
      string authenticated, int categoryID, int productID)
    {
        try
        {
          XmlWriterSettings settings = new XmlWriterSettings();
          settings.Indent = true;
          string fileName = System.Guid.NewGuid().ToString() + ".xml";
          XmlWriter writer = XmlWriter.Create(@"C:\Projects\Wrox\Drop\" +
              fileName, settings);
          writer.WriteStartDocument(false);
          writer.WriteComment
             ("This file represents information collected for reporting purposes");
          writer.WriteStartElement("ReportInfo", null);
          writer.WriteElementString("Browser", browser);
          writer.WriteElementString("RequestType", requestType);
          writer.WriteElementString("Authenticated", authenticated);
          writer.WriteElementString("CategoryID", categoryID.ToString());
          writer.WriteElementString("ProductID", productID.ToString());
          writer.WriteEndElement();
          writer.Flush();
          writer.Close();
        }
        catch (Exception ex)
        {
          Response.Write(ex.Message);
        }
        return true;
    }
</script>
```

Listing 15-17 is similar to the `CategoriesListing.aspx` page in that it also relies on a local XML file named `Products.xml` for the data displayed through the `FormView` control `formProductDetails`. The place where it is different is where it creates the XML file using a method named `CreateXmlDocument()`. The `CreateXmlDocument()` method is invoked at the end of the `Page_Load` event. Before calling the `CreateXmlDocument()` method, you store the parameters related to the current request into a local variable.

```
string browser = Request.UserAgent.ToString();
string requestType = Request.RequestType.ToString();
string authenticated = Request.IsAuthenticated.ToString();
```

Call the `CreateXmlDocument()` method passing in the values of the local variables.

```
CreateXMLDocument(browser, requestType, authenticated,
   categoryID, productID);
```

The `CreateXmlDocument()` method creates an XML file in a specific directory using the `WriteXXX()` methods of the `XmlWriter` object. The name of the XML file is generated by the call to the `NewGuid()` method of `Guid` class.

A typical XML file created by the `CreateXmlDocument()` method looks as shown in Figure 15-10.

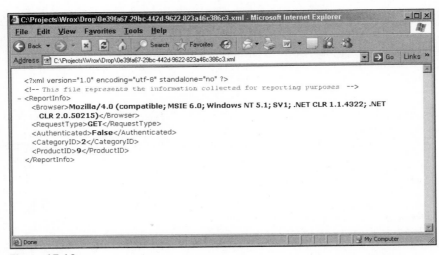

Figure 15-10

Now that the `ProductDetails.aspx` page is capable of generating the dynamic XML file, the next step is to add the required code to the Windows service so that it can process the files generated by the product details page.

Adding Monitoring Capability to Windows Service Using FileSystemWatcher

To add monitoring capabilities, drag and drop a `FileSystemWatcher` component to the design surface of the `PollingService` that is part of the `WinInformationPollingService` project. Now modify the `OnStart()` method to look as shown in Listing 15-18. Listing 15-18 also implements two additional methods: `OnChanged()` and `SaveReportInfo()`.

Listing 15-18: Adding Asynchronous Reporting Data Collection Support to Product Details Display Page

```
protected override void OnStart(string[] args)
{
AutoResetEvent autoEvent = new AutoResetEvent(false);
//Create the delegate that invokes methods for the timer
```

```
    TimerCallback timerDelegate = new TimerCallback(GetData);
    //Create a timer that signals the delegate to invoke GetData method
    //immediately, and every 10 seconds thereafter
    stateTimer = new Timer(timerDelegate, autoEvent, 0, 10000);
    //Configure the FileSystemWatcher to watch for changes
    fileSystemWatcher1 = new FileSystemWatcher();
    fileSystemWatcher1.Path = @"C:\Projects\Wrox\Drop\";
    //Set the Filter to watch for .xml files
    fileSystemWatcher1.Filter = "*.xml";
    //Filter for Last Write changes
    fileSystemWatcher1.NotifyFilter = NotifyFilters.LastWrite;
    fileSystemWatcher1.IncludeSubdirectories = false;
    //Add event handlers
    fileSystemWatcher1.Changed += new FileSystemEventHandler(OnChanged);
    //Enable the component to begin watching for changes
    fileSystemWatcher1.EnableRaisingEvents = true;
}

private void OnChanged(object source, FileSystemEventArgs e)
{
//Read the contents of the file and save it to the database
SaveReportInfo(e.FullPath);
}

private void SaveReportInfo(string path)
{
try
{
    XmlReader reader = XmlReader.Create(path);
    XmlDocument document = new XmlDocument();
    document.Load(reader);
    XmlNode reportInfoNode = document.DocumentElement;
    ReportInfo report = new ReportInfo();
    //Get all the values from the XML document into the ReportInfo object
    report.Browser = reportInfoNode.ChildNodes.Item(0).InnerText;
    report.RequestType = reportInfoNode.ChildNodes.Item(1).InnerText;
    report.Authenticated = reportInfoNode.ChildNodes.Item(2).InnerText;
    report.CategoryID =
      Convert.ToInt32(reportInfoNode.ChildNodes.Item(3).InnerText);
    report.ProductID =
      Convert.ToInt32(reportInfoNode.ChildNodes.Item(4).InnerText);
    ReportDB reportDB = new ReportDB();
    reportDB.InsertReportInfo(report);
    reader.Close();
}
catch (Exception ex)
{
    throw ex;
}
}
}
```

In the OnStart() method, you configure the relevant properties of the FileSystemWatcher component so that it can start monitoring the "C:\Projects\Wrox\Drop" for creation of new XML files.

```
fileSystemWatcher1 = new FileSystemWatcher();
fileSystemWatcher1.Path = @"C:\Projects\Wrox\Drop\";
//Set the Filter to watch for .xml files
fileSystemWatcher1.Filter = "*.xml";
//Filter for Last Write changes
fileSystemWatcher1.NotifyFilter = NotifyFilters.LastWrite;
fileSystemWatcher1.IncludeSubdirectories = false;
```

You then hook up the `Changed` event of the `FileSystemWatcher` to a method named `OnChanged()`.

```
fileSystemWatcher1.Changed += new FileSystemEventHandler(OnChanged);
```

Finally, you enable the component to begin watching for the creation of new files by setting the `EnableRaisingEvents` property to true.

```
fileSystemWatcher1.EnableRaisingEvents = true;
```

Now that you have enabled the `FileSystemWatcher` to watch for new files, whenever a new file is created, the `OnChanged()` method will be called. In the `OnChanged()` method, you simply invoke a helper method named `SaveReportInfo`, which reads the contents of the generated XML file and stores that in the database.

As the name of the method suggests, `SaveReportInfo` method reads the contents of the XML file into a `ReportInfo` object, and invokes the `SaveReportInfo` method of the `ReportDB` object passing in the `ReportInfo` object as an argument. Now recompile the `WinInformationPollingService` and redeploy it using the Windows installer.

Putting It All Together

Now that you have constructed the different parts of the application, it is time to exercise the functionalities of the application by going through the following steps.

❏ If the `PollingService` is not already running, start the service through the Service Control Manager. After the service is started, the service will begin monitoring the `C:\Projects\Wrox\Drop` directory for creation of new files in addition to refreshing the contents of the local XML files with the latest data retrieved from the XML Web service.

❏ Now if you navigate to the `ShoppingAssistant` Web site and browse through the Categories and Products Web pages, the latest information from the local XML files will be used to display the information.

❏ While navigating to the product details page, you will find that all the details related to the displayed product are added to the `ReportInfo` table, which can be later used for reporting purposes. This is made possible due to the combination of the following operations. The Web page that displays the product details page creates an XML file and drops it on to the `C:\Projects\Wrox\Drop` directory that is being monitored by the `FileSystemWatcher` (that is hosted on a Windows service). Because the `FileSystemWatcher` monitors the directory for the creation of new files, an event is automatically raised as soon as a new XML file is created. The Windows service captures the event, reads the contents of the XML file, and then stores that information in the `ReportInfo` table in the database through the methods of the `ReportDB` class.

Summary

This case study has discussed the following features:

❑ The new event-based programming model for asynchronous invocation of Web service

❑ How to leverage the XML serialization capabilities of the `XmlSerializer` class to serialize the contents of an object into an XML file and vice versa

❑ How to effectively leverage the asynchronous Web service invocation capabilities in a Web application

❑ How to utilize the features of the `FileSystemWatcher` to asynchronously process the XML files

❑ How to use master pages to create consistent look and feel for the entire Web site

Although the application that was demonstrated was simple in functionality, it should provide a solid foundation for understanding how to build high-performance, scalable, flexible, and reliable Web applications using the asynchronous features of the .NET framework such as XML-based Web services, and `FileSystemWatcher`. If your application consumes a lot of external Web services and the application allows some tolerance in terms of the staleness of the data it gets from external services, the asynchronous Web service invocation capabilities could very well be an excellent feature to use.

Index

Index